WEBSTER'S NEW WRLD™
STUDENT WRITING HANDBOOK

Fourth Edition

by Sharon Sorenson

Webster's New World™ Student Writing Handbook, Fourth Edition
Copyright © 2000, 1997, 1992, 1988 by Sharon Sorenson

This edition is a major revision of *Webster's New World™ Student Writing Handbook*, Third Edition, copyright © 1997, 1992, 1988 by Sharon Sorenson

IDG Books Worldwide, Inc.
An International Data Group Company
919 E. Hillsdale Blvd., Suite 400
Foster City, CA 94404

A Webster's New World™ Book

WEBSTER'S NEW WORLD is a trademark of IDG Books Worldwide, Inc.

LIBRARY OF CONGRESS CATALOGING-IN-PUBLICATION DATA
Sorenson, Sharon.
    Webster's New World student writing handbook / by Sharon Sorenson.— 4th ed.
     p. cm.
    "A Webster's New World book"—T.p. verso.
    Includes index.
    ISBN 0-7645-6125-1
    1. English language—Rhetoric—Handbooks, manuals, etc. 2. Report writing—
Handbooks, manuals, etc. I. Title: Student writing handbook.

    PE1408.S6577 2000
    808'.042—dc21   00-042644
                                                        CIP

ACKNOWLEDGMENTS

Customarily, in the front pages of a book, an author lists the people who have helped see the manuscript to completion. In this case, the list is more than customary. The names here are those of truly special people. They offered advice, references, experience, and wisdom. But most of all they offered time–in every case, a precious commodity. To all, I extend my sincere appreciation, not just for what they did but for who they are: dear, kind professionals who are also my friends, especially Valda Alsop, William Asbury, Rick Barter, Viola Blaser, Robert Edelman, Rosemary Ewing, James Gardner, Dr. Virginia Grabill, Mary Lou Heeger, Dr. Ed Jenkinson, Athalene Klein, Joyce Marlin, Charlotte Mason, Ninalea McIntosh, Rosemarie Norrick-Urash, Marcia Onnybecker, June Purcell, Ralph Rothert, John Russell, Jack Schriber, Sue Schriber, Dr. Ann Stuart, Edmund Sullivan, Virginia Thrasher, Sharon Tuggle, Dr. Laura Weaver, Susan Wolf, Jim Wootton, and many others who answered questions, offered opinions, made suggestions, and otherwise provided moral support.

Others agreed to allow their work to be included as models. A special thanks to those for their cooperation and willingness to help: Hillary Altekruse for her literary analysis, "Alone in a Crowded World: Emily Dickinson and Her Poems"; David Ciepley for his short story, "Spud"; Jo Ann McCulley for her literary analysis, "Sylvia and the White Heron"; Jack B. Schriber for his poem, "Ode to a Tupperware Container"; Ann Commons Weil for her research paper, "Mother Goose: A Devoted Teacher"; and Jerome Welte for his laboratory report, "The Effects of Acid Rain on the Growth of Bulbous Plants."

Finally, a warm note of gratitude to Linda Bernbach, the editor who suggested the idea for this handbook, who answered hours of long-distance questions, who guided me through two previous projects, and whose exemplary professionalism should be a standard in the publishing industry.

TABLE OF CONTENTS

To Charlie…
who has made all the difference.

INTRODUCTION

This book began with an ambitious goal: to meet the writing needs of all students. Acknowledging that "students" are not confined to a classroom, the idea was to develop a reference book that would assist readers in any situation, academic, personal, or professional. It would offer guidance for writing assignments across the curriculum, from accounting to zoology. And for personal reference, the book would help with resumes and letters as well as scholarship, college, and job applications. The book would include all kinds of writing, creative or technical, formal or informal. It would address all problems, no matter whether writers needed to study a model; find a quick definition and example in the Glossary; solve a grammar, usage, or mechanics problem; or follow an extended step-by-step explanation from the text. No matter whether students were writing, revising, or proofreading—or only preparing to write—the book would meet every writer's every need.

It was, indeed, an ambitious goal. This fourth edition attests to the book's continued success.

Having worked with students in both high school and college for over 30 years, I sincerely believe this book can guide you through every writing situation you will face. Others agree, including the many teachers and students I consulted about the various kinds of writing assignments, in and out of the classroom. Here's why we think the book works:

- The book is a reference work, a guide, a kind of "dictionary" of writing, not meant for cover-to-cover reading. You can pinpoint needed information with little reading.
- The alphabetical arrangement allows you to find quickly the sections that meet your specific needs. Cross-references refer you to related sections if you need additional help.
- The five parts of the book include
  - a discussion of writing basics, including planning, writing, revising, and proofreading good sentences, good paragraphs, and good multiple-paragraph papers,
  - a study of the ten methods for developing any kind of writing,
  - a description of virtually every kind of writing, both academic and personal,
  - a grammar, usage, and mechanics reference,
  - short definitions and brief examples in the Glossary.

- Step-by-step instructions help alleviate the fear of facing writing assignments. These instructions tell you what to do, how to do it, and how the finished product should look. The instructions also include guidelines and checklists along the way to ease you through the task.
- Analyzing 55 types of writing, the book covers writing for all kinds of assignments in all major content areas and test situations as well as for personal needs.
- The discussion of each type of writing examines
  - its characteristics,
  - the process for developing it, including prewriting, writing, revising, and proofreading,
  - writing samples to illustrate the characteristics and process,
  - analyses of the writing samples describing their important features.
- The book includes the following six kinds of samples to aid writing across the curriculum:
  - English
  - Social Sciences
  - Science
  - Mathematics
  - Work-Place Writing
  - Technical Writing
- Wherever appropriate, all six samples for a specific kind of writing deal with the same general topic. The result illustrates how to tailor your writing for a specific audience.
- The samples may also feature parallel topics to further understanding. For instance, using the same novel as the subject to illustrate a book review, a literary analysis of a novel, a synopsis, and a book report for the major disciplines makes clear how one kind of writing *differs* from another.
- The practical, readable writing samples range from single paragraphs to full-length research papers and address a wide variety of contemporary subjects. High school and college students have written many of the samples. Teachers in the respective disciplines agreed to the writing samples' success.
- The book includes numerous illustrations, examples, notes, hints, and warnings that help clarify solutions to common writing problems.

- Cross-references within the book emphasize the relationships among the many facets of writing and help you understand terms or concepts that may otherwise hinder you.
- Frequent references to computer searches and data banks acknowledge the technical and electronic world in which you work.

As a result of its organization, many cross-references, and thorough treatment of each topic, this book should answer any need in any writing situation. I hope you agree. But more importantly, I hope that what you find in these pages improves your writing—in school, on the job, and in your personal life. When that happens, this book will have met its goal.

PART I

BASICS OF GOOD WRITING

Good writing starts with process. So we'll begin by telling you how to go about writing. How to get ideas. How to put them together. How to get them on paper. How to polish them into a fine piece of writing. Those are the four broad steps in writing anything: prewriting, writing, revising, and proofreading.

- **Prewriting**: The prewriting process refers to the kinds of things you do to get ready to write. Helpful hints to suggest how to think. How to plan. How to make choices. Prewriting prepares you to write freely.
- **Writing:** Suggestions for writing follow with details about how to use the building blocks of good writing:
  - Good sentences
  - Good paragraphs
  - Good multi-paragraph papers.
- **Revising:** Then we help you with probably the toughest part of writing: polishing your paper. Improving content. Improving structure. Improving emphasis. Improving continuity.
- **Proofreading:** Finally, we show you how to eliminate those bothersome mechanical errors.

Refer to this basics-of-writing section regularly, no matter what you write. In fact, you can find cross-references to this section throughout the book, suggesting that you use it to supplement the book's step-by-step processes.

Prewriting

Throughout Parts II and III of this book, you can find series of steps labeled *Prewriting*. The term generally refers to any kind of activity that helps you loosen up, think about your topic, focus on purpose, analyze your audience, and otherwise prepare to write. The prewriting steps vary with the kind of paper you are planning. Some papers are obviously more complicated than others, and so some steps for getting ready to write are also more complicated. For instance, one paper may require thorough primary or secondary research, while another may demand nothing more complicated than selecting and organizing appropriate details. In either case, prewriting activities lay the groundwork for a great paper.

Usually, the prewriting activities help you find a good topic, narrow topics that are too broad, and look at purpose. You should finish the prewriting activities with at least a sentence and a list. Or you may have something as formal as a three-part thesis sentence and a fully developed outline. Either way, you'll have laid the groundwork.

STEP 1   **Gathering Thoughts and Information**
What we write depends on what we think about. What we think about usually depends on what has happened to us, perhaps as a result of what we have read, what we have heard, what we have seen. The first part of prewriting demands that we focus on our thoughts, perhaps expanding them by seeking additional information. Probably a dozen or so different general activities help in finding a topic, but here we look at the following most common activities:

- Reading (specific assignments, general background, and research)
- Discussion (group and interview)
- Personal reflection
- Journal writing
- Brainstorming
- List making
- Graphic organizers
- Daily experiences (what you see, hear, and do)

Reading: Specific Assignments. Reading is one way to prepare for writing. Perhaps you have a reading assignment to which you must respond. Perhaps you are summarizing the assignment, reacting to it, or in some other way showing that you have read and understood it. The assignment may also be a springboard from which you can make mental leaps to topics of related but special interest to you.

Reading: General Background. Frequently, however, the reading material is something other than a specific assignment. At one extreme, it may be general, almost casual reading that merely relates to classroom work and only indirectly applies to specific daily assignments. This reading material may be in the form of periodical articles or books, perhaps by authors renowned in their fields. But as these topics attract your interest, they suggest writing topics.

Reading: Research. General background reading at the other extreme may be so comprehensive as to be labeled *research*. Your research may require the use of various periodical indexes, a card or computer catalog, electronic data searches, or any other of the many guides to sources found in the library or on the Internet. In these prewriting situations, you are responsible not only for the additional reading but also for finding the sources.

All these reading activities—specific assignments, general background, and research—fall in the category of prewriting. The reading keeps your mind active, introduces new ideas, provides specific information, and helps you think of suitable writing topics.

Discussion: Group. Prewriting activities may also be oral and may include formal or informal discussion, in class or out. With classmates and friends familiar with the subject matter, you may discuss not only possible topics for your paper but also the possible content of your paper.

Discussion: Interview. Of course, discussion can also take place in the form of an interview. While the interview may be similar to an informal discussion, it differs in that you will have sought out the authority with whom you are speaking. His or her comments may become the basis for your paper. As a result, you can still consider it a research paper even though the source is primary rather than secondary and oral rather than printed. [*See* primary research *and* secondary research *in the Glossary.*]

Personal Reflection. Prewriting activities may also be in the form of personal reflection. If it is to result in writing, however, reflection usually needs direction. You can reflect on all manner of things, but without a general topic of concern or a specific assignment to address, reflection may be more akin to daydreaming than to prewriting and may never result in writing. Many writers use a variety of means for directing personal reflection, including journal writing, brainstorming, and list making.

Journal Writing. Serious writers frequently keep daily journals. They write about whatever attracts their attention, seems worthy of note, merits observation. Ironically, they find that the more they record, the more they observe. Thus, they argue, keeping a journal makes them more observant and helps them generate ideas about which to write. The idea of journal writing may suggest a goal of creative writing, such as short stories or poetry, but that is not necessarily the case. Journalists, copywriters, even students who must respond on a regular basis to written assignments find that keeping a journal helps them stay in shape, so to speak, to write the most vigorous articles or papers.

Brainstorming. Brainstorming also helps focus personal reflection. Brainstorming involves offering ideas freely, without fear of criticism, allowing one idea to suggest another and another. You can brainstorm alone, but obviously the process is more effective in a group. As one idea generates another idea, you come up with new approaches to old ideas. The trick to brainstorming effectively is to allow the mind the freedom to make connections between ideas, no matter how strange the connections may seem at the time. And the freedom is encouraged by not discouraging any idea.

List Making. As a result of brainstorming, you may be able to generate lists that suggest composition topics and supporting ideas; however, lists evolve by other means as well. Generating lists helps you look critically at ideas and their relationships. You can create all kinds of lists:

- Lists of main ideas
- Lists of supporting details
- Lists of examples
- Lists of arguments
- Lists of reasons

All these topics can be parts of a composition. A list that is revised and arranged in logical order is, for all practical purposes, an outline. In many of the prewriting activities in Parts II and III, you find that generating lists is a primary way to pick out main ideas and then to find appropriate supporting ideas. As a prewriting activity, list making helps you collect your thoughts, plan and arrange them in logical order, and clarify the direction of your paper. The result is organized, unified writing. But more on that later. [*See Step 7.*]

Graphic Organizers. Some writers work better with graphic organizers than with lists. Graphic organizers are drawings or maps that show how ideas connect. Using them will help you generate ideas and begin to put your thoughts on paper. Consider the example in Figure 1.1.

FIGURE 1.1

Organizing your ideas graphically may help you generate more ideas.

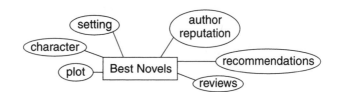

Daily Experiences: What You See and Hear. Other kinds of prewriting activities occur almost as a coincidence of living. Sometimes you may be stimulated to write as a result of something you have seen: a film, an art exhibit, an accident, an animal in distress, a busy highway, a lonely farm pond, a thoughtful gesture, a construction site, a rare flower, a criminal act, a rude driver, a mime, a tornado, or a champion swimmer. For example, films frequently have a powerful message that leaves you sad, joyful, remorseful, even furious, a feeling that may be worthy of a description, a comparison-and-contrast, a classification, or a persuasion paper. Television viewing may evoke similar kinds of reactions. You may react to news commentators and their methods of reporting the nightly news. You may react to a special report on a world crisis that evokes empathy and helps you write an opinion paper, or you may react to a variety show that stimulates your sense of humor and helps you write effective dialogue.

Daily Experiences: What You Do. Likewise, sometimes you may be stimulated to write as a result of something you have done: visiting a city dump, watching a track meet, sitting in the rain, falling out of a boat, suffering from loneliness, facing tragedy, enjoying success, completing a task, dieting, building a hang glider, catching a big fish, finding a lost wallet, helping a stranger, having an accident, or being friends with someone special. For instance, sometimes having a conversation with someone particularly motivating may help you sort through your own feelings enough to react in written form.

In summary, day-to-day activities, given attention, help you collect thoughts, gather information, and promote ideas for writing.

Doing something as simple as taking an afternoon walk may suggest a dozen topics about which you can write. For example, children playing in the street invite danger by their behavior. You wonder why they have nowhere else to play. A driver coasts through a stop sign, neglecting the clear response that the traffic sign demands. His behavior makes you wonder about accident causes in your neighborhood. The neighbor's dog bounces out to wag his greeting. You wonder how dogs have become the domesticated "man's-best-friend." Within a few minutes' walk, you discover three possible topics to explore.

STEP 2   Finding a Topic

After exploring possible subjects by reading, talking, listening, observing, and thinking, choose a topic that is right for you. Perhaps you must tackle an assigned topic; perhaps you have the freedom to choose anything of interest. Name the topic.

STEP 3   Narrowing the Subject

After choosing a general topic, narrow your subject to suit the length of the paper you plan to write. Most writers have trouble narrowing a subject sufficiently for full development in a paragraph or multi-paragraph paper. The following questions can help you limit your subject:

- How many divisions are included with this topic? Will any one division better serve as a topic for a full paragraph? Or do I need a multi-paragraph paper to talk about several divisions? For instance:

  Topic: the best popcorn
  Divisions:
  > black—tiny kernels, hull-less
  > yellow—large kernels, some hulls
  > white—moderate kernels, buttery flavor

- What attitude toward this subject do I want to share with my reader? (If I have more than one attitude, I must write more than one paragraph.)

  Topic: the best popcorn
  Attitudes:
  > best popping
  > favorite eating
  > best keeping
  > easiest to raise
  > most readily available
  Single attitude: favorite eating

- Can I narrow the subject by putting it in a specific time and place? (For instance, if I want to describe my father in one paragraph, I must limit the description to a single incident.)

STEP 4 **Determining Purpose**

An earlier section suggested gathering ideas from an afternoon walk. You may wonder why the children are playing in the street, why they have nowhere else to play. Assume you decide to write about that. First, however, decide what you hope to accomplish as a result of your writing. Do you simply want to report information on the assumption that others may be interested? Do you hope to analyze the problem in an effort to find an answer? Do you want to persuade local government to do something about the problem? Do you want to offer suggestions for alternate play areas? Do you want to warn the children about the dangers of playing in the street? In other words, you must decide why you are writing.

What is your purpose? Put it in a sentence.

STEP 5 **Analyzing the Audience**

Directly related to purpose is audience. For example, if writing about the children's play area, will you write to local government officials, to the children, to the newspaper editor, or to parents? Your audience determines dozens of details about your writing: vocabulary, sentence structure, formality, psychological appeals, organization, and approach. If you are writing about a technical subject to an audience of laypersons, you must use layperson's vocabulary. If you are writing about a formal subject to an academic audience, your sentence structure should mirror the formality. If you are expressing an opinion to readers who will likely disagree, you should use different appeals and a different organization than you would with readers who will likely agree. You should tailor your writing about a political debate for an audience of politicians differently than you would for an audience of apathetic voters.

Who is your audience? Name it. Analyzing audience is part of the prewriting process.

STEP 6 **Writing the Topic or Thesis Sentence**

Now you should be prepared to write a topic or thesis sentence. You know your purpose and you understand your audience, so what will you say to achieve your purpose with this particular audience? Write a sentence that states your topic. For a paragraph, that sentence is called a *topic sentence*. For a multi-paragraph paper, it's called a *thesis sentence.* [*For details about writing topic and thesis sentences, see* Writing a Paragraph *or* Writing a Multi-Paragraph Paper *later in this part.*]

STEP 7   Organizing the Material

Finally, before you can write an effective paper, you must have some plan for presenting your main ideas. That plan is called *organization*. You may have a list developed from Step 1. If so, you are well on your way toward organizing your paper. Now you need to rearrange that list so that it becomes a plan for your paper. If necessary, you can transform that list into an outline. [*See* Outlines: For a Paper *in Part III for a discussion of list making and formal outlining.*]

Generally, the organization should follow one of three plans: chronological order (as arranged in time), spatial order (as arranged in space), or some order of importance (as arranged by any measure of significance). The specific method of development [*as suggested in all the entries in Parts II and III*] also determines organization.

PREWRITING SUMMARY

Prewriting activities should result in two products: a topic or thesis sentence and a list or outline. Together, they guide you smoothly through the writing process.

Most writers go through a prewriting process, begin writing and stop writing from time to time to think again about the results of their prewriting activities. Thus, because writers often move from prewriting to writing to prewriting again until they achieve their goal, the term we will use occasionally in this book is the *yo-yo approach*. Sometimes writing does not move as smoothly as you had hoped; you need additional preparation, additional thought, additional research, additional experience, additional reflection, additional discussion before your ideas form a unified, comprehensive piece of writing. If you use the yo-yo approach as you work, the writing process will be less painful, and the prewriting activities will provide more inspiration for the writing process ahead.

Writing

Having completed the prewriting steps, your writing should move along smoothly. Whether your prewriting activities result in a list, a scratch outline, or a formal outline, the process of writing the first draft is nothing more than the development of your prewriting-activity products. During the writing steps, you should feel free to express your ideas without worrying about mechanical details, sentence structure, and other formal writing techniques. Those details can be left as part of revising and proofreading.

This section of Part I follows the logical building blocks for

- Good Writing Habits
- Writing Sentences
- Writing a Paragraph
- Writing a Multi-Paragraph Paper

GOOD WRITING HABITS

The following steps suggest a good plan for gathering all those words in your head and getting them onto paper.

STEP 1   **Getting Situated**
Situate yourself in a comfortable spot, free from distractions, in whatever surroundings are most stimulating to your own creative process. For some writers, any kind of sound—music, voices, street noise—proves distracting. For other writers, background noise helps drown out other distractions. In any case, arrange to work in the situation most comfortable for you.

STEP 2   **Following the Plan**
Follow the organization plan you developed during the prewriting process. Begin with the topic or thesis sentence and add the supporting details suggested in your list or outline.

STEP 3   **Using the Yo-Yo Approach**
If the organization plan you developed during the writing process is not working well for your purpose, then, using the yo-yo approach, go back to the prewriting steps that dealt with organization and try a different plan. Implement the plan, using the thesis sentence and/or topic sentences as developed during the prewriting process. Add the supporting details in logical order as you rearrange them.

STEP 4   **Letting Thoughts Flow**
As you write, concentrate on allowing your thoughts to flow. Here's how:

- Do not struggle with words or spelling or punctuation or other mechanical details.

- Do not act on the urge to reread, restructure, and rewrite. Rather, concentrate on getting your main ideas on paper, writing quickly, perhaps even informally.

STEP 5 **Following Paragraphing Techniques**

As your thoughts flow, frame them into paragraph structures. Even though you will polish structure during the revising process, the conscious concern over paragraph structure at this point may save some agony later. [*See* Writing a Paragraph *later in this part.*]

STEP 6 **Sticking to the Subject**

Be sure you stick to your subject, thus maintaining unity. Avoid the temptation to wander off into interesting examples that do not support your topic or thesis sentence. Those examples will not help your purpose! As you think of them, use transitions to connect your ideas and to show relationships between and among ideas.

STEP 7 **Ignoring (for the Moment) Technical Details**

It should be obvious that what happens while you are writing is merely the result of using the products you developed in your prewriting work. All other kinds of technical work—the mechanics, grammar, usage, sentence structure, the fine points of parallelism, emphasis, and formal structure—can be left for the revising and proofreading processes.

STEP 8 **Writing the Rough Draft in One Sitting**

Make every effort to complete the first draft in a single sitting in order to maintain a consistent tone and smooth continuity with less effort.

When you complete the first draft, you have passed a major hurdle. You have your thoughts on paper. You have developed the plan established in the prewriting activities. But this is the first draft—the rough draft, if you prefer. Rough drafts need polish. The polishing comes with revising and proofreading. So when you have the first draft finished, take a well-deserved break and come back ready to be objective about your work.

WRITING SENTENCES

You've written sentences since you were in elementary school, so why take the space here to talk about writing good sentences? Because not all sentences are created equal, good writers don't just spew out sentences and consider the job done. Instead, they consciously manipulate sentence structure, word choice, sentence length, and emphasis. While paragraphs are the building blocks for every multi-paragraph paper, sentences make up the foundation. We all know that if a foundation crumbles, the building blocks come crashing down. So, here is your guide to writing good sentences.

CHARACTERISTICS

Good sentences follow these characteristics:

- Accurately exhibit one of four structures: simple, compound, complex, or compound-complex
- Use strong words, including specific nouns and verbs
- Include variety in their beginnings, structure, and length
- Use parallel structures for parallel ideas
- Put the main idea in the main clause and subordinate ideas in subordinate clauses
- Place the most important idea at the end, the second most important idea at the beginning, and tuck other information in the middle
- Follow the rules of grammar, mechanics, and usage

STEP 1   **Building Basic Sentences**

Sentences are built using one of four structures:

Simple. A simple sentence has a subject and verb. Either may be compound, and both may have words and phrases that modify them. For example:

The pad fell.
> Simple sentence; subject *pad*, verb *fell*

The red personalized mouse pad fell off the desk and onto the floor.
> Subject: *pad*
> Verb: *fell*
> Words modifying the subject: *the, red, personalized, mouse*
> Phrases modifying the verb: *off the desk, onto the floor*

The mouse pad and mouse fell off the desk.
> Compound subjects: *pad* and *mouse*
> Verb: *fell*
> Words modifying the subject: *the, mouse*
> Phrases modifying the verb: *off the desk*

Compound. A compound sentence is made of two simple sentences joined together. A comma marks where the two simple sentences are joined. For example:

The mouse pad fell on the floor, and the mouse landed on top.
> First simple sentence: *The mouse pad fell on the floor.*
> Second simple sentence: *The mouse landed on top.*

Complex. A complex sentence is a simple sentence with a subordinate clause added. [*See Part IV, Section C:* Phrases and Clauses *for explanations about subordinate clauses.*] For example:

The mouse pad fell on the floor when the cat jumped on the desk.
> Simple sentence: *The mouse pad fell on the floor.*
> Subordinate clause: *when the cat jumped on the desk*

Compound-Complex. A compound-complex sentence has two simple sentences and at least one subordinate clause. For example:

When the cat jumped on the desk, the mouse pad fell on the floor, and the mouse landed on top.
> First simple sentence: *The mouse pad fell on the floor.*
> Second simple sentence: *The mouse landed on top.*
> Subordinate clause: *when the cat jumped on the desk*

STEP 2   **Choosing Strong Words**

Any sentence structure is strengthened by strong words. Consider these suggestions:

Use strong nouns and verbs in order to eliminate wordy adjectives and adverbs.

Don't write:
> The young boy walked slowly across the yard.

Instead write:
> The toddler inched his way across the yard.

Use more action verbs than linking verbs. [*See definitions and examples for both in the Glossary.*]

Don't write:
> He was tall and handsome.

Instead write:
> The tall, handsome man caught her eye.

Use active voice more frequently than passive voice. [*See definitions and examples of each in the Glossary.*]

Don't write:
   The child was bitten by a snake.

Instead write:
   A snake bit the child.

Use figurative language for creative sentences. [*See figure of speech in the Glossary.*]

Don't write:
   She ran home as quickly as she could.

Instead write:
   She flew home like the wind.

STEP 3   Varying Sentences

Repeated sentence structures, no matter how good, bore your reader. Variety, as the cliché goes, is the spice of life; so spice up your writing accordingly. Follow these suggestions:

Vary sentence beginnings. If every sentence begins with the subject that is followed by the verb, you create monotony. Instead, begin sentences with these common variations:

- With a prepositional phrase, such as *After dinner last night....*
- With a participial phrase, such as *Walking home alone....*
- With an infinitive phrase, such as *To put her best foot forward....*
- With an adverb clause, such as *After we ate dinner last night....*
- With an introductory word, such as *Yes....*
- With a transitional word, such as *Thus....*
- With a transitional phrase, such as *No matter the results....*

Commas usually follow these kinds of introductory phrases and clauses. [*Check the rules for commas in Part IV, Section D.*]
[*To learn more about phrases and clauses, study Part IV, Section C.*]

Vary sentence structure. Consider these variations:

- If you use predominantly simple sentences, your message seems simple (and if your audience is young readers, that may be your intent).

- If you use mostly compound-complex sentences, your message seems complicated and difficult to understand.
- If you use a mixture of sentence structures, you can create emphasis. Put the many background details in a series of compound, complex, and compound-complex sentences; put the conclusion in a simple sentence. The simple sentence packs emphasis. (Compare these last two sentences for an example.)

Vary sentence lengths. Consider two examples of the power of varied lengths:

- A series of very short sentences surrounded by longer sentences can create a staccato-like rhythm that hits hard. For example:

  We hoped for gorgeous weather during our two-week vacation to the beach. We wanted sun. We wanted hot. We wanted breeze. Unfortunately, we wanted more than Mother Nature would give us.

- Long sentences followed by a single short one generally build to a powerful emphasis. Consider the following:

  The two candidates spoke eloquently about preserving the environment, including legislating wetlands protection and national and state forest protection. According to their messages, environmentally minded voters could cast their votes for either candidate and find satisfaction. One message was false.

STEP 4   Using Parallel Structures

When you have a series of parallel ideas, write sentences that put those ideas in parallel structure:

We wanted sun. We wanted hot. We wanted breeze.
Various passersby offered to drive her home, to change the flat tire, or to call a cab.

STEP 5   Placing Ideas

For the clearest message and greatest emphasis, place ideas in sentences according to their importance. Put the main idea in the main clause, and subordinate ideas in subordinate clauses. For example,

Don't write:
Because Marty hoped to find the floral delivery person at her door, she smiled when the doorbell rang.

Instead write:

> When the doorbell rang, Marty hoped to find the floral delivery person at her door.

STEP 6   Placing Important Words

Any public speaker, advertiser, or coach will tell you that the last word spoken is the most important. The last word of a speech lingers on the listener's ear just a few seconds longer than those words that came before. The last word on a television or radio commercial (usually the product name) floats just a bit in the listener's mind. And when the coach sends the team out to the playing field, it's with a command to give it their best.

The most important word in any sentence is the last. So be sure to put *your* most important word last! The second most important is the first. The rest tends to get buried in the middle.

Don't write:

> I was sure, with the telltale signs throughout the house, that Brian had been there.

Instead write:

> Telltale signs proved Brian had been in the house.

Using these steps will help you consciously control your own sentences and build a solid foundation into everything you write.

WRITING A PARAGRAPH

Writers use paragraphs to group their thoughts and to help the reader follow those groups of thoughts. While the paragraph can stand alone as a unit of writing, it is frequently combined with other paragraphs to create a larger work.

The paragraph that stands alone is written somewhat differently than one that is a building block for a longer piece of writing. [*See* Writing a Multi-Paragraph Paper *later in this part for a discussion of paragraphs as building blocks in a longer paper*.] Certain characteristics almost always appear in the standalone paragraph.

CHARACTERISTICS

The following elements appear in a standalone paragraph:

- A subject narrowed sufficiently to be treated as a single idea.
- A topic sentence that announces the subject of the paragraph (often appearing as the first sentence, though it may appear later).

- A specific and consistent attitude toward the subject [*see Step 3 in* Prewriting *earlier in Part I*].
- Supporting details that explain or illustrate the topic sentence.
- Transitions that bridge the details to each other and to the topic sentence [*see* transitions *in the Glossary*].
- A concluding statement that shows the writer's completed thoughts.

STEP 1   Writing a Topic Sentence

As a result of the prewriting process, you have a topic, either chosen or assigned. Be certain your topic is narrow enough to be developed in a single paragraph. [*Review* Prewriting *earlier in this part for tips on narrowing a subject.*] Next, write a topic sentence. As the name implies, a topic sentence states the topic of a paragraph. Compare your topic sentence with the following examples:

Too Broad:

Guitar music offers a variety of sounds.

Improved:

The bass-guitar accompaniment in this composition offers real challenges, even for an accomplished guitarist.

Too Broad:

Some students enjoy participating in peer social groups.

Improved:

I enjoy participating in the annual sorority Spring Sports Fling.

Too Broad:

Senator Joe Glick deserves to be reelected.

Still Too Broad:

Because of his stand on environmental issues, Senator Joe Glick deserves the support of environmentally concerned voters.

Improved:

Senator Glick's stand on the issue of acid rain helps voters understand his general attitude toward environmental issues.

STEP 2   Selecting Subtopics

Adequate supporting details yield a good paragraph. Usually the support comes in the form of subtopics: reasons, causes, examples, illustrations, steps, comparisons, differences, or other explanations. No magic number of supporting details makes a perfect paragraph; the details, added together, must clarify the topic and leave the reader satisfied.

In order to think through the logical subdivisions of your topic, divide either the subject or the predicate of your topic sentence. [*See* subject *and* predicate *in the Glossary*.] For instance, consider the following examples and notice from which part of the topic sentence the accompanying subtopics come.

Topic Sentence:
Utility bills seem to reflect household activities.

Subtopics:
Bills rise when school is out for the summer.
Bills rise when school is out for spring recess.
Bills rise during the winter holiday season.

Note that the subtopics divide the parts of the predicate referring to household activities.

Topic Sentence:
Getting away from it all makes primitive camping a preferred vacation for many.

Subtopics:
getting away from news media
getting away from telephones
getting away from job responsibilities
getting away from household responsibilities

Here, note that the subtopics divide the part of the subject referring to getting away from it all.

Jot down evidence or ideas to support your topic. Use words, phrases, or complete sentences in order to get your ideas on paper. Your list may look something like this:

Topic Sentence:
Pulling out of the water on skis requires complex muscular coordination.

Subtopics:
squatting position, ski tips out of the water, rope between knees
back muscles lean against boat's power
leg muscles keep skis in position
arm muscles give balance against towrope as rise to standing position

These four subtopics, each listing some part of the muscular coordination and each explaining the attitude *complex*, will make up the main points of the paragraph.

Hint: If you have difficulty dividing your topic, reexamine the topic sentence. It may be too narrow or too broad.

STEP 3   **Arranging the Details**

Next, arrange your list in some kind of logical order: chronological, spatial, or an order of importance. [*See entries for each in the Glossary.*] For example, the details about the water skier in the preceding step are arranged chronologically, the order in which the skier must react.

Number the items on your list in the order in which you will write about them.

STEP 4   **Developing the Notes**

Using the organized list of details from Step 3, you should be able to develop the paragraph quickly. Follow these steps:

- Begin with the topic sentence unless you have a good reason for saving it until later. Note these possible reasons:
  - If an introductory statement is necessary, the topic sentence may follow the brief introduction, which should include an attention-getter.
  - If you address a highly controversial subject, the topic sentence may work better as the conclusion, when readers are more likely to accept your idea.
  - If the paragraph builds to a surprise, the topic sentence may appear at the end.
  - The topic sentence may never appear but only be implied. Be cautious if you use this approach that the topic sentence is clearly implied; otherwise the reader will be left wondering.
- Use an effective transition to move from your topic sentence to the first subtopic or supporting detail. [*See* transitions *in the Glossary.*]
- Use specific supporting details. Show, don't tell, the reader your message. [*See* Description *in Part II for a good explanation of specific details. Also see* Revising: Sample Revision for Specific Detail *later in Part I.*]
- Use good sentence structure and work toward sentence variety and emphasis. Balance long sentences with short, complicated with simple. [*See* Revising: Sample Revision for Sentence Variety *and* Revising: Sample Revision for Emphasis *later in Part I.*]
- Aim for specific word choice appropriate for the audience. [*See* Revising: Sample Revision for Specific Detail *later in Part I.*]
- Use effective transitions to move on to additional supporting details. [*See* Revising: Sample Revision for Transition *in Part I.*]

- Maintain consistency, both in verb tense and point of view. [*See* point of view *and* tense *in the Glossary. Also see Step 5 in* Revising *later in Part I for additional details on checking consistency.*]
- Conclude with an effective clincher or ending statement. Some paragraphs can end with a final statement that merely finishes the final subtopic rather than with a true clincher sentence. The reader, however, must have a sense of completion and not be left to feel that the writer simply quit.

SAMPLE INDEPENDENT PARAGRAPH

The following paragraph, written as an independent composition, serves as a sample for analysis for this section. You can find numerous examples of other independent paragraphs throughout Parts II and III.

From Sitting to Standing

Pulling out of the water on skis requires complex muscular coordination. The simplest part of the coordinated effort occurs when the skier positions himself on his skis behind the towboat. He assumes a squatting position, toes of the skis just above the water's surface, and the towrope between his knees. As the towboat idles forward to keep the towrope taut, the skier uses both leg and body muscles to keep himself in a ready position, squarely behind the skis. All muscles work against the steady pull. Then, as the towboat accelerates, back muscles work together with leg muscles, and the skier leans against the boat's power. As the pull intensifies, muscles from the toes to the hips work to keep the skis parallel, pointed forward, tips above the surface. Finally, the towboat's full thrust tests the skier's arm muscles. With his skis climbing to a plane and his body rising above the water, the skier must flex his arms to provide a counter-balance against the lessening drag behind the towrope, thus pulling himself to a standing position. Once a skier experiences this complex muscular coordination, it is like that for riding a bicycle: It comes without thinking and never leaves.

 Analysis of the Sample Independent Paragraph. The preceding sample represents a good independent paragraph. While paragraph structure can vary widely, the following typical characteristics appear:

- A topic sentence begins the paragraph.
- Four subtopics divide the topic sentence predicate and emphasize the attitude complex.
- Each subtopic provides specific details to help the non-skier understand the complexity of the muscular coordination.

- Sentences vary both in length (from seven words to 38 words) and complexity (from simple to compound-complex).
- Transitions connect the subtopic sentences into a smoothly flowing paragraph.
- The concluding statement refers back to the topic sentence and suggests the longevity of the experience.

For additional examples, read other independent paragraphs and their accompanying analyses in Parts II and III.

WRITING A MULTI-PARAGRAPH PAPER

Multi-paragraph papers, often called *themes*, use any method of development suitable to the topic. [*See* development, methods of, *in the Glossary*.] They usually contain an introductory paragraph, a concluding paragraph, and separate body paragraphs for each main idea of the thesis. Because they often follow a rather formal structure, themes typify expository writing.

A theme is frequently the traditional five-paragraph paper; yet themes may contain as few as two and as many as several dozen paragraphs. Because the five-paragraph theme readily illustrates the concept, this section will treat it as the model. [*Sample papers throughout Parts II and III illustrate themes of varying lengths*.]

CHARACTERISTICS

The five-paragraph theme represents a common denominator among the various kinds of expository writing. In general, a theme

- contains an introductory paragraph, three body paragraphs, and a concluding paragraph,
- begins with an introductory paragraph that includes any one of a number of devices to attract reader attention [*see* attention-getter *in the Glossary*],
- concludes the introductory paragraph with a thesis sentence that states or implies the topics to be developed in each of the body paragraphs,
- shows in the thesis sentence the order in which the body paragraphs will be developed,
- includes a separate body paragraph for each main idea,
- includes in each body paragraph a topic sentence derived directly from the thesis sentence,
- relies on careful use of transitional words and phrases to connect ideas within and between paragraphs,

- employs, on occasion, transitional sentences to connect ideas between paragraphs,
- follows a logical plan, using any one of the orders of development [*see* order, in paragraph development *in the Glossary*],
- concludes with a paragraph that summarizes, emphasizes, or otherwise brings the paper to a satisfying end,
- includes the characteristics peculiar to the chosen method of development [*see Part II for* Analogy, Cause and Effect, Classification, Comparison and Contrast, Definition, Description, Narration, Opinion, Persuasion, *and* Process Analysis].

Shorter or longer themes include many of the same characteristics, but they follow somewhat different patterns. Listed in the paragraphs that follow are characteristics peculiar to themes of different lengths.

The two-paragraph theme includes a brief introduction, thesis sentence, and supporting details for the first main idea in its first paragraph. The second paragraph includes supporting details for the second main idea and a concluding sentence. [*See Sample for Social Sciences in* Definition *in Part II for an example.*]

The three-paragraph theme begins with a paragraph containing a brief introduction, a thesis sentence, and supporting details for the first main idea. The second paragraph develops the second main idea. The third paragraph develops the third main idea and adds a concluding statement. [*See Sample for English in* Classification, *and Sample for Science in* Process Analysis *in Part II, and Sample for a Poem* in Literary Analyses *in Part III for examples.*]

The four-paragraph theme usually contains two main ideas. It follows the same pattern as the five-paragraph theme but develops only two body paragraphs. The introductory paragraph concludes with the thesis sentence; each of the two body paragraphs develops a main idea; the concluding paragraph summarizes or reiterates the main ideas and refers back to the original thesis. [*See Sample for Science in* Classification *and Sample Work-Place Writing in* Comparison and Contrast, *both in Part II, for examples.*]

The six-paragraph theme also follows the basic pattern of the five-paragraph theme but develops four body paragraphs. [*See Sample for Social Sciences in* Classification *and Sample Work-Place Writing in* Process Analysis, *both in Part II, for examples.*]

The longer paper, a paper with more than six paragraphs, follows the basic pattern of the five-paragraph theme but develops more complicated main ideas. Even when a paper has only three main ideas, more paragraphs may be required for support purposes. In addition, a longer paper may also include paragraphs that serve only as transitions (that is, the paragraphs summarize the ideas presented to that point and so lead into the next idea). [*For examples and more thorough discussions of longer papers, see Sample for a Symbol in* Literary Analyses, *the sample paper in* Research Paper, *and the sample lab report in* Technical Report, *all in Part III.*]

STEP 1   **Choosing the Focus**

You must decide what you want to say about your topic. For instance, if you write about your favorite hobby, building model gliders, you must decide what to emphasize. Do you want to focus on the skill that making gliders requires? How you became involved with them? Why you build them? Their aerodynamics? How to paint them? Flying them? Narrowing your subject in this way will help give you a manageable topic.

Having narrowed your topic, like *how to paint model gliders*, decide next how to explain things to the reader. In other words, how do you want to treat your subject? Do you want to describe the process of painting gliders? [*See* Process Analysis *in Part II.*] Do you want to describe common designs and patterns? [*See* Description *in Part II.*] Do you want to compare painting methods? [*See* Comparison and Contrast *in Part II.*] Can you best support your topic by analogy? [*See* Analogy *in Part II.*] Will the reader understand your topic better if you classify the various kinds of painting? [*See* Classification *in Part II.*]

Most writers decide by making lists of approaches, ideas, examples, or illustrations.

So, select your focus and make a list of the points you want to make. Your list may look something like this:

Narrowed topic:
> How to paint model gliders

Ideas:
> Use startling over/under patterns
> Use humorous color combinations
> Use simple two-tone combinations

Complete your list before going on to Step 2.

STEP 2   **Writing the Thesis Sentence**

The thesis sentence states each of the major topics in a multi-paragraph paper. It has two characteristics:

- It states or suggests the topics of each of the body paragraphs. Thus, a five-paragraph theme will have a thesis sentence suggesting three ideas.
- It states or implies the order in which the ideas will appear. In other words, the subtopic appearing first in the thesis sentence appears in the first body paragraph.

Consider these sample thesis sentences:

A diamond broker must have expertise in color, clarity, and cut.
A serious bird watcher knows to search for birds according to their habitat, foraging habits, and nesting sites.
Whether in spring, summer, autumn, or winter, hiking in the Red River Valley offers challenges.

Develop the list from Step 1 into a thesis sentence. Then compare with the following examples:

A model-glider builder may paint a simple two-tone combination, but a more creative builder will develop a startling over-under pattern or even a humorous color combination.

Three points:

1. two-tone combination
2. over-under pattern
3. humorous combination

Working with pets requires tedious daily routines, occasionally heartbreaking responsibilities, and frequent loving attention.

Three points:

1. tedious daily routines
2. occasionally heartbreaking responsibilities
3. frequent loving attention

A diamond broker must have expertise in color, clarity, and cut.

Three points:

1. color
2. clarity
3. cut

Note that each example includes three points. Each point will become the subject of a body paragraph. Revise your thesis sentence as suggested by reading these models.

STEP 3   Choosing the Order

In organizing paragraphs and themes, writers use one of three orders: spatial, chronological, or order of importance.

Spatial order presents topics as they appear in space: left to right, top to bottom, front to back. Useful transitional phrases in a left-to-right spatial order would include:

At the far left...
Next to that...
Near the center...
Just right of center...
At the far right...

Chronological order presents topics as they appear in time. Useful transitions include:

Yesterday...
Late last evening...
This morning...
An hour ago...
Now...

Orders of importance present topics in one of three ways:
From most to least important
From least to most important
From second most, through least important, to most important

Useful transitional phrases include:
One important idea...
Less important but equally interesting...
Another important factor...
Most importantly...

Select the order you think best. If necessary, rearrange your thesis sentence to reflect this order. For instance, you may have written a thesis sentence arranged chronologically, from winter to spring to summer, like this:

The refuge attracts a wide variety of visitors during the hunting season, during the fishing season, and during the birdwatching season.

You may decide, however, that you can write more effectively if you describe visitors according to what brings most of them to the refuge. So you rewrite the thesis sentence like this, arranging your subtopics from the least to the most popular reasons for visiting:

The refuge attracts visitors during the birdwatching season, during the hunting season, but most of all during the fishing season.

STEP 4   Writing the Topic Sentences

With the thesis sentence in place, you can easily write a topic sentence for each body paragraph. Study the following:

> **Thesis sentence:**
> Caring for pets requires tedious daily chores, sometimes heartbreaking tasks, and loving attention.
>
> **Topic sentence for first body paragraph:**
> Tedious chores are necessary for a pet's good health and demand daily routines.
>
> **Topic sentence for second body paragraph:**
> Caring for a sick or injured pet can be heartbreaking and demands even more time than the normal routines.
>
> **Topic sentence for third body paragraph:**
> The joy of pet care lies in the constant loving attention owner and pet heap upon each other.

Using this as a guide, develop topic sentences for each of your body paragraphs. With their completion, your theme will be well under way.

STEP 5   Selecting the Method of Development

A theme can be developed in at least a dozen ways. Choose any of the methods included in this handbook [*see* development, methods of, *in the Glossary*] or any combination of methods. Each body paragraph may follow a different method. Use the one most appropriate to the subject and purpose.

Make a tentative list of the method(s) you will use in each body paragraph.

For the pet care example earlier in this section, the list might appear as follows:

> **First body paragraph**
> Method of development: *description (daily chores)*
> Organization: *chronological order*
>
> **Second body paragraph**
> Method of development: *cause and effect (pet's illness or injury and resulting care)*
> Organization: *order of importance*
>
> **Third body paragraph**
> Method of development: *comparison (pet's point of view and owner's point of view)*
> Organization: *order of importance*

STEP 6   **Drafting the First Attempt: The Introduction**

Some writers prefer to begin writing with the introductory paragraph. Others prefer to begin with the body paragraphs. Use whichever method suits you.

No matter when you write it, your introduction must attract the reader's attention and set the tone for the paper. You may choose to use one of the following approaches:

- Say something startling, either by making a statement or by giving statistics. For example:

  To form one cubic inch of stalactite, that stone icicle found hanging from cave ceilings, nature requires about 100 years.

  This statistic startles the reader who has seen stalactites the diameter of a human body dropping 20 or more feet from a cave ceiling.

- Describe a compelling scene or situation:

  One week before St. Patrick's Day, the plane touched down at London's Heathrow International Airport. A train was there to take the tour group to Devonshire, the land of rolling hills and centuries-old stone fences. Settled into their coaches, the group relaxed and let busy London glide past them as they slipped into something more comfortable—the rural, pastoral English spring.

  The scene helps the reader identify with the mood and perhaps arouses some curiosity. What happens to the tour group?

- Refer to an event, either historical or current, perhaps in the form of a story or conversation:

  A year ago today, Jerrod Hunt graduated from high school. He and his friends celebrated even before the formal ceremony, but the real celebration came afterward. Today, Jerrod is trying desperately to learn to walk again.

  The reader anticipates what has happened to Jerrod.

- Show a controversy, contradiction, or unusual opinion.

  Despite computerized technology and presorted, zip-coded mail, most of us open an envelope with a handwritten address first.

  A contradiction is posed between technology and the personal touch.

- Ask a question:

  What keeps woodpeckers from destroying their brains when they pound relentlessly on wood?

  A thought-provoking question is asked about a common occurrence.

- Use a quotation, adage, or proverb:

  It's not what you know but who you know.

  The reader wonders whether the writer will agree or disagree with this adage.

Other methods will serve as well. These offer a place to start.

Finally, conclude your introductory paragraph with the thesis sentence.

STEP 7   **Drafting the First Attempt: The Body**

In Step 4, you wrote topic sentences for the three body paragraphs of the theme. Now write a transition that will move readers from the thesis sentence of the introduction to the topic sentence of the first body paragraph. [*See* Revising *later in Part I for a discussion of types of transitional devices*.] The topic sentence may be the first sentence of the paragraph and include the transitional device, or it may appear later in the paragraph. In either case, develop the first paragraph using the method of development that seems most appropriate. Conclude the first paragraph with a reference to the topic sentence or with a clincher statement.

Next, develop the second body paragraph. Again, begin with a transition. Develop the topic with adequate supporting details. Add a conclusion.

Develop the third body paragraph in the same manner.

In summary, body paragraphs should have the following characteristics:

- An opening transition that connects it to the preceding paragraph
- A topic sentence derived from the thesis sentence
- Supporting details, such as explanations, illustrations, examples, or reasons, to clarify the topic sentence
- Internal transitions to carry the reader's thought from one supporting detail to another
- A final statement, or conclusion, which may also act as a transition into the following paragraph

STEP 8   Drafting the First Attempt: The Conclusion

A transitional device must connect the final body paragraph with the conclusion. The conclusion itself should summarize or reemphasize the main idea; it will probably also refer to the thesis sentence. But most importantly it should refer to the attention-getter used in the introductory paragraph. This approach gives the best sense of completeness, a feeling of having seen the full picture.

SAMPLE MULTI-PARAGRAPH PAPER

The following five-paragraph theme includes the traditional introductory paragraph, three body paragraphs, and a concluding paragraph. Once you have finished your own theme, compare its structure with the one following.

Land of the Free and the Wild

A great horned owl hoots across the quiet water and then glides through the stand of bald cypress along the eastern side of the swamp. Whip-poor-wills call; bullfrogs croak; mosquitoes hum. Darkness creeps across the swamp. Hovey Lake, Indiana's cypress swamp, protected as a wildlife refuge, greets visitors with night sounds common to the uncommon 1,400-acre environment. Offering a different set of treats every season, the refuge attracts a wide variety of visitors during the hunting season, during the fishing season, and during the birdwatching season.

Because the swamp is situated along the Mississippi flyway, it offers refuge to 40,000 to 50,000 waterfowl each winter. Canada geese far outnumber other waterfowl, but snow geese, blue geese, and occasionally white-fronted geese winter there, too. Nearly every variety of duck, diver and puddle, reside in the quiet, smaller sloughs. As a result, the swamp attracts hunters in early winter, goose hunters to the pits and duck hunters to the blinds. The hunters' closely regulated success is the result of hundreds of acres of corn left standing by Posey County farmers, who rent the rich bottom land between the lake and the river by sealed bid. The farmers' contracts require them to leave 25 percent of the harvest as food for the thousands of waterfowl, encouraging them to stay. The encouragement works, much to the hunters' delight.

In spring, however, the fishermen replace the hunters on Hovey Lake waters. Attracted by the spring crappie run, fishermen haul in hefty stringers of slabs and return to fish for bluegill. Evening campfires turn skillets full of fresh fillets into plates full of succulent morsels. Then sunrise sends the bass fishermen scurrying to secret waters, some to return with empty bags. One fisherman, however, boats three, one weighing in at eight pounds two ounces. Later in the day, a few trotlines yield spoonbill catfish, those prehistoric monsters weighing 30 pounds or more, as long as a man is tall. In late afternoon or early evening, a jug fisherman occasionally bags perch, catfish, or even a wily gar, long, slender, and sharp-toothed. Spring moves into summer, and summer moves into autumn. Only then, when the lake is closed for waterfowl migration, do the fishermen leave.

The most experienced hunters and fishermen at Hovey Lake, however, are not human. They are avian. Boasting a greater variety of bird life than almost any other spot in Indiana, the swamp attracts bird watchers twelve months a year from a dozen states. With powerful binoculars, they scan the bald cypress trees and standing dead timber, known to attract woodpeckers, including the pileated, red-headed, red-breasted, downy, and hairy. Other tree dwellers, from grumpy-looking owls to scurrying swifts, stake out territory in the swamp growth. During the warbler migration, the trees house whole orchestras, but the prothonotary warbler stays most of the summer, flashing yellow among the yew-like lower branches of the cypress. Flocks of martins, cowbirds, and grackles fly in and out seasonally. In the more inaccessible parts of the swamp, the great blue herons and great white egrets wade the shallows near one of the last stands of bamboo-like cane this far north or perch high in treetops from which they can see the Ohio River. In winter, the bald eagles and ospreys soar among the thousands of geese and ducks, surely a testimony to the value of this wildlife sanctuary.

Boasting none of the amenities of modern campgrounds, Hovey Lake nevertheless attracts 90,000 visitors a year, visitors who hunt and fish and watch the birds. They come to appreciate the swamp for what it is, a precious ecological system struggling to survive man's intrusion. They hear the owls, the whip-poor-wills, the frogs, even the mosquitoes, and know that in the chain of this uncommon swamp life, every link must stay intact.

 Analysis of Sample Multi-Paragraph Paper. The sample illustrates the basic characteristics of the five-paragraph theme. Note the following specifics, broken down by paragraph.

In the first paragraph:

- The introduction uses the attention-getter to set the scene. The reader will readily identify with the lure of the swamp.
- The thesis sentence appears as the last sentence, to which the paragraph has led smoothly.
- The thesis sentence names the topics of the three body paragraphs in the order in which they will be discussed.

In the second paragraph:

- A long introduction and series of transitional devices precede the fourth, the topic sentence.
- Supporting details explain why the hunters come and are successful.
- The concluding sentence refers back to the topic sentence and ties together the ideas in the paragraph.

In the third paragraph:

- The first sentence serves as both a transition and a topic sentence.
- The supporting details show the kinds of fishing and the kinds of fish without giving the reader the feeling of reading a list.
- The concluding sentence shows the fishermen leaving.

In the fourth paragraph:

- Two sentences of transition tie the description of hunters and fishermen to that of the birds.
- The third sentence serves as the topic sentence.
- Supporting details are piled one after another to emphasize the variety of bird life. The writer finds no need to repeat the information given about waterfowl in the first body paragraph.
- The concluding sentence in the last body paragraph ties together not only the paragraph but the general idea as well.

In the fifth paragraph:

- The reference to the thesis sentence does not simply repeat the thesis.
- Reference is also made to the scenic description of the introductory paragraph, concluding with an analogy between the uncommon environment and a chain.

Note, too, some characteristics about the writing style:

- The method of organization emphasizes the writer's message. The writer clearly thinks wildlife preservation to be more important than hunting and fishing; thus, his last body paragraph deals with birdwatching, and his conclusion carries an ecological message.
- Organization within the paper is roughly seasonal, moving from winter (hunting) to spring (fishing), summer (fishing), and autumn (fishing); references to all-season birdwatching round out the structure.
- Within the paragraph on fishing, the organization is chronological from evening to evening.
- In the birdwatching paragraph, the writer follows the birds from spring to winter (though perhaps only someone familiar with migratory birds would recognize the organization).
- The writer employs specific, concrete language, including strong verbs.

- Good sentence variety is evident throughout, from three-word sentences to lengthy, complicated sentences with multiple appositives and subordinate clauses.
- Figures of speech enhance the quality of the writing. [*See* figure of speech *in the Glossary*.]
- The paper maintains unity throughout, offering only details directly related to the topic.
- The paper includes dozens of descriptive and factual details to help the reader "see" the writer's point of view. [*See* imagery *in the Glossary*.]

The characteristics and process described here along with the model and analysis should help you write a dynamic theme. In addition you will want to refer to the sections describing specific kinds of themes in order to take advantage of the various methods of development illustrated. [*Additional examples of multi-paragraph papers are to be found throughout Parts II and III*.]

Revising

You have finished the prewriting and writing steps. You have learned how to write good sentences, good paragraphs, and good multi-paragraph papers. Now you are ready to learn to revise.

During the process of revising, the really tough part of writing takes place. True, you have worked hard to write your paper, and now you are merely making changes. The writing that occurs during the revision process, however, makes a mediocre paper a good paper. Revision adds variety, emphasis, coherence, transition, and detail. Revision eliminates wordiness, irrelevancies, and inconsistencies. Revision polishes, hones, and perfects. Thus, most professional writers agree that the real work comes in the revising. It's where they spend the bulk of their time.

So what happens in the process of revising? A writer looks at virtually everything involved in the process of writing: structure, organization, and emphasis. He thinks about ways to make his paper more interesting, either by content or by structure.

In this section, you look at the parts of revision one at a time. As you revise any paper, follow not only the suggestions for revision for that particular kind of paper as outlined in the respective sections of

Parts II or III, but make sure you consider each of these general revision principles as well.

Cross-references are listed in most of the following steps. Thus, if you need additional information, you will know where to look.

STEP 1   **Checking Structure: Multi-Paragraph Papers**

If you have written a multi-paragraph paper, ask yourself the following questions to check its structure:

- Does the multi-paragraph paper begin with an introductory paragraph that includes an attention-getting device? [*See* Writing a Multi-Paragraph Paper *earlier in Part I and* attention-getter *in the Glossary*.]
- Does the paper include a thesis sentence? [*See* Writing a Multi-Paragraph Paper *earlier in Part I for a thorough discussion of effective thesis sentences and their development*.]
- Does the thesis sentence state or imply the content of each of the body paragraphs that follow it?
- Does the thesis sentence establish the order of the body paragraphs?
- Does the theme maintain unity throughout?
- Are there adequate transitional devices to connect the paragraphs? [*See* Sample Revision for Transition *later in this section*.]
- Does the theme follow a logical order? Do the body paragraphs follow a logical order? [*See* order, in paragraph development, *in the Glossary*.]
- Does the conclusion reflect the thesis sentence and offer a summary, final statement, or final observation that relates to the thesis sentence?

As you examine your paper's structure, also think specifically about its development. Ask yourself these questions:

- Have I used the most logical and effective means of development? [*See the methods of development detailed in Part II, or check a quick definition in* development, methods of, *in the Glossary*.]
- Are there additional methods of development that may add more specificity to my paper and help the reader better understand my point?

STEP 2   Checking Structure: Paragraphs

If you have written only a single paragraph, you must examine the paragraph structure as a single unit of composition. If you have written a theme, you must examine the theme structure in terms of individual paragraphs.

As you examine the structure of a paragraph, whether as a single unit of composition or as part of a larger composition, ask yourself the following kinds of questions:

- Does my paragraph include a topic sentence, either stated or implied? [*See* Writing a Paragraph *earlier in Part I for a discussion of effective topic sentences.*]
- If the paragraph is part of a multi-paragraph paper, does it begin with a transitional word, phrase, or sentence to tie it in with the previous paragraph? [*See* Sample Revision for Transition *later in this section.*]
- Does my paragraph include sufficient specific details that support or explain the topic sentence? [*For an example, see* Sample Revision for Specific Detail *later in Part I.*]
- Have I used the most appropriate means of developing that paragraph? [*You can use any means of development as described in Part II or any combination of these methods. For a quick reference, see* development, methods of, *in the Glossary.*]
- Have I included specific rather than abstract details? [*See* abstract *and* specific detail *in the Glossary. Also see* Sample Revision for Specific Detail *later in this part.*]
- Have I maintained unity throughout my paragraph? That is, have I included any material that does not directly support the topic sentence? [*See* Sample Revision for Unity *later in Part I.*]
- Does my paragraph follow a logical method of organization? [*See* order, in paragraph development, *in the Glossary.*]
- Have I included adequate transitional devices to connect the ideas within the paragraph? [*See* Sample Revision for Transition *later in this part.*]
- Does my paragraph end with a clincher or concluding statement?

STEP 3   Checking Structure: Sentences

Finally, no matter whether you have written a multi-paragraph paper or a single paragraph, you want to check the sentence structure. Ask yourself the following questions:

- Have I included a variety of sentence types? Simple sentences? Compound sentences? Complex sentences? Compound-complex sentences? [*See* Writing Sentences *earlier in Part I and* Sample Revision for Sentence Variety *later in Part I.*]
- Do my sentences begin in a variety of ways? For instance, do some sentences start with the subject while others start with an introductory phrase or introductory clause? [*See* Writing Sentences *earlier in Part I.*]
- Have I used a variety of modification structures? [*See* Writing Sentences *earlier in Part I.*]
- Do my sentences vary in length? A mere word count gives a quick answer. Because many writers tend to write sentences of similar length, varying the length usually requires a conscious effort.

Another means of adding strength to sentences is to choose specific details and use strong nouns and verbs. In an effort to check your work for strength, ask yourself these questions:

- Have I used specific words, the most precise words for the purpose? [*See* Revision for Specific Detail *later in this part.*]
- Have I used strong, specific nouns instead of weak, general ones? Have I talked about a 15-year-old star on the girls' cross-country team as opposed to a high-school athlete?
- Have I used strong, specific verbs as opposed to weak, general ones? Have I said, for instance, *The dog loped across the yard*, instead of *The dog walked across the yard*?
- Have I omitted excessive adjectives and adverbs that could be replaced with stronger nouns and verbs? For instance, instead of saying, *He walked slowly*, have I said, *He ambled*?
- Have I used active-voice as opposed to passive-voice verbs? [*See* active voice *and* passive voice *in the Glossary and in Part IV, Section A,* Verbs.] Of course, under certain circumstances, passive voice is preferable. Those special circumstances appear in the discussion of those respective writing samples in Part III, especially in technical writing and in instances when the doer of a deed is unknown.

- Have I, wherever possible, substituted strong action verbs for weak linking verbs? [*See* action verb *and* linking verb *in the Glossary and in Part IV, Section A,* Verbs.]
- Have I used appropriate vocabulary for the subject? Is the language too technical for my audience? Is it technical enough to be appropriate for the subject? Have I avoided colloquial and slang expressions? [*See* colloquial expression *and* slang *in the Glossary*.] Have I avoided other expressions too informal for the subject or the audience?
- Have I avoided trite expressions? [*See* trite *in the Glossary*.]
- Have I included figures of speech and imagery wherever appropriate to show maturity in writing and to add reader interest? [*See* figure of speech *and* imagery *in the Glossary*.]

Finally, check your sentences for wordiness. The most powerful papers make significant points in few words. [*See* Sample Revision for Wordiness *later in this part*.] Think about every sentence, phrase, and word. Are you repeating yourself? Do you say *free gift*? What other kind of gift is there? Do you say *hot water heater*? There is no cold water heater. Do you refer to *Easter Sunday*? Is there an Easter Thursday? Be critical of your writing as you study every word. Eliminate excess.

STEP 4   **Checking Emphasis**

In addition to structure and organization, look at your paper for proper emphasis. [*See* emphasis, in sentences *in the Glossary for a quick reference, and see* Sample Revision for Emphasis *later in this part*.] Emphasis begins at the sentence level. If sentences carry proper emphasis, chances are the entire paper shows proper emphasis. Ask yourself the following questions about emphasis:

- Do I have the main ideas in the main clauses? [*See* clause, main, *in the Glossary and Part IV, Section C,* Clauses.]
- Do I have supporting ideas in subordinate clauses? [*See* clause, subordinate, *in the Glossary and Part IV, Section C,* Clauses.]
- Have I put the most important ideas at the end of my sentences?
- Are the second most important ideas at the beginning of my sentences?
- Is the information in the middle of the sentences least important or worthy of the least emphasis?

You create special emphasis by using particular structures. For instance, the use of a series establishes a rhythm. Parallel structures, especially, help the reader remember the items in the series. [*See* series *and* parallel structure *in the Glossary*.] Other kinds of structural emphasis can occur, too. As a result, ask yourself the following questions:

- If I have used items in a series, are they structurally parallel?
- If I have listed several items in the course of several sentences, could I improve the listing by putting the items in a parallel series?
- Have I avoided dangling modifiers? [*See* dangling modifier *in the Glossary*.]
- Have I avoided ambiguous modifiers? [*See* ambiguity *in the Glossary*.]

STEP 5   Checking Consistency

The next thing you should check is consistency: consistent point of view and consistent verb tense. [*See* shifts, confusing, *in the Glossary*.] If, for instance, you begin a formal essay with a third-person point of view, you must maintain this point of view throughout. A short story, of course, allows certain options in shifts in point of view [*see* Short Story *in Part III*], but expository writing allows no such shift. The questions you should ask about consistent point of view include the following:

- Have I used the point of view most appropriate for the purpose of my work? For instance, using a second-person point of view results in didactic writing, a style which may not endear you to your audience. A third-person point of view appears more formal, less personal. A first-person point of view is usually reserved for narratives or short stories, usually too informal for classroom work.
- Have I maintained a consistent point of view throughout the writing? Or if I have switched point of view, have I done so with a purpose and within the framework of accuracy and acceptable style?

Next, check for consistent verb tense. For instance, if you began your paper in the present tense, then unless you are using a flashback, you must maintain the present tense throughout the paper.

A NOTE ABOUT THE SAMPLES

Now that you are familiar with the process of revision, study the following samples, which apply some of the more complicated steps above. The examples show changes in specific detail, unity, transition, sentence variety, and emphasis, and then analyze the reasons for these changes. Note that the revisions read more smoothly, with greater clarity and emphasis.

SAMPLE REVISION FOR SPECIFIC DETAIL

The following passage [*an excerpt from the sample paper included in* Writing a Multi-Paragraph Paper *earlier in Part I*] illustrates the difference between a paragraph with and without specific detail.

Original Passage

In spring, the fishermen replace the hunters on Hovey Lake waters. They come to catch big stringers of fish in the early spring. Some are more successful than are others. They use all kinds of methods to try to catch fish. Only when the lake closes do the fishermen leave.

Revised to Add Specific Detail

In spring, the fishermen replace the hunters on Hovey Lake waters. Attracted by the spring crappie run, fishermen haul in hefty stringers of slabs and return to fish for bluegill. Evening campfires turn skillets full of fresh fillets into plates full of succulent morsels. Then sunrise sends the bass fishermen scurrying to secret waters, some to return with empty bags. One fisherman, however, boats three, one weighing in at eight pounds two ounces. Later in the day, a few trot lines yield spoonbill catfish, those prehistoric monsters weighing 30 pounds or more, as long as a man is tall. In later afternoon or early evening, a jug fisherman occasionally bags perch, catfish, or even a wily gar, long, slender, and sharp-toothed. Spring moves into summer, and summer moves into autumn. Only then, when the lake is closed for waterfowl migration, do the fishermen leave.

 Analysis of the Sample Revision for Specific Detail. The original passage omits any reference to specifics. Note the following kinds of revisions:

- Specific kinds of fish are named in the revised passage. Rather than appearing in a list, however, the specific species' names are interwoven with additional details.
- Specific methods of fishing are named.
- Times of day and seasons are named.

- Specific word choice adds detail. Strong verbs such as *haul, boats,* and *bags* as well as specific and colorful nouns such as *stringers, slabs, succulent morsels,* and *monsters* enhance the details.
- Specific size descriptions add detail, including phrases such as *eight pounds two ounces* and *as long as a man is tall.*

SAMPLE REVISION FOR UNITY

The following paragraph lacks unity. The writer fails to stick to his topic as indicated in his topic sentence. Instead, he allows his paragraph to hop from one idea to the next, as if he is reporting the wanderings of his own mind. Each sentence seems to remind him of a new topic! The revised paragraph, however, maintains unity. Every detail supports the topic sentence.

Original Passage

Nearly every community tries to combat the problems pigeons create. While pigeons are docile and provide enjoyment in the parks for those who like to feed them peanuts and popcorn, they also create a health hazard where they most frequently roost. Some experts try simply to change the roosting place. Of course, that only causes the health hazard to relocate. In fact, one year, officials used chicken wire to close off a favorite roosting place; so the pigeons began roosting in our garage. They created not only a health hazard but a financial burden as well. We had to have the car repainted as a result of the frequent stains on the hood. In spite of that, I really like pigeons. In fact, we used to raise pigeons when I was a child. Some of them are quite beautiful, not only because of their colors but also because of the ruffs around their necks or the long feathers along their legs. Of course, these are special breeds. Other special breeds are racing pigeons and those that fly in groups called kits, tumbling and diving to the spectators' delight.

Revised to Maintain Unity

Nearly every community tries to combat the problems pigeons create. While docile pigeons provide enjoyment for those who like to feed them peanuts and popcorn, they also create a health hazard where they most frequently roost. In addition, they deface buildings, monuments, and other public and private properties. To alleviate the problems, some communities erect wire barriers around the pigeons' favorite roosting places. Nearly invisible, the wire tends to be the least offensive relief measure. Other communities try various noisemakers to scare the birds from their roosts. Sirens, clappers, gunshots, and mild explosions send the pigeons on their way. Of course, the noise disturbs human residents as well, so to some the solution seems more unpleasant than the problem. With either means of combating the problem, however, the pigeons simply move elsewhere. As a result, the problem does not go away; it merely relocates.

Analysis of the Sample Revision for Unity. The revised paragraph maintains unity throughout. Note how this happens:

- Every sentence directly supports the subject named in the topic sentence: combating problems pigeons create.
- To establish the link between each sentence and the topic sentence, the revised paragraph uses transitions such as *while, also, in addition, of course,* and so on.
- Repetition of key words or their synonyms, as well as pronouns that refer to those key words, clearly indicate unity: *problem, solution, it, pigeons, they, their.*

No sentence refers to extraneous details that detract from the topic of combating the problems the pigeons create.

SAMPLE REVISION FOR TRANSITION

Transitions are words, phrases, clauses, and sentences that connect ideas. Transitions help the reader understand relationships such as time, space, addition, emphasis, example, comparison-and-contrast, and cause-and-effect. For instance, *consequently* shows effect, *on the other hand* shows contrast, *eventually* shows time, and *in fact* shows emphasis.

Sometimes transitions appear as whole sentences. In that case, they connect major ideas between paragraphs in a full-length paper.

Finally, transitions can be entire paragraphs. In a long paper, such as a research paper, a transition paragraph connects ideas between major points. While a single major point may be supported by several paragraphs, a transition paragraph helps the reader summarize the subtopics before moving to the next major point. In other words, the transition paragraph summarizes what has come before and introduces what is still to come. [*See* Research Paper *in Part III for an example.*]

The following paragraph omits almost all transitions. The revision that follows [*an excerpt from a sample* Opinion *paper in Part II*] illustrates the frequency with which good writers use transitional devices to help their readers follow the logic and organization.

> **Original Passage**
> Candidates see the depressed economy as a major issue in the eighth district. Brolliette proposes tax incentives to lure big businesses into the area. The Republican incumbent voted for the huge tax incentive that brought two moderate-size businesses to the area. Citizens have been hit with major increases in their personal property tax bills. The businesses offered over 1,200 jobs. Almost all the jobs have gone to employees who accepted a transfer. One business' plant closed in the Southwest. Irate local citizens are footing the tax bill for jobs not open to them. Brolliette defends the position. Kinsingtonne warned City Council and County Council members that citizens would resent the increase. He fought for citizen protection before he announced his candidacy for office. He understands the working man's plight and the ramifications of big business on the little man's pocketbook.

> **Revised to Include Transitions**
> <u>Each</u> candidate sees the depressed economy as a major issue in the eighth district. Brolliette proposes tax incentives to lure big businesses in the area. The Republican incumbent, <u>in fact</u>, voted for the huge tax incentive that brought two moderate-size businesses to the area. <u>Suddenly, however</u>, area citizens have been hit with major increases in their personal property tax bills, <u>some as much as double</u>. <u>Although</u> the businesses have offered over 1,200 jobs, almost all have gone to employees who accepted a transfer <u>as a result of</u> one business' plant closing in the Southwest. <u>So</u> irate local citizens are footing the tax bill for jobs not open to them. Brolliette <u>continues</u> to defend the position. Kinsingtonne, <u>on the other hand</u>, warned City Council and County Council members that citizens would resent the increase. He fought for citizen protection <u>even</u> before he announced his candidacy for office. <u>Apparently</u> he understands the working man's plight and the ramifications of big business on the little man's pocketbook.

 Analysis of the Sample Revision for Transition. The preceding revision includes single-word transitions and transitional phrases. The underlined transitions mark the revisions. Note that as a result of the added transitions, the paragraph now makes more sense.

SAMPLE REVISION FOR SENTENCE VARIETY

The following sample paragraph lacks sentence variety. Most sentences are about the same length and follow a similar structural pattern: subject/verb/modifiers.

The revised paragraph [*a sample paragraph from* Cause and Effect *in Part II*] illustrates improved sentence variety. The structures include simple, compound, complex, and compound-complex sentences, and the lengths vary from a few words to several lines.

Original Passage

Biologists have been studying the balance of nature at Isle Royale National Park. It is an unusual experiment. The park contains 210 square miles of wilderness. Scientists can study animal relationships there. The animals are not disturbed by man or other animals. Moose arrived on the island early this century. They probably came by swimming from the Canadian shore. The moose multiplied because they had no predators. They literally ate themselves out of house and home. They could not leave the island. They starved. They died in large numbers. A fire in 1936 nearly eliminated the browsing food moose eat. It was a disaster. The fire, in turn, opened large areas for new growth. The new growth was just the right diet for the huge animals. The herd grew. It outgrew its supply of food again. A severe winter in 1948–1949 caused an ice bridge to form. It bridged the Minnesota mainland to Isle Royale. A small pack of Eastern Timber wolves ventured across the ice. They found the island and the moose. Wolves are the only natural predators of moose. Scientists have watched the moose population grow and thrive. The moose population dwindles. The wolves die from lack of food. The moose population increases. The environment of the island is controlled. It includes a relatively small geographical area. Scientists can thus keep actual head counts. They can study the moose-wolf balance in detail. The balance of nature theory has proven itself accurate. What a lesson for man to learn! One scientific observer said, "The island's uniqueness lies in its complex yet simple system of natural processes.... In such a system a delicate balance is struck in which no one animal or organism is more important than another. And man's part? We must leave this balance to natural law, observing but not manipulating."

Revised to Include Sentence Variety

For the past 50 years, biologists have been studying the balance of nature by means of a unique experiment conducted in the self-contained laboratory called Isle Royale National Park. The park, an island consisting of 210 square miles of wilderness, affords scientists the opportunity to observe animal relationships in an environment completely undisturbed by man. Sometime early in this century, moose arrived on the island, probably by swimming from the Canadian shore. Proliferating without predators, the moose herds by the early 1930s literally ate themselves out of house and home. Limited by the boundaries of the island, they starved, dying in large numbers. A disastrous fire in 1936 nearly eliminated the browsing food moose eat; but in turn, the fire opened large areas for new growth, just the right diet for the huge animals. So the herd grew. Again it outgrew its supply of food. Then in 1948–1949, the severe winter caused an ice bridge to form from the Minnesota mainland to Isle Royale. By chance, a small pack of Eastern Timber wolves ventured across the ice, found the island, and found the moose. Wolves are the only natural predators of moose. In the course of the next several decades, scientists have watched the wolf population grow and thrive until the moose population dwindles. Then the wolves die from lack of food, and the moose population increases. As a result of the controlled environment of the island and the relatively small geographical area involved, scientists can keep actual head counts and study the moose-wolf balance in detail. The balance of nature theory has, in the decades of study there, proven itself accurate. What a lesson for man to learn! As one scientific observer said of the park, "The island's uniqueness lies in its complex yet simple system of natural processes.... In such a system a delicate balance is struck in which no one animal or organism is more important than another. And man's part? We must leave this balance to natural law, observing but not manipulating."

 Analysis of the Sample Revision for Sentence Variety. The preceding revision includes sentences that vary both in length and in structure. Note these particulars:

- The sentences vary in length from 4 words to 30 words. Interestingly, the longest and shortest sentences appear next to one another. The result is a significant emphasis on the idea in the short sentence.
- The sentences vary in structure from simple sentences to compound-complex sentences. [*See entries in the Glossary to identify kinds of sentences*: simple, compound, complex, *and* compound-complex *and see* Writing Sentences *earlier in Part I.*]
- The sentences include a wide variety of modifiers: single-word modifiers, phrase modifiers, and clause modifiers.

- The sentences begin in a variety of ways: with prepositional phrases, with participial phrases, with subjects, with transitional words and phrases, with relative pronouns, with introductory clauses.
- The sentences include both exclamatory and interrogatory sentences, although typically most are declarative.

SAMPLE REVISION FOR WORDINESS

Eliminating wordiness presents a challenge to some writers. The following two paragraphs [*taken from the first draft of the sample in* Letters, Editorial *in Part III*] illustrate in the revision an effective elimination of wordiness.

Original Passage

Do we want continuing increased property taxes? Do we want to ignore drug-pushers and users? Do we want a "yes" man representing us in Congress? To answer "no" to these questions is to vote for Jerrald Kinsingtonne. Here's why.

When Republican incumbent Rodney Brolliette urged local authorities to provide tax incentives to lure businesses into our community, he ignored the cry from private citizens that they would pay with increased property taxes. Democratic candidate Jerrald Kinsingtonne spoke on their behalf, but no one in the Republican-controlled Council listened. Now, strapped with property tax bills double last year's rate, citizens know who they need to support. When Kinsingtonne pleaded their case, he wasn't a candidate. Now he is.

Revised to Eliminate Wordiness

Shall we increase property taxes? Ignore drug-pushers? Elect a "yes" man for Congress? To answer "no" is to vote for Jerrald Kinsingtonne. Here's why.

When Republican incumbent Rodney Brolliette fought for tax incentives to lure businesses here, he ignored Kinsingtonne's plea that private citizens would pay with increased property taxes. Now, strapped with tax bills double last year's rate, citizens know who they need to support.

 Analysis of the Sample Revision for Wordiness. The preceding revision eliminates words, phrases, even whole sentences. As you compare the two passages, you see that no ideas are omitted, but the revision gives the main idea greater emphasis. To reduce nearly 120 words to just over 60 words, the writer used phrases and clauses to combine ideas into single sentences. He used strong nouns and verbs to eliminate the need for modifiers. As a result of eliminating wordiness, the writer has secondarily improved his sentence variety.

SAMPLE REVISION FOR EMPHASIS

The following passage, an early draft of this chapter on revising, illustrates revision to achieve emphasis.

Original Passage

It is in the process of revising a paper that real writing takes place. That may sound strange because after all you wrote your paper and now you are merely making changes. Of course, that's true. The writing that takes place during the process of revision, however, is the writing that makes the difference between a paper and a good paper, between a good paper and a superior paper. Most professional writers will tell you the real work comes in the revising.

Revised to Add Emphasis

During the process of revising, the really tough part of writing takes place. True, you have worked hard to write your paper; and now you are merely making changes. The writing that occurs during the revision process, however, makes a mediocre paper a good paper. Revision adds variety, emphasis, coherence, transition, and detail. Revision eliminates wordiness, irrelevancies, and inconsistencies. Revision polishes, hones, and perfects. Thus, most professional writers agree that the real work comes in the revising.

 Analysis of the Sample Revision for Emphasis. The preceding revision illustrates a number of revision techniques, all of which enhance emphasis. Note the following particulars:

- Main ideas appear in the main clauses. For instance, in the original passage, the first sentence swallowed the main idea in a subordinate clause, *that real writing takes place.* In the revision, the main idea appears in the main clause, *the really tough part of writing takes place.* [*For explanations about main clauses and subordinate clauses, see Part IV, Section C,* Phrases and Clauses.]
- Subordinate ideas appear in subordinate positions. In the first sentence, for instance, the phrase *during the process of revising* appears as an introductory prepositional phrase that functions as an adverb. The modifier merely places a time limit on the main clause, further emphasizing *tough part.*
- The most important words, words that need emphasis, appear at the ends of sentences. Note the emphasis on *making changes, good paper,* and *revising.*
- Parallel series add emphasis to the concept of revising. Three parallel sentences begin with the word *revision.* Each sentence, however, emphasizes a different part of revision. The first says

revision adds; the second says *revision eliminates*; the third says *revision polishes, hones, and perfects*. Note, too, that each sentence itself includes parallel structures: The first sentence includes a series of five nouns; the second, a series of three nouns; and the third, a series of three verbs.

- Further sentence strength is achieved by the elimination of linking verbs. In the original passage, all sentences but the last include a linking verb. The revision eliminates all linking verbs.

- Even though the second passage carries a stronger message, it is nearly the same length as the original passage.

Using these revision techniques should help you polish your own compositions. You can find additional suggestions for revising in Parts II and III. These suggestions give you a good set of guidelines for thorough and effective revision, the really tough part of writing!

Proofreading

When you have revised the paper so that the content and structure are as accurate and concise as you can make them, then you are ready to prepare the final draft. Whether you prepare the final draft at the computer or by writing it out by hand, you need to proofread it for accuracy.

Use the following questions in addition to those included in the proofreading sections for the specific paper you are writing.

STEP 1   Checking for Punctuation and Mechanics

Use the following questions to check for possible punctuation or mechanics problems:

- Have I punctuated my sentences accurately so that I have avoided major sentence errors like fragments and run-ons? [*See references to each of the marks of punctuation in the Glossary and Part IV, Section D,* Punctuation.]

- Have I included accurate punctuation so that the meaning of sentences is clear?

- If I used semicolons and colons, have I used them accurately?

- Have I used accurate capitalization?

- If documentation is required, have I documented accurately? [*See* Research Paper *in Part III.*]

- Is the documentation note complete and accurate, including its punctuation?
- Is the corresponding bibliography complete and accurate and punctuated correctly?
- Have I spelled all words correctly? Refer to *Webster's New World Dictionary* for preferred spellings.

STEP 2   Checking for Grammar and Usage

Use the following questions to help you spot possible grammar or usage problems:

- Do all of my subjects and verbs agree? [*See* Usage, Agreement of Subject and Verb, *in Part IV, Section B.*]
- Do nouns and pronouns agree both in number and gender? [*See* Pronoun Usage *in Part IV, Section B.*]
- Have I used the correct verb forms, especially for irregular verbs?
- Have I used the objective case accurately where it is required? [*See Part IV, Section B.*]
- Do I maintain the use of the nominative case after a linking verb? [*See* Pronoun Usage *in Part IV, Section B.*]
- Have I avoided using the adjective form when the adverb form is required? [*See* Adjective and Adverb Usage *in Part IV, Section B.*]

These questions, answered positively, should allow you to proofread successfully and, therefore, produce an accurate final copy.

The many steps from prewriting to proofreading may suggest that writing must be a nearly insurmountable task. Not so! The more you write, the more these general guidelines will play in your mind. And the more that happens, the easier it is to spot weaknesses on your own.

The sections in Parts II and III provide specific step-by-step processes for writing by a particular means of development and for writing a particular product. Applied to specific situations, the process described in this part takes on new emphasis. Your understanding of these general guidelines for prewriting, writing, revising, and proofreading can help you whisk through those specific situations.

PART II

METHODS OF DEVELOPMENT

No matter what you write, you must choose a means for developing what you say. This part of the handbook details and illustrates ten common methods of development. In alphabetical order, they are as follows:

- **Analogy** strives to simplify something complicated by comparing the complicated with the simple, such as comparing how a computer works with how a sewing machine works.
- **Cause and effect** explains the why something happened, such as why a war was won or lost, or what happened as a result of something, such as what happened to the economy in the South as a result of the Civil War.
- **Classification** puts things together that belong together, such as talking about the hiking trails in Yellowstone by grouping them according to their difficulty.
- **Comparison and contrast** shows how one subject is similar to or different from another, such as how one athletic team is similar to another or how one DVD system is different from another.
- **Definitions** explain terms, sometimes in just a sentence as part of a larger written piece, and sometimes as the entire piece, such as responding to the question, "What is chemotherapy?"
- **Description,** either technical or literary, gives details so that others see, hear, smell, taste, or feel what you do.
- **Narration** "tells the story," either in fact or fiction.
- **Opinion** expresses your own thoughts about a subject, such as abortion, but must be supported with facts and statistics.
- **Persuasion** attempts to convince others of your opinion.
- **Process analysis** explains how something was or is done, such as how a war was won or how to use a lathe to turn a table leg.

Because you must use these methods to develop any paper you write, consult this section frequently. And keep in mind that any one piece of writing may use several methods of development. For instance, a piece that explains how to use a lathe to turn a table leg will be developed primarily by process analysis. However, the piece may also include any or all of the following:

- **Definition:** What is a lathe?
- **Description:** What does a turned leg look like?
- **Comparison and contrast:** How is it different from any other table leg?
- **Cause and effect:** What happens if you don't use the lathe properly?
- **Opinion:** Is there a certain wood that is better for the project than another kind?

Use this section to find models for every kind of development method you're likely to use, no matter what you must write. Study the analyses that follow each model for clues about what works and why. Then apply what you learn to the more than 40 kinds of writing explained and illustrated in Part III.

Analogy

An analogy explains an idea by making a comparison. The analogy may explain how something works, how something looks, what something means. Usually, an analogy compares something hard to understand with something easy to understand. It makes the complex simple. As a result, analogy is a popular means of developing all or parts of many kinds of written products.

How does an analogy differ from a simple comparison? While the analogy explains the likenesses between two things, usually these two things do not belong to the same group. For instance, an analogy would not compare two kinds of apples. That is merely a comparison. [*See* Comparison and Contrast *later in Part II*.] Instead, an analogy would compare making long-term investments in the stock market with planting an apple orchard, showing how long each takes to develop into a profitable venture and how many dangers lurk along the way. Such an analogy compares something abstract or complicated (making long-term investments in the stock market) with something concrete or easy to understand (planting an apple orchard).

CHARACTERISTICS

An analogy includes characteristics that set it apart from a simple comparison. A good analogy

- presents an extended comparison of two things in different classes,
- differs from a simple comparison, which serves only to clarify relationships between or among items in the same class,
- compares the complicated with the simple, the unfamiliar with the familiar,
- functions to explain or clarify a complicated or unfamiliar item or idea,
- resembles a metaphor but is extended and serves to explain or to clarify,
- can add drama, humor, and/or interest to an explanation,
- shows imagination on the part of the writer,
- stimulates the readers' imagination and interest.

PROCESS

The following steps help you develop a successful analogy.

STEP 1   **Prewriting • Choosing a Topic**

To develop a good analogy, begin with a complicated concept that you can compare to something simple. To help you come up with the comparison, brainstorm, perhaps with a fellow student, to think of comparisons in other, probably unrelated, fields. [*See* Prewriting *in Part I for additional suggestions for ways of gathering ideas*.]

As you brainstorm, remember that an analogy is simply an aid to explain or clarify. Consider it a word game that allows you to help your readers use their imaginations to deal with a difficult concept.

Example: You must explain how stalactites form. You imagine several possibilities for an analogy:

- Stalactites grow from a substance like molten lava.
- Stalactites form the way an ice-cream machine fills cones.
- Stalactites form the way icicles form.
- Water dripping from a cave ceiling is like sap dripping from a tree, both forming columns of hardened materials.
- Stalactites grow longer the same way a blue wasp's nest grows longer.

Write out several similar comparisons for your own topic. As you think of possible topics for an analogy, keep in mind two suggestions:

- Avoid choosing a comparison that breaks down after only a brief correlation. In order to choose an effective subject for your analogy, you need at least three points of comparison. As a result, you may have to try several topics. If you find only one or two comparisons, you need a better topic.
- At the other extreme, avoid searching for a comparison that will never break down. The comparison set out in an analogy will, by its very nature, eventually break down. The purpose of the analogy is to offer an explanation; it will not withstand critical, logical evaluation in an argument.

On this basis, evaluate the comparisons you chose. Select the one most suitable.

STEP 2   **Prewriting • Planning the Comparisons**
Make a parallel set of lists, one for each of the two parts of the analogy. List every basis for comparison you can find. Use the following example to help you create your lists:

Formation of Stalactites	Formation of Icicles
from ceiling of cave	from eaves of house
residue	freezing
cause of "freezing"	cause of freezing
speed of drip	speed of drip

STEP 3   **Prewriting • Choosing Vocabulary**
Look for words that describe both items. Using a parallel vocabulary effectively and subtly extends the comparison, creating a more imaginative and interesting analogy.

For example, in the comparison in Step 2, some words common to both topics come to mind:

freezing	dripping	ceiling
droplets	icicles	formations
water	running	grow
growth	form	trickle

We can use any of these words to talk about the growth of stalactites or icicles. A parallel vocabulary enhances the analogy.

STEP 4   **Prewriting • Organizing and Considering the Possible Plans**

Arrange the comparisons in logical order. Probably you will choose one of the following:

- If you are explaining how something works, organize the analogy in chronological order. Let the readers follow the process from beginning to end. [*See* chronological order *in the Glossary*.]
- On the other hand, if you are trying to explain an idea or define an abstract term, organize the analogy in order of importance, either from the most to the least obvious comparison or from the most to the least important. [*See* order of importance *in the Glossary*.]

Arrange your points of comparison in the most suitable order for your subject and your purpose.

STEP 5   **Prewriting • Organizing and Planning the Whole**

Whether you organize chronologically or by order of importance, the analogy must take on either a part-by-part or whole-by-whole organization. The usual pattern is to explain the familiar or the easy-to-understand first, followed by the unfamiliar, complicated, difficult-to-understand. Consider each of the methods of organization:

Part-by-part organization requires the writer to explain a single point or part of the comparison, first for one topic of the analogy and then for the other topic. Next the writer explains the second point, or part, of the comparison for each topic of the analogy, and so on until he completes the analogy.

By contrast, **whole-by-whole organization** allows the writer to explain all points of one topic of the analogy and then all points of the other topic.

The following outline best illustrates the two patterns:

Part-by-part organization	Whole-by-whole organization
Point 1	Topic A
Topic A	Point 1
Topic B	Point 2
Point 2	Point 3
Topic A	Topic B
Topic B	Point 1
Point 3	Point 2
Topic A	Point 3
Topic B	

Now you can put part-by-part and whole-by-whole organization together with chronological order or one of the orders of importance discussed in Step 4.

First, consider part-by-part organization. If it is also organized chronologically, then Point 1 will come first in time. Both Topic A and Topic B will be included in Point 1. Following will be Point 2, the second item in time order, and so on.

Consider a chronological, part-by-part analogy to compare the stock-market index to a roller-coaster ride:

Point 1: January
    Topic A: roller-coaster ride
    Topic B: stock-market index

Point 2: June
    Topic A: roller-coaster ride
    Topic B: stock-market index

Point 3: December
    Topic A: roller-coaster ride
    Topic B: stock-market index

If the part-by-part analogy is organized by order of importance, Point 1 will represent the item of greatest importance.

Now consider the whole-by-whole organization. If the whole-by-whole analogy is also organized chronologically, then again Point 1, this time in Topic A, will be the first item to appear in time. Upon completion of Topic A, the pattern will repeat for Topic B.

A chronological whole-by-whole analogy comparing the stock-market index for the past 12 months to a roller-coaster ride might read like this:

Topic A: roller-coaster ride
    Point 1: beginning of ride—thrills
    Point 2: middle of ride—chills
    Point 3: end of ride—spills

Topic B: stock-market index
    Point 1: January—beginning of ride
    Point 2: June—middle of ride
    Point 3: December—end of ride

Similarly, if the analogy is organized by order of importance, Point 1 will still be the item of greatest importance. The pattern will repeat itself for Topic B.

With these patterns in mind, choose the one that best suits your topic and purpose. Also consider which pattern will have the greatest impact on your audience. Try several patterns until you find the one that works best.

STEP 6   Writing • Implementing the Plan

Now you are ready to prepare the first draft of your analogy. The following suggestions may help:

- Begin with a topic sentence or thesis sentence that states the analogy. [*See* Writing a Paragraph *in Part I for a discussion of topic sentences. See* Writing a Multi-Paragraph Paper *in Part I for an explanation of thesis sentences.*]
- Using the organizational plan selected in Step 5 earlier in this section, develop the analogy, maintaining unity within each division of the paper. [*See* Revising: Sample Revision for Unity *in Part I.*]
- Use details and vocabulary that help readers follow subtle parts of the analogy as well as the more obvious stated parts. [*See* specific detail *in the Glossary for a quick reference, and see* Revising: Sample Revision for Specific Detail *in Part I for explanations and examples.*]
- Aim for good sentence variety and adequate emphasis. [*See* Revising: Sample Revision for Sentence Variety *and* Revising: Sample Revision for Emphasis *in Part I for examples.*]
- Make sure the parallels are adequately developed and clarified by transitions so that readers follow a smooth development. [*See* Revising: Sample Revision for Transition *in Part I.*]
- Conclude with a summary or clincher that ties together the analogy. [*See* conclusion *in the Glossary.*]

STEP 7   Revising • Checking the Content

As you revise your first draft, ask yourself these questions to guide possible rewrites:

- Does my topic sentence (or thesis statement for a theme) clearly state the analogy?
- Does the topic sentence (or thesis statement) appear at or near the beginning of my paper?
- Does the organizational pattern follow throughout the analogy so that readers are not confused?
- Do transitions develop smooth parallels between the two topics being compared? [*See* Revising: Sample Revision for Transition *in Part I.*]
- Do the details provide sufficient comparison?

- Do all the details support the topic so that I have maintained unity throughout the paper? [*See* Revising: Sample Revision for Unity *in Part I.*]
- Is the vocabulary suitable for the analogy and for the audience?
- Have I used strong nouns and verbs and avoided flowery modifiers?
- Are sentences varied in both length and structure, and are they appropriate for both the subject and the audience?
- Have I used the appropriate tone and mood for the topic? [*See* tone *and* mood *in the Glossary.*]
- Does the paper conclude effectively?

STEP 8   **Proofreading • Checking the Details**

Next, prepare the final draft. Check for punctuation, grammar, mechanics, usage, and spelling. [*See Part IV for rules and examples.*]

A NOTE ABOUT THE SAMPLES

The following samples illustrate part-by-part and whole-by-whole organization, chronological order and order of importance, and fully developed paragraphs and an analogy used to introduce a longer paper.

SAMPLE FOR ENGLISH

Students in an English class were asked to explain how people learn to write well and how they recognize when their writing is effective. One student decided that the abstract explanation of good writing is elusive, so he chose to develop his explanation by means of an analogy.

Writing: The Baker's Plan

Writing well is like baking well. Recipes for each abound; but the true professionals, the ones who make their living at their craft, rely on their experience and a kind of sixth sense to alter the recipes. The baker does more than mix flour, eggs, shortening, and leavening; he uses his senses—sight, taste, and touch—to get the proportions right. So the writer does more than mix nouns, verbs, modifiers, and punctuation marks; he uses his senses—sight, sound, and touch—to get the emphasis right. Each strives for the right consistency, the right texture, the right effect, perhaps with just a touch of the dramatic, a spice, an herb, a well turned phrase. Each acknowledges that timing is all, timing the rising and baking, timing the sentence and the conclusion. In the end, each achieves the palatable product.

Analysis of the Sample for English. The preceding paragraph illustrates the use of an analogy to explain an abstract idea (*writing well*) in terms of a concrete, more familiar idea (*baking well*). Note the following:

- The paragraph begins with a topic sentence that states the analogy.
- The part-by-part organization allows readers to follow the analogy in chronological arrangement from start to end.
- Each point about the baking reminds readers of a similar point in writing: *a touch of the dramatic, a spice, an herb, a turn of phrase.*
- The vocabulary suggests subtle comparisons and conjures elements shared by the two subjects: *consistency, texture, effect, the dramatic*—all words applicable either to baking or writing.
- The conclusion uses *palatable* denotatively in the sense of *taste* and connotatively in the sense of *acceptability*. The sense of taste, of course, becomes one not just of physical but also of judgmental, aesthetic taste.

One can argue, of course, that extending the comparison much more will cause it to break down. Writing, after all, is more difficult than baking. Remember, however, that the analogy serves only to explain or clarify, not to define or defend. All analogies, carried too far, will ultimately break down. Such is their character.

SAMPLE FOR SOCIAL SCIENCES

While studying a unit in economics, students concentrated on the law of supply and demand and its effect on the economy. As part of an assignment, they were asked to explain how the law works. One student decided, as a supplement to more specific examples, to include an analogy that would not only indicate her thorough understanding of the principle but also heighten excitement in what may otherwise be only an average paper. Here is the analogy she used.

Seesaw Economy

The effect on prices of the law of supply and demand is somewhat like the effect of two children on a seesaw. When one child is down and gives a strong push to go up, the other child must necessarily come down. With careful, light pushes and mutual attention to balance, however, the two children can stop the seesaw parallel to the ground. Only a slight movement on the part of either child will send the seesaw pivoting on its fulcrum, but the balance is possible. So it is with supply and demand. If demand is up and supply is down, the prices soar. A big push from supply, however, may soon send the supply end of the seesaw well above demand. Prices plummet. The market, the fulcrum, determines the rise and fall. Finally, when the perfect balance exists between supply and demand, then prices, too, level, a point which economists call equilibrium.

 Analysis of the Sample for Social Sciences. This comparison of the law of supply and demand with children on a seesaw illustrates most of the principles of a good analogy. Think about the following points:

- The topic sentence establishes the analogy.
- The paragraph uses the whole-by-whole method of organization, from the most important comparison to the least. By first showing the children on the seesaw and allowing them to balance themselves, the writer prepares the reader to visualize the ups and downs of supply and demand.
- While shared vocabulary is somewhat limited in these two comparisons, the final use of the word *level* does draw strength from the earlier *parallel*. The common use of *push* for both topics of the comparison further enhances the analogy on a less obvious plane.
- Sentence variety and vocabulary suit subject, analogy, and audience.
- Transitions such as *when, however, so it is with,* and *finally* help the reader move smoothly from one topic to the other, following the organizational plan.

True, the analogy will break down with further examination. The law of supply and demand includes more complicated principles than does a simple seesaw. Still, the analogy works; it serves, you will remember, only as an introduction to a longer piece.

SAMPLE FOR SCIENCE

After studying the creation of caves and the formations in them, students were asked to write a paragraph explaining how stalactites form. One student decided to explain the process by means of an analogy, comparing the formation of stalactites to that of icicles.

Icicles of Rock

Stalactites form in caves much the way icicles form from the eaves of houses. When sunshine melts the snow on the roof, water begins dripping. Because the air temperature is well below freezing, however, the droplets turn to ice. As additional droplets form and refreeze on their way to running the course of the preceding droplets, the icicle begins to form. During the warmest times of the day, the icicle lengthens: the droplets trickle faster and thus travel farther before they refreeze. During cooler times, the icicle grows larger at its base, the droplets running more slowly and freezing quickly. Each tiny droplet, however, adds to the size, either to the length or the circumference, of the growing icicle. So it is with stalactites, one of the carbonate speleothems. As rainwater seeps through the ground, the carbonic acid in the rainwater dissolves the limestone, forming calcium carbonate. Trickling into caves where no sandstone cap blocks their path, the droplets fall from the cave roof to the floor. As each droplet falls, a tiny deposit remains, "frozen" to the ceiling. What causes the "freezing"? The water loses carbon dioxide to the cave air, rendering the water less acidic. For this and other reasons, the water cannot retain as much calcium carbonate; therefore, some calcium carbonate precipitates, leaving minute deposits on what is to become a stalactite. The faster the drip, the longer the stalactite grows, becoming more conical. As a result, the deposits "freeze" into colorful stone-like icicles, forming one cubic inch of stalactite in about a hundred years.

Analysis of the Sample for Science. The preceding analogy explains a complicated process by means of an everyday phenomenon. The following points show what makes the analogy effective:

- The topic sentence announces the analogy.
- The organization is whole-by-whole, with the discussion of the familiar, the icicle, coming first, followed by the discussion of the more complex, the stalactite.
- Chronological order appears in both topics.
- The parallel vocabulary includes *trickle* and *freeze,* but the scientific section uses quotation marks around *freeze* to emphasize its uncommon (in this case, unscientific) use.
- Other parallel vocabulary adds subtle comparisons in the analogy: *eaves* and *roof* both suggest structures from which the formations hang; *air* affects both formations; and, because both topics relate to water, words common to a discussion of water aid the analogy.
- Transitions such as *because, however, as, during, so it is, as a result, similar to,* and *like,* combined with the repetition of key words, clarify relationships.
- The conclusion, which in this paragraph merely makes a final statement, functions as a clincher for the comparison.

SAMPLE FOR MATHEMATICS

Math students were asked to compare learning mathematics to some other real-life situation. One student wrote the following:

> **Math as a Box of Tools**
>
> A thorough knowledge of mathematics is like a flail box of mechanic's tools. If you have all the tools—like the knowledge of fractions, percentages, ratios, and algebraic operations—you are equipped to do any job that comes along, whether that job is determining the trajectory of the ball in a football game, gas mileage for an automobile, the power requirements for a piece of machinery, the interest earned on a bank account, the ratio of insecticide to water in a spray mix, or the cost of a long-term loan. The tools not only enable the user to cope with daily problems, they also appreciate in value with increased understanding and experience on the part of the mechanic.

 Analysis of the Sample for Mathematics. The following characteristics appear in the preceding analogy:

- The first sentence states the analogy.
- The remainder of the paragraph gives examples to support the analogy, and the examples illustrate real-life situations.
- The final sentence suggests the present and increasing value of the mathematics "tools."
- This model paragraph represents an excellent journal or learning log entry. [*See* Journal *in Part III.*]

SAMPLE WORK-PLACE WRITING

Students were asked to describe what makes a good manager. Because being a good manager requires many abstract qualities, one student developed an analogy comparing a good manager with a good gardener.

The Gardener in the Office

A good manager is like a good gardener. Each begins by looking at the conditions under which he or she must work. Given a specific climate and specific working conditions, each must adjust. Within the given environment, however, both the manager and the gardener can choose the right commodities: the right personnel, the right plants. Because not all people and all plants react the same to the environment, however, a good manager as well as a good gardener will attend to the differences. Some people work well under pressure; others do not. Some plants produce well in partial shade; others do not. Nurturing people as well as plants can improve production. Even when harvest time comes, the gardener knows to expect a higher yield from a tomato plant than from a corn stalk; but knowing that, he planted more corn than he did tomatoes. Likewise, the manager knows to expect a different yield from people with different responsibilities; so she hires accordingly. Finally, when the crops are sold, the gardener does not measure each bean's worth; he considers the total garden's yield. So the manager measures the department's worth. Granted, though, if the eggplant does not produce anything, the gardener will not replant it next year; and if a worker does not produce, the manager must consider eliminating that employee. If, on the other hand, the gardener feels he should have tended the eggplant more carefully, sprayed it for insects, watered it, or fertilized it, then he may consider replanting, hoping that with better care, the eggplant will be a better producer. Likewise, the good manager may realize she has not tended the worker as much as she might, talking with him about problems, offering suggestions for improved output, or altering the worker's responsibilities. She may give the worker another opportunity. So, managers, like gardeners, reap what they sow.

Analysis of the Sample Work-Place Writing. By using an analogy to talk about good management, the writer describes characteristics without belaboring the point. The creative approach adds interest to the subject.

Consider these additional points that make the preceding analogy a suitable one:

- The topic sentence clarifies the analogy.
- The part-by-part organization allows the writer to discuss each point in terms of both the manager and the gardener.
- The generally chronological order moves from planting to harvesting.
- The vocabulary furthers the analogy with such mutual ideas as working conditions, attending, production, yields, reaping, and sowing.

- Transitions clarify the development, especially words such as *both, each,* and *likewise,* as well as the repetition of the key words.
- The concluding sentence ties together the two subjects and uses an adage to complete the comparison.

SAMPLE TECHNICAL WRITING

When asked to explain how to select a piece of lumber, one student wrote the following analogy. The passage, written as an introduction, allows the writer to make some important points about wood selection.

Choices

Choosing the right piece of wood for a project is like choosing a friend. Although a person may not choose the same friend for a fishing buddy that he does for a date at the homecoming dance, he usually has a reason for selecting the friend he does. For instance, a fisherman may prefer the companionship of another experienced fisherman, but fishing ability has nothing to do with dancing ability. So it is with selecting a piece of wood for a project. A piece of bird's-eye maple may be desirable for a gunstock but impractical for a bookcase. The woodworker chooses lumber for its ability to hold weight, resist splitting or warping, finish well, and show good grain.

Analysis of the Sample Technical Writing. The preceding analogy clarifies that one selects different kinds of lumber for different projects. The following characteristics appear in the model:

- The topic sentence establishes the analogy.
- Organized whole by whole, the analogy first discusses the familiar subject, friends, and then the less familiar subject, choosing the right lumber.
- The analogy serves as an introduction for a longer paper.

The preceding models and their analyses should help you develop an analogy suitable to whatever situation you confront. You may choose to use an analogy only as an introduction, as a single point in a longer paper, or as a paper in itself. In any case, you follow the same developmental process set out in this section.

Cause and Effect

The cause-and-effect method of development works well for analyzing a situation from one of two directions. First, it works for examining the cause or causes of a situation. A writer may be answering questions such as, "What caused these rock formations?" "How did the incumbent lose the election?" "Why did the City Council reject the petition for rezoning?" "What makes a lathe work?" The result is known, and cause and effect is the best method of development to explain what brought it about—the cause, the why, the how.

Second, the cause-and-effect method of development works well for examining the effect or effects of a situation. A writer may be answering questions such as, "What will happen if PCBs are spilled into the river above the city's water intake?" "How do FCC regulations affect what the television viewer sees?" "What happens if I overdraw my checking account?" "How will safety glasses protect me during certain industrial processes?" The cause is known, and cause and effect is the best method of development to explain the result, the effect.

CHARACTERISTICS

Usually a cause-and-effect paper, either a paragraph or longer, includes

- An analysis of the cause or causes of a specific effect,
- An analysis of the effect or effects of a specific cause, or, in a really complicated paper,
- An analysis of both the cause(s) and the effect(s) of a specific situation, and, in any case,
- Evidence of clear, logical relationships.

In addition to clearly established cause-and-effect relationships, a cause-and-effect paper also

- begins with a good introduction,
- includes a clear topic or thesis sentence [*see* topic sentence *and* thesis sentence *in the Glossary*],
- shows clear organization,
- uses effective transitional devices [*see* transitions *in the Glossary*],

- develops clear supporting details [*see* specific detail *in the Glossary*],
- maintains unity [*see* unity *in the Glossary*],
- demonstrates effective sentence variety,
- builds effective emphasis,
- uses vocabulary appropriate for the subject and the audience,
- concludes logically.

PROCESS

The following steps can help you use cause and effect to develop a paper, either a short, paragraph-length analysis or a full-length paper. [*See* Writing a Paragraph *in Part I for an analysis of paragraph structure and* Writing a Multi-Paragraph Paper *in Part I for details about writing a full-length paper.*]

STEP 1   **Prewriting • Finding a Topic**

This section assumes that you have been asked to develop a paper using the cause-and-effect method. If you must choose your own topic, think of subject matter you have studied recently. Without worrying about order or logic, jot down 10 or 15 topics as quickly as they occur to you. In an economics class, for instance, the list of topics may include these items:

> Monopolies
> Oligopolies
> Perfect competition
> Capitalism
> Production
> Supply and demand
> Inflation
> Socialism
> Communism
> Distribution equilibrium point

Once you have topics, the cause-and-effect situations become evident. For instance:

- How do monopolies form? (causes)
- What happens to the price of products produced by a monopoly? (effects)
- What factors are involved in production? (causes)
- When production slows, what happens to the economy? (effects)

- What brings about inflation? (causes)
- How does inflation affect the stock market? (effects)
- What happens to production during periods of high inflation? (effects)

Any of these topics call for a cause-and-effect analysis.

After you have generated a list of topics, pick one that interests you and formulate a question similar to those in the preceding list. The purpose of your paper is to answer that question.

STEP 2   **Prewriting • Deciding on Cause or Effect**

When you have a topic, either assigned or selected by the process above, decide whether your analysis will examine causes or effects. If you are not sure, try restating the question so that you use the word *cause* or *effect*. For instance, the question above, "When production slows, what happens to the economy?" can be reworded to ask, "When production slows, what are the *effects* on the economy?" The rewording clarifies that you will be writing about effects. On the other hand, the question, "How do monopolies form?" can be reworded to ask, "What *causes* monopolies?" Then you understand that you will be analyzing causes and explaining how monopolies come into being.

STEP 3   **Prewriting • Selecting the Main Ideas**

With your topic stated as a question, jot down as many answers as you can. To answer a complicated or technical question, you may need to do research, but these steps assume that you already know the answers. The word "answers" takes a plural form under the assumption that your chosen topic will not have a simple, single cause or effect. If it does, it probably does not merit an analysis.

Use the following example to help you develop a list of answers. Assume that a writer is developing a paper to explain why various groups of people have come to a remote island, called Isle Royale, in Lake Superior. That writer's list of answers may look like this:

To study the wolf population
To study the moose population
To harvest lumber
To explore
To sightsee
To fish commercially
To hike
To mine copper

List answers to your own question now.

STEP 4   **Prewriting • Narrowing the Topic**

When you have listed all the answers you can think of, decide which three or four are most important. Set them aside before going on to Step 5.

For instance, the writer working with the preceding list chose to narrow his topic to deal only with early groups of people who came to Isle Royale. As a result, he limited his answers to these three:

> To harvest lumber
> To fish commercially
> To mine copper

STEP 5   **Prewriting • Adding Supporting Details**

Using the list of answers as topics, add three or four supporting details to each item. The supporting details may be examples, illustrations, definitions, analogies, comparisons, contrasts, or other explanations. Use the following sample list as a guide for developing your own:

> To mine copper
> > Prehistoric people
> > First settlers
> > Last miners
> To fish commercially
> > Early success
> > Declining success
> > Present success
> To harvest lumber
> > In the 1890s
> > In the 1920s

This list is, in fact, a scratch outline. [*See* Outlines *in Part III.*]

STEP 6   **Prewriting • Organizing the Details**

You must choose a pattern of organization appropriate for your subject. For instance:

- A paper analyzing the economic results of slowed production may take a chronological approach (What happens first? What happens next?) or an order of importance approach (What is the most important effect? The next most important? The least important?).

- An analysis of the impact of World War II on an industry may take an order of importance approach (either from most important to least or least important to most).
- A descriptive analysis of the effects of a tornado may take a spatial approach, following the path of destruction (for example, from southwest to northeast).

Select the organizational plan that best suits your subject: chronological order, spatial order, or one of the orders of importance. [*See the entry for each in the Glossary.*]

STEP 7   Prewriting • Checking the Logic

The following flaws in thinking can occur in the development of a cause-and-effect paper:

- A cause-and-effect relationship based only on a time relationship,
- A cause-and-effect relationship based upon coincidence,
- A cause-and-effect relationship simplified by citing only the immediate causes when more remote causes are equally important.

To deal with these potential logic problems, try these three suggestions:

Suggestion 1. Sometimes Situation B appears to be caused by Situation A simply because A happened before B. But merely because an earthquake occurred immediately after a heated argument does not mean that the argument caused the earthquake! Be sure the cause-and-effect relationship you analyze depends on more than a time relationship.

Suggestion 2. Sometimes an analysis breaks down because the writer finds what seems to be more than a time relationship but in fact is merely coincidence. A court of law would label such analyses as circumstantial. For instance, if a monkey plays with a camera long enough, it may manage to take a decent picture. The picture, however, is not proof that the monkey has learned how to take pictures. It is only coincidence. Do not include what may be coincidence as primary evidence of causes or effects.

Suggestion 3. Certainly any analysis must cope with recent and more remote causes and effects. The length of your paper determines how far back or forward you can take your analysis. The real problem, however, occurs when the writer looks at remote causes or distant effects instead of recent ones. While indeed a serious automobile accident was ultimately caused by the invention of the automobile, such a remote cause is ridiculous in light of the immediate cause: The driver ran a stop sign. Be sure your analysis deals with recent causes and effects, delving into the remote past or distant future only as logic and space allow.

STEP 8   **Writing • Following the Plan**

As you develop your cause-and-effect paper, follow the organization established in the preceding steps. [*See* Writing a Multi-Paragraph Paper *in Part I if you are writing a full-length paper, and see* Writing a Paragraph *in Part I if you are writing a shorter paper.*]

STEP 9   **Revising • Checking the Content**

Use the following questions to determine where your paper may need revision:

- Have I clearly established the cause-and-effect relationship by using transitional devices?
- Have I avoided logical fallacies?
- Does the paper begin with an effective introduction? Does it give something of the background and include a thesis or topic sentence? [*See* thesis sentence *or* topic sentence *in the Glossary.*]
- Is the paper well structured? [*See* Revising: Checking Structure *in Part I.*]
- Have I maintained unity by omitting unrelated ideas? [*See* Revising: Sample Revision for Unity *in Part I.*]
- Does each body paragraph include a topic sentence? Does it relate directly to the thesis statement? [*See* Writing a Multi-Paragraph Paper *in Part I for a complete explanation.*]
- Is my conclusion effective? [*See* conclusion *in the Glossary.*]
- Have I used good sentence structure and achieved effective sentence variety? [*See* Revising: Sample Revision for Sentence Variety *in Part I.*]
- Do my sentences generate appropriate emphasis? [*See* Revising: Sample Revision for Emphasis *in Part I.*]

If you cannot honestly answer "yes" to each of these questions, you have discovered areas in need of revision.

[*In addition, see* Revising *in Part I for general information, including a more detailed list of questions for guiding your revision.*]

STEP 10   Proofreading • Checking for Details

Read your paper for accurate mechanics, usage, and grammar. [*Refer to Part IV for rules and examples.*] Check for accurate spelling and word choice.

A NOTE ABOUT THE SAMPLES

The following cause-and-effect papers all deal with a single subject: Isle Royale National Park. By using one topic, we can illustrate how to select specific topics to relate to specific content areas and for specific purposes.

Some samples deal with causes, some with effects, and some with both. Some are a single paragraph while others are full-length, five-paragraph themes. You may want to compare to see how structure affects content.

SAMPLE FOR ENGLISH

Students in an English class were asked to analyze a specific vacation spot. In other words, the question they were to answer is as follows: What causes some people to choose _____ as a vacation spot? The following cause-and-effect paragraph is one student's analysis.

Choosing a Vacation Spot

Some people choose vacation spots because their friends went there last year or because the advertisements make the place look luxurious. Others choose spots that meet their special interests. For instance, some people prefer a vacation spot away from tourists or bustling crowds. The only crowds they want to see are crowds of wildlife—flora and fauna. They do not demand luxurious accommodations but enjoy a quiet view of the water. Sunrises and sunsets fascinate them more than neon lights and glittering marquees. A lone wolf or loon call drifting over the steady slap of waves on the rocks lulls them to sleep far more readily than rumbling trucks on a nearby interstate. They do not mind the inconvenience of a five-hour boat trip to reach a place where these phenomena greet them, for they appreciate the fact that no tourist can come jouncing in in an automobile, adding noise and air pollution to a virtually pristine environment. Most important, however, they welcome the absence of outside stress: no radios, no television, no roads, no vehicles, no contact with the outside world for as long as they choose to stay. These people choose to vacation at Isle Royale National Park.

Analysis of the Sample for English. The cause-and-effect paper exhibits many typical characteristics:

- The writer enumerates the causes for visiting Isle Royale National Park.
- The organization permits the writer ample opportunity to build to the topic sentence, here the last sentence of the paragraph.
- Organized by order of importance, from least important to most important, the writer begins with the second most important reason for choosing the park as a vacation spot: few people. Next he lists the least important reason, the comfortable but not luxurious accommodations; and finally he concludes with the most important cause, the absence of stress from the outside world. While some writers may arrange the materials differently, this writer suggests personal preferences by the order of his arrangement.
- Although the writer does not begin by saying, "These issues caused us to choose Isle Royale National Park for our vacation spot," the readers recognize by the end of the paper that these have been the guiding issues for the analysis.
- Being subtle, the writer lists issues and then indicates that the chosen vacation spot fulfilled the preference.
- The conclusion, without elaborating, tells the reader what to expect at Isle Royale.
- The cause-and-effect logic follows smoothly.
- The varied sentence structure provides easy reading.
- Specific details create clear mental pictures.
- Grammar, mechanics, and usage are accurate.

In general, then, the paragraph generates an effective causal analysis.

SAMPLE FOR SOCIAL SCIENCES

The following five-paragraph cause-and-effect paper analyzes what caused various early groups of people to come to what is now Isle Royale National Park.

The Riches of Isle Royale

Isolated in the far reaches of Lake Superior, Isle Royale has lured people to its mysterious shores for centuries. Over the past 4,000 years, only three natural resources have merited man's battle with the isolation and climate; and in every case, the battle was at worst sporadic and at best relatively short-lived.

The lumber industry fought the shortest-lived battle. During only two periods did the lumber industry attack the island, first in the 1890s and again in the early 1930s. In each case, a natural disaster halted operations. In the earlier period, a flood, which caused the log barrier to break, scattered the entire year's harvest into Lake Superior; and during the second period, a fire burned nearly a quarter of the island, leaving the lumber company's assets in ashes. Fortunately, at least for the island's ecology, its isolation and thin soil, which will not support tall stands of trees, discouraged the lumber industry from doing further damage to the ecosystem.

The second natural resource that caused man to come to Isle Royale was the abundance of fish. Commercial fishing began before 1800 and continues today, albeit in a considerably reduced manner. Early on, nearly every protected cove had a fish house or fisherman's cottage, although most fishermen and their families occupied the island only seasonally. Now, plagued by a decline of fish and increase in expense, commercial fishing only suggests what once was. Primarily an individual enterprise, commercial fishing in the area enjoys the protective coves and inlets abundant in the archipelago. While catches of the prized whitefish have declined for unknown reasons, the fishermen also face man-made disruptions of the area's fishing. Sea lampreys and smelt, both introduced by man or as a result of man's interference, have significantly affected the fish population. The remaining fishermen, mostly park service employees, attempt to maintain the vocation as part of the island life.

The primary attraction to Isle Royale, however, has been its potential for precious copper. Prehistoric Indians, like most others who came after them, explored the island during the short summer season, leaving the whipping subzero winds to batter only the trees and rocks. Although experts do not know exactly when or why Indians first crossed the water to Isle Royale, carbon dating indicates they were there by 2000 B.C. In their search for copper, they used the beach cobbles to hammer away the rock and expose the copper veins. Prized for spear points, implements, and decorative ornaments, the copper attracted Indians to the island for over 1,000 years. Their occupation sites indicate their peak activity period from 800 to 1600 declined until by the 1840s the Indian culture in the entire Lake Superior area diminished. When white miners came in the 1840s, only two Indian camps remained. Copper mining activity, still only sporadic after the Indians left, resulted in only small quantities of the precious metal. As the largest operation, the Minong Mine employed nearly 150 miners during the late 1800s. They and their families established the largest white man's settlement on Isle Royale. When that mine went out of business, it left behind piles of "poor rock," some yawning pits, and little else. Nothing remains of the town.

> Now people come to Isle Royale for only one natural resource: wilderness. Protected by the National Park Service, the island is as close to primeval North woods as any other land in the United States. That may be a more precious commodity than the natural resources any copper, fish, or lumber industry has sought.

 Analysis of the Sample for Social Sciences. While the sample causal analysis for English was paragraph length, the analysis here for social sciences is a typical five-paragraph paper. Note these specifics:

- The first paragraph sets out the cause-and-effect relationships to be examined: What caused people to come to Isle Royale?
- Secondarily, almost coincidentally, the paper also looks at causes for the people's leaving.
- The introduction includes the thesis sentence, the final sentence in the first paragraph.
- The introduction establishes the order in which the body paragraphs will be developed.
- Each paragraph examines one cause for their coming: lumbering, fishing, and mining.
- Each paragraph includes ample supporting details to develop the main ideas.
- The paragraphs are obviously arranged by order of importance, from least important to most important.
- Effective transitions help readers follow the organization and recognize the order of importance.
- The intent of the analysis is to describe why people have come to the island over the centuries. Following logically, however, are other cause-and-effect relationships.

Note that in discussing the three industries on Isle Royale, the writer suggests other causal relationships suitable for further analysis and leaves certain questions unanswered. Still, she has written what she set out to write. On the other hand, these remaining analyses and questions show how complicated most cause-and-effect relationships really are. Be prepared to find such open-ended situations when you try to analyze a complicated subject.

SAMPLE FOR SCIENCE

The following cause-and-effect paragraph, also dealing with Isle Royale, illustrates a topic appropriate for a science class. While a number of subjects suitable for a scientific cause-and-effect paper appeared in the preceding discussion for the social science paper, the following subject emphasizes the effects rather than the causes.

**The Significance of Balance-of-Nature Studies
at Isle Royale National Park**

For the past 50 years, biologists have been studying the balance of nature by means of a unique experiment conducted in the self-contained laboratory called Isle Royale National Park. The park, an island consisting of 210 square miles of wilderness, affords scientists the opportunity to observe animal relationships in an environment completely undisturbed by man. Sometime early in this century, moose arrived on the island, probably by swimming from the Canadian shore. By the early 1930s, proliferating without predators, the moose herds literally ate themselves out of house and home. Limited by the boundaries of the island, they starved, dying in large numbers. Then a disastrous fire in 1936 nearly eliminated the browsing food moose eat; but in turn, the fire opened large areas for new growth, just the right diet for the huge animals. So the herd grew. Again it outgrew its supply of food. Then, in 1948–1949, the severe winter caused an ice bridge to form from the Minnesota mainland to Isle Royale. By chance, a small pack of Eastern timber wolves ventured across the ice, found the island and found the moose. Wolves are the only natural predators of moose. In the course of the next several decades, scientists have watched the wolf population grow and thrive until the moose population dwindles. Then the wolves die from lack of food, and the moose population increases. As a result of the controlled environment of the island and the relatively small geographical area involved, scientists can keep actual head counts and study the moose-wolf balance in detail. The balance-of-nature theory has, in the decades of study there, proven itself accurate. What a lesson for people to learn! As one scientific observer said of the park, "The island's uniqueness lies in its complex yet simple system of natural processes. . . . In such a system a delicate balance is struck in which no one animal or organism is more important than another. And man's part? We must leave this balance to natural law, observing but not manipulating."

Analysis of the Sample for Science. In a single paragraph, the causal analysis explores the effect on the moose population when wolves moved onto the island, a dynamic cycle usually expressed by biologists in terms of natural balance. The writer deals effectively with the explanation. Note these specifics:

- In order to succeed with her explanation, the writer had to deal with both causes and effects. For instance, she explained what caused the moose population to expand and decline and then repeat the cycle before the wolf population was introduced. Already the natural balance existed. She had at least to suggest what caused the wolves to arrive on the island and what caused them to thrive and then decline and thrive again. In the process of examining causes, the writer tied together sufficient information to indicate the effects of wolves on the moose population, and vice versa.

- The chronological organization flows smoothly, allowing readers to follow the rise and fall of populations.
- The logical relationships avoid the potential pitfalls. The frequent repetition of the rise-and-fall pattern over the past decades emphasizes the evidence.
- Sentence structure, varied but appropriately technical for its scientific nature, offers clarity and good detail.
- No extraneous material destroys unity.

In short, the paper offers a sound analysis suitable for a science class.

SAMPLE FOR MATHEMATICS

Math students were to respond to the following problem: In order to increase the water storage capacity from 5,000 to 10,000 gallons, workers on Isle Royale built a new cylindrical tank the same height but twice the diameter of the old one. When filled, the new tank held much more than 10,000 gallons. What caused the problem?

Water Storage Problem

The volume of a cylinder is calculated by multiplying the area of the base by the height. Since the new tank was the same height as the old one, the only change occurred in the area of the base. In this case, the diameter was doubled, which at first glance may appear to double the area. In fact, however, doubling the diameter quadruples the area of the base. Here's why. Since the area of a circle is calculated by using the formula πr^2, the area varies as the square of the radius. When the diameter doubles, the radius also doubles. When the doubled radius is squared, the area increases by four since $\pi(2r)^2 = 4\pi r^2$. When this new area is used to figure the volume of the cylinder, whose height remains the same, the volume quadruples. Thus the new tank holds 20,000, not 10,000 gallons.

 Analysis of the Sample for Mathematics. The preceding paragraph explains the cause for a given effect and also illustrates a problem-solving technique.

- The first sentence states the principle in the problem and prepares readers to follow the logic behind the solution.
- The formulas are accompanied by explanations that clarify the cause of the tank's too-large capacity.
- The final sentence presents the logical conclusion.

SAMPLE FOR WORK-PLACE WRITING

The following cause-and-effect analysis was prepared to illustrate writing appropriate for the work place. The assignment was to examine the causes for a particular business's failure.

The Failure of the Copper-Mining Industry on Isle Royale

The copper-mining industry on Isle Royale may have been doomed to failure even before it began. With a number of natural obstacles facing a mining operation on an isolated island, expenses soared. Situated in the northwestern part of Lake Superior, Isle Royale lies 15 miles from Minnesota and nearly 70 miles from Michigan's Upper Peninsula. Any industry located there must necessarily deal with both the frigid, unyielding winters and the isolation. The mining industry was, of course, no exception. Three interrelated causes probably joined forces to destroy the industry.

First of all, miners and their families living on the island faced total dependency on water transportation for every need. While some game and an abundance of fish provided food, few men could be spared from the mine to hunt or fish. The severe climate and short growing season all but eliminated any other potential food supplies on the island. As a result, any needs—clothing, supplies, parts, livestock, fuel, or staples—depended on the boats' timely and safe arrival. During the long winter months, ice blocked boats from entering the harbors or even nearing the island. As a result, miners may have gone months at a time without parts or tool replacements necessary for their work. They and their families no doubt faced a grim life, choosing to leave as soon as possible.

Second, water transportation also provided product export. Without boats, the copper ore merely accumulated at the mine site. The waters around the island chain, notoriously treacherous and frequently stormy, often claimed the boats before they reached their destinations. Such maritime accidents no doubt took their toll on the mining operation.

Third, added to the serious problems of isolation, the island mines faced the same problem as other mines of the period: declining prices. Many mines could increase production and thereby offset the price decline. On Isle Royale, however, copper quantities appeared to be insufficient to make increased production practical. Furthermore, the mines at Isle Royale had to deal with the added expenses unnecessary at other mine sites. No doubt few alternatives remained but abandonment.

So, as a result of the expensive dependency on dangerous and sometimes unreliable shipping combined with the decline of copper prices, Isle Royal bears only ghostly reminders of a once-busy industry.

Analysis of the Sample Work-Place Writing. The preceding causal analysis model speculates on three reasons for the failure of the copper-mining industry on Isle Royale. The following details suggest how the writer succeeds:

- The theme's organization relies on order of importance, but at the same time the cause developed in each paragraph is part of the overall cause: the island's isolation.
- While the writer is careful to use qualifying words such as *no doubt, probably,* and *may,* the causal analysis flows logically.
- Varied sentence structure, good emphasis, and accurate grammar, mechanics, and usage combine to create a good theme.
- Because the writer follows the tight organization established in the introduction and presents each of three interrelated causes, the theme also maintains unity.
- The writer develops good structure throughout his paper. [*See* Revising: Checking Structure *in Part I.*]
- Specific details enhance the paper and give readers a clear understanding of the writer's intent.
- Effective transitions help the paper flow smoothly.

SAMPLE TECHNICAL WRITING

The following sample paper shows the effects of isolation on the skills required of Isle Royale maintenance personnel, thus exploring a technical topic.

Working on Isle Royale

Isle Royale National Park, located in Lake Superior, is the most isolated of all the national parks. Its location results in peculiar problems, especially for maintenance personnel. A supply boat makes the run to the island once a week, weather permitting, but the only other contact the staff has with the mainland is via two-way radio. As a result, Isle Royale workers must be prepared to meet any emergencies and have on hand whatever parts, tools, and equipment they may need. The island generates its own electricity, so maintenance personnel must be able to solve any electrical problems or else the entire community is in the dark. Furthermore, the island maintains its own water supply. So maintenance people must understand the workings of the supply, purification, and pumping systems. And what comes in must go out. Maintenance personnel are also responsible for the garbage disposal and waste-water treatment systems. Complicated by the island's location, the maintenance problems at Isle Royale reach limits unknown to most park-maintenance workers.

 Analysis of the Sample Technical Writing. The effects described in the preceding paragraph result from the single cause established in the opening sentence. Note these additional details:

- The writer has presented the effects from most obvious to least obvious.

- Sufficient detail allows the reader to acknowledge the complications inherent in even minor repairs.
- Because the writer deals only with the effects of isolation on the skills required by maintenance staff, he maintains unity.

By using these samples, you should be able to develop a satisfactory cause or effect paper. Be sure to clarify your purpose and organization in the topic or thesis sentence and then maintain unity with supporting details.

Classification

If you need to clarify relationships, you can develop your writing by means of classification. That method of development examines the parts and their relationships so that readers may better understand the whole.

To develop a piece of writing by means of classification, a writer divides his subject into logical groups. In an English class, for instance, he or she may group authors by the period in which they wrote or group poems by their theme. In a social science class, the writer may group leaders according to the causes they represented or group eighteenth-century immigrants according to the geographical areas in which they settled. In a science class, where scientific method relies heavily on classification, the writer may group animals according to their habitat or group plants according to their reproductive means.

In addition to developing a paper whose sole purpose is to classify, a writer often needs to use classification along with other methods of development. For instance, a paper that examines the economic opportunities in a geographical area may classify opportunities into two kinds: investment opportunities and employment opportunities. When readers see the parts in relationship to the whole, they understand the subject. Using classification helps achieve that end.

CHARACTERISTICS

A paper developed by classification usually exhibits most, if not all, of the following characteristics:

- A clear statement of the subject
- An identification of the means by which the subject will be divided into smaller groups

- A statement of the number of smaller groups the writer will address
- An explanation of each of the smaller groups, which identifies the groups and distinguishes between or among them
- Clear transitions that help readers identify and follow the explanation of each of the divisions
- A clear organization that limits the discussion of a single division to a single paragraph or single section of the paper
- Logical order appropriate for the subject
- A conclusion that restates or draws attention to the subject, means of division, and number of groups in the classification

PROCESS

The following steps can help you plan, organize, develop, and revise your classification paper.

STEP 1 **Prewriting • Choosing a Topic**

If you must select your own topic, begin by brainstorming, possibly with a fellow student, listing topics you have studied recently. [*See* Prewriting *in Part I.*] Try completing the following statement:

Recently, we have studied different kinds of _____.

Whatever words fit in the blank may be suitable topics for your classification paper. You may have completed the statement above with words such as these:

business letters	computer keyboards
lettering styles	watercolor methods
advertising	leavening agents
poetry	pest control
production means	points of view
recession	taxes

These topics may suggest others as you brainstorm your own class situation.

STEP 2 **Prewriting • Choosing a Means of Division**

With a topic in mind, you are ready to decide on possible divisions. First, decide the means by which you will divide the subject. Consider these examples:

- Business letters divided according to purpose
- Computer keyboards divided according to ease of use
- Watercolor methods according to wetness of brush

- Advertising according to media
- Pest control according to application method

Choose the means that best suits your subject.

STEP 3   **Prewriting • Naming the Divisions**

When you have decided on the means of division, jot down the two, three, or four divisions you have chosen. For instance, examine the topics and their divisions below:

- Poetry divided by rhyme scheme: haiku, sonnet, and villanelle
- Point of view divided by person: first-person, second-person, third-person
- Production means divided by automation: piecework, assembly line, robotics
- Recession divided by degree: creeping, galloping, and runaway
- Taxes divided by application: property, income, inheritance
- Leavening agents divided by ingredients: yeast, baking soda, baking powder

Be sure your divisions are logical. Sometimes divisions overlap. For instance, look at the following illogical example:

schools divided by grades: elementary, middle, junior high, and senior high

Because middle school, which usually includes grades six through eight, overlaps junior high school, which usually includes grades seven through nine, the divisions are illogical. Instead, divide schools into these logical classifications:

schools divided by grades: elementary, middle, and high school
schools divided by grades: elementary, junior high, and senior high

STEP 4   **Prewriting • Writing the Topic or Thesis Sentence**

Now you are ready to write the topic or thesis sentence. [*See* topic sentence *and* thesis sentence *in the Glossary.*] This sentence should list the subject, the means of division, and the number. Study the following thesis sentence:

When applying pesticides, one must understand the differences among the four formulations: liquids, dusts, wettable powders, and emulsions.
    Subject: pesticides
    Means: formulations
    Number: four

Write your own topic or thesis sentence now and check for subject, means, and number.

STEP 5   **Prewriting • Listing Details**

Next, develop a list for each of the items you will classify. In the lists, name the specific details you will discuss for each.

Three general kinds of advertising bombard the unsuspecting consumer: print, television, and radio.

Subject: advertising
Means: medium
Number: three

print	television	radio
magazines	moving image	sound effects
print size	sound effects	good voice
copy	visual	copy
visual design	copy	timing
photographs	timing	anyplace
readable	auditory	auditory

STEP 6   **Prewriting • Organizing and Thinking about the Parts**

Using the lists you prepared in Step 5, organize the details. Look for similar categories in each of the lists to help you group ideas. In the advertising example, for instance, two lists included "auditory" and two included "visual." The column headed "television" included both terms. Study the following reorganized lists to see how other terms have been grouped and reorganized. Note also that some items from the original list have disappeared from the reorganized list.

print	television	radio
visual	visual and auditory	auditory
copy	copy	copy
availability	availability	availability

Now the lists are parallel. [*See* parallel structure *in the Glossary.*] They include the same number of items, and the items appear in the same order on each list. The reorganization suggests logical divisions for the discussion of each of the topics.

Reorganize your lists to show logical divisions and parallel structure.

STEP 7   **Prewriting • Organizing and Thinking about the Whole**

A classification paper must have a logical organization that the reader can follow. For instance, if advertising is classified according to medium (print, television, or radio), which will you discuss first? Why? The answer determines your choice of organization. [*See* chronological, spatial, *and* order of importance *in the Glossary.*]

First, you may organize the kinds of advertising by some order of importance.

- From most to least expensive
- From smallest to largest audience
- From most to least effective
- From most to least creative

An equally appropriate option is the reverse of any of these orders of importance.

Likewise, you may choose to organize advertising media from the oldest to the newest, thus relying on chronological order.

So, which do you use? That depends on the purpose of your paper. If you want to present a historical perspective, chronological order is best. If you want to convince a client to spend the money for a multimedia advertising campaign that your advertising firm will develop, then you will probably use one of the orders of importance.

No matter how you organize the overall classification paper, however, keep these two suggestions in mind for each of the subtopics:

- Show your organization in the topic or thesis sentence by listing the topics in the order in which you will discuss them. For example:

  Advertising uses different techniques in each of the three media: radio, print, and television.

  The thesis sentence implies the writer will discuss radio advertising first, then print advertising, and finally television advertising.
- Discuss each of the parallel subtopic details (listed in Step 5) in the same order for each topic. For radio, for instance, discuss visual/auditory details first, then copy details, and finally availability details. Repeat the same order for print and then for television advertising.

STEP 8   Writing • Following the Plan

With the preparation and planning behind you, you are ready to prepare the first draft of your classification paper:

- Begin your classification with the topic sentence (for a paragraph) or introductory paragraph and thesis sentence (for a theme).

- Develop each of the topics in the order in which they appear in the topic or thesis sentence.
- Follow the organizational plan you chose in Step 7.
- Be sure to include sufficient details so that the reader can identify each item separately and, when finished, see the relationship of each to the whole.
- Use a vocabulary and sentence structure appropriate to your audience.
- Use effective transitions to make the paper flow smoothly. [*See* transitions *in the Glossary*.]
- End with a conclusion that effectively ties together the ideas in your paper. [*See* conclusion *in the Glossary*.]

STEP 9   Revising • Checking the Content

As you reread your classification paper, ask yourself these questions to see what revisions may be needed:

- Does my topic or thesis sentence clearly state the subject, the means of classification, and the number of items into which the subject is classified?
- Are the divisions logical?
- Does the topic or thesis sentence appear at or near the beginning of the paper?
- Are the details sufficient for clarity? [*See* Revising: Sample Revision for Specific Detail *in Part I*.]
- Have I maintained unity throughout the paper? [*See* Revising: Sample Revision for Unity *in Part I*.]
- Did I organize the paper effectively, probably according to some order of importance? [*See* Revising: Checking for Organization *in Part I*.]
- Have I included effective transitions to help readers move smoothly from one sentence to the next, from one paragraph to the next? [*See* Revising: Sample Revision for Transition *in Part I*.]
- Do my transitions help show the relationships between the subtopics and the general subject of my classification?
- Are my words and sentences appropriate for my audience?
- Have I used strong nouns and verbs and avoided flowery modifiers? [*See* Revising: Sample Revision for Wordiness *in Part I*.]

- Are the sentences varied both in structure and in length? [*See* Revising: Sample Revision for Sentence *Variety in Part I.*]
- Do my sentences and paragraphs create the appropriate emphasis for my subject? [*See* Revising: Sample Revision for Emphasis *in Part I.*]
- Is the tone appropriate? [*See* tone *in the Glossary.*]
- Does the paper conclude effectively?

STEP 10   **Proofreading • Checking the Details**

When you have completed the revising process in Step 9, prepare your final draft. Then, check it for punctuation, grammar, mechanics, and usage. [*See Part IV for rules and examples.*] Check word choice and spelling.

A NOTE ABOUT THE SAMPLES

Each of the following samples deals with some aspect of the general topic of Mammoth Cave National Park. Note that specific topics are tailored for specific content areas. In addition, note that the five sample classification papers include single-paragraph papers and three-, four-, and six-paragraph themes. The samples illustrate both order of importance and chronological order. By comparing the five samples, you should gain a broad understanding of the classification method of development.

SAMPLE FOR ENGLISH

Students in an English class were asked to classify some aspect of a hobby or activity they enjoyed. One student classified basketball games by back-alley, intramural, and interscholastic competition; another classified recreational reading by best-seller novels, classical literature, and periodicals. Yet another student classified hiking trails both by location and by difficulty. This double classification shows clear organization, as seen in the following.

Hiking at Mammoth Cave National Park

While the average tourist goes to Mammoth Cave National Park to walk through part of the cave, the avid hiker discovers two very different kinds of hiking in the park: below ground and above ground. Even in those two locations, he can find anything from easy ambling to rugged adventure.

Below ground, in the cave system, the trails range from wide, gentle paved paths softly illuminated with indirect lighting to muddy crawl holes dimly lit by hand-carried kerosene lanterns. The easy trails, sometimes only a half-mile long, require little effort along their paved meanderings. The moderate trails, usually a mile or more long, include steps with handrails and sometimes short but steep hills. The rugged trails, however, usually several miles long, require climbing and endurance along hundreds of steps or ladders, over steep sometimes slippery hills, and through narrow passages that bang elbows. The really tough trails, called "adventure trails" in the park literature, may take most of the day to traverse and include long stretches of crawl spaces unsuitable for anyone with even a tinge of claustrophobia. Scrambling over boulders and across muddy streams with only the dim helmet lights and smoky lanterns to show the way, hikers come above ground at the end muddy, perhaps a bit ragged, but glowing with excitement for having shared the cave's secrets.

Above ground, the hikers can select again from easy, broad trails to rugged endurance tests. The easy trails meander for a mile or so through hardwood and cedar forests and along cliffs that drop a sheer hundred feet or more to Green River. With little effort, hikers can enjoy the flora and fauna. A moderate trail, perhaps a mile or so long, may include some hills, but scenery across the nearly mountainous vistas make the mild effort worth the exertion. The rugged trails, long and steep, demand dirty-knee climbing, bottom-dirty sliding, and body-tiring huffing and puffing. Hikers snake up limestone cliffs and struggle over house-sized boulders. They trudge along sandy river banks and climb steep forested hills. They explore sinkholes and intriguing little caves scattered throughout the park. They finish the trail tired but enriched by the variety of experiences. So above ground or below, the land that boasts the longest known cave in the world offers two very different kinds of hiking, either kind with as little or as much challenge as the hiker prefers.

Analysis of the Sample for English. The preceding sample paper includes the general characteristics of a classification paper:

- It includes a clear statement of the general topic (hiking at Mammoth Cave National Park) and indicates the number (two) and the means (by location, below and above ground) of the classification.
- To help the reader follow the organization, the writer adds a sentence to explain that both kinds of hiking, below and above

ground, include another classification: from easy to rugged. Thus, the organization of the entire paper is explained in the introduction.

- Each of the two subgroups is discussed in its own paragraph, below-ground hiking in the second paragraph and above-ground hiking in the third.
- The organization, by order of importance from more well known (below ground) to less well known (above ground), is whole-by-whole. [*See* whole-by-whole organization *in the Glossary.*] The four kinds of trails below ground are discussed in the second paragraph, and the three kinds of trails above ground are described in the third paragraph, in each case from the easiest to the most difficult (another kind of order of importance).
- Images such as *house-sized boulders, dirty-knee climbing, crawl spaces unsuitable for anyone with even a tinge of claustrophobia* help the reader see the different kinds of trails.
- Because no extraneous details appear, the paper maintains unity. [*See* Revising: Sample Revision for Unity *in Part I.*]
- Transitions help the reader follow the organization. Words such as *below ground, above ground, easy, moderate,* and *rugged* are repeated to provide transition from one idea to the next. Other transitions include words such as *however, at the end,* and *again.*
- The sentences flow smoothly and use a direct, simple vocabulary that suits the subject.
- The conclusion reiterates the introduction and adds a spark of interest about the *longest known cave in the world.*

SAMPLE FOR SOCIAL SCIENCES

The following six-paragraph theme, developed by classification, meets an assignment for an anthropology unit in a history class. Using the same general topic of Mammoth Cave National Park, the specific narrowed topic now reflects social science content. After reading the model, study the analysis.

The People and the Cave

Mammoth Cave, the longest cave in the world, has one unusual finger of history outside its geological and environmental history, and that is the history of its people. In general, the people fall into four historical groups: the prehistoric Indians, the early Kentucky settlers, the tourists, and the serious explorers.

Over 4,000 years ago, prehistoric Indians made use of the cave's shelter during winter. The constant 54-degree temperature in the dry cave preserved their remains so well that archaeologists have learned not only about their implements and clothing but also about their agricultural and mining habits. For some unknown reason, however, the Indians left the cave about the time of the birth of Christ, and the cave system remained uninhabited and undisturbed until nearly 1800.

Legends describe the discovery of the cave in 1797 by an early Kentucky hunter named Houchin, who was chasing a bear. His discovery led early settlers to the cave's riches, for unlike the prehistoric Indians who used the cave primarily for shelter, the settlers sought the minerals. Not until the War of 1812, though, did this group of people receive much notice. At that time, the enterprising settlers mined a seemingly endless supply of nitrate for the production of gunpowder, an operation conducted with the aid of slaves.

By the 1830s, the ownership of the cave changed, and that brought the next group of people, the tourists. The new owner brought three black slaves to the cave, and because of their significant exploration, discoveries, and charming personalities, they popularized the cave. Tourism grew. Then another new owner, with money for promotional activities, added a posh hotel, which attracted wealthy visitors, some of them famous, who found it the vacation place. Over the decades, tourists continued to swarm to Mammoth Cave, first by stagecoach, then by train, and now by automobile and every imaginable recreational vehicle. They come to see the cave's magnificent formations, its multiple levels, its hugeness. They want ease of walking and electric lighting, a well informed tour guide, and a sense of the spectacular. Certainly, they get it all.

In the midst of the early stages of tourism, another group of people, the serious explorers, came, first out of curiosity and then out of serious scientific research. Today, the explorers remain. In 1972, a major discovery referred to as the Big Connection placed the Mammoth Cave system on the charts as the longest cave in the world. Discoveries continue. As recently as 1983, another cave system was found to connect with Mammoth Cave, and authorities believe there is the potential for at least another 500 miles of passages to be discovered. Explorers, curiosities whetted by the suspicions of additional undiscovered, unexplored passages, regularly undertake expeditions to be the first to walk through uncharted territory, perhaps the final frontier on this earth.

Obviously, then, the cave system will continue to attract people, both tourists and explorers, for years to come.

 Analysis of the Sample for Social Sciences. The preceding classification theme varies considerably from the example for English. Note these particular features:

- The thesis statement includes the topic (people at Mammoth Cave), the means (historical groups), and number (four).

- Each of the four groups is discussed in a separate paragraph, and the paragraphs appear in the same order in which the groups are listed in the thesis statement.
- Organization follows a chronological pattern, using the whole-by-whole method.
- The details for each group include two kinds of information: when they came to the cave and why they came. Note that the details are thus somewhat different from those in the English sample. The historical significance takes a prominent place in a paper for a history class.
- The writer maintains unity by omitting details that may be interesting but are not relevant to one of the four groups.
- Transitions both between and within paragraphs let the reader move smoothly through the composition. Note the repetition of such words as *Indians, settlers, tourists,* and *explorers* to carry out the organizational plan. Other transitions include words such as *first, however, until, unlike, though, then,* and *while,* and phrases that show time progression such as *over 4,000 years ago, by the 1930s, in 1972,* and *as recently as 1983.* All are effective transitions.
- Sentences vary in length from quite short to fairly long and vary in structure from simple to compound-complex.
- Vocabulary appropriate to the subject and audience includes specific images.
- The paper concludes with a single sentence, carrying the last two groups, the tourists and the explorers, into the future.

The classification theme for social science achieves its purpose. If it has a fault, it may attempt to cover too much in too short a space, but perhaps the assignment offered little alternative.

SAMPLE FOR SCIENCE

The nature of scientific study suggests the importance of classification in a science class. Scientists regularly sort, show relationships, and classify. The following paper illustrates classification development suitable for a science class.

Animals in Mammoth Cave

In Mammoth Cave, biologists have identified nearly 150 animal species, but only about 30 can be considered common. These cave-dwelling animals fall into two groups: Part-time cave dwellers, called trogloxenes, who move freely from inside to outside, and permanent cave dwellers, which include both troglophiles and troglobites.

The trogloxenes depend less on sight than do other animals and thus can find their way in and out of the cave in the dark. They rely on the cool, constant temperatures and the high humidity for protection either in winter or summer. These animals, all of which feed outside the cave, include raccoons, pack rats, cave crickets, and bats. Animals such as raccoons spend only brief periods in the cave for protection. Pack rats and cave crickets spend part of every day in the cave and reproduce there, both of them using chemical trails to find their way to and from their shelters. The most generally recognized cave animals, the bats, use the cave primarily for hibernation, depending on the cold-air drafts from outside to slow their metabolism so that their fat reserves will last through the winter.

Of greater interest to scientists, however, are the permanent cave dwellers, those animals that can survive in the dark environment where lack of plant life severely limits the food chain. Troglophiles can live outside the cave, but the environment outside the cave must be similar to that inside. For instance, they can survive under rocks and undercut banks or under the tree litter in the forest. Over the centuries, however, certain troglophiles have evolved so that those that remained inside caves became a separate species, the troglobites. They have evolved for survival, so they can detect minute food sources and use little energy for survival. For instance, they have lost seeing eyes and any coloration. Because of the constant temperature and humidity in the changes, the evolutionary process has given them large sensory structures which can detect water movement or air movement, a sense which helps protect them from predators and obstacles and helps them locate prey. As a final evolutionary quirk, their reproduction depends on the added food supply brought as a result of seasonal flooding. Because length of daylight cannot trigger an annual biological calendar, the troglobites must be ready to reproduce quickly. As a result of these evolutionary changes, they are literally confined to the cave. The permanent cave dwellers include beetles, spiders, millipedes, mites, springtails, bristletails, fish, crayfish, shrimp, isopods, amphipods, and flatworms.

The animals at Mammoth Cave provide obvious examples for scientific study. Some animals use the cave as only a part of their environment while others depend entirely upon the cave for their survival. Evolutionary changes within the full-time cave residents provide curious examples for scientific investigation.

Analysis of the Sample for Science. The whole system of scientific identification is based on classification, and the preceding sample indicates the appropriateness of the classification method of development for a science paper. The following comments point to the general success of the approach:

- The topic sentence indicates that the classification of cave animals will be divided according to their dependency on the cave (means) and divided into two groups (number).
- Each of the two body paragraphs describes one of the groups.
- Details for each group separate one from the other, clearly establishing that one group is really a cave visitor while the other depends on the cave for survival.
- Within the second group, two subdivisions are identified, further evidence that classification is of particular benefit to the scientific paper.
- The writer maintains unity in each body paragraph and throughout the entire paper.
- Transitions help the reader move from sentence to sentence and from paragraph to paragraph. Specific transitions include the repetition of words such as *animals, cave dwellers,* and the pronouns that refer to them such as *they, these,* and *those.* Other transitions include words and phrases such as *thus, however, greater interest, but, inside, outside, for instance, over the centuries, so, as a result,* and *while.*
- The use of technical terms is appropriate to the scientific subject matter and the audience.
- Numbers appear in Arabic rather than word form, a typical treatment in a scientific paper. Some formal papers may include both words and numerals to eliminate any possible misreading.
- The sentences vary both in length and structure.
- As a conclusion, the final paragraph restates the main idea and indicates its importance to the subject matter.

The paper for science meets the general requirements for a good classification paper. Its suitability for the science class is obvious.

SAMPLE WORK-PLACE WRITING

The classification paper often appears in work-place settings. For instance, while introducing new products, a report may discuss the kinds of sales approaches necessary for different kinds of clients. Likewise, a company executive may prepare a report enumerating the kinds of money-saving techniques he plans to implement during the next year.

The following classification paper addresses business principles. The writer develops the subject in a single paragraph, so note how this single-paragraph classification paper differs from the longer sample papers earlier in this section.

Business Opportunities around Mammoth Cave

While Mammoth Cave National Park is a business within itself, controlled and operated by the National Park Service, the area surrounding the park offers a multitude of business opportunities. Four general categories of opportunities meet the needs of tourists. First, tourists have basic needs, one of which is lodging. Only a limited variety of hotel and motel accommodations, from luxurious to economical, exists in the immediately adjoining areas, and so potential business opportunities exist in that field. Because many tourists arrive with their own accommodations in the form of tents or recreational vehicles, however, other lodging needs offer alternate business opportunities. For these people, campgrounds with and without hook-ups come at a premium during peak seasons. Second, whether they come as hotel/motel guests or as campers, tourists need food. Restaurants, from gourmet to fast-food, now far from readily available, may offer potential business. For those tourists who prefer to cook on their own, packaged goods and fresh fruits and vegetables are simply unavailable nearby. Third, because of the atypical climate in the cave—a constant cool, damp 54 degrees—many tourists come without appropriate wearing apparel. Nowhere in the immediate vicinity can one buy a sweater or sweatshirt, jeans, or long socks for comfort in the cave. Fourth, in spite of the opportunities available in the park, tourists who stay more than a couple of days will seek other recreational opportunities. A canoe livery could enhance water sports on the Green River. For those less inclined toward the rugged exercise necessary for extensive enjoyment of the park, a miniature golf or par-three golf course could offer a viable alternative. Even a few tennis courts, theaters, or small theme park may offer alternate business opportunities. In short, for the entrepreneur, opportunities exist. Further market research and investment analysis will determine which has the greatest potential.

Analysis of the Sample Work-Place Writing. This sample classification paper, a single paragraph, follows the general characteristics set out in the beginning of this section. Study the following analysis:

- The first sentence discusses the general idea of the paper, but the second sentence, the topic sentence, establishes that the paper will deal with four classes of business opportunities based on tourist needs (means).
- The four classes are emphasized with numeric transitions, first, second, third, and fourth.
- Organization moves from the most obvious tourist need to the least.
- Transitions, including the numeric ones, help the reader move smoothly through the paragraph.
- Specific nouns name specific business ventures.
- The writer maintains unity throughout.

- Vocabulary and sentence structure, appropriate for the subject, aim at a business-oriented audience.
- The conclusion acknowledges the writer's cursory examination of the subject and admits need for far more careful analysis prior to investment.

SAMPLE TECHNICAL WRITING

The following sample classification paragraph deals with the use of Mammoth Cave for the production of gunpowder. The writer develops the topic in a single paragraph.

Saltpeter Operation in Mammoth Cave

Used for making gunpowder during the War of 1812, the saltpeter operation at Mammoth Cave required, in addition to the cave's supply of nitrate, two kinds of natural resources available in the hills of Kentucky: wood for construction and wood for burning. The wood for building the square vats and for making pipes required long, straight grain. Tulip poplar trees, abundant in the surrounding hills and ravines, met the requirement. Constructing the vats required little special skill, but forming the wood pipes required special tools and patience. Workers used hand augers to bore out the centers of the typically straight poplar logs. Then they tapered the end of one log and reamed out the end of the next log, thus permitting the two logs to slip together. The system of log pipes carried water from the nearby Green River into the cave for production of the saltpeter. The second kind of wood, however, served an entirely different purpose in the saltpeter operation. In fact, the wood was not used as wood; it was used as ash. It provided potassium. So, by burning hickory and oak, both rich in potassium, the workers produced an ash that, when the nitrate solution trickled through it, caused the calcium nitrate to become potassium nitrate, or saltpeter. Thus, the natural resources above the cave allowed the useful conversion of a mineral inside the cave.

 Analysis of the Sample Technical Writing. The paragraph follows the prescribed general characteristics. Furthermore, it includes a suggestion of process [*see* Process Analysis *in Part II*], and includes some characteristics of a cause-and-effect paper [*see* Cause and Effect *in Part II*]. Note the following classification characteristics:

- The topic sentence tells the reader the general topic (natural resources), the means (aboveground), and the number (two).
- The organizational pattern uses chronological organization (from construction to operation) in the whole-by-whole pattern (wood for construction in the first part of the paragraph and wood for burning in the second part).

- The details explain the reason for the selection of the particular woods (straight grain, high potassium content).
- The writer maintains unity by omitting irrelevant details.
- Transitions move the reader smoothly from one sentence to the next. Especially notable is the transition from the first idea (wood for construction) to the second (wood for burning). Note that the transition is really two complete sentences.
- Sentence structure, vocabulary, and tone are all appropriate to the technically minded audience.
- The conclusion ties together the two parts of the classification and shows the relationship to the whole.

The explanation of characteristics and process along with the sample papers and their analyses should give you a solid background for developing all or part of any paper by means of classification.

Comparison and Contrast

Writing developed by the comparison-and-contrast method shows similarities in otherwise unlike subjects and differences in otherwise similar subjects. Usually, a writer does not analyze similarities in subjects already recognized as similar or differences in subjects recognized as different.

Some assignments may require you to compare or contrast certain ideas: Compare the attitudes of the North and the South immediately prior to the Civil War. Compare the poetry of Walt Whitman with that of Carl Sandburg. Contrast two methods of accounting and indicate which is the better method for specific purposes.

Sometimes an essay test will include questions that require a comparison-and-contrast answer: Contrast the economic principles of socialism with that of capitalism. Compare and contrast two Shakespearean sonnets that describe or seem to refer to the Dark Lady. [*See also* Essay-Question Responses *in Part III.*]

The comparison-and-contrast method of development almost always incorporates other methods of development as well, including analogy, definition, description, cause and effect, narration, or process. [*See entries for each elsewhere in Part II.*]

CHARACTERISTICS

A paper developed by means of comparison or contrast usually includes the following characteristics:

- A subject suitable for comparison or contrast so that a comparison shows similarities of generally unlike subjects and a contrast shows differences of generally similar subjects
- A topic or thesis sentence that establishes the general comparison or contrast [*see* topic sentence *and* thesis sentence *in the Glossary; see* Writing a Paragraph *and* Writing a Multi-Paragraph Paper *in Part I for discussion and examples*]
- A clearly developed whole-by-whole, part-by-part, or similarities-differences organization
- Details that clarify the similarities or differences
- Precise transitions that help the reader single out the differences or similarities [*see* transitions *in the Glossary*]
- Unity within individual paragraphs and, in the case of a theme, within the entire paper [*see* unity *in the Glossary*]
- A conclusion that reiterates the purpose of the paper, to show comparisons or to show contrasts, or, in rare occasions, to show both [*see* conclusion *in the Glossary*]

PROCESS

The following steps can help you plan, organize, develop, revise, and proofread any writing developed by comparison and contrast.

STEP 1   **Prewriting • Selecting Suitable Subjects**
Subjects suitable for comparison-and-contrast development must meet two of these three qualifications:

- The two subjects to be compared must be generally different so that the writer can establish similarities:

  Potatoes and onions, while obviously different, show similarities as root crops: planting procedure, harvesting, storing.

- The two subjects to be contrasted must be generally similar so that the writer can establish their differences:

  Catalpa and white-pine lumber, both soft woods, differ in weathering qualities, rot resistance, and usefulness indoors and out.

- The comparison or contrast must be of significance to the reader. For example, the differences between dogs and cats as pets are so obvious that readers will not waste time reading about them.

In many cases, the subject will be assigned, such as in an essay test. In other cases, you may have to select the subject yourself. In order to select a suitable comparison-and-contrast subject, think of content-related topics you have recently studied:

two economic theories
two contemporary poets
two mathematics principles
two similar chemical compounds
two Impressionistic artists
two political figures in the same office
two political figures running for the same office
two thematically similar stories
two kinds of hardwood lumber
two kinds of lathes
two recipes for whole-wheat bread
two approaches to disciplining children

Make a list of potential subjects. Think through each of them in terms of similarities and differences. Select one that seems to offer the greatest potential for a paper.

STEP 2   **Prewriting • Choosing Details**
Next, decide whether you can most effectively show similarities or differences. A third alternative may be to show both similarities and differences. Although the organization becomes more complicated when you show both, this third alternative may be the best in some situations.

Jot down three or four major similarities or differences or both. Your list may look like this:

Topic: **Methods of Disciplining Children**
Approach: Differences
Details: Nonverbal message
                   Verbal message
                   Reward/reinforcement

STEP 3   **Prewriting • Organizing the Whole**
Comparison-and-contrast pieces may be organized according to one of three patterns: whole-by-whole, part-by-part, or similarities-differences. Which organization you use depends entirely on which works best for the subject. In some cases, one method may be as effective as another. Following are brief summaries of each of the three methods:

Whole-by-Whole Pattern. Using the whole-by-whole pattern of organization, the writer explains all of one subtopic before she discusses the second. For instance, from the list in Step 2, the writer discusses one method of discipline in terms of each detail, nonverbal messages, verbal messages, and reward/reinforcement. Then, she discusses the second. The general outline looks like this:

First method of discipline
  Nonverbal messages
  Verbal messages
  Reward/reinforcement

Second method of discipline
  Nonverbal messages
  Verbal messages
  Reward/reinforcement

[*For sample papers developed by the whole-by-whole pattern, see the* Sample for Social Sciences *and the* Sample for Science *later in this section.*]

Part-by-Part Pattern. Using the part-by-part pattern of organization, the writer explains the main point of both subtopics before introducing the next point. For instance, using the same preceding example, the writer discusses nonverbal messages in the first method of discipline and then in the second. Then, the writer discusses verbal messages and, finally, reward/reinforcement. The general outline looks like this:

Nonverbal messages
  First method of discipline
  Second method of discipline

Verbal messages
  First method of discipline
  Second method of discipline

Reward/reinforcement
  First method of discipline
  Second method of discipline

[*For sample papers developed by the part-by-part pattern, see the* Sample for English *and the* Sample Technical Writing *later in this section.*]

Similarities-Differences Pattern. Using the similarities-differences pattern of organization, the writer deals with both comparisons and contrasts. In this pattern, the writer discusses in one paragraph all the similarities of the two methods of discipline and in another paragraph all the differences. The general outline may look like this:

Similarities

Nonverbal messages
    First method of discipline
    Second method of discipline
Verbal messages
    First method of discipline
    Second method of discipline
Reward/reinforcement
    First method of discipline
    Second method of discipline

Differences

Nonverbal messages
    First method of discipline
    Second method of discipline
Verbal messages
    First method of discipline
    Second method of discipline
Reward/reinforcement
    First method of discipline
    Second method of discipline

Or, the general outline may look like this:

Similarities

First method of discipline
    Nonverbal messages
    Verbal messages
    Reward/reinforcement
Second method of discipline
    Nonverbal messages
    Verbal messages
    Reward/reinforcement

Differences

First method of discipline
    Nonverbal messages
    Verbal messages
    Reward/reinforcement
Second method of discipline
    Nonverbal messages
    Verbal messages
    Reward/reinforcement

[*For a sample paper developed by the similarities-differences pattern, see the* Sample Work-Place Writing *later in this section.*]

How items are organized within the specific patterns determines the paper's emphasis. [*See* emphasis *in the Glossary.*]

STEP 4   **Prewriting • Organizing the Parts**

Next, determine which details you will discuss first and last. Think about the set of subjects and details listed earlier in this section. The writer must decide whether nonverbal messages are more important than verbal messages and whether reward/reinforcement is most or least important. The internal organization, then, may be one of the orders of importance. [*See* order of importance *in the Glossary.*]

Whichever order you choose, keep these guidelines in mind:

- The topic you discuss last will have the most impact on your reader.
- The topic you discuss first will have the next greatest impact on your reader.
- The details in the middle attract less attention and sometimes are nearly buried, a situation that may or may not be beneficial to your subject.

These general guidelines apply both to the overall organization of the broad topics and to the internal organization of the details.

[*See the* Sample for Science *and the* Sample Work-Place Writing *later in this section for examples of orders of importance.*]

Chronological organization or spatial organization may also be appropriate for the internal organization of comparison-and-contrast papers. [*Note the spatial organization in the* Sample for English *and the* Sample for Social Sciences *and the chronological order in the* Sample Technical Writing *later in this section.*]

Choose the internal organization that best suits your subject and enables you to achieve the greatest emphasis.

STEP 5   **Prewriting • Developing the Topic or Thesis Sentence**

With the organizational plan in place, you are ready to develop the topic sentence, or, in the preparation of a theme, the thesis sentence. The topic or thesis sentence should indicate not only the general subject and whether the paper will deal with comparisons or contrasts but also the organization. For example:

Two methods of disciplining children show vast differences between the verbal and nonverbal messages as well as the reinforcement techniques.

The preceding topic sentence indicates the subject (*two methods of disciplining children*), establishes a purpose of contrast (*vast differences*), and indicates the order (*a discussion of verbal and nonverbal messages will be followed by a discussion of reinforcement techniques*). The implication of the topic *reinforcement techniques* appearing last is that it illustrates the greatest differences between the two methods of discipline and, perhaps, offers the best means for determining which method to choose.

STEP 6   **Writing • Developing the First Draft**

Following the organization plan selected in Steps 4 and 5, develop the first draft of your comparison-and-contrast paper. Be sure to use techniques of good writing:

- If you are developing a paragraph, begin with the topic sentence. [*See* Writing a Paragraph *in Part I.*]
- If you are developing a theme, begin with a suitable introductory paragraph that concludes with the thesis sentence. [*See* Writing a Multi-Paragraph Paper *in Part I.*]
- Follow the organizational plan. If your plan does not work, go back to Steps 4 and 5, alter the plan, and begin again.
- Add sufficient details to clarify the differences and/or similarities.
- End with a concluding statement or concluding paragraph that restates or summarizes your topic.

STEP 7   **Revising • Checking the Content**

As you reread your comparison-and-contrast paper, ask yourself the following questions to pinpoint possibly necessary revisions:

- Does my topic or thesis sentence clearly state my subject and the organization of my paper?
- Do I follow the organization established in my topic or thesis statement?
- Is the organizational pattern the most effective for my subject and purpose? [*See* Revising: Checking Organization *in Part I.*]
- Does the order of my paper best emphasize the most important points? [*See* Revising: Sample Revision for Emphasis *in Part I.*]
- Does the paragraph structure follow my organizational plan? [*See* Revising: Checking Structure *in Part I.*]

- Have I provided sufficient details to support the topics? [*See* Revising: Sample Revision for Specific Detail *in Part I.*]
- Have I maintained unity by omitting unrelated details from the paper? [*See* Revising: Sample Revision for Unity *in Part I.*]
- Are my transitions precise and adequate to clarify and emphasize the comparisons or contrasts to readers? [*See* Revising: Sample Revision for Transition *in Part I.*]
- Are my words and sentences appropriate to the subject and the audience?
- Have I used strong nouns and verbs and avoided flowery modifiers? [*See* Revising: Sample Revision for Wordiness *in Part I.*]
- Is the sentence structure of my paper varied? [*See* Revising: Sample Revision for Sentence Variety *in Part I.*]
- Is the tone of my paper appropriate for the subject? [*See* tone *in the Glossary.*]
- Does the conclusion end my paper effectively? [*See* conclusion *in the Glossary.*]

[*See also* Revising *in Part I for additional general guidelines for the process of revising.*]

STEP 8   **Proofreading • Checking the Details**

When you have completed the revisions suggested by your analysis in Step 7, proofread your paper for accuracy. Check punctuation, grammar, mechanics, and usage. [*See Part IV for rules and examples.*] Check spelling word choice.

A NOTE ABOUT THE SAMPLES

The following samples and their analyses help crystallize your understanding of the comparison-and-contrast method of development. The samples, which include single-paragraph papers and a four-paragraph theme, all deal with the general topic of clothing. Note, however, that specific topics relate directly to the content purpose.

SAMPLE FOR ENGLISH

The following single-paragraph paper was developed for a drama class. The assignment asked students to prepare an introductory paragraph to accompany illustrations of period costumes.

His and Hers Clothing

Over the centuries, as men's clothing has changed, so has women's. When men wore hats for dress, so did women. While men's hats were generally the stereotypical black top hats, women's were plumed, flowered, veiled, broad-brimmed, and bright. When men wore celluloid stand-up collars, women wore high-necked dresses. Even though the men's collars were all alike, women's were decorated with lace, buttons, and jewelry. When men wore gloves, so did the women, not for warmth but as part of the coordinated whole. When men wore high-topped, high-buttoned shoes, women wore the same with a high heel added. Although most shoes were black, the women's sported pointed toes and stitched or cut patterns. So, while the dress of men and women has made simultaneous changes, the women's fancier details added femininity.

Analysis of the Sample for English. The preceding comparison-and-contrast paragraph illustrates some of the characteristics discussed in this section:

- The topic sentence, the first in the paragraph, establishes the subject and the comparison.
- The general organization is part-by-part as the writer talks first about men's hats and then women's, next about men's collars and then women's. (A whole-by-whole organization would have required the writer to talk about men's apparel and then, when he finished that, to talk about women's apparel.)
- The specific order is spatial—from head (*hat*) to foot (*shoes*).
- As the writer compares the simultaneous changes, he also points out some specific differences, always showing the women's apparel as fancier, more decorative.
- The transitions clarify the change, especially with words such as *when* and *while*. Other transitions emphasize the more decorative women's apparel, words such as *even though* and *although*.
- The sentence structure maintains the balance of the comparison. Equal numbers of sentences apply to each subtopic in the paragraph.
- The conclusion ties together the comparison and sets out the contrast.

SAMPLE FOR SOCIAL SCIENCES

As part of a unit on the American Revolution, students wrote papers about some human aspect of the war. The following single-paragraph paper compares the clothing worn by American and British soldiers.

Clothing the Soldiers

During the American Revolution, the American and British soldiers wore different kinds of uniforms. Most American soldiers, straight from their homes and fields, wore what they had: hand-stitched jackets, homespun shirts, leather suspenders, drop-front pants, and homemade shoes. Their hats were as varied as the hat makers. They made do with their lack of similar dress, understanding that rank had its privileges, but making no effort to document it with stripes or stars or bars. They presented a motley group. Unwittingly, however, they wore what, by comparison, was nearly camouflage. On the other hand, the British soldiers were attired in the smart English uniform: red coats, white pants, knee-high black boots, and cocky hats. Their commanders' uniforms marked their prestige. In the fighting field, however, which was home to the American farmers and hunters, the British found their white pants dirty, their boots muddy, and hats knocked askew. What is more, the red and white gleamed like a beacon in any forest or meadow, making amazingly easy-to-spot targets. In fact, the two white belts that crossed their chests made perfect targets. One could debate whether the war was won or lost because of the soldier's clothing.

Analysis of the Sample for Social Sciences. The social sciences sample provides an interesting comparison with the sample for English in several respects. Study the two and note the following:

- The topic sentence, the first sentence in the paragraph, clarifies the subject and the purpose.
- The general organization is whole by whole. First the reader learns about the American soldiers' dress and then about the British soldiers'.
- The order is generally from top to bottom. The reference to the headgear returns the reader to the top.
- Transitions move the reader in an orderly fashion from one topic to the next, an entire sentence providing the transition from the American soldier to the British.
- The order is consistent throughout the paragraph. The topic sentence mentions first the American soldier's clothing, which indeed is discussed first in the paragraph. And because jackets are mentioned first for the American soldier, they are likewise mentioned first for the British soldier. Even later, the order remains as the writer refers to *red and white* as opposed to *white and red.*

- Sentences vary both in length and structure.
- Active voice adds emphasis. [*See* active voice *in the Glossary*.]
- The conclusion emphasizes the differences and leads to speculation.

SAMPLE FOR SCIENCE

As part of a laboratory experiment, students tested the flammability of various substances. Each student reported on a part of the experiment. The student whose paper appears following compared the flame resistance of three fabrics common in clothing.

A Comparison of Flame Resistance among Fabrics

In the process of determining flame resistance among three common fabrics, the experimenter carefully measured two controlled variables: the time the fabric was exposed to flame and the distance of the fabric from the flame. As a result, all test measurements were consistent. Under these controls, three fabrics were tested: polyester, cotton, and wool. Results indicated that the least flame-resistant fabric was polyester. Within 30 seconds' exposure to the flame, the polyester sputtered, melted, and then extinguished itself, leaving a blackened, charred sample. The second least flame-resistant fabric was cotton. It scorched badly when exposed to flame, but it did not burn unless held in the flame for a minimum of 45 seconds. The most flame-resistant fabric was wool. It would not burn unless held steadily in the flame for more than one minute. The results of this test suggest that those people who plan to be near open flame, such as a campfire, would be safest wearing wool.

Analysis of the Sample for Science. Because the science paper is typically very different from an English or social sciences paper, the preceding sample merits attention, especially in terms of the following specifics:

- The topic sentence, which appears first, indicates the basis of the comparison—a laboratory test. Because of the nature of a science paper, it must account for the testing process, even if only briefly, as in this paragraph.
- The general organization follows the whole-by-whole pattern, giving all details for one fabric before moving to the next.
- The internal pattern of organization follows an order of importance, from the least flame-resistant fabric to the most.
- Each comparison includes a one- or two-sentence summary of test results as a basis for comparison.
- Vocabulary and sentence structure are appropriate to the subject and the audience.

- Transitions move the reader smoothly through the organization, especially with words such as *least, next, more,* and *most.*
- The report maintains the third-person point of view by referring, appropriately, to *this experimenter.*
- The conclusion clarifies the comparison by extending the meaning of the test results to daily living.

SAMPLE FOR MATHEMATICS

A clothing designer wanted a pattern spaced on a length of fabric in geometric sequence. Math students compared arithmetic and geometric sequences. The following is one response:

Arithmetic and Geometric Sequences

An arithmetic sequence has numbers arranged so that each number in the list has the same difference between it and the one before. For instance, an arithmetic sequence can be 1, 4, 7, 10, 13, and the difference between any number and the previous number is three. Another arithmetic sequence can be 2, 6, 10, 14, 18, and the difference between any two adjoining numbers is four. On the other hand, a geometric sequence has numbers arranged so that each number in the list is multiplied by a constant value to get the next number in the list. For instance, a geometric sequence can be 3, 6, 12, 24, 48, where the constant multiple is two. Another geometric sequence can be 4, 16, 64, 256, 1024, where the constant multiple is four.

Analysis of the Sample for Mathematics. In comparing arithmetic and geometric sequences, the writer used the following techniques:

- The first part of the paragraph explains arithmetic sequence and gives two examples.
- The comparison is introduced by the phrase, *on the other hand.*
- The second part of the paragraph explains geometric sequence and gives two more examples, thus showing readers the difference between the two kinds of sequences.

SAMPLE WORK-PLACE WRITING

As part of a study on advertising, students compared advertising campaigns from competitive companies. The following four-paragraph paper compares three mail-order clothing companies.

A Comparison of Leading Clothing Catalogs

Mail-order catalogs generate big business in the clothing industry. As a result of the direct-to-the-door competition, the catalogs have become subjects of intense study in terms of advertising techniques. Three such catalogs, apparently equally successful in their respective marketing campaigns, embody significant similarities while at the same time illustrate astounding differences.

Each of the three catalogs uses only full-color photographs. No black and white photographs or line drawings appear in any of them. The paper quality, nearly equal in all three, suggests a "slick" advertisement. All catalogs feature high-fashion items, sportswear, lingerie, and limited footwear. In every case, the item descriptions carry typical advertisers' buzzwords, obviously selected to give the product the best image without obvious misrepresentation. Finally, all three include some kind of general guarantee of "satisfaction or your money back," a toll-free number for information or ordering, and an order blank that accommodates charge customers.

On the other hand, each catalog embodies astounding differences. One is size. The catalogs vary from standard $8\frac{1}{2}$" x 11" to a mid-size 5" x 7" to a half-size 4" x $5\frac{1}{2}$". While the smallest catalog includes eight more pages than the largest, the total number of items listed is just over half that of the largest catalog. Second, the photographic backgrounds for the models range from shabby to sleek. The mid-sized catalog uses nondescript backgrounds, including wood-paneled walls that reflect glare from lights, windows with poorly hung drapes, and painted walls that, under the intense camera light, show imperfections as shadowy effects. At the other extreme, the smallest catalog uses all career-oriented backgrounds, with models standing beside or in front of executive desks, wooden filing cabinets, computer systems, airline ticket counters, or other CEO-related settings. The models carry briefcases, gold pens, computer disks, legal pads, and calculators. Finally, the models' facial expressions and body positions vary considerably. The largest catalog uses models whose expressions are cold, impersonal, distant, maybe even arrogant. The mid-sized catalog's models seem untrained, most assuming an amateur grin, eyes on camera, body pose less than advantageous either for the model or for the clothing. The models in the smallest catalog, however, assume relaxed expressions and poses, almost too relaxed for the business atmosphere in which they are photographed.

In short, then, the mail-order clothing business has reached massive proportions, so much so that catalogs compete in sensitive, subtle ways for the home buyer's business. One who understands the psychology of advertising can sort through the various messages the three catalogs send to their customers.

Analysis of the Sample Work-Place Writing. This theme-length comparison-and-contrast business paper illustrates several options we have not yet seen. Note the following specifics:

- The opening paragraph sets the scene and concludes with the thesis sentence. The reader is prepared to read about both similarities and differences in the three catalogs.
- The general organization of the comparison-and-contrast theme follows the similarities-differences pattern. All similarities are set out in the first body paragraph while all differences appear in the second.
- The specific order within the general pattern follows an order of importance. Both body paragraphs move from the most obvious to the least obvious.
- Abundant transitions help the reader move from the broad category of similarities to the broad category of differences. The transitions also help the reader sort through the differences among the three catalogs. (For actual class purposes, you would cite the catalogs by name, providing a clearer reference for the reader.)
- Vocabulary and sentence structure are appropriate to the subject and the audience.
- The paper maintains unity throughout, each paragraph dealing only with details supporting its topic sentence.
- Specific details allow the reader to see both similarities and differences, including details about color, background, clothing types, model's attitudes, and general descriptions.
- The conclusion, set out in a separate paragraph as theme organization would have it, returns the reader's attention to the popularity and business impact of the subject. At the same time, the conclusion admits that the *astounding differences* require a skilled analyst to determine the total message.

SAMPLE TECHNICAL WRITING

In a clothing class, students wrote papers to compare or contrast two sewing techniques. The single-paragraph paper below compares two kinds of seams.

The Differences between Two Common Clothing Seams

Two common seams appear in both men's and women's clothing: the plain seam and the flat-felled seam. The two kinds of seams require different sewing methods and result in different appearances and different strengths. The plain seam requires the seamstress merely to place two pieces of fabric, right sides together, and run a single row of stitches 5/8" from the raw edges. The flat-felled seam, on the other hand, requires the seamstress to place the pieces of fabric, this time wrong sides together, and stitch a plain seam. At this point, however, she is far from finished. Next, she must press open the seam allowances and trim one seam allowance to 1/8". After turning under the raw edge of the remaining seam allowance, she presses it over the trimmed edge. Finally, she topstitches the pressed seam to the garment close to the folded edge. When these two kinds of seams are finished, they present very different appearances. The plain seam shows only a single line where the fabric joins, but no stitching shows. The two raw edges are hidden inside the garment. On the other hand, the flat-felled seam shows two rows of stitching on the right side of the fabric and no raw seam edges appear inside or out. It adds a classic detail that enhances sportswear. Finally, the seams can be compared by their strength. A plain seam with its single row of stitching is necessarily weaker than two rows of stitching. The added width of fabric between the two rows of stitching on the flat-felled seam further enforces the seam strength. And the flat-felled seam cures fraying edges, another strengthening feature. In short, the plain seam, because it is easy to sew, is more frequently used; but the flat-felled seam, although it requires greater sewing skill, adds strength and classic detail to the garment.

Analysis of the Sample Technical Writing. The preceding comparison-and-contrast paragraph effectively contrasts two kinds of seams. Think about the following specifics as you evaluate the sample yourself:

- The topic sentence names the subject and the three major differences.
- The part-by-part organization permits the writer to discuss the sewing method, the appearance, and the strength of each kind of seam.
- The chronological order allows the reader to follow the organization from sewing to finished product.

- In every case, to follow the pattern of organization, the writer discusses first the plain seam and then the flat-felled seam.
- Transitions move the reader from step to step and from detail to detail.
- Vocabulary and sentence structure fit the subject and the audience.
- The conclusion makes a final statement in support of the flat-felled seam.

After studying the samples and their analyses, you should be able to use the comparison-and-contrast method to develop your own writing.

Definition

A definition paper is particularly useful in dealing with abstract terms such as *democracy, love, hope,* and *ethics.* In some cases, when a special term requires a definition, the dictionary definition will suffice. In other cases, however, a whole paragraph or even a full-length theme may be necessary. For instance, a single-sentence definition of artificial intelligence may be adequate for the lay person, but the scientific community involved in the research may provide a several-page definition. Be sure you understand to what extent the instructor expects you to define. [*See also* Essay-Question Responses: Essay Test Questions *in Part III.*]

The scope of the definition depends on the purpose, and the purpose generally depends on the audience.

CHARACTERISTICS

In general, regardless of length, a definition

- identifies the term to be defined,
- identifies the class to which the term belongs,
- identifies the difference between this term and all others in the class. For example:

  A computer catalog *(term to be defined)* is an index *(class to which the term belongs)* of all the books in a given library *(difference between computer catalog and all other indexes).*

- uses terminology suitable for the audience, reducing technical terms to lay terms for the lay audience,

- sometimes uses the negative to identify what the term is not,
- may include examples by way of explanation,
- may include process analysis [*see* Process Analysis *later in Part II*],
- may include cause and effect [*see* Cause and Effect *earlier in Part II*],
- may include comparison, especially to show the unfamiliar in terms of the familiar [*see* Comparison and Contrast *and* Analogy *earlier in Part II*],
- may include description [*see* Description *later in Part II*].

PROCESS

The following process can help you plan, organize, write, and revise a definition. You need to use the same process whether you write a single sentence or a full-length theme; this section uses a middle ground, the paragraph, by way of example.

STEP 1   Prewriting • Putting the Term in Its Class

When you define a term, either within the context of another paper or as a paper in itself, you must first put the term in its class. In other words, to what larger group does this term belong? Consider the examples below:

Term	Class
conifer	tree
capitalism	economic philosophy
hypothalamus	part of the brain
gross income	income
acrylic	paint

Now, for the term you must define, list the class to which it belongs.

STEP 2   Prewriting • Deciding the Difference

After you have named the class to which the term belongs, you must decide how this term is different from all others in its class. Study the following examples:

Term	Class	Difference
conifer	tree	stays green year-round
capitalism	economic philosophy	encourages free enterprise
hypothalamus	part of the brain	controls metabolism
gross income	income	before expenses are deducted
acrylic	paint	works like oil but dries quicker

Now write a sentence in which you put the term in its class and show the difference between it and other members of its class. For example:

A conifer is a tree that stays green year-round.

This sentence may become the topic or thesis sentence for your paragraph or theme. [*See* topic sentence *and* thesis sentence *in the Glossary for quick reference, and see* Writing a Paragraph *and* Writing a Multi-Paragraph Paper *in Part I for a complete discussion of paragraph and theme structu*re.]

STEP 3   **Prewriting • Choosing Explanatory Details**

If your definition requires more than a single sentence, then you need to determine which details will best complete the definition. Think about the following possibilities:

Analogy or Comparison. You may define the *law of supply and demand* by comparing the price fluctuations with the behavior of children on a seesaw. [*See* Analogy *and* Comparison and Contrast *earlier in Part II.*]

Process or Structural Analysis. A *kiln* can be defined by structural analysis, describing how it is constructed, and by process analysis, describing how it is used. [*See* Process Analysis *later in Part II.*]

Cause or Effect. To define *mulch* as *any organic matter that smothers unwanted vegetation and, as it deteriorates, enriches the soil* is to define by effect. The definition explains how the mulch affects what it covers.

Description, Details, Examples. You can best define *technical report* by describing its contents and appearance and by offering an example of a typical technical report.

Negation. By establishing what is not, you can define what is. To say that a *fireplace is not an efficient means of heating* is to define by negation.

Combination of Methods. *Photosynthesis* can be defined by explaining the process (process analysis), by showing the effects of the process (cause or effect), and by describing the effect when the process breaks down (description, example, cause or effect, and negation).

Choose the most appropriate means of defining the term and list as many details as you can using that means.

STEP 4   **Prewriting • Organizing the Details**
Next, arrange the details in some logical order. You may choose chronological order, spatial order, or some order of importance [*see entries for each in the Glossary*] according to the demands of your subject.

STEP 5   **Writing • Making the Definition Clear**
As you write your first draft, think of your audience:

- Will they understand the terminology?
- Will they be able to follow the organization?
- Do transitions help them see relationships among the subtopics?
- Are the details sufficient to explain the term?

STEP 6   **Revising • Checking the Content**
As you reread your definition, ask yourself these questions to check for areas for possible revision:

- Does the topic sentence put the term into its class and then show the differences between it and all other members of its class?
- If the term is abstract, does the definition include specific details and examples to help the reader understand the abstraction? [*See* Revising: Sample Revision for Specific Detail *in Part I.*]
- If the term is technical, does the definition reduce the term to lay person's language or provide specific examples the lay person will understand?
- If the term names a process, does the reader learn about the process?
- If the term names a situation, does the reader learn about the situation and its causes and effects, as appropriate?
- If possible, does the reader see the unfamiliar in terms of the familiar, perhaps by means of a comparison, a contrast, or an analogy?
- Can the reader follow a clear organization with the help of effective transitions? [*See* Revising: Sample Revision for Transition *in Part I.*]
- Does the conclusion satisfy the reader with all he or she should know about the term? [*See* conclusion *in the Glossary.*]

[*In addition, see* Revising *in Part I for general guidelines for improving structure and polishing style.*]

STEP 7 **Proofreading • Checking the Details**

When you have completed the revising process in Step 6, you are ready to prepare your final draft. Then check your work for grammar, mechanics, usage, and punctuation [*see Part IV for rules and examples*] and check spelling and word choice.

A NOTE ABOUT THE SAMPLES

The following single- and two-paragraph definitions illustrate definition by description, example, effect, process analysis, structural analysis, negation, comparison, and combinations of methods. Study the samples and the analyses that follow.

SAMPLE FOR ENGLISH

The following definition, developed for a drama unit in a literature class, uses a combination of methods, including comparison, description, example, and effect.

> **The Proscenium Arch**
>
> Originated in 1618 in Parma, Italy, at the Farnese Theater by an architect name Aleotti, the proscenium arch gave the audience a new kind of theater experience. The proscenium arch is a style of stage construction that frames the performing area as if with a picture frame. Its development has been labeled as the beginning of the modern stage; as such, the frame-like structure, for the first time, literally separated the audience from the actors. The separation physically and psychologically enhanced the impact of the performance. Until this time, many performances occurred on platforms, some of them makeshift affairs set up in the town square. The typical platform, even in a fine theater, simply sat in front of an ornamented facade. With the development of the proscenium arch that placed the action behind the "picture frame," the architect permitted the visual expansion of the stage. Using the arched structure, Italian set designers experimented with linear perspective and soon added movable sets to change scenery, thus, giving the audience the illusion of expansive settings. Indeed, stages sometimes are as much as 100 feet deep and need little illusion. Still, the proscenium-arch theater opened new vistas to the set designers, the actors and actresses, and the audience.

Analysis of the Sample for English. The preceding single-paragraph definition illustrates a number of the principles discussed in the writing process:

- The topic sentence, the second in the paragraph, names the term to be defined (*proscenium arch*), puts it in its class (*style of stage construction*), and identifies the difference between this and others in its class (*"frames" the stage*).

- Clearly intended as introductory remarks, the definition uses such technical terms as *facade, set designers, movable scenery,* and *linear perspective.* The terms, however, probably have some meaning for the audience.

- Enhancing the definition, a comparison with earlier stage construction and the analysis of two structures help the reader recognize the significance of the proscenium-arch development.

- An explanation of the effects (in a cause-and-effect relationship) also clarifies the impact of the arch design.

- The frame analogy allows the reader to compare the unfamiliar term with the familiar.

- The conclusion makes a final statement about stage construction and summarizes its impact.

SAMPLE FOR SOCIAL SCIENCES

The following two-paragraph paper explains a kind of tax. Prepared to meet an assignment in an economics class, the definition relies primarily on process analysis and comparison.

Value-Added Tax

Value-added tax is a kind of corporate tax that taxes each step of production only for the proportionate value it has in the final product. It is an alternate means of taxing industrial processes and, according to some political analysts, encourages business and additional employment. Consider, for instance, the aluminum industry. Under present corporate tax laws, the ore is mined, sold to the smelters, and taxed. Then the ore is smelted, sold to the aluminum companies, and taxed. Next the aluminum is cut into sheets, sold to can producers, and taxed. Then the sheets are formed into cans, sold to beverage companies, and taxed. Finally, the cans are filled with fruit juice, sold to consumers, and taxed.

Value-added tax eliminates the standard tax at each step and taxes only the amount of value that step adds to the final product, in this case, the canned drinks. For instance, if a piece of ore is worth $1.00, and the smelted aluminum from that ore is worth $3.00, the smelter pays tax on the $2.00 value added. If the piece of aluminum now valued at $3.00 forms aluminum cans worth $5.00, the can maker pays the tax not on the $5.00, but on the $2.00 value added. Finally, the $5.00 worth of cans, filled with beverage, are now worth $15.00, so the beverage company pays tax on the $10.00 added value. The consumer pays no tax except, of course, indirectly in increased prices.

Analysis of the Sample for Social Sciences. The preceding definition follows many of the process suggestions:

- The thesis sentence, the first sentence in the paragraph, identifies the term (*value-added tax*), the class (*a kind of corporate tax*), and the difference between it and others in its class (*taxes each step of production only on the value added toward the final product*).
- The remainder of the first paragraph uses the aluminum industry by way of example to describe the present taxing method.
- The second paragraph illustrates the differences in the value-added taxing method.
- The comparison-and-contrast development follows the whole-by-whole approach. [*See* Comparison and Contrast *earlier in Part II, and see* whole-by-whole organization *in the Glossary*.]
- Parallel construction enhances the organization and provides smooth transition for the reader. [*See* parallel structure *in the Glossary*.]

SAMPLE FOR SCIENCE

The following paragraph responds to an essay question on a chemistry test in which students were to define quantum numbers in a well-developed paragraph. [*See also* Essay-Question Responses: Essay Test Questions *in Part III*.]

Quantum Numbers

Quantum numbers are numerical descriptions that, when taken together, describe a given electron in a given atom. There are four quantum numbers for every electron. The first, called the principal quantum number, describes the energy level of the electron. The second, called the orbital quantum number, describes the shape of the orbit in which the electron moves. The third, called the magnetic quantum number, describes the electron's orientation in space. The fourth, called the spin, describes the clockwise or counterclockwise spin of the electron around its own axis. Together, the four numbers describe an electron, and no two electrons in an atom can have the same four quantum numbers.

 Analysis of the Sample for Science. The preceding definition is written for an audience with some understanding of electrons and their function; most beginning chemistry students have that understanding. Thus, the definition uses technical terms appropriate for the content area. Specifically it includes these features:

- The topic sentence identifies the term to be defined (*quantum numbers*), the class (*numerical description*) and the difference between it and others in its class (*describe an electron*).
- The definition separates the term into its four parts, and by analyzing each of the parts, defines the whole.
- The organization follows an order of importance. [*See* order of importance *in the Glossary*.]
- Transitions effectively separate the four kinds of quantum numbers and help show the distinctions among them. [*See* transitions *in the Glossary*.]

SAMPLE FOR MATHEMATICS

Students in math class were asked to define scientific notation. The following is one student's response.

> ### Scientific Notation
>
> When writing extremely large or small numbers, you may sometimes have so many digits that you cannot read them or even pronounce whatever words it may take to say them. (What comes after trillions?) To more easily write those very large or small numbers, mathematicians use a method called scientific notation. To write a number in scientific notation, you move the decimal point from its present location one place to the right of the first digit that is not a zero. In other words, you write the number so that it has a value between 1 and 10, rounding off as necessary. Then you multiply the number by 10 raised to the power equal to the number of places that the decimal point was moved. If you move the decimal point from the right to the left, the exponent is positive. For example, 9,238,648,500 written in scientific notation is 9.24×10^9. On the other hand, if you move the decimal point from the left to the right, the exponent is negative. For example, .00000092 written in scientific notation is 9.2×10^7. So scientific notation makes numbers shorter and easier to read and mathematical operations easier to complete.

Analysis of the Sample for Mathematics. As a definition, the preceding paragraph uses several special techniques:

- The topic (third) sentence identifies the term (*scientific notation*), the class (*method*) and the difference between it and others in its class (*for writing very large or small numbers*).
- The explanation of the process for writing scientific notation (*see also* Process Analysis *later in Part II*) helps readers further understand the definition.

The examples clarify scientific notation, including both positive and negative exponents.

SAMPLE WORK-PLACE WRITING

The following paragraph defines net profit by using negation and process analysis.

Net Profit

When a business must determine success or failure, it looks at net profit. Net profit is the money made after all expenses are deducted. It is not a measure of sales or income. That is gross profit, or how much money actually came into the business. Beginning with gross profit, the business deducts salaries and wages, cost of employee benefits, cost of raw materials, cost of manufacturing or production, cost of maintenance and depreciation, and all other business expenses, either direct or indirect, for the year. When all expenses are deducted from the gross profit, what is left is net profit. That is the traditional "bottom line."

 Analysis of the Sample Work-Place Writing. The sample definition follows the general guidelines for the process:

- The topic sentence includes the term to be defined (*net profit*), the class (*money*), and the difference between it and others in its class (*what is left after expenses are paid*).
- The term is negated, that is, explained in terms of what it is not.
- The remainder of the paragraph lists some of the major deductions from gross profit to show that what is left is net profit.
- The simple, straightforward organization, from what is not to what is, makes the definition easy to understand.

SAMPLE TECHNICAL WRITING

The following paragraph defines a specific kind of roof. The paragraph is one student's response to an assignment in an architectural design class.

The Gambrel Roof

The gambrel is a kind of roof that has a double pitch. The traditional roof, shaped like an upside-down V, has one pitch, each side sloping toward the ground at the same angle. The gambrel roof, which the British call a mansard roof, has a second pitch about halfway down the slope. The second pitch is always much steeper than the first, sometimes nearly straight. So the roof looks something like a small upside-down V standing on stilts. The gambrel roof is often put on barns or other buildings to afford a second story without building two-story exterior walls.

Analysis of the Sample Technical Writing. As a definition, the preceding paragraph uses several special techniques:

- The topic sentence identifies the term (*gambrel*), the class (*roof*), and the differences between it and others in its class (*has a double pitch*).
- The comparison of the gambrel with the traditional roof enables the reader to visualize the differences.
- The comparisons with the upside-down V help readers to follow a verbal description visually. Often diagrams accompany such definitions.
- Finally, the explanation for the purpose of the roof helps the reader think not only about the outside appearance but the inside structure.

The preceding samples should help you write effective definitions. The principles of developing a good definition remain constant, regardless of the length or your paper.

Description

Certain situations require papers that are completely descriptive. You may be asked to describe the setting for a novel or a microscopic specimen. In addition, almost all papers require some description. For instance, how could a writer talk about the process by which something is made without describing the steps in the process? Cause and effect, comparison and contrast, definition, narration, analogy—almost anything you write may include description. [*See separate entries for each of these methods of development in Part II*.]

Description relies on the five senses. The reader should see, hear, taste, smell, and feel. [*See* imagery *in the Glossary*.] At the same time, however, good description is synonymous with clarity. It conveys information accurately.

This section assumes that you need to develop an entire paper using description. As you use description to develop parts of other papers, of course, you will employ the same techniques but perhaps in abbreviated form.

CHARACTERISTICS

A descriptive paper serves only to describe. Usually, however, the paper includes the following general characteristics:

- A subject worthy of description
- An emphasis, either direct or indirect, on the five senses
- Use of figures of speech, especially to enrich the description and spark reader interest
- A topic or thesis sentence that names the subject to be described and establishes the attitude toward the subject [*see* tone *in the Glossary*]
- One of three patterns of organization: chronological, spatial, or order of importance
- A single, consistent tone and mood [*see* mood *in the Glossary*]
- Details that support the tone and mood
- Unity within the paragraphs and the paper as a whole
- Vocabulary that clarifies
- Varied sentence structure, which enhances the general attitude and adds appropriate emphasis
- An effective conclusion

PROCESS

In order to plan, organize, write, revise, and proofread your description, use the following process.

STEP 1   **Prewriting • Choosing a Topic**

Ordinarily almost any topic can lend itself to description. Think about the subjects you have studied most recently in various content areas:

cooking utensils
machines
audiovisual equipment
globes, maps
writing techniques
art supplies
wiring harnesses
keyboard position
rough-cut lumber
radio-script writing
chemical reactions
camera functions

As you think about the subjects, choose one that fits the purpose. [*See also* Prewriting *in Part I.*]

STEP 2   **Prewriting • Narrowing the Topic**

The subjects listed in Step 1 are too broad for a single descriptive paper. In order to narrow the topic, list subtopics for each general topic. Use the following example as a pattern:

General subject:	**globes, maps**
Subtopics:	outline maps
	regional maps
	resource maps
	topographical maps
	political maps
	world maps

As you list the divisions of your subject, you should find a topic narrowed enough for a descriptive paper. In the preceding list, for instance, you may choose topographical maps for a descriptive paragraph.

Select the narrowed topic before you go on to Step 3.

STEP 3   **Prewriting • Determining the Purpose**

Next, think about what you hope to accomplish with your description. Who will read it? What purpose do you hope to achieve by it? (If the topic has been assigned, the purpose is probably stated or implied in the assignment.)

Stop now and determine the purpose. State your purpose in a single sentence. For example:

The description of a topographical map will explain the purpose of its lines and symbols, especially as they are helpful to hikers.

The statement of purpose will help you select relevant details.

STEP 4   **Prewriting • Selecting the Details**

After you have narrowed the topic and determined your purpose, you must select appropriate details for your description. Assume, for instance, that you have chosen to develop a description of a topographical map. You may list the following details:

snake-like contour lines
elevation indicated
ridges, valleys
increasing versus decreasing elevation
exploration
good for hikers, backpackers
help plan routes

Now, select details that specifically support your purpose. In the preceding example list, for instance, the details about hikers, exploration, and planning routes are only of secondary importance to the purpose of the paper. Revised to meet the purpose of the paper, the list now looks like this:

Indicates rate of incline
    Increasing elevation
    Decreasing elevation
Indicates ridges
Indicates valleys

STEP 5   Prewriting • Organizing the Details

Next, arrange the details in some order. If the subject is set in time, use chronological order, perhaps including a flashback. [*See* chronological order *and* flashback *in the Glossary.*] For a different kind of subject, use an order of importance. [*See* order of importance *in the Glossary.*] Or, for a description of a setting or scene, use spatial order. [*See* spatial order *in the Glossary.*]

The preceding example can be organized by an order of importance, describing first the most obvious characteristics of the topographical map (the snake-like contour lines) followed by the less obvious characteristics (degree of incline or decline).

Select the method that seems most logical for your subject and number the details in that order.

STEP 6   Prewriting • Developing the Topic or Thesis Sentence

Finally, you are ready to write a topic or thesis sentence. [*See* topic sentence *and* thesis sentence *in the Glossary for quick reference, and see* Writing a Paragraph *and* Writing a Multi-Paragraph Paper *in Part I for complete details and examples.*]

Use the statement of purpose developed in Step 3 to develop your topic or thesis sentence. If you are writing a paragraph, your topic sentence should include these specifics:

• Stated subject to be described
• Attitude toward subject

Examine the following topic sentence and then develop one for your own descriptive paper.

The topographical map may look like a child's inept efforts to follow the lines, but a closer look shows three purposes for the squiggly dividing marks.

STEP 7   **Writing • Following the Plan**

To prepare your first draft, begin with the topic or thesis sentence and develop supporting details in the order you selected in Step 4. As you write, try to include techniques that will enhance your description:

- Use colorful language, specific nouns and vigorous verbs, especially those that create images of the senses.
- Where appropriate, make a conscious effort to include figures of speech, allowing subtle comparisons to spark the reader's imagination.
- Include adequate supporting details to clarify the subject being described. [*See* specific detail *in the Glossary*.]
- Conclude with a clincher that adds a final bit of descriptive imagery.

STEP 8   **Revising • Improving the Content**

When you have completed the first draft, revise. Every paper can be improved, so examine your description using the following questions to suggest possible improvements:

- Does my topic or thesis sentence clearly state my subject and identify the attitude of my description?
- Do I follow a specific organizational plan?
- Is the organizational plan effective, or would my paper be better using a different one?
- Does my paper maintain a consistent tone throughout? [*See* tone *in the Glossary*.]
- Have I added adequate details to clarify the subject being described? [*See* Revising: Sample Revision for Specific Detail *in Part I*.]
- Do the details stimulate the reader's five senses, or at least most of them?
- Where appropriate, do figures of speech enhance the description?
- Does the vocabulary suit the subject, attitude, and audience?
- Does the sentence structure add emphasis or variety? [*See* Revising: Sample Revision for Sentence Variety *in Part I*.]
- Does the paper maintain unity? [*See* Revising: Sample Revision for Unity *in Part I*.]
- Are transitions adequate to move the reader smoothly from sentence to sentence and from paragraph to paragraph? [*See* transitions *in the Glossary and* Revising: Sample Revision for Transition *in Part I*.]

- Does the paper avoid flowery modifiers, using instead strong nouns and verbs? [*See* Revising: Sample Revision for Wordiness *in Part I.*]
- Does the conclusion end the paper effectively? [*See* conclusion *in the Glossary.*]

[*For additional, more general guidelines, see* Revising *in Part I.*]

STEP 9   **Proofreading • Checking the Details**

When you have completed revising, proofread your paper for accuracy. Check punctuation, grammar, mechanics, and usage [*see Part IV for rules and examples*]. Check spelling and word choice.

A NOTE ABOUT THE SAMPLES

The following samples and their analyses apply the process described in this section. Each describes some feature of cedar, as a tree or as lumber, appropriate for the subject or purpose. Descriptions vary according to their purpose. What is suitable in a literary description, for instance, is not suitable in a scientific description.

SAMPLE FOR ENGLISH

Students in an English class studied descriptive-writing techniques and then wrote single-paragraph descriptions.

The Stately Cedar

A gnarled cedar clutches the limestone cliff. Its trunk twisted and bent, the stalwart has bowed and sighed in decades of mock worship to the wind, never budging from its king-of-the-mountain perch. In the searing sun, its incense drifts across the wind-clean rock, and the feathery dark blue-green foliage casts only thin shadows on the gray-white floor. Forever stirring breezes across the cliff top trade mindless whispers with the Ancient One. It stands as the Maker's champion of endurance.

 Analysis of the Sample for English. The preceding paragraph includes many characteristics of a good literary description. Note the following specifics:

- The topic sentence, which is also the conclusion in this paragraph, names the topic (*champion,* which the reader understands now to be the cedar tree) and indicates the attitude (*endurance*).
- Images to affect four of the five senses appear throughout the paragraph:

- **Sight**: gnarled, twisted, bent, bowed, king-of-the-mountain perch, searing sun, feathery dark blue-green, thin shadows, gray-white floor
  - **Sound**: sighed, stirring breezes, whispers
  - **Touch**: gnarled, clutches, limestone, twisted, searing sun, wind-clean, feathery, stirring breezes
  - **Smell**: incense
- Figures of speech add subtle interest to the description:
  - **Personification**: clutches, twisted and bent, bowed and sighed in . . . worship, never budging, king-of-the-mountain perch, breezes . . . trade mindless whispers, Ancient One, champion
  - **Allusion**: stalwart, king-of-the-mountain perch, Ancient One, champion
  - **Alliteration**: clutches the cliff, bent and bowed, searing sun . . . incense
  - **Onomatopoeia**: sighed, searing, whispers
  - **Metaphor**: stalwart, wind-clean rock, gray-white floor, mindless whispers, champion
- Organized chronologically, from distant past to today, the description also moves from physically distant to close.
- The transitions, primarily repetition of words and phrases and their respective pronouns, connect the sentences smoothly.
- Use of active voice and action verbs throughout makes the description more powerful. [*See* active voice *and* action verb *in the Glossary.*]
- Sentence structure varies from simple to complex, including complex series.
- The conclusion, which is also the topic sentence, ties together the details in the paragraph, all of which illustrate endurance in spite of obstacles.

SAMPLE FOR SOCIAL SCIENCES

Students in a United States history class were asked to describe typical furnishings in an American home in the late 1800s. After visiting a living museum, one student prepared the following description of a hope chest. Appropriately for a social sciences class, the description also incorporates a cultural statement. By describing the contents of a bride's hope chest—often made of cedar—the writer is able to describe prized home furnishings. Note, too, that as a result of the writer's approach, the description takes on a narrative quality. [*See* Narration *later in Part II.*]

The Cedar Chest: A Cultural Statement

As she propped open the hinged lid carved with the traditional hearts and doves, the sweet aromatic cedar scent wafted up, filling the room like incense with a home-at-last comfort. Inside the cedar chest lay the material realities of the bride's dream for a happy home. In the far left corner, a Trail to Dublin quilt lay folded, its tiny stitching attesting to the work of family quilting bees, its red and white now dimmed in the candlelight. Crowded against it as if for protection, a pair of pewter candlesticks, still free from wax, waited like sentinels to grace the bride's table. An Aladdin oil lamp, its chimney wrapped in tissue, squatted against the quilt but closer to the front, away from the pewter. The lamp's shining nickel bowl distorted the reflection of the embroidered table runner, folded carefully on top of the knotted comforter to the right. In the far right corner, the precious family heirlooms lay linen-wrapped, awaiting the new bride's home: a hand-carved springerle board, the family Bible, an ivory comb and brush set, and a floral picture made of hair. She closed the lid to the chest and traced with her finger the date carved on the front: 1892.

Analysis of the Sample for Social Sciences. The preceding paragraph includes fewer figures of speech than did the sample for English; however, it includes enough imagery and figurative language to make what could be a lackluster paper into an interesting one. Consider the following characteristics:

- The topic sentence appears as the second sentence in the paragraph: *Inside the cedar chest lay the material realities of the bride's dream for a happy home.* It states the subject (*material reality*, that is, contents of cedar chest) and the attitude (*dream for a happy home*).
- Images affect most of the five senses. The absence of the taste and sound senses seems reasonable in light of the topic. Note these images:
  - **Sight**: carved, traditional hearts and doves, Trail to Dublin quilt, tiny stitching, red and white dimmed, candlelight, pewter, free from wax, Aladdin oil lamp, wrapped in tissue, squatted against the quilt, closer to front, shining nickel, distorted reflection, embroidered, knotted comforter, linen-wrapped, hand-carved springerle board, Bible, ivory comb and brush set, floral picture made of hair, date on front read 1892
  - **Smell:** aromatic cedar scent
  - **Touch**: propped, carved, crowded against it, tissue, shining lamp bowl, knotted comforter, traced date

- Although this paragraph includes fewer figures of speech than did the sample for English, it does include images that help the reader see more than the specific details:
  - **Simile**: like incense, like sentinels
  - **Personification**: attesting to, crowded, squatted, lay, awaiting
  - **Alliteration:** sweet cedar scent, happy home, pair of pewter, reflection of runner, lay linen-wrapped
- Details are sufficient to clarify the subject.
- Active voice and action verbs add emphasis.
- Organization follows a spatial order, from left to right.
- Transitions help the reader follow the order, from the opening of the lid, from left to right inside the chest, and then to the outside front. [*See* Revising: Sample Revision for Transition *in Part I.*]
- Sentence structure varies from simple to complex. [*See* sentence structure *in the Glossary.*]
- Because a single attitude prevails, it helps maintain unity throughout the paragraph. [*See* unity *in the Glossary.*]
- The conclusion helps the reader focus on the reference in the title to cultural statement.

SAMPLE FOR SCIENCE

In a botany class, students wrote scientific descriptions of a species of tree. They were to include growing conditions and ecological relationships as well as physical descriptions of shape, size, leaves, trunk, fruit, and root system.

Red Cedar, the Stalwart Tree

The red cedar, *Juniperus virginiana,* sometimes called red juniper or, simply, cedar, grows in dry, rocky areas from Nova Scotia and Ontario south to Florida and west to the Dakotas, Nebraska, and Oklahoma. While it prefers hills, it does not grow at high altitudes and will grow as well along lakes and streams. Usually no more than 40 feet tall with a trunk no more than 20 inches in diameter, it generally takes a rather conical shape unless quite aged. Mature trees spread wider and become round-topped or, in inhospitable climates, even distorted, particularly when exposed to harsh winds as on a cliff or shoreline. The red cedar's ridged or lobed trunk, often buttressed at the base, has a light reddish-brown bark that hangs in shreddy strips, fringed at the edges. The four-sided twigs, green from the covering of minute leaves, support dark green or reddish-brown leaves 2 mm or less long, scale-like, opposite in pairs. The leaves, which stay on for several years, closely overlap and are generally oppressed, rounded, glandular.

> Crushed, they emit an aromatic odor, and the oil from these leaves is used as perfume. The fruit, about the size of a small pea, fleshy, dark blue, tasting sweetish with a resinous flavor, provides food for songbirds, turkey, grouse, quail, fox, and opossum. The tree's worst enemy is fire, and even a small fire will damage its root system, which lies close to the soil surface. Although few insects bother the red cedar, it is the bridging host for apple rust. As a result, orchard growers make up the minority that strives to rid their area of these tough, stalwart, and often picturesque trees.

 Analysis of the Sample for Science. The descriptive paragraph prepared for a science class includes notable differences from other descriptive paragraphs. Note the following peculiarities:

- Scientific description requires a distinctive terminology. As a result, such terms as *Juniperus virginiana, ridged, lobed, buttressed, opposite in pairs, oppressed, glandular,* and *bridging host* may not be completely familiar to lay readers but are appropriate for the scientific description.
- In spite of the scientific emphasis, words that appeal to the senses do appear:
  - **Sight**: conical, wider, round-topped, distorted, ridged, lobed, buttressed, reddish-brown, shreddy, fringed, four-sided, green, 2 mm long, scale-like, pairs, overlap, rounded, glandular, dark blue
  - **Smell**: aromatic odor, perfume
  - **Taste**: sweetish with resinous flavor
  - **Touch**: shreddy strips, fringed, fleshy
- Figures of speech are limited, but some words suggest comparison: *conical, buttressed, shreddy, scale-like, fleshy,* and *about the size of a small pea.* Scientific descriptions rely on precise, often technical, wording and seldom include specific use of figures of speech.
- Details support the areas of useful scientific description: *habitat, overall appearance, bark, twigs, leaves, berries,* and *enemies.*
- The organization is in order of importance, from general to specific, from overall to minute. [*See* order of importance *in the Glossary.*]
- The single attitude, that of objective viewer, helps maintain unity.
- Sentence structure and vocabulary meet the needs of the subject and the audience, including technical terms and some rather compact, complicated sentences.
- The clincher sentence, which offers a final statement, takes the reader back to the general.

SAMPLE FOR MATHEMATICS

One student created a cedar jewelry box but wanted to add an elliptical piece to decorate the top. In order to cut the piece, he first had to mathematically describe the ellipse so that it would fit on the 10" x 16" rectangular lid. The following is his description.

Creating an Ellipse

In order to create an ellipse that would just fit the 10" x 16" lid, I started a graph by drawing intersecting axes *x* and *y*:

From the center of the lid, the distance to the right edge was 8", and the distance to the top was 5". Then I used the mathematical formula for an ellipse to plot points on the graph:

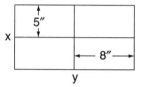

$$\frac{x^2}{a^2} + \frac{y^2}{a^2} = 1, \text{ where } a = 8 \text{ and } b = 5$$

By solving the equation for *y* in terms of *x* and substituting values for *x*, I created the following table, which, when plotted on a graph, creates a description of a perfect ellipse.

x	8	6	4	2	0	-2	-4	-6	-8
y	0	±3.31	±4.33	±4.84	±5	±4.84	±4.33	±3.31	0

Analysis of the Sample for Mathematics. A mathematical description varies considerably from most other kinds of descriptions. In this sample, the student explains the process [*see* Process Analysis *later in Part II*] for generating a mathematical description of an ellipse. Note that the description is in the form of a formula solved.

SAMPLE WORK-PLACE WRITING

Business students were asked to describe some factor that affects the value of a property. The student whose paragraph follows chose to describe the use of cedar as a building material and its effect on the value of the building.

Building for Value: Use Cedar

When deciding to invest in buildings, one must, of course, consider their durability. If construction materials include wood, the wary investor rightfully throws up his guard. Cedar, however, allows him to drop his guard, at least a little. As a construction material, cedar has been tested to be 80 percent as strong as white oak; its fine grain resists warping or shrinkage. More importantly, it resists rotting; so exposure to weather, soil, and water will not result in rapid decay. Cedar fence posts, for instance, often stand longer than the men who set them. The wood also weathers to a soft patina, so cedar shingles look warm and natural on rustic structures. Cedar channel-lap siding with its knots accenting the weathered patina will add a rustic look as well. Inside, rough-cut, unstained aromatic cedar panels give the room a reddish-cream warmth. Inside closets, the planed cedar scares away moths and silverfish, providing protection to woolens without offensive mothballs or insect sprays. Inside or out, cedar adds strength, beauty, endurance, and, therefore, value to a structure.

 Analysis of the Sample Work-Place Writing. By describing the characteristics rather than just the appearance of cedar, this sample offers yet another use of description. Note, however, that the descriptive approach is nearly the same. Think about the specifics listed in the analysis below:

- The topic sentence, the third in the paragraph, specifies the subject and clarifies the attitude: *Cedar, however, allows him to drop his guard, at least a little.*
- The description includes images that affect the senses:
  - **Sight**: fine grain, soft patina, warm and natural on rustic structures, knots, weathered patina, rough-cut, unstained panels, reddish-cream, planed
  - **Smell**: aromatic cedar, offensive mothballs or insect sprays
  - **Touch**: fine grain, rough-cut, unstained panels, warmth, planed
- This paragraph, unlike the other examples, describes characteristics, such as weather resistance, protection against insects, and durability. These kinds of descriptions do not rely heavily on sensory images or figures of speech. Subtle comparisons can, however, help the reader understand a point:
  - **Allusion**: throws up his guard, drop his guard
  - **Comparison**: 80 percent as strong as white oak, cedar fence posts stand longer than the men who set them
  - **Personification**: posts stand, cedar scares away and provides protection

- Active voice and mostly action verbs create effective emphasis.
- The organization, arranged in spatial order, moves from outside to inside, and then to inside closets.
- Transitions help the reader follow the organization.
- Sentence structure varies from simple to complex. [*See* Revising: Sample Revision for Sentence Variety *in Part I.*]
- The single attitude throughout the paragraph helps maintain unity. [*See* Revising: Sample Revision for Unity *in Part I.*]
- The conclusion, which refers to the organization, inside or out, ties together the main points: strength, beauty, endurance, and value.

SAMPLE TECHNICAL WRITING

To describe the qualities of cedar in the construction of furniture is to apply description to technical writing.

The Charm of Finished Cedar

Any piece of cedar—in furniture, a chest, or a tiny jewelry box—takes on an unmatched appearance. No other wood, stained or unstained, can equal the creamy-red color unique to red cedar. Coloration ranges from a deep purplish rose-red to a cream with only a hint of pink. Over the largest surface, however, red-ochre dominates. The light, close, straight grain revealed in an edge-grained cut contrasts dramatically with the sweeping Vs and gentle flares of a flat-grained cut. The grain pattern, its color heightened by satin varnish, plays like dancing flames in the mind's eye. While the wood is not especially hard and will therefore mar easily, and while it does tend to splinter and have little or no bending strength, it is exceedingly easy to work and is among the most warp-resistant woods known. Having once been used for skiffs and other light boats, it is still used for trim and finish in luxury canoes, motor boats, and yachts. With its primary use in making lead pencils, red cedar touches literally everyone's life. Specialty cedar articles, however, are still guaranteed to make a treasured gift.

 Analysis of the Sample Technical Writing. As a descriptive paragraph, this sample deals with content effectively. Consider the specifics:

- The topic sentence names the subject (*cedar*) and the attitude (*unmatched*).
- Arranged in an order of importance, the details move from overall color to predominant color to specific markings. The details support the attitude.
- The sensory images are primarily sight: *creamy-red, deep purplish rose-red, cream with hint of pink, red-ochre, close and*

straight grain, grain's sweeping Vs, gentle flares, heightened by satin varnish.

- One figure of speech, a simile, adds to the reader's interest: *plays like dancing flames in the mind's eye.*
- The sentences are mostly simple, but they include compound parts. As a result, sentence length varies considerably.
- The conclusion reiterates the topic sentence and applies the understanding to treasured gift.

These samples and their analyses, along with the explanation of process, should prepare you to write effective descriptions suitable for any purpose.

Narration

A narration (or *narrative*) tells a story. Sometimes narration is used as a means of development whereby a writer explains his purpose. Sometimes narration appears as part of other means of development, such as character sketches, autobiographies, biographies, and short stories. [*See* Character Sketch, Autobiography, Biography, and Short Story *in Part III*.] Other than an expository paper that uses narration as its total means of development, the short story probably relies most heavily on narration.

CHARACTERISTICS

Whether for the development of an entire paper or only a segment of a paper, narration has certain characteristics. A narration will

- tell a story,
- have a theme rather than a topic sentence [*see* theme, *as it relates to short story, in the Glossary*],
- be written in the first person,
- tend to be factual,
- include description [*see* Description *earlier in Part II*],
- include dialogue [*see* Dialogue *in Part III*],
- rely on sensory details for impact [*see* specific detail *and* imagery *in the Glossary*],
- utilize the techniques of storytelling [*see* Short Story *in Part III*],
- follow a chronological organization [*see* chronological order *in the Glossary*].

PROCESS

The process for developing narration is much like that of writing a description or short story. The following steps should help you develop a successful narration.

STEP 1   **Prewriting • Planning the Narration**
Topics for narrations are usually personal experiences that relate an event of interest to the reader; but in the course of telling about the event, the writer makes a point. Think about interesting situations or events in which you have been involved. Maybe you witnessed an automobile accident, found a stray puppy, bought a new car, were interviewed for a job, met an unusual door-to-door salesperson, or experienced a frightening carnival ride. Any of these can result in a narration. [*See* Prewriting *in Part I for additional suggestions*.] The purpose of your narration may be to entertain, teach a lesson, or create an impression.

So now, write a sentence summarizing the point of the narration you plan to write.

STEP 2   **Prewriting • Planning the Details**
When you have selected a topic, plan the details. List the events you want to include. Remember that narration is usually developed in chronological order, so as you develop your list, arrange it in the order of occurrence. Of course, narration can employ some of the characteristics of storytelling, such as flashbacks, foreshadowing, or other variations of chronological order to enhance the storytelling qualities. [*See* flashback *and* foreshadowing *in the Glossary*.]

Complete your list of events before you go on to Step 3.

STEP 3   **Writing • Following the Plan**
Writing the narration is a matter of telling the story from beginning to end. As you write, include certain techniques to generate interest for the reader. Consider the following:

- Write good description. Show the reader what happened, don't tell. [*See* Description *earlier in Part II.*]
- Dialogue helps the reader see the characters in lifelike situations. [*See* Dialogue *in Part III.*]
- Use specific details, especially those that provide sensory images. [*See* specific detail *and* imagery *in the Glossary. Also see* Revising: Sample Revision for Specific Detail *in Part I.*]

- Employ the techniques of short-story writing, particularly those of character development, setting, and plot. [*See* Short Story *in Part III*.]
- Because a narration is not actually a short story, aim toward brevity and maintain a first-person point of view.

STEP 4 **Revising • Polishing the Content**

A narration, like any other writing, should include good writing techniques. To revise your narration, ask yourself these questions and make any revisions needed so that you can answer "yes":

- Have I told a story from a consistent, probably first-person point of view?
- Does my story follow chronological order?
- Have I used the techniques of storytelling: sensory images, specific details, dialogue, and elements of characterization, setting, and plot?
- Have I divided paragraphs appropriately according to change in speaker or topic?
- Have I put main ideas in main clauses?
- Does my sentence structure emphasize ideas? [*See* Revising: Sample Revision for Emphasis *in Part I*.]
- Are my sentences varied in length and structure? [*See* Revising: Sample Revision for Sentence Variety *in Part I*.]
- Have I maintained the reader's interest?
- Does my narration reach a satisfactory conclusion?
- If my narration has a message, is it clear?

STEP 5 **Proofreading • Checking the Mechanical Details**

Proofreading should involve two steps. First, check for grammar, usage, and mechanics problems. [*See Part IV for rules and examples.*] Check punctuation in dialogue. Second, check for accurate spelling and word choice. Remember that strong nouns and verbs are superior to weak, wordy adjectives and adverbs.

SAMPLE NARRATION

The following narration exemplifies the characteristics and process set out in the preceding steps. Study the sample and the analysis that follows.

The Chinese Birth Party

"The party is at 6:00," Yim said. "Will you be there?" I had made a commitment. Now it was time. I had never before attended a Chinese party, and this was a special one for Yim and his family, a celebration of the birth of their first child.

According to Chinese custom, the mother and child remain in seclusion for one month after the birth of the child. At the end of the month, the joyous birth-party celebration replaces all the traditional American parties known as showers, brunches, and luncheons for mother and expected child. And what a replacement it is!

Over 150 of us crowded into the Canton Inn, the popular restaurant Yim and his family operate. In the midst of our "oohing" and "ahhing," the new mother glowed with understandable joy over her sleeping baby, a bundle of black hair and pink blankets, wearing a jade pendant and a gold-coin pendant from Grandmother in Hong Kong. She slept blissfully unaware, first in her mother's arms, and then in her paternal grandmother's arms.

The restaurant tables, arranged in two long rows, were already set with cold roast duck and chunks of specially prepared pork with a crunchy crust. We nibbled. Soon to follow were bowls and bowls of Cantonese shrimp, jumbo shrimp dipped in a batter that when deep-fried came out fluffy and crisp. Traditional plum wine accompanied the appetizers.

For us Americans, whose idea of Chinese appetizers is limited to egg rolls, these appetizers brought wide-eyed interest. We soon replaced our interest with wide-mouthed grins. Surprised by the chilled roast duck and infatuated by the contrast with the crunchy pork and the piping-hot shrimp, we devoured the appetizers—minus any sign of egg rolls—with relish and reckless abandon.

We shouldn't have. Before the dozens of ducks and bowls of pork and shrimp disappeared, a steady stream of main-course dishes filled and finally overfilled the tables. Surely far more dishes loaded the tables than there were people present. First, a stir-fried chicken-and-almond dish with pea pods, bok choy, mushrooms, and water chestnuts tempted us. But fast-following dishes of stir-fried shrimp and sweet-and-sour pork distracted me from my usual favorite. The platter of squid and octopus prepared with onion and those black, almost filmy Chinese mushrooms wafted exotic past my nose, and I shoved the idea of squirmy squid to the back of my mind as I sampled the delicacy. It made the beef and broccoli dish taste mundane. We washed the exorbitance down with pots and pots of aromatic hot tea.

Ah, but we weren't finished, yet. Each of us received a red egg. "Eat the egg. Bring baby good luck," we were instructed.

Surely you jest, I thought to myself. Eat a hard-boiled egg after I've just glutted myself with this gourmet meal? I slipped mine, I hope unobtrusively, into my pocket. "I'll eat it later," I promised myself.

Then came dessert. No fortune cookies. Dessert. These dessert things looked rather like turnovers, pastry-covered somethings. "One has a meat filling; the other, a sweet filling," someone said who had just returned from the kitchen.

> Meat for dessert? I opted for the sweet. Actually, I opted for half of a sweet and shared the other half with a new acquaintance to my left. What was the "sweet"? I have no idea. Maybe a combination of pureed fruit? With taste buds so overwhelmed by so many new flavors, they simply grew numb. A final cup of tea, thank you, and my stomach screamed, "No more!"
>
> And the baby slept through it all. What a joy, I thought to myself, that the Chinese feel the birth of a child merits a celebration of this degree. Ironically, at least to Americans, the only other Chinese celebration of equal magnitude is the celebration of their elders' birthdays.

Analysis of the Sample Narration. The preceding sample narration tells of the writer's attending a party. Certain characteristics make the sample particularly interesting:

- The narration appears in the first-person point of view.
- It tells a factual story of the writer's experiences.
- It employs elements of the short story, including some dialogue and good description that tantalizes the senses.
- It follows chronological order.
- The writer shows rather than tells about the festive activities. For instance, we do not read that the dishes were tasty but see the dishes and imagine the taste. The writer does not say he is full, only that his stomach screams.
- The paragraphs change when the topics change or, in the case of dialogue, when the speakers change.
- The paragraphs do not include topic sentences, nor does the paper include a thesis sentence.
- A theme, however, does emerge, particularly in the final paragraph in which the writer shares his thoughts about the festive occasion.

By imitating the process, characteristics, and model above, you should be able to develop a good narration.

Opinion

Because an opinion, by definition, cannot be proven, a writer who expresses one has an important responsibility. The writer must somehow show that she or he has examined all the facts, angles, possibilities, and, as a result, has made a judgment or formed an opinion.

The opinion paper serves many purposes, from sharing ideas to stimulating thinking. It may explain the writer's reasons for certain actions or reactions, thus playing a big role in interpersonal relationships. Or it may get the reader to accept an argument and change his or her mind.

The opinion paper and the persuasion (or argumentative) paper bear some similarities; however, the persuasion paper tries to change the reader's mind. [*See* Persuasion *later in Part II.*]

A letter to the editor is a specific kind of opinion paper, some trying to persuade readers, many merely expressing an opinion. [*See* Letters: Editorial Letters, *in Part III.*]

CHARACTERISTICS

The opinion paper should include a number of specific kinds of details. Generally, the opinion essay should

- deal with a subject that cannot be proven,
- deal with a topic worthy of the writer's effort and the reader's time, that is, express an opinion not widely held,
- express an opinion likely to cause opposition,
- indicate the writer's careful examination of the available facts,
- provide details, illustrations, statistics, examples, comparisons, contrasts, definitions, descriptions, causes, effects, and analogies to support the opinion [*see* detail, statistics, *and* example *in the Glossary and* Comparison and Contrast, Definition, Description, Cause and Effect, *and* Analogy *earlier in Part II*],
- avoid phrases such as *I believe, I think,* or *in my opinion,* because the paper's purpose is to express opinion,
- anticipate the reader's point of view and thereby include the most appropriate supporting material,
- stop short of simply telling the reader to accept the writer's opinion or take some action.

PROCESS

Developing an opinion paper calls for an objective examination of all information available and a careful analysis of your opinion. The following process should help you plan and develop an effective opinion paper.

STEP 1   Prewriting • Thinking About the Subject
Even though we all have opinions, most of them are probably not well founded. For instance, we may be quick to express the opinion that heating with wood offers few advantages to modern households.

But what do we really know about heating with wood? Do we know how to regulate room temperature with wood heat? Do we know how a house feels that is heated with wood? Or do we have some preconceived notion that conjures up images of sitting around a potbellied stove, roasting one side while freezing the other? If so, we are expressing an unfounded opinion. We really do not know all the facts.

Thinking about your subject demands that you determine objectively what you know and what you do not. [*See* Prewriting *in Part I for additional suggestions.*] Is research necessary? Will your reader have information that you do not? If you make obvious errors, including errors of omission, you may look ridiculous; your credibility will suffer.

So, do whatever research is necessary. Know what you are writing about.

STEP 2   Prewriting • Stating the Subject

After careful thought and thorough research, you should be able to express your opinion in a single sentence. Consider the following examples:

> Florida is the worst possible winter vacation spot.
> Cats understand what we say to them.
> Football players make more money than they are worth.

 As you write your sentence, check that you have a topic really suitable for an opinion paper. Avoid any subject that can be proved or disproved with statistics, research, or experimentation. Consider these examples:

Poor example: The Freedom Festival attracts more visitors to Kingston than any other activity the city sponsors.

Counting visitors can prove or disprove that.

Better example: The Freedom Festival is more enjoyable than any other activity sponsored by the City of Kingston.

More enjoyable is a matter of opinion that cannot be proven or disproven.

Write a single sentence that states the opinion you will develop in your paper.

STEP 3   Prewriting • Determining Your Audience

Knowing your audience helps you know what you need to include. Do you expect strongly antagonistic readers? Or are they apt to read without really reacting one way or the other? If you anticipate antagonism, you should approach the organizational plan differently than if you anticipate idle interest.

Likewise, think about the readers' personal interest in your subject. Does the subject affect their pocketbook, eating habits, health, family, lifestyle, job, ability to work, recreation, or hobbies? Capitalize on whatever personal involvement may develop.

STEP 4   **Prewriting • Selecting Details**

Select details appropriate for your audience. Referring to Step 3, select details that matter. You do not want the reader to finish your paper and say, "So what?"

Make a list of possible supporting details. Consider the following:

Radio stations should be prevented from airing local sports events.
    Interferes with gate receipts
    Interferes with simultaneous out-of-town broadcasts
    Intensifies feelings of ill will when two local events occur simultaneously
    Causes added confusion in the announcers' booth
    Causes traffic congestion when radio truck must park near stadium
    Ties sports events to commercial sponsors
    Interferes unnecessarily with regular radio programming
    Antagonizes regular listeners who are not sports enthusiasts

Develop your own list of details now. List anything that will help you explain or support your opinion.

STEP 5   **Prewriting • Organizing the Details**

You will decide that not every detail on your list merits equal attention and eliminate some. For instance, cut details that represent different points of view. In the preceding list, some details express the view of the sports fan (*interferes with gate receipts; interferes with simultaneous out-of-town games*) while others represent the view of those uninterested in sports (*interferes unnecessarily with regular radio programming; antagonizes regular listeners*). Limit your supporting details to the three or four most relevant.

Next, organize the list logically. Most opinion papers follow some order of importance. [*See* Prewriting *in Part I and* order of importance *in the Glossary*.] Keep the reader in mind. How can you most likely gain and retain his or her attention? Apply those thoughts to the order of importance. For instance, if you can support your opinion with details concerning tax dollars, environmental issues, and human rights, the reader is most personally and immediately affected by taxpayers' dollars—in the pocketbook. Only if you can show the reader a direct personal stake in environmental issues (for instance, that air pollutants will destroy the paint on an expensive new car) will he or she be actively interested. The same holds true for the vague term *human rights*; the reader must see the effects on his or her daily life. A reader will be attracted first and foremost by what seems immediate and personal, in this case, taxes.

Now, organize the list. You will probably use the following order of importance:

Detail one: second most important
Detail two: least important
Detail three: third most important
Detail four: most important

This organization allows you to begin with something important enough to catch the reader's attention but still save the whopper for last, when the reader will most likely accept it.

STEP 6   **Writing • Following the Plan**

As you write, follow the organizational plan you established above. Use the items listed in the Characteristics section. In addition, try to include the following writing techniques:

- Begin with an effective introduction, one that includes a topic or thesis sentence and attracts the reader's attention. [*See* Writing a Paragraph *and* Writing a Multi-Paragraph Paper *in Part I. See also* topic sentence *and* thesis sentence *in the Glossary*.]
- If your subject is highly controversial, your topic or thesis sentence may appear at the end of your paper. By withholding your statement of opinion, you can prepare the reader throughout the paper's development to more readily accept your opinion.
- As you follow the organizational plan, maintain a single idea in a single paragraph. [*See* unity *in the Glossary*.]
- Provide adequate supporting details for each main idea. Use as many methods of development as your topic warrants.
- Include transitions—words, phrases, or sentences—both within and between paragraphs to help the reader follow your thoughts and see the relationships among your ideas. [*See* transitions *in the Glossary*.]
- Remember that you are explaining why you hold your opinion. You are not attempting to persuade the reader to think as you do.

- In order not to offend the reader, maintain a third-person point of view. You should not include such phrases as *I believe* or *in my opinion.* At the same time, to use the second-person point of view (*you*) is to risk putting the reader ill at ease.
- Conclude with a reference to the topic or thesis sentence. A summary of your main points may also serve effectively as a conclusion.

Write quickly to get your ideas on paper. Do not worry about sentence structure, mechanics, grammar, and other technical details. Think about content. Think about the best examples or details to explain your opinion. Just write.

STEP 7   **Revising • Improving the Content**

Rereading the draft will help you see trouble spots that need revision. To help, ask yourself these questions:

- Does my introduction attract the reader's attention?
- With a subject likely to create antagonism, have I begun with details least apt to turn away the reader?
- Have I organized the details in the most effective manner? Do I attract interest early, maintain it, and build to the most significant supportive details?
- Does the topic or thesis statement appear in the introduction or, in the case of a highly controversial subject, in the conclusion?
- Do the details support the opinion I am trying to express? Have I maintained unity?
- Have I included effective transitions both between and within paragraphs? [*See* Revising: Sample Revision for Transition *in Part I.*]
- Are the supporting details specific? Have I used specific words, clear examples, good illustrations, effective explanations? Can the reader identify with the supporting details? [*See* Revising: Sample Revision for Specific Detail *in Part I.*]
- Are my sentences varied in length and structure? Have I maintained good emphasis within the sentences, putting the main ideas in the main clauses? [*See* Revising: Sample Revision for Sentence Variety *and* Revising: Sample Revision for Emphasis *in Part I.*]
- Is the conclusion effective?

Using these questions as guidelines, make revisions so that you can answer "yes" to the questions above. Then compare your essay with the sample and its analysis below.

STEP 8   Proofreading • Checking the Details

When you have revised to the best of your ability, prepare your final draft. Then, check for punctuation, grammar, mechanics, and usage. Refer to Part IV for rules and examples to guide your proofreading process.

SAMPLE OPINION PAPER

The following opinion essay adheres to the characteristics set out above. [*Compare with the* Sample for Social Sciences *in* Persuasion *later in Part II and with* Letters: Editorial Letters, *in Part III. These samples show how the same subject is handled for different purposes.*]

The Eighth District Congressional Race

Two qualified candidates have conducted their equally active campaigns to influence the voters of the Eighth District. Democrat Jerrald Kinsingtonne and Republican Rodney Brolliette represent their parties well and have conducted themselves as gentlemen in what historically has been a sometimes less than gentlemanly race. Both deserve commendations for that. One man, however, has offered voters in the Eighth District at least three reasons to earn their support.

As a conservative, Brolliette has taken a tough stand against illegal drugs, demanding unannounced testing of all city, state, and federal employees. Kinsingtonne, while also opposing illegal drug use, believes the drug testing proposed by his opponent may well be illegal. His respect for individual rights and concern for innocent victims makes him wary of possibly illegal measures. He cites test cases in which non-drug users tested positive as a result of recent surgery or as a result of legal, doctor-prescribed medications. At the same time, known users tested negative because they bought "legal" urine and made a quick transfer of specimens. Instead of such testing, then, Kinsingtonne believes a crackdown on illegal drug dealers—more arrests and stiffer penalties—may better serve to halt the drain on the nation's economic resources. His alternative protects honest citizens from undue harassment.

As a result of the recent controversy over a proposed hazardous-waste incinerator to be located in the heart of the Eighth District, voters have had the opportunity to examine the environmental position of the two candidates. Kinsingtonne announced his opposition early, risking the ire of construction workers who would likely build that plant as well as the ire of the general public who looked forward to 30 additional jobs in the area. As local environmentalists explained to the public the inherent dangers of the incinerator and pointed out its proximity to a major earthquake fault and the water supply for over half of the district, citizens joined the opposition. Only then, when it seemed popular, did Brolliette take a position, ironically one mirroring the apparently successful Kinsingtonne stand. Perhaps only the more aggressive candidate will help successfully fight the proposed plant.

Finally, each candidate sees the depressed economy as a major issue in the Eighth District. Brolliette proposes tax incentives to lure big businesses into the area. The Republican incumbent, in fact, voted for the huge tax incentive that brought two moderate-sized businesses to the area. Suddenly, however, area citizens have been hit with major increases in their personal property tax bills, some increases as much as double. Although the businesses offered over 1,200 jobs, almost all have gone to employees who accepted a transfer as a result of one business's plant closing in the Southwest. So irate local citizens are footing the tax bill for jobs not open to them. Brolliette continues to defend the position. Kinsingtonne, on the other hand, warned City Council and County Council members that citizens would resent the increase. He fought for citizen protection even before he announced his candidacy for office. Apparently he understands the common man's plight and the ramifications of big business on the little man's pocketbook.

Surely little doubt remains who will make the best representative for the Eighth District. Kinsingtonne understands the impact of proposals on individual rights, on local environment, and on taxpayers' pocketbooks. He identifies with the individual and risks unpopular positions to do what he knows is right. That's good.

Analysis of the Sample Opinion Paper. The preceding sample paper follows the guidelines for a good opinion paper. In addition to effective organization and good theme structure, note the following:

- The introduction compliments both candidates but concludes with the intentionally vague thesis sentence alluding to three reasons the writer prefers one candidate over the other.
- Each paragraph explains an issue or a situation in which Kinsingtonne has, in the writer's opinion, proposed a better plan or behaved in a better way than Brolliette.
- While the paper gives the reader some individual issues with which to identify, the personal involvement is not as direct as that in a persuasive paper or in a letter to the editor.
- The comparison-and-contrast approach allows the writer to discuss first Brolliette's position or proposal and counter it with the "better" Kinsingtonne position or proposal. [*See* Comparison and Contrast *earlier in Part II, for a discussion of organizational patterns*.]
- The conclusion states the writer's position without asking readers to vote for Kinsingtonne or to agree.

Compare the sample opinion paper with your own and apply the techniques to your own work. You should have a successful opinion paper.

Persuasion

A persuasive (or *argumentative*) paper convinces. It may try to convince the reader to follow a certain course of action or accept a belief or position and thus relies on reasoning and clear logic. Persuasion is part of every facet of our lives: Convincing a potential employer to hire us, a neighbor to keep his dog from ruining our shrubbery, the electric company that the house meter is faulty, the appliance store that we paid the bill on time. Others use persuasion to convince us to vote for them, to buy or use their products, to invest in their schemes, to follow their religious beliefs, or to accept their points of view.

Many kinds of writing may include elements of persuasion: letters (especially letters to the editor), short stories, comparison and contrasts, even biographies. Likewise, different means of development can be used in a persuasive paper: definition, analogy, cause and effect, comparison and contrast, opinion, classification, and description. [*See entries for each earlier in Part II for additional details.*] A competent writer finds persuasion to be one of the most versatile tools available.

CHARACTERISTICS

The following characteristics should be evident in a persuasive paper. In general, a persuasive paper

- deals with an appropriately debatable subject,
- assumes the reader to be antagonistic,
- begins on some common ground so that reader and writer have a point of agreement,
- anticipates the reader's concerns and opposing point of view,
- refutes opposing arguments,
- presents supporting details, including statistics, examples, cause-and-effect relationships, and so on,
- places the topic or thesis sentence at the beginning or the end, depending on the intensity of the reader's antagonism,
- follows an organizational plan that anticipates objections by the reader,
- relies on logical reasoning,
- uses subtle emotional or psychological appeals,
- depends in large part on the writer's credibility for acceptance,
- avoids a second-person point of view so as to avoid antagonizing the reader,

- avoids a first-person point of view to help the reader focus on the subject, rather than on the writer,
- uses effective transitions to move the reader smoothly through the evidence,
- concludes with a logically reasonable statement of what the reader should do or think.

PROCESS

Use the following steps to successfully plan, write, and revise a persuasive or argumentative paper.

STEP 1   **Prewriting • Focusing on the Subject**

The subject for a persuasive paper must be debatable. It makes little sense to write a paper to persuade a reader to pay taxes. There would be no point in reading it. Likewise, there is little debate that we should eat balanced meals, observe the law, or exercise regularly.

In most cases, you probably already know the general topic of your persuasive paper. You have a reason for writing. In order to focus on that subject, however, you should first write a sentence that indicates what you ultimately want the reader to do or think. Consider the following examples:

> Attend the Homecoming activities.
> Vote for Gerald Morrison for Eighth District Representative.
> Write to the governor and local representatives to show opposition to
>   relaxed air pollution laws.
> Attend a meeting to support a rezoning proposal.
> Buy only U.S.-made products.
> Invest in the stock market.
> Use vitamin supplements with caution.

Now write a sentence that indicates what you want your reader to do or think. This sentence will direct your topic or thesis sentence. [*See* topic sentence *and* thesis sentence *in the Glossary, and see* Writing a Paragraph *and* Writing a Multi-Paragraph Paper *in Part I.*]

STEP 2   **Prewriting • Studying the Reader's Positions**

Because the persuasive or argumentative paper assumes an antagonistic reader, put yourself in your reader's place. Anticipate his or her needs by answering the following questions:

- What is the reader's current position?
- What information does the reader have or not have that is relevant to the issue?
- What objections does the reader have toward your position?

• How will the issue affect the reader personally? In the pocketbook? At the dinner table? On the job? In his or her children's future?

Jot down the answers to these questions before you go on. If you must do research in order to answer these questions, continue to Step 4.

STEP 3   Prewriting • Thinking Through the Arguments

With the reader's position defined, begin planning your arguments. Answer the following questions concerning your point of view:

• What information can I give the reader to make his or her current position uncomfortable? Will something happen to the reader—to his or her job, home, or children as a result of this current position?
• What facts, statistics, examples, or illustrations will help the reader see the importance of changing his or her position?
• What information can I include that will negate the reader's counter-arguments?
• What personal appeal will most likely cause the reader to take action?

Answers to these questions will help you select appropriate details. Yes, the persuasive paper relies on reason and logic to make a point; but never underestimate the need for clever psychology to get the reader's attention and to deal with his or her emotions.

Note that you may need to do research to answer some of the questions. If so, combine your efforts in seeking answers with Step 4 immediately following. As you seek answers, you can also seek supporting details.

Based on your work in Steps 2 and 3, write the three or four main points for your persuasive paper.

STEP 4   Prewriting • Doing the Research

If your topic so requires, do any necessary research. Get the facts and illustrations to support your argument. Find authorities that support your point of view. Make note not only of their identity but also of their reasoned arguments. Read opposing arguments as well; understand the opposition's point of view, the better to refute it. [*See* Notes: For a Paper, *in Part III for suggestions on effective note taking. See also* Precis *and* Paraphrase *in Part III for help with writing effective summaries.*] Take notes on ideas that support your cause. Also, note specific arguments your paper must refute.

STEP 5 **Prewriting • Using the Right Appeals**

The writer must somehow appeal to the reader in order to change his or her position or opinion. Logic is certainly one way. Emotional appeal is another. Credibility is a third. A combination of these three will most likely persuade the reader. Look at each appeal:

Logic. You can use a number of approaches to logic, many of which are specifically addressed in other sections of this manual. Consider the following:

- Analogy, in which a simple situation is compared with a complicated one to make clear the general concepts of the more difficult situation [*See* Analogy *earlier in Part II, including the section describing its limitations.*]
- Cause-and-effect relationships, in which one event is proved to be the cause or effect of another [*See* Cause and Effect *earlier in Part II.*]
- Facts, examples, and illustrations that support or explain a given situation or idea
- Judgments or opinions that support ideas that cannot be proven statistically [*See* Opinion *earlier in Part II.*]

Emotional Appeal. Persuasive writing must somehow help the reader become personally involved in the argument. If a situation or belief will not affect the reader's life in some way, he or she will have little reason to respond, positively or negatively. Consider these possible emotional appeals:

- Physiological needs, such as food, drink, and shelter
- Psychological needs, such as the need to be loved, or to feel attractive, accepted, successful
- Emotions, such as love, hate, guilt, fear, loyalty, pride, self-esteem

Credibility. An author's credibility in large part determines the reader's reaction. A credible writer is one who approaches the reader as an equal, avoids logical fallacies, uses only subtle emotional appeal, and shows clear understanding of his topic, either as a result of firsthand knowledge or objective research. Content that enhances writer credibility enhances persuasiveness.

Choose the appeals most suitable for your topic and your audience. List them.

STEP 6   Prewriting • Organizing the Approach

The organization of a persuasive paper will vary somewhat depending on how adamant the reader's opposition will be. The firmer the objection, the more carefully you must present the argument. Consider these two possibilities:

For a persuasive paper that merely asks the reader to write to his or her Member of Congress or to show support for an issue, the most adamant opposition may be nothing more than his ignoring you. In that case, the organization may follow a straightforward plan such as the following:

- Begin with the topic sentence or, in the case of a longer paper, with the thesis statement. [*See separate entries in the Glossary if you need help with topic or thesis sentences.*] The topic or thesis sentence will state both the subject and your attitude.
- Present the two, three, or even four arguments supporting the topic or thesis statement. Arrange them in some order of importance, probably from second most to most important. Thus, you present your most powerful argument last, hoping the reader has begun accepting the lesser arguments earlier. [*See the Glossary entry for* order of importance *for additional details.*]
- Conclude by requesting specific action.

On the other hand, a persuasive paper may elicit strong reaction and deal with a controversial subject. For instance, you may argue to make a change that will enable employees to arrange vacation time with the rest of their families. The proposal is important to you but will meet with resistance from those with greater seniority. Presented the wrong way, the arguments may turn the reader against the proposal before he or she finishes reading—and in fact may not finish reading. Thus, use a different plan of organization, such as the following:

- Begin with general statements about the topic without stating a particular position. The opening remarks should serve only to indicate the subject under examination.
- Acknowledge the strongest opposing point of view and present counter-arguments. You may use phrases such as *some people sincerely believe* to introduce opposing points of view. When switching to the counter-arguments, use transitions such as *on the other hand* or *under careful analysis, however.*

- Then acknowledge the second strongest opposing argument and present your rebuttal. Use transitions similar to those suggested above.
- Follow the pattern until you have negated the opposition's positions.
- When your rebuttal is completed, continue with additional points of persuasion. Use whatever psychological techniques are appropriate. Organize these points in the order of their importance, concluding with the most convincing argument.
- Because of the sensitivity of the argument, your topic or thesis statement should probably appear at the end. In fact, the concluding statement that calls for the reader's action may be the topic or thesis statement, appearing here for the first time.

Select the better plan for your topic and develop a tentative outline. Use the lists you developed in Steps 3, 4, and 5. [*See also* Outlines: For a *Paper in Part III*.] You may decide to change the organization slightly as you write, but the outline will serve as a reminder of where you have been and where you must go with the arguments.

STEP 7 **Writing • Getting the Arguments on Paper**
Use the prewriting notes and outline developed above to write your persuasive paragraph or paper. Strive to include logical and emotional appeals in proper balance and to maintain your own credibility.

STEP 8 **Revising • Analyzing the Content**
As you think through your first draft, ask yourself questions to pinpoint possible weaknesses:

- Is my subject appropriately debatable and therefore suitable for a persuasive paper?
- Does the paper begin on some common ground so that the reader and I begin with a point of agreement?
- Have I included a clear topic or thesis statement, either at the beginning or at the end?
- Have I followed an appropriate plan determined by the reader's probable antagonism?
- Is the organization clear? In a multi-paragraph paper, have I developed a single argument in each paragraph? Does each paragraph have a topic sentence, supporting details, and a conclusion? Have I used suitable transitions both within and between paragraphs to move from one argument to another

or from the opposing view to my own? [*See* Revising: Checking Structure *and* Revising: Sample Revision for Transition *in Part I.*]

- Is the content easy to follow with clear, concise sentences? Are the sentences developed with the main ideas in the main clauses and the subordinating ideas in the subordinate clauses? [*See* Revising: Sample Revision for Emphasis *and* Revising: Sample Revision for Sentence Variety *in Part I.*]
- Are the supporting arguments logical? Have I included facts, statistics, examples, or other supporting details to develop the arguments? [*See* Revising: Sample Revision for Specific Detail *in Part I.*]
- Have I refuted the major opposing arguments and responded with additional supporting arguments? Have I dealt with the major arguments and eliminated from my paper unimportant, even petty ones?
- Is the tone appropriate to the subject? [*See* tone *in the Glossary.*]
- Have I carefully balanced the logical appeals with the more subtle emotional appeals?
- Do I maintain my credibility by avoiding hasty generalizations, faulty logic, propaganda techniques, and heavy emotional appeals? Do I show a broad understanding of both points of view?
- Does the conclusion specifically call for action? Is the reader apt to take that action based on the arguments included in the paper?

As you answer these questions you may find reason for revision.

STEP 9   **Proofreading • Checking the Details**

When you have revised the content, check for mechanics, usage, and grammar details. [*See Part IV for rules and examples.*] Check spelling and precise word choice.

A NOTE ABOUT THE SAMPLES

The following sample papers include formal and informal papers, paragraphs and longer papers, all illustrating the characteristics of persuasive papers. Although each paper focuses on an argument for leading a better life, other subtle emotional appeals will be evident. Watch to see how the emotional and logical appeals interact.

SAMPLE FOR ENGLISH

The following persuasive paper, developed as a single paragraph, illustrates the characteristics described in this section:

Why Get Involved?

The first commandment of contemporary society lays down the law: Don't get involved. Somehow, though, we ignore the axiom sure to follow: If you don't get involved, you never grow, personally or professionally. Sure, the usual arguments come roaring to the defense: "I don't have time to get involved" or "I have enough problems of my own." True, we're busy, and we all have problems, some far more serious than others. But look at what the experts say. Using the buzzword "networking" to refer to the activity of meeting and working with others, authorities believe an activity that allows us to reach out to others allows us to benefit from others' experiences. In other words, by reaching out to others, we may learn not only to solve our own problems more easily but also to put those problems in perspective. Working with others helps prevent self-centered tunnel vision. Thus, networking becomes time well spent. In addition, however, the experts maintain that the reaching out improves humanizing qualities buried by the don't-get-involved approach. For instance, meeting with our professional peers may help us locate new business contacts and discover that a company across town boasts a superior office manager for whom it is a pleasure to work. Working voluntarily with social agencies may allow us to enjoy opportunities for improving interpersonal relationships and to understand why a deaf child resents being labeled "handicapped." Serving on church, school, and civic committees may develop an understanding of contemporary problems and their consequences like the impact an alternate bus route has on the city budget. Simply meeting and working with more people from different walks of life may even help us recognize alternatives to business, social, and personal dilemmas—new ways to deal with a power-hungry boss, with a terminally ill parent, or with a puppy that refuses to be housebroken. Someone with whom we network can offer suggestions. We can grow. If these goals sound like platitudes, nevertheless the result is singular: Meet people, get involved with their situations and see their problems, and we become better persons because of it. So it's time to break the first commandment of contemporary society. Get smart. Get the benefits. Get involved.

 Analysis of the Sample for English. The preceding paragraph follows the guidelines for a good persuasive paper. Especially note the following points:

- The paragraph begins on common ground. The reader can agree with, or at least recognize having heard, what seems to be a common law of contemporary society.
- The second sentence suggests the writer's point of view and implies the topic sentence. (The topic sentence

actually appears at the end, the last three sentences combined.)

- Immediately the writer deals with the opposition's two major arguments and rebuts them in the next couple of sentences. The rebuttal also allows a smooth transition into the writer's basic argument for getting involved.

- The writer maintains an informal approach, using dialogue, contractions, first- and second-person points of view, and a didactic approach that, while the approach departs from the general recommendation under the list of characteristics earlier in this section, allows the writer to emphasize the informality.

- While the paragraph uses primarily a first-person plural (we/our) point of view, the use of the second person at the beginning and at the end permits a more personalized, didactic approach. Note that a more formal paper, as detailed earlier in this section in the list of characteristics, will rely entirely on a third-person point of view. [*See the following* Sample for Social Sciences *for a formal third-person point of view approach.*]

- The emotional appeals suggest that personal success, personal growth, personal happiness, and other "humanizing" qualities can come as a result of getting involved. In the conclusion, the general term *benefits* appears.

- Specific details follow more general ones. For instance, the readers can *improve interpersonal relationships*, a generally positive sounding goal made more specific by *understanding why a deaf child resents being called "handicapped."* Even a *puppy that refuses to be housebroken* provides a somewhat amusing detail, one with which the reader can identify even if not by personal experience.

- The series of four illustrations helps the reader see why he should get involved. The illustrations, in their specificity, promote the reader's personal involvement.

- The organizational plan moves the reader from the second most important reason (*business contacts*) to the most important (*personal support*). While another writer may choose a different order of importance, the intent here appears to be to support individual growth.

- The conclusion, actually a series of three short sentences, demands specific action. Using the second-person point of view (with the implied *you* as the subject), the writer involves the reader in a personal command.

SAMPLE FOR SOCIAL SCIENCES

The following persuasive paper aims to convince voters to cast ballots for a specific candidate. Compare this persuasive paper with the sample opinion paper [*see* Opinion *earlier in Part II*] and with the sample letter to the editor [*see* Letters: Editorial Letters *in Part III*], all with the same subject but developed to meet the unique characteristics of the specific writing form. In addition, compare this more formal paper with the preceding informal one, noting the characteristics that suggest formality or a lack of it.

The Eighth District Congressional Race

Two qualified candidates have conducted their equally active campaigns to influence the voters of the Eighth District. Democrat Jerrald Kinsingtonne and Republican Rodney Brolliette represent their parties well and have conducted themselves as gentlemen in an historically sometimes less than gentlemanly race. Both deserve commendations for that. The voters, however, must select only one man to serve, preferably the better man.

While Brolliette is a conservative and Kinsingtonne a liberal, labels may offer little help for voters. Actions, however, illustrate the labels. As a conservative, Brolliette has taken a tough stand against illegal drugs, demanding unannounced testing of all city, state, and federal employees. Kinsingtonne, while also opposing illegal drug use, believes the drug testing proposed by his opponent may well be illegal. His respect for individual rights and concern for innocent victims makes him wary of possibly illegal measures. He cites test cases in which non-drug users—ordinary employees in area businesses—tested positive as a result of recent surgery or as a result of legal, doctor-prescribed medications. At the same time, known users, people having been arrested for possession, tested negative because they bought "legal" urine and made a quick transfer of specimens. Instead of such testing, then, he believes a crackdown on illegal drug dealers—more arrests and stiffer penalties—may better halt illegal practices and at the same time protect innocent employees from undue harassment. Do Eighth District voters want on-the-job harassment?

As a result of the recent controversy over a proposed hazardous-waste incinerator to be located in the heart of the Eighth District, voters have had the opportunity to examine the environmental position of the two candidates. Kinsingtonne announced his opposition early, risking the ire of local construction workers who would likely build the plant as well as the ire of the general public who looked forward to 30 additional jobs in the area. As local environmentalists explained to the public the inherent dangers of the incinerator and pointed out its proximity to a major earthquake fault and the water supply for over half of the district, citizens joined the opposition. Only then did Brolliette take a position, ironically one mirroring the apparently successful Kinsingtonne stand. A bandwagon approach to issues of such magnitude reflects poorly on a congressional candidate. Do Eighth District voters want a "yes" man representing them in Congress?

Finally, each candidate sees the depressed economy as a major issue in the Eighth District. Brolliette proposes tax incentives to lure big businesses into the area. The Republican incumbent, in fact, voted for the huge tax incentive that brought two moderately sized businesses to the area. Suddenly, however, area citizens have been hit with major increases in their personal property tax bills, some increases as much as double. Although the businesses offered over 1,200 jobs, almost all have gone to employees who accepted a transfer as a result of one business closing a plant in the Southwest. So irate local citizens are footing the tax bill for jobs not even open to them. Brolliette continues to defend the position. Kinsingtonne, on the other hand, warned City Council and County Council members that citizens would suffer the consequences and predicted the now-realized increase. He fought for citizen protection even before he announced his candidacy for office, again taking an initially unpopular position because he recognized the long-term burden in the plan. The common man's plight facing the ramifications of big business caused Kinsingtonne to fight for the common man's pocketbook. Do Eighth District voters want to continue paying increased taxes to provide outsiders with employment?

Little doubt remains, then, who will make the best representative for the Eighth District. Kinsingtonne has shown his concern for individual rights and will be aggressive enough to take a stand that may initially appear to be unpopular. He has an uncanny understanding, however, of what is best for the most, and he is willing to take risks to fight for the most. So the issues boil down to three simple questions: Do you want on-the-job harassment? Do you want a "yes" man in Congress? Do you want increased personal property taxes? If your answer is a resounding "no" to those questions, you will vote a resounding "yes" for Kinsingtonne next Tuesday. Vote for a better life for all of us in the Eighth District.

 Analysis of the Sample for Social Sciences. The preceding five-paragraph theme illustrates most of the characteristics of a good persuasive paper. Note these specifics:

- The general title omits any reference to the writer's point of view, thus enticing proponents of both sides to read on.
- Beginning on common ground, the writer makes positive comments about both candidates. The objective approach in the opening paragraph does not antagonize the reader. On the other hand, most political battles are just that—battles. So the writer correctly assumes antagonism from at least half of the audience.
- The thesis sentence, the last in the introductory paragraph, makes a purposely vague reference to *one man,* thus avoiding the potential of turning off the reader before the writer has an opportunity to persuade.

- The organization, following an order of importance, begins with the opposition's strongest argument, the strong stance against illegal drugs. After refuting that argument, the following points move to the strongest argument for Kinsingtonne. [*See* order of importance *in the Glossary*.]
- Using a comparison-and-contrast approach [*see* Comparison and Contrast *earlier in Part II*], the writer uses only positive comments, never slandering or name-calling. She merely establishes the relative strengths of Kinsingtonne.
- By the time she reaches her final argument, the writer has appealed to the voter's sense of self-worth, pocketbook, sense of justice, sense of morality, and fear of the future.
- A number of words suggest underlying issues: *air and water pollution, increased taxes, civil rights, unemployment, economic depression.*
- A topic sentence may be either implied or held until the end of a paragraph. Both techniques allow the writer subtlety in approaching an antagonistic reader.
- A real thesis sentence never appears, but we can write one: *Kinsingtonne deserves your vote because of his approach to the illegal-drug dilemma, his active concern in environmental issues, and his understanding of the plight of the common man in issues of big business.*
- The conclusion comes close to stating a thesis sentence and specifically asks for reader action. Only at this point does the writer rely on the second-person point of view in order to draw her reader personally into the argument.
- The paper assumes primarily a formal tone, using a third-person point of view until the end. Sentence structure supports the formal tone as do organization and word choice.

SAMPLE FOR SCIENCE

The following persuasive essay opposes a coke-processing plant and illustrates the potential strength of a persuasive paper.

A Coke-Processing Plant: What Results?

Fir River Resources, Inc., has preliminary approval to build a coke-processing plant just 3$\frac{1}{2}$ miles southwest of our town. There may be something you don't know about the proposed plant, some things that may cause concern.

If the proposed coke-processing plant is built, Posey County, as well as the neighboring counties, is likely to see an increased rate of death by lung cancer as a result of the plant's pollutants. In two independent studies carried out in the U.S., coke-oven workers exhibited a rate of lung cancer $2^{1}/_{2}$ to 10 times greater than that in other workers. In another study made in southern Ohio, scientists found that people living near coke-processing plants had significantly higher death rates from lung cancer than persons in other areas. Several counties also showed high death rates from cancer of the large intestine, liver, and bladder. In the same study, surrounding counties showed increased death rates from lung cancer. In yet another study, scientists discovered that by exposing mice to coke-processing plant emissions for a period of 50 weeks, 93 percent of the mice developed at least one cancerous tumor. Scientists believe that two kinds of chemical compounds, initiators and promoters, work together to cause cancer. The coking plant will emit benzo(a)prene, an initiator. The phenol plant, located near the proposed coke-processing plant, emits phenolics, which are promoters. The combination may lead to a significant increase in the possibility of cancer among local residents and phenol plant workers. Finally, particulate emissions from coke plants have been found to be 500 times more cancer causing than are the particulates in cigarette smoke.

If the coke-processing plant is built, we might expect other kinds of effects. For instance, we might expect to see a rise in mutations in babies. Some of course could die because of serious malformations; others will live, maybe a worse fate. The scientific data is so clear that it appears in college textbooks. The emissions from coking plants interfere with the development of DNA, that biological compound that makes us all different. Interference in that development causes mutations. In addition, we might expect to see some crop damage. Fir River says the proposed plant will cause no damage to crops. On the other hand, the plant's nine smokestacks, each only 50 feet tall, will emit 30,000 pounds of sulfur dioxide per day. Annually, the plant will emit 5,700 tons of sulfur dioxide, 1,181 tons of particulates, and 199 tons of nitrogen oxide. Finally, studies of other potential problems have not yet been completed. Scientists do know, however, that other kinds of pollution will occur; but they cannot, with the statistics Fir River has supplied, determine total impact. For instance, water pollution will occur from the quenching operation. Coal-pile run-off produces pollutants that will flow into the Ohio River. Increased truck and rail traffic will have a significant impact on the community. The proposed plant will ship in 750,000 tons of coal annually and will ship out 540,000 tons of coke annually. This leaves over 1 million pounds of waste per day in Posey County.

Finally, the pollutants could cause Posey County to become economically stagnant. While the proposed plant will provide 70 more jobs, the plant will consume 87 percent of the county's pollution increment for sulfur dioxide. Because it may lead to a violation of the National Ambient Air Standard for Particulates, it could severely hamper further industrial expansion. As a result, present companies like General Electric will be unable to expand. Mead Johnson, which recently announced plans for a major new warehouse complex north of the highway in anticipation of a major manufacturing expansion, could be prevented from further industrial expansion. SIGECO, responsible for providing the tri-state area with power, may be unable to pursue plans to expand. Additional industries may not be allowed to locate in Posey County. In the future, then, as our county's population increases, one of two things will happen: Either unemployment will increase, or residents will be forced to leave the county to seek employment.

Whether your concern is for your personal health, your children's future, the economic future of the community, or the future of the world's environment, you cannot afford to ignore this proposed coke-processing plant. Your influence will help. Attend the hearing next Thursday, 7:00 p.m., in the high-school auditorium to show mass concern. We must fight politics in the political way—with the force of the multitudes.

Analysis of the Sample for Science. This five-paragraph theme relies on scientific evidence to support the arguments. Hard evidence makes the persuasive paper all the more convincing. Note, too, these details:

- The introduction appeals to the reader's concern, suggesting that, armed with the facts, he or she may feel a need to fight the proposed facility.
- While the paper does not acknowledge any major arguments from the opposition and so does not appear to be building rebuttals, in fact the paper is a rebuttal to the entire process that has allowed the plant to gain preliminary approval.
- The rebuttals focus on three major points, each developed in a separate paragraph and organized in order of importance.
- Supporting details establish the author's credibility and emphasize facts, statistics, studies, and authorities.
- Emotional appeals are subtle until the concluding paragraph in which the writer specifies the reader's possible concerns.
- Note the use of "guarded" words that enhance the writer's credibility but at the same time protect him against any potential liability: *is likely to see, believe, might expect, could, may.* Such vocabulary is essential in the scientific community where stronger words could be questioned on the basis of scientific evidence.
- The conclusion switches to the second-person point of view to involve the reader and ask for specific support by attending a meeting.

- The final sentence includes a first-person point of view so that the writer can include himself, not set himself apart with a didactic *you*.
- Remaining sections of the paper maintain a third-person point of view and suggest a rather formal approach.
- The vocabulary reflects the technical nature of a science paper.

SAMPLE WORK-PLACE WRITING

The following paragraph, supported by explanations of business principles, illustrates most of the characteristics of a persuasive paper. Because the writer does not assume the reader to be antagonistic, no rebuttal appears in the early part of the paragraph. The points are organized merely to explain why the investment seems wise.

Investing in Utility Stocks

Investing in the stock market is a matter of judgment and risk. Certainly, however, good judgment can minimize risk. Most investors who shy away from serious risk prefer to invest in relatively safe stocks. Many of those investors turn to utility stocks. Here's why. First, utility companies are stable. Essentially monopolies, they can raise rates as costs go up leaving the consumer no choice but to pay the increased rates. The rate increases can virtually guarantee a profitable company, so utility companies stand as stalwart businesses. Second, although the consumer has little or no recourse but to pay increased rates, from the investor's point of view the utility company thus guarantees steady profit. Then, as a result of the steady company profit, utility stocks offer high dividends and slow but steady growth. Although an increase in interest rates usually results in a decline in virtually all stock prices, utility stock remains as one of the safest, most stable stocks on the market. Investing in them at the right time can offer a significant financial advantage.

 Analysis of the Sample Work-Place Writing. The preceding single paragraph, short and to the point, offers two reasons for investing in utility stock, both showing dollars-and-cents logic. Consider, too, the following characteristics peculiar to a persuasive paper:

- The introductory sentence acknowledges what most people fear about the stock market. By acknowledging but without dwelling on that fear, the writer progresses directly to his point. Note that each sentence connects with the previous sentence and moves smoothly to the next idea.
- The cause-and-effect relationships are closely knit and clearly presented.

- Organization is emphasized by transitions such as *first* and *second* as well as by the many transitions used to show relationships: *thus, as a result, then, although.* The paragraph moves chronologically to follow the cause-and-effect relationship.
- To maintain his credibility, the writer admits that stock prices usually drop when interest rates decline and that buying at the right time still determines stock growth potential.
- Appeals to logic and to the emotional desire for success mesh so well that they seem as one.
- The conclusion offers a guarded recommendation, guarded to avoid any potential liability. Good business practice suggests such approaches.

SAMPLE TECHNICAL WRITING

The following persuasive paragraph, less formal than the work-place writing sample, offers a reasonable comparison with preceding samples.

When Should You Change Oil in Your Car?

Most automobile owner's manuals suggest an oil change every 7,500 miles. Many mechanics suggest your engine will last longer, however, if you change the oil at least every 3,000 miles. I know what you're thinking: The mechanics just want more business so that they can rake in more dollars from the unsuspecting car owner. Well, certainly mechanics don't mind additional business or extra dollars, but the only thing unsuspecting about the car owner is his blind faith that engine oil changed every 7,500 miles will effectively lubricate his engine. In fact, as you drive, the lubricating oil picks up tiny particles from engine wear, particles so fine you can barely feel the grittiness when you rub it between your fingers. The tiniest piece of grit, forced between the piston and engine wall, creates more wear, more particles. Added to the particles, chemical contamination of the oil further increases engine wear. Moisture droplets, excess fuel from occasional incomplete combustion, and acid from the combustion itself all dissolve in the oil. Obviously the longer you drive without an oil change, the more particles and the more chemical contamination the oil contains. You are merely forcing the residues through the engine, creating abrasion, in effect running oily sandpaper through the valves and pistons. As the heavy particles react with engine heat, they create a buildup, commonly known as sludge. Engines hampered by sludge deposits perform poorly and ultimately must be rebuilt or discarded. So maybe it costs a few dollars extra to change oil more frequently, but in the long run you'll save dollars by extending the life of your engine.

Analysis of the Sample for Technical Writing. This single paragraph illustrates a slightly different kind of persuasive paper than earlier samples discussed. Note these characteristics:

- The paragraph begins on common ground, immediately indicates the writer's position, and admits the first argument. The remainder of the paragraph rebuts the argument.
- Facts, comparisons, and illustrations offer supporting details for the argument.
- Organization follows order of importance while suggesting cause-and-effect relationships as well.
- The informal style, especially the use of *I* and *you* and the use of contractions, appropriately matches the subject matter.
- The conclusion refers again to the opposition's primary argument and extends the emotional fear of unjust cost to the emotional fear of greater cost.
- Emotional appeals accompany logical appeals, but the logic far outweighs the fear or subtle threats in convincing the reader of the importance of more frequent oil changes.

The characteristics and process described here should enable you to develop a successful persuasive paper. Compare your own writing with the samples and their respective analyses.

Process Analysis

A process analysis paper explains how something is or was done. You can explain how to build a bird feeder (present time) or how a bird feeder was built (past time). In either case, you take readers step by step through the process.

The process paper serves to instruct, so that readers can complete a similar process, or to inform, so that they can develop a deeper understanding or appreciation of some process.

For instance, a process analysis may tell readers how to fill out tax forms, how to dry wall a new room, how to refinish furniture, how to drive safely in heavy traffic, or even how to antagonize a younger sister. In each case, by following the instructions, readers may complete the process on their own.

Similarly, a process analysis may explain how a spacecraft provides oxygen during an extended flight, how a fuel-injection system works, how a cancer patient coped with his terminal illness, or how the perfect crime was committed. In these cases, readers need not plan to complete the process personally. The paper broadens understanding for the process and, in some situations, appreciation for the people involved. It can even become the basis for a television program or bestseller!

CHARACTERISTICS

A process analysis paper takes many forms and numerous directions but in general

- demonstrates the writer's familiarity with the subject,
- gives step-by-step directions or explanations,
- clarifies cause-and-effect relationships [*see also* Cause and Effect *earlier in Part II*],
- follows a chronological order [*see* chronological order *in the Glossary*],
- includes illustrations, examples, and other specific details [*see* specific detail *in the Glossary*],
- includes ample transitions to allow the reader to follow the logical steps [*see* transitions *in the Glossary*],
- uses terminology appropriate for the audience, but avoids overly technical words.

PROCESS

The following steps can help you develop a suitable process analysis paper.

STEP 1   **Prewriting • Focusing on the Subject**
A satisfactory process analysis deals with a subject narrow enough for a thorough discussion within the paragraph or pages planned. For instance, to analyze the process of building a house, a writer must plan for a nearly book-length manuscript. On the other hand, a writer can analyze the process of building footings for a house in a few pages.

To focus on your own subject, complete the following sentence:

My paper will explain how _____.

Now look at your sentence. Are you planning a paragraph or a book? Is your subject appropriate to the length? If not, adjust it to be narrow enough, or broad enough, to suit your purpose.

STEP 2   Prewriting • Determining Essential Details

When you have a focus for your paper, jot down the steps in the process. In addition, must the reader anticipate other problems? Consider these ideas:

If the reader may actually complete the process,

- Are certain materials or equipment required to complete the job? Protective clothing or goggles? Tools? Special materials? Perhaps you can prepare a shopping list for the reader.
- Must certain conditions prevail, either for satisfactory results or for safety reasons? For instance, must the temperature lie between 50 and 75 degrees? Is humidity detrimental? Should the workspace be well ventilated?
- How long will the process take? A few minutes? Several hours? A week? Offer guidelines so that the reader can better decide how, or if, to follow the process.
- Does he or she need additional terminology? Should you supply definitions or technical explanations? [*See* Definition *earlier in Part II.*]
- Which parts of the process will be most difficult to understand? Can you provide clarifying examples, illustrations, and comparisons? [*See* Analogy, Classification, *and* Comparison and Contrast *earlier in Part II.*]

As you jot down steps, add notes for whatever other information the reader needs to understand the process.

Complete the list of steps before you go on to Step 3.

STEP 3   Prewriting • Organizing the Details

Using the list of details from Step 2, group the details into three, four, or maybe even five divisions. By forcing yourself to put related ideas together into no more than five steps (and preferably fewer), you can present an easy-to-follow process. Imagine the frustration of trying to remember 15 steps for anything!

After the items are grouped logically, organize them chronologically. Rarely in process analysis will any other form make sense. Be sure, of course, to include supporting details in your chronological plan. [*See* chronological order *in the Glossary.*]

STEP 4   **Prewriting • Creating the Topic or Thesis Sentence**

Write your topic or thesis sentence. [*See* topic sentence *and* thesis sentence *in the Glossary. See also* Writing a Paragraph *and* Writing a Multi-Paragraph Paper *in Part I.*]

As you write your topic or thesis sentence, give your reader a clue about the complexity of your topic. Use the following examples as guides:

> Onscreen instructions permit even first-time users to work successfully with the library's computer catalog.
>
> Building a doghouse requires materials, common tools, and three general steps in construction.
>
> Making sure a diesel engine will start in cold weather requires certain precautionary steps.

After you have a good topic or thesis sentence, list the details that support your sentence. If necessary, convert the list into an outline. [*See* Outlines: For a Paper *in Part III.*]

STEP 5   **Writing • Getting the Process on Paper**

With the prewriting steps completed, you should have little trouble with the actual writing. Use the following guidelines to help:

- Begin each paragraph with a topic sentence.
- Begin a longer paper with an introductory paragraph and thesis sentence.
- Follow the chronological order you mapped out in Step 3.
- Use the outline or list from Step 4 to determine subtopics (for paragraphs) or paragraphs (for full-length papers).
- Include transitions to help the reader follow your explanation. Common transitions used in process include the following: *next, then, once, afterward, until, when, later, first, second, furthermore, now, simultaneously, at this time, following this, similarly.* [*See* Revising: Sample Revision for Transition *in Part I.*]
- Show the importance of the process in the concluding sentence or paragraph, but avoid merely reiterating the steps.

STEP 6   **Revising • Polishing the Writing**

After you have finished the first draft, use the following guidelines as you look for areas for improvement:

- Does my introduction establish the importance of the process? If not, will it be self-evident?

- Are the topics grouped into three or four (but no more than five) divisions, so the reader can easily remember the main points?
- Does each division of the subject correspond to a structural division in my paper? [*See* Revising: Checking Structure *in Part I.*]
- Have I organized my paper chronologically so that the reader can follow it logically?
- Have I included adequate transitions to help the reader follow the organization?
- Is my vocabulary appropriate for the intended audience? Have I defined any unfamiliar technical words? Do my definitions include meaningful examples or illustrations?
- Are adequate details provided? Have I used comparisons, analogies, and illustrations to clarify the parts of the process? [*See* Revising: Sample Revision for Specific Detail *in Part I, and see* Comparison and Contrast *and* Analogy *earlier in Part II.*]
- Have I maintained unity by omitting irrelevant material? [*See* Revising: Sample Revision for Unity *in Part I.*]
- Have I used good sentence variety and emphasis? [*See* Revising: Sample Revision for Sentence Variety *and* Revising: Sample Revision for Emphasis *in Part I.*]
- Does the conclusion offer a sense of completeness to the paper?

Use the answers to these questions to guide your revisions.

STEP 7   **Proofreading • Checking the Details**
As you check your final copy, look for grammar, mechanics, and usage problems. [*See Part IV for rules and examples.*] Check spelling and word choice.

A NOTE ABOUT THE SAMPLES

The following samples, all dealing with some topic of photography, illustrate the different approaches a process analysis paper can take. Note that while some subjects can be developed in a single paragraph, others require longer papers. Note also that some subjects are more technical than others—but that all are aimed at a similar audience.

SAMPLE FOR ENGLISH

The following paragraph on editorial photography illustrates process analysis appropriate for a journalism class. The narrowed subject, suitable for a single paragraph, deals only with how to frame an editorial photograph. The term *frame* is a photographer's word for selecting and arranging the subject matter in the camera's viewfinder. Thus, this paper is aimed at the aspiring editorial photographer. Watch for the typical characteristics of a process analysis paper.

How to Frame Editorial Photographs

Thought-provoking photographs grab reader attention. Anything that grabs reader attention necessarily helps sell newspapers, and *that* grabs editors' attention. So the aspiring photojournalist will do well to move beyond news photographs and work toward editorial photographs, those photos that evoke emotional response or rouse the typical reader from his stupor. Probably the most important concern in editorial photography is framing. Three steps aid a technically accurate photographer in the process of capturing that all-important meaning on film. First, he frames for details. Requiring close-up photographs, such framing probably calls for something other than the normal 50-mm lens. For instance, by using a normal lens, the photographer snaps a photo showing a political candidate from the waist up, waving to the crowd. The picture has no real meaning, no message, only the typical politician-and-crowd photo. On the other hand, by using a 105-mm lens, the photographer gets a headshot that captures a puzzled frown or a satisfied smirk. Then, when he has framed for details, he next seeks a meaningful point of view. Too much photography is from shoulder height, eight feet away. Instead, he moves down to shoot up, or he climbs up to shoot down. Maybe he walks all the way around the subject to find the most meaningful approach. While he avoids dramatic angles for the mere drama, he will depend on unusual point-of-view framing to heighten meaning. Photographing from the shoulder a block-long stretch of a potholed street hardly heightens the driver's plight, but a photo from street level showing the sharp edges gouging an automobile tire evokes reader reaction. Finally, third, he frames to omit extraneous matter. Every detail in the photograph must have purpose, meaning. Even though the subject should rarely be centered in the viewfinder, neither will the careful photographer allow irrelevant details to creep into focus around the corners and edges. Thus, the photojournalist frames to create editorial comment rather than click-click, name-place-date pictures.

 Analysis of the Sample for English. The preceding paper describes the process a photographer may use to frame a specific kind of photograph. Note these characteristics:

- The introduction sets the scene, beginning broadly and then narrowing to the specific topic.
- The thesis sentence, the fifth in the paragraph, states the specific focus.
- Chronological order helps the reader follow the organization, with single-word transitions such as *first, second, third, finally, then,* and *thus;* transitional phrases such as *such framing* and *on the other hand;* and transitional clauses such as *when he has framed for details* and *while he avoids dramatic angles for the mere drama.*
- Each of the main points is supported by details. The first two include specific illustrations with which the reader can identify.
- The writer maintains a third-person point of view, referring to the photographer and using the masculine pronoun *he,* thus avoiding *you.*
- The conclusion, a single sentence, is tight and to the point; it emphasizes the importance of the process by which a photographer may avoid mundane photographs.

SAMPLE FOR SOCIAL SCIENCES

The following paragraph includes characteristics similar to those found in the preceding sample. But notice here the changes brought by a different point of view. The writer uses the first person and an implied second person to talk directly to the reader.

Analyzing Historical Photographs

Confronting historical photographs in books and magazines sometimes leaves readers with little or no reaction. Worse, the reaction is one of "Why put that silly picture in here? What's the point?" By contrast, however, we can learn a great deal about history by merely studying photographs of the period. The photographer will have had a general purpose for taking a picture, and an editor will have had a specific reason for including a picture in the text. Almost always, the people in the picture, their clothing and accessories, will date the picture and locate its historical perspective. Beyond that, however, we can often glean other interesting bits of historical perspective if we know how to study the background in the photograph. Using an old photograph taken outdoors, try this process. First, look for indications of the state of technology. Are there utility poles visible? What about streetlights? Are there gaslights? What kind of transportation is evident? Are there hitching posts and water troughs for horses? Can you see evidence of automobiles or trains? Are there trolley tracks or overhead wires? Is the road or street surfaced? Next, study any printed matter that shows in the photograph, perhaps using a magnifying glass to enhance the letters. Look for signs above doorways or on windows that name or advertise businesses. Look for phone numbers. If they appear, count how many digits they have. What does all this tell you about the period? Next, look for packaging materials. Are commodities stored in barrels, cloth bags, wooden crates, cardboard boxes, or paper sacks? Remember that cardboard boxes and paper sacks are relatively recent additions to the retail market; and the more substantial storage methods better withstood the rigors of rough shipment. Finally, look at the materials with which buildings are constructed. Are they mostly wood? Is stone or brick readily available in the area? Is there evidence of concrete? Can you spot aluminum or plastic? Does glass seem to be readily available? Of course, these guidelines limit application to outdoor photographs, but at the same time they suggest the broader process of evaluating any photograph for its historical clues.

Analysis of the Sample for Social Sciences. The paragraph employs most of the characteristics of a good process analysis paper. The following items are particularly worthy of note:

- The introduction establishes the importance of the topic.
- The topic sentence, the seventh in the paragraph, narrows the focus to a single topic.
- The structure of the paragraph is an example of the rather unusual situation in which chronology is not the primary means of organization. While the paragraph suggests a chronology by which the reader should apply the process, the process may in fact be completed in any order. Thus, an order of importance development makes most sense.
- The use of the second person, especially the implied *you* [*see* point of view *in the Glossary*], allows the writer to address the reader directly. While formal writing generally requires use of the third person, this process analysis lends itself naturally to a less formal approach.
- The ample use of transitions moves the reader smoothly through the material.
- The use of questions helps focus the reader's attention on details.
- The conclusion restates the importance of the process and broadens its applicability.

SAMPLE FOR SCIENCE

The following paper continues the informal approach suggested in the preceding sample. This sample, however, has a precise chronological order.

Photographing Microscopic Specimens

Photographing microscopic specimens permits simultaneous large-group study of a single slide, a situation otherwise impossible. The photography process requires basic equipment: a prepared slide, a microscope, a single-lens reflex camera, and a microscope attachment that accepts the camera body. This attachment, available through most scientific supply companies, comes with either a screw mount or a bayonet mount; and the choice, of course, depends on the type of lens mount on the camera.

The following steps should lead to a successful photograph:

1) Remove the camera lens from the camera.
2) Fasten the microscope attachment to the camera.
3) Remove the eyepiece from the microscope.
4) Slip the camera's microscope attachment into the microscope.
5) Place the slide under the microscope.
6) Focus the microscope for a clear image through the camera viewfinder.
7) Adjust the light coming through the microscope so that a clear image appears through the camera's viewfinder.
8) Adjust camera speed based on light-meter readings, and bracket shots to assure success. (The use of an automatic camera will eliminate the need for light-meter readings and camera-speed adjustments.)

These steps should result in crisp, clear photographs that can be enlarged or projected as slides.

Analysis of the Sample for Science. The paper gives specific directions in numerical order. The steps are clear. This approach represents one way to give precise, uncluttered instructions. Note these details:

- The paper begins by explaining why the procedure is important and what results it can yield.
- The second sentence, almost in lab-experiment style, lists the necessary equipment.
- The third sentence offers additional information about the microscope attachment.
- The body of the paper appears as a list. Each item is an imperative sentence that begins with a verb. [*See* imperative sentence *in the Glossary.*] The use of such lists is especially appropriate in a scientific writing.
- The steps are arranged chronologically.
- The brief conclusion emphasizes the results of the procedure without taking a persuasive approach.

SAMPLE FOR MATHEMATICS

A photographer has a poster-size print 20" high and 30" wide, but she wants to reduce it to 15" high. Assuming she will maintain the same proportions for her new print, she must know how to figure the width of the reduced print. Students were asked to explain to the photographer how to figure the width of the new print. Here is one student's how-to explanation:

Figuring Proportions

In order to figure the height of the new print, the photographer must set up a proportion and solve it. The relationship between the width and the height of a print is a ratio. A proportion, which compares two ratios, sets up the relationship of the width and height of the original print to the width and height of the new print. The proportion would read this way: The unknown value is to 30 inches as 15 inches is to 20 inches. The photographer wants to find the unknown value. Mathematically, the proportion looks like this:

x : 30 inches :: 15 inches : 20 inches

To solve the proportion, she would follow these steps:

Set up the proportion.

$$\frac{x}{30} = \frac{15}{20}$$ where x = height in inches

Then cross multiply to solve the proportion.

$$20x = (15)(30)$$

Next, solve the proportion for x.

$$x = \frac{(15)(30)}{20}$$

So, $x = 22.5$

Therefore, to maintain the same proportions as the old print, the width of the new print will be $22\frac{1}{2}$ inches.

Analysis of the Sample for Mathematics. The math sample includes typical techniques for creating effective process analysis papers:

- The first three sentences give background and define terms. The writer assumes readers are familiar with the photographer's problem.
- The next three sentences set up the problem. The writer assumes an audience is generally familiar with setting up and solving simple equations and uses terminology accordingly.
- The remaining sentences and illustrations explain, in step-by-step order, how to solve the problem and reach the solution. Transitions such as *then* and *next* clarify the chronological order.

SAMPLE WORK-PLACE WRITING

The following full-length paper illustrates a process analysis that covers too much material to limit itself to a single paragraph. Note that the introductory paragraph outlines the steps of the process and explains why their particular order is the only sensible one.

Building the Photographer's Advertising Plan

The portrait photographer's business does not just happen. He builds his business as carefully as a contractor builds an office complex. The advertising plan to promote that business develops in exactly the same way. The photographer starts with an evaluation of his needs, lays a solid foundation, builds the basic structure, and then adds the amenities. Any step without the preceding ones makes the advertising plan—and maybe the business—sure to topple.

Initially, the portrait studio has two basic advertising needs in order to survive. The cliche "hanging out the shingle" probably best summarizes the first advertising step, displaying a sign that announces the business location. The sign may be nothing more than a placard on the door or a name painted on the window, but customers must feel they are entering a place of business, not just a temporary setup in an empty room. The second basic advertising need is a listing under "photographers" in the yellow pages of the telephone directory. The listing need not be elaborate; the basic name-address-phone gives an official ring to the business.

After the essentials are met, a successful portrait photographer must build the foundation for his advertising plan. A solid foundation comes from quality work. Going the proverbial extra mile to create fine work, above and beyond what competitors offer, will allow a portrait photographer's work to serve as the most powerful advertising campaign of all. Portraits must more than satisfy; they must delight the customer. Wedding albums must more than record; they must recreate the high emotion of the moment. Certainly masterful technique plays a large part in that kind of quality, but personal touch helps create quality as well. Courtesy, friendliness, and cooperation, even in the face of thoughtless, grouchy customers, help establish a quality advertising image.

Atop the foundation of quality, three basic structures of outside-the-studio advertising can be put in place. First, as an extension of the studio itself, attractive window displays foster public awareness. The window display is just as much a part of advertising as anything else the portrait photographer does. A potential customer walks or drives past every few minutes. Because people usually look without stopping, the overall impression of the display creates a business image. If it is neat, colorful, and tasteful, it creates a very different image from the one created by a cluttered and sloppy display. In addition, window displays that carry a monthly theme can entice new business. For instance, if March is Pet Month, maybe some customers will decide they want their member-of-the-family pet photographed. Without the suggestion from the window display, however, the thought may never have occurred to them! A second basic advertising medium can reach the potential customer via the mail. In the advertising business, a good direct mailing will bring in two percent of the recipients, but carefully selected mailing lists will assure profits. For instance, lists of graduates from the local high schools and universities will provide an excellent mailing list for commencement portraits and employment application photographs. Then a third basic advertising approach contacts the potential customer amid other businesses aimed at weddings. Bridal shows give the portrait photographer an opportunity to display his work, to provide competitive price sheets, and to introduce himself personally to brides-to-be. Sometimes only two or three bookings will more than pay for the show's exhibit fee.

Finally, when the basic advertising structure stands firm, the portrait photographer can add the amenities in advertising. Maybe it is time to consider radio or television spots, newspaper advertising, or a big splash in the yellow pages of the telephone directory. Maybe a billboard during strategic times of the year could attract anniversary and family portraits. These kinds of advertising, however, cost dearly. Probably only the most successful studios can afford the fees; and in view of the success, perhaps then the amenities are unnecessary.

So the advertising program for a successful portrait photographer's studio should build with the business and build in a logical, economical process. Beginning with a few essentials and then building a solid foundation allows the photographer to begin with a solid structure and then—only then—add the amenities of advertising.

 Analysis of the Sample Work-Place Writing. This six-paragraph composition clearly sets out the process of planning an advertising campaign for a portrait studio. Because it is more detailed than the single-paragraph and three-paragraph samples, you should note its specific characteristics:

- The introductory paragraph attracts attention with an analogy [*see* Analogy *earlier in Part II*]. The writer carries this analogy through to the conclusion.
- The thesis sentence alludes to the four parts of the analogy: *essential needs, foundation, structure,* and *amenities.*
- Separate paragraphs develop the parts, with several subtopics in each. The continuing analogy helps the reader remember the four parts and see the importance of the chronology.
- Transitions help clarify the order and show relationships.
- Specific illustrations clarify the steps of the process.
- The conclusion emphasizes the importance of the process and completes the analogy.

- The use of the third-person point of view maintains throughout a more formal tone than a second-person point of view, as represented by the social sciences and science samples.

SAMPLE TECHNICAL WRITING

Although this sample is a single paragraph, it illustrates some fresh points about process analysis papers. Watch for the differences between this and the earlier single-paragraph process analysis samples.

How to Use Aperture Settings

Using the aperture settings effectively on a 35-mm camera requires only three basic steps. The aperture setting, otherwise called "f-stops," determines how much light the lens lets into the camera when the shutter trips. How wide the lens opens determines how much light hits the film. Too much light overexposes and washes out the photograph while too little light underexposes and leaves the photograph dark. So the first step in choosing the aperture setting is to determine available light. Many cameras have a built-in light meter that, as it registers the intensity of the light, will give an aperture setting to correspond with a particular shutter speed. Using that or some similar meter will suggest a reasonable aperture setting. A light meter, however, can misread the real situation. For instance, a light reading will vary wildly from reflected light (from snow, water, or fog or heavy bright/dark contrasts on a brilliantly sunny day) and will gauge light only where the sensory "eye" is aimed. As a result, a careful photographer must move the light meter or camera lens left and right, up and down to see if the meter fluctuates. If so, she takes an average reading. After determining a reasonable reading, the photographer must next translate that reading into an aperture setting. To create a light picture, she will use a lower f-stop number, say 8 instead of 16. If she wants the picture darker, perhaps to compensate for glare, she will use a higher f-stop number, say 8 instead of 4. While the numbers move in the reverse of what seems logical, the rule is that the higher the f-stop number, the smaller the hole in the lens through which the light can travel. Finally, the third step in the effective use of aperture settings applies the readings to a series of shots, a practice called "bracketing." Bracketing calls for using at least a half stop, perhaps as much as one and a half stops, on either side of the suggested reading. Thus, the photographer shoots at least three shots of every subject—one shot at the suggested reading as well as one shot a half stop above and one shot a half stop below. She may even choose to shoot two additional exposures: one a full stop below and one a full stop above the suggested reading. Effective use of the aperture settings determines photographic success.

Analysis of the Sample Technical Writing. The paragraph includes significant techniques for developing effective process analysis papers:

- The introduction is brief and to the point and offers no enticement beyond the reader's need for information.
- The topic sentence, the second in this paragraph, focuses on the subject and helps the reader think in terms of three.
- The terminology assumes that the audience is at least roughly familiar with modern 35-mm cameras.
- Chronological order, essential to the organization of the paragraph, allows the reader to follow, step by step, to completion.
- The transitions move the reader smoothly through the organization.
- The conclusion provides a sufficient ending to the single paragraph and at the same time suggests the importance of the process described.

With the help of these samples, you should be able to write effective process analyses. Be sure to consult the cross-references in other parts of this book for help with specific problems.

PART III

TYPES OF WRITING

This section discusses over 50 specific types of writing, listed under 30 general categories. The types of writing are arranged alphabetically for quick reference, and appropriate cross-references offer additional help.

The discussion for each type of writing follows a similar format:

- An *overview* defines and explains the general purpose of the designated kind of writing.
- The list of *Characteristics* names the typical features found in the specific kind of writing.
- The *Process* section takes you step-by-step through the method of preparing the particular kind of paper and includes:
  - *Prewriting* steps, which help you find ideas, select good details, and organize your thoughts
  - *Writing* steps, which direct your thinking toward the development of a good paper
  - *Revising* steps, which show you how to check content and structure
  - *Proofreading* steps, which focus on mechanics, grammar, usage, and spelling
- *Sample Papers* illustrate two kinds of features:
  - The typical features of the individual kind of paper
  - The appropriate emphasis for papers of this kind when developed for different curricular purposes
- *Analysis* of each sample points out two kinds of qualities:
  - Typical features of the certain kind of writing
  - Structural and stylistic techniques enhancing the work
- *Cross-references* to other parts of the book offer frequent opportunities for additional clarification.

Advertising

Advertising, a lucrative, multimedia business, probably provides writers with more opportunities for employment than virtually any other kind of writing except, perhaps, journalism. People who write for advertising agencies or write advertising material on a freelance basis write what is commonly referred to as *copy*. Advertising copy is designed to sell a product, create an image, or generate good will or a good company name. Because its purpose differs so radically from that of other kinds of writing, advertising copy, often called simply *ad copy*, has unique characteristics.

CHARACTERISTICS

Catching the reader's eye, the listener's ear, and the television viewer's attention demands copy that relies on psychological impact as well as on powerful writing techniques. In general, advertising copy

- uses concise, powerful structures,
- frequently employs sentence fragments, even single words or short phrases written as if they were sentences,
- relies on imagery, sound, and wordplay,
- relies heavily on psychological appeals,
- may be limited in number of words by space allowed in an overall layout or by seconds allowed in a commercial [*see also* Scripts: Radio *and* Scripts: Television *later in Part III*],
- frequently relies on titles, headings, captions, or words and phrases otherwise appearing in different-sized print to attract attention to main ideas,
- studiously avoids any extra words,
- may include paragraphs that act as thought groups but not paragraphs in the traditional expository sense.

PROCESS

Use the following steps to develop advertising copy.

STEP 1 **Prewriting • Studying the Product and the Image**
In order to identify the saleable features of a product or a company image, a copywriter must learn about the product or the company. This step calls for interviewing the client and/or product users, using the product, reading about the product, and talking with the people involved with the product's design or production. Sometimes the

client has an idea that he or she wants to pursue—a sales approach, campaign, or manner in which the product or company image should be promoted. At other times, the sales campaign is the product of the advertising agency, perhaps in direct cooperation with the copywriter. If the copywriter is responsible for creating the idea, then he or she must spend ample time discussing, planning, thinking, rethinking, and evaluating whatever plan he or she and other members of the agency can create.

The brainstorming that takes place in these sessions helps you focus on approaches the client may like. By the time you finish learning about a product and the image that the client hopes to create, you should have a list of general ideas. Your list may include sales features, product features, or the company's versatile attributes.

In general, you are looking for distinctive features or qualities in this product or company that are unmatched by competitors. Ask yourself the following questions:

- How is this product or company different from others of its kind?
- What does this product or company claim to have that other products or companies of a similar nature do not claim?
- What benefits does this product or company offer its customers?

Refine your list to include answers to these questions.

STEP 2   **Prewriting • Defining the Audience**

No matter how much you know about the product or the company, if you do not clearly identify the audience, your copy will fail. If you are selling a product to a housewife with five children, you need an approach very different from one used to sell that same product to an executive assistant at a large corporation. Both persons may be convinced to use the product and may find it the most satisfactory product on the market to meet their needs, but their needs differ. Therefore, the advertising campaign for each audience will differ.

To help you identify the audience, answer these questions.

- Will the copy be used in a mass-marketing campaign across all media? A direct-mail flier? In a catalog mailed to selected potential customers? Find out from the client.
- Next, think about what influences the audience. Is it most interested in economy? Quality? Reputation? Creativity? Long-term usefulness? Product availability?

When you can answer these questions, you understand your audience.

STEP 3 **Writing and Revising • Developing the Copy**

Most copywriters admit that they struggle with every word and sometimes throw out every word and start over. Thus, for ad-copy writing, which is best developed with an ongoing writing-revising cycle, use the following questions to guide you through the process:

- Is my copy concise, omitting any words or phrases not absolutely essential?
- Does my copy rely on very short sentences, perhaps even fragments of only a word or two?
- Have I omitted all long sentences?
- Have I arranged longer copy in paragraph form, not as a paragraph in expository writing, but as a group of words expressing a single thought?
- Have I used especially powerful nouns and verbs?
- Have I used the most precise word in every instance? A good thesaurus, such as *Webster's New World Thesaurus*, can help you with word choice.
- Have I used effective wordplay?
- Have I relied on writing techniques that attract attention by creating imagery and sound, such as parallel structures, items in series, innuendo, figurative language, rhythm, or other similar devices? [*See* parallel structure, series, imagery, figure of speech, *and* rhythm *in the Glossary*.]
- Have I created the most positive image possible for the product or the company without misrepresentation?
- Have I used the most effective psychological appeal to address the intended audience?
- If my copy is designed to fit a specific layout, will it, in fact, fit the space provided?
- Likewise, will the copy enhance the theme of the layout?
- If my copy is designed for a radio or television spot, can it be read—with expression—in the typical 30-second or 60-second time frame?

Make any revisions suggested by these questions. Remember, you should be able to answer an honest "yes" to each question.

STEP 4   **Proofreading • Checking the Final Product**

With the prewriting/writing/revising steps complete, check the copy for precision—in spelling, punctuation, and technicalities. While copywriters often break the traditional rules of grammar, mechanics, and usage, they do so only to achieve a greater goal. Examine your work carefully for any violation of the rules. If you include such a violation, make sure it results in improved copy.

Strive for precise words. Then check punctuation. Copywriters use punctuation more freely than do other professional writers, but be sure your punctuation helps rather than clutters.

Finally, make sure your copy reflects the format it ultimately will follow, either print or audio.

SAMPLE ADVERTISING COPY

The following is part of a corporate-image brochure that aims to sell the company's image rather than a specific product.

> If you're working for your personal computer, you're caught in an eternal trap.
> Your PC should work for you.
> Do what you want done.
> The way you want it done.
> Without compromise.
> With you in control.
> That's the ultimate key to personal computer utilization. The key to success.
> MBI gives you that control.
> Efficiently.
> Quickly.
> MBI. Masters working with masters.
> Meeting your computer needs.
> Talking success.

 Analysis of the Sample Advertising Copy. The ad copy above sells a corporate image. The product is service for businesspeople who use computers and programs designed to meet their needs. The ad copy includes these key ingredients:

- Short, punchy word groups, mostly fragments, hit hard the key ideas.
- The psychological appeal to business principles—efficiency, control, effectiveness, success—attract the intended audience.
- The arrangement of the copy makes it read quickly.
- The writing is tight, with no extraneous words or punctuation marks.

- Paragraphing follows thought groups, sometimes including only a word or two.

The best way to develop a thorough understanding of advertising is to study print ads and television and radio commercials. You will gain understanding of the subtleties of the work.

Analysis

An analysis paper examines or interprets. The writer may discuss the various parts of something to show their relationship to a whole, or he may discuss the results of something to show benefits, effects, or causes. Because *analysis* is such a broad term, this book examines several kinds of analyses. The list below directs you to the specific section most helpful for your purpose.

You may be preparing an analysis that

- examines the cause of a condition or situation,
- interprets the effects of a condition or situation,
- analyzes a problem, or
- explains how a condition or situation came into existence.

[*If so, see* Cause and Effect *in Part II.*]

You may be preparing an analysis that

- interprets a piece of literature, or
- evaluates the results of a literary technique or condition.

[*If so, see* Literary Analyses *in Part III.*]

You may be preparing an analysis that

- analyzes how to do something,
- discusses how something was done, or
- examines the meaning, implication, or reason for a condition or situation.

[*If so, see* Process Analysis *and* Description *in Part II.*]

Announcement

An announcement serves to let people know about significant events: meetings, policy changes, new information, forthcoming appearances. Through announcements, we learn about everything from upcoming meetings to weather conditions, from promotions to layoffs, from war to peace. Because announcements often have a significant impact on most people's lives, it is mandatory that they be clear, complete, and accurate.

CHARACTERISTICS

A good announcement should

- give all the pertinent details: who, what, why, when, where, and how,
- use clear, simple language,
- be complete but concise,
- offer an explanation for unusual or unexpected events.

PROCESS

Use the following plan to prepare an announcement.

STEP 1 **Prewriting • Getting the Basic Information**
On separate lines, list the pertinent questions to be answered by the announcement: who, what, why, when, where, and how. Then, answer each of the questions in the simplest, most direct way you can.

STEP 2 **Prewriting • Organizing the Details**
Ordinarily, an announcement is so brief that organization is relatively unimportant. Sometimes, however, the length or content of the announcement suggests a particular organization:

- If the announcement is lengthy, you can use an inverted pyramid organization, listing all the important ideas first (who, what, why, when, where, and how), adding explanatory notes later.
- Sometimes, the explanation—the *why*—must precede the pertinent items simply because the reader or listener has no reason to react unless he hears the explanation. For instance, an announcement to attend a meeting at a certain time and

place will get little or no reaction if it fails to attract the attention of its intended audience. Sometimes, then, the *why* and the *who* must precede the other essential details.

Plan the organization of your announcement to meet the needs of the situation.

STEP 3   **Writing • Developing the First Draft**
Combine all the information from the lists into good sentences. Group similar kinds of information together into sentences or put related ideas together into one sentence. Develop sentences that put main ideas in main clauses and thus emphasize your main ideas. [*See* Revising: Sample Revision for Emphasis *in Part I.*]

STEP 4   **Revising • Checking Content**
Check for completeness. Ask yourself these questions:

- Have I included all the details from my list?
- Have I added explanations where necessary?
- Have I anticipated the reader's or listener's questions and answered them?

Revise so that you can answer "yes" to the above questions.

Then, read the completed announcement aloud to check for clarity. As you read, think about these possible problems:

- Are the sentences too long and rambling for clear reading or listening? Or have I written short, clear sentences?
- Do all of the sentences sound alike and create a monotonous reading? Or have I created variety in the sentence structure to emphasize main ideas?
- Are some details buried in a hodgepodge of words? Or have I used a simple style so that readers or listeners will catch all the details?

Tighten your message until it is as concise as possible while still maintaining clarity. [*See* Revising: Sample Revision for Wordiness *in Part I.*]

Revise until you can honestly answer "yes" to the second question in each of the three preceding list items.

As a final check, count the words in each sentence. Do you have sentences with more than 15 or 20 words? If so, shorten them. Put the main ideas in the main clauses and the supporting ideas in subordinate clauses. [*See* Revising: Sample Revision for Emphasis *in Part I.*]

Finally, have someone unfamiliar with the situation read the announcement and react to it. Is there anything missing that readers or listeners need to know? Ask the pertinent questions (*who, what, why, when, where,* and *how*) of your reader. Are the answers obvious? Revise as necessary for clarity, completeness, and accuracy.

STEP 5   **Proofreading • Taking a Critical Look**

Double-check your accuracy. Carefully note every detail and ask yourself basic questions:

- Are dates, both days of the week and days of the month, accurate?
- Are times accurate, indicating Central Standard Time, Eastern Time, Pacific Daylight Time, and so on?
- Are places clearly identified, including street addresses or simple directions for finding a location?
- Are names included where necessary, and are these people identified by title as well?
- Are other details accurate?

SAMPLE ANNOUNCEMENT

The chairman of the board of a local company released the following announcement to the news media:

> **News Release**
>
> On June 10, Karson Manufacturing will break ground for a $6 million expansion. Lamont Karson, chairman of the board, announced the expansion will provide additional employment for 230 workers by late next year. The addition to their present location will allow the company to increase production of its current stamping operation. Increased sales and anticipated additional increases over the next year warrant the expansion, and current profits will help finance the addition. The information was made public at today's stockholders' meeting.

Analysis of the Sample Announcement. Here is a critical look at the preceding sample announcement:

- It answers the pertinent questions:
  - Who? *Lamont Karson, chairman of the board.*
  - What? *Announced a $6 million expansion of Karson Manufacturing.*
  - Why? *Because of increased sales and anticipation of additional increases.*

- ◆ When? *Breaking ground on June 10 and in operation late next year.*
- ◆ Where? *At their present location.*
- ◆ How? *By using current profits for expansion.*
  We have to assume spelling is accurate, titles are correct, and other matters are accurate.
- The sentences are short, none more than 20 words. The main ideas appear in the main clauses.
- While there may be further questions, such as what kinds of profits did the company show and how long has the expansion project been in the planning stages, the purpose of the announcement is fulfilled. Additional information may well appear in a news article, but the announcement is complete as it is. [*For comparison, see* News Article *elsewhere in Part III, which develops the topic of the preceding sample announcement into a full-length article.*] A comparison of the two samples will help you better understand how to maintain brevity in an announcement.

Argument

To present an argument is to persuade someone to agree with you. An argument gives reasons. [*If you are writing a paper that will simply express an opinion, see* Opinion *in Part II. If the purpose of your paper is to persuade readers to follow a certain course of action, see* Persuasion *in Part II.*]

Autobiography

By definition, an autobiography is the story of the writer's life. Unlike a biography, in which a writer researches and reports on someone else's life, the autobiography reveals what the writer chooses to tell about himself. An autobiography, however, unless it is book length, does not tell about the writer's life from birth to present; rather, it focuses on some significant event, object, or person that reveals something important about the writer. An autobiographical sketch may be as short as a paragraph or as long as a book. Whatever its length, however, it should read like a good piece of nonfiction, even a good short story, but certainly not like a list of events.

CHARACTERISTICS

Most commonly, an autobiography includes a rather definite set of characteristics. An autobiography

- reveals an understanding of one or more personality traits of the writer,
- limits itself, unless of book length, to describing a particular event, object, or person that has influenced the writer,
- explains, perhaps indirectly, the effect or result of the influence [*see* Cause and Effect *in Part II*],
- reads almost like fiction, certainly maintains interest, and maybe even provokes,
- may follow the same characteristics as a narrative [*see* Narration *in Part II*],
- often includes many characteristics of good fiction: setting, plot, characters, flashback, figurative language, symbolism, and so on [*see* Short Story *in Part III and* setting, plot, characterization, flashback, figure of speech, *and* symbol *in the Glossary*],
- includes dialogue, as necessary or as it enhances the telling of the story [*see* Dialogue *in Part III*],
- permits the writer's unique style to offer additional subtle self-revelations.

PROCESS

Assuming that you are developing a multi-paragraph autobiography, use these steps to plan and develop your paper.

STEP 1   **Prewriting • Thinking about the Subject**
Jot down a dozen questions about yourself. The questions may refer to your reactions, emotions, and behavior. Use questions that ask about particular situations:

Why did I say angry things to my mother last evening?
Why did I pass the test I thought I'd failed?
Why do I hate snow?
Why am I always afraid I'll be late for class, work, or appointments?

If your autobiography is for a specific audience, gear your questions accordingly. For instance, if you are writing for a group of fellow youth-group members, you may list such questions as these:

Why do I need the support of my peers when I make a decision?
Why am I usually sitting on the fringes of the group, participating mentally but not physically?

STEP 2   Prewriting • Narrowing the Subject

From your list, choose one question that seems the most interesting. Do not worry about whether or not the question is important to the world, only whether or not it is interesting enough that you want to explore the possible answers.

Next, list a half dozen or so possible answers. Be open-minded and creative in your approach, being careful not to rule out any option. Consider objects, events, and people that may have influenced your answer.

Now select one answer that seems most accurate.

 The inexperienced writer almost invariably attempts to cover too much material in one simple autobiographical sketch. To avoid that possible pitfall, make sure that you select only *one* of the questions about which to develop your autobiography. If, during the course of developing the sketch, you feel your question is too narrow, you may choose to broaden it. Before you do so, however, you should consider first whether or not you have included sufficient details in responding to the chosen question.

In any case, do not expand the concept by adding another question. That will merely confuse both the issue and the readers and ultimately destroy the organization of your autobiography.

STEP 3   Prewriting • Choosing the Organizational Plan

The organization of an autobiography is usually either chronological or cause and effect. Of the two options explained in the following sections, select the organization most effective for your purpose.

Chronological. Chronological organization lets you write an autobiography much the way you tell a story. The paper begins at the beginning and tells the story in a straightforward manner through a series of events directly to the conclusion. The conclusion offers some revelation about the writer's actions, behavior, or beliefs. A more sophisticated narrative may also include a flashback [*see* flashback *in the Glossary*], a technique that allows the author to skip back in time to offer insight on a current situation.

Cause and Effect. The cause-and-effect organization [*see* Cause and Effect *in Part II*] forces the writer to deal more specifically with events, situations, objects, or people and how they affected reactions, behaviors, and beliefs. In this case, the writer uses one of two approaches:

- In one approach, he begins with the effect and shows how it came to be. For instance, he may admit that he always feels a kind of nagging terror when he drives across the two-mile-long suspension bridge near his home. Readers are left with the expectation that an explanation will follow. The remainder of the autobiography relates information about some event, situation, object, or person that explains the long-term nagging terror.
- In the second approach, the writer reverses the process and chooses to relate information about some event, situation, object, or person, allowing the reader to follow in suspense. The suspense comes from the expectation of a new insight into the writer.

Choose the organization most effective for your purpose.

STEP 4   **Writing • Following the Plan**
Develop your autobiographical sketch according to the plan you selected in Step 3. Include details that allow readers to feel what you have felt, see what you have seen, think what you have thought. In other words, use good description to involve readers in your own experiences. [*See* Description *in Part II and* Revising: Sample Revision for Specific Detail *in Part I.*]

Use whatever techniques of good fiction seem appropriate for your sketch. [*See* Short Story *in Part III.*]

STEP 5   **Revising • Improving the Content**
Next, reread for content. Ask yourself these questions to determine if certain parts may benefit from revision:

- Does my introduction grab the reader's attention in the same manner as a good short story?
- Does the introduction help the reader focus on the narrowed subject of the sketch, a particular event, object, or person that has influenced me?
- Does the sketch read almost like fiction, maintaining interest, even suspense, while offering nonfiction details?

- Will dialogue, or additional dialogue, make the sketch more readable, more real, more human?
- When the reader finishes the sketch, will he or she understand why or how the event, object, or person influenced me?
- Does the sketch conclude or merely quit? Does an effective clincher tie together the contents? [*See* conclusion *in the Glossary*.]
- Have I used a personal style that offers additional insight for the reader?
- Have I varied my sentences, both by length and by structure? [*See* Revising: Sample Revision for Sentence Variety *in Part I*.]
- Have I maintained effective emphasis? [*See* Revising: Sample Revision for Emphasis *in Part I; see also* Revising *in Part I for additional suggestions for general revision*.]

STEP 6   Proofreading • Checking the Details

Finally, check for mechanics, grammar, and usage. [*See Part IV.*] If you have used dialogue, be sure to double-check punctuation and paragraphing of the quotations. Check word choice and spelling.

SAMPLE AUTOBIOGRAPHY

Following the preceding steps, the writer has prepared the suggested list of questions, examined them, and chosen the following question on which to base her autobiography: Why did I enjoy being alone in a crowd? Notice that the question itself never appears in the autobiography, but the answer is obvious by the end of the sketch.

Alone in a Crowd

Last year, just prior to our community's annual Fall Festival, the small weekly newspaper that I work for gave me what I thought was the ideal assignment. I was to spend as much time as possible during the week-long festivities capturing those so-called human-interest photographs. My mind reeled. The Fall Festival! A whole week to select the choicest foods from the hundreds of booths! A whole week to see over 800,000 people who would flock to the festival! A whole week to see friends I hadn't seen since last year's festival! I'd stuff myself with all the fried, sugared, salted junk until I was miserable; and in the process, I'd catch up on all the gossip. And I'd get paid for doing it. What a life!

The first afternoon, camera in hand and camera bag slung across my left shoulder, I headed toward the kiddie rides. Children, joyous and uninhibited, always provide great human-interest shots; these proved no different. The toddler in the pink sweat suit, terrified by the merry-go-round, didn't hesitate to scream her fears. A great picture, her grubby fist knuckling a tear-stained face. The pint-sized cowboy in boots and ten-gallon hat obviously found riding the bumper cars every bit as good as riding the range. Another great picture, her hat flopping over her eyes after a resounding bump from behind.

That's when Alan showed up. "Hey, look at you in the kiddie park! Fancy meeting you here. What's up?" Alan was chaperoning his kid sister for a few hours, looking for his own entertainment. Apparently I was it. But then, wasn't I looking forward to meeting old friends?

"Hi, Alan. Gosh, long time no see. What are you doing these days?" For some reason I didn't care how he answered, or if he answered. Frankly, I don't remember what he said. Fortunately, his sister was taking her turn in the bumper cars, so I managed to escape without his following me.

From the kiddie rides, I hit the first block of food booths. The smell intoxicated me. Bratwurst, fudge, elephant ears, kuchen, pizza, apple cider—anything to tempt the taste buds. Oh, but just look at the people queued up to buy whatever tidbit rewarded them at the end of the long line! Changing to a 105-mm lens to photograph them unaware, I stood back, watching. There! The woman with a string of caramel draped at least a foot from her lips to the caramel apple she was eating. Then that guy with the sauerkraut dangling from the corner of his mouth. And that kid taking his first bite from that wonderfully buttery, cinnamon-sugared elephant ear—elephant ear from ear to ear! What shots!

"Hey, Hotshot, what's with the camera bit when there's all this wonderful food?"

I turned to the voice I recognized, tempted to take Sherry's picture, too. Indeed, she would have made quite a picture, a cup of apple cider wedged in the crook of her left arm, a stacked ham sandwich, half eaten, in her left hand, and a bag of three French waffles swinging from her right hand.

"Hey, Hotshot, yourself," I responded, trying to sound casual. "Just on assignment, that's all. What's with the horde of food? You on a diet?" I tried to be funny, an effort to cover up my tension. Why was I frustrated? Sherry, of all people. One of my best friends. We should share a few jokes, revel in our mutual joy of finding each other at the festival, and head out to have a great evening together.

I couldn't wait to get away.

So that day melted into the following ones. By week's end, I had taken 12 rolls of film and cranked out some exciting candid shots. The editor's rare moment of praise added a satisfied glow to the week's work. Lurking in the shadows, though, was something less than a glow. It gnawed and irritated, like a stone in a shoe. I'd spent the week at the festival, seldom eating and rarely speaking to anyone. I had resented any intrusion—for that's the way I came to view it—on my privacy. I had detached myself from the crowd, watched the crowd as individuals, studied their expressions, their mannerisms, absorbed in and by the sensations. Alone in the crowd. And I had grown.

Analysis of the Sample Autobiography. The preceding autobiography answers why the writer enjoyed being alone in a crowd. The following points make it work:

- The multi-paragraph sketch follows a chronological organization.
- It bears many of the characteristics of a narrative. [*See* Narration *in Part II*.]
- The informal style offers further insight into the author's personality.
- The dialogue included, appropriate for the informal style, sounds natural, not contrived.
- The paragraphing helps the reader follow change of speakers.
- Vocabulary and sentence structure suggest not only an informal style, but casual characters and a casual situation. Note that only informal writing permits the use of incomplete sentences.
- The dialogue uses accurate punctuation, including commas setting off the interrupting phrases and quotation marks indicating exact words.
- Sentence fragments, usually inappropriate in nonfiction, serve a specific purpose here. [*See* fragment *in the Glossary*.] Their use, however, should not be misconstrued to mean that sentence fragments are appropriate for all autobiographies. Not so. Here, the fragments show further informality of style; but more importantly, the fragments suggest the author's staccato series of impressions. In other words, the fragments are used for stylistic purposes. Furthermore, their use makes the sketch read more like fiction, one characteristic sometimes apparent in an autobiography. By contrast, an autobiography written in a formal style will not include sentence fragments.
- Paragraph development [*see* Writing a Paragraph *in Part I*] is typical of fiction, not of expository writing. The paragraphs lack topic sentences and carefully structured development. Instead, they follow the narrative form, a change in time or character determining a change of paragraph. Again, a more formal autobiography will take a more formal approach, including a formal paragraph structure.

This autobiography succeeds. The writer answers the questions she asked of herself. Granted, we don't know how old she is, where she was born, who her parents are, where she went to school, or where she lives. On the other hand, we have a general idea of her age; we know how she feels about people; we understand her mixed attitudes toward the Fall Festival; and we understand her new insight into her own professional responsibilities and what they require of her.

Biography

A biography is the story of a life. It may vary in length from a paragraph to a book. Most frequently, however, when students are asked to write a biography, the expected product ranges from a well-developed paragraph to a research paper. [*See* Research Paper *later in Part III*.] This chapter looks at the short biographical sketch. The steps, organization, and pitfalls, however, are the same whether you write a long or short account of a life.

CHARACTERISTICS

Although a biography is the story of someone's life, unless it is book length, it cannot recount the details of a full lifetime. In addition, because the writer is describing someone else's life, he cannot write without research, either primary or secondary. [*See* primary research *and* secondary research *in the Glossary*.] As a result, a carefully prepared biography should include

- an effective introduction that includes background information that places the subject in a specific setting,
- a focus on the subject that allows the writer to limit the lifetime material to a manageable subject [*see* focus *in the Glossary*],
- an approach appropriate for the audience,
- details that support the specific focus, including effective anecdotes and quotations [*see* specific detail *in the Glossary*],
- evidence of research or knowledge of the subject,
- clear, logical organization,
- effective transitions to help readers follow the organization [*see* transitions *in the Glossary*],
- consistent style, assuring the omission of plagiarism [*see* plagiarism *in the Glossary*],
- interesting reading, not a list of facts and figures.

PROCESS

Students who prepare biographies usually do so as part of a class assignment. If the subject is not assigned, the content area suggests the subject and emphasis. Use the following steps to plan and develop a biography, regardless of its length.

STEP 1   **Prewriting • Doing the Secondary Research**

Assuming you have identified the subject of the biography, complete the secondary research by consulting available sources:

- If the subject is included in a general encyclopedia entry—print, electronic, or online—begin with that. Usually encyclopedia information serves as a guide for further research.
- Check specialized encyclopedias and other reference books, particularly *Current Biographies*.
- After your preliminary search, consult the library's card or computer catalog or computer-search facilities for further references. For instance, you may find the subject's autobiography, or you may find books and articles by other biographers. [*See* card catalog *and* computer catalog *in the Glossary*.]
- Check the *Reader's Guide to Periodical Literature*, either the print or electronic version, for magazine articles that provide additional kinds of information, including bibliographies.
- The vertical file may include some information. [*See* vertical file *in the Glossary*.]
- Newspaper articles, especially those accessible through the Internet, may also include interesting highlights. Research in other areas will suggest dates and newspapers most likely to yield any material.
- If you have access to special collections, usually housed in museums or in special-collections library rooms, examine the subject's personal effects: mementos, personal letters, and diaries or journals.

Many students think they can read a single encyclopedia article and develop an adequate biography. Before you can write sensitively about another human being, however, you must understand him or her—the personality, the frustrations, the joys, the motives, the goals, the strengths, the weaknesses, the contributions, the failures. Seek out as many potential sources as you can.

The greater the variety of source material you have, the more complete, accurate, and interesting your biography will be.

STEP 2   **Prewriting • Doing the Primary Research**

Complete whatever primary research you can. How much you do depends on several factors: the extent of the biography, the availability of secondary research, the availability of primary-research sources, and the time allotted for research.

Obviously, an extensive biography relies on every possible source available and requires months—maybe even years—of thorough research. Most of you will not be delving that deeply to develop a biography. The availability of secondary research, then, may determine how much time you can devote to primary research. Consider these two situations:

Situation One. Even though your subject may have had books and articles written about him or her, you gain a different insight into your subject through primary research. Here's what to do:

- If your subject is still living, you should try to interview him or her at length.
- Find people who know the subject, worked with or are related to him or her. Talk with these people to get a broader perspective of your subject.
- Talk with a recognized authority or scholar who has studied your subject extensively. Compare his or her comments with the results of your own research.

Situation Two. If the subject of your biography has received no journalistic coverage, all of your research will be primary:

- If he or she is still living, you must interview your subject.
- In addition, you must locate his or her friends, neighbors, and relatives.
- For the sake of perspective, you should interview your subject's enemies—or at least his or her opponents. They will most likely broaden your perspective.

STEP 3   **Prewriting • Selecting a Focus**

Research completed, select a focus for your biography. An especially lengthy research paper may successfully develop more than one focus, but probably not more than three.

In order to select a single focus, think about those aspects of the subject's life most directly related to the content of a course you are taking, especially if you are writing the biography as an assignment for that course. If, for instance, you are doing a biography on Benjamin Franklin for a social-science class, you will probably focus on his work as an ambassador. If you choose the same biographical subject for a science class, however, you will probably focus on his work as an inventor. For an English class, you will probably discuss his writing and his wit.

You may, on the other hand, select the single focus to show a broader understanding of your subject. For instance, while writing for a social-science class, you may acknowledge Franklin's expertise as an ambassador but dwell on his contributions to the shipping industry as a result of his work as an oceanographer who discovered the Gulf Stream.

STEP 4   **Prewriting • Listing the Details**

After you have selected a focus, make a list of the details which will illustrate it. The details may include the following:

> personality traits
> business experiences
> comments by critics
> self-evaluation
> educational background
> contributions to his or her field(s) of endeavor
> effects of those contributions
> any other details which introduce readers to your chosen focus on the
>   subject's life

Write your own list now.

STEP 5   **Prewriting • Organizing the Details**

Arrange the details in a logical order. For biographies, the order is almost always chronological.

STEP 6   **Prewriting • Developing the Setting**

To help readers locate your subject in an historical time frame, jot down details about the period in which the subject lived. Note locations, dates, and historical events. For instance, was the subject struggling through college during World War I, or was he being schooled by a private tutor at home during the Golden Age of Greece? By weaving these details into the context of the biography, readers better understand your subject.

Prepare a brief list now of possible details to establish the setting for your subject's story.

STEP 7   **Writing • Developing the Introduction**

The introduction for a multi-paragraph biography does not rely on the time element. Rather, it follows a separate plan:

- The introduction sets the time and place and introduces the subject of the biography. Refer to the list you developed in Step 6. The reader will appreciate, however, a creative introduction, not just a list of names, dates, and places. The introduction may include, for instance, a quotation attributed to the subject, a perceptive comment from a critic, or merely the writer's reaction to the subject.
- The introduction should conclude with a thesis sentence. The thesis sentence narrows the subject of the biography and indicates the writer's focus. [*See* thesis sentence *in the Glossary for a quick reference, and see* Writing a Multi-Paragraph Paper *in Part I for a thorough explanation of effective thesis sentences.*]

In a paragraph-length sketch, the introduction may be only a sentence or two; but in a long paper, the introduction will be a full paragraph. [*See* Writing a Multi-Paragraph Paper *in Part I for a clear explanation and example of an introductory paragraph.*]

STEP 8   **Writing • Building the Body**

Take note of three items as you develop the body paragraphs of the biography:

First, using the lists developed in Steps 4–6 as a result of your primary and secondary research, select details for the body paragraphs that support the topic sentence. Some hints:

- Be selective; choose only the most telling details.
- Discuss details in chronological order, or establish cause-and-effect relationships as appropriate. [*See* Cause and Effect *in Part II.*]
- Use a variety of methods to develop the paper—examples, comparison and contrast, cause and effect, perhaps analogy and definition, as well as description [*see these methods of development discussed under their separate entries in Part II*]. Whichever method of development you choose, the development should be organized chronologically.

Second, as you develop the body paragraphs, remember that the details must be adequate to support the focus. Some hints:

- Be reasonable. Two or three details will be insufficient to explain Benjamin Franklin's contributions as an ambassador.
- At the same time, however, be careful not to stray into a discussion of sidelights. They may be interesting; but if they do not support or explain the selected focus, they do not belong in the biographical sketch. [*See* unity *in the Glossary and* Revising: Sample Revision for Unity *in Part I.*]

Third, the sketch may be enhanced by anecdotes or quotations to add variety and interest. Some hints:

- Anecdotes and quotations must support or explain the focus.
- To include them just to add a bit of human interest is to lose unity in the paper.
- Give credit to your sources for the anecdotes, quotations, and other information. A formal paper requires some kind of formal documentation (parenthetical notes, endnotes, or footnotes, as well as a bibliography) for all information sources. An informal paper, however, may use a text reference and omit other formal means of documentation. [*See* Research Paper *in Part III for additional information on documentation.*]

STEP 9　Writing • Adding the Conclusion

Conclude the biography with an emphasis on the focus established in the introduction. Obviously, a biography need not end with the subject's death. The subject may still be living! The reader will respond with greatest interest to a conclusion that dwells on the subject's significant contributions rather than on the bare facts of names, dates, and places.

STEP 10　Revising • Checking the Contents

Reread your completed paper to look for possible weaknesses. [*See* Revising *in Part I for a thorough explanation of revision techniques.*] In addition, ask yourself these questions to help you spot weaknesses peculiar to a biography:

- Have I researched thoroughly and carefully to avoid writing a biography that misrepresents the subject?
- Does my biography reflect the research accurately?
- Have I avoided personal bias so that I do not misrepresent the subject?
- Did I avoid too much name-date-place information?
- Have I included meaningful details to support the focus?
- Are names, dates, places, and details accurate?

- Does the biography read well, or does it sound like a list of facts and figures?
- Does the reader get a good glimpse of the subject?

You should have answered "yes" to each of the preceding questions. If you cannot, use the questions to which you answered "no" as a guide for revising weaknesses in the biography.

STEP 11 **Proofreading • Checking for Accuracy**

When you have finished revising, check for final details. Check spelling and word choice. Double-check sources for any inconsistencies in dates or details and for accuracy in documentation. Then read for grammar, mechanics, and usage errors. [*See Part IV for rules and examples.*]

A NOTE ABOUT THE SAMPLES

All of the following sample biographies deal with John James Audubon. As you study the sketches, however, note that the focus changes in each. The writers took into consideration their respective content areas and audiences. Thus, the focus parallels the subject matter: The paper for English class talks about Audubon as a writer; for social sciences, as a man of the frontier; for science, as an ornithologist; for work-place writing, as a businessman; for technical writing, as a man using his skills to earn a living.

SAMPLE FOR ENGLISH

The following biography, developed as a single paragraph, focuses on John James Audubon as a writer. Compare it with the others that follow to see how the emphasis changes to meet the needs of the content area.

Woodsman Audubon as a Writer

Most people worldwide recognize John James Audubon as an artist, the self-trained painter of birds who was the first to depict them life-sized and in motion. As an artist whose life spanned the years roughly between the American Constitutional Convention and the beginning of the Civil War, Audubon studied his subject more carefully than any other of his contemporary ornithologists. In addition to his painting, however, Audubon also wrote about the birds, their habits, and their habitats. His constant struggle to write effectively endears him to the hearts of modern readers who lack his otherwise genius-like characteristics. For instance, in the *Ornithological Biography*, a five-volume text to accompany his paintings, Audubon wrote with telling insight about the subject to which he devoted the last half of his life. As Michael Harwood points out, Audubon, like many other struggling writers, called on information from his "old journals and memorandum books, which were written on the spot" (Audubon, quoted in Harwood, *Audubon Demythologized,* New York: National Audubon Society, n.d., 10). From the beginning, he indicated that the work would not be a scientific one; he had inadequate training for that. Little did he know, however, what an effort he would face in order to produce even an unscientific work. In fact, the final work that was published for the buying public probably bears little resemblance to the first several drafts. Because he included many stories of the wilderness, as one critic notes, while the books were a pioneering work, "they were flowery, rich with moralizing and anthropomorphizing. That reflected his time, in which educated men looked to nature for spiritual messages" (Harwood 10). Audubon wrote with the flair and flamboyance he learned as a child growing up in France, but he had the wisdom to hire William MacGillivray, a Scottish ornithologist, to edit his work and add anatomical descriptions. MacGillivray, like a good critic, regularly and repeatedly argued with and questioned Audubon, forcing him to write with greater accuracy; however, Audubon's lifelong habits of exaggerating and embellishing were difficult to break. As a result of his critics, though, including MacGillivray and other academic naturalists, Audubon finally forced himself to restrain his flowery style. His diaries nevertheless retain the embellished style. So even though he called himself "the American Woodsman" who liked simply to tramp in the woods and watch the birds, he wrote with a woodsman's style far from simple. Like other writers, he struggled to change to make his work acceptable to the buying public. As a result, genius artist that he was, Audubon's struggles as a writer give him a humanizing quality worth empathy.

 Analysis of the Sample for English. The preceding biographical sketch focuses on Audubon's writing. The writer selected that focus, of course, because he was preparing the sketch for an English class assignment. Note these additional details:

- As suggested in Step 3 earlier in this section, Audubon's renown as an artist is acknowledged in the first two sentences, but the focus of this biographical sketch, his writing, is introduced in the third sentence.
- The fourth sentence suggests the writer's attitude toward Audubon's struggles.
- The details are in order, from most important to least. Because the details relate to only two works, the *Ornithological Biography* and Audubon's diaries, there is little on which to base chronological organization. Instead, the writer emphasizes the larger work and concludes with a reference to the smaller work. The writer can emphasize Audubon's struggle to refine his style by pointing to the diaries.

- The use of quotations, both from Audubon and from a critic, adds interest and further details. The full publication information in parenthetical notes credits the source, adequate for the brevity of this paper.
- Without mentioning specific dates or places, the writer lets readers know when and where Audubon lived.
- The conclusion ties together the significance of the focus chosen for this English class assignment.

SAMPLE FOR SOCIAL SCIENCES

The following sample biographical paragraph focuses on John James Audubon as a frontiersman, a focus appropriate for the content area.

Audubon, the Frontiersman

Artist John James Audubon, recognized ornithologist, embodied what contemporary Americans refer to as the American frontiersman. Born two years before the Constitutional Convention, he died shortly before the Civil War. During those rugged developmental years, French immigrant Audubon left Pennsylvania, crossed the mountains, and made his way down the Ohio River to settle first at Louisville and then at Henderson, Kentucky, at that time the rugged, untamed edge of the frontier. When he brought his girl-next-door bride, Lucy, from Pennsylvania to a log cabin in Henderson, she grieved at leaving her family and fine comforts behind. Perhaps she had a right to grieve, for the trip across the mountains by a tumultuous stagecoach ride and, at times, on foot or on horseback, demanded far more of her than any other experience Lucy had ever had. Then, after a sojourn in Louisville, when they finally reached what would be their home, Audubon himself, in his journal, described Henderson as "one of the poorest spots in the Western Country." Although the life there was painful for Lucy, the rest of the world can be grateful for that "poor spot." As a result of his experiences there, Audubon began the work that finally brought him ongoing fame: painting birds. The wilderness rich with wildlife gained Audubon's nearly full-time attention, and he dedicated himself to a goal of painting every bird he encountered. The frontier offered species no one else had studied, and Audubon is credited with "discovering" a number of new birds. His travels along the frontier, up and down the Mississippi from Louisville to New Orleans, allowed him to see birds from north to south and to sight water birds, land birds, and birds of prey. Treks up the Missouri River into a farther Western wilderness provided even more species for Audubon's brush. Reading Audubon's diaries recounting his ventures into the frontier offers modern Americans a glimpse of the time when the West (now the Midwest) was a different place—an environment alive with birds now extinct, an almost impenetrable wilderness without roads, where transportation was an exercise in torture, and where the waterways provided the easiest means of getting from one remote point of population to another. As a result, to understand Audubon's life is to gain an inside view of the frontier life.

Analysis of the Sample for Social Sciences. The Audubon biographical sketch developed for a social science class examines his life as a representative of the American frontier. Note these specifics:

- The first sentence states the focus.
- The remainder of the sketch, organized chronologically, gives details to support the idea of frontiersman representative.
- A quotation from Audubon's diary adds interest to the supporting details. Because the writer indicates the source of the quotation within the text, no further documentation is required in this informal paper.
- The conclusion draws the readers' attention again to the specific focus of the biography.
- When readers are finished, without having read lists of dates, names, and places, they know when and where Audubon lived and gain insight into how reading Audubon's diaries can teach them even more about the American frontier in the early nineteenth century.

While the biography ignores Audubon's contributions to science and his failure as a businessman, readers were told in the first sentence that the emphasis would be on the frontiersman idea. To include details supporting other ideas would cause the sketch to lose unity.

SAMPLE FOR SCIENCE

The writer of the following John James Audubon biography focuses on Audubon's contributions as an ornithologist. The focus parallels appropriate subject matter for a science paper.

Artist Audubon as Ornithologist

Two hundred years after his birth, John James Audubon continues to gain world acclaim as a painter of birds. As an ornithologist, however, he made equally significant but less widely acclaimed contributions to the world of science. During Audubon's life, birds now extinct soared the skies in pest-like abundance. Audubon's diaries speak of hordes of annoying passenger pigeons killed in masses and left lying where they fell for the hogs to eat. He wrote of bald eagles and trumpeter swans readily sighted. He described marshes, woods, and skies thick with birds. More importantly, however, he wrote in detail about their habits and habitats. Unlike other ornithologists who studied dead specimens in a laboratory and whom Audubon called "closet naturalists," Audubon studied birds alive in their natural environments. While scientists and artists, including Audubon, commonly shot their specimens for close study, Audubon always first studied the birds alive, watching their behavior, even studying their migratory habits. He may well have been the first to band birds to see if the same individuals returned to the same habitat each spring. As a result, when Audubon wrote the *Ornithological Biography* to accompany his paintings, he noted, "No man living knows better than I do the habits of our birds ... and with the assistance of my old journals and memorandum books, which were written on the spot, I can at least put down plain truths, which may be useful." The details in both his writing and in his painting illustrate superiority to anything produced by his contemporaries. He made the mistake, however, of including in the bird biography some tall tales about his life on the frontier. The inclusion affected his reputation as a reliable observer. As a result, his contributions to the field of ornithology were shrouded by criticism from his colleagues, much the result of what one critic calls "quirks in his personality and style." Critic Robert Cushman Murphy suggests the bird biographies "have become a half-forgotten treasure ... surely replete with information that compilers of later works have not yet used." The world has more to learn about Audubon the scientist.

 Analysis of the Sample for Science. Audubon the scientist becomes the focus for this biography. Written for a science class, it includes these characteristics:

- The sketch points out first the differences between Audubon and his contemporary ornithologists. By clarifying Audubon's pioneering effort, the writer can then deal with the biography chronologically.
- The writer discusses Audubon's method of research, then his writing, followed by his unscientific anecdotes, concluding with his discredit in the scientific community.
- By ending the biographical sketch with a critic's words about the potential wealth of important information remaining in the many volumes, the writer places Audubon in a scientific niche, which aids the readers' understanding.
- The writer enables readers to draw assumptions without being spoon-fed. For instance, readers know Audubon was born 200 years ago and that he experienced a very different environment along the then-frontier from the one Midwesterners know today.
- Because the writer indicates the sources of his quotations within the text of his paper, he omits further documentation. In some classes, with some instructors, this kind of documentation will be sufficient. Follow your instructor's requirements. Hard scientific data needs more complete documentation.

Without being critical, the writer explains the historical period of which Audubon was a part, when passenger pigeons were slaughtered as pests, when gentlemen scientists did not favor field research, when the infant field of ornithology provided rich opportunities for study and discovery. The result is a biographical sketch that reveals more than just facts on the surface.

SAMPLE WORK-PLACE WRITING

The following biography focuses on John James Audubon's experiences as a businessman and entrepreneur.

Giving Up Business for the Birds

John James Audubon gained well-deserved recognition as an artist and ornithologist. As a frontiersman, he evoked the interest of his European contemporaries fascinated with the wild America. As a businessman, however, Audubon provided his biographers with room for argument. Many critics claim he was too busy frittering away the hours chasing birds in the woods to be a successful businessman, but other critics say the struggling nation's forces over which he had no control created his downfall. Whatever the case, he landed in debtors' prison, leaving his penniless wife alone with two children. Audubon's business problems began when he and a fellow Frenchman set up an importing business in Louisville. Shortly thereafter, as a result of the Napoleonic Wars and their effect on American shipping, Congress passed the Embargo Act in 1807 and cut off overseas trade. Thus ended the import business and the partnership. While his partner blamed Audubon's frequent forays into the woods as the cause of failure, surely the embargo affected an import business, too. Audubon returned to Henderson, Kentucky, where he owned land, slaves, and a sturdy log cabin, and there he became a shopkeeper. He took risks. As critic Michael Harwood wrote, "That sort of thing was characteristic of the place and time: Every man stood a chance to make a fortune if he simply dared to try for it" (*Audubon Demythologized*, New York: National Audubon Society, n.d., 4). Audubon tried, but when the war with England caused blockades to be set up at the ports of entry, he failed again. After the war, Audubon built a steam mill in Henderson, a gigantic affair with significant potential. The community failed to grow the way Audubon had anticipated it would, so the mill failed, too. Then the banks failed. Like many other businessmen, Audubon was in debt, and the failing banks cost him his business and personal property. He declared bankruptcy and faced debtors' prison. As a result of his disastrous business affairs, however, Audubon gave the world far more than he was ever paid. Only when Audubon had nothing else to turn to did he begin painting birds with a serious goal—to earn money. Like many other artists, he struggled financially for most of his life. Sadly, his story is one of business decisions affected both by divided attention and economic factors beyond his control and even beyond his understanding. In the end, however, he gave the world his art treasures, one collection of which sold recently for well over $1.5 million!

Analysis of the Sample Work-Place Writing. The preceding biographical sketch focuses on Audubon as a businessman. Note these details:

- The first two sentences acknowledge his other, more famous, contributions; the third sentence establishes the focus of this sketch.
- In order to set the scene, the writer introduces the conflict among biographers who examine Audubon's businesses and then tells her readers the outcome: debtors' prison.
- The remainder of the biographical sketch, organized chronologically, details Audubon's business experiences and ultimate failure. By noting that the business failures caused Audubon to begin painting, the writer suggests the world can be grateful for them.
- Some indirect information shines through the direct retelling of the facts. For instance, by using a narrative approach, telling a story of Audubon's business ventures, the writer lets the reader see the man in his time.
- Using parenthetical documentation permits the writer to credit her source for the quotation. The brevity of the paper suggests this simple documentation form, thus omitting the need for a bibliography. Use whatever documentation your instructor requires.
- By concluding with the positive contribution of the artist to the business of the contemporary art community, the writer softens the characterization of Audubon as a failure. Simultaneously, she extends the business point of view in Audubon's biography from the nineteenth century to the twenty-first century.

SAMPLE TECHNICAL WRITING

The following biography of John James Audubon focuses on his ability to use his skills to earn a living. The technical focus shows a side of Audubon not included in the earlier biographical samples.

Audubon's Worldwide Fame

As an artist, John James Audubon earned worldwide fame for his daring new approach to painting birds. Although he began teaching himself to draw birds in his early manhood, not until mid-life did he assume the serious goal of painting every specimen he could find. Roaming the American frontier during the early nineteenth century, he discovered a wealth of subject matter. Because he studied the birds alive in their natural surroundings, even though he painted the details from a dead specimen, he depicted the birds in a lifelike pose unmatched by that in the work of any of his contemporaries. Other artists used static side views, recalling a kind of bird-like imitation of Egyptian art. Critic Michael Harwood explains that to aid himself in depicting the lifelike poses, Audubon "devised a method of wiring up a freshly killed bird—giving the model an armature, as if it were a piece of sculpture—which permitted him to pose it as he recalled it in life." Audubon's real contribution to bird art, however, was his insistence that every bird, whether hummingbird or bald eagle, be painted life-sized. So his paintings took a huge format, referred to as the "elephant folio." Yet another characteristic developed as Audubon grew with his art. The background detail gave critics as much to study as did the birds. Often enhanced with other creatures and an abundance of plant life, the paintings attempted to put the full-sized lifelike birds in natural settings. When the paintings were finished, Audubon had 435 plates. Today, a single set of those prints, bound in the elephant folio, will bring about $1.5 million, not a bad price for an artist who spent most of his life in poverty.

 Analysis of the Sample Technical Writing. By focusing on Audubon as an artist, the biography deals with Audubon's claim to fame. Note these details:

- The writer begins with an overview to explain why Audubon differed from his contemporaries. The entire sketch focuses on the distinctive differences.
- Readers follow Audubon from his youthful self-instruction to his midlife beginning of a serious career. The time sequence continues as further Audubon trademarks emerge.
- As the artist expands his career, readers follow, up to the estimated current value of his works. So while the biography focuses on the technical trademarks of Audubon's work, chronological organization remains loosely in place.
- Selected details support the paper's focus adequately but without burden.
- Readers know who, what, why, when, and where without any list-like rendering of names, dates, and places.
- The expository approach lets the writer show Audubon's style without losing good organization and without relying on narrative. A story-telling approach here could weaken the writer's credibility in regard to an understanding of Audubon's art.
- The conclusion enhances the point of view and brings readers back to the present, better informed about the value of Audubon's work.

- Because the writer credits the source of quoted material within the text of the paper, further documentation is omitted.

These sample biographical sketches and their analyses should help you develop a biography limited by a suitable focus.

Book Report

A book report summarizes and offers a reaction to a book. While it always includes certain details, a book report is usually tailored to its reader. Thus, a book report written for an English class has very different content from one written for a social science or technical class. As opposed to a book review [*see* Review *later in Part III*], the book report strives only to report what the book includes, reflecting only briefly, perhaps indirectly, the reader's reaction to it. Emphasis usually falls on those aspects of the book directly related to the subject matter of the class for which the report is prepared. In fact, a book report is often used to prove that the writer has gained knowledge from outside reading in the subject area.

CHARACTERISTICS

Book reports usually follow a rather simple format that includes

- the title of the book,
- the author's name,
- the characters, setting, and point of view in a work of fiction [*see* characterization, setting, *and* point of view *in the Glossary*],
- a one-paragraph synopsis of the book [*see* Synopsis *later in Part III and in the Glossary*],
- the topic or theme of the book as it relates to the subject matter of the class for which the report is being written [*see* theme *in the Glossary*],
- the writer's reaction to the book, particularly as related to anything he or she may have learned from reading it,
- direct quotations from the book to support general statements.

PROCESS

Realistically, a book report cannot deal with every aspect of a book. Use the following steps to plan, organize, write, and revise a successfully focused book report.

STEP 1   **Prewriting • Narrowing the Topic**

Complete a careful reading of the book, making notes as you read. Notes may include important names, dates, incidents, and significant ideas, as well as a notation of the page numbers on which you find those incidents and ideas introduced. Take note of significant passages that may be useful for supporting detail in the book report.

When you've finished reading, sort through your notes for subject-matter ideas. A subject-matter idea is one directly related to the subject of the class for which you are preparing the report. Check the two or three most important subject-matter ideas. These will be the ideas on which your report will focus.

For example, after reading a work of fiction, *The Clan of the Cave Bear*, for a science class, a writer checked the two following subject-matter ideas as most important:

> Biology of prehistoric plants and animals
> Fictionalized representation of the theory of evolution

Note that the preceding subject-matter ideas relate directly to the science class for which the writer is preparing the book report. Selecting these subject-matter ideas determines the emphasis of the report.

STEP 2   **Prewriting • Selecting Details**

Think about the book's two or three subject-matter ideas listed in Step 1. List three or four details that explain the book's contribution to that subject matter. Remember to direct your choices toward the content of the class for which you are preparing the report.

For instance, the writer can support the subject-matter ideas listed in Step 1 with the following details:

> Biology of prehistoric plants and animals:
>> Life at edge of glacier
>> Animals such as woolly mammoth, cave bear, horses
>> Medicinal and edible plants
> Fictionalized representation of the theory of evolution:
>> Neanderthal people's characteristics
>> Destiny of Neanderthal
>> Cro-Magnon's characteristics

Complete your own list of details. This list will serve as a scratch outline for the body of your book report. [*See* Outlines: For a Paper *later in Part III.*]

STEP 3   Prewriting • Checking the Author

Check to see whether the author has written other books, noting especially those of similar subject matter. (Note: The book itself usually lists the author's previous books, but you may need to check the card or computer catalog.) If the author has written additional books, is the book for your report the most recent or one of the earlier books? Making note of earlier or later books by the same author lends perspective to your report.

Next, check the author's background and make note of anything that particularly relates to this book's subject matter.

STEP 4   Prewriting • Organizing the Overall Plan

The book report usually reflects a simple pattern of organization. Use the following plan:

Introduction. The introduction includes the basic information: the book's title, author, and topic or theme. In a work of fiction, the introduction may also identify major characters and setting.

If the author has written other books of a similar nature, include that notation either here or in the concluding paragraph. Likewise, either here or in the conclusion, include a sentence or two about any pertinent details regarding the author's background.

Body Paragraphs. A book report usually includes three or four body paragraphs. The first body paragraph is a synopsis of the book, organized in the same order as the book itself. [*See* Synopsis *later in Part III for an example and explanation of the process for developing the summary.*]

The next two or three body paragraphs explain the two or three topics you listed in Steps 1 and 2. Develop a separate paragraph for each, using incidents, examples, and supporting quotations from the book. These paragraphs will probably be organized in order of importance. [*See* order of importance *in the Glossary.*]

Conclusion. The final paragraph summarizes the book's contribution to the subject area and includes the reader's reaction to the book, particularly as it relates to the subject matter. This paragraph should be arranged so that the report's most important evaluative comment is the final one, a kind of concluding remark for the entire report.

When writing book reports, inexperienced writers tend to sum-marize the book rather than write a synopsis and then deal specifi-cally with the theme or topic as it relates to the subject matter of the class for which the report is being written. Remember that the bulk of your report should explain the two or three subject-matter ideas selected in Steps 1 and 2. The synopsis is only about one-fifth of an effective report.

STEP 5   **Writing • Following the Plan**

Write your report based on the organizational plan spelled out in Step 4. Pay attention, also, to the following general guidelines:

- Make the synopsis concise.
- Include sufficient supporting details from the book to develop your two or three subject-related paragraphs. [*See* Revising: Sample Revision for Specific Detail *in Part I.*]
- Provide adequate transitions to help the reader move easily from sentence to sentence and idea to idea. [*See* Revising: Sample Revision for Transition *in Part I.*]
- Maintain unity within each paragraph and within the report as a whole. Omit irrelevant details. [*See* Revising: Sample Revision for Unity *in Part I.*]
- Use vocabulary and sentence structure appropriate for the subject and the audience.
- End with an effective clincher. [*See* Writing a Multi-Paragraph Paper *in Part I for a discussion of effective conclusions.*]

STEP 6   **Revising • Checking the Content**

When you have finished the first draft, check the content of your book report against the following guidelines:

- Does the first paragraph include the basic information: the book's title, author, and topic or theme?
- Does the first paragraph include a thesis sentence [*see* thesis sentence *in the Glossary and* Writing a Multi-Paragraph Paper *in Part I*] and any pertinent information about the book's preparation or the author's background?
- Is the one-paragraph synopsis concise?
- Are the two or three subject-related ideas developed in separate paragraphs?
- Are the subject-related ideas supported by details and quotations from the book?

- Are all details relevant to your thesis? [*See* Revising: Sample Revision for Unity *in Part I.*]
- Are quotations from the book included to provide support and authenticity?
- Do transitions connect ideas within and between the paragraphs? [*See* Revising: Sample Revision for Transition *in Part I.*]
- Do word choice and sentence structure seem appropriate to the subject and the audience? [*See* Revising: Sample Revision for Emphasis *in Part I.*]
- Are sentences varied, both in length and structure? [*See* Revising: Sample Revision for Sentence Variety *in Part I.*]
- Does the organization emphasize the report's main ideas?

[*For additional general suggestions for revision, see* Revising *in Part I. Combining these suggestions with those in this section should provide guidelines for thorough revision.*]

STEP 7   **Proofreading • Checking the Details**

When you have completed the revisions and prepared your final draft, check for accurate spelling and good word choice. Using Part IV of this book, check also the grammar, mechanics, usage, and punctuation for accuracy. Especially check to see that all quotations are accurately enclosed in quotation marks and accurately punctuated. Make any final corrections necessary.

A NOTE ABOUT THE SAMPLES

Following are book reports, all of the same novel, developed for five purposes. Recognize that some books are far more appropriate for certain classes than are others. In fact, your teacher or instructor may assign a specific book or give you a reading list from which to choose a book. The following samples should not be misconstrued to mean that any book is appropriate for any class or subject area. After you have read the five reports, however, you should be better prepared to write effective reports. [*See also* Review, *elsewhere in Part III, to compare a book report with a book review, and see* Literary Analyses: Sample for a Novel, *also in Part III, to compare a book report with a literary analysis of a novel. The same novel serves as the subject of the book report, the book review, and the literary analysis.*]

SAMPLE FOR ENGLISH

Students in an English class were asked to read and report on books set in a time period other than the present. Students were also asked to relate themes in the book to subject matter discussed in class. The writer whose book report appears below tailored the report to meet that assignment.

Language and Logic: Cave Woman Style

The Valley of the Horses fictionalizes the beginning of civilization in the Asian area north of the Beran Sea. Like two of Jean M. Auel's other books, *The Clan of the Cave Bear* and *The Mammoth Hunters*, this one gets its foundation from archaeological research supporting the evolution of man. In this unusual historical novel, the reader follows Ayla, a child of the Others, who has been reared by the Clan of the Cave Bear and then ejected from the Clan when she violates customs she can neither understand nor accept. In exile in the valley of the horses, she survives five years alone until she meets Jondalar, a man of the Others. They face a major obstacle: They cannot communicate. Ayla has no verbal language, and Jondalar cannot understand the nuances of her gestures and facial expressions.

Ayla faces a lonely struggle for survival after her death curse by the Clan. To solve basic survival problems, she must use logic: Alone, how can she kill, butcher, and process an animal large enough to feed her through the severe winter; alone, how can she provide clothing, cooking utensils, sleeping skins, and shelter for protection; alone, how can she protect herself from the dangers around her? Her training as a medicine woman and her knowledge of hunting, coupled with the large brain characteristic of the Others allow her to succeed. Also as a result of her background, she saves Jondalar's life after a lion mauls him and kills his traveling-companion brother. Jondalar is the first of the Others that Ayla has seen. After Ayla's medicinal powers help Jondalar regain his health, the two of them suffer from their inability to understand each other's customs. Jondalar finally teaches her to speak, however, and they establish a strong bond, sharing their creative ideas to reach solutions for both the physical and mental problems they face as a team.

Among the many concepts about the development of civilization that Auel weaves into her novels to stimulate the reader's imagination and curiosity, one of the most intriguing is the development of language. Without writing a history of the development of language, Auel forces the reader to deal with the transition from nonverbal to verbal to written communication. The Clan, characterized as Neanderthals, used only grunts, facial expressions, and gestures to communicate. As Jondalar notes in one encounter, he was "aware, peripherally, that the young flathead (Clan member) and the female were waving their hands and making gutteral sounds." He adds that he "had an impression they were communicating." By contrast, the Others use almost entirely a spoken language. In fact, when Ayla tries to explain to

Jondalar how she guides her horse, she can only say, "Whinney just knows where I want to go." The horse senses her muscular nudges and reactions and knows where Ayla wants to go, a phenomenon Jondalar has difficulty understanding. Written language, however, is unknown to either of them. While Jondalar explains sculpture to Ayla, neither of them draws representations as a preliminary written language. On the other hand, Ayla does make marks on sticks to keep track of the days and months. Interestingly enough, though, she cannot count the many marks she has made; Jondalar calculates her lonely stay at over five years.

Another intriguing idea presented in *The Valley of the Horses* to stimulate the reader's imagination about the development of civilization deals with the importance of logic for survival. Much of the development of the various civilizations was aided by the people's ability to reason and solve problems. The Clan people, described by Auel to resemble the forerunners of *Homo sapiens,* had memories but could not learn anything new. They could not reason. They did whatever they did because it was all they knew. Necessarily, then, Ayla was feared. As a woman, she learned on her own to hunt, something no Clan woman could or would think of trying to do. Because the Others had a larger brain, they could learn new things, adapt to their surroundings, and, yes, verbalize. In one instance, when Ayla discovers by accident that striking together two pieces of flint can produce fire, the author says of the accident: "That was the serendipity. Ayla supplied the recognition and the other necessary elements: she understood the process of making fire, she needed fire, and she wasn't afraid to try something new." The implication, of course, is that the Others succeeded and thrived; the Clan died.

Auel suggests other topics for thought about man's development: how Ayla first learns to start a fire with flint, how she learns to use a horse to help her, how she learns to communicate in a kind of extrasensory way with animals, how Jondalar learns to construct a craft to move on water. All are woven into the plot as naturally as any other event in a historical novel. The difference between this and more typical historical novels is merely setting; but the research—biological, geographical, geological, zoological, anthropological, sociological, and archaeological—exhibited by the author makes for astounding, thought-provoking reading. As the second book of the series, however, *The Valley of the Horses* undoubtedly evokes the greatest comment on the development of languages and the importance of the ability to reason in the development of civilizations. That Auel could do all of this and still maintain suspense and drama in a complicated plot significantly credits her creative ability.

 Analysis of the Sample for English. As you study the preceding sample book report, consider the following items:

- The introductory paragraph includes the necessary information: title, author, characters, setting, and theme. Readers learn, too, that the author has written two other books in the series; they are named but not discussed.

- The second paragraph presents a synopsis of the 550-page book in one paragraph. Probably the most difficult part of the book report to write, the synopsis must do what it does here, give only a sketch of what happens.
- In the third and fourth paragraphs, the writer narrows the discussion to topics most appropriate for an English class, language and logic. While obviously the writer could say much more about the book, its theme, its plot, or its development, he must somehow limit the report. By choosing two significant, subject-related topics for a brief discussion, the writer makes good use of the book-report format.
- The fifth paragraph suggests additional points of interest which further develop the theme, indicates the breadth of the research, and concludes with a reference to the points made in paragraphs 3 and 4, emphasizing the creativity evident in this unusual historical novel.
- Distinctive terms are included to merge style with the content area, words such as *fictionalize, historical novel, nonverbal* and *verbal communication*, as well as other references to a novel's structure.
- Direct quotations from the book, accurately set apart with quotation marks, support the general statements and lend authenticity to the report.
- Other characteristics of effective theme development are evident throughout the paper.

Without a doubt, the preceding book report could have taken several approaches for an English class. On the other hand, a book report is neither a critical analysis [*see* Literary Analyses *later in Part III*], nor a review [*see* Review *later in Part III*]. A book report merely tells what the book is about and relates it to the subject area.

SAMPLE FOR SOCIAL SCIENCES

In a sociology class, students were asked to read and report on books, either fiction or nonfiction, that examine cultural habits, particularly as those habits can create prejudices. Note that some introductory parts of the book report for social sciences remain the same as that for English. At the same time, note how the book report is refocused in order to be appropriate for the different curricular content.

Prehistoric Prejudice

The Valley of the Horses is a historical novel, which fictionalizes the beginning of civilization in the Asian area north of the Beran Sea, an area in which many anthropologists locate the beginnings of civilization. Like two of Jean M. Auel's other books, *The Cave of the Clan Bear* and *The Mammoth Hunters*, this one gets its foundation from archaeological research supporting the evolution of man. The reader follows Ayla, a child of the Others who has been reared by the Clan of the Cave Bear, as she meets Jondalar, a man of the Others. The Clan characterizes the end of the Neanderthal people, and the Others characterizes the beginning of the Cro-Magnon people. Set 25,000 years ago near the end of the Ice Age, the book clarifies the differences between the two peoples.

Ayla faces a lonely struggle for survival after her death curse by the Clan. To solve basic survival problems, she must use logic: Alone, how can she kill, butcher, and process an animal large enough to feed her through the severe winter; alone, how can she provide clothing, cooking utensils, sleeping skins, and shelter for protection; alone, how can she protect herself from the dangers around her? Her training as a medicine woman and her knowledge of hunting, coupled with the large brain characteristic of the Others allow her to succeed. Also as a result of her background, she saves Jondalar's life after a lion mauls him and kills his traveling-companion brother. Jondalar is the first of the Others that Ayla has seen. After Ayla's medicinal powers help Jondalar regain his health, the two of them suffer from their inability to understand each other's customs. Jondalar finally teaches her to speak, however, and they establish a strong bond, sharing their creative ideas to reach solutions for both the physical and mental problems they face as a team.

It is the couple's inability to understand each other's customs that creates the conflict in the last half of the book. Jondalar, one of the Others who looks down on the Clan as animals, is outraged when he finds that Ayla, obviously also one of the Others, has lived with the Clan and has even had a child by one of them. His outrage stems from his background. As a youth, he had shared in whispered conversations and rude jokes about the Flathead females, as the Others referred to the Clan women. "You know the one about the old man who was so blind, he caught a flathead female and thought it was a woman...." Flatheads were to be feared and territory was to be protected from them. As one stocky leader suggested, "Maybe we should get up a flathead hunting party and clean the vermin out." Jondalar knew that Flatheads could walk upright, but only with a bowlegged, slightly bent shuffle. They had only crude spears, fashioned from sharpened sticks. They merely wrapped skins around them, neither cut nor stitched to fit. Quite simply, he saw them as "half-animal, half-human abominations."

His outrage at learning about her relationship to the Clan leaves Ayla confused and frustrated. Tall and blonde, quite different from the short, stocky, dark, hairy Clan people, Ayla grew up believing she was ugly.

Different was ugly. So she accepts the Clan—both the people and their ways—as normal. She has seen no other human until Jondalar. Because she understands the Clan's humanness, their sensitivity, their customs, and their interpretation of the spirit world, she cannot understand Jondalar's reaction. It is only after several highly emotional scenes and obvious innocence on her part that Ayla is gradually able to give Jondalar enough insight into the Clan world that he begins to see his error. He struggles with reason. "Could Ayla be that? Could she be defiled? Unclean? Filth? Evil? Honest, straightforward Ayla? With her Gift of healing? So wise, and fearless, and gentle, and beautiful." Ultimately, when he acknowledges that animals don't recognize a spiritual world, Jondalar is able to accept the fact that maybe—only maybe—Clan people are human.

The obvious parallel of these two representatives of opposing cultures with contemporary society leads the reader to wonder whether civilization has made much progress in the area of human relations and willingness to accept and understand other cultures. Indeed, Auel has dealt with a delicate subject in such a distant context that some readers may find the parallel invalid. With other themes readily a part of the trilogy, a reader may well choose to discuss them instead. The obvious intent of the plot of *The Valley of the Horses*, however, surely must be to help the readers see what Jondalar sees: Without thorough understanding and insight, without walking in the other fellow's moccasins, so to speak, one cannot understand his ways. Too often, what is different is ugly; what is different is wrong. It is called prejudice.

Analysis of the Sample for Social Sciences. The following specific analytical comments emphasize the difference between a book report for an English class and one of the same book for a social sciences class:

- The first two paragraphs in the social sciences book report are very similar to those in the book report for English. The differences are subtle: a reference to the area *where archaeologists believe civilization began,* and the omission of such phrases as *unusual historical novel.* Certainly the plot, summarized in paragraph 2, will be the same for any subject area.
- The obvious differences begin in paragraphs 3 and 4. The writer approaches this complicated novel via the sociology strand. By dealing specifically with the understanding the two characters must gain from each other about their respective cultures, the writer tailors her report to the social science subject area. The paragraphs merely summarize those specific areas of conflict; they do not evaluate or respond critically.

[*For a comparison, see* Literary Analyses *and* Review *later in Part III.*]

- The conclusion further enhances the social science emphasis. By concluding with a reference to paragraphs 3 and 4 and acknowledging the presence of other themes, the writer first broadens the scope and then zeros in on her main idea, ending with an application of the theme to contemporary society.
- Note that direct quotations, punctuated accurately, help support the general ideas.
- Effective transitions help readers move smoothly within as well as between paragraphs.

Note that the social science book report follows the same organization and structure as did the English book report. The difference comes from the choice of subject matter for discussion. As always, the subject matter must relate to the content area of the course for which the report is being prepared.

SAMPLE FOR SCIENCE

As part of a biology class, students were asked to select a book from a list of works of fiction and report on the use of scientific knowledge as it helps develop either the plot or the background of the book. Note that the science book report follows the same organization and structure as did the English and social sciences book reports, but the choice of subject matter differs. Again, the subject matter must relate to the content area of the course for which the report is being prepared.

When Science in Fiction Is Not Science Fiction

The Valley of the Horses fictionalizes the beginning of civilization in the Asian area north of the Beran Sea. Like two of Jean M. Auel's other books, *The Clan of the Cave Bear* and *The Mammoth Hunters*, this one gets its foundation from the archaeological research supporting the evolution of man. The reader follows Ayla, a child of the Others who has been reared by the Clan of the Cave Bear only to be ejected from the Clan when she violates customs she cannot understand or accept. In exile in the valley of the horses, she survives five years alone until she meets Jondalar, a man of the Others.

Ayla faces a lonely struggle for survival after her death curse by the Clan. To solve basic survival problems, she must use logic: Alone, how can she kill, butcher, and process an animal large enough to feed her through the severe winter; alone, how can she provide clothing, cooking utensils, sleeping skins, and shelter for protection; alone, how can she protect herself from the dangers around her? Her training as a medicine woman and her knowledge of hunting, coupled with the large brain characteristic of the Others allow her to succeed. Also as a result of her background, she saves Jondalar's life after a lion mauls him and kills his traveling-companion brother. Jondalar is the first of the Others that Ayla has seen. After Ayla's medicinal powers help Jondalar regain his health, the two of them suffer from their inability to understand each other's customs. Jondalar finally teaches her to speak, however, and they are able to establish a strong bond, sharing their creative ideas to find solutions for both the physical and mental problems they face as a team.

The obviously well-researched novel brings to life a number of scientific aspects of the prehistoric world. For instance, the reader gains an understanding of life at the edge of a glacier. How interesting to learn that because of the severe cold and resulting air turbulence above the glacier, lands adjoining the ice field are dry and nearly barren. The glacier feeds the rivers with its spring melt, and readers see the rampage and the ravages. Plants and animals native to the prehistoric setting, many of which are now extinct, also come to life for the reader. "Many of the animals were huge— bison and cattle half again as large as their later counterparts; giant deer with eleven-foot racks; woolly mammoth and woolly rhinoceros." The relative size of the woolly mammoth startles the reader when he sees a human standing above the mammoth's eye. Likewise, the reader learns about plants and their uses. "Her collection of beargrass, cattail leaves and stalks, reeds, willow switches, roots of trees, would be made into baskets, tightly woven or of looser weave in intricate patterns, for cooking, eating, storage containers, winnowing trays, serving trays, mats for sitting upon, serving or drying food." Thus the biological and botanical details of the Ice Age make a formidable impact on the reader.

In addition to the biology and botany of the prehistoric world, Auel includes significant references to the theory of evolution. The reader meets Clan people who, although they can walk upright, walk bowlegged and slightly bent. They are short, stocky, dark, and hairy, their foreheads sloping backward from their eyebrows, all characteristic of scientific evidence distinguishing the Neanderthal man. Their short necks and lack of a chin make Ayla, born of the Others, appear to them to be deformed. She is tall, with long, straight legs, blonde hair, and blue eyes that water, characteristic of scientific evidence distinguishing the Cro-Magnon man. She assumes she is ugly. Because her arms are long and straight, however, she can use a sling more effectively than any of the men of the Clan, a fact that ultimately costs her a place in the society. When Ayla violates a taboo and invades the secret ritual meeting of the men, the medicine man, called the Mogul, claims that tradition indicates such violation will be the end of the Clan. The prediction is Auel's way of dealing with the death of one branch of the human tree.

While the book is fiction, the scientific principles encompassed in the plot, setting, and characters make much of prehistoric theory and archaeological evidence real to the mind's eye. Then, to pick up the newspaper and read of another discovery of an ancient skeleton somewhere in Asia makes the parallels more obvious and the reading of both more interesting. Quite simply, the scientific reality woven into the historical novel makes the nonfiction aspects more readable and more memorable.

Analysis of the Sample for Science. The biology book report must, obviously, focus on scientific issues and concerns. Although paragraphs 1 and 2 are similar to those paragraphs in the English and social sciences reports, note these differences:

- Paragraph 3 points out the specific insights a reader gains from Auel's descriptions of prehistoric situations related to glaciation, particularly the geology and plants and animals.
- Paragraph 4 points out the insights related to and supported by archaeological research on evolution.
- The concluding paragraph emphasizes the value of the book, not as a scientific document but as a realization of theories and concepts. By concluding that *the scientific reality woven into the historical novel makes the nonfiction aspects more readable and more memorable*, the author points out both the value and the weakness of the book in the field of science.
- Direct quotations enhance the report, not only for support but to illustrate the thoroughness of the research.
- Effective transitions move readers through the report.
- Other characteristics of a good theme are evident throughout the report. [*See* Writing a Multi-Paragraph Paper *in Part I.*]

SAMPLE WORK-PLACE WRITING

Typically, work-place reading is entirely nonfiction. However, for the purposes of comparison, this sample uses the same fiction book as previous reports but focuses on a work-place concern. A report on a nonfiction work should follow the same principles.

The Early World of Barter

The Valley of the Horses fictionalizes the beginning of civilization in the Asian area north of the Beran Sea. Like two of Jean M. Auel's other books, *The Clan of the Cave Bear* and *The Mammoth Hunters*, this one gets its foundation from archaeological research supporting the evolution of man. The reader follows Ayla, a child of the Others who has been reared by the Clan of the Cave Bear, to her meeting with Jondalar, a man of the Others.

Ayla faces a lonely struggle for survival after her death curse by the Clan. To solve basic survival problems, she must use logic: Alone, how can she kill, butcher, and process an animal large enough to feed her through the severe winter; alone, how can she provide clothing, cooking utensils, sleeping skins, and shelter for protection; alone, how can she protect herself from the dangers around her? Her training as a medicine woman and her knowledge of hunting, coupled with the large brain characteristic of the Others allow her to succeed. Also as a result of her background, she saves Jondalar's life after a lion mauls him and kills his traveling-companion brother. Jondalar is the first of the Others that Ayla has seen. After Ayla's medicinal powers help Jondalar regain his health, the two of them suffer from their inability to understand each other's customs. Jondalar finally teaches her to speak, however, and they establish a strong bond, sharing their creative ideas to find solutions for both the physical and mental problems they face as a team.

The novel provides insight into one of business' most basic principles: barter. The Clan people, by whom Ayla was reared, do not barter. While the division of labor is clear within the Clan and as long as enough members exist in a Clan they can survive, they depend only on their immediate surroundings for resources. As a result, when resources dwindle, the Clan people move; they do not seek alternative resources or alternative sources. On the other hand, Jondalar's people maintain trade with other tribes, not only for natural resources but also for skills. For example, Jondalar as a young man lives with another tribe to learn from the most respected craftsman the techniques of making flint tools. In another example, he trades two extra fine pieces of flint from a faraway area for the promise of hospitality on his return visit. When his host exclaims, "I was going to visit . . . next year to get some flint from the Lanzadonii mine. There is no better stone," Jondalar responds, "I have some Lanzadonii flint with me . . . . I'd be happy to give it to you if you'd like it." Concerned over the value of the flint, Jondalar's host counters with, "I'd be happy to take it, but I'd want to give you something in return. I don't mind getting the better side of a good trade, but I wouldn't want to cheat you." And so the trade is completed.

The most complicated form of barter evidenced in *The Valley of the Horses,* however, is a trade system developed by two tribes so closely dependent upon one another that intermarriages can occur only in pairs. "Maybe we need to find him a river woman so he can become a Ramudoi. It's only fair . . . ." The Ramudoi is a hunting tribe that lives in wooden shelters; the other is a boat-building tribe. Because each can offer to the other skills and services as well as resources like fish and game, the two tribes have intertwined so thoroughly that relationships are too complicated for the visiting Jondalar to understand. During his visit there, however, they teach him their refined boat-building skills. He learns that the principle of building their boats "was to enclose a pocket of air within a wooden shell. It was a significant innovation." He repays their instruction with labor and new tools, the only resource he has to offer at the time. As they say of him, "It's not the boats, it's the tools we use to make them. Jondalar, you'll always be a toolmaker at heart."

> Even though the book is fiction, Auel's assumptions about the beginning of civilizations are obviously couched in careful research. Although "business" as a term seems hardly appropriate to the prehistoric cultures, the concepts were beginning to develop. To examine with Auel how barter affected the ultimate existence of a tribe clarifies the reader's understanding of the importance of the division of labor enriched by barter.

 Analysis of the Sample Work-Place Writing. Like the previous sample book reports, this one is tailored for a specific purpose. Following the organizational plan set forth in the beginning of this section, this book report includes these characteristics:

- In the introductory paragraph, the reader finds all the pertinent information.
- Paragraph 2 contains a synopsis of the plot.
- Paragraphs 3 and 4, like those in the earlier reports, tailor the report to the purpose and, in this case, deal with a discussion of barter, a basic work-place principle.
- The conclusion, echoing the content of the previous two paragraphs, attempts to place the book's treatment of the subject in perspective.
- Direct quotations add supportive detail.
- Transitions function well, moving readers through the report.

SAMPLE TECHNICAL WRITING

The book report that follows is refocused in order to address the technical aspect of the discovery or invention of a work-saving device.

> ### Learning by Necessity
>
> *The Valley of the Horses* fictionalizes the beginning of civilization in the Asian area north of the Beran Sea. Like two of Jean M. Auel's other books, *The Clan of the Cave Bear* and *The Mammoth Hunters*, this one gets its foundation from the archaeological research supporting the evolution of man. The reader follows Ayla, a child of the Others who has been reared by the Clan of the Cave Bear, to her meeting with Jondalar, a man of the Others.
>
> Ayla faces a lonely struggle for survival after her death curse by the Clan. To solve basic survival problems, she must use logic: Alone, how can she kill, butcher, and process an animal large enough to feed her through the severe winter; alone, how can she provide clothing, cooking utensils, sleeping skins, and shelter for protection; alone, how can she protect herself from the dangers around her? Her training as a medicine woman and her knowledge of hunting, coupled with the large brain characteristic of the Others allow her to succeed. Also as a result of her background, she saves

Jondalar's life after a lion mauls him and kills his traveling-companion brother. Jondalar is the first of the Others that Ayla has seen. After Ayla's medicinal powers help Jondalar regain his health, the two of them suffer from their inability to understand each other's customs. Jondalar finally teaches her to speak, however, and they establish a strong bond, sharing their creative ideas to reach solutions for both the physical and mental problems they face as a team.

It is Ayla's struggle to survive alone that gives the reader the greatest insight into how new work-saving techniques may have come into being. First, as Ayla faces the problem of killing, butchering, and processing a large animal, she stumbles into a long-term situation that eventually eases her workload. With the aid of a pit trap, she kills a horse. Only after the slaughter is complete does she realize the mare has a colt. Because her instinct as a medicine woman is to care for living beings, she takes the colt back to her cave, raises it, and, in the course of time, learns to ride it and rely upon its speed to hunt from it. "The ride was a thrill she could hardly contain. The very idea of going along with a horse when it galloped filled Ayla with a sense of wonder. She had never dreamed such a thing was possible. No one had." Later, after another big kill, Ayla is faced with the problem of getting a deer carcass back to her cave, a distance of several miles. She discovers quite by accident how to use two poles, harnessed to the horse, to function like a sled. In short, her experiences exhibited one principle: "Only in the animal called human did survival depend on more than strength and fitness. Already puny compared with their carnivorous competitors, mankind depended on cooperation and compassion to survive."

In addition to her rather remarkable discovery of using animals to help with her work, she also discovered new kinds of tools. By accident, she learned that two pieces of flint, struck together, would produce a spark. By experiment, she learned that attaching flint tools to a wooden handle improved their usefulness.

By necessity, she experimented with plants to find the right combination to help a lion cub and later Jondalar regain their health. Finally, by watching Jondalar and studying his clothing, she learned to use bone needles to stitch hides, thus creating more form-fitting garments.

Auel presents a fascinating story for even the most casual reader. Furthermore, however, she includes thought-provoking details about the development of tools and other discoveries that reduced work. In fact, Ayla seems to embody the maxim "Necessity is the mother of invention." The details seem almost afterthoughts to the plot development, but in fact they generate some of the best reading. Certainly the reader can appreciate from this prehistoric perspective the phenomenal assistance man now has to ease his labors.

Analysis of the Sample Technical Writing. Tailored for technical content, the preceding book report follows the general outline given earlier in this section:

- Paragraph 1 gives the pertinent introductory information. Paragraph 2 gives the synopsis of the book.
- In paragraphs 3 and 4, the writer directs his attention to technical matters: finding tools to complete a job. Each paragraph develops one idea.
- The paragraphs include support from direct quotations from the book.
- Finally, the conclusion indicates that while necessity is the mother of invention, the book adds a certain perspective to the advantages of modern labor aids. In brief, the book report emphasizes the content appropriate for technical content.

After studying the sample book reports and analyses and by following the process set out at the beginning of this section, you should be able to develop a satisfactory report for any content area.

Character Sketch

A character sketch, sometimes called a *characterization* or *profile*, focuses on one or two dominant features of a real or imaginary person. The sketch reveals a character trait or traits that the writer believes readers will find informative or at least interesting. Frequently used by both magazines and newspapers, character sketches attract attention (and encourage sales) because most people like to read about other people. Sometimes, too, teachers ask for a characterization of a real or fictional person you have been studying: a major historical figure, an inventor or scientist, a leader of some cause, the protagonist or antagonist in a novel, short story, or drama. In addition, fiction writers sometimes write sketches of their major characters for a planned short story or novel. The sketches help develop consistent characters.

CHARACTERISTICS

A character sketch usually includes the following kinds of information:

- a character who is in some way unusual,
- a single focus on the character,
- details about the character that help the reader understand the focus,
- character actions that help the reader understand the focus,
- character conversations which help the reader understand the focus,
- direct or indirect descriptions of the character.

PROCESS

The following planning and writing steps can help you complete a satisfactory character sketch.

STEP 1   **Prewriting • Selecting a Subject**

Sometimes the subject of a character sketch is assigned; other times the writer selects the subject. If you select the subject, begin by brainstorming and creating a list of names. [*See* Prewriting *in Part I for additional suggestions*.] You may head your list with phrases such as these:

> people at work
> people at my family reunion
> people who live on my block
> people on my athletic team

When you have a list of a dozen or so people, think about each person individually. Ask yourself questions such as these:

- What is his or her most unusual characteristic?
- How is this person's view of life different from that of most other people?
- How are this person's habits, demeanor, and other characteristics different from most others like him or her?
- What would someone who meets him or her for the first time be most likely to notice—or least likely to notice?

These questions and others like them will give you a basis for choosing a subject for your character sketch.

STEP 2   **Prewriting • Determining the Focus**

Now that you have selected a person about whom you can write, list all the possible characteristics you can think of that make this person interesting or unusual. You may have a list something like this:

> called "world's oldest hippie"
> considers self a medical healer
> invents "contraptions"
> built own house
> eats strange herbs and plants
> makes violins
> raises own food—garden, goats, bees
> usually looks dirty

From your list, select one idea on which to build a character sketch. Put that idea in a sentence:

> My neighbor, whom we call "the world's oldest hippie," considers himself a healer, using strange herbs and plants, all of which he raises himself.

In a single sentence, write the one idea on which you think you can build your character sketch.

STEP 3   **Prewriting • Showing Your Reader**

The most important part of writing an effective character sketch is showing, not telling, about your subject. Ask yourself at every sentence, "Am I telling, or am I showing?" If you write *Richard loved children*, then the reader must simply take your word for it. Instead, show that Richard loved children. Write something like this:

> Richard always met the neighborhood children at the bus stop. Even at 72, he was spry enough to bat balls, throw Frisbees, and play a short game of basketball. But when he met us at the bus, he always had some new trick to show us—a wooden top that would spin for minutes without toppling, a wooden doll-like creature that would climb a pair of ropes, a wooden man that turned flips. Always wooden. Carved and sanded and assembled in his cluttered little shop. He gave them away to whoever seemed to show the greatest fascination with the trick of the day.

Not once does the writer say that Richard loved the children, but readers know.

Select a situation in which you can best *show* your chosen character to readers.

STEP 4   **Prewriting • Choosing a Means of Characterizing**

You can show, rather than tell about a character by using one or a combination of means. Consider any or all of these options:

Description. To help the reader see and know the character, describe any significant features about him or her or the surroundings of the sketch. Indirect description can be more effective than direct description. And remember, even in the course of describing, to show rather than tell. [*See* Description *in Part II.*]

Weak

Telling: He was sloppy.

Better

Showing: He dragged his sleeve through the spaghetti sauce.

Action. Rather than tell readers about the character, show the character in action. By watching people's behavior, we can learn about them.

Weak

Telling: She was glad to see me.

Better

Showing: When she saw me, she ran, arms open, to give me that wonderful bear hug hello.

Dialogue. Let your character talk. Use the same kinds of words and sentence structure in the dialogue as the character really uses. You will, of course, enclose the dialogue or monologue in quotation marks. [*See* Dialogue *later in Part III.*]

Weak

Telling: Jeremy seemed nervous.

Better

Showing: "No. I'm okay. Don't bother." Jeremy's tight voice left me unconvinced. "It's just.... Well, no, I'm okay. Really." He studied his fingernails.

Often these three means—description, action, and conversation—are combined in a narrative style resembling an excerpt from a short story. [*See* Narration *in Part II. For fictional character sketches, see* Short Story *later in Part III.*]

STEP 5   Prewriting • Determining the Point of View

Next, decide from which point of view to present your character sketch. [*See* point of view *in the Glossary.*] A first-person point of view permits you to describe the character by being a part of the description. You become the "I." A third-person point of view allows you to stay outside the description. The reader sees the character more objectively.

Select the point of view which will best enable you to present the character to your reader.

STEP 6   **Writing • Putting It All Together**

Now, as you write, follow a clear organization. [*See* order, in paragraph development *in the Glossary*.] A character sketch can follow nearly any organization. Certainly one of the orders of importance could function well. Often a sketch will read almost like a piece of fiction, so time order may be appropriate. Because of its similarity to fiction, the sketch may also include flashbacks, especially if you want to develop the sketch stylistically. [*See* flashback *in the Glossary and other details about fiction in* Short Story *later in Part III*.]

Write the sketch now, including description, dialogue, and action, showing rather than telling.

STEP 7   **Revising • Checking for Content**

When you have completed your first draft, consider the following questions as you reread to spot possible weaknesses:

- Does my character become real to the reader?
- Have I made him or her sound special rather than stereotypical?
- Have I maintained a single focus rather than rambling about all kinds of interesting details? [*See* Revising: Sample Revision for Unity *in Part I*.]
- Do all details—descriptions, actions, dialogues—support the single focus?
- Are details logically organized?
- Does the reader hear and see the character?
- Does the dialogue reflect the character? [*See* Dialogue *later in Part III*.]
- Because actions speak louder than words, does the reader see the character in action?
- Are details subtle rather than blunt and bold? [*See* Revising: Sample Revision for Specific Detail *in Part I*.]
- Do I show rather than tell what the character is like?
- Do I maintain good emphasis, putting main ideas in main clauses? [*See* Revising: Sample Revision for Emphasis *in Part I*.]

Any questions to which you cannot answer an honest "yes" may suggest areas for revision.

STEP 8   Proofreading • Checking the Details

As you proofread, check punctuation, especially in conversations. [*See* Dialogue *later in Part III.*] Correct any grammar, mechanics, or usage problems you find. [*See* Part IV *for rules and examples.*] Check the Glossary for quick definitions, examples, and further cross-references. Finally, check spelling and vocabulary.

SAMPLE CHARACTER SKETCH

The following character sketch exhibits most of the characteristics listed in this section. As you read, watch for "showing" words and phrases.

> **Mr. Biddleman: He Is What He Eats**
>
> "Come into the kitchen with me. I'm eating just now." A hint of British accent added a musical quality to his old-man voice. "Let me get you some tea."
>
> A fine old bone-china plate sat on the painted wooden table piled high with books and junk mail. Whatever was on the plate—unrecognizable by local standards—smelled like a wild combination of garlic and sage.
>
> "Shove the books over; I've your tea here." He placed on the table a cup and saucer that matched the plate. On another saucer were two brownish cookies or thin cakes. "I must say it's so great to see you, my boy. What brings you around to my humble abode?" A glance around the room emphasized humble but not poor. Books tumbled over one another on every sitting place but one, the ladder-back rocker in the corner by the window.
>
> "Just visiting. What are you reading lately?"
>
> "Most recently I've been reading up a bit on the ancient herbal medicines. You know the Incas...."
>
> Listening to the details of his past day's reading helped put the room in perspective. The plants on the windowsill, the aroma from the oven, the cookie-cakes on the table, the food in his plate, the trays of dried leaves on the refrigerator, the strings of dried flowers and pods hanging from the ceiling light, the bags of dried grains in the corner, and the fresh vegetable cuttings in the sink wove their way into his recounting of his latest reading.
>
> "It's all in what you eat, you know. Eat up." The cookie-cake things seemed to grow uglier by the minute. He wiped his plate clean with some kind of dark brown bread, stuffed the hunk in his mouth, and wiped the dribble from his chin. "Eat up, my boy, eat up!"
>
> Only when the door slapped shut on squeaky hinges after his final goodbye did the overwhelming sensory bombardment drift away with the air. Ah, fresh air.

 Analysis of the Sample Character Sketch. The preceding character sketch achieves a description of a peculiar neighbor without telling the reader that he is peculiar. Note how:

- The writer shows the character's eccentricities by allowing readers to see a series of seemingly incongruous characteristics:
  - The man uses fine bone china but eats in clutter on an old painted table.
  - His speech and the abundance of books tumbling on every sitting place suggest an educated man with an eccentric lifestyle.
  - Readers see the kitchen, full of herbs living, drying, and dried, and make the connection with the old man's reading.
  - Although readers do not know for sure, they suspect the old man may have only recently become fascinated by the effect of certain herbs on one's physical and/or mental being.
  - The visitor, obviously unprepared for the experience, finds the situation a bit more than he can bear.
  - The writer shows that the visitor is eager to leave, shows that the old man's conversation causes the boy's mind to wander, and shows that the cookie-cakes are unappetizing. A good characterization, you will recall, shows; it does not tell.
- The methods of development obviously include all three mentioned in Step 4: description, action, and conversation:
  - The readers witness the descriptions, see the room, the clutter, the details. They see books, a ladder-back rocker, foods, china, painted table, refrigerator, sink, and so on. All these descriptions aid in characterizing the eccentric old man.
  - The readers see the old man in action, not just what he's doing during the visit but what he's been doing prior to the visit.
  - The readers hear his voice, his words, his accent.
- The writer chooses a third-person point of view. Notice, however, that readers see the old man from the boy's point of view.
- The mechanics of writing this particular characterization call for accurate use of quotation marks and accurate paragraphing to indicate change of speaker. Inaccuracies here will confuse the reader and cause the characterization to fail.

With the process, suggestions, sample, and analysis in this section, you should have a good idea now how to develop a successful character sketch of your own.

Classified Ad

A classified advertisement, commonly called a *classified ad*, appears in a newspaper or magazine for the purpose of selling goods or services or recruiting employees. Because the cost of these ads varies according to the number of words, the ad writer aims for brevity. Unlike other kinds of writing we have examined, the classified ad frequently does not include complete sentences, uses abbreviations, and follows an unusual organization.

CHARACTERISTICS

A classified advertisement usually includes

- a word or phrase concisely naming the goods or services offered for sale or sought,
- words or phrases to form a concise description of special features of the goods or services, especially those features that set this product or position apart from similar ones,
- the price of the goods or services,
- the phone number or address to which interested persons should make inquiries.

PROCESS

The following steps can help you plan and compose a classified advertisement:

STEP 1   **Prewriting • Selecting the Name**
In most cases, the name of the goods or services will be evident. For instance, if you are selling a used sofa, the name is obvious: *sofa*. If you are seeking someone to fill the position of night clerk, the name is obvious: *night clerk*. In some cases, however, the writer must determine a name.

For example, assume you are selling a set of plans to build a patio. The plans include a blueprint, step-by-step instructions, progressive diagrams, and a list of materials, tools, and equipment needed for the job. You need a concise name for the product. You may choose *complete patio plans*.

Write the concise name for your product or position.

STEP 2 **Prewriting • Choosing Descriptive Words**

In order to distinguish your product or position from others similar to it, you need something referred to as *sales features*. In the example in Step 1, the sales features include the blueprint, the step-by-step instructions, the diagrams, and the list of materials, tools, and equipment. These are the specific items that will help sell your product or position.

Write a list of descriptive words that will help sell your product.

STEP 3 **Prewriting • Adding Other Details**

Make a separate list of the additional necessary details. These include a phone number or address. You may choose to include a price. You may include other specifics such as, but not limited to, the following:

- Time of day phone number is in service (Example: *between 8 a.m. and 5 p.m.*)
- Response time needed (Example: *allow three weeks for delivery*)
- Method of selection (Example: *applications accepted*)

STEP 4 **Prewriting • Considering the Reader**

Most people read classified ads quickly, noting only the first few words. Thus, the words for the entire ad must be arranged in order of importance. Use this general method:

- First, give the product or position name.
- Next, give descriptive sales features.
- Finally, add details.

STEP 5 **Writing • Including the Essentials**

When you write the classified ad following the preceding steps, omit any words not absolutely necessary. The ad need not include complete sentences: phrases, even single words, are acceptable as sentences in a classified ad. Abbreviations are appropriate.

STEP 6 **Revising • Checking for Conciseness**

When you have finished the ad, use the following guidelines to revise it:

- Cross out any words not absolutely necessary. If the magazine or newspaper for which you are preparing the ad includes a base rate for up to a specific number of words, you may wish to limit your ad to that number.

- Omit articles and prepositions. [*See* articles *and* preposition *in the Glossary*.]
- Check to see that essential information is included.
- Make sure that you have begun with the most important words and followed them with the least important words and phrases.
- Check for possible abbreviations or shortened word forms. The following examples may help you:
  - Use *phone* instead of *telephone*.
  - Use *call* instead of *phone*.
  - Use *in person* instead of *personally*.
  - Use *SASE* instead of *self-addressed stamped envelope*.
  - Use *after 5:00* instead of *call after 5:00*.
  - Use *applications accepted* instead of *applications being accepted*.
  - Use *negotiable* instead of *price is negotiable*.

STEP 7   Proofreading • Checking for Accuracy

Be absolutely certain to check the following details for accuracy. An inaccurate ad wastes your money!

- Is the phone number, including the area code, accurate?
- Is the address, including zip code, accurate?
- Is the essential information included? Is it accurate?
- Is the punctuation accurate to separate words and phrases in place of sentences?
- Does the ad include sufficient information to eliminate needless calls or unnecessary correspondence?
- Is the ad as concise as it can be?

SAMPLE CLASSIFIED ADS

The following classified advertisements follow the characteristics suggested in this section. After you have studied the ads, compare your thoughts with the analyses below.

Part-time assistant, retail clothing. Hours flexible; some benefits. Apply in person. 240 Main.

Antique dining table, six chairs, cherry, needlepoint seats. $1,200, delivered in area. 763-1432.

Complete patio plans, instructions, diagrams, materials list. SASE, $4.50. PLANS, 410 E. Ridgewood, Oakfield, GA 56842.

Analysis of the Sample Classified Ads. The following analyses refer to the preceding sample classified ads. Compare the samples with your own:

- All three ads begin with the name of the goods, product, or position. In the first ad, the position named is *part-time assistant*. In the second ad, the goods named are *antique dining table, six chairs*. In the third ad, the product named is *complete patio plans*.
- The descriptive words follow. In Ad 1, the descriptive words include *retail clothing* and *hours flexible; some benefits*. In Ad 2, the descriptive words are *cherry* and *needlepoint seats*. Ad 3 includes a series of sales features: *instructions, diagrams, materials list*.
- The added information varies with the purpose of the ad. Consider these specifics:
  - In Ad 1, the only added information indicates the applicant should apply in person at the given address. No wages are listed, perhaps because the position offers minimum wage or because the wage is negotiable. No city is listed in the address because the ad appears in a local newspaper.
  - In Ad 2, the added information names the price, indicating that it includes delivery in the area and gives a phone number, thus suggesting that further information is available by phone. No area code is included.
  - Ad 3 includes several bits of added information. *SASE* is a common abbreviation meaning to *send a self-addressed stamped envelope*, in this case along with $4.50, to the listed address. The address is complete, including zip code.
- None of the ads includes a complete sentence.
- All of the ads use punctuation to separate words and phrases describing or giving added information:
  - Commas separate words of equal modification.
  - Semicolons separate larger thought units.
  - Periods separate sections.
- Abbreviations are included as appropriate.

These analyses should help you evaluate your own classified ad and, perhaps, help you save money when you place it in a newspaper or magazine.

Dialogue

Dialogue is conversation. Narratives, character sketches, autobiographical sketches, biographies, and short stories all depend on dialogue to stir the readers' imagination and promote their understanding of character. Drama exists entirely on the basis of dialogue. Politicians win or lose elections based on their spoken word. Teachers and pastors make their points via the spoken word. Marriages thrive or disintegrate with the spoken word. So writers use dialogue to make characters, either real or imaginary, live for the reader.

CHARACTERISTICS

Writing successful dialogue demands special attention to the techniques. In general, dialogue

- shows the speaker's exact words by enclosing them in quotation marks,
- includes spelling clues to indicate dialect or speech patterns,
- produces natural-sounding conversation, usually using short sentences and contractions,
- may include sentence fragments to illustrate a speaker's exact words or to enhance style [*see* fragment *in the Glossary*],
- uses phrases such as *he yelled* or *she snarled* to allow the reader to "hear" the words in the context of the situation,
- relies heavily on accurate punctuation, including commas, end marks, and apostrophes as well as quotation marks,
- shows a change in speaker by a change in paragraphing,
- includes description, not just of voice and expression but also of mannerisms and other nonverbal means of communication.

PROCESS

Use the following prewriting, writing, revising, and proofreading steps to produce successful dialogue.

STEP 1   **Prewriting • Listening to the Character**
If you are writing about a real person, you have a responsibility to quote accurately. If using a tape recorder is not possible, use the following guidelines. Make notes as you listen:

- What is the person's usual vocabulary? Does word choice suggest education or lack of it? Are certain words or phrases often repeated, such as *actually, generally speaking,* or *well, I declare*?
- Are the sentences short and choppy or moderately long? Does the person answer *Yep* instead of *Yes, I think so*?
- What tone of voice does the speaker use? Does he or she shout, whisper, rasp, hiss, or whine? How would you describe the voice?
- Does the character occasionally use poor grammar?
- Does the person drop word endings, saying *walkin'* for *walking* or *talk* for *talked*?
- Does pronunciation reflect a dialect, words such as *cain't* or *musta* for *can't* or *must have*?
- If the character is fictional, listen in your mind. Ask yourself the same questions, and then make the speech pattern consistent with the character. For instance, a well-educated character is not likely to use poor grammar, but an uneducated character may not use poor grammar either. He may have learned by listening. If you show evidence of the character having learned other things by listening, it may be out of character for him to use poor grammar.

STEP 2   Prewriting • Watching the Character

Dialogue also includes description of mannerisms and other nonverbal means of communication. As a result, as you listen, you must also watch. Make notes as you ask yourself questions such as these:

- How does the character stand or sit? Does he or she slouch, lean on a cane, prop chin in hands? How else can you describe the character's posture?
- What does the character do with his or her hands? Does he jab the air with a pipe-filled fist; does she unceasingly rub her thumbs together or twist her wedding band?
- How can you describe the person's eyes? Are they clear or cloudy, sparkling or dull? Do they pierce the listener or wander off into an undefined distance?
- What visual evidence is there of facial reaction to comments? A frown, a fading dimple, a grin, a cocked head, a dropped jaw?

- What visual evidence is there of other physical reaction to comments? A shifting of position, a crossed leg, folded arms, leaning forward?

If your character is fictional, think through these same questions. Maintain a description appropriate for—and consistent with—his or her personality.

STEP 3 **Writing • Recording the Conversation**

Regardless of the context in which the dialogue appears, the writing process is the same:

- Write the exact words of the speaker, including spellings that help the reader hear the pronunciation of the words.
- Use sentence fragments as appropriate or necessary to enhance characterization or maintain style.
- Unless you are writing a script, enclose the speaker's words in quotation marks. [*See* Scripts *elsewhere in Part III.*]
- If a speaker's words fall into two or more paragraphs, omit the close quotation marks at the end of all but the last paragraph. Open quotation marks, however, should appear at the beginning of every paragraph. Study the sample dialogue to see paragraph modeling.
- Add descriptions that help the reader hear the tone of voice or vocal inflections.
- Add descriptions that help the reader see the speaker's nonverbal reactions.
- Start a new paragraph each time a new character speaks. Because a new paragraph (followed by close quotation marks) indicates a change in speaker, you can eliminate many of the repetitious *he said* and *she said* tag lines. Study the sample dialogue to see paragraph modeling.

STEP 4 **Revising • Checking the Content**

Read the dialogue aloud, perhaps with a friend or friends who will read other characters' parts. Listen carefully to the dialogue, asking yourself these questions:

- Does the conversation sound natural? Have I avoided a stilted, awkward, uncharacteristic speech pattern?
- Does the conversation fit the character? Are his words and sentences appropriate for his age, sex, education, environment, occupation, and emotional attitude?
- Will the reader be bored with too much irrelevant conversation, or is every part essential to furthering the plot or the characterization?

- Is the dialogue snappy, to the point, avoiding lengthy speeches or lengthy sentences?

Revise to improve the natural conversation flow and achieve your purpose.

STEP 5   **Proofreading • Checking the Techniques**

Certain techniques peculiar to writing dialogue require attention beyond the usual checks for grammar, mechanics, and usage:

- Check paragraphing. You may include description relating to the character or the situation in the same paragraph, but you must begin a new paragraph when another character begins speaking. [*See* Scripts *later in Part III for writing description relating to characters or situations in plays, television, or radio scripts.*]
- Check quotation marks. Have you enclosed the speaker's words, but not his thoughts, in quotation marks? If the speaker's words run more than one paragraph, have you started each new paragraph with quotation marks but ended only the last paragraph with them?
- Are commas, question marks, and exclamation marks used in correct relationship with the quotation marks? Study the following two rules and their respective examples:
  - Always put commas inside quotation marks.

    Example: "Never open an e-mail attachment unless you're certain of its contents," my brother warned.
    (The comma belongs inside the quotation marks.)

  - Put question marks and exclamation marks inside quotation marks if the quotation is a question or exclamation. Put question marks and exclamation marks outside quotation marks if the complete sentence is a question or exclamation.

    Examples: "Why are you standing in the rain?" Marty asked.
    (The quoted words form a question; thus the question mark goes inside the quotation marks.)
    Did Kirsten say, "I love standing in the rain"?
    (The quoted words do not form a question; rather, the complete sentence is a question. Thus, the question mark goes outside the quotation marks.)

- Are apostrophes used to show omission of letters or dropped endings?
- Are spellings appropriate for the dialogue, words in some cases spelled to indicate pronunciation?

- Do capital letters begin not only your sentences but also the sentences of the speakers?
- Are any grammar or usage errors within the dialogue intentional, designed to characterize the speaker?
- Are narrative and descriptive sections free from grammar or usage errors?

If you use the process indicated in these steps and proofread carefully, you should be able to develop a satisfactory dialogue.

SAMPLE DIALOGUE

The following sample dialogue is appropriate for fiction or for character sketches, autobiographical sketches, narratives, or biographies.

Watching

Clarence leaned into the oars, looking at but not seeing the pink polish on Irene's bare toes. The wind tore at the boat's direction, aiming it to the east of the inlet.

"Don't you think we'll be gettin' there afore long?" An edge of fear slipped into her words, belying her masked smile.

"Aye, we'll be there soon." A long silence bore down between them, lengthened by the distant rumble, the screech of oarlocks, and the seemingly interminable rhythm of dip-splash, dip-splash, dip-splash. "Yep, we'll be there soon."

She studied his face, his eyes averted, and wondered if he was lying. The western sky roiled. He watched her pink-painted toes grip her sandals. No use looking up. He knew too well the creases between her eyebrows and the worry lines on her forehead, even the weak smile that usually accompanied her worry lines.

"We have some water left," she said, "in the thermos here. Don't you want a drink? You're working so hard." He knew she was trying to be helpful, supportive, in spite of her fears. But he couldn't dare stop rowing, the wind as it was.

"Not just yet. But have some yourself," he added.

She loosened the top, tipped up the thermos, took two swallows and wiped the dribble from her chin. She wasn't thirsty, and the water had no taste. "It's still cold. Sure you don't want some?" He shook his head; she closed the thermos.

The sky, like some smothering blanket, hung above them, threatening. She looked over her shoulder, allowing the bluster to wrap her hair across her face. "We're almost there!"

He heard the relief in her voice. "Yep, we'll make it now." She heard the "now" and knew.

Analysis of the Sample Dialogue. The preceding dialogue, while it relates only a minor incident, includes examples that illustrate what dialogue can do:

- The actual words in the conversation are minimal.
- The dropped endings and word choices help the reader "hear" the conversation, the voices, the inflections, and the dialect.
- Sentence fragments aid in developing a natural-sounding conversation.
- Facial expressions, nonverbal mannerisms, and characters' thoughts tell more than the words. The reader can infer all kinds of details: The couple know each other well; he knows what her face looks like without looking; he sees her toes give away her fears; each recognizes the underlying unspoken messages behind the other's words; she suspects when he's lying; she recognizes the *now* as an affirmation of his effort to comfort her earlier.
- The paragraphing allows the reader to follow the speakers without *he said* or *she said* after every set of quotation marks.
- Description and narration, developed in the paragraph structures, show the meanings behind the words—the fears, suggestions, and mindless comments.
- Good description, that which shows rather than tells [*see* Description *in Part II*], helps the reader see, hear, feel, and taste the details.
- Accurate punctuation and capitalization help the reader follow the dialogue.

Using the process, sample, and analysis in this section, develop dialogue that follows these suggestions. You should have a satisfactory product.

Directions

You may be asked to write directions that explain how to do something or how to reach a destination. [*In either case, see* Process Analysis *in Part II*.]

Editorial

An editorial expresses an opinion. As part of the editorial page of a newspaper or magazine, the editorial differs significantly from news or feature articles. [*See* Feature Article *and* News Article *later in Part III*.] Concise and direct, an editorial takes a position on a controversial issue, offers evidence and reasons to support the position, anticipates counter arguments, and frequently calls for specific action.

Editorials usually receive a more prominent placement in the newspaper or magazine than do the opinions expressed by the general public in letters to the editor. [*See* Letters: Editorial Letters *later in Part III*.] In fact, editorials frequently sway voters to decide issues, force public officials to change positions, cause injustices to be righted, and influence labor and management to settle differences. Sometimes, of course, editorials take unpopular positions and raise the ire of readers; but fortunately, the right of freedom of the press permits reader response. [*Because the editorial expresses an opinion and often seeks to persuade, see* Opinion *and* Persuasion *in Part II*.]

E-Mail

Electronic mail (or *e-mail*) can transmit any kind of writing, personal or professional, and is sent electronically over the Internet. *You've got mail* is a familiar message to millions of writers. The mail may be a simple *hello* to a friend, or it can hold one or more attachments transmitting large amounts of data.

Because e-mail is transmitted over the Internet, it is public. You may think you are sending a personal note to your best friend, but you should know that problems can erupt. Sure, the server can be down or the download time slow, but even at warp speed, e-mail still has its good and bad features.

CHARACTERISTICS

The good characteristics are that e-mail messages

- can be received almost instantaneously; thus, personal and business matters move almost as quickly as they would via a phone conversation.

- are dated and timed; thus, e-mail can corroborate timely responses and document business details.
- move 24 hours a day; thus, your message can be sent or received at an hour when you wouldn't dare phone.
- can be accessed at the recipient's convenience; thus, you don't have to worry about getting only someone's answering machine or voice mail or calling at an inopportune time.

The bad characteristics are that e-mail messages

- can be forwarded to anyone anywhere, either accidentally or intentionally; thus, a sensitive personal or business message can end up in the wrong hands.
- can be intercepted and read by those who know how; so, especially if you are using a school or company e-mail service, know that your messages can—and probably will—be monitored.
- offer no proof that the message was sent unless you or the recipient prints a copy; thus, to use e-mail for important business transactions can cause problems later unless you keep a print file of all transmissions.
- provide no proof that the intended recipient actually received the transmission; thus, the lame excuse that *the check's in the mail* now becomes *it never came through.*
- may not be able to be formatted to show italics or boldface; thus, if necessary surround the word(s) with underscores or asterisks. For example, *Check the _Writer's Encyclopedia_ for that information.* Or *Use the word *unique* correctly.*

PROCESS

The following steps, combined with those found elsewhere in this text, can help you send good e-mail messages.

STEP 1   **Prewriting • Getting Ready**

Have the recipient's e-mail address handy. If you've not used it previously, you may want to test it to make sure it's accurate. There's nothing more frustrating than working diligently on a message, resting assured that the message is in the recipient's hands, only to find it returned the next morning as *Unable to Deliver.* If you don't know the e-mail address for the intended recipient, call or check an Internet locator search database.

STEP 2   **Prewriting • Planning an Attachment**

If you have already completed a large document that you plan to attach to your e-mail, make sure beforehand that the recipient can retrieve it. If not, and if your attachment isn't too long, you may want to copy and paste the document into the e-mail message.

STEP 3   **Prewriting • Planning the Content**

Creating an effective e-mail message requires the same process and skill as writing that same message for delivery by any other means. See the sections in Parts II and III most appropriate for the e-mail you intend to send. Follow the writing process outlined there.

STEP 4   **Writing and Revising • Writing the Draft**

As you follow the process suggested in Step 3, compose your first draft off-line. Edit and polish off-line. When you are satisfied with the final draft, use the *Edit* command to copy the text, and then close your word-processing program.

STEP 5   **Writing and Revising • Maintaining Netiquette**

Netiquette is a newly coined word that refers to *network etiquette*. Just as you follow good etiquette when writing a business letter, you follow good etiquette on the Internet when you send or respond to e-mail.

- Don't flame. A *flame* is a personal attack. Because e-mail can be made public, you'll probably regret any such personal attacks.
- Don't spam. *Spam* on e-mail is the same as junk mail in your mailbox. If you send the same message to hundreds of people, you are spamming, and most recipients will not take kindly to your message.
- Don't shout. To use all capital letters LIKE THIS is considered shouting on e-mail. Don't be rude.
- Don't send unnecessary messages. People don't like to waste their time reading messages that don't pertain to them.
- Unless you're in first grade, omit the smileys, those cute little faces that read left to right, like this: :-).

STEP 6   **Writing and Revising • Entering the Preliminaries**

When you have opened your e-mail program, enter the recipient's address. Every e-mail message automatically includes your name, date, and time of message; however, you must enter a subject line, a brief description of your purpose. If your message is a reply to an earlier e-mail, then change the subject line to reflect your response.

If you are e-mailing a business letter, the e-mail message lines labeled *Return-Path, From, To, Subject,* and *Date* serve as the heading and inside address. Thus, you can begin with "Dear ____" followed by the appropriate punctuation.

STEP 7   **Writing and Revising • Pasting the Message**
With the preliminaries completed, use the *Edit* command to paste your final draft into the message box.

STEP 8   **Proofreading • Checking One Final Time**
Before you hit *Send,* proofread once more to eliminate any grammar, usage, or mechanics errors. Make sure the e-mail address is accurate, and then send your message.

Refer to samples throughout Parts II and III for guidelines in preparing the message you plan to e-mail.

Essay

The term *essay* refers to any short piece of writing that analyzes or interprets something in a personal way. Many class assignments call for essay writing.

Because so much of what you write is likely to be in essay form, this book discusses nearly a dozen kinds of essays. See the specific section that most accurately describes the kind of essay you must write. Clue words from the assignment can help you select the most helpful reference section. For instance, if your essay must *show relationships,* your essay should classify or possibly compare or contrast. If your essay must *describe,* you should use description. If you must *convince readers to follow a course of action,* you should use persuasion. If you must *explain why you feel as you do,* you should use opinion.

Depending on your assignment, you can develop your essay using one of the following methods, which are detailed and modeled in Part II:

Analogy	Description
Cause and Effect	Narration
Classification	Opinion
Comparison and Contrast	Persuasion
Definition	Process Analysis

The following types of essays are described in Part III:

Essay-Question Responses
Literary Analyses
Research Paper
Review

[*If you need more general help with developing a basic paragraph or theme, see* Writing a Paragraph *and* Writing a Multi-Paragraph Paper, *both in Part I, for a thorough explanation of structure and sample papers for comparison.*]

Essay-Question Responses

Students must frequently prepare essay responses. A science test may require students to *explain the process of photosynthesis.* A scholarship or college admission application may ask applicants to *explain how a book you have read recently affected your attitude toward man's relationship to the environment.* Contest sponsors will award *a $1,000 prize to the contestant preparing the best 100-word answer to the question, "What makes you most proud to be an American?"*

Being able to write good essay responses, then, can be—quite literally—a valuable asset.

CHARACTERISTICS

Any essay response includes some basic characteristics. Keep in mind, however, that various kinds of responses (as discussed in this section) require different emphases. In general, an essay response

- is directed toward a specific audience,
- maintains a tight focus on the question or topic,
- relies on transitional devices to clarify the focus,
- uses formal but not unnatural structure, vocabulary, and style,
- shows command of the subject matter,
- follows a clear plan of organization,
- includes specific examples to support the topic or thesis statement,
- shows, rather than tells.

This section examines four kinds of essay-question responses. The preceding characteristics apply to all four kinds of responses, but you can also find additional characteristics peculiar to the specific responses.

COLLEGE-ADMISSIONS APPLICATION ESSAYS

Purpose. While test scores, letters of recommendation, grades, and lists of activities [*see* Short Answers: Lists *later in Part III*] all influence college-admissions personnel, virtually every college or university requires as part of its admissions application at least one essay. Some require several. In every case, the admissions personnel look for two qualities: content and evidence of writing ability.

The admissions staff want to see how you handle challenging topics, how—or if—you can think, and how well you can use the language.

Note two implications of what you've just read:

- You should remember the audience. You are writing for the admissions people. They read thousands of essays, many dull and poorly written. Make yours lively, personal, and polished, and you will attract their attention.
- You should write honestly. The student who writes to sound impressive, using five-syllable words and circuitous sentences, attracts attention, but it's the wrong kind.

Do not write:
It is uppermost in my mind to walk the hallowed halls of Some University and share great thoughts with the world's greatest minds.

Instead, say what you really mean:
I have been interested in Some University since the day I read about Dr. Important and learned that he and his student-research teams have contributed to the world's understanding of black holes.

In short, the college-admissions essay response should

- keep in mind its readers, and
- talk to them honestly and specifically.

Types of College-Admissions Application Essays. The types of college-admissions application essays vary, but most fall into these general categories:

- Essays about yourself, your interests, or your activities
- Essays explaining why you want to attend that college or university
- Essays responding to a thought-provoking statement, a book, or a contemporary problem

Essays about yourself, your interests, or your activities seek a better understanding of you as an individual. The essay topics may have wording similar to the following:

- What are your career preferences?
- Tell us anything about yourself, your activities, your interests, or your goals that will help us know you as a person.
- If you were to describe yourself in terms of a fictional character, who would it be? Explain your answer.

Sometimes the topic is broad enough to allow the student to choose his own avenue of response:

> In reading and evaluating your application, we hope to gain as complete a picture of you as possible, but our knowledge of you is necessarily limited to the information provided us. Why not, then, use this opportunity to tell us about anything you think we should know. . . (Brown University).

Whether the required response permits broad interpretation (as in the topic immediately preceding) or merits a more specific approach (as in choosing a fictional character to explain yourself), the essay demands specific details. Only through showing, not telling, can the admissions people learn about you. Obviously the toughest part is deciding which details to include. The approach is much like that for the autobiographical sketch [*see* Autobiography *earlier in Part III*]. Use the same process and the same means of limiting your subject.

For instance, because you should write about some aspect of your life that shows readers who you are, you may choose to focus on how your work backstage gave you an appreciation for the importance of behind-the-scenes work in any job. Perhaps as a result of four years of baby-sitting with the same three children, you have learned how familiarity affects discipline. Or perhaps your experiences when your best friend moved away helped you realize that real friendships must be cultivated; they don't just happen.

No matter your subject, your responsibility is to show who you are and give insight to your personality, interests, or aspirations. Choose details that permit you to do so. Above all, remember that readers are looking for evidence of your ability to think and write.

Essays explaining why you want to attend a particular university, beyond seeking evidence of your ability to write and show an effective command of the language, probe your understanding of the school to which you are applying. The questions are usually direct:

- Why do you think our school is appropriate for you?
- How did you become interested in our school?

- Why do you think our school can best meet your career preferences?
- Why do you believe our school can best fulfill your academic interests?

Obviously, your answers must be specific and reflect an accurate understanding of what the school is all about. For instance, does the school offer a degree in your area of interest? Are there reasons beyond academics that attract you to the school? What does this school offer that other schools do not?

In order to respond effectively to these kinds of essay questions, you should

- Study the catalogs, brochures, courses of studies, and any other printed information available regarding the school, its curriculum, and its activities.
- Talk to students currently enrolled and ask about the courses, instructors, and school in general. Ask about extracurricular activities, campus life, and areas of special interest to you. Recent alumni may also provide good insight.
- Visit the campus, if possible, before you develop your essay or report for an interview. References to your visit will help you include specific details.

With your homework behind you, you can get on with the essay.

Avoid general kinds of responses:
Blank University will provide the best education for me because it has fine courses in the area in which I hope to major.

Instead, aim for details, for showing, not telling:
Blank University attracted my attention as soon as I saw the cyclotron and talked with two of the professors doing independent research with it.

[*See also* Short Answers: Brief Responses *later in Part III for a sample short answer to a similar question.*]

Essays responding to a thought-provoking statement, a book, or a contemporary problem look for personal reaction to thought-provoking topics and probably allow you to tell more about yourself—albeit indirectly—than the topics that ask for specific responses. The questions may read something like these:

Compose a letter to your U.S. Congressional Representative in which you express your opinion on a public policy issue of current importance. In your letter you should include a brief factual description of the issue, your views on the issue, and the reasons why you believe as you do. Remember that

the influence your letter will carry depends on the clarity of your views and
the soundness of your argument. (Earlham College)
What book or author has particularly impressed you? Please explain the
significance of your choice. We encourage you to incorporate plot elements
only as necessary to support your thesis. (DePauw University)
Imagine the year is 1881. You may expect to live for another thirty-five
years. What person would you most want to know well during that time? For
what reasons? (Swarthmore College)

Topics such as these require essay responses similar to those
already developed. The first example, for instance, asking for a persuasive letter, should use the method of development detailed in the
Persuasion section in Part II. The second example is a type of literary
analysis and should follow the format and process set out in the Literary Analyses section later in Part III. The third example, a what-if
fictional situation, should focus on reasons, and so the essay may be
an opinion or cause and effect and follow the method of development
detailed in Opinion and Cause and Effect in Part II.

No matter the topic or your approach to it, keep in mind that the
purpose of any written response on an application form is twofold:

- To help the admissions people get to know you as a person
- To help them better understand your academic abilities,
  especially your writing ability

PROCESS

No matter which kind of essay you write, you should follow the same
general process of prewriting, writing, revising, and proofreading.
The following guidelines should be helpful.

STEP 1 **Prewriting • Thinking About the Topic**
As you narrow your focus, make lists and ask yourself questions. The
following questions help you think of suitable topics and suggest
other appropriate questions:

- What activities have I participated in during the last four
  years? Which activities have brought me the greatest
  satisfaction? Why? Have I grown as a result of those activities?
  How?
- In what community projects have I participated? How have
  they affected me or my interest in civic pride and
  responsibility? Did I learn to understand or appreciate

government or social conditions? Did I have my eyes opened to some alarming or exciting facility or situation?

- Which academic classes maintained my interest? Why? How has that affected my aspirations? What additional research have I done beyond the confines of the classroom to further my interest or explore the possibilities of the class subject?
- What goal was the most difficult for me to attain? How did I overcome that difficulty? Did I gain some insight about myself or my surroundings as a result?
- Who has most influenced my life? A real person or a fictional one? How has he or she influenced me and how have I changed as a result? Is the change good?
- Where have I traveled? What did I see or do there that most impressed me? Why was I impressed? Did the experience affect my attitude toward someone or something?
- What happens at home that most affects me? How? Does that help me grow, help me become more self-disciplined?
- What have I read that has affected the way I think or what I do? What effect has it had? What part of the reading caused me to react as I did?

Once you have these lists and responses in front of you, you are well on your way toward developing a specific focus for your essay.

STEP 2　　Prewriting • Developing a Focus

After you have considered options such as those in Step 1—as well as any others you may think of—talk with friends, teachers, counselors, or alumni about possible responses. Sometimes their reactions to possible topics help you gain objectivity in your planned response.

With their suggestions in mind, select the specific approach you will use. Write in a single sentence what you want your essay response to accomplish. Consider these examples:

Do not say:
My response will explain why I want to attend Blank University.

Write instead:
Blank University includes three world-renowned musicians among its faculty, and they can help me pursue my goal as a master of wind instruments.

Do not say:
I read a book recently that has influenced my ideas about midlife career changes.

Write instead:
The biography of John James Audubon helped me understand that midlife career changes, while sometimes financially painful, often bring deep personal satisfaction.

The sentence you write will serve as a thesis sentence for your essay response.

STEP 3   **Prewriting • Choosing Details**
With your thesis sentence in front of you, list the specific details that help you explain your idea. Remember that details help your essay stand out among the thousands that the admissions people read.

STEP 4   **Writing • Getting the Ideas on Paper**
As you write the first draft, forget about spelling and mechanics. Get the ideas down in support of the thesis sentence. Do not be afraid to include ideas that seem not to fit. Maybe they belong somewhere else in the essay, or maybe they do not belong in it at all; but you can always take them out or move them during the revision process. For now, get them on paper so that you do not lose them.

STEP 5   **Revising • Adding and Deleting Ideas**
Next, get away from the job for at least a day. Then reread the topic and your response to it. Ask yourself these questions:

- Do I respond specifically to the topic?
- Do my details support specific parts of the topic? [*See* Revising: Sample Revision for Specific Detail *in Part I.*]
- Have I maintained unity? [*See* Revising: Sample Revision for Unity *in Part I.*]
- Is there an obvious order to my essay, or do I wander aimlessly as thoughts occur? [*See* order, in paragraph development *in the Glossary.*]
- Is the essay consistently lively, clear, and descriptive?
- Have I avoided the deadly trap of trying to sound sophisticated by using five-syllable words and circuitous sentences? [*See* Revising: Sample Revision for Wordiness *in Part I.*]
- Does the essay reflect my personality and my interests? Is it personal?
- Does it show thought? Have I avoided vague and empty sentences?

These questions give a basis on which to make revisions. Ask the same questions after your revision. If you can, ask a peer to read your essay and respond to the same questions.

STEP 6   Revising • Polishing the Writing

Finally, you are ready to polish the essay. [*See* Revising *in Part I for questions to guide your general revision*.] Use the following questions to guide revisions particularly important to the college-admissions application essay:

- Do I use transitions effectively to show relationships between and among ideas? [*See* Revising: Sample Revision for Transition *in Part I*.]
- Have I varied both the length and structure of my sentences? Do I show sophisticated writing techniques? [*See* Revising: Sample Revision for Sentence Variety *in Part I*.]
- Does my sentence structure show effective emphasis? [*See* Revising: Sample Revision for Emphasis *in Part I*.]
- Is my vocabulary appropriate for the subject and the audience?
- Have I chosen the most powerful or most effective words?

STEP 7   Proofreading • Checking the Details

The necessity of proofreading should be obvious. Your accuracy with spelling, mechanics, grammar, and usage will reflect your command of the language.

Depending on the college or university, your final copy may be submitted electronically or in print. Follow their guidelines.

SAMPLE COLLEGE-ADMISSIONS APPLICATION ESSAY

This sample essay is a response to the following college-admissions application topic: Discuss some issue of local or national concern and its importance to you.

Last year our community destroyed part of its own heritage when the wrecking ball brought down the ornate Gothic structure that was once the railroad station. Such was the media's wording: The wrecking ball brought it down. In fact, we, the citizens of this community, brought it down. Mincing words to avoid blame falls short of accepting reality. Although city officials purportedly made an attempt to locate potential developers, many of us questioned their seriousness. Deadlines, extended twice, came and went with "not even a nibble" of interest. So now the old railroad station is gone. Its demolition testifies that historic preservation, only a fancy word for some local individuals with stately old homes, lacks meaning for the general citizenry. How sad. For instance, many contemporaries living in the fast lane lack the roots that give stability and sense of direction from the perspective of where they have been. In contrast, the picture in our family album shows Mother, aged twelve, standing in the crowd waiting at the railroad station for debarking passengers, steam puffing from beneath passenger-train cars. Grandma and Grandpa stand together, their suitcases pried against a post, waiting for Uncle Frederick's approaching surrey. That is "heritage." That is where I came from, my family, a picture that tells me more than names and places. Their lifestyle spills out for me. But the station is gone. My children will never see what they should not have been denied. They will not walk through waiting rooms or hallways where their great-grandparents walked; they will not share the heritage. The sabotage hangs as a sin on this community's shoulders.

Analysis of the Sample. The preceding essay response achieves what is discussed in the explanation and process analysis in this section. Note these specifics:

- The response to the topic takes a local approach and adds personal interest. The destruction of a railroad station has obviously affected the writer; so as a result, the essay gives her an opportunity to respond specifically to an issue that matters.
- Specific details abound. Readers see the structure of the station (*Gothic*), learn about the family (*through the details in the photograph*), and recognize the writer's reaction (*should not be denied, sin on community's shoulders*).
- The response allows a glimpse of the writer's personality. (Do you not have an idea now what the writer's interests are?)
- The writer uses a good variety of sentence structures and an effective vocabulary to demonstrate command of the language.

College-admissions people who read these kinds of essays take note of the writers!

CONTEST ESSAYS

Purpose. Contests have sponsors. Sponsors have inherent interests. To win a contest, you must, within the framework of the contest rules, say what the sponsors want to hear, something in line with their interests. Such contest sponsors look for people with philosophies similar to their own.

Usually the topic blatantly suggests the sponsor's purpose or interest:

In an essay of no more than one typewritten page, explain why you are proud to be an American (contest sponsored by the Veterans of Foreign Wars). Define good citizenship in 100 words or less (contest sponsored by the Daughters of the American Revolution).

Develop an essay that explains how our community can best attract visitors (contest sponsored by the Chamber of Commerce).
In 100 words or less, share with our readers your most memorable holiday experience (contest sponsored by the local newspaper).

If you plan to develop a contest essay, keep in mind the following suggestions:

- Stick to the topic.
- Be precise and concise.
- Cling to specifics, especially the dramatic or touching.
- Read the contest rules carefully. You'll usually find them detailed (sometimes in fine print) with the application or submission form.
- Be certain to follow all rules exactly. If a word count is included, abide by it. You will be disqualified if you neglect the rules. (When counting words, you need not count the articles *a*, *an*, and *the*. Some contests, however, expect you to count every five spaces as a word.)
- Look for a unique approach. Something different will attract the attention of judges exhausted from reading hundreds of ho-hum entries.

PROCESS

As you plan a contest-essay response, use whatever process is appropriate for the kind of essay required. For instance, if you must define good citizenship, check the method for developing Definition in Part II. If you must develop an essay expressing an opinion, follow the method of development illustrated in the section in Part II labeled Opinion. You may also need to use other methods of development, such as Description, Persuasion, Classification, or Analogy, all found in Part II. To the processes outlined in these respective chapters, add the suggestions of this section for contest essays. The result should yield an effective—perhaps winning—essay response!

SAMPLE CONTEST ESSAY

A local newspaper contest asked readers to explain in 100 words or less a memorable family experience. Because the contest announcement appeared in early summer, the topic implied family vacation or at least family summer activities. One reader prepared the following essay:

Family Reunion

Memorable family reunions signify family-favorite dishes at the carry-in dinner. Uncle Ned roasts a whole pig in his homemade cooker, and Grandma brings hot German potato salad, a recipe in which the first ingredient is twenty pounds of potatoes. Aunt Millie's corn salad earns the only rave reviews among the dozens of relishes and vegetable salads. Everyone, though, saves room for a wedge of Aunt Georgia's black-walnut angel-food cake, her own closely guarded recipe. That and a dollop of Uncle Pat's hand-churned ice cream add the final touches to a feast. I can taste it all now, even though it's been six years since both Grandma and Uncle Ned died.

Analysis of the Sample. The less than 100-word essay seems appropriate for the contest on these points:

- It focuses on the contest topic but includes a bit of drama to heighten reader attention.
- By using present tense throughout, the writer maintains a feeling of *now* even though readers learn in the final sentence that the memories are six years old.
- Details offer good images [*see* Description *in Part II*].
- The essay follows the few rules required for the contest. (For the word count, hyphenated words and proper names were counted as single words and articles were not counted.)

SCHOLARSHIP APPLICATION ESSAYS

Purpose. While much of a scholarship application is devoted to grades, test scores, and letters of recommendation, and while part of the application requires mere lists or brief statements [*see* Short Answers *later in Part III*], another part of many scholarship applications requires you to develop an essay response to some general topic. Topics range from the very broad (*Why is a good education important?*) to the highly personal (*What peculiar family problems suggest need for financial assistance?*).

Scholarship applications, like college-admissions applications, establish your identity, setting you apart from the hundreds or thousands of other applicants. As a result, your essay response should accomplish two purposes:

- Allow your reader to know you personally, to see you as an individual among the hundreds or thousands of other applicants.
- Prove that you are mentally alert, fluent, and personable.

Both goals can be met by a well-written, carefully developed essay response.

PROCESS

In the case of a specific, personal question, your job is clearly defined. Answer to the point, with specific details, statistics, and examples. Be straightforward, honest, and candid. And be concise but complete. Follow the same process as for any paragraph or theme. [*Refer to appropriate sections in Part II of this handbook*: Description, Definition, Cause and Effect, Process Analysis, *and so on*.]

In the case of a broad topic use the same process as outlined for the College-Admissions Applications Essay responses earlier in this Part. Follow the same warnings, avoiding chronological listings or dryly recounting facts in dull thoughtless prose. Use specifics; be personable; keep it lively.

SAMPLE SCHOLARSHIP APPLICATION ESSAY AND ANALYSIS

Because the scholarship essay is very much like that of the College-Admissions Application Essay, see the sample and analysis in that section. [*For more about scholarship application answers, see* Short Answers *later in Part III*.]

ESSAY TEST QUESTIONS

Purpose. Requiring students to respond with essays allows an instructor to find out how well they really understand a subject. Students can write easily about what they understand. In test situations, however, you must plan carefully what you will say. Time limits demand that you structure your response to present your understanding in the best possible manner.

Types of Essay Test Questions. Certain clue words identify the kind of response your teacher is seeking. The following list indicates appropriate responses.

- **ANALYZE** Show parts in relation to a whole. [*See* Cause and Effect, Process Analysis, Comparison and Contrast, *and* Description *in Part II, and* Literary Analyses *later in Part III*.]

  Example: Analyze the relationship between state and local governments.
  Other clue words: show the process, explain the means by which, describe the effects, clarify the causes, criticize

- **COMPARE**   Show the similarities of two or more things. [*See* Comparison and Contrast *in Part II*.]

  Example: Compare two of Shakespeare's sonnets in terms of their references to the Dark Lady.
  Other clue words: similarities, resemblances, likenesses, comparison, alike

- **CONTRAST**   Show the differences between two or more things. [*See* Comparison and Contrast *in Part II*.]

  Example: Contrast direct current with alternating current.
  Other clue words: differences, contrasting, differ, different

- **CRITICIZE**   Discuss the strengths or merits of a given topic. [*See* Literary Analyses *later in Part III*.]

  Example: Write a critical analysis of the structure of the following sonnet.
  Other clue words: point out the strengths and weaknesses, critical analysis, evaluate, analyze

- **DEFINE**   Clarify the meaning of a given topic. [*See* Definition *in Part II*.]

  Example: Define metamorphosis as it applies to the German cockroach.
  Other clue words: definition, explain the meaning, clarify

- **DESCRIBE**   Give details. [*See* Description *and* Process Analysis *in Part II*.]

  Example: Describe the process of developing black-and-white film.
  Other clue words: explain, show, description

- **DISCUSS**   Elaborate upon the specific details involved in a general idea. [*See* Description, Process Analysis, Opinion, Comparison and Contrast, *and* Cause and Effect *in Part II*.]

  Example: Discuss the impact of tax reform on limited partnerships.
  Other clue words: explain, discussion, talk about

- **DEMONSTRATE**   Show an aspect of something by giving details. [*See* Process Analysis *or* Description *in Part II*.]

  Example: Demonstrate the importance of safety devices in a metal-working shop.
  Other clue words: show, illustrate, explain, describe

- **EXPLAIN**   Give reasons for a thing being as it is. [*See* Description, Persuasion, *and* Opinion *in Part II.*]

  Example: Explain how a bill becomes law.
  Other clue words: show, why, what, how

- **ILLUSTRATE**   Explain a main idea through use of specific examples. [*See* Comparison and Contrast, Description, Process Analysis, Opinion, and Cause and Effect *in Part II, and* Literary Analyses *later in Part III.*]

  Example: Define *deus ex machina* and illustrate from at least six plays.
  Other clue words: show, give illustrations, give examples, how

- **INTERPRET**   Indicate the meaning or significance of a given topic. [*See* Literary Analyses *later in Part III and* Description, Cause and Effect, Comparison and Contrast, *and* Process Analysis *in Part II.*]

  Example: Interpret Hamlet's soliloquy that begins, "To be or not to be . . . ."
  Other clue words: analyze, interpretation, significance, meaning of, show influence of, analyze

- **PREDICT**   Indicate a logical outcome of an action or condition. [*See* Cause and Effect *and* Opinion *in Part II.*]

  Example: Predict the results of pH variables on soil in terms of vegetation growth potential.
  Other clue words: anticipate, prediction, if . . . then, what . . . if

- **SUMMARIZE**   State concisely the main points of a topic. [*See* Precis, Paraphrase, *and* Synopsis, *all later in Part III.*]

  Example: Summarize the issues involved in the Populist Movement.
  Other clue words: state briefly, brief review, give the main points, discuss the main ideas

- **TRACE**   Follow a series of events in chronological order. [*See* Cause and Effect, Description, Narration, *and* Process Analysis *in Part II*, and Literary Analyses *later in Part III.*]

  Example: Trace the development of adding machines.
  Other clue words: follow, follow the development, outline

These essay-question clues will help you know what your instructor expects in your answer. Use the clue words to shape your essay's content.

PROCESS

Answering questions on an essay test requires more, however, than knowing what the teacher or instructor expects in your answer. Planning takes the driver's seat. Here's how:

STEP 1   **Prewriting • Planning Your Time**

When you get your test copy, first look through the test. Look for answers to these questions:

- What kinds of questions are there?
- How many questions are there?
- Do the directions say that I must answer all questions, or do I answer only some of them?
- How much time do I have for the entire test?

When you have answers to these questions, plan a schedule for yourself. If the test includes one section of 25 multiple-choice questions and another of two essay questions, you must allot sufficient time for each of the essay questions. Perhaps you have an hour in which to take the test. You may plan a schedule such as this:

20 minutes   25 multiple-choice questions
40 minutes   2 essay questions

This kind of schedule allows slightly less than one minute per multiple-choice question and 20 minutes apiece for the essay questions.

Next, plan how to spend the 20 minutes allotted to each essay question. For example:

4 minutes   planning
13 minutes   writing
<u>3 minutes</u>   <u>checking, revising</u>
20 minutes   total time

STEP 2   **Prewriting • Planning the Content**

During the four-minute planning period, follow these steps:

- Read the question (frequently stated as a command rather than a question) carefully and look for clue words that indicate what your teacher or instructor wants. Consider the following three sample questions:

Example 1: What are quantum numbers?

Note that the clue words are *what are,* so you must define the term in all its parts. [*See* Definition: Sample for Science *in Part II for a model response to the question.*]

Example 2: Analyze the predominant image in Emily Dickinson's poem, "She Sweeps with Many-Colored Brooms."

Note that the clue word is *analyze,* so you must state the predominant image and support with details from the poem how the image works. [*See* Literary Analyses: For Literary Elements, Sample for an Image, *later in Part III, for a model response to the question.*]

Example 3: Explain who you think is the better candidate for the 8th District and why.

Note that this question includes two key parts, *explain who* and *why.* These double key parts—especially when the second part is *why*—are common in longer questions. When you are faced with a two-part question, you must be certain to fully answer both parts. [*See the sample in* Opinion *in Part II for a complete model response to this question.*]

- Make a list or scratch outline of the main ideas. [*See* Outlines *later in Part III.*] For the preceding three sample questions, scratch outlines may look like the following:

Example 1:   q.n. = numerical descriptions

         4 for each elec:

            principal q.n.

            orbital q.n.

            magnetic q.n.

            spin

(Note the simple list and use of abbreviations.)

Example 2:   prom. = domestic

         why? (M. Nat. - friend)

            sweeping)

            dusting) connect w/ sunset

            sewing)

         key wds: apron, shreds, duds, threads, ravelings

(Note again the simple list, the use of abbreviations, and the illustration that three terms in the poem are all connected with sunset. The writer also reminds herself that certain key words from the poem will help support her idea.)

Example 3:   3 issues:

            stand on drugs (B = testing; K = dealers)

            environ. (B = late; K = strong, early)

            econ. (B = tax incen.; K = no)

(Note the writer has chosen only three issues on which to base his response and shows parenthetically each candidate's position.)

- Organize the list by numbering the items in the order in which you will include them in your essay response. When you compare the three sample lists earlier in this section with the completed responses, you see that the respective writers address the ideas in the order in which they are listed here.
- Reread the question for accuracy and decide whether you have included in your list everything required by the question.
- Anticipate the time you can spend on each item. If, for instance, you have 4 main items and 13 minutes, you can spend 3 minutes on each item. Obviously, you must plan to be concise.

STEP 3   Prewriting • Organizing the Response

You have already organized the main ideas in Step 2. Now you must organize each response. In general, follow this plan:

- Give an introductory statement, usually beginning with the same words as or words similar to those in the question. For instance, refer once again to the first sentence in each response to the three examples earlier in this section:

  Example 1:   Quantum numbers are numerical descriptions that, when taken together, describe a given electron in a given atom.
  Example 2:   Emily Dickinson's poem, "She Sweeps with Many-Colored Brooms," works well because of a predominant image.
  Example 3:   Two qualified candidates have conducted their equally active campaigns to influence the voters of the 8th District.

- State your topic sentence if the answer requires only a single paragraph. [*See* topic sentence *in the Glossary, and see* Writing a Paragraph *in Part I for detailed explanation and examples.*]
- Give your thesis statement if the answer requires a several-point response. [*See* thesis sentence *in the Glossary, and see* Writing a Multi-Paragraph Paper *in Part I for detailed explanation and examples.*]
- Present the main ideas and the specific support.
- Conclude the response, restating the general topic.

STEP 4   Writing • Keeping to the Point

As you write, follow your plan carefully. You have no time to be distracted or go off on tangents. Try to remember these guidelines:

- Keep to the point. Avoid padding with unrelated details or allowing stray ideas to get in your way.
- Follow the outline you planned in Steps 2 and 3.
- Be specific. Use dates, names, places, formulas, details—whatever concrete evidence best supports the topic.
- Watch the time so you do not overextend in one area and slight another. You'll lose valuable points for incomplete answers.

STEP 5   **Revising and Proofreading • Checking Your Response**

Because you have only three minutes planned for checking your response, you will do any quick revising and proofreading as a single step. Check for spelling; accurate names, dates, and details; omissions; repetitions; and grammar, usage, or mechanical errors. Your instructor understands that you do not have time to recopy, so make your corrections as neatly as possible.

SAMPLE TEST ESSAYS AND ANALYSES

Sample papers appear alphabetically by type of essay throughout Parts II and III. To help you find the most appropriate example, refer to Types of Essay Questions earlier in this section. References listed parenthetically refer to sections in Part II where methods of development are detailed and to sections in Part III where you can find sample essays and their respective analyses. Thus, if an essay test question requires a definition, you can find sample essays in the section labeled Definition.

Fax

A fax, the shortened term for *facsimile*, is the exact reproduction of any graphic matter by wire. Using telephone lines, fax machines let writers share instantly any document that will feed through the machine. For instance, your doctor can have a lab report faxed to her from across town or across the country while you finish dressing. An East Coast business can fax a West Coast customer a product information sheet while customer and salesperson continue talking on the other line.

Because you can fax literally any document to any fax machine, there are a few guidelines that apply:

- Unless the fax machine is in the recipient's home, you can assume that any given transmitter serves several people, maybe even several offices. Thus, because a fax coming in can be read by whoever happens to be nearby, avoid sending anything personal, confidential, or sensitive.
- Don't send unnecessary fax transmissions. Your efforts will be unappreciated. You'll waste the recipient's time and money replenishing paper in the machine.
- Every fax should have a cover page. That page should include the following details:
  - Name of recipient
  - Business name and room number, if applicable
  - Fax number of recipient
  - Name of sender
  - Business name and room number, if applicable
  - Fax number of sender
  - Phone number of sender in case of transmission problems
  - Date
  - Subject
  - Number of pages, including the cover page
  - Optional comments

To include the cover page is to insure that the intended recipient does, in fact, receive your fax. It also provides adequate information in case the recipient wants to respond by fax.

Feature Article

The feature article gives information of human interest. The label *feature* covers a broad range of newspaper or magazine articles that include everything except straight news, editorials, and advertising. [*For comparison, see* News Article, Editorial, *and* Advertising *elsewhere in Part III.*] Generally, feature articles attempt to involve the reader emotionally.

Because of its human-interest approach, the feature article allows the writer considerable opportunity for creativity. While the subject of a feature may be related to a news item, the article will not follow the pyramid structure of a straight news piece. Rather, it is more likely to include conventions of fiction: plot, character, dialogue, and symbolism. [*See separate entries for each in the Glossary.*] A feature is a creative article that deals with real events, issues, and trends; but unlike straight news articles, it places emphasis on the people involved rather than on the facts of news.

CHARACTERISTICS

A feature article generally

- evokes an emotional reaction: joy, sympathy, anger, frustration, contentment, or some other emotion,
- gives depth and meaning to complicated issues or news items, thus clarifying and interpreting events,
- follows the techniques of good creative writing [*see* Short Story *later in Part III*],
- avoids the pyramid structure of a straight news story,
- follows an organization appropriate for the subject [*see* order *in the Glossary*],
- uses an introduction (or lead) that attracts readers,
- uses a tone and style appropriate to its subject,
- achieves success by being researched and brightly written.

PROCESS

Use the following steps to develop a feature story.

STEP 1   **Prewriting • Finding the Story**

If you are not assigned a subject, your search begins with finding the right topic, one related to breaking news or current issues or trends. Seeing a good topic for a feature article in the midst of the so-called "hard" news depends on your curiosity. In short, your creativity determines how you will deal with a subject.

For instance, if the breaking news deals with tornado damage to the school, your feature story may recount the teacher's story who spotted the twister, sounded the alarm, and prevented widespread injuries. Or your feature story may spring from a tour of the building, noting damage to the classrooms, reporting pencils jammed into concrete-block walls, and observing pine needles pinning pages to bulletin boards. Feature articles usually evoke some kind of emotion.

STEP 2   **Prewriting • Gathering the Information**

Whether the information comes from your own account, interviews with eyewitnesses, or printed sources, you must gather as much information as possible. Even though a feature article is not a straight news story, its facts must be accurate and its message valid.

STEP 3   **Prewriting • Determining the Type of Feature**

Your purpose determines the type of feature you will write. Features are limited only by the writer/reporter's imagination; however, a few basic types are suggested by the general purpose.

The Human-Interest Feature. The most common of the feature articles, the human-interest feature does what it says: describes some unusual aspect of the life of an ordinary human being, an aspect that makes him or her interesting. The story may tell about success in spite of great odds, recall a tragic predicament, or share a continuing struggle supported only by hope and faith.

The Personality Feature. A human-interest feature that takes on greater depth turns into a personality feature. In many respects, the personality feature resembles a characterization. [*See* Character Sketch *earlier in Part III*.] The main character may or may not be known but will have done something of interest to others. Maybe the person developed a product that has become an international retail item; learned to overcome shyness and became a political candidate; travels to school each day on roller skates. Usually the personality feature shows how a person gained recognition.

The How-To Feature. The how-to feature is not much more than a process analysis article [*see* Process Analysis *in Part II*], but it usually takes a do-it-yourself approach.

The Past-Events Feature. Sometimes features focus on historical events or celebrations. Supported by library research, such features provide human-interest history lessons. The story of a Japanese-American citizen's imprisonment in the United States during World War II helps readers see the complexity of human emotion during war. Published on December 7, the anniversary of Pearl Harbor, the story takes on added emotional impact.

The News Feature. A human-interest focus on breaking news results in a news feature, an article that adds personal involvement to what may otherwise be a distant, seemingly unimportant current event. An interview with the parents of a soldier wounded in an overseas battle brings personal emotion into the report of an event in which readers may have no other involvement.

Determine the kind of feature you plan to write.

STEP 4   **Prewriting • Choosing the Single Focus**

When you have determined your purpose (and, thus, the kind of feature you plan to write), force yourself to write a single sentence that explains the specific focus the article will take. Although this sentence probably will not appear in the article, it will help you frame your thoughts. The sentence may look something like this:

Tara's mouse-like dolls began as whimsical gifts from her sewing room but have become a million-dollar-a-year international business.

The feature article, a human-interest piece, will explain how Tara achieved success.

STEP 5   **Writing • Determining the Organization**
Decide how you can best present the information in your feature. Will an order of importance be best? [*See* order of importance *in the Glossary.*] Will a flashback [*see* flashback *in the Glossary*] work better? Will chronological order be better? [*See* chronological order *in the Glossary.*]
Choose the approach most effective for your purpose.

STEP 6   **Writing • Drafting the Lead**
The lead, or introduction, must catch the reader's attention and make him or her want to read more. Use any attention-getting device [*see* attention-getter *in the Glossary*] suitable to your topic. Make sure, too, that the lead sets the tone for the article. [*See* tone *in the Glossary.*]

STEP 7   **Writing • Drafting the Body**
Following the organizational pattern you selected in Step 5, develop the body of the feature article. Keep in mind the creative nature of the feature and realize that your best tool for writing is an inquisitive mind. Use techniques appropriate to short-story writing [*see* Short Story *later in Part III*] and strive to achieve an easy writing style.

STEP 8   **Writing • Drafting the Conclusion**
The conclusion of a feature article is much like the conclusion of a short story: it gives an air of finality and ties together any loose ends. It may also refer back to the lead. It usually does not, however, end with a summary or conclusion in the manner of a traditional expository composition.

STEP 9   **Writing • Preparing the Headline**
Sometimes feature writers have the opportunity to develop their own headlines; in other cases, someone else assumes this responsibility. If you develop your own, or if someone else accepts your suggestions, you should add a headline that attracts reader attention and pinpoints the focus of your article.

STEP 10 **Revising • Checking for Good Writing Techniques**

Because the feature article is more nearly creative writing than anything else, revise the piece according to these suggestions:

- Does the article reflect careful, complete research?
- Do I attract my reader's attention in the opening paragraph?
- Does the article maintain interest throughout?
- Did I follow a logical organization to achieve my purpose?
- Have I maintained unity? [*See* Revising: Sample Revision for Unity *in Part I.*]
- Have I varied sentence structure in keeping with the tone and purpose? [*See* Revising: Sample Revision for Sentence Variety *in Part I.*]
- Are transitions sufficient to guarantee smooth reading? [*See* Revising: Sample Revision for Transition *in Part I.*]
- Does the word choice show freshness and originality?
- Have I eliminated wordiness? [*See* Revising: Sample Revision for Wordiness *in Part I.*]
- Do I use good story-writing techniques? [*See* Short Story *later in Part III.*]

STEP 11 **Proofreading • Checking the Details**

In the journalistic trade, writers refer to *copy reading* rather than *proofreading*. Copy reading occurs in the newspaper business when the writer completes his final copy. He reads to correct his own errors. On the other hand, proofreading takes place after the printed proof is ready. Then the writer reads for others' errors.

Whatever you call it—copy reading or proofreading—be sure to check your final copy carefully for grammar, mechanics, and usage errors. If the publication for which you are writing has its own style manual, check it for stylistic details.

SAMPLE FEATURE ARTICLE

Compare this feature news article with the sample in News Article later in Part III to note the differences between a news article and a feature article.

Community Grows as Karson Grows

Together, the employer and the employees pay over a million dollars in state and local taxes each year. Together, they provide materials for about one-fourth of the automobiles produced in the United States. Together, they have showered stockholders with over a half-million dollars in dividends in the past five years. Together, they make up Karson Manufacturing, the area's largest employer.

Karson Manufacturing began as a garage operation when, in 1932, the late Rodney Karson started machining parts for local businesses. As business expanded, he moved to the current location on Oak Road. But the site was hardly the same then as today. Photographs in the 1942 edition of the *Daily News* show the company as little more than a series of one-story brick buildings, obviously added as needed. Not until 1962 did the present facility begin to take shape. Additions in 1969 and 1978 resulted in the current facility.

George Hatman, vice-president of manufacturing, began with the company in 1938. "I still remember my interview with Mr. Rodney Karson. He wore a blue work shirt, sleeves rolled up, with black suspenders holding up his work pants. He looked like all the rest of the workers except for his hat. He wore this funny felt bowler with a red hat band. Usually he kept a pencil stuck in the hat band. Don't know why. Never saw him use it. But that's the way he showed up for the interview. Funny, but I'd worn my best suit. Thought I should try to impress him.

"We didn't talk long. Asked me a few questions about experience. I didn't have any but I was willing to work. So you know what he said? He said, 'Well, get yourself home, son, and put on some work clothes. Come back this afternoon and we'll see what you're made of.' That's what I did. And I'm still here."

Hatman believes that Karson's philosophy made the company what it is today. "He figured if you wanted to work, you were a good man to have on the team. And that's what we have here—a team. We all pull together, work together, make decisions together, show success together. It's a heck of a team to be on!"

And together, the Karson team today announced a six-million-dollar expansion. As a result, the local community as well as Karson will grow. Together.

 Analysis of the Sample. As a feature article, the sample above includes the characteristics that make it a satisfactory representation. Note the following specific details:

- The sample falls into the "past-events" category but also includes a personality profile. It would probably run the same day as the news story [*see sample in* News Article] announcing the Karson expansion.
- The organization is roughly chronological, beginning with the present, jumping back to the company's origins, and moving forward.
- The introduction (or lead) catches the reader's attention, sets the tone for the article, and introduces the theme, togetherness.
- Paragraph structure follows short-story writing techniques.

- Dialogue generates the emotional impact of the piece. By using the speaker's words, the writer permits him to share personal experiences that shed light on the elder Karson's personality.
- The article maintains a single focus, showing how togetherness has helped the company grow.
- The conclusion makes a final statement without summarizing or restating.

Journal

A journal, sometimes called a *learning log*, records—or logs—what you have learned. Usually kept on a daily basis in a spiral notebook as informal personal writing, the journal may be a voluntary learning tool or a required part of a course. Generally, a writer's journal holds responses to assignments, notes on class discussion, or summaries of outside reading.

CHARACTERISTICS

The characteristics of a journal vary from class to class, teacher to teacher, and student to student. Usually, however, journal entries

- are made on a regular basis, often daily, and are dated for identification,
- respond to a prompt, usually given by the teacher or found within the assigned reading,
- record what you have learned, or struggled to learn, in a given class,
- include summaries, responses, reactions, definitions, questions, or unsolved problems you have about assignments, discussions, or outside reading,
- may include entries that are sentences, lists, paragraphs, diagrams, illustrations, or charts,
- are considered informal writing, usually not evaluated as a piece of writing, and thus,
- generally ignore the formal processes of prewriting, writing, revising, and proofreading (though, in fact, the journal may serve as a prewriting activity for certain future writing assignments).

PROCESS

Because journals or learning logs are usually written as informal responses to learning situations, they lack the formal process of other written products. Instead, you will most likely be asked to respond to a prompt such as one of the following:

In English class:
In what ways are Sylvia and the heron alike in the short story, "The White Heron"? [*Later in Part III, see* Literary Analyses: Sample for a Short Story *for a sample response.*]

In social sciences class:
Colonial brides kept what they called a "hope chest." Based on your reading, what items do you think might be included? [*See* Description: Sample for Social Sciences *in Part II for a sample response.*]

In science class:
If a farmer wants to quit using pesticides, what can he do to improve insect control? [*See the sample in* Notes: For a Class *later in Part III.*]

In math class:
What is the difference between an arithmetic sequence and a geometric sequence? [*See* Comparison and Contrast: Sample for Mathematics *in Part II for a sample response.*]

In work-place writing:
Imagine that you own a photography studio. What kinds of advertising do you think you should use? [*See* Process Analysis: Sample for Work-Place Writing *in Part II for a sample response.*]

In technical writing:
Explain in one sentence the purpose of a bulkhead. [*See the sample in* Short Answers: Definitions *later in Part III for a sample response.*]

As these examples illustrate, a journal entry may be a single sentence, a list, a paragraph, or several paragraphs. Unlike these samples, however, the journal entry frequently is not polished writing. It often serves, on the other hand, to organize thoughts or to find (or form) ideas for later finished products.

Lab Report

A laboratory report, commonly called a *lab report*, details the procedures and findings of primary research in a laboratory situation. [*See* primary research *in the Glossary*.] While most lab work is scientific, you may be asked to develop a lab report in the work place or in a technical class. In any case, the report requires attention to minute details of equipment, procedure, and analysis, all examined carefully with logical, critical detachment.

Because a lab report is a kind of technical report, see Technical Report later in Part III for a complete sample and analysis.

Letters

By means of letters, we communicate with our friends, our enemies, our business associates, our government. In addition, many people choose to express their opinions regularly in letters to newspaper and magazine editors.

Everyone at one time or another finds it necessary to write business and social letters. It is probably safe to say that the most important writing we do over the course of our lives is letter writing. Letter writers deal with everything from huge financial transactions to delicate personal emotions.

Letters follow a unique but simple format. This section discusses the following kinds of letter writing:

- Business letters, including
  - Personal business letter
  - Request for information
  - Letter of complaint
  - Letter to accompany a resume
- Editorial letters
- Social letters

BUSINESS LETTERS

Business letters deal with innumerable matters, but most fall into one of two groups: those that relate to our professional lives and those that relate to business matters in our personal lives. By discussing business letters in general and then showing specific variations, this section guides you through successful business-letter writing.

CHARACTERISTICS

First, a business letter must look business-like. Immaculate appearance is essential, so the business letter should

- be printed on 8½" x 11" plain white paper, preferably at least a 20-pound bond,
- be printed in a clear, easy-to-read font, such as Courier or Times Roman,
- maintain ample margins with an even left margin and a right margin as even as possible and with top and bottom margins reasonably equal,
- use a header on all pages beyond the first, a header that includes the name of the addressee, the date, and the page number.

Second, the business letter should include the following seven parts:

- A letterhead or heading.
  If you don't have printed letterhead, use a three-line heading giving your street address; city, state, and zip code; and the date.
  Or, if you don't have printed letterhead, create your own by using a 14- or 16-point bold font. On three or more lines an inch from the top, include
  - your name,
  - street address,
  - city, state, and zip code.
  As part of their printed letterhead, some businesspeople also include
  - business phone number,
  - cell phone number,
  - fax number,
  - e-mail address.
- The date on which the letter is written.
- The inside address, three or more lines made up of
  - recipient's name,
  - recipient's title or position, if known,
  - company name,
  - company's street address,
  - company's city, state, and zip code.

- A salutation, such as *Dear Mr. Glatter, Dear Dr. Hansen*, or *Gentlemen*, followed by a colon.
  Note: Use the name if you know it: *Dear Mr. Smith*. If you do not know a name but only a title, use *Dear Chairperson, Dear President, Dear Secretary, Dear Sir, Dear Madam*, or whatever is appropriate. If you know neither a name nor a title, use *Gentlemen, Ladies*, or *Ladies and Gentlemen*. The salutation should agree with the inside address.
- The body of the business letter, arranged in paragraph form.
- A closing, such as *Yours truly* or *Sincerely yours*, followed by a comma.
  Note: Use the following closings for the following purposes:
  - *Yours truly* (with or without *very*) when the salutation is the impersonal *Gentlemen* or *Dear Sir* and when the tone of the letter is cold and formal, or when you are in doubt about what to use.
  - *Sincerely* or *Cordially yours* (with or without *very*) when the addressee's name appears in the salutation and the tone of the letter is personal and friendly.
  - *Respectfully yours* (with or without *very*) when the letter is addressed to a person of high rank.
- The writer's signature, written (not printed) in ink, followed by the typewritten name.

Third, the business letter may include the following items:

- An attention line, used when a letter is addressed only to a company or to a department rather than to an individual. *Note:* The attention line appears immediately after the inside address and before the salutation. It begins with the word *Attention* followed by a colon and the name of the specific department to which the letter should be forwarded, such as *Attention: Sales Department*. Never use a person's name in the attention line. If you know the person's name, use it in the inside address and omit the attention line.
- A subject line, which appears immediately after the salutation. The subject line begins with the word *Subject* followed by a colon and a few words or a phrase to state the subject of the letter, such as *Subject: Past-Due Payment*. Use initial capital letters to name the subject.
- A writer's identification, which appears immediately below the typewritten signature and identifies the writer's title or position. *Note:* The writer never signs his name with a title or position preceding or following his name.

- Reference initials, which appear at the left margin below the typewritten signature line and identify the typist, such as *kjs* for *Kirsten Joo Seng.*
- Enclosure notation, which appears immediately below any reference initials and indicates something is enclosed with the letter. *Note:* If you have more than one item enclosed, use one of the three appropriate messages: *Enc., 2 Enclosures,* or *Enc. 2.*
- Copy notations, which appear immediately after any enclosure notation and indicate who will receive copies of the letter, such as *cc: Sales Department.*
- A postscript (**PS**), which appears immediately after any copy notations. *Note:* A postscript is always the last item in a letter. It allows the writer to include something he forgot to mention in the body or sometimes to call attention to an important detail.

Fourth, the parts of the business letter should be arranged in one of three styles:

- Block style, which begins every line in every part of the letter at the left margin.
- Modified-block style, which uses no indentation and which begins all lines in the heading and closing at the center of the page (a style often referred to as *standard format*).
- Modified-block style with indented paragraphs, which follows the same format as the modified-block style, with the addition of an indentation for every paragraph.

[*Examples of each of these styles appear in the Samples and Analyses later in this section.*]

Fifth, the good business letter maintains characteristic standards of writing, so it

- follows standard grammar, mechanics, and usage rules,
- follows standard spelling,
- maintains courtesy and diplomacy,
- displays clear, precise writing,
- avoids complex, convoluted sentences,
- omits ambiguous words, phrases, or sentences,
- eliminates excess words, phrases, or sentences.

PROCESS

Developing a business letter goes quickly after a few preliminary preparations. Follow these steps for best results.

STEP 1   **Prewriting • Gathering the Necessary Information**

To work efficiently, gather the necessary names, titles, addresses, records, or other papers you need to develop the letter. Verify that titles and addresses are current, perhaps with a quick phone call. Usually, a business switchboard operator or receptionist can give you the information you need. Using current, accurate information justifies even a long-distance call, especially for important matters.

STEP 2   **Prewriting • Planning the Body of the Letter**

Because much of the business letter form requires only that you put accurate information in certain parts of a prescribed format, the only planning necessary is for the body of the letter.

First, write a single sentence that says what you want this letter to accomplish. Start with the phrase: "The purpose of this letter is to . . . ." Then complete the sentence. Develop a sentence similar to one of the following examples:

> The purpose of this letter is to direct the exchange of a sweater ordered from a mail-order company for the same sweater in a larger size.
> The purpose of this letter is to get information about the tourist attractions in and around Denver.
> The purpose of this letter is to apply for the position of sales manager in the company.

Next, list the important ideas you want to include, most notably the following:

For a Personal Business Letter

- The account or other identification number, as applicable
- The date of the transaction, contractual agreement, conversation, or other business contact
- Any necessary background information
- A direct statement of what you want of the reader: a reply, an appointment, or, perhaps, no action

For a Request for Information

- Specific details about the information you are requesting: dates, places, and general-interest areas for tourist information; specific areas of inquiry for printed information
- Details about payment
- Directions for forwarding the requested information: to whom, where, by what means, at whose expense

For a Letter of Complaint

- The order, identification, serial, catalog, or part number of the consumer item
- The name of the consumer item
- The date of purchase or of the agreement, contract, lease, or other business dealing
- A specific explanation of the problem
- The name and/or title of any company representative with whom you have previously talked regarding the problem
- A reference to any guarantee or warranty agreement
- An explanation of what you want done to correct the problem
- Photocopies of any information that may aid the resolution of your complaint
- An attitude of courtesy and tact, regardless of your frustration or anger

For a Letter to Accompany a Resume

- An inside address and a salutation naming the specific person who makes personnel decisions
- A polite reference to the company, its product line, its reputation, or, if you have met, a polite reference to the person addressed
- A reference to the accompanying resume
- Emphasis on your areas of greatest strengths as a potential employee
- An expression of willingness to learn new skills, travel, relocate, work irregular hours, begin with a part-time position, and so on

STEP 3 **Writing • Developing the Ideas into a Letter**

With the preliminary work completed, developing the body of the letter should go quickly. As you write, remember a few guidelines:

- Get to the point immediately.
- Provide any necessary details to clarify your point for the reader.
- Be concise.
- End with a courteous sentence.

STEP 4 **Revising • Checking the Content**

Check the content of your letter for accuracy. Ask yourself the following questions as a guide for possible revision:

- Does the first sentence state the purpose of the letter?
- Are adequate details included in order that the addressee can understand my point and, if necessary, respond?
- Have I avoided excess verbiage and complicated sentences?
- Is my letter courteous, polite, business-like?
- Does the final sentence conclude the letter courteously without compromising my position?

Make revisions. Then follow the guidelines in Step 5 as you type a final copy.

STEP 5 **Revising • Typing the Final Copy**

As you type the final copy of your letter, ask yourself these questions to address accuracy and appearance. Check additional details in the proofreading section that follows.

- Does the letterhead begin an inch from the top of the page?
- Does the correct date appear at least a double space below the letterhead?
- Does the inside address begin four to ten spaces below the date to adjust for appearance?
- Is the inside address accurate and complete, including a current title or position of the addressee?
- Does the salutation begin two spaces below the inside address?
- Are all words in the salutation capitalized accurately?
- Is the salutation appropriate for the occasion and followed by a colon?
- Does the body begin two spaces below the salutation and follow a consistent format?
- Is the body typed single-spaced with a double space between paragraphs?

- Are the left and right margins nearly equal, the left margin even and the right margin as nearly even as possible?
- If my letter runs onto a second page, have I avoided having only three or four lines on the second page?
- If I must divide a paragraph at the bottom of page one, have I included at least two lines of the paragraph on page one and at least two lines on the top of page two?
- Does the second page begin one inch from the top with a heading that includes the name of the addressee, the page number, and the date?
- Have I started page two of the body of the letter three lines below the heading?
- Have I maintained the same side margins on the second page as on the first?
- Does the closing appear two lines below the body?
- Is only the first word of the closing capitalized?
- Is the closing appropriate and followed by a comma?
- Is my signature in blue or black ink, signed, not printed?
- Does the typewritten signature appear four lines below the closing in order to allow room for the written signature?
- Does my written signature omit all titles or references to position, such as *Mr., Dr., Ms., Professor,* or *Manager*?
- Is the typewritten signature accurate, including any necessary designations of title or position?
- Are any other necessary notations included, such as copy lines, attention lines, subject lines, and so on?
- Is the format consistent, either in block form or in one of the two modified-block forms?
- Are the top and bottom margins nearly equal?

Make any necessary revisions based on the preceding guiding questions. If necessary, for the sake of an immaculate, business-like appearance, reprint the letter.

STEP 6   **Proofreading • Checking the Technical Details**
Check grammar, mechanics, and usage. [*See Part IV for rules and examples.*] In addition, consider the following questions as you proofread:

- Have I punctuated the letterhead correctly, using a comma between the city and state but no punctuation between the state and zip code?
- Did I include a comma between the day of the month and the year?

- Have I punctuated the inside address correctly, using a comma to separate the name of the addressee from his title or position if both are listed on the same line? Did I punctuate the address correctly?
- Have I maintained accurate capitalization throughout?
- Do I use accurate terminology throughout the letter?
- Is my spelling absolutely correct? In the case of alternate spellings, do I use the preferred spelling? See *Webster's New World Dictionary* as a final reference.
- When you have typed a final copy, proofread it carefully and sign it. The letter is ready to prepare for mailing.

STEP 7 **Proofreading • The Final Step**

In order to maintain an immaculate, business-like appearance, this section discusses three final points: addressing the envelope, folding the letter, and sending the letter.

Addressing the Envelope. Follow these steps:

1. Use a plain white envelope, preferably letter-size.
2. Put your return address, including your name, in the upper left corner of the envelope, using the same style as you used in the heading of the letter.
3. Begin the mailing address on line 14 of a letter-size envelope and on line 12 of a small envelope. Start at the vertical center of the envelope. The mailing address should appear exactly as it does in the inside address of the letter.
4. Be sure to add sufficient postage.

Folding the Letter. If you are using a long envelope, fold your letter in thirds, folding the bottom third toward the top and then the top third down. Insert the letter in the envelope with the open end of the letter toward the top of the envelope. [See Figure 3.1.]

FIGURE 3.1

Folding a letter in thirds.

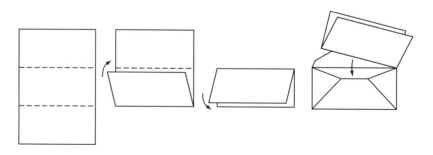

If you are using a short envelope, first fold your letter in half, bringing the bottom up to the top. Then fold that into thirds by bringing the left third toward the right and the right third over the left. Again, insert the letter in the envelope with the open end of the letter toward the top of the envelope. [See Figure 3.2.]

FIGURE 3.2

Folding a letter for a smaller envelope.

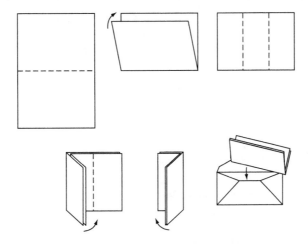

Finally, seal the envelope and check for sufficient postage.

Sending the Letter. If you are sending the letter through the U.S. Postal Service, you can mail the letter first class at any postal-service box. If you are sending it as certified mail (which, if a return receipt is requested, provides a record of delivery) or as registered mail (which provides top security for valuable or hard-to-replace items), then you need to mail it from a post office. If you are sending it as express mail (for guaranteed one-day delivery), you can, if you have in hand the necessary forms, mail it from an express mailbox. Private carriers also deliver letters and parcels—some overnight, some within a day, some within two days. Of course, you pay extra for the speedy service.

Study the following sample business letters and their analyses for further guidelines.

SAMPLE PERSONAL BUSINESS LETTER

The following letter verifies in writing an important telephone conversation. The purpose in such a letter is to record a specific event. As telephone conversations are subject to your-word-against-theirs arguments, it is wise, in important matters, to verify them.

F. Brody Kleindorf
1234 Shortridge Road
Catharge, NM 98765-4321

July 29, 20—

Mr. Wilbur Offenberg
Vice President of Accounts
Finner, Hopewell, and Finner Securities
7890 Jarrell Financial Center
Irontown, WA 56789-0123

Dear Mr. Offenberg:

I am writing to confirm our telephone conversation this morning regarding my account No. 567890 with Finner, Hopewell, and Finner Securities. As you recall, I requested that $5,000 be moved from account No. 567890 into my joint account No. 123456.

In the course of our conversation, you agreed to make that transaction immediately in order for me to take advantage of the improved interest rate effective August 1. At the same time, I agreed to sign a withdrawal/deposit slip and forward it to you in today's mail. You will find the slip enclosed, requesting the $5,000 transfer of funds.

I appreciate your help in this matter. This kind of service makes it a pleasure doing business with Finner, Hopewell, and Finner.

Respectfully yours,

F. Brody Kleindorf

F. Brody Kleindorf

Enc.

Analysis of the Sample Personal Business Letter. The personal business letter follows the standard format (modified-block style). Note that the left margin is flush except for the centered letterhead, closing, and signature. Compare this with the following two letters that illustrate the block and the modified-block with indented paragraphs.

In addition, note these characteristics:

- The six parts of the letter are evident: heading, inside address, salutation, body, closing, and signature.
- An enclosure notation shows that the withdrawal/deposit slip is enclosed.
- The letterhead and inside address use the standard two-letter abbreviations for states. Follow the same form on the envelope.
- A colon follows the salutation.
- The two body paragraphs discuss a single idea each. Each is concise.
- The final paragraph represents a good courtesy paragraph.
- The closing is appropriate and followed by a comma.

SAMPLE REQUEST FOR INFORMATION

The following letter requests information. Written in block style, the left margin is flush throughout the letter.

Gerald Kleimann
1803 State Highway 43 North
South Plaine, OH 48691-4968

November 18, 20—

Mr. Glenn K. Yonkers
Midwest Regional Tourism Division
1400 North Cross Street
Nashville, TN 48815-5188

Dear Mr. Yonkers:

Our family is planning a two-week trip through Kentucky and Tennessee during the summer of 20—. Please send a brochure or pamphlet listing the scenic attractions of eastern Tennessee and a highway map for the state. Because we are photography buffs and avid hikers, we are interested specifically in geographic scenery, not man-made attractions.

Please send the two items to me at the address above. I understand this is a service you provide for those planning vacations in the area.

We're looking forward to our visit to your part of the country.

Sincerely yours,

Gerald Kleimann

Gerald Kleimann

Analysis of the Sample Request for Information. The preceding sample follows the general characteristics of a good business letter. As a model of a block-style letter, note that the left margin is straight throughout, except, of course, for the letterhead.

In addition, note these particular features:

- The heading and inside address use the approved two-letter abbreviation for the state followed by the zip code.
- The salutation and closing are appropriately business-like.
- The body of the letter, brief and specific, covers the basic requirements for a letter of request.
- The courtesy sentence is neither too gushy nor too cold.
- The signature line is accurate.

SAMPLE LETTER OF COMPLAINT

The following letter maintains the modified-block style with indented paragraphs. Note that it maintains courtesy in spite of the writer's obvious unhappiness.

Claudette McMooney
4157 Southland Drive
Oxmoore, SC 61842-5073

January 23, 20—

Customer Relations Office
Kalaxton Manufacturing Company, Inc.
12700 Broadmore Way
New Richland, AL 38741-2763

Gentlemen:

Six weeks ago on December 15, I purchased a Kitchen Kit Appliance Aid, model A-4001-6, at the Trenton Store in Oxmoore. I have tried for several weeks now to understand the operator's manual, but so far I have been relatively unsuccessful. As a result, I don't know whether I am operating the Appliance Aid improperly or whether it is malfunctioning. When I try to cut French fries, for instance, I get grated rather than cut potatoes. Likewise, when I use the slaw cutter, what comes out looks more like mush than slaw.

I have talked with the retailer at Trenton who claims he knows nothing about the Appliance Aid's operation. Could you tell me, please, where I can find someone in the Oxmoore area who can demonstrate the Aid and who can also tell me whether my Aid is malfunctioning or whether I am, in fact, operating it improperly.

I am looking forward to your response.

Very truly yours,

Claudette McMooney

Claudette McMooney

Analysis of the Sample Letter of Complaint. The preceding letter appears in modified-block style with indented paragraphs. Although the form is not as popular as the two previous letters, certain businesses still prefer it.

Note these additional features:

- Because the writer did not have the name of a specific person at Kalaxton Manufacturing Company, she could write only to Customer Relations. Generally, this title will get your letter where it needs to go.
- The salutation is appropriate.
- The two body paragraphs give the company representative sufficient information to know which appliance the writer has, its model number, its date and place of purchase, and the customer's problem.
- By asking for a specific response, the writer lets the addressee know exactly what she hopes to accomplish. She is not asking for a replacement or repairs; she is not asking for a refund.
- The final courtesy sentence appropriately expresses a business-like attitude.
- The closing and signature are accurate and appropriate.

SAMPLE LETTER TO ACCOMPANY A RESUME

The following letter, written in modified-block style, probably the most popular of the three styles, serves to introduce the writer to a potential employer. The accompanying resume [*see* Resume *later in Part III*], lists the applicant's qualifications.

Kevin L. McDermitt
12806 South Pike Road
Mt. Simon, LA 23306-1229

September 4, 20—

Ms. Krista McGallahan
Personnel Manager
Feagley Electronics Company
3468 Longway Drive
Judson, Virginia 43210-3210

Dear Ms. McGallahan:

Having worked with Feagley computers regularly in various computer centers for the past three years, I am looking forward to an opportunity to work with the company as a full-time employee.

Experienced in both software programming and alteration to meet customer needs and in tutoring clients, I am qualified as a software-hardware technician, able to alter software to make it compatible with most brands of hardware, including that developed by Feagley. As you can see from the accompanying resume, I also have an associate degree in business with a minor in computer education.

I am looking forward to an interview for a position with Feagley Electronics. I will call in a week for an appointment.

Sincerely yours,

Kevin L. McDermitt

Kevin L. McDermitt

Enc.

Analysis of the Sample Letter to Accompany a Resume. The preceding letter accompanies the resume sample found in Resume, later in Part III. Compare letter and resume samples to better understand the relationship of the cover letter to the resume itself. In addition, note these features:

- Like any other business letter, the letter to accompany a resume must maintain an immaculate, businesslike appearance and follow proper form.
- In addition, the letter is really another opportunity to sell yourself as a potential employee. Saying something nice about the company certainly will not spoil anything. Note the effect of this process in the first paragraph of the sample.
- Finally, do not repeat all the information included in the resume, but do point out the most impressive qualifications and put your best foot forward.

The characteristics, processes, samples, and analyses in this section should enable you to develop satisfactory business letters.

EDITORIAL LETTERS

In a letter to the editor, you can express your opinion about relevant issues and expect to have a wide audience. While all letters to the editor express an opinion, some aim to convince; others to inform. Some express appreciation or condolences; others question. Some hope to destroy apathy; others unwittingly create it. Generally, however, people write letters to the editor to voice opinions on issues that to them, at least, merit the time and effort, and in which the readership may share an interest.

CHARACTERISTICS

A letter to the editor includes some of the same characteristics as a business letter; but to meet its purpose, the letter to the editor must meet certain other criteria. In general, a good letter to the editor should

- be brief, including no more than 300 words in its body (where a word equals five characters),
- address a timely subject,
- attract the reader's attention, thus increasing the chances of its being published,

- express clearly, probably in the first sentence, your opinion,
- provide details adequate to support your opinion,
- anticipate the reader's point of view and potential questions,
- indicate thorough knowledge of the subject,
- follow an organizational plan that best attracts reader attention,
- suggest, if possible, a solution to the problem or issue and offer as well a means of implementation,
- omit phrases such as *I think, in my opinion, it seems to me,* or *I, for one* as a letter to the editor is already recognized as your opinion,
- avoid name-calling, sweeping generalizations, and unfair accusations,
- maintain a courteous, polite tone,
- include your signature and typewritten name as newspapers and magazines rarely publish anonymous letters,
- include a phone number where you can be reached, preferably during the day, for verification,
- follow either a business-letter format or a less formal but more easily read format as described in Step 6 later in this section.

While the organization of letters to the editor vary as much as the writers themselves, good writing techniques enhance any letter. Thus, using a comparison or contrast, cause and effect, analogy, description, definition—or any of the other methods of development—will improve the letter's effectiveness. [*See* Comparison and Contrast, Cause and Effect, Analogy, Description, Definition, *and entries describing other methods of development in Part II.*]

Similarly, good sentence structure and accurate grammar, usage, and mechanics will likewise improve your letter's effectiveness. [*See* Revising *in Part I and rules and examples for grammar, usage, and mechanics in Part IV.*]

PROCESS

Writing a letter to the editor requires much the same process as developing an opinion paper. [*See* Opinion *in Part II.*] Because it may also try to convince the reader to reach agreement, it follows a process similar to that for developing a persuasion paper. [*See* Persuasion *in Part II.*] The following summarizes the steps.

STEP 1   Prewriting • Stating Your Purpose

Before you write the first word, think about what you really want to say. Recognizing that a letter to the editor must be brief (no more than 300 words, preferably fewer), you should be able to put your idea into a single sentence. If not, then you may have the basis for more than one letter. Consider the following examples and then write your own main idea. Omit opening phrases such as *this letter will serve to convince . . .* or *the purpose of this letter is to . . . .* Instead, state your opinion.

> The County Council should initiate action to merge city and county governments for the sake of economic stability.
> Local media have distorted the reasons for Fire Chief Daikerson's dismissal.
> The recent article entitled "Minding Your Own Business" omitted two potentially serious stumbling blocks for someone who is considering establishing his own business.

Does your one-sentence statement of purpose follow these models?

STEP 2   Prewriting • Planning the Supporting Details

Planning the supporting details calls for two thought processes. First, with your statement of purpose in front of you, think about the examples, situations, illustrations, descriptions, comparisons, analogies, causes, or effects that will help you explain your point of view. Make a list of them.

Next, think about the newspaper or magazine reader. What will attract the reader's attention? With what can the reader most easily identify? What message hits closest to home? Make a list of these ideas.

Finally, survey your two lists. How can they best fit together? If your audience identifies with the problem of unemployment, then what situation, illustration, or cause will best serve that identification?

Compare the writer's following two lists with his completed letter to the editor at the end of this section:

List of examples:	B's tax incentives; K's warnings
	B's drug testing; K's crackdown
	K's incinerator fight; B's nothing
Ideas to attract the reader:	increased taxes—hit pocketbook
	drug test harassment
	"yes" man

Analyzing the lists will help you select supporting details.

Because the letter must be brief, select only those details that most directly affect the reader. You may need no more than two or three details, certainly no more than four. (Remember the 300-word limit.)

STEP 3 **Prewriting • Organizing the Details**

Choose a logical plan of organization. Here's how. First, see chronological order, spatial order, and order of importance in the Glossary so that you understand the general plans of organization.

Next, think about the many kinds of development available to you as a letter writer. Will your letter have a greater impact using one method of development over another? [*See Part II for a variety of development methods*.]

Third, think again about the audience analysis you completed in Step 2.

Now, using all that information, list the details in their most effective order. Try several plans to find the most effective one.

STEP 4 **Writing • Following the Plan**

As you write, keep in mind the items listed in the Characteristics section earlier. Begin with some means of catching the reader's attention. Justify what you have to say.

Follow with a statement of your opinion and proceed with the supporting details as you organized them in Step 3. Stick to the point; avoid excess verbiage.

As part of the conclusion, suggest either a course of action, a solution to the problem, or a means by which to implement the solution.

STEP 5 **Revising • Polishing the Content**

Getting your ideas on paper puts you over the hurdle. Now you can polish those ideas and put them in the best light for your reader. As you revise the content, ask yourself the following questions:

- Have I presented my opinion clearly? Will the reader understand exactly how I feel?
- Do I give enough examples, illustrations, situations, and other details? Will the details help the reader feel the same way? [*See* Revising: Sample Revision for Specific Detail *in Part I*.]
- Would different details improve the explanation of my opinion?

- Have I been concise? Have I omitted insignificant details? Have I avoided getting carried away by my emotions? [*See* Revising: Sample Revision for Wordiness *in Part I.*]
- Are sentences polished, placing emphasis on the most important ideas? Are main ideas in the main clauses? [*See* Revising: Sample Revision for Sentence Variety *in Part I.*]
- Have I used the techniques of emphasis? [*See* Revising: Sample Revision for Emphasis *in Part I.*]
- Do transitions connect and show relationship among the ideas? Have I used the most effective transitions? [*See* Revising: Sample Revision for Transition *in Part I.*]

Revise so that you can answer "yes" to the preceding questions. [*See* Revising *in Part I for additional, more general guidelines for polishing.*]

STEP 6   **Revising • Typing the Final Draft**

Next, type a final copy of your letter. In order to prepare the inside address, find the editor's name on the editorial page.

You may use a typical business-letter format [*see* Letters: Business Letters *earlier in Part III*], or, as some editors prefer, you may type your letter on a single, standard 8½" x 11" sheet of paper, double-spaced, maintaining standard margins. Although this format permits you to omit a formal heading and inside address, you should begin with the salutation *Dear Editor* to identify your purpose. In addition, your name and address must appear on the page, preferably at the end. Most papers will not print your address or phone number, but the editor must have this information for verification. (It's for your protection. Someone else could submit a letter with your name and cause undue embarrassment.) Editors almost never print anonymous letters.

STEP 7   **Proofreading • Checking the Mechanics**

Before you mail your letter, check for mechanical details. [*Check Parts I and IV for explanations and examples of writing techniques.*] Finally, check spelling and word choice.

If you used a business-letter format, ask yourself the following specific questions regarding the form of the letter:

- Have I used an accurate and complete letterhead, adding today's date, properly punctuated?
- Have I included an accurate and complete inside address, including the editor's name and title, all properly punctuated?

- Did I use an appropriate salutation followed by a colon?
- Is the spacing accurate between the letterhead and the inside address, between the inside address and the salutation, and between the salutation and the body of the letter?
- Is the closing appropriate for a letter to the editor?
- Have I signed the letter?
- Have I included my daytime phone number?
- Is the spacing accurate between the body of the letter and the closing and between the closing and the signature?
- Have I followed a consistent style, either the block, the modified-block, or the modified-block style with indented paragraphs?
- Is my letter neat and business-like?

If you used the less formal format, ask yourself these questions:

- Did I begin with the salutation *Dear Editor* to identify my purpose?
- Have I limited my letter to a single page?
- Did I maintain standard margins (2" at the top, 1" at the left, right, and bottom)?
- Is my letter double-spaced, neat, and free from typing or printing errors?
- Does my name appear on the page, preferably at the bottom, along with my address and daytime phone number?

You should be able to answer "yes" to these questions.

When you are satisfied, fold the letter and mail it in a properly addressed envelope. [*See Step 7 in* Letters: Business Letters *for tips.*]

SAMPLE EDITORIAL LETTER

The following letter to the editor expresses the writer's opinion regarding an upcoming congressional election. Compare the letter with the persuasive essay [see Persuasion *in Part II*] and the opinion essay [*see* Opinion *in Part II*], both of which deal with the same subject. By comparing the three, you can better understand the letter to the editor.

Norman K. Blackwade
3456 Georgetown Road
Salt River, Kansas 77068-6695

October 23, 20—

Mrs. Paulette Henry, Editor
The Salt River Journal and Times
100 Second Street
Salt River, Kansas 77069-6651

Dear Editor:

Shall we increase property taxes? Ignore drug pushers? Elect a "yes" man to Congress? To answer "no" is to vote for Jerrald Kinsingtonne. Here's why.

When Republican incumbent Rodney Brolliette fought for tax incentives to lure businesses here, he ignored Kinsingtonne's warning that private citizens would pay with increased property taxes. Now, strapped with tax bills double last year's rate, citizens know whom to support.

Both candidates oppose illegal drug use. Brolliette proposes unannounced testing. Let's pretend for a minute. You go to work one morning and discover you must submit to a test. You had the flu two weeks ago; the doctor prescribed medicine. You took it. As directed. Now, you test positive. You're a drug user. Period. Kinsingtonne proposes instead a stiff crackdown on dealers: more arrests, stiffer penalties. Should you be harassed for others' wrongdoings? Kinsingtonne doesn't think so either.

In the controversy over a proposed hazardous-waste incinerator here, Kinsingtonne took an early stand to fight the plan, even before a majority joined him. Finally, Brolliette announced "me too" opposition. Too little, too late. Kinsingtonne risks what he must for what is right. And he does it now.

So there's little question of how to vote next Tuesday. Think about a "yes" man in Congress. Think about harassment over drug testing. Think about your tax bill. See what I mean?

Yours truly,

Norman K. Blackwade

Norman K. Blackwade

Analysis of the Sample Editorial Letter. The preceding sample exhibits the characteristics of a good letter to the editor. Note particularly the following items:

- The letter consistently follows the modified-block style and exhibits good format—even margins; accurate spacing; and complete and accurate letterhead, inside address, salutation, body, closing, and signature.
- The body of the letter clearly presents the writer's opinion.
- The opening paragraph catches the reader's attention. Anyone is interested in his pocketbook, and taxes hit the pocketbook. Most people feel frustrated about excessive illegal drug use. And the idea of a yes-man does not please many. So the writer uses these three approaches to attract readers.
- The opening paragraph also states the writer's point of view.
- The following three paragraphs present details to support the writer's opinion, each paragraph providing illustrations and examples to explain one point.
- The paragraphs eliminate all wordiness. [*To see how to achieve brevity, see* Revising: Sample Revision for Wordiness *in Part I.*]
- By the final paragraph, the reader may agree with the writer, but the writer forces him or her to think once again about three major issues. The writer reverses the order so that he concludes with the issues closest to home—the tax bill.

Compare this letter with the Sample for Social Sciences in Persuasion in Part II, and with the sample paper in Opinion, in Part II. Note that the editorial letter blends many of the characteristics of the two. At the same time, however, note these differences:

- While the writer used a formal style for the persuasive and the opinion essays, he's more informal in his letter to the editor. Note the use of *you*, the frequent contractions, and the sentence fragments (such as *Period.* and *Too little, too late.*).
- The letter omits many of the supporting details used in the persuasive and opinion essays. It includes only the most important details. Brevity characterizes a letter to the editor.
- In addition, the arrangement of details varies from that in the two essays. The letter discusses taxes first, in case the reader fails to finish the letter. Most people put their pocketbooks before the environment and illegal-drug use. Tax bills hit home!

- The letter relies on personal reaction. In the third paragraph, for instance, the writer directs the reader's attention to his or her own situation if Brolliette's proposal were approved. By putting the reader in an uncomfortable situation, the writer better illustrates his point.

With these points in mind, you should be able to write an effective letter to an editor. Compare yours with this sample and its analysis. Then mail it!

One final warning: Because letters to the editor may appear in print as soon as a few days or as late as six weeks after you send it, you may want to recall your letter if it no longer deals with current events.

SOCIAL LETTERS

Social letters, sometimes called *friendly letters*, bear little resemblance to business or editorial letters. Rarely is a social letter written on letterhead. None use an inside address, but do, of course, include the date. The salutation usually addresses the reader by first name, and the closing suggests personal relationships. Social letters are rarely typed, although busy people who rely on their word processors are likely to type them, insisting that a letter via a word processor is better than no letter at all!

Apart from format and style, the content of a social letter also bears little resemblance to business or editorial letters. In general, a social letter serves one of the following purposes:

- To correspond with a friend or relative in lieu of a personal conversation
- To thank someone for a gift, entertainment, or other kindness
- To congratulate someone for an achievement
- To offer condolences
- To extend an invitation
- To accept or decline an invitation

While e-mail is more popular, quicker, and in many respects easier than writing and mailing a social letter, it is never a socially acceptable substitute for the purposes listed here.

CHARACTERISTICS

Although the social letter is less structured than other letters, certain characteristics are usually evident. Most social letters

- omit a heading or letterhead form unless the receiver needs to be reminded of your return address,
- include a date, usually for later reference (sometimes friends keep personal letters for years!),
- use an appropriate, friendly salutation followed by a comma,
- follow an informal style, like written conversation, unless the subject of the letter, such as an invitation to a rather formal affair or an expression of condolence, requires a somewhat more formal style,
- use an appropriate, friendly closing, followed by a comma,
- include a signature line but no typewritten name, even if the letter for some reason is printed,
- follow the same style on the envelope as in the letter, either handwritten or typewritten.

PROCESS

The process of writing a social letter follows a more relaxed approach than virtually any other piece of writing.

STEP 1 **Prewriting • Getting Ready to Write**

If you are writing a friendly letter just to keep up to date with friends and family, you may want to jot down a list of items you want to be sure to mention. This will keep you from forgetting some detail you wanted to share.

If you are writing a thank-you note, a note of condolence, or an expression of congratulations, you probably have only brief comments and need nothing more than to try a couple of drafts until the note sounds just the way you want.

If you are writing an invitation, put the vital information in a list to make sure you do not omit any essential details: date, time, place, purpose, dress, and an R.S.V.P., if necessary. (R.S.V.P. is an abbreviation for the French *répondez s'il vous plaît*, which means *please respond*. Such a notation on invitations requires recipients to let you know whether or not they will attend, thus enabling you to make appropriate preparations.)

STEP 2 **Writing • Putting Your Thoughts on Paper**

With no more effort than suggested in Step 1, you will probably be ready to write. Because friendly letters usually reflect your personality, you should write from the heart. While some general organization will help your friends and family follow your thoughts, you need not depend on outlines or formal paragraph structure. Do use good grammar. Do write effective sentences. Do make your letter interesting. Do use accurate spelling and mechanics. Do follow good usage. At the same time, however, aim for a conversational style, as if you were talking face to face with your reader.

STEP 3   Revising and Proofreading • Checking the Letter

Before you mail a social letter, do what you would do with any piece of writing: check it over. Sometimes we omit words or word endings, sometimes we misspell words; sometimes a sentence does not sound the way we thought it would when we wrote it. Check for these kinds of problems. Sometimes the reader is offended by a written remark that you intended as humor. Sometimes the reader may misinterpret your intentions by the way you word a sentence. Try reading the letter aloud to yourself to catch any possible problems.

When you are satisfied with the letter, fold it, put it in a properly addressed envelope, and mail it! [*See Step 7 in* Letters: Business Letters *for tips.*]

SAMPLE SOCIAL LETTER

The following social letter, an invitation to an outdoor cookout, illustrates one of several kinds of social letters.

July 8, 20—

Dear Gretchen,

Before these delightful summer evenings grow short, Bob and I are looking forward to an outdoor picnic with a group of our dearest friends—you, of course, among them! On Saturday, July 23, we hope you'll join us for an old-fashioned barbecue at our home, with appetizers at 5:00 and dinner at 6:30. Dress casually, since we'll be on the lawn. And maybe a sweater, in case the evening breeze grows cool.

Please let us know we can expect you!

Love,

Allison

 Analysis of the Sample Social Letter. The social invitation includes the essential details: time, date, place, purpose, dress, and a request for a response. Note that the style maintains a friendly, informal air, including a sentence fragment (*And maybe a sweater . . . .*). Note the date but the absence of a heading or letterhead form and inside address. The salutation greets the addressee by her first name. The closing expresses a personal relationship; and the signature, first name only, indicates a close friendship.

Literary Analyses

Students are asked to write literary analyses most often in literature classes. The assignment may require a critical overview of the author; an analysis of literary elements; or a well-organized evaluation of a literary work, such as a novel, short story, drama, poem, or nonfiction article or essay. No matter its purpose, an effective analysis of any piece of literature must demonstrate thorough understanding of the literary work under discussion.

Writers face three kinds of analyses—of an author, of literary elements, or of specific works. Within those three, however, the options vary significantly. For instance, the writer may discuss a specific poem in terms of the author's characteristic use of literary devices, thus combining the three general kinds of analyses into one. Likewise, a writer may develop a thorough analysis of a short story merely by discussing its theme. While working through the octopus-like literary analysis, then, you will study the main characteristics and then add some variations found in typical analyses.

FOR AN AUTHOR

The analysis of an author presumes familiarity with an author's work; thus, it is probably the most demanding of all the types of literary analyses. While an author analysis may require formidable research, you can write a good paper by narrowing the topic to deal with one or more short representative works with a common theme. Or, by treating an atypical work, you can develop a good analysis showing how that work differs from the author's usual style or subject matter.

Following are the general characteristics for a literary analysis for an author.

CHARACTERISTICS

While some of the following characteristics are peculiar to an analysis for an author, others should be included in most any literary analysis. A good literary analysis of an author should

- show evidence of a broad understanding of an author's work, including style and general themes,
- include a topic or thesis sentence narrow enough to develop fully within the scope of the paper [*see* topic sentence *and* thesis sentence *in the Glossary for quick reference, and see* Writing a Paragraph *and* Writing a Multi-Paragraph Paper *in Part I for detailed explanation and examples*],
- include details from specific works to support general statements in the topic or thesis sentence,
- enclose all direct quotations in quotation marks,
- paraphrase long passages when citing from the author's works [*see* Paraphrase *later in Part III*],
- show evidence of research, including documentation, particularly in a long or complicated paper [*see* Research Paper *later in Part III for information on documentation*],
- follow a rather formal writing style, including the use of third-person point of view [*see* point of view *in the Glossary*],
- use the present tense to discuss the work but the past tense to discuss the literary or historical period or author's background,
- conclude with a general statement about the author supported by the content of the paper [*see* conclusion *in the Glossary*].

PROCESS

Use the following process to develop a literary analysis of an author.

STEP 1   **Prewriting • Reading the Author**
In order to write an analysis, the primary—and forever ongoing—demand is for a careful reading and thorough understanding of the author's work. If you have not read all of it, then be certain that you have read at least all representative works. In many cases, more than one reading may be necessary.

STEP 2   **Prewriting • Doing Necessary Research**
A lengthy paper may call for not only your own analysis but also that of others. Be sure you understand what is expected of you. If research is part of the job, be thorough in your examination of others' evaluations. Your paper could, in fact, analyze contrasting reactions to the author.

[*If research is part of your task, see* Research Paper *later in Part III for an explanation of the research process, particularly note-taking and documentation. In addition, see* Paraphrase, Precis, *and* Notes: For a Paper, *also in Part III.*]

STEP 3   **Prewriting • Narrowing the Subject**

Writing a literary analysis of an author requires a thoughtful narrowing of the subject. You cannot say everything there is to say about any author in a short paper, so your purpose is your guide. Clearly, if the purpose of the analysis is to discuss the author's favorite literary devices, the devices must be part of the analysis. If you propose a unique interpretation of the author's work, then your discussion details evidence supporting your position.

In any paper, space limits what you can say. While you must support every idea with adequate details, forget trying to include everything you know about an author. Resist the temptation to include unusual details just because you think they're interesting.

So, to narrow the subject of your paper, jot down your main idea. Then, ask yourself which three or four supporting ideas will explain, clarify, or illustrate your main idea. List them.

STEP 4   **Prewriting • Writing the Topic or Thesis Sentence**

A carefully worded topic or thesis sentence must—absolutely must—clarify the direction and purpose of the paper. In Step 3, you narrowed your subject, wrote a main idea, and listed three or four supporting ideas. Now, using this information, develop a topic or thesis sentence. [*See* Writing a Paragraph *in Part I for a careful explanation and examples of the topic sentence. See* Writing a Multi-Paragraph Paper *in Part I for a careful explanation and examples of the thesis sentence.*]

Compare your topic or thesis sentence with the following examples:

Topic sentences:

Neil Simon's light-hearted one-liners make his plays box-office successes. (A series of examples from a half dozen successful plays will support the topic sentence.)

Alvin Toffler predicts a future worth fearing. (Examples from *Future Shock* and *The Third Wave* will show fearful futures.)

Thesis sentences:

Susan Howatch attracted contemporary readers with three books exhibiting her prowess as a Gothic novelist. (Each of the three body paragraphs will illustrate the Gothic characteristics of separate Howatch books: *Penmarric, Sins of the Fathers,* and *The Rich Are Different.*)

Herman Wouk uses his understanding of the phenomenon of war to build exceedingly long, complex, and poignant novels. (Two supporting paragraphs will deal with the complexity and poignancy of *The Winds of War* and *War and Remembrance*.)

STEP 5   **Prewriting • Choosing a Method of Development**

A literary analysis can be developed by a variety of methods, including comparison and contrast, cause and effect, and opinion. [*See entries for each in Part II*.] Parts of the paper may also include definition, description, and analogy. [*See entries for each in Part II*.] Think about the possible ways by which you can develop your topic or thesis sentence.

For instance, if you plan to show how events in an author's life influenced her to write certain novels, then a cause and effect development may be the most useful. If you plan to explain your admiration for an author's style, then an opinion paper may best serve your purpose.

Select the method that seems best for your purpose.

STEP 6   **Prewriting • Organizing the Paper**

Next, develop a plan for the paragraph or paper by organizing the list of details developed in Step 3. Use chronological order or some order of importance. [*See* chronological order *and* order of importance *in the Glossary*.]

If you are developing a longer paper, list two, three, or four supporting ideas under each of the main ideas. For all practical purposes, you have developed a scratch outline. [*See* Outlines *later in Part III*.] Your outline should give a miniature view of your completed paper.

STEP 7   **Writing • Following the Plan**

The careful planning you have done in Steps 1–6 will pay off now with relative ease in writing. Begin with your introductory statement and topic or thesis sentence. Develop your ideas in accord with your outline, changing the outline as needed if the order seems faulty. As you write, try to include the following:

- Specific supporting details from the work itself, either quoted and enclosed in quotation marks or paraphrased
- Transitions to bridge ideas and paragraphs [*see* transitions *in the Glossary*]

As you write, be sure to avoid the following:

- Giving a mere summary of the plot rather than a discussion of your ideas
- Quoting the author's works without accurate use of quotation marks
- Using glittering generalities—words, phrases, or whole sentences—without the support of examples or details

Finally, add a conclusion that effectively ties together your main ideas with a clincher (in a paragraph) or a concluding paragraph (in a longer paper). [*For additional help with conclusions, see* Writing a Paragraph *or* Writing a Multi-Paragraph Paper *in Part I.*]

STEP 8   Revising • Polishing the Content

If you have followed the suggestions in these steps, your first draft will be in reasonably good shape. Take time now to review the items in Step 7, checking to see that you have indeed heeded their advice.

When you feel satisfied, ask yourself the following questions to check for other areas of possible weakness:

- Have I used good sentence structure?
- Does the structure emphasize main ideas? [*See* Revising: Sample Revision for Emphasis in *Part I.*]
- Is the structure varied? [*See* Revising: Sample Revision for Sentence Variety *in Part I.*]
- Have I maintained a consistent third-person point of view?
- Have I used the present tense to discuss the author's work and the past tense to describe the author's background?
- Have I used specific rather than general words and phrases? [*See* Revising: Sample Revision for Specific Detail *in Part I.*]
- Have I avoided plagiarism by using quotation marks around words not my own? [*See* plagiarism *in the Glossary.*]
- Have I eliminated any materials that do not support my main idea? [*See* Revising: Sample Revision for Unity *in Part I.*]
- Have I included adequate transitions to provide coherence between sentences and paragraphs? [*See* Revising: Sample Revision for Transition *in Part I.*]

Revise your first draft so that it reads smoothly and follows good writing style.

STEP 9   Proofreading • Checking the Mechanical Details

When you have the content molded into a solid, well-developed composition, make a final check for the mechanical details. Be particularly careful in checking quotations or references from outside sources. Check not only for accuracy in quotations and in their punctuation, but also for accuracy in documentation. [*See* Research Paper *later in Part III for additional information.*]

SAMPLE LITERARY ANALYSIS FOR AN AUTHOR

The following sample paper uses three representative poems to discuss the characteristic style of poet Emily Dickinson.

Alone in a Crowded World: Emily Dickinson and Her Poems

Emily Dickinson lived a solitary life, maintaining little communication with people and the outside world. In fact, she preferred nature and the Deity over people and things of this earth, so the extensive travels to which her poems refer took place only in her mind. Three representative poems indicate how Dickinson related her lonely life in her work.

Her solitary life reflects a personal choice. "This is my letter to the World/That never wrote to Me," Dickinson writes while expressing her resentment toward society. The only "person" who truly understands her, Dickinson says, is Mother Nature. Although Dickinson admits she cannot see the actual person, she nevertheless remains convinced that Mother Nature is real and sincerely cares for her children, Dickinson concludes. As a result, the poet sees little need to communicate with the less faithful outside world.

Perhaps because of her identification with Mother Nature, Dickinson also expresses a fondness for nature and the supernatural. She admits preferring to be alone with the birds and the trees in her garden to attending a gala event with hundreds of people. As part of her belief in the supernatural, however, she faces the reality of death and often wonders what follows. While she admits that she has never spoken with God, she believes she is assured of a place in Heaven. In "This World Is not Conclusion" she states, "A Species stands beyond—/Invisible, as Music—/But positive, as Sound." Throughout the poem, Miss Dickinson talks about the attempts man has made through the years to explain the metaphysical and how he has failed, so in this manner she affirms her belief in nature and the supernatural.

Because she maintained a solitary life, however, she used her imagination to explore the outside world. In the poem "I Never Saw a Moor," Dickinson embarks on a mental journey admitting that while she has never seen many places, she knows "how Heather looks/And what a Billow be," referring to the moors and the seashores of England. Her solitary life, then, did not close her mind to the outside world, no matter how sadly it reflected itself to her. An avid reader, Dickinson no doubt traveled through her books as well as through her obviously active mind.

> Poems such as these give us a clear picture of Emily Dickinson's beliefs, choices, and lifestyle. Dickinson, who preferred to see no adults other than her own family, expressed her characteristic attitudes in her poetry: her reciprocal love of Mother Nature, her corresponding belief in the supernatural, and her delight in mental voyages. While the people of her era described her as eccentric, unethical, even rebellious, she has proved to be one of the greatest poets of all time.

Analysis of the Sample Literary Analysis for an Author. The preceding five-paragraph theme illustrates a literary analysis using representative works to discuss the author. The three poems, each addressed in a separate paragraph, serve to introduce the author. Note these specific characteristics:

- The first paragraph introduces the three ideas developed successively in the following paragraphs. The final sentence of the first paragraph functions as the thesis sentence. The reference to three poems, as yet unnamed, suggests the means by which the ideas of solitary life, respect for nature and the spiritual, and mental travel will be developed.
- Quotations from the three poems, enclosed in quotation marks, support the writer's main ideas.
- The slash, or diagonal mark (/), shows where lines of poetry end.
- References to other ideas in the poems, paraphrased rather than quoted, further support the main ideas.
- The organization of the body, in order of importance from most to least important, follows the order set out in the introduction.
- While the first paragraph, discussing Dickinson's life, is written in the past tense, paragraphs discussing her works are in the present tense. Because the works still exist but Dickinson does not, the change in tense is logical.
- Likewise, the fourth paragraph begins and ends in the past tense, discussing her life, while the middle paragraphs use the present tense, discussing her work as it continues to exist.
- The conclusion, like the introduction, uses past tense to reflect on Dickinson's life.
- Sentence variety, both in structure and length, credits the writer with good style.
- Transitions link sentences as well as paragraphs into a smoothly flowing composition.

Compare this sample paper with others in the section for a thorough overview of writing about literature.

FOR LITERARY ELEMENTS

An analysis for literary elements explores or evaluates a technical aspect of a literary work. Probably the most common approach to writing about literature, the analysis of a literary element thoroughly examines some literary device that helps weld together the mosaic of the entire work. Common elements include the following:

characterization	rhyme
setting	imagery
plot	figures of speech
theme	symbol
dialogue	tone
point of view	mood
rhythm	

CHARACTERISTICS

Following are two lists of characteristics. One shows elements included in virtually any analysis of literary elements. The other shows elements included in the specific topics. A combination of the lists will give a thorough description of the respective approaches to this kind of analysis.

First, any analysis of literary elements should

- show a thorough understanding of the work as it gains meaning from the literary elements,
- include an introduction naming the work and its author,
- include a topic or thesis sentence that names the literary elements to be discussed and at least implies the means by which you will develop the discussion [*see* Writing a Paragraph *and* Writing a Multi-Paragraph Paper *in Part I for a detailed explanation and examples*],
- follow a clear plan,
- support your ideas with details from the work, either quoted [*see* quotation marks *in the Glossary*] or paraphrased [*see* Paraphrase *later in Part III*],
- explain how the literary elements affect the interpretation of the literature,
- document any references to outside sources,
- follow a rather formal writing style, limiting point of view to third person,
- use the present tense to discuss the work but the past tense to discuss the literary or historical period or the author's background,

- conclude with a reaction to the literary elements as they expand the work's meaning.

To effectively address certain literary elements, include these additional analytical characteristics:

For character:

- An analysis of what the character says, thinks, and does, pointing out any discrepancies
- An analysis of what others say about the character
- An analysis of any differences between what the reader observes of the character and what others say about him or her
- An evaluation of any direct description by the author about the character
- A statement of position as protagonist or antagonist [*see* protagonist *and* antagonist *in the Glossary*]

For setting:

- An evaluation of the relationship of setting to the work's mood [*see* mood *in the Glossary*]
- An evaluation of the setting as it reflects the work's theme [*see* theme *in the Glossary*]
- An evaluation of the setting's impact on the characters
- An analysis of the setting's impact on the conflict [*see* conflict *in the Glossary*]
- An explanation of change in setting as it affects change in mood, characters, or conflict

For plot:

- An analysis of the exposition, or beginning, of the story, drama, or novel
- An evaluation of the rising action [*see* rising action *in the Glossary*]
- An analysis of the climax, or high point [*see* climax *in the Glossary*]
- An analysis of the falling action [*see* falling action *in the Glossary*]
- An examination of special techniques of plot, such as foreshadowing and flashback [*see the corresponding Glossary entries*]

For theme:

- A statement of the major idea or theme of the story, drama, or novel
- An analysis of evidence supporting the theme

For dialogue:

- A description of the dialogue's purpose
- An analysis of its appropriateness, considering word choice, sentence length, and cadence
- An analysis of its impact on characterization [*refer to the earlier section of this list* For character]
- An analysis of its impact on the plot [*refer to the earlier section of this list* For plot]

For point of view:

- A description of the point of view: first, second, or third person, including the third person omniscient [*see* point of view *in the Glossary*]
- An analysis of the impact of the point of view on theme, plot, conflict, or characterization

For rhythm:

- A description of the rhythm's pattern [*see* rhythm *in the Glossary*]
- An analysis of the impact of any departure from the pattern
- An evaluation of the impact of rhythm on word or thought groups
- An evaluation of rhythm as one of the many sound devices available to a poet, including its interaction with the other devices to create an overall impact

For rhyme:

- A description of the pattern, including internal rhyme if any [*see* rhyme *in the Glossary*]
- An analysis of the impact of any departure from the pattern
- An evaluation of the impact of rhyme on word or thought groups
- An evaluation of rhyme as one of the many sound devices available to a poet, including its interaction with the other devices to create an overall impact

For imagery:

- An indication of the specific image or images being analyzed [*see* imagery *in the Glossary*]
- An explanation of the development of the image or images throughout the work
- An analysis of the importance of the image or images to the meaning or enjoyment of the work
- An evaluation of the interrelationship between the image or images and other literary elements

For figures of speech:

- An indication of the specific figure(s) of speech being analyzed [*see* figure of speech *in the Glossary for a list and examples of the most common figures of speech*]
- An explanation of the use of the figure(s) of speech throughout the work
- An analysis of the importance of the figure(s) of speech to the meaning or enjoyment of the work
- An evaluation of the interrelationship between the figure(s) of speech and other literary elements

For symbolism:

- A careful explanation of the development of the symbol [*see* symbol *in the Glossary*]
- A symbolic interpretation of the work, including citations of specific instances throughout the work
- An evaluation of the overall impact of the symbol on the work's theme or underlying message

For tone:

- A description of tone as it appears throughout the work or within a specified section of the work [*see* tone *in the Glossary*]
- An analysis of how the author achieved this tone
- An explanation of the impact of the tone on the work's theme

For mood:

- A description of mood as it appears throughout the work or within a specified section of the work [*see* mood *in the Glossary*]
- An analysis of how the author achieved this mood
- An explanation of the impact of the mood on the work's theme

PROCESS

Use the following process to develop an analysis of a particular literary element within a work.

STEP 1   **Prewriting • Reading for Analysis**
With any literary analysis, careful reading precedes any other activity. Once you decide which of the many elements you will discuss in a given work, whether as a result of an assignment or personal preference, reread the work searching for examples. Study the element's relationship to other parts of the work and its impact on the work.

As you reread, make notes. If you are using your own copy of the book, you may wish to pencil in notations of important words, phrases, and passages. If you are using a copy not your own, take notes on note cards, separate sheets, or gummed note sheets that can later be removed from the page without marring the print. [*See* Notes: For a Paper *later in Part III.*]

STEP 2   **Prewriting • Narrowing the Topic**
When your careful reading is finished, you are ready to narrow the focus of your paper. If, for instance, you want to write about the setting of a short story, you must decide what you will develop as your main idea. Will you discuss how it enhances the theme, how it puts hardships on the characters, how it suggests the mood? Or if you want to write about an important image in a poem, will you discuss how the author develops it, the effect it has on the poem's meaning, what it means?

Narrowing the topic to a single focus comes most easily by looking for repeated ideas in your notes from Step 1. The focus must lend itself to thorough development within the limits of your paper and deal with some important aspect of the work.

Determine the direction your topic will take. Write a sentence or two stating the focus. For example:

Emily Dickinson's biographer said she domesticated the universe. Her images make the spiritual world as familiar as household items.

STEP 3   **Prewriting • Planning the Paper**
Next, list examples from the work that support your topic. Use the notes you developed in Step 1. Your list may look something like this:

Dickinson's domestic images:
"housewife" items
    broom
    dusting
    sewing items—thread, ravelings, and so on

apron
scattered duds
sweeping

Then organize the items in some logical manner. The organization may show relationships, cause and effect, comparisons or contrasts, or opinion. [*See* Cause and Effect, Comparison and Contrast, *or* Opinion *in Part II*.] Or you may arrange the items by some order of importance or perhaps by the chronological order of the appearance in the literary work. [*See* chronological order *and* order of importance *in the Glossary*.]

Completed, the organized list may look like this:

Dickinson's Domestic Images:
1. "Housewife" chores
   a. Sweeping
   b. Dusting
2. Seamstress items
   a. Thread
   b. Ravelings
   c. Duds

The organization in the preceding outline follows the chronological organization of the poem from which the examples come. Some items from the original list have been reworded or omitted. You may need to make similar changes in your own list. [*For further examples, see* Outlines: For a Paper *later in Part III*.]

 Because the student's most frequent error in writing any kind of literary analysis is summarizing plots instead of analyzing, be certain to develop a plan similar to the one here in Step 3. Then follow it! So doing will prevent your falling into this common trap.

STEP 4   **Prewriting • Checking Other Sources**

If your assignment requires outside research, use the plan you developed to guide your reading. It is quite possible, however, that you need not do research other than reread the literary work itself. Follow your instructor's suggestions.

If you do outside research, take careful notes, making sure to include quotation marks around an author's exact words. When you transfer this material to your own paper, you must be able to document accurately in order to avoid plagiarism. [*See* Research Paper *later in Part III for a complete discussion of note-taking, quotations, and documentation. See also* Notes: For a Paper, Precis, *and* Paraphrase *later in Part III for help with note taking*.]

STEP 5 **Writing • Following the Plan**

Write the first draft by following the plan you completed in Step 3. Begin with an introductory statement or an introductory paragraph, depending on whether you are writing a single paragraph or a multi-paragraph paper. Include in the introduction the following:

- Title of the work
- Author's name
- Specific literary element to be discussed
- An indication of that element's importance in the overall work

Follow the introductory segment with your topic or thesis statement.

Develop the subtopics or the body paragraphs, following the plan established in Step 3 or revising the plan as necessary. Try to include the following kinds of details:

- Examples sufficient to clarify your ideas
- Supporting details from the work, either quoted or paraphrased
- Transitions from one supporting idea to another and from one main idea to another
- Transitions that help your reader follow your organization and the relationships among your ideas [*see* transitions *in the Glossary*]

Finally, add a conclusion that refers to your topic or thesis statement and makes some general statement about the literary element as it lends importance to the work.

STEP 6 **Revising • Improving the Content**

In order to revise, ask yourself the following questions:

- Is the introduction effective and complete?
- Is the plan clear?
- Are transitions adequate and effective? [*See* Revising: Sample Revision for Transition *in Part I.*]
- Have I developed paragraphs adequately with sufficient supporting details, including specific details from the work, either quoted or paraphrased? [*See* Revising: Sample Revision for Specific Detail *in Part I.*]
- Have I avoided plagiarism by using quotation marks around words not my own and documenting accurately? [*See* plagiarism *in the Glossary.*]

- Do the main ideas work together to say something about the literary element as it affects the entire work?
- Have I avoided retelling the story?
- Have I maintained a rather formal writing style, using the third-person point of view and accurate verb tense?
- Is the vocabulary, including appropriate literary terms, accurate?
- Are my sentences varied both in length and in structure? [*See* Revising: Sample Revision for Sentence Variety *in Part I*.]
- Do my sentences carry the most effective emphasis for their respective subjects? Are the main ideas in the main clauses? [*See* Revising: Sample Revision for Emphasis *in Part I*.]
- Does the conclusion refer to the topic or thesis sentence and at the same time make a general statement about the effect of the specific literary element on the work as a whole? [*See* conclusion *in the Glossary*.]

Make necessary revisions until your paper satisfies all the preceding suggestions.

STEP 7 **Proofreading • Checking Details**

As you read your final draft, check for details of grammar, mechanics, and usage. [*See Part IV for rules and examples*.] Finally, check spelling and word choice.

A NOTE ABOUT THE SAMPLES

Now that you know what an analysis of a literary element should include and what process you should follow to develop an effective analysis, study the three following examples and their respective analyses. The first sample traces the images in a Dickinson poem, the second analyzes the characters of a short story, and the third, a full-length paper, examines the development of a single symbol in a novel. By comparing these and other sample papers throughout this section, you will better understand the various kinds of analyses.

SAMPLE LITERARY ANALYSIS FOR AN IMAGE

The following single-paragraph analysis of an image in a poem illustrates the characteristics of an analysis of a literary element. Compare this example with a three-paragraph analysis of the same poem in the sample for literary works, later in Part III.

Mother Nature Domesticated

Emily Dickinson's poem, "She Sweeps with Many-Colored Brooms," works well because of a predominant image. An extended metaphor, which is sustained throughout the poem, generates the domestic image. Because Emily Dickinson lived as a recluse and because she felt Mother Nature was her only real friend, many of her images domesticate Mother Nature in a manner that makes the spiritual familiar. In "She Sweeps," Dickinson uses common household images to describe Mother Nature creating a sunset. The apron-clad housewife sweeps but forgets to dust. A careless sweeper, she "leaves the shreds behind." She also leaves scattered duds and threads and ravelings from her sewing strewn across the eastern sky. The clouds, which she sees as flying aprons, stay until the "brooms fade softly into stars." By using the sweeping-dusting-sewing images, Dickinson makes the universal sunset the result of a careless housewife; thus, as some critics view Dickinson, she domesticates the universe.

 Analysis of the Sample Literary Analysis for an Image. The preceding single paragraph includes the basic characteristics of an analysis of a literary element. Note these details:

- The introductory segment includes a topic sentence as the first sentence.
- Details both paraphrased and quoted from the poem support the main idea. Adequate details appear without retelling the poem's story or paraphrasing the entire work.
- Varied sentence structure enhances the formal style.
- The present tense appears accurately throughout the discussion of the work.
- Transitions effectively connect ideas.
- The paragraph follows clear organization.
- The conclusion refers not only to the topic sentence but also to the importance of the image in Dickinson's style. [*See the earlier section* For an Author *to compare this comment with a literary analysis of Dickinson as an author*.]

Compare this sample with the later sample addressing the same poem. [*See* For Literary Works *later in this section*.]

SAMPLE LITERARY ANALYSIS FOR CHARACTER

The following analysis, also a single paragraph, contrasts two characters in a short story as the contrast affects theme. Thus, the paragraph follows the organization of a comparison-and-contrast paper [*see* Comparison and Contrast *in Part II*] but follows the content plan for a literary analysis.

Chee and Old Man Fat: A Study in Contrast

Juanita Patero and Siyowin Miller in "Chee's Daughter" depict the two main characters so that their contrasts emphasize the story's theme. Chee and his father-in-law, Old Man Fat, exhibit significant personality differences. For example, Chee works and lives on his farm, while Old Man Fat works in a small trading post near the highway. Chee is strong and hard-working; he enjoys being outdoors, working on his farm. On the other hand, Old Man Fat shows nothing but laziness. He stays inside the trading post and does as little work as possible. In addition, Chee depends only on himself and the land. To earn money, he sells the crops he grows on his farm. Old Man Fat, in contrast, depends on the trading post and on other people. He charges tourists to see his Navajo mother-in-law weaving and to see the inside of a "real" Navajo home. Perhaps, though, their personalities show the greatest differences in their general attitudes. Chee, the very caring and generous person, loves his farm with all his heart. He believes that "a man took care of his land and it in turn took care of him." In contrast, Old Man Fat, greedy and selfish, does not care about land or anyone else; he cares only about himself and making money. The difference between the two characters underlines the story's theme: Land, the most precious natural resource, will not forsake a man who shares the "feeling of wholeness and of oneness with the sun and earth and growing things." It is caring for land that allows Chee to finally regain his daughter from Old Man Fat, caring for land that, unlike people, does not cheat.

Analysis of the Sample Literary Analysis for Character. The preceding single paragraph illustrates an analysis of a literary element developed by means of contrast. These special effects bear noting:

- The introductory sentence includes the essential information.
- The topic sentence, here the second sentence of the paragraph, establishes the contrast to be developed.
- The organization flows smoothly with the use of the part-by-part plan. [*See* Comparison and Contrast *in Part II for methods of organizing comparison and contrast papers, and see* part-by-part organization *in the Glossary.*]
- Effective transitions move the reader smoothly through the paragraph and maintain clear parallel contrasts, using such phrases as *for example, while, on the other hand, in addition, by contrast,* and *though.*
- Details from the story provide adequate support for the three subtopics.
- The analysis avoids the common pitfall of retelling the story.
- The conclusion refers to the topic sentence and identifies how the literary element affects the work as a whole.

SAMPLE LITERARY ANALYSIS FOR A SYMBOL

The following multi-paragraph paper analyzes the use of a single symbol in a long novel. A complex paper discusses a complex text, and it illustrates both creativity and understanding of one element of a highly complex novel. Compare this paper with others in this section, not only in terms of development but also in terms of content and structure.

Melville, the Weaver

In the course of his novel *Moby Dick*, Herman Melville sets out three basic parts of a complex motif of weaving. By careful examination of each in the order in which they appear, one can see a beautifully structured motif emerging.

> The first part of this motif appears in the chapter "The Mat-Maker": As I kept passing and repassing the filling or woof of marline between the long yarns of the warp, using my own hand for the shuttle, and as Queequeg, standing sideways, ever and anon slid his heavy oaken sword between the threads . . . it seemed as if this were the Loom of Time, and I myself were a shuttle. . . . The straight warp of necessity, not to be swerved from its ultimate course; . . . free will still free to ply her shuttle between given threads; and chance, though restrained in its play within the right lines of necessity, and sideways in its motions directed by free will, though thus prescribed to by both, chance by turns rules either and has the last featuring blow at events.

Melville leaves no question in his reader's mind at this point. Every symbol of the larger motif is spelled out: *Necessity, the warp, is being woven with free will, the woof.* Though restrained by both necessity and free will, chance, the force behind the shuttle, yields the final result.

Now that Melville has introduced the motif, he becomes more symbolic in "As Bower in the Arsacides":

> . . . the industrious earth beneath was as a weaver's loom, with a gorgeous carpet on it, whereof the ground-vine tendrils formed the warp and woof, and the living flowers the figures . . . .Through the lacings of the leaves, the great sun seemed a flying shuttle weaving

the unwearied verdure. . . . Now amid the green, life-restless loom of that Arsacidean wood the great, white, worshipped skeleton lay lounging—a gigantic idler! Yet, as the ever-woven verdant warp and woof intermixed and hummed around him, the mighty idler seemed the sunning weaver; himself all woven over with the vines. . . . Life enfolded Death; Death trellised Life; the grim god wived with youthful Life, and begat him curly-headed glories.

A paradox seems to emerge: Both the sun, traditionally a life force, and the gigantic idler, an obvious death symbol, are named as weavers—the gigantic idler a "sunning" weaver, at that! The last line, however, resolves the apparent paradox: The grim god, here obviously Death, and youthful Life are wedded. They have become one and act together as the force behind the shuttle, that force already recognized as chance. Man, therefore, has no control over life or death. He cannot, within Melville's symbolism, use his free will to weave the pattern of life as he wishes: He lacks "the last featuring blow at events." Indeed, Ishmael did state, "It seemed as if I myself were a shuttle," but the word "seemed" offers the key. Even Job knows (Job 7:6) that "My days are swifter than a weaver's shuttle." People cannot control their days.

Melville wants his readers to recognize that this search for the whale, this quest in the open sea, and, more figuratively, this lifetime quest for answers is in some way fated. In "Faustine," Charles Swinburne puts it this way: "For in the days we know not of/ Did fate begin/ Weaving the web of days that wove/ Your Doom." Similarly, in *Moby Dick's* epic qualities creeps a constant awareness of foreboding, a repetition of premonitions, the divinity but at the same time the terror of whiteness: the bleached ship *Albatross* reminiscent of the becalmed, scorching, death-filled trip of Coleridge's "Rime of the Ancient Mariner," the symbolic third day of the chase, the third time down for the whale, the third time out for Fate's lieutenant. Fate is interwoven through the entire novel. All of this evidence of fate, this quest for answers, however, is a major part of life. Oedipus sought answers; but he knew he could not get them all, was warned that he should not. Santiago pushed too far and was almost unable to return to society. So Ahab pushed too far. Because Ahab pushed too far does not mean, though, that Melville would prefer the stagnation of the lee shore. The full life comes only with that spark of divinity which causes man to search.

Carrying the motif to its final major part, Melville, in "The Gilder," shows the reader the real magnitude of this symbolic mat:

> But the mingled, mingling threads of life are woven by warp and woof: calms crossed by storms, a storm for every calm. There is no steady unretracing progress in this life; we do not advance through fixed gradations, and at last one pause. . . . Our souls are like orphans whose unwedded mothers die in bearing them: the secret of our paternity lies in their grave, and we must there to learn it.

The original woven mat of "The Mat-Maker" has, then, emerged finally as a symbol of man's life on the one hand and the pattern of all life on the other, both made up of storms and calms, of troubles and solutions, of evil and goodness. Melville would not have his reader forget that there is both evil and goodness, and he thus emphasizes that there is a calm for every storm. Shakespeare, in fact, in *All's Well That Ends Well* (Act IV, Scene 3) emphasizes that same idea: "The web of our life is of a mingled yarn, good and ill together."

How the final motif emerges can be represented this way:

Part	Warp	Woof	Weaver
1	Necessity	Free Will	Chance
2	Vines	Vines	Sun/Life/Chance
2	Vines	Vines	Skeleton/Death/Chance
3	Storms	Calms	Chance

Thus, as Queequeg's wooden sword by chance packed tightly or loosely the woof of free will through the warp of necessity, so the sun, by chance, caused the vines to wrap themselves around the idler's skeletal ribs. Nevertheless, since death is part of life, i.e., since "Life enfolds Death," the mat of life cannot be completed until death occurs. As Thomas Gray puts it in his "Ode for Music," "Weave the warp and weave the woof,/ The winding-sheet of Edward's grave." Thus, even though death is equated to chance, it is a chance that will inevitably come—fate, if you will—and it is only when the mat is completely woven; only after necessity, free will, and chance have intermingled into one piece; only after death can one see the full pattern of life. Only then is the quest for life's answers finished. So Starbuck notes as his end is near that "Strangest problems of life seem clearing." His mat is ready to be bound.

Numerous other incidents within the novel carry out the motif as well. Perhaps one of the most obvious is the warp and woof of Ahab's charts, the lines representing longitude and latitude. Certainly, Ahab exerts free will in plotting the course of his ship across such warp and woof. "The Chart" would seem to indicate that his calculations were quite scientific; but the element of chance, the fact that the White Whale may not be there, is never denied. So

Ahab plots his life across his charts never knowing where death may chance to come. He knows, however, that his death has been predicted as coming only by means of hemp. How interesting to note that hemp, too, is woven. Indeed, Ahab is said to weave the rope's yarns around the pole of his specially made harpoon. "This done, pole, iron, and rope—like the Three Fates—remained inseparable. . . ." Again, the element of chance, the famous three sisters, is paralleled with the weaving motif.

The three mates of the *Pequod* could, perhaps, suggest yet another weaving motif. Flask, who never questions, imagines, or thinks, could represent the limited and calculated variation of the warp. Starbuck, the one who "bucks the stars," who would oppose necessity and chance, obviously represents the woof of free will. Stuff, who professes the postulates of fatalism, represents chance. Together, they weave the mat of the voyage.

Melville's weaving motif stands, then, as a representation of a philosophy of man's life in particular and in intermingling, interacting, multifaceted life in abstract.

Analysis of the Sample Literary Analysis for a Symbol. The preceding multi-paragraph paper includes certain characteristics not otherwise addressed in this section. The following characteristics are unique to a longer paper:

- Long quotations, supporting the major points of the paper, are set in from the left margin and typed single-spaced. Even though they are direct quotations, no quotation marks are used. The format replaces the punctuation.
- Documentation is omitted for quotations from the novel. Some instructors may ask that the numbers of the pages from which the quotations are taken appear parenthetically after the quoted passage. Follow your instructor's preference.
- Frequent references to other pieces of literature, although optional, enhance a literary paper, particularly for more advanced classes. References that indicate other authors' use of similar techniques broaden the reader's literary understanding.
- Parenthetical notes show outside sources, a quick, easy means for limited documentation.
- A chart helps the reader visualize the writer's ideas. An optional device, the chart provides a clever, if unconventional, way to summarize the paper's ideas to this point.

Other aspects of the paper are typical. The paragraph structure, supporting details, organizational plan, transitional devices, sentence structures, and formal style all follow the characteristics of a satisfactory literary analysis. While certainly *Moby Dick* provides ample materials for thousands of additional pages of analysis, the writer has dealt suitably with a single symbol and showed its effect on the novel.

FOR LITERARY WORKS

When asked to analyze an entire literary work—either a long, complicated novel or a single-page poem—you should take a systematic approach. The analysis of a literary work focuses on several related ideas or elements, traces them throughout the work, and illustrates how those ideas or elements affect the work as a whole.

Because literary analysis may take so many directions, however, you should best examine its possibilities by looking first at its general characteristics and the general process for writing it, and then at a series of examples.

The examples for drama, nonfiction, and poetry, like those earlier for author and for literary elements, focus on Emily Dickinson. By comparing these examples, you will better be able to see how various kinds of literary analyses take separate approaches, even when they deal with similar subjects. In addition, each example includes its own analysis. Together, the examples and analyses in this section and in the preceding sections combine to present a solid foundation on which to build your own analysis.

CHARACTERISTICS

A literary analysis of a complete work will be similar to that of an analysis for literary elements; however, certain additional details usually appear. In general, a literary analysis of a specific work

- shows evidence of a thorough understanding of the entire work as a representative of its genre,
- includes an introduction naming the work and its author, and, as necessary, naming the type within the genre, such as Elizabethan, contemporary, musical, or morality (types of drama); biography, article, essay, or journal (types of nonfiction); historical, science fiction, fantasy, or Russian (types of novels),
- analyzes a combination of literary elements as they relate to one another or as they work together to achieve an overall effect,
- includes a topic or thesis sentence that states the approach of the analysis and at least implies the organizational plan [*see* Writing a Paragraph *and* Writing a Multi-Paragraph Paper *in Part I*],
- follows a clear organizational plan,
- includes specific details from the work, either quoted [*see* quotation marks *in the Glossary*] or paraphrased [*see* Paraphrase *later in Part III*], which support the topic or thesis,
- includes, if necessary, background research,
- follows a rather formal writing style, including the use of a third-person point of view,
- uses the present tense to discuss the work but the past tense to discuss the historical or literary period or author's background,
- concludes with a reaction to the work as a representative of its genre, but limits the reactions to only those topics discussed in the paper.

PROCESS

Use the following process to develop a literary analysis discussing a literary work.

STEP 1   **Prewriting • Determining the Topic**

After you have read the entire work, determine the approach your paper will take. One of the most frequent mistakes students make in writing an analysis is venturing off the analysis to simply retell the plot. As a result, be particularly cautious to select a topic and develop it, using elements of the plot only as they support your topic and your ideas.

If you have not been assigned a specific topic, use these questions to help you select a general topic:

- Does the work rely on some unusual characteristic for its success? Are there shortcomings as a result of this atypical characteristic? Advantages?
- Does the work exhibit some particularly strong characteristic that elevates it as a model of its genre?
- Does the work exhibit some unique characteristic that sets it apart from its genre?
- Are certain literary elements particularly attractive to readers' interests (or to your interest in particular)?
- Do certain literary elements combine in an unusual manner to further enhance the work's theme or overall impact?
- Are underlying elements, less obvious to casual readers, helpful in furthering the work's impact?
- Will unraveling complicated symbols or images enhance the reader's enjoyment of the work?
- Do certain characteristics of the work attract your attention because of their relationship to other works?

These questions should help you find a topic that interests you. In a sentence or two, write your topic. Then list ideas from the work that support that topic, as in the following example.

General topic:

The play, "The Belle of Amherst," uses only a single character to depict the biography of Emily Dickinson. By doing so, the dramatist can allow Emily to do what most characters in a play cannot.

Details:

have conversations with those offstage
share secrets with audience
show her impishness

STEP 2   **Prewriting • Reading for Analysis**

Next, reread the work, skimming for specific examples that support your idea. Either take notes on separate note cards or mark the pages of the work with slips of color-coded paper (using different colors to mark supporting details for different topics). If you are using your own copy of the book, you may also choose to mark specific passages directly in the book.

As you read, add to or delete items from your list of supporting topics; thus, you can add important details and delete less supportive details. Revise or expand your list as necessary.

STEP 3   **Prewriting • Planning the Paper**

Now develop a topic or thesis sentence suitable for your paragraph or paper. Then arrange the revised and expanded list of details in a logical order. The order may show relationships, opinion, cause and effect, or comparison and contrast. [*See* Opinion, Cause and Effect, *and* Comparison and Contrast *in Part II*.] You may also use chronological order or some order of importance. [*See* chronological order *and* order of importance *in the Glossary*.]

Next, make some final decisions about your list. Are some items so insignificant that you will have trouble developing them well? Are some too broad to develop in only a single paragraph? If so, what logical divisions can you see? Do you have too many subtopics to develop in a single paper? If so, can you choose the three or four most important or most telling in terms of your general topic? Change the list as necessary.

When you finish, you will have a scratch outline of your paper. If your assignment requires it, develop a formal outline from this informal list. [*See* Outlines: For a Paper *later in Part III*.]

Revise your statement of purpose (as written in Step 1) so that you have a well-written topic or thesis sentence.

STEP 4   **Prewriting • Doing Research**

If your assignment requires outside sources, use the statement of purpose to guide your reading. Take careful notes so that you can document accurately. Be certain to enclose any words not your own in quotation marks. Such precautions will help you avoid plagiarism in your final work. [*See* plagiarism *in the Glossary. Also see* Research Paper, Notes: For a Paper, Precis *and* Paraphrase *later in Part III for additional help as needed*.]

STEP 5   **Writing • Following the Plan**

Now you are ready to write the first draft of your analysis. Begin with an introductory statement or an introductory paragraph. Include in the introductory segment the following specifics:

- Title of the work
- Author's name
- Specific kind of work within the genre [*see the list of* Characteristics *earlier in this section*]
- Perhaps an indication of the work's importance within the literary world or within the author's career

Next, include the topic or thesis sentence you developed in Step 3.

Develop the subtopics in your paragraph or the supporting body paragraphs in your full-length paper. As you do, try to include the following content:

- Sufficient examples to clarify your ideas
- Supporting details taken from the work, either quoted or paraphrased
- Specific supporting detail, if necessary, from outside sources, either quoted or paraphrased and accurately documented
- Transitions that connect one supporting idea with another and one main idea with another [*see* transition *in the Glossary*]

Finally, add a conclusion that refers to your topic or thesis statement and makes some general statement about the work as it represents the genre. Limit the general statement, of course, to only those matters discussed in your paragraph or longer paper.

STEP 6   **Revising • Improving the Content**

As you read your draft, use these questions to pinpoint areas of possible weakness:

- Have I included the necessary information in the introduction?
- Does the introduction give the reader a reason for reading the analysis?
- Can the reader follow my plan or do I need to improve it?
- Are transitions adequate to show relationships among ideas? [*See* Revising: Sample Revision for Transition *in Part I.*]
- Have I developed paragraphs adequately with sufficient supporting details, including specific details from the work, either quoted or paraphrased? [*See* Revising: Sample Revision for Specific Detail *in Part I.*]

- Have I avoided plagiarism?
- Do the main ideas work together to say something about the work as a whole?
- Have I avoided retelling the story, instead referring only to elements that support my main ideas?
- Have I maintained a rather formal writing style, using a third-person point of view and accurate verb tense?
- Is the vocabulary, including appropriate literary terms, accurate?
- Are my sentences varied both in length and in structure? [*See* Revising: Sample Revision for Sentence Variety *in Part I.*]
- Do my sentences carry the most effective emphasis for their respective subjects? Are the main ideas in the main clauses? [*See* Revising: Sample Revision for Emphasis *in Part I.*]
- Does the conclusion refer to the topic or thesis sentence and at the same time make a general statement about the work? [*See* conclusion *in the Glossary.*]

Make necessary revisions until your paper satisfies all the preceding suggestions.

STEP 7   Proofreading • Checking Details

As you read your final draft, check for distracting problems, such as problems with grammar, mechanics, usage, spelling, and word choice. [*See Part IV for rules and examples.*]

A NOTE ABOUT THE SAMPLES

Now that you know what an analysis of a literary work should include and how you go about writing it, study the following examples and their respective analyses for further understanding. You will find examples for a drama, a nonfiction piece, a novel, a poem, and a short story. They vary from single-paragraph, to three-paragraph, to five-paragraph papers.

SAMPLE LITERARY ANALYSIS OF A DRAMA

A literary analysis of a drama frequently deals with such specific literary elements as character, dialogue, setting, plot, and theme. It never deals only with a single element; rather, it shows the relationships among those elements. It also frequently deals with the techniques of drama, such as staging, props, costumes, or lighting, discussing how they make the play effective—or not. The fact that meaning, form, techniques, and background interrelate to make a play work gives the writer ample choices for developing an analysis. Showing interrelationships, you will remember, helps distinguish between an analysis of a literary work and an analysis of a literary element.

The following sample analysis for a drama illustrates the writer's examination of a combination of elements that makes the unusual characteristics of this play particularly suitable for its theme.

When a Belle Is Not a Belle

Because "The Belle of Amherst" by William Luce is a one-person dramatized biography, it bears little resemblance to most plays. On the other hand, because Luce uses only the single character, he is able to dramatize the solitary life of Emily Dickinson. As the only character in the play, Emily tells her own story in dialogue directed toward the audience, with whom she shares "secrets;" in conversation with offstage characters, which allows the audience to glimpse her daily life with her family; and in examples of her impishness, which show the audience something other than the strange recluse she seemed to be.

The play opens with Emily talking directly to the audience about her fear of seeing so many people at one time. "I never see strangers and hardly know what I say," she explains. The reclusive poet of Amherst, Massachusetts, shares secrets with the audience, which sees possible reasons for her apparently strange behavior. "Why should I socialize with village gossips?" she asks, adding that "I give them something to talk about. I dress in white all year round, even in winter." The audience must chuckle at her antics, especially when, later in the play, she adds, "I've never said this to anyone before, but I'll tell you. I do it on purpose. The white dress, the seclusion. It's all—deliberate." She even shares with the audience the recipe for her famous black cake, thus letting them in on yet another "secret."

In order for the audience to share Emily's point of view, they also see her on her home turf. Although they never glimpse other members of the household, they do learn about them during Emily's conversation with these offstage characters. For instance, the audience learns that her brother, Austin, has received eleven valentines. The audience witnesses a conversation with an unseen suitor, one whom she may choose to escort the Belle of Amherst. Likewise, her conversation with an unseen Mr. Higginson, the poet who she hopes will be her mentor, seems a fantasy, a reliving of those important moments in her life. So, while the conversations with characters offstage enhance the audience's understanding of Emily's life, they add to the strange aura of her life.

The strangeness, however, is tempered by her impishness. What else can one call her behavior? She must assume a sly smile when she says, "I'm told one woman in Amherst is imitating me now. Probably Clarissa Cartwright. Just what Amherst needs—another eccentric." She mimics the

> village gossips, poking fun at their poking fun at her. Of one of the gossips, she says, "To spare the expense of moving, I directed her to the cemetery." Even her own family is the butt of her impish comments. Of her sister Vinnie, Emily says, "She snores like a poker and shovel and pair of tongs." The humor tempers the strange.
>
> In short, then, "The Belle of Amherst" describes a most unlikely belle. Only in her fantasies is the poet the society belle. Instead, in an unusual play that doubles as a biography and in a play that includes but a single character, Luce shows his audience a warm, humorous recluse who plays a game with an unknowing Amherst society. Only the audience is in on the secret. The insight makes the recluse more human.

 Analysis of the Sample Literary Analysis of a Drama. The sample literary analysis of a drama illustrates most of the general characteristics and includes some specific details worth noting. Consider these features:

- The introduction names the play and the author and establishes its unique position among drama forms, that it is biographical and that it includes only a single character.
- The introduction leads to the thesis statement that names the paper's three main ideas in the order in which they will be discussed, from the most to the least obvious.
- Supporting details are quoted directly from the play, enclosed in quotation marks, or paraphrased.
- The paper avoids retelling the plot.
- The three main ideas combine to describe the literary work as a whole and discuss its ability to succeed in spite of its peculiar approach and form.
- The paper relies heavily on, but does not deal only with, character. Because it mentions techniques of staging (dialogue directed at the audience and conversations with offstage characters) and Luce's unusual approach to the genre, the paper meets the more general qualifications of a literary analysis of a work.
- The language and structure are formal, and the verb tense is appropriately present in the discussion of the work.
- Sufficient references help readers understand ideas indirectly related to the paper. For instance, the title is explained without the writer ever saying, *The title refers to the fact that Emily Dickinson, who lived in Amherst, Massachusetts, hoped to be a belle of the ball but in actuality achieved that only in her fantasies.*

- Transitions help clarify the organization. Both words and phrases as well as entire sentences serve to join the paragraphs and the sentences within the paragraphs.
- An effective conclusion makes a reference to the thesis sentence without repeating it and reaches some general conclusions about the play.

SAMPLE LITERARY ANALYSIS FOR NONFICTION

The *nonfiction* label applies to more than a half dozen kinds of writing, each of which follows its own technique and/or form: essays, biographies, autobiographies, speeches, letters, journals, and diaries. Even newspaper and magazine articles fall into the nonfiction genre. Frequently, then, a literary analysis of a nonfiction work will focus on author style—the characteristics of sentences and paragraphs and their effect.

The following sample analysis illustrates this very kind of analysis. The subject, like that in the preceding literary analysis of a drama, is the biography of Emily Dickinson. The writer focuses on the techniques of writing nonfiction.

Emily Dickinson: The Peculiar One

In his biography of Emily Dickinson, Van Wyck Brooks uses a vocabulary that enhances his obvious attitude toward Dickinson, that she is peculiar. His expressions suggest the mysterious. "She spoke from the shadows," he writes, and follows with, "These letters were also peculiar," thereby suggesting that speaking from the shadows is peculiar. He includes a description of clipped and pasted letters used to address the envelopes and thus reinforces the attitude. Descriptions of her meeting Colonel Higginson, the poet who she hoped would be her mentor, include her "soft, breathless voice" toward a man certain "there was something abnormal about her." Other phrases Brooks uses include a description of Emily as a "hurrying whiteness," and a reference to her vanishing "like a ghost or an exhalation." The reader sees Emily "fluttering about the porch like a moth in the moonlight," a woman with a "microscopic eye" whose "imagination dwelt with mysteries and grandeurs." While Brooks no doubt reports on his research accurately, his vocabulary creates what is an apparently conscious effort to mystify rather than demystify Emily Dickinson to his readers.

 Analysis of the Sample Literary Analysis for Nonfiction. The single paragraph analyzing Brooks' style is a typical example of a literary analysis of a piece of nonfiction. While nonfiction often includes characters, plot, setting, and many of the other literary elements, much of what makes nonfiction successful (as the author must rely on unalterable facts) is author style. The preceding paragraph includes these characteristics:

- The topic sentence, here the first, combines with other details to introduce the paragraph.
- The many details in the paragraph support the purpose announced in the topic sentence.
- By showing, through details both quoted and paraphrased, rather than telling, the writer allows the reader to draw his or her own conclusions.
- Varied transitional devices prevent tedium.
- A concluding sentence makes reference to the topic sentence without repeating it and also clarifies the writer's point about Brooks' biography.
- Sentence structure maintains a formal style and simultaneously shows variety both in structure and length.
- The present tense, maintained throughout, serves the analysis well.

SAMPLE LITERARY ANALYSIS OF A NOVEL

A literary analysis of a novel probably offers more options than any other kind of analysis. Some writers react to a novel based on their own involvement with it, particularly if it has had some personal impact on them. Other writers remain more objective and deal with literary elements and techniques, especially as they develop a theme or message. Still other writers focus on the full meaning of the novel—the overt message as well as the underlying themes, symbols, and implications. They react to the author's broad comments about the world, its people, its societies, its cultures. Any of these approaches fit the general characteristics of a literary analysis of a novel. Be cautious, however, that you do not lapse into a literary review [*see* Review *later in Part III*] if the assignment is to prepare a literary analysis.

The following sample and analysis permits you to compare a book report, a book review, and a literary analysis of a book. Because the same novel is the subject in all three sections [*see also* Book Report *and* Review *elsewhere in Part III*], you can see how writers approached the novel to meet the characteristics of each of the three kinds of writing. Studying the differences and similarities will further your understanding of a literary analysis.

Ancient Science Fiction

Transporting readers across 25,000 years to an alien civilization sounds like the topic of a good science-fiction novel. Tradition usually requires that science fiction move its readers ahead, not back; yet in Jean Auel's *The Valley of the Horses,* prehistory becomes a sub-genre of science fiction. Set in the convergence of Neanderthal and Cro-Magnon civilizations, *Valley* illustrates a nontraditional approach to science fiction. Auel's extensive scientific research for the series, referred to as the Earth Children series, generates the science-fiction quality. Readers learn about prehistoric biology, geology, and human anatomy, all based on hard scientific data. Combined with Auel's fictionalized speculation of the society, its people, its culture, its spiritual beliefs, the novel allows readers to glimpse an alien world. Combined, the backward-time leap to an alien society, the scientifically accurate environment, and the speculative, even hypothetical but still fictionalized aspects generate a solid argument to categorize *Valley* as science fiction.

Alien societies characterize many works of science fiction. *Valley* throws the reader back 25 millennia to a civilization as strange as any developed by Isaac Asimov. The Neanderthals are aliens, described as subhuman, animal-like creatures, dark, hairy, and chinless, with ridged eyebrows and flat heads. In spite of their subhuman characteristics, however, the clan members follow a highly ritualistic spiritual tradition, far more complicated and symbolic than that of the Cro-Magnon people. Auel also endows the Neanderthals with Memories, an expanded brain capacity that enables them to know everything their ancestors knew but that renders them incapable of learning anything new. As a result, to modern readers the alien society takes on an additional aura of mystery.

In spite of its hypothetical, speculative society, the novel, like others in the series, shows rich scientific detail. Auel traveled all over the world to study archeological sites, to talk with experts on wolves, to sleep in an ice cave, to learn to knap flint, to study glaciers. Her ongoing research gives the reader technical details about medicinal plants, poisonous plants, even birth-control plants; details about woolly mammoths, wild horses, cave lions, wolves, and hyenas; details about glacier flow, glacier melt, and glacier atmosphere. Her characters can discuss in detail the attributes of certain flint for certain tools. Through the characters, the reader also learns how to hunt certain game, find plants for food, store both to sustain life during the long, excruciating winters, and provide for other necessities of life: clothing, footwear, bedding, cooking and storage utensils, shelter, and fire. Every amenity must be found, caught, processed, drilled, woven, braided, cut, or somehow altered to suit the purpose. It is the science of prehistoric man: botany, biology, geology, anatomy, and archaeology.

Within the scientific research, however, Auel emphasizes that all three novels' events grow from her imagination. *Valley* represents Auel's fictionalized version of how people first learned all manner of skills: to ride a horse, to make fire with flint, to hunt animals too big and too fast to kill with sling or spears, to use animals to help carry a heavy load, to traverse wide rivers, to make boats, to improve shelters from simple caves to man-made structures, to make more sophisticated tools. *Valley* also represents Auel's fictionalized version of evolution, including the reason for the demise of the Neanderthals and the success of the Cro-Magnons. Auel's guess as to how tribes moved across Europe and Asia during the last Ice Age in the midst of the changing geography makes fascinating reading. Her speculation of their relationship with the spiritual world, their burial customs, their preparation for the afterlife, their use of hallucinogens for contacting the spirits—all show Auel's imagination at play with sketchy facts. Her interpretation of anthropological evidence lays the foundation for the novel.

Indeed, *The Valley of the Horses* as well as other books in the Earth Children series may be the most unusual example of science fiction to appear on modern book shelves. Taking the reader to a fictionalized, alien civilization situated in a scientifically correct environment, *Valley* does what Auel says she likes in books: "I like stories that pick me up and put me down somewhere else. 'What if'—that's the great thing fiction writers work with." The "what if" in *The Valley of the Horses* results in a blend of science and fiction of a different vintage!

Analysis of the Sample Literary Analysis of a Novel. The literary analysis of a novel can include dozens of aspects. The preceding sample presents an argument for thinking of a novel as a special kind of science fiction. Thus, the analysis does several jobs at once: It presents an argument supported by details from the book; it presents an analysis of science-fiction characteristics as they appear in the book; and it includes the general characteristics for a literary analysis of a novel. Note the following details:

- The introduction includes the vital information and establishes the basis for the argument that the book is a special kind of science fiction.
- The thesis sentence points out, in the order to be discussed, the three main ideas the writer will develop in the three body paragraphs.
- Each paragraph is supported by details from the novel, all of which appear as paraphrases, even list-like series. Quotations are omitted for brevity.
- Transitions provide clear connections between ideas.
- Sentence structure maintains a rather formal writing style and simultaneously illustrates good variety. Complicated sentences, some of which include complicated series, contrast with short, simple sentences.
- The present tense appears appropriately in the discussion of the work.

- A concluding paragraph not only refers to the thesis sentence but also states the author's attitude. The quotation by the author probably appeared on a jacket cover; thus the writer did not document its source.

SAMPLE LITERARY ANALYSIS OF A POEM

To write a literary analysis of a poem, a writer must select a combination of elements that, peculiar to that poem, create some significant impact on the poem's meaning. An analysis of a poem may consider sound devices, structure, tone, mood, theme, imagery, figure of speech, symbol, point of view, setting, perhaps even character. [*See entries for each in the Glossary*.] It may offer comparisons, contrasts, description, cause and effect, and opinion. [*See entries for each in Part II*.] Unlike an analysis of a single literary element [*see the earlier section* For Literary Elements], the analysis of a poem must deal with the overall effect of the work. Compare the following analysis with the earlier example [*in* For Literary Elements].

Mother Nature Domesticated

Emily Dickinson's poem, "She Sweeps with Many-Colored Brooms," serves as a typical representative of Dickinson's style. The extended metaphor, sustained throughout the poem and emphasized by the absence of a clear rhyme pattern, enables her to achieve the compact multiple meanings for which she is recognized. Because Dickinson lived as a recluse and because she felt Mother Nature was her only real friend, much of her poetry domesticates Mother Nature in a manner that makes the spiritual familiar. In the poem, "She Sweeps with Many-Colored Brooms," Dickinson uses the common household words to describe Mother Nature's sunset. Mother Nature uses a broom, dusts, and wears an apron. She also leaves shreds, ravelings, and threads as she litters the eastern sky with duds. On the literal level, then, Mother Nature is, indeed, the housewife, emphasized by the line, "Oh, housewife in the evening west." The poem suggests the vivid colors—purple, amber, emerald—that Mother Nature has painted the sunset sky, colors Dickinson obviously enjoys until "brooms fade softly into stars—/ And then I come away."

The extended metaphor, however, suggests some underlying questions the reader must consider. Mother Nature shows herself less than a tidy housewife. She leaves shreds behind, does not dust the pond, drops ravelings and thread, and litters. Even her brooms are spotted. That Dickinson refers to the untidy housewife may suggest irreverence, but it may also suggest a mature awareness that few mothers are perfect. In fact, the adoration for the sunset's loveliness more clearly illustrates a daughter's love than it does a lack of respect.

Probably, in fact, Dickinson admires the variations Mother Nature sweeps into the sunsets, variations like those in Dickinson's own poem. The rhyme is sprung to avoid a singsong effect, and the result emphasizes Dickinson's message. For instance, in verse one, "behind" almost rhymes with "pond," and in verse two, "thread" almost rhymes with "emerald," but in verse three, "fly" fails completely as a rhyme with "away." Instead, as the reader listens for a near rhyme, thinking "fly," his thought, jolted by the absence, carries "fly" with "away." Dickinson, the recluse, relied on the spiritual world to take her away from the domestic, and watching the sunset made her own spirit soar until the stars emerged. Then she returned to this world, her garden, her home, her own room. As biographer Van Wyck Brooks said, Dickinson domesticated the universe.

Analysis of the Sample Literary Analysis of a Poem. The preceding three-paragraph composition analyzes a single poem. Note some of the specific features in this paper:

- As a three-paragraph paper, the sample illustrates a format unlike others this section examines. The first paragraph is both an introduction and the development of the first point.
- The thesis statement, the second sentence in the first paragraph, suggests the three topics to be discussed.
- The paper follows an order of importance, beginning with the most important idea, the extended metaphor, and building other ideas on that.
- By looking at a combination of extended metaphor, potential problems with meaning (such as irreverence), and the impact of missing rhyme, the analysis deals adequately with the poem's total effect. In this manner, too, it sets itself apart from an analysis that deals with only a single literary element.
- Transitions help the reader see connections between ideas within and between paragraphs.
- Varied sentence structure enhances the quality of the paper. The main ideas appear in main clauses.
- The paper maintains a formal style, aided by the consistent use of a third-person point of view and accurate verb tense, the present to discuss the work and the past to discuss the background.
- The conclusion, the final part of the third paragraph, not only emphasizes the points in the paper but also broadens its message by applying the techniques evident in this one poem to much of Dickinson's poetry.

SAMPLE LITERARY ANALYSIS OF A SHORT STORY

A short story analysis can take almost as many approaches as that for a novel. For instance, it can trace the development of a character and show the relationship between the development and the theme. Or it can show how point of view creates sympathy for a character. It can describe the setting and show its effect on mood and, in turn, show how mood affects theme. It can deal with structure, tone, style, and theme. It can express opinion or cause and effect.

In the interest of providing yet another kind of literary paper, however, this section looks at a sample that develops a comparison. The following literary analysis combines the organizational pattern of a comparison-and-contrast paper with the content of a literary analysis [*see* Comparison and Contrast *in Part II*]. Compare this paper, too, with the short story analysis that deals only with setting [*see the earlier section* For Literary Elements].

Sylvia and the White Heron: A Comparison

An interesting comparison in Sarah Orne Jewett's short story, "The White Heron," enhances the reader's understanding of the author's message. The comparison between one of the main characters, a young girl named Sylvia, and the white heron allows the reader to better understand their similar personalities. For instance, both find comfort in the outdoors, especially the wilderness. Just as the white heron naturally inhabits the woods and water, Sylvia, although less naturally, spends nearly all of her time in the same setting. As the reader learns, "it seemed as if she never had been alive at all before she came to live at the farm." In addition, both characters are shy. For example, Sylvia has a difficult time relating to and getting along with other people. Likewise, the white heron, frightened, flies away if only an annoying pair of catbirds approaches. Perhaps, however, the most significant similarity between the two is that both of them keep secrets well. The white heron, ever silent, never attracts the attention of others, thus keeping its nesting site a mystery. Similarly, even though Sylvia sees the nest of the somewhat rare bird, she never reveals the secret, not even to a young man who offers a princely ten-dollar reward for the information. Thus, Sylvia and the white heron possess certain traits that cause the reader to think in terms of mirror images, each character enhancing the other. Seeing the characters in juxtaposition helps the reader react positively to Sylvia's behavior as she reflects the heron's natural behavior. Thus the reader comes to better appreciate Jewett's message: All living beings are children of nature, and all share a common bond. The preservation of that bond can have no selling price. For Sylvia to give away the heron's secret is to give away his life; and because Sylvia has become one with the heron, to give away his life is to give away her own.

Analysis of the Sample Literary Analysis of a Short Story. In a single paragraph, this analysis develops a comparison that does more than merely analyze character. In this respect, the paragraph follows the characteristics of an analysis for a literary work. Note these specifics:

- The topic sentence specifies the purpose of the paragraph.
- The three supporting details, each in turn supported with examples from the short story, including one quotation, clarify the main idea.
- Effective transitions show relationships among the ideas throughout the paragraph.
- Arranged in order of importance, the ideas build from most obvious to least obvious, from least impact to greatest impact. The culmination of the comparison illustrates the strength of Sylvia's character.
- Varied sentence structure maintains an effective and rather formal style.
- A third-person point of view and a consistent present tense in the discussion of the work also aid in developing an effective formal style.
- The conclusion reemphasizes the introduction. In addition, it permits the writer to make a more general comment about the effect of the comparison.

The many explanations, examples, and analyses in this section should provide an ample foundation on which to build your own literary analysis. Regardless of topic, length, or kind of work you must analyze, you will surely find an example here to guide your work.

Memorandum

A memorandum or memo (plural: *memoranda*) is a letter designed to be used within a department, or between the departments or branches of a business. Frequently, a printed form or e-mail determines the format [*see* E-Mail *earlier in Part III*]. In other cases, employees follow the approved format explained later in this section.

CHARACTERISTICS

A memo

- follows a format that includes a heading with *To, From, Subject*, and *Date*,
- conveys a company-related message about anything from sales to the company bowling league,
- is written like a business letter, with the main idea in the first paragraph followed by necessary details and finally, if required, a request for action or response,
- is usually more informal than formal,
- records or requests an action (implying the sender keeps a copy),
- follows a standard format which calls for single-spaced, block paragraphs [*see* Letters: Business *earlier in Part III*], two spaces between paragraphs, and three between the heading and the body.

PROCESS

Use the following steps to develop an accurate, business-like memorandum.

STEP 1   **Prewriting • Recognizing a Need**

Before you write a memo, know exactly why you are writing it. Consider some of these possible reasons:

> You are requesting action. Perhaps you want to confirm the dates for your vacation with your superior.
> You are confirming an action. If your supervisor asks you to file a report by the end of the month, a memo on the 25th noting that the report has been filed shows that you have followed through.
> You are summarizing the results of a committee meeting.
> You wish to announce a departmental meeting.

While we cannot begin to list every purpose of a memo, these ideas will help you determine the specific purpose of your communiqué.

STEP 2   **Prewriting • Preparing the Heading**

By developing the heading first, you focus your attention on the audience and force yourself to name your subject in a few words. Answer these four questions:

To whom, specifically, is the memo addressed?
From whom is the memo coming? You? Your department?
What is the subject of the memo? Put it in a few words.
What is the complete date of the memo's distribution?

By answering these questions, you can complete the heading. Use one of these forms:

To:	Name
From:	Name
Subject:	Title
Date:	Date

(The names, title, and date begin two spaces to the right of the colons.)

To:	Name
From:	Name
Subject:	Title
Date:	Date

(The names, title, and date begin two spaces to the right of the longest line.)

Note that in one form the colons are aligned. In the other form, the headings align on the left margin. In both cases, the names, title, and date are aligned.

While companies often preprint memo forms, more likely you will have a memo format on your word-processing program. Either case eliminates the necessity of your setting up a format. Or at least you won't need to set it up more than once!

STEP 3   Prewriting • Planning the Message

Now you need to organize your thoughts before you write. The message should appear in three parts. Use the following plan to make notes for your message:

- Paragraph 1 should include the main idea. What, in one or two sentences, do you need to convey? Are you announcing a new policy? Jot down the main points.
- Paragraph 2 gives details. If you are announcing a new policy, how will it affect the reader? If you are requesting suggestions, why do you need them? Why should the reader respond?
- Paragraph 3, if necessary, requests action or response. If the reader must complete some form, spell out what to do. If the reader is to put a suggestion in writing, say to whom to address the comments and by when.

STEP 4   **Writing • Completing the Memo**

When you have planned the details, follow the organization set out in Step 3 and write the memo. Use clear language and simple sentences. Be direct and informal. Avoid stilted language and trite expressions.

STEP 5   **Revising • Checking Content**

As you reread your memo, ask yourself these questions:

- Is the heading clear, precise, dated accurately and completely?
- Will my reader understand the message?
- Are the details sufficient to support the main idea? Is the explanation adequate?
- Have I included deadlines, specific actions, names, and places as necessary?
- Are my sentences simple and clear?
- Have I used a conversational vocabulary, or have I resorted to buzzwords and stilted language?

Use these questions to guide revision. When you believe the content is accurate and complete, print a copy and sign your initials beside your name in the heading.

STEP 6   **Proofreading • Checking the Mechanics**

When the final copy is printed, proofread it carefully. Make sure you have made no omissions or typing errors. Check the spelling. Read for grammar, usage, and mechanics precision.

SAMPLE MEMORANDUM

The following memo follows the process set out above and illustrates one reason for writing a memo.

V*I*P

VIDEO INSTRUCTIONAL PRODUCTS

To: Mearl Evans, Sales Department Manager
From: Sara Davidson
Subject: New Product Proposal
Date: November 8, 20—
CONFIDENTIAL

The New Products Committee hopes to present a proposed new product to the VIP Board of Directors at their December meeting. The first draft of the proposal outlines the product concept, potential sales, and cost estimates for a new industrial training video.

The new training DVD production follows the design of earlier products used in the industry on videocassette recorders. It will focus on the pest-control industry. Its primary purpose will be to train pest-control technicians to eradicate pests in residential and commercial properties while maintaining safety standards for both the PC technician and personnel working or living in the area. The product, an innovation in both pest control and in training, appears to have good market potential.

The committee looks forward to presenting the proposal to you and your staff prior to the December Board meeting. We think you will have valuable contributions to make to the overall plan and can suggest methods by which the proposal can best be presented to the Board. By next Friday, please suggest a time most appropriate for our discussion.

Analysis of the Sample Memorandum. The preceding memorandum serves the purpose of maintaining communication between departments and involving personnel at all levels in the development of a potential new product. Note these specifics about the memo itself:

- The company name and logo are preprinted at the top of the memo form, as are the words *To, From, Subject,* and *Date.*
- The heading lists a title for the addressee but no title for the writer. The tendency is to be more formal with the addressee than with the writer.
- The heading concisely indicates the subject matter. Note the initial capitals.
- The complete date is essential for future reference.
- The *Confidential* notation emphasizes what employees already know: Competition requires secrecy about the development of new products.

- The message follows the typical organization, with the main idea in paragraph 1, details in paragraph 2, and a request for action in paragraph 3.
- While the vocabulary uses business terminology (*cost estimates, pest-control technician, eradicate,* and *residential* and *commercial properties*), the language is not stilted or filled with buzzwords.
- Sentence structure is simple and clear.
- The tone is polite and suggests professional courtesy, especially in seeking interdepartmental cooperation.

Good memos are really a matter of courtesy. People working together do a more effective job if they understand their respective roles. Communication goes a long way to maintain that relationship. Memos help serve that purpose.

Minutes of a Meeting

If you are elected secretary of a club or organization, your primary responsibility will be to take notes of what happens at any membership meeting. These notes are called *minutes*. They simply record the official business that occurs during a meeting. If the club or organization is relatively large, the meetings will be more formal than if the organization is small. The more formal the meeting, the more formal the minutes. Regardless of formality, however, certain characteristics are evident in the minutes of any meeting.

CHARACTERISTICS

The minutes of a meeting should include

- the date, time, and place of the meeting,
- the name of the person who calls the meeting to order,
- a list of those present, or, in a large group, the number of members present,
- a notation of handling of the minutes of the previous meeting,
- a notation of committee reports and actions,

- a list of unfinished business,
- a record of elections or appointments,
- an explanation of any business transacted, including any motions made (sometimes, but not necessarily, the names of the persons who propose and second the motion) and any actions taken,
- a list of important dates and facts,
- an indication of the next meeting date, time, and place,
- the time of adjournment,
- your signature and typewritten name, along with the date (sometimes preceded by *respectfully submitted*, a phrase now considered outdated).

PROCESS

The following steps will help you prepare accurate and complete minutes of a meeting.

STEP 1   Prewriting • Planning for the Meeting

Before the meeting, you should complete two preliminary steps:

- Study the agenda, if there is one. The agenda [*see* agenda *in the Glossary*] serves as a skeleton outline for your minutes.
- Prepare a list of the items to include in your minutes. Use the preceding list of characteristics to develop your list, and allow enough room to take notes. In some cases, a line will be ample, but for reports, unfinished business, and new business, you may wish to allow a full page.

STEP 2   Prewriting • Taking Notes

Arrive early and seat yourself in the front of the room near the presiding officer.

Using your prepared list as a guide, take careful notes of everything that happens. Strive for accuracy, asking as necessary for a motion to be repeated or for the names of those who make and second motions.

To avoid inaccuracies, you may wish to read a motion aloud directly from your notes just prior to the president's asking for a second or just prior to the vote. This will give everyone, including you, a chance to agree on wording and to understand the motion.

STEP 3   Writing • Preparing the First Draft

As soon after the meeting as possible, at least within the next day or two, write out the minutes in rough draft. Waiting too long after the meeting will add to the difficulty of maintaining accuracy:

- Your notes will get "cold," and you may have trouble remembering what your abbreviations mean.
- You may have trouble reading your own handwriting. Notes written in haste sometimes become indecipherable after several days, simply because you cannot remember the general context in which they were taken.
- Your recollection of specific details will fade with time.

So, even though you may not have to read the minutes for a month, prepare them as soon as possible.

While the format for minutes is somewhat flexible, the organization is always the same: chronological. [*See* chronological order *in the Glossary*.] Even if the order of business [*see* order of business *in the Glossary*] varies from the agenda, you will record the minutes as the events actually occurred. Normal order of business is as follows:

Meeting called to order
Minutes read and unanimously approved, approved as corrected, or approved as submitted
Reports presented by committees
Unfinished business discussed
Elections held
New business presented
Announcements made
Next meeting date, time, and place established
Meeting adjourned

Finally, when you have completed the minutes, you need to check for accuracy.

STEP 4   **Revising • Checking for Accuracy**

The most common errors in minutes result from one of two causes:

- Inaccurate information
- Incomplete information

For instance, you may misunderstand a motion and record it inaccurately. Or maybe you mistakenly write *not* for *now*, thus changing the meaning of a motion. On the other hand, you may simply neglect to include such important information as the names of those making and seconding motions, the voting results, and any inconclusive discussions that became unfinished business.

Ultimately, accurate minutes require complete notes taken throughout a meeting. Even if you take such detailed notes that you later decide some minor points of the discussion need not be included, you should have adequate details to prepare accurate, complete minutes.

Finally, when you have revised the minutes and made a neat final copy, sign your name and record the date.

STEP 5   **Proofreading • Checking for Details**

When you have completed the final draft, read it for mechanical details: typographical errors, misspellings, inaccurate punctuation. These errors can cause the minutes to be misread and in extreme cases create the potential for legal action. Legal cases have been won or lost over the use of a comma. Your responsibility is not to be taken lightly.

Ultimate proofreading occurs as you read the minutes for approval. Whatever revisions the membership demands are made on the final copy and noted as revisions in the next meeting's minutes.

SAMPLE MINUTES

The following sample of minutes and the analysis that follows illustrate the characteristics described in this section.

JUNIOR CIVITAN CLUB
Regular Monthly Meeting

The regular monthly meeting of the Junior Civitan Club was called to order on Tuesday, January 28, 20—, 3:00 PM in Room 29 at Central High School by President Staci Marlin. Twenty-seven members answered roll call. Three were absent.

The minutes of the December meeting were read and approved as corrected. The treasurer reported a balance of $104.86 in the treasury.

The membership committee reported positive reaction to the membership drive held during the two weeks' period from January 6 through January 17. Eight new members will join the club at the February meeting. During discussion, it was suggested that the club plan an informal reception at the end of the next meeting to welcome the new members. The membership committee will consider the suggestion.

Little progress was reported by the apple-sale committee. The sale is scheduled for the third week of May, and the current emphasis is on scheduling workers to sell the apples at the afternoon and evening athletic events. Ron Richards, chairman, indicated he expected to have the schedule completed by the March meeting.

A slate of officers was presented by the nominating committee in preparation for the election of new officers during the March meeting. The nominees were Francis Wittington, President; Jerome Hudson, Vice-President; Gaila Schwartz, Treasurer. The current secretary has another year remaining in office.

In matters of unfinished business, President Marlin reported that the food donations collected by the club were well received at the local food bank during the Christmas season. The club donated nearly $400 worth of staples. In other unfinished business, Yolanda Wong requested that the club reach a decision about Civitan Scholarship applicants since time is nearing for the application deadline. She made a motion, seconded by Joyce Kozlowski, that at the regular February meeting the club select by secret ballot a representative from the organization to apply for the $500 scholarship, representation to be based on club participation and club support. The motion passed.

No new business came before the membership. Members were reminded of the dates for the Junior Achievement exhibit next weekend, February 3 and 4, since Civitan members like to support fellow students' activities. In addition, Lanny Collins, student athletic director, suggested members watch for posters announcing dates for spring sports meetings.

The next regular meeting of the Central High School Civitan Club will be held February 25, 20—, at 3:00 PM in Room 29 at Central High School. The meeting was adjourned at 4:15 PM.

Brandon Hartwell
Brandon Hartwell
January 31, 20—

Analysis of the Sample Minutes. The sample minutes include all the vital information. For instance:

- We know by the heading the title of the meeting and that it was a regular meeting.
- The introductory statement, paragraph 1, includes the date, time, and place of the meeting, the name of the presiding officer, and a report of attendance.
- Paragraph 2, a single sentence, indicates how the minutes of the previous meeting were handled.
- Then begins a series of three paragraphs about three reports. Paragraph 3 describes the report from the membership committee, including discussion from the membership. Because no motions were made, names of those commenting are not listed. Paragraph 4 describes the report from the apple-sale committee, and paragraph 5 describes the report from the nominating committee. Specific names are listed only where needed.
- Paragraph 7, dealing with unfinished business, summarizes the discussion, indicates a motion made, and, although unnecessarily, states by whom and by whom seconded. We know that the motion passed. The motion, obviously somewhat complicated, is worded to include all matters of importance because of the impact on future action in the club.
- Although no new business was transacted, notation of that fact is necessary in paragraph 8 to avoid the possible misunderstanding that such business was simply omitted from the minutes.
- In paragraph 9 are the announcements and reminders to members. While not part of the club's actual business, these items are of general interest.
- Paragraph 10 specifies the date, time, and place of the next regular meeting.
- The final paragraph gives the time of adjournment.
- Finally, the secretary omits a complimentary close and instead merely adds his signature and printed name. The date is not the date of the meeting, but the date on which he completed the final copy of the minutes.

If you follow this sample when you take minutes for your own club or organization, you will prepare good minutes.

News Article

News articles provide current information to newspaper and magazine readers. Most follow a specific plan to ensure brevity. [*Compare the news article with* Feature Article, *elsewhere in Part III. A news article reports straight news, while a feature article focuses on human interest.*] Because most news-article writing appears in daily or weekly newspapers, this section focuses on newspaper, rather than magazine, articles.

Most who have occasion to write a news article do so because of a responsibility as a publicity person for a club or organization or perhaps because of work in a public relations department for a business. In either case, unlike journalists who earn their livings writing news articles full time, these writers need to-the-purpose guidelines by which to prepare the article.

CHARACTERISTICS

News articles follow an inverted-pyramid plan. They are written to "rest" on an opening statement the way a pyramid, turned upside down, rests on its point. Sentences coming after the first statement (or lead) expand and broaden the topic, but the points made in them are ever less important. This structure is used because editors often shorten articles to fit the space available. Editors can cut the end of a news story written as an inverted pyramid without losing its shape or meaning.

In general, then, the news article should

- report news, not advertise [*see* Advertising *earlier in Part III*],
- begin with the essentials: *who, what, why, when, where*, and *how*,
- add details in order of importance, most important first,
- include relevant details which may help answer anticipated questions [*see* detail *in the Glossary*],
- avoid the sensational just for the sake of sensation,
- maintain the integrity of the writer and the publication,
- report information objectively, free from all opinion, judgment, and assumption,
- limit details to the facts, thus maintaining brevity,
- follow the standard rules of grammar, mechanics, and usage,
- begin a new paragraph for each new idea, often using paragraphs of only a sentence or two,
- be printed double-spaced,

- be directed to a specific person at the newspaper, a person whose name a receptionist usually gives you.

Compare these characteristics with those for an announcement [*see* Announcement *earlier in Part III*]. The news article extends and elaborates the idea presented in an announcement.

If you are not an employee of the publication, you should include certain additional information in a cover letter or on a separate sheet of paper:

> Your name and title, or the name and title of someone else who, as a company or organization representative, can verify the information
>
> Your mailing address
>
> The telephone number at which you can be reached during the day

This information is critical to an editor who, working under deadline, must contact you to clarify or to verify the facts. Without it, your article may go unpublished or be published too late. If you do not want your address and phone number published, be sure to write *Do Not Publish* alongside that information.

PROCESS

In order to develop a satisfactory news article, follow these steps.

STEP 1   **Prewriting • Gathering the Basic Information**
On separate lines, list the basic questions: *who, what, why, when, where,* and *how.* Then answer each in as few words as possible. These responses make up the basic information that appears first in the inverted-pyramid construction.

STEP 2   **Prewriting • Adding Details**
Next, decide what additional information to include. Think in terms of reader interest. What impact will the news have on the community? Does the impact need further explanation? What additional information will the reader need to understand the importance of the news? In other words, what makes your article noteworthy?

Make notes of additional and directly related facts that can be included. Omit judgment, opinion, and assumption.

List the details your article should include.

STEP 3   **Prewriting • Planning the Inverted Pyramid**
Next, arrange the details in order of importance. Note that order of importance may not be the same as order of interest. And it may not be the same for you as for the reader. Follow the order of importance

from the point of view of the reader. Because the editor may need to shorten the article, he will cut from the end without revising. So be objective so that the reader gets the important details first.

Arrange your list of details in the order of their importance.

STEP 4 **Writing • Developing the First Draft**
Begin with a single sentence that includes as many of the answers to the basic-information questions as possible. If you need a second sentence to include all—the *who, what, why, when, where,* and *how*—use it. But use no more than two sentences.

Next, add information following the inverted-pyramid plan. Avoid rambling. Omit unnecessary details. Omit irrelevant information.

STEP 5 **Revising • Polishing the Content**
When you have finished the first draft, check for completeness. Ask yourself these questions:

- Have I included who, what, why, when, where, and how?
- Have I included explanations where necessary?
- Will the reader have questions I have not addressed? Can I anticipate and reply?

Next, check for good writing techniques:

- Are my sentences short and simple?
- Have I used a clear, nontechnical vocabulary?
- Have I begun a new paragraph for each new idea, recognizing that a newspaper paragraph is very unlike an expository paragraph?
- Do I follow the inverted-pyramid organization? Or will the reader lose vital information if the editor cuts the end of the article?

Make necessary corrections and improvements.

STEP 6 **Proofreading • Taking a Critical Look**
Check for accuracy. Consider the basic questions:

- Are dates accurate?
- Are times accurate, indicating Central Standard Time, Eastern Daylight Time, Pacific Time, and so on?
- Are places clearly identified, including street addresses and business locations?

- Are names included where necessary and are these people identified by title or position?
- Are other details accurate?

In addition, check for grammar, mechanics, and usage details. [*See* Revising *in Part I and all of Part IV for rules, explanations, and examples.*] Check spelling and word choice.

Finally, read the following sample news article and its accompanying analysis. Together, they should help you develop your own article.

SAMPLE NEWS ARTICLE

The public relations director of a local company submitted the following news article to the newspaper. Compare it with the announcement on the same subject released by the chairman of the board of the same company [*see* Announcement *earlier in Part III*].

News Release

On June 10, Karson Manufacturing will break ground for a $6 million addition at its present location according to Lamont Karson, chairman of the board. The expansion will allow the company to increase production of its current stamping operation to meet increased sales.

As a result of the expansion, Karson expects to employ an additional 230 workers by late next year.

The information, made public at today's stockholders' meeting, confirms local business analysts' expectations of significant company profit margins. As sales increase, said Karson, profits "will be returned to the company."

The Karson stamping operation currently provides sheet-metal parts to both the automotive industry and to the small-appliance industry. The new expansion will allow the company to meet the increasing demands in both industries.

In addition, the company expects to begin operations that will serve the lawn-care industry. With the recent expansion of Jayne Lawn Equipment Manufacturing in adjoining Perigo County, Karson expects to take advantage of that growing market.

Karson explained that recent plant closings of three small area stamping operations have resulted in increased sales for Karson Manufacturing.

Because current land holdings adjoining the present manufacturing site permit extensive expansion, no residential or business properties will be affected by the plans. Ample transportation systems currently serve the site.

Analysis of the Sample News Article. The sample news article includes the following:

- The first two sentences provide the basic information: *who, what, why, when, where,* and *how.*
- The most important details appear first, followed by less and less important information. The final paragraph could easily be omitted without serious damage to the article.
- The writer has anticipated the reader's questions and answered them: about additional employment, increased profits, future potential, and impact on nearby homes and businesses.
- The paragraphs, unlike those in expository writing, include only a few sentences so that only a single idea appears in each.
- The relatively short sentences read easily and clearly.
- The article follows the standard grammar, mechanics, and usage rules.
- The article maintains an objective point of view—although another writer might have interviewed a representative from the labor community, the construction business, the stockholders' list, a competitive company, or neighboring households and businesses.

When you are ready to submit your own article, follow these suggestions:

1. Give your name, address, and phone number so the editor can reach you.
2. Submit the article in advance so that it can be handled on a "future" basis. Then, a few days before you want the article printed, call the editor for an opportunity to clear up questions and put your item in the forefront.
3. Understand that what you submit will probably be changed to conform to newspaper style. In fact, some newspapers print only material an employee rewrites. The better your work, the better your chances that the article will carry the message and emphasis you want.

Notes

Notes serve two purposes: First, they help you concentrate on what you hear or read. Second, they help you remember what you have heard or read. Taking effective notes, either for a class or in preparation for writing a paper, requires you to pick out main points and supporting details.

Sometimes your task is complicated by a poorly organized speaker or writer who is hard to follow. In other cases, a writer includes head notes to indicate what each chapter covers, headings and subheadings to locate specific main ideas, and chapter summaries to emphasize the relationships among the main ideas. Similarly, a good speaker or lecturer tells you in the beginning what he or she intends to talk about and list his or her main points.

This section discusses two kinds of note-taking: for a class and for a paper. The tasks differ.

FOR A CLASS

One kind of note-taking is in preparation for a class. You may be taking notes from assigned reading materials or from orally presented class materials.

CHARACTERISTICS

Notes for a class fall into two categories: notes on reading and notes on oral material. General characteristics exist for either kind. Usually, good notes

- should be brief but thorough,
- appear in shorthand or notehand or in a self-styled abbreviated form,
- may appear in formal outline style [*see* Outlines: As a Summary *later in Part III*], as a list, or as a series of phrases, according to the writer's purpose,
- include the main points,
- provide enough supporting details to show the significance of the main points,
- provide a chance to review the contents of the course prior to testing,
- stimulate recall of additional details and relationships among ideas discussed in class.

Frequently, notes taken in class are written hurriedly and in such an abbreviated form as to become meaningless later. As a result, some notes, particularly those taken in class, should be reread as soon as possible. Explanatory words, phrases, and supporting details should be added so that the notes later retain their meaning.

PROCESS

The process for taking notes is primarily a mental one. Preparation for taking notes is, therefore, primarily mental. Attentiveness and concentration are the two qualities most important to taking effective notes. This section looks at the process step by step.

STEP 1   **Prewriting • Getting Ready to Take Notes**
If you are getting ready to take notes from reading materials, gather the essential tools—the reading matter, paper, and pen or pencil—and find a comfortable place to work. While some people do take notes at the keyboard, there is a tendency then to write too much and to write it in the language of the reading material. You'll do better to write in your own words.

Next, look through the assigned reading. Is there a head note that describes the topics to be discussed? Are there headings? Subheadings? Section summaries? Chapter summaries? If so, read them through. This kind of preparation, sometimes called *surveying*, lets you know what to expect and helps you concentrate on and watch for major points.

If you are preparing to take notes in class, again be prepared. Preparation assumes not only that you have the necessary materials but also that you have studied the assignment. As a result, notes you take on reading matter will prepare you for note-taking in class. Some students, in fact, like to take notes in a notebook using the left-hand side of the page for assigned reading notes and the right-hand side of the page for parallel in-class discussion notes.

STEP 2   **Writing • Picking Out the Main Ideas**
In order to take effective notes, you must be able to pick out main ideas. The main ideas in reading matter are easier to pinpoint than the ones in oral presentations. The reasons are simple: Most written matter is more carefully organized and constructed than is an oral presentation. In addition, you can reread as many times as necessary to find the main ideas. Together, these two conditions simplify note-taking from printed material. Understanding any preceding assignment, however, should

help you select main ideas from a discussion. Certainly any topic that was important in a reading assignment will be important to the in-class discussion.

So concentrate on picking out main ideas in written matter. You know from your own writing experience that paragraph structures revolve around main ideas. While professional writers sometimes do not include a topic sentence in every paragraph, a good reader should be able to pick out the main idea from a paragraph and put it into a sentence. As you take notes from reading matter, then, select one idea from each paragraph to include in your notes.

Include the main ideas in the order in which they appear in the reading matter.

As you write, watch for specifics: names, dates, and statistics you know the instructor will stress. Be sure this kind of information is in your notes.

If the reading matter includes charts, diagrams, tables, figures, graphs, or maps, study what they mean. Include this information in your notes as well. These kinds of details will help you later, as you review for an in-class discussion or exam.

Remember that notes can take varied forms, from formal outlines, to word lists, to phrases, to whole sentences. Use whichever form best suits your purpose.

STEP 3   **Revising and Proofreading • Checking Legibility**

Because note-taking is highly personal, it need not follow a particular style or form. There is little responsibility for revising and proofreading. But there is one exception: Many times during an oral presentation, notes must be taken rapidly; the results may be less thorough than you would like. In such cases, words or phrases are jotted down to remind you of whole ideas. And while using words or brief phrases is the best way to take notes under such conditions, two days later (and almost certainly, two weeks later) the notes may make little sense. As a result, it is imperative to read over the notes as soon as possible. In the course of reading, add new details to help you later review for a test or prepare for a discussion.

SAMPLE NOTES FOR A CLASS

The following reading was assigned for class. Following the reading are notes taken on the reading. [*For an example of notes on the same reading matter, prepared in a formal outline style, see* Outlines: As a Summary, *later in Part III.*]

Original Passage

The food habits of birds make them especially valuable to agriculture. Because birds have higher body temperatures, more rapid digestion, and greater energy than most other animals, they require more food. Nestling birds make extremely rapid growth, requiring huge amounts of food. They usually consume as much as or more than their own weight in soft-bodied insects every day.

Young robins have been observed to gain eight times their original weight in the first eight days of their life.

Insect-eating birds must fill their stomachs five to six times daily because they digest their food so fast and because of the large amount of indigestible material in insects.

One young robin, weighing three ounces, consumed 165 cutworms weighing $5\frac{1}{2}$ ounces in one day. If a ten-pound baby ate at the same rate, he would eat $18\frac{1}{3}$ pounds of food in a day.

Of course, birds cannot control insects completely, but they are of great value. By using soil- and water-conserving practices, farmers and ranchers could probably double the population of helpful birds. Field and farmstead windbreaks, living fences, shrub buffers, grass waterways, and farm ponds are only a few of the many land use practices useful in attracting and increasing beneficial forms of wildlife.

Notes

Birds help control insects:
—eat more than weight
—fill stomach 5–6 times/day
—much indigest. stuff in insects.

Comparison: 10-lb. baby would eat $18\frac{1}{3}$ lbs./day.

To increase bird population:
windbreaks
living fences
shrub buffers
grass waterways
farm ponds

Analysis of the Sample Notes for a Class. The brief notes help the note-taker remember the contents of the reading matter. A few characteristics bear mentioning:

- The form includes phrases and lists rather than whole sentences, yet the notes present information clearly and completely.
- Certain stylistic gimmicks appear: the use of dashes, the substitution of the / mark to mean *per*, and abbreviations for

long words. Each helps the writer take notes more quickly without clouding the content.

- The notes include all the main ideas from the reading matter and several, but not all, illustrations to show the significance of the main ideas.

Someone else's notes on the same reading matter would likely vary in form and style. Still, as long as the essential details appeared, the notes would serve their purpose: to quickly remind the reader of important information.

FOR A PAPER

The second kind of note-taking is used for developing a lengthy paper that requires research; such a paper is frequently called a *term, research,* or *library paper.* [*See* Research Paper *later in Part III.*]

CHARACTERISTICS

The characteristics of note-taking for a paper differ considerably from that for class assignments or in-class lectures. Notes taken in preparation for writing a paper require a great deal of attention to two details:

- Maintaining careful records in order to document your sources of information
- Exercising extreme caution to avoid plagiarism [*see* plagiarism *in the Glossary*]

As a result, notes taken in preparation for writing a paper should

- appear on 3" x 5" or 4" x 6" note cards,
- include only one idea on a card,
- acknowledge the source from which the note is taken, including the author, the title, and the page number [*see* Research Paper *later in Part III for documentation forms*],
- include quotation marks around any words taken directly from the source,
- paraphrase any technical information [*see* paraphrase *in the Glossary and later in Part III*],
- include words, phrases, lists, or sentences that summarize main ideas [*see* precis *in the Glossary and later in Part III*],
- be concise,
- address the main ideas,
- treat examples, illustrations, or other supporting details only when these are particularly telling,

- include a slug, or title, that names the topic of the note, one that helps the writer arrange the note cards later according to an organizational plan. [*See* Research Paper *later in Part III.*]

Although note cards can, of course, be written at the keyboard, you should maintain the flexibility of the card system. Adjust your printer commands to accept either the 3" x 5" or 4" x 6" cards and follow the preceding guidelines.

PROCESS

The process of taking notes for a paper is considerably more complicated than for other reading matter. Notes for a paper must be preceded by the development of a preliminary outline and some reading in the general subject area. [*See* Research Paper *later in Part III.*]

Even though these steps start with prewriting, understand that other tasks have been completed: selecting, narrowing, and determining the direction of the topic; reading the preliminary sources; preparing a preliminary bibliography; and developing the preliminary outline.

Look now at the steps in the actual note-taking process.

STEP 1   **Prewriting • Getting Ready**

You need a preliminary outline, the research material, 3" x 5" or 4" x 6" note cards, and an ink pen. Using ink helps keep your note cards legible through the extensive handling required to organize your paper.

The preliminary outline includes the words and phrases that become the slugs for your note cards. A *slug* is a title or topic for a note card, and it appears on the top line of the card. Accurate, descriptive slugs help you organize your cards later. Remember, however, that the outline undergoes constant revision. You will no doubt add topics and subtopics, and you may well decide to eliminate some. Using slugs lets you change the organization as you please.

To begin, check the table of contents and index of any books, looking for parts that seem pertinent. Refer to these sections or chapters and read for relevant details.

Keep your numbered bibliography cards nearby. [*See* Research Paper *later in Part III.*] Use the numbers on the cards to code the source of your notes. For instance, if you are reading from page 56 in a magazine whose bibliography card you have numbered 8, then the code 8-56 goes in the upper-right corner of your note card. If you omit this code, you may be unable to document later. Most instructors react harshly to sloppy documentation.

STEP 2 **Writing • Selecting the Details**

As you find information in your reading matter that helps you develop main points or subpoints in your outline, take notes. Begin by noting the source of the material. Use either a code number, as discussed in Step 1, or the author's last name and the page number. Put this information in the upper right corner of your note card.

Write only one idea on each card, even if that idea is only a few words. If you include more than one idea, the cards become useless when you begin to arrange them for your paper.

Put your notes in your own words. You may use a list, paraphrase, or precis form. [*Follow the suggestions in* Paraphrase *and* Precis *elsewhere in Part III for writing accurate summaries*.]

Avoid copying words from the text as if they were your own. Put quotation marks around words taken directly from the source. In order to avoid plagiarism, you must be scrupulously careful with your note cards. Omitting quotation marks around an author's words at this point will obviously cause you to omit them later, when you transfer the information from the cards to your paper. The price of such carelessness may be higher than you are willing to pay: Your instructor will fail papers that include plagiarism. Be careful.

STEP 3 **Revising and Proofreading • Checking the Note Cards**

Because the notes you take are for your own use, the format and style are generally unimportant. As long as you include the necessary information, your note card will be satisfactory. To assure accuracy, proofread and revise each card before you turn it aside to begin another one. Ask yourself the following questions about each card:

- Does the card give the source from which it is taken, including author, title, and page number?
- Does it note the subject, preferably as a slug, taken directly from the preliminary outline?
- Have I avoided plagiarism by placing quotation marks around any words not my own?
- Does my paraphrase or precis accurately express the point of view of the author from whom I took the note?
- Have I correctly spelled the names of people and places?
- Have I accurately recorded dates, statistics, or other numbers?

When you finish checking one note card, go on to the next. Failing to check before turning a card aside is begging for a long search later to find a forgotten page reference, the end of an incomplete quotation, or the accurate spelling of a name.

SAMPLE OF NOTES FOR A PAPER

The following notes, taken from the original passage quoted in the Sample of Notes for a Class, illustrate three general concepts:

- Notes for a paper take a form very different from those for a class.
- Notes for a paper frequently use a type of summary called a *precis*.
- A single note card includes only one idea.

[*Compare* Precis: Sample for Science, *later in Part III, with the following notes.*]

The following notes would be included in a paper discussing environmentally safe ways of controlling insects that are agricultural pests.

---

4 - 16

Control—birds

Because of their rapid metabolism, birds daily eat more than their own weight. Since insects are not fully digestible, birds eat nearly twice their weight.

---

4 - 17

Control—birds

will "fill their stomachs 5 to 6 times daily" so eat large amounts—much of insect not digestible.

4 - 18

Control—birds

Comparison: 10-lb. baby would eat 18'/₃ lb. per day

(Do own comparison with adult, same proportions.)

4 - 19

Control—birds—encourage more

Add "windbreaks, living fences, shrub buffers, grass waterways, and farm ponds" to encourage insect-eating birds to stay.

 Analysis of the Sample Notes for a Paper. The preceding note cards, taken from the same passage as the notes for a class, emphasize the differences between the two kinds of notes. Consider these items:

- Each card begins with a slug, or title, to show where the note fits into the overall topic. Each card deals with *Control—birds*, but the last adds a subdivision to the slug to help the writer organize the cards later.
- Each includes a single idea: some as words and phrases, some by complete sentences, some with direct quotation, some entirely in the note taker's own words.

- Each includes a code number in the upper-right corner. The code tells the writer in which book and page the information was found. The number 4 refers to the bibliography card the writer has designated 4; thus the number becomes shorthand for both the name of the author and the title of the book. The second number, (e.g., 16) indicates the page number on which the specific information is to be found.

Use these guidelines to take accurate and useful notes. They will help you avoid plagiarism and allow you to gather information from many sources without confusion—the two hurdles that the successful note-taker must overcome.

Outlines

Outlines serve several purposes, primarily as summaries for something we have read or are about to develop into a paper or speech. They are somewhat like skeletons: the bare bones on which to hang the muscle of a composition. Sometimes their formality intimidates writers, but in reality they are merely lists that show the arrangement of details. In this section, you look at an outline as a summary of reading matter, in preparation for a paper, and in preparation for a speech. While all follow the general characteristics, each takes a slightly different approach to suit its purpose.

CHARACTERISTICS

The outline includes certain characteristics. An outline

- includes a title,
- may begin with a thesis statement or, in the case of a speech, an introductory statement,
- includes topics or sentences, but not both,
- follows a parallel structure [see parallel structure in the Glossary],
- uses a combination of Roman numerals, upper- and lower-case letters, and Arabic numbers to show relationships,
- shows the logic of development so that the summary of the parts of any one subdivision equals the topic of that division,
- includes topics that are mutually exclusive,
- includes at least two divisions at any level so that an item designated 1 will be followed by 2, and an item designated a will be followed by b,

- guides the paragraph structure of a written paper, with each main idea or subheading representing a separate paragraph,
- uses periods and parentheses to set number and letter designations apart from the outline topics or sentences,
- follows a pattern of indentation to show the relationship of ideas,
- capitalizes only the first word of each topic in a topic outline,
- omits periods after topics in a topic outline,
- capitalizes the first word of the sentence in a sentence outline,
- includes a period at the end of each sentence in a sentence outline.

A fully developed outline that includes numerous details should follow the pattern shown below:

Title

I.
   A.
   B.
      1.
      2.
   C.
      1.
      2.
II.
   A.
      1.
         a.
         b.
      2.
   B.
      1.
      2.
         a.
            1)
            2)
               a)
               b)
            3)
         b.
      3.
III.
   A.
   B.

Note that the preceding sample outline form illustrates characteristics peculiar to the form:

- The Roman numerals have a ragged left margin so that the periods after them align vertically.
- The number-letter designation follows this pattern:
  - Roman numerals
  - Capital letters
  - Arabic numbers
  - Lower-case letters
  - Arabic numbers followed by close parenthesis
  - Lower-case letters followed by close parenthesis
- Each number or letter is followed by a period or a close parenthesis.
- Each level is represented by equal indentation. Thus, all items designated by a capital letter appear at the same left margin.
- The total of the subpoints equals the main point. Thus, in the section labeled with a Roman numeral II, item B equals the total of subpoints 1, 2, and 3. Likewise, item 2 equals the total of subpoints a and b, and item a equals the total of subpoints 1), 2), and 3).
- Divisions should be mutually exclusive. For instance, if you divide *college students* into *male*, *female*, and *nontraditional*, then you have a problem with mutual exclusion. *Nontraditional students*, those older than most, are either *male* or *female*. The divisions overlap. To solve the problem, divide *college students* into *traditional* and *nontraditional*. Those two subdivisions could in turn be divided into *male* and *female*. Then each division is mutually exclusive.
- Because outlines follow a parallel structure, you should note that items within categories are parallel to each other. Thus items listed after Roman numerals must be parallel. In addition, items A, B, and C in I must be parallel, but they need not be parallel with A and B in either II or III. [*See* parallel structure *in the Glossary.*]

These general characteristics should help you develop an outline to meet the most demanding needs. Follow every detail with exceeding care if you are submitting a formal outline as part of a paper. Pay less attention to details if you are taking notes for your eyes only.

Recognizing those acceptable differences, this section focuses on the specific purposes of outlines and how you can develop outlines for each of those purposes.

AS A SUMMARY

Frequently, as you read or listen, you need to take notes. While the approach to note-taking varies from individual to individual and situation to situation [*see also* Notes *elsewhere in Part III*], one form of note-taking is outlining.

The outline, while rather formal in appearance, permits a writer to show relationships among ideas. By keeping track of those relationships as they develop, either as you read or listen, you can always see how one idea relates to another or how an example explains a general concept.

PROCESS

The process of taking notes by means of an outline is only slightly different from taking any other kind of notes. The biggest difference is form.

STEP 1   **Prewriting • Getting an Overview**

If you are taking notes from reading matter, skim the chapter or section and pick out its main points. Write them down, perhaps on separate sheets of paper, allowing ample space for supporting details.

If you are taking notes from a lecture, listen carefully for the speaker's clues. He or she may say something like, "This afternoon we will discuss three methods for approaching the potentially irate client." You know, then, to look for three main ideas. In addition, listen for clues such as *first, second, one of the reasons, another,* and other similar transitional devices that signal main and supporting ideas.

Having a general overview should help you determine which supporting details belong with which main ideas.

STEP 2   **Writing • Showing Relationships among Ideas**

Designate main headings by Roman numerals. As you read or hear about details that support or explain those main ideas, list them as subheadings, using capital letters. If additional supporting examples or illustrations appear as support for the subheadings, then indent for another "layer" of details.

Listing topics in their appropriate levels of relationship should help you better understand the material you are studying.

STEP 3   **Revising and Proofreading • Checking for Accuracy**

As you reread your outline, think about the relationships of ideas as your outline expresses them. For instance, start with the supporting ideas in one section. Do the ideas listed as subpoints really explain the topic under which you have them listed? In other words, do subtopics 1, 2, and 3 under B really illustrate, explain, list the parts, or make up the whole of topic B?

If you find illogical levels of support, revise the outline until you are certain it accurately reflects what you have read or heard.

SAMPLE OUTLINE AS A SUMMARY

The following outline summarizes reading material. For comparison's sake, this sample shows the outline first in topic form and then in sentence form. Use whichever best serves your purpose.

For the text from which the following outline was made, see Notes: Sample Notes for a Class, elsewhere in Part III. In addition, in that same section, you can compare the less formal notes appearing with the original text in Notes and the more formal notes appearing as an outline here.

Topic Outline

Birds as Insect Controllers

I. How birds help
  A. Have high metabolism rate
  B. Eat nearly twice weight
      1. 3-ounce to $5^1/_2$-ounce ratio in birds
      2. 10-pound to $18^1/_3$-pound ratio in humans

II. How environment helps
  A. Vegetation
      1. Windbreaks
      2. Living fences
      3. Shrub buffers
  B. Water
      1. Farm ponds
      2. Grass waterways

Sentence Outline

Birds as Insect Controllers

I. Birds eat insects.
   A. The birds have a high metabolism rate.
   B. The birds eat almost twice their own weight.
      1. A 3-ounce baby bird will eat 5$^1/_2$ ounces of insects.
      2. A 10-pound human baby would have to eat 18$^1/_3$ pounds of food.

II. The environment attracts birds.
   A. Planting the right vegetation attracts birds.
      1. Windbreaks provide birds protection.
      2. Living fences provide birds nesting and roosting sites.
      3. Shrub buffers provide birds protection.
   B. Developing water sources attracts birds.
      1. Farm ponds provide birds with water and food.
      2. Grass waterways attract birds of different varieties.

Analysis of the Sample Outline as a Summary. The preceding sample outline, which appears in both topic and sentence form, should help you see the importance of an outline in showing relationships among ideas. If you compare this outline with the notes [*see* Notes *earlier in Part III*] on the same reading material, you can see how ideas take on a new meaning when grouped by relation. Notice these characteristics about the two forms of the outline above:

- Each of the main headings is supported by two subheadings. Although such perfectly even distribution is not essential, it does indicate that the note taker has not given undue attention to one main idea while neglecting the others.
- Each division includes at least two items, thus following the logic that nothing can be divided into less than two.
- The subtopics, taken together, explain, illustrate, or provide other supporting detail to fully develop their respective main topics.
- Both the topic and sentence outline follow a parallel structure. Note that the main headings are parallel and that the subheadings are structurally parallel with the other subheadings in that same division. [*See* parallel structure *in the Glossary.*]
- The outlines use proper punctuation and indentation.
- The number-letter combinations establish relationships between and among ideas.

- The topic outline uses capital letters for only the first word in each topic.
- The topic outline does not include periods after the topics.
- The sentence outline follows the rules of capitalization for any sentence, and of course, each sentence ends with a period.

FOR A PAPER

Writing an outline for a paper requires a different thought process than writing an outline as a summary. When you outline as a summary, you reduce someone else's ideas to a bare-bones skeleton; however, when you outline in preparation for a paper, you must generate the bare-bones skeleton and then add the muscle. The process demands your creativity.

Developing a formal outline may not be necessary for all papers, but you will almost always develop a kind of outline, even if it is nothing but a loose listing of ideas you want to include. You will notice throughout this book, in the course of the prewriting work, we develop lists. We do not call them outlines, but in fact they are scratch outlines. To make them into formal outlines requires adding only the formality: the proper number-letter combinations, indentation pattern, capitalization and punctuation necessities, and parallel structures.

Study now the process for turning a loose listing into a formal outline.

PROCESS

Assume, for the sake of practicality, that you are about to write a paper that requires a formal outline. It might be a research paper, a technical paper, or a long paper of unusual formality. Follow these steps for developing the outline.

STEP 1   **Prewriting • Looking at the Lists**

As you work through the prewriting stages of your paper, you will develop one or more lists. From these lists you will develop your outline. One list may include your main points. You probably have put that list into some kind of order. [*See* organization *in the Glossary for an explanation of the main kinds of order.*] You may have another list of the supporting details you plan to use to explain your main ideas: illustrations, examples, and so forth. These lists, reorganized and rearranged, will make up the outline.

STEP 2   **Writing • Putting the Lists into Outline Form**

Begin by writing your thesis statement. [*See* thesis statement *in the Glossary.*] The prewriting activities for the particular kind of paper will have helped you develop that statement.

Next, list your main ideas either on separate sheets of paper or on a single sheet with ample space beneath each main topic. Designate these main ideas with Roman numerals.

Now begin adding the items from your list of supporting details, the A, B, C part. Quite likely, an outline for a five-paragraph paper will go no farther than the second level of division. If you do have supporting ideas listed that actually develop a second-level topic, such as 1 and 2 to develop A, then of course you will want to add them.

 For a five-paragraph theme, you should have no more than three Roman numerals. For a longer paper, you should have a separate Roman numeral for each main idea you will develop, five, six, or even more. Two hints:

1. The introduction and conclusion generally do not appear on the outline.
2. The Roman numerals usually represent body paragraphs. Thus, three Roman numerals designate three body paragraphs in a five-paragraph theme. [*See* Writing a Multi-Paragraph Paper *in Part I for a complete discussion.*]

Consider these possible problems:

- You may have designated something less than a main idea by a Roman numeral. If you cannot develop at least a full paragraph for each Roman numeral, you have divided illogically.
- Your topic may be too broad. As a result, your main topics may include far more material than you can support in a single paragraph. While subheadings can also designate independent paragraphs, they usually do not, except in particularly long papers.

Note: When subheadings designate independent paragraphs, the main headings under which they appear do not represent paragraphs. For instance:

    I. Traditional college students
        A. Male
        B. Female
    II. Nontraditional college students
        A. Male
        B. Female

If you develop one paragraph for *traditional male students* and another for *traditional female students*, then the two paragraphs together equal the topic represented in the Roman numeral designation I.

STEP 3   Revising • Polishing the Outline

When you have listed all the supporting ideas in logical order under their respective topics, you are ready to polish the outline. Ask yourself the following questions about logic and organization:

- Together, do the main headings provide adequate support for the thesis sentence?
- Are the divisions logical? Are the items within a division mutually exclusive?
- Is the outline a suitable skeleton on which to build a paper? If you develop paragraphs according to the main headings or subheadings in the outline, will you have a satisfactory development of your paper?

STEP 4   Proofreading • Checking the Peculiar Details

When the content is accurately and logically represented, you should attend to the peculiar characteristics of the outline form itself. Check these points:

- Does the outline follow a parallel structure?
- Are the number-letter combinations in correct sequence?
- Is each number or letter followed by a period and, in the case of fifth-level divisions or greater, by a parenthesis?
- Does each topic or sentence begin with a capital letter?
- Is the indentation accurate and consistent?
- Does each sentence in a sentence outline end with a period? (And, by the same token, are periods omitted after topics in a topic outline?)
- Are sentences in a sentence outline structured accurately and punctuated appropriately?
- Is spelling accurate throughout?

When you can answer "yes" to all these questions, you should have an accurate outline.

SAMPLE OUTLINE FOR A PAPER

The following outline was used to develop the cause-and-effect sample paper for social studies. [*See* Cause and Effect: Sample for Social Sciences, *in Part II.*]

Isle Royale's Riches

Thesis: Only three natural resources have merited man's battle with Isle Royale's isolation and climate.

I. Lumber
   A. Destroyed by flood
   B. Halted by fire

II. Fish
   A. Commercial activity
   B. Individual activity
           1. Decline by unknown causes
           2. Decline by man-made causes

III. Copper
   A. Indian miners
   B. White settlers

Analysis of the Sample Outline for a Paper. The preceding sample illustrates the general characteristics of an outline used to develop a paper, in this case a five-paragraph theme. [*See* Writing a Multi-Paragraph Paper *in Part I.*] Note these particular features:

- The thesis statement, which also appears as the last sentence in the introductory paragraph of the paper, serves as a guide to the writer. It sets a tone (*battle with isolation and climate*) and suggests the kinds of details needed.
- Introductory paragraph matter does not appear in the outline.
- The three main divisions, designated by the Roman numerals, suggest the body paragraphs of the paper. [*Compare the outline's divisions with the actual paper in* Cause and Effect: Sample for Social Sciences, *in Part II.*]
- The outline indicates the order of development: the first body paragraph will discuss the lumber industry; the second, the fishing industry; the third, the copper industry. The order is one of importance, the most important last.
- Each of the main divisions is structurally parallel, each being a noun.

- The first level of a division, designated by a capital letter, represents the subtopic sentence of each paragraph. The paper's first body paragraph will discuss the flood that ruined the first business attempt by the lumber industry; then it will discuss the fire that destroyed the second attempt.
- Each pair of subtopics is parallel, but the three pairs are not (and need not be) parallel to each other.
- Each body paragraph includes two subtopics, A and B; one subtopic includes two subtopics of its own, 1 and 2.
- The outline suggests that the three body paragraphs will include nearly equal amounts of detail. Thus, the writer assures a balanced development.
- The conclusion does not appear in the outline.

FOR A SPEECH

Although the outline for a speech resembles—logically so—the outline for a paper, most speech instructors suggest a few additional details that help the speaker deliver a successful extemporaneous speech. Think through the following process.

PROCESS

Although this handbook is not designed to help you prepare a speech, we can certainly help you write a suitable outline that in turn may at least start you in the right direction!

STEP 1 **Prewriting • Planning the Contents of the Speech**
Probably you must prepare a specific kind of speech: introductory, demonstrative, informative, persuasive, and so on. No doubt you have suggestions for possible topics, either from a textbook, from the instructor, or from the person who has asked you to make the speech.

Use the same kinds of prewriting activities as you would for writing a paper. [*See* Prewriting *in Part I and refer to specific sections in Parts II and III.*] When you have developed lists of main and supporting ideas, you are ready to begin your outline.

STEP 2 **Writing • Developing the Body of the Speech**
As you prepare your outline, do not concern yourself with the introduction or conclusion. Think only about the main ideas of the speech.

List your main ideas on separate note cards. Arrange them in order but, for the present, omit number or letter designations. On each card, under the main idea, list the supporting points you want to include. Use the indented form. When you have listed all the necessary supporting details, arrange them in order. Finally, when you feel satisfied with the content and organization, add number and letter designations.

STEP 3   **Writing • Forming the Introduction and Conclusion**

Many speakers make an effort to memorize their opening and closing statements. They believe that by so doing they can get into the speech smoothly and so proceed extemporaneously. Likewise, rather than risk a rambling search for just the right concluding words, they memorize the final sentence, and so they present a smooth, concise end.

As a result, many speakers develop a special outline form that permits them to include the introduction and conclusion. Here's a sample format:

Title

Purpose: (A sentence here indicates the purpose of the speech, which may be, for instance, to persuade the audience to vote for a specific candidate for class office. Think of this sentence as a thesis sentence for a speech.)

I. Introduction: (The introductory sentences appear here, written out word for word.)

II. (First main point of the body appears here, followed by supporting details as necessary.)
  A.
  B.

III. (Second main point of the body appears here. Use as many main points and supporting points as necessary, adding divisions to the outline as necessary.)
  A.
  B.
  C.

IV. Conclusion: (The concluding remarks are written out here, word for word.)

As you compose your introduction, include it in the outline as suggested in this step. Treat the conclusion in the same way.

STEP 4   **Revising and Proofreading • Putting the Outline on Note Cards**

When you think the outline works well for your speech, transfer it to note cards. Most speakers put their introductory statements on a single card and each of the main ideas on a separate card, with the concluding remarks on a single card. Write or type the cards, perhaps using all capital letters or a large font. Do whatever you can to make the cards easily legible from a lectern.

When you finish, reread the note cards carefully to check for mis-spelled words that may cause you confusion or for the omission of key words necessary to help you remember what you plan to talk about. Be sure to practice your speech using the outline in note form so that you will be comfortable during the actual presentation.

SAMPLE OUTLINE FOR A SPEECH

The following outline uses the special format many speakers prefer.

Planning Your Garden by Computer

Purpose: The audience will learn how computers help gardeners plan their space for best productivity.

I. Introduction: Early last spring on a warm, sunny day my father and I headed for our 10' by 10' garden. He carried a bag of fertilizer, the hoe, and a rake. I came along behind with the stakes, string, packages of seed . . . and a computer printout.

II. Source of printout
A. Questionnaire
B. Procedure
C. Result

III. Contents
A. Direction of rows
B. Spacing between rows
C. Arrangement of varieties
D. Spacing between plants

IV. Results
A. Fewer plants
B. Greater production
C. Second plantings

V. Conclusion: It seems a little strange to trudge to the garden with a computer-printed diagram of how to plant. As a result of last year's experience, how ever, we will continue to rely on the computer's brain to do what we've been doing for years. But now we get results!

Analysis of the Sample Outline for a Speech. While the outline includes most of the characteristics of that for a paper, note the three distinguishing features:

- The Purpose statement replaces the thesis sentence.
- The introduction not only appears in the outline but also is written as a full sentence (or sentences) even though the outline is a topic outline.
- The conclusion likewise appears in the outline, written out as full sentences.

The information in this section should help you to develop a suitable outline for whatever purpose you face, whether it be to take notes on reading matter or from an oral presentation, to prepare a long paper, or to plan a speech. Consult cross-references for thorough understanding.

Paraphrase

A paraphrase is a kind of summary. A paraphrase restates a passage in your own words. In one sense, it is a summary because you are "translating" technical or complicated material into your own vocabulary. In another, however, it is not a summary, because it is usually the same length, or nearly the same length, as the original. [*A summary that is shorter than the original passage, is called a* precis *or synopsis. See those sections elsewhere in Part III for comparison.*]

You may be asked to paraphrase passages to show you have read and understood them. You may be asked to paraphrase scientific results as part of a research project. You may write paraphrases for your own benefit, to clarify complicated passages. Whatever the reason for writing them, paraphrases provide a means of simplifying complicated, technical passages.

CHARACTERISTICS

A paraphrase usually

- reflects the paraphraser's own vocabulary,
- reduces the original only slightly, usually by less than one-fourth,
- displays careful reading of the original,
- represents the original idea accurately and completely, without reflecting personal bias,
- uses clear, effective sentences as well as good mechanics, usage, and grammar.

PROCESS

To write a paraphrase, use the following procedure.

STEP 1   **Prewriting • Reading the Material**

Read the original passage several times to be sure you understand its meaning.

Next, before you begin writing, jot down the main ideas in the order in which they appear. Use only the key words or phrases, not sentences.

STEP 2   **Writing • Drafting the First Summary**

Once you have the material clearly in mind, put aside the original passage. Refer only to your list of main ideas, and write the summary in your own words. It is important to do so in order to avoid lifting whole phrases and sentences from the original. The temptation to plagiarize is the result of lazy thinking; by picking up an author's phrases and sentences, the paraphraser need not struggle to put the ideas into his or her own words. [*See* plagiarism *in the Glossary.*]

Beneath the obvious theft of plagiarism lies a deeper problem. Because the very purpose of the paraphrase is to simplify and reduce difficult passages, the ultimate futility of using the author's words should be self-evident.

STEP 3   **Revising • Checking for Accurate Content**

Once you have completed your paraphrase, reread the original and compare it with your version. Ask yourself these questions:

- Have I included all the important ideas? If I haven't, how can I best include them?
- Have I avoided all insignificant and unnecessary ideas?
- Have I accurately represented specifics and generalities? If not, what can I change to produce an objective paraphrase?
- Have I developed each idea the same relative length as in the original? If not, how can I best adjust the imbalance?
- Have I placed the same emphasis on each idea as in the original? If not, how can I resolve the difference?
- Have I used a simple, straightforward vocabulary?
- Have I used clear, effective sentence structure?
- Have I plagiarized? If so, how can I rephrase things?
- Make any additions, deletions, or changes necessary to maintain accuracy.

Be absolutely certain that you do not take phrases or sentences directly from the original. Read through the original passage again, line by line, comparing it with your paraphrase.

STEP 4   **Proofreading • Correcting the Mechanics**

Make sure that spelling, punctuation, grammar, usage, and mechanics are accurate. [*See Part IV for rules and examples*.] Check for accurate vocabulary.

Check the sentence structure. Have you used effective sentences? Have you varied their structure? Are they easy to read? Finally, check one more time that you have not committed any of the deadly sins of paraphrase writing. Be certain that you have not

- misrepresented or changed the emphasis of an idea from the original source, or
- relied too heavily on the wording of the original passage and allowed plagiarism to creep into your work.

Use the following sample paraphrase to test your understanding of the process and the expected result. An analysis of the sample follows.

SAMPLE PARAPHRASE

The original passage that follows uses technical language to discuss the way in which we learn. The paraphrase simplifies this technical language and sentence structure. Note evidence of the preceding process steps.

Original Passage

Recent research has determined that humans tend to fall into one of four quadrants according to their learning styles. Quadrant one learners tend to be divergent thinkers and need personal and emotional involvement in order for learning to take place. As idea people, they function through social integration and strive to bring unity to diversity. Quadrant two learners are assimilators, needing systematic learning via a logical and intellectual approach. As analytic learners, they reflect on ideas to create concepts and models. Quadrant three learners tend to be convergent thinkers who are practical, problem-oriented people. Pragmatic decision makers, they restrict judgment to concrete things. Quadrant four learners are accommodators needing random patterns of learning. They aim to bring action to concepts and exercise authority through common vision, hesitating to make decisions affecting others.

Paraphrase

As learners, we fall into four groups. The first kind of learner needs to be caught up in an idea physically and personally. His personal involvement and concern for others make him seek harmony. He's emotional. The second kind of learner absorbs all the information around him, categorizes it, and reasons out the results. He will seek the data gathered to develop an ideal. He's systematic. The third kind of learner is opposite the first kind. He tends to be less emotional, more utilitarian. His thorough analysis results in a valid decision. He's practical. The fourth kind of learner needs numerous approaches to learning something new. As an opposite to the second kind of learner, he relies more on instinct than on logic. When decisions must be made, he doesn't like to interfere with others' lives. He's an accommodator.

Analysis of the Sample Paraphrase. Note the following characteristics regarding the sample paraphrase:

- The paraphrase presents the same ideas as the original passage and is nearly the same length.
- Its vocabulary is quite different from that of the original. This change marks its most important function: to reduce technical or complicated writing to simpler, easier-to-understand prose. For instance, the technical term *quadrant* is omitted, as are words such as *divergent, convergent, assimilators, analytic learners,* and *pragmatic.*
- Complicated ideas are presented in simple sentences to make them easier to understand. In the original passage, quadrant one learner is defined by means of a sentence with a compound predicate. In the paraphrase, first kind of learner is defined by a simple sentence.
- The paraphrase and the original are nearly the same length, though the original includes nine sentences to the paraphrase's fifteen since the sentences in the paraphrase are much shorter than those in the original.
- Words are shorter in the paraphrase. While words tend to be three syllables in the original, those in the paraphrase tend to two syllables.
- The paraphrase shows careful reading and thorough understanding of the original. No plagiarism has crept in.
- Sentence structure, mechanics, usage, and grammar are accurate.

Following these step-by-step procedures and heeding these suggestions should enable you to create an equally successful paraphrase.

Poetry

Poetry takes many forms—indeed sometimes apparently no form—and employs special kinds of language. Consequently, describing how to write poetry is somewhat like describing how to make snowflakes. No two poems are quite alike, and even poets cannot succinctly define poetry or explain how they write it. The following section, then, introduces poetic characteristics and offers suggestions for general poetic techniques.

CHARACTERISTICS

Poems vary from two-liners to book-length epics. Likewise, the forms vary from carefully metered and rhymed verse to seemingly unstructured and unrhymed word groups that look very much like prose. [*See* poem *in the Glossary for a list of different kinds of poems*.] Any list of the characteristics of poetry must necessarily be general; nevertheless, the following may prove helpful to aspiring poets. Generally, a poem

- expresses the writer's feelings about a subject,
- relies on imagery [*see* imagery *in the Glossary*] to stimulate the reader's thoughts, thus conveying a larger message,
- relies on figurative language [*see* figure of speech *in the Glossary*], especially metaphor and simile [*see* metaphor *and* simile *in the Glossary*] to tease the ear and mind,
- builds language in multiple layers of meaning, thus making every word count more than once,
- may include a rhyme pattern [*see* rhyme *in the Glossary*],
- may follow a specific rhythmic pattern called *meter* [*see* meter *in the Glossary*],
- uses nontraditional punctuation to clarify meaning and show relationships among ideas,
- may include lines grouped together to form stanzas.

PROCESS

Although it is virtually impossible to tell someone how to write a poem, this section looks at the process by which a poem can be developed.

STEP 1   **Prewriting • Finding Ideas**

Ideas for poetry, like ideas for any other writing, come from observation and experience. Immediate surroundings and the intimate details of life's daily struggle are the stuff of poetry. To find poetic ideas, most poets keep journals, making daily—even multiple daily—entries. They record thoughts, observations, reactions, or images that they will turn to for inspiration. Writing daily helps you become more observant, more thoughtful, more aware. [*See also* Prewriting *in Part I for additional suggestions.*]

After you keep a journal for some time, you find ready ideas for your poems.

STEP 2   **Prewriting • Selecting Images**

An idea that expresses your pleasure, joy, fear, disgust, or perhaps irony, surprise, or awe is a perfect starting point for a poem. Select images that best convey your primary message. For example, if you think a certain kind of home is distasteful, you won't say *distasteful*. Instead, you can use images that picture distaste. Show plastic flowers and bleach-bottle ornaments, and let the reader decide for him or herself.

So, list possible images. Journal ideas may stimulate your thinking. Perhaps just concentrating on your subject and your reaction to it will stimulate thinking. You may need several days to think of just the right images.

STEP 3   **Writing • Working on the Poem**

Few poets sit down to write a poem saying, "Now I'm going to write a four-stanza poem with iambic pentameter and a rhyme scheme of abba/cddc/effe/ghhg." Rather, they allow the subject to determine the poem's form. Forcing yourself to write in a particular form is a superb discipline and often the basis for a class assignment. But in reality, creative poets don't follow this practice.

Developing the poem, then, becomes a trial-and-error process. The struggle to write a poem is lessened if you "let go," writing freely the ideas, images, figures of speech, even series of descriptive words without fighting for rhyme, rhythm, or form. Get the ideas on paper. Save the frustration for later!

STEP 4   **Revising • Fighting for Form**

Once the ideas are on paper, think about form, rhyme, and rhythm, never losing track, of course, of your content and your message.

Review the list of characteristics earlier in this section. The layers of meaning and the imagery and figurative language stimulate the reader's senses and imagination, and these become part of a poem only by conscious effort on the part of the writer. Work to add them. For instance, if you can personify a computer program that is giving you nightmares, the reader can identify with that "person" who chases you using its power cord as a whip!

Use the images and figures of speech that best enhance the message.

Next, improve rhythm. Even unrhymed poems usually have a rhythm that heightens their message. If your poem rhymes, check its pattern for consistency. Then see if you can improve the form, perhaps by altering stanzas or rearranging them for better flow and clarity.

Finally, check every single word in the poem. Is each necessary? Does each carry an important, or at least worthwhile, meaning? Can you eliminate any without affecting meaning? Remember that strong nouns and verbs eliminate the necessity for weak, generally wordy, modifiers. This is as true of poetry as it is of prose.

STEP 5   **Proofreading • Checking the Final Details**

Obviously, you want your poem's presentation to be accurate. Therefore, check your spelling carefully. A misspelled word suggests a lack of attention to detail, and poetry is synonymous with detail.

Next, check punctuation. Remember that punctuation in a poem does not follow the general rules; rather it often serves to separate and show relationships between ideas. Make the punctuation work for you.

Finally, add a title and sign your name!

SAMPLE POEMS

The following poems represent two very different kinds of verse. One is freeform, and the other is highly structured. Compare the two poems and their analyses with your own work. Perhaps some of the ideas—either in the poems or the analyses—will serve as springboards for improving your own work.

Ode to a Tupperware Container

Through a plastic-flower grotto
Mary offers peace and tranquility.
Clorox-bottle topiary trees welcome silver-balled stands,

Snow White, Bambi, and bird baths.
No resemblance of nature left.
Plush-green-carpet-lawn, astroturf.

The tinker-toy community, all the originality of tonka-toy blocks,
Bedecked in aluminum siding, adorned with
Precious carriages.
Precise. Exact. Car-ported. These monuments to man
Reveal more than they hide.

Afternoon Tea

The women sit and sip their tea
And gossip about some absentee,
Cite some authors in plebeian slur:
Whitman, Rousseau, and Joyce Kilmer.

"Wouldn't it be swell to get
Heston to read the great Hamlet
And selections from the poems of Edgar Guest?"

("I finally passed my driver's test—I wore a knit dress!"
"Her daughter's sick."

"Betty's failed arithmetic!")

"I wish we could get Ogden free
Of charge to read his poetry."

"He's the greatest since Guthrie!"

The pseudos sit and sip their tea.

 Analysis of the Sample Poems. The preceding poems show, at least in brief, the vast range of possibilities open to poets—vast subject matter, varied form, different approaches. Look closer at them:

- "Ode to a Tupperware Container" does not rhyme and includes two stanzas, the second broken by a separated line to enhance its meaning.

- "Afternoon Tea," on the other hand, follows a rhyme pattern of aabb/ccdd/eeaa/aa and includes four stanzas, the last three broken by the spacing in order to show changes in speaker.
- "Ode" expresses the writer's attitude toward modern suburban houses and what they say of their occupants.
- "Tea" expresses the writer's attitude toward groups of women who feign literary interest when, in fact, they spend more time gossiping.
- "Ode" contrasts words such as *grotto* and *topiary trees* with *plastic flower* and *Clorox bottle*. These contrasts startle the reader into recognizing the poem's message.
- "Tea" uses phrases such as *plebeian slur*, and references to *passing a driver's test*, to set the tone of the "pseudos" sitting and sipping their tea.
- "Ode" alludes to common trappings: *Snow White* and *Bambi* to ceramic yard decorations; *tonka-toy blocks* to houses set tightly together in suburban neighborhoods; *precious carriages* to the decorative pieces that appear on the sides of houses or above garage doors.
- "Tea" alludes to literature: the names *Whitman* (the American poet), *Rousseau* (a French philosopher and social reformer), and *Joyce Kilmer* (another American poet) point to a wide variety and quality of work. *Ogden* refers to the poet Ogden Nash, *Guthrie*, to an author of Wild West stories. Knowing these authors' works helps the reader understand the "pseudos."
- "Ode" is punctuated for emphasis, especially in the next-to-the-last line. Note how the periods force the reader to focus on each word.
- "Tea" uses punctuation and new lines to show change in speaker. The series of unrelated bits of gossip helps the writer to show the wide variety of topics discussed at this literary tea. Enclosing these quotations in parentheses separates them from the literary references in the rest of the poem.

The two poems illustrate diversity. As you begin writing verse, study poetry—all kinds of poetry. The more you read, the more creative your writing will become. Use this section of your handbook as a guide to begin your first poetic efforts. Then read, study, and write more!

Precis

A precis (pronounced *pray-see*) is a kind of summary. [*Compare the precis with two other kinds of summaries, the* Paraphrase *and the* Synopsis. *See those entries elsewhere in Part III.*] The purpose of a precis is to provide a shortened version of a piece of writing. You may be asked to write precis (plural, pronounced *pray-sees*) to show that you have read and understood chapters or passages. You may be asked to write precis to present concisely the results of your research in a special project. You may write precis for your own benefit, as a kind of note-taking.

A precis, then, is a short restatement of the main points of a piece of writing. A precis of one page may well summarize the points presented in 25 pages of carefully supported detail. Similarly, a precis of 100 words may restate what an author explains in three pages. Finally, a precis of a single sentence may summarize a paragraph or two.

CHARACTERISTICS

A precis usually

- omits details, illustrations, and subordinate ideas, presenting instead the major ideas,
- reduces the original passage by at least two-thirds,
- indicates careful reading of the original passage,
- portrays the original author's concept accurately, without adding personal bias,
- follows the guidelines of standard grammar, usage, and mechanics—using strong, effective sentence structure.

PROCESS

To write an effective precis, follow these steps.

STEP 1   Prewriting • Reading the Material
Read the passage quickly to grasp the general idea and purpose. Look up any unfamiliar words or references.

Read the passage again, more slowly, to detect details as they relate to the main points.

Jot down the main ideas in your own words.

Reread the original passage, comparing your skeleton outline with the text. Revise as necessary to maintain accuracy or correct omissions.

STEP 2 **Writing • Preparing the Precis**
Without referring to the original, write the summary in your own words, following the skeleton outline developed in Step 1.

Use the following guidelines as you write:

- Organize your precis the same way as the original passage.
- Include only the bare essentials. If the original passage is well organized, you should be able to select a single main idea from each paragraph.
- Be sure, however, to include all the main points from the original passage, perhaps even using the passage's key words. The expression *key words* refers to terms or expressions unique to the subject. Take pains to avoid plagiarism. [*See* plagiarism *in the Glossary.*]

STEP 3 **Revising • Checking the Content**
Once you have completed your precis, ask yourself the following questions:

- Have I reduced the content by at least two-thirds?
- In the process of reducing volume, have I presented the main ideas, all the essentials?
- Have I omitted nonessential details and information?
- Does the precis honestly reflect the original passage, or have my own biases crept in?
- Have I avoided plagiarism?
- Have I written simply and clearly, with unadorned vocabulary?
- When the reader finishes the precis, will he or she understand the intent of the original work?

If you answer "no" to any of the above questions, revise the precis to solve the problems suggested.

STEP 4 **Proofreading • Checking for Accuracy**
Once you have completed the revisions, check the final copy for misspellings, punctuation and grammar errors, usage problems, and mechanical inaccuracies. [*See Part IV for rules and examples.*]

A NOTE ABOUT THE SAMPLES

The following samples offer models for an examination of the results of the precis process. Each sample includes the original passage from which the precis was written and is followed by an analysis.

SAMPLE FOR ENGLISH

A student writing a research paper for an English class has chosen to write about automobile-induced air pollution. She has found a passage in "Autos and Air Pollution," a brochure published by the United States Environmental Protection Agency. The original passage appears, followed by her precis. Once you have studied both, read the analysis that follows.

Original Passage

The use of leaded gasoline in vehicles designed for unleaded gasoline can increase tailpipe emissions 200 to 800 percent, EPA has determined. More than 1 million tons of hydrocarbons and 12 million tons of carbon monoxide were spewed from the tailpipes of cars with defective emission control systems during Fiscal Year 1983.

Studies show that most people who engage in fuel switching do so to save money—about 7 cents a gallon. However, these people are victims of faulty economics, according to Joe Cannon, EPA's assistant administrator for Air and Radiation. "In the long run, the use of leaded gas in the car will more quickly foul the spark plugs, wear out the exhaust system, degrade the oil, and foul the oxygen sensor in new cars, in addition to ruining the catalytic converter," he said.

Cannon estimates that people who substitute leaded for unleaded gasoline will end up paying 12 cents a gallon in extra maintenance and repairs.

Precis

Using leaded instead of unleaded gasoline contributes to a 200 to 800 percent increase in air-polluting emissions. According to Joe Cannon, EPA assistant administrator for Air and Radiation, while consumers save about seven cents a gallon at the pumps, they ultimately pay twelve cents a gallon more to repair the resulting damage to the car's ignition, exhaust, and lubricating systems.

Analysis of the Sample for English. The preceding precis follows the general guidelines for content, organization, and structure. Note the following specifics:

- The precis reduces the original passage of approximately 120 words to less than 60 words.
- Six sentences in the original passage become two in the precis.

- The choice of material included in the precis is determined by the general purpose of the research paper in which it is to be included. For instance, the information about the amount of pollutants emitted into the atmosphere as a result of defective emission-control systems is omitted, because the writer plans to deal only with problems resulting from the use of leaded gasoline.
- The choice of vocabulary is consistent with the original, especially as the original lacks technical terms needing simplification.
- The main ideas appear in the same order as in the original.
- EPA administrator Cannon is included to enhance the authenticity of the seven-cent/twelve-cent comparison; however, the writer chooses not to use his exact words. The summary of his comments is accurate and makes the same point more concisely.

Thus, a precis achieves its purpose and reduces a significant passage to a manageable size for use in a paper.

SAMPLE FOR SOCIAL SCIENCES

To explain government regulations and their effect on business, one student needed a concise definition of the Clean Air Act. He found an explanation in a brochure published by the United States Environmental Protection Agency and decided to summarize it in his paper. The original passage, its precis, and an analysis of the precis follow.

Original Passage

The Clean Air Act of 1970, amended in 1977 and 1981, is one of the basic laws under which EPA operates. Its purpose is "to protect and enhance the quality of the nation's air resources so as to promote the public health and welfare and the productive capacity of its population."

In order to do that, Congress authorized a national research and development program to prevent and control air pollution. The act also provided for EPA to assist state and local governments in the development and execution of their air quality programs.

The Clear Air Act required EPA to set national primary and secondary ambient air quality standards for certain air pollutants. The law also required emission standards for mobile sources of air pollution (vehicles), and for new stationary sources such as smokestacks. In addition, the act called for regulation of hazardous air pollutants for which no ambient air quality standard is applicable.

Another section of the law was designed to protect air quality in national parks, wilderness areas, monuments, seashores, and other areas of special national or regional natural, recreational, scenic, or historic value, and to prevent significant deterioration of air quality in those areas.

Precis

The Clean Air Act, designed to protect air quality, provides a means for studying and building a program to solve air-pollution problems. The program decides when pollutants become problems by establishing and applying standard levels permissible for various emissions, from moving and stationary sources. The act also addresses clean air standards in protected natural areas such as wildernesses and seashores.

Analysis of the Sample for Social Sciences. The precis achieves the goals set for a good summary. Note these specific characteristics:

- An original of over 150 words is reduced to about 60 in the precis.
- Eight sentences in the original are reduced to three.
- Every major idea is included.
- The precis maintains the same organization as the original.
- Sentence structure and vocabulary are appropriate for the audience.

SAMPLE FOR SCIENCE

In an ecology class, one student researched insect control, seeking a means of controlling insect damage without upsetting nature's balance. She found useful information in the booklet, "Teaching Soil and Water Conservation," published by the United States Department of Agriculture. Her precis and an analysis of it follow. [*For further comparison, see* Notes *and* Outlines: For a Class, *elsewhere in Part III, for sample notes taken from the following passage. Compare the notes with the precis that follows.*]

Original Passage

The food habits of birds make them especially valuable to agriculture. Because birds have higher body temperatures, more rapid digestion, and greater energy than most other animals, they require more food. Nestling birds make extremely rapid growth, requiring huge amounts of food.

They usually consume as much or more than their own weight in soft-bodied insects every day.

Young robins have been observed to gain eight times their original weight the first eight days of their life.

Insect-eating birds must fill their stomachs five to six times daily because they digest their food so fast and because of the large amount of indigestible material in insects.

One young robin, weighing three ounces, consumed 165 cutworms weighing 5¹/₂ ounces in one day. If a 10-pound baby ate at the same rate, he would eat 18¹/₃ pounds of food in a day.

Of course, birds cannot control insects completely, but they are of great value. By using soil- and water-conserving practices, farmers and ranchers could probably double the population of helpful birds. Field and farmstead windbreaks, living fences, shrub buffers, grass waterways, and farm ponds are only a few of the many land use practices useful in attracting and increasing beneficial forms of wildlife.

Precis

Because of their rapid metabolism, birds daily eat more than their own weight. Because insects are not fully digestible, insect-eating birds may eat nearly twice their weight in these pests. Residents can double the numbers of insect-eaters by providing coniferous trees, dense and thorny shrubs, and ponds to attract them to an area.

Analysis of the Sample for Science. The precis achieves the purpose of a summary. By condensing the long original passage to a manageable paragraph, the writer prepares to incorporate the information directly into her report. Note these specifics:

- The original passage is reduced from over 200 words to 55 words.
- Eleven sentences are reduced to three.
- The supporting details of the original, explaining specifics about nestlings and young robins, do not appear. While the details are interesting, they are unnecessary to convey main ideas.
- Scientific references not mentioned in the original appear in the precis. For instance, *windbreaks* becomes *coniferous trees*; and *living fences* and *shrub buffers* become *dense and thorny shrubs*. The student recognized windbreaks and living fences as such.
- The precis is developed with the ultimate goal of supporting the main idea in the paper. This goal helps determine which ideas go into a precis, and thus reflects editorial judgment. The materials still mirror the content and emphasis of the original. Nothing is distorted, or taken out of context, to meet the goals of the proposed paper.

SAMPLE WORK-PLACE WRITING

Students in a business class were asked to consider the businesses that rely on a single resource. One student chose to look at wood. In researching, he discovered a passage on its many uses. This passage, from a Department of Agriculture booklet, follows, after which you'll find the precis and its analysis.

Original Passage

Wood is a universal material, and no one has ever been able to make a satisfactory count of its many uses. The Forest Products Laboratory, a research institution of the United States Forest Service, at Madison, Wisconsin, once undertook to make an official count of wood uses. When last announced, the number was more than 5,000, and the argument had only started over how general or how specific a use had to be to get on the list.

Just one well-known wood-cellulose plastic, including its conversion products, claims 25,000 uses—among them such different items as dolls' eyes and advertising signs. The use of wood fiber as the basis for such products is increasing every day.

Another important use of wood is paper for printing our books, magazines, and newspapers. A high point in our culture came less than a century ago with the discovery that wood fiber could take the place of cotton or linen in paper manufacture. Today we use more than 73 million tons of paper and board each year. Of this amount, each person's annual share of all kinds of paper and board is about 660 pounds. When paper was made chiefly of rags, each person's annual share was less than 10 pounds.

Container board accounts for about a fourth of our paper and board use. Newsprint accounts for an additional 17 percent of paper use. The rest is used in a myriad of forms—writing paper; sanitary cartons for prunes, cereals, butter, ice cream; paper cups, plates, disposable napkins, towels, handkerchiefs; wrapping paper for groceries, meats, dry goods.

Precis

The Forest Products Laboratory, a research institution of the United States Forest Service, suggests over 5,000 uses for wood, but admittedly no one knows how to set the limits of specificity for the list. For instance, some wood fiber products alone can boast over 25,000 uses, including dolls' eyes and billboards. In another example, wood supplies annually over 73 million tons of paper and board, used for everything from containers to newsprint, amounting to over 40% of paper use.

Analysis of the Sample Work-Place Writing. The precis achieves the usual goals of a summary and does some additional things as well. Notice these characteristics:

- It reduces the original by about two-thirds.
- While it includes several specific examples (*dolls' eyes, billboards, containers to newsprint*), it mostly confines itself to main ideas.
- Statistics and sources are considered *key words* and thus appear in the precis just as they did in the original.
- The writer has achieved some organizational patterns not evident in the original and used transitions to clarify relationships. Note particularly the transitions *for instance* and *in another example* that alert the reader that these two show examples of how hard it is to quantify the uses of wood. Thus, the precis-writer achieves what the author of the original passage did not: helps the reader reach a conclusion about the various facts and figures.

SAMPLE TECHNICAL WRITING

A student studying food preservation chose to investigate the history of canning. She remembered her great-grandmother's tales of working over a woodstove all day, only to have the food spoil three days later. The student wondered what went wrong. The following material is summarized in a precis that follows.

Original Passage

Not until the nineteenth century did canning become a part of food preservation. Until then, foods were dried, salted, or smoked. In 1795, during the Napoleonic Wars, the French government offered a reward to the first person who could preserve food satisfactory for military use. In 1809, M. Nicholas Appert won the 12,000 francs and earned recognition as the father of canning. Although he used glass bottles, sealed with cork and processed in a hot-water bath, he did not know why his process worked. Ultimately, Louis Pasteur determined why improperly processed foods spoil. Microorganisms found in the air, and on all objects, cause spoilage as soon as they come in contact with food. Only proper sterilization, found Pasteur, could kill these microorganisms.

Prior to 1850, the only sterilization method known to farm women called for canning—first in tin cans and later in glass jars, both of which had a groove around the top, into which a tin lid fit. Hot food, placed in hot cans or jars and topped with a hot lid, was sealed with hot sealing wax—a hard red wax, quite unlike today's paraffin. When dry, the brittle wax seal was broken only by pelting the wax with a blunt object, usually a knife handle. In 1858, John L. Mason invented a glass jar that could receive a screw-on zinc lid sealed by a rubber gasket. For the first time, home canning became easy, economical, and popular. By 1903, Alexander H. Kerr perfected the two-piece lid, a snap lid and a ring, still in use nearly 90 years later. Home canning literally snapped forth a new option for homemakers.

Precis

M. Nicholas Appert first canned food in 1809 in cork-sealed glass bottles processed in a hot-water bath. Pasteur's discovery that sterilization killed microorganisms and kept food from spoiling explained Appert's success. As a result, women learned to can successfully in tin and glass, using a hard wax to seal the hot food. Then, in 1858, John L. Mason sealed glass jars with a screw-on lid and rubber gasket. Finally, in 1903, Alexander Kerr developed the two-piece lid still in use.

Analysis of the Sample Technical Writing. The preceding passage exhibits the general characteristics of a good precis:

- The original has been reduced by two-thirds.
- Virtually no supportive details are included.
- Transitions show relationships between ideas: *as a result, then, finally*.
- Every major idea, represented by a paragraph in the original passage, is included.
- Key words such as *processed, hot-water bath, sterilization, microorganism, hard wax, screw-on lid, rubber gasket,* and *two-piece lid* are included accurately.
- The writer conceals any personal prejudice.
- The writing is concise, bare of supportive or illustrative material.
- The writer avoids plagiarism.
- Sentences read well, and the paragraph flows well as the result of internal transition.

Using similar techniques will enable you to develop successful precis for your own work.

Research Paper

A research paper, sometimes called a *term* or *library* paper, reports research findings. Most often, the research is a literal *searching again* through what others have written on a subject. In some cases, when the paper reports entirely on primary research [*see* primary research *in the Glossary*], the writer may find a laboratory or technical report more suitable than a research paper.

Research papers may either report research or evaluate research information. If the paper reports your research, it tells what you have read, either from a single source or from many sources. If the paper evaluates research information, it addresses *why* or *how*; thus, it is usually either a comparison-and-contrast or cause-and-effect paper. [*See* Cause and Effect *and* Comparison and *Contrast in Part II.*] More likely, it is this evaluative paper that you will be asked to write. As an evaluative paper, it requires numerous sources, and it assumes a writer's ability to show originality and imagination.

CHARACTERISTICS

An effective research paper

- indicates careful, comprehensive reading and understanding of the topic,
- establishes, in its introduction, a thesis to be developed during the course of the paper [*see* thesis statement *in the Glossary and* Writing a Multi-Paragraph Paper *in Part I*],
- follows a clear organization [*see* organization, chronological order, spatial order, *and* order of importance *in the Glossary*],
- employs the principles of good composition,
- includes direct quotations, paraphrases, or precis that support the thesis [*see* Paraphrase *and* Precis *earlier in Part III*],
- includes parenthetical notes, endnotes, or footnotes,
- includes a list of works cited,
- exhibits careful, thorough documentation of sources of ideas,
- includes direct quotations in support of its thesis,
- follows a carefully prescribed format.

PROCESS

The step-by-step development of a research paper sounds rather simple and direct. The research process, however, always requires a kind of yo-yo approach: rather than completing one step and moving neatly to the next, you will find that you confront problems that either cause you to go back to a previous step or to think ahead to the next. Just when you think you have completed the research, you may discover that you need new information to fill a gap or add support. And just when you think you have completed a sensible outline, you may find that the paper does not flow smoothly, given its method of organization. So you must go back—rethink, reread, rewrite. The yo-yo process continues until you have printed your final draft.

The following process works well if you understand—and accept as a fact of the research life—the yo-yo approach.

STEP 1   **Prewriting • Selecting a Suitable Subject**

In some cases, you may be assigned a broad research topic; in other cases, you may be free to select whatever topic you wish. Selecting the right topic often determines the success of the paper.

Begin with general, broad topics that interest you. [*See* Prewriting *in Part I for suggestions for sources of topics*.] In order to select one topic, narrow it, and wed it to the paper's purpose, do exploratory reading in the general area. Browse through encyclopedias, magazines, reference books, and online research for thought-provoking ideas. Read quickly. Then, put your general subject in the form of a question. Answers to this question will suggest narrowed topics, some of them possibly suitable for your research paper.

General topic:
    What influenced us as children to become the kinds of young adults we are?

Narrowed topics:
    television, parents, neighborhood, siblings, games, toys, books, food, friends, relatives

Perhaps, after exploratory reading in the area of child psychology, you're intrigued by an authority's claim that parents influence a child by what they read to him or her. You decide to pursue this subject.

Further reading, however, convinces you that the topic is still too broad. You list all the kinds of books you can think of that parents read to their children:

fairy tales	classical stories
jingles	rhymes, poetry
fantasy	picture books
number books	nonfiction
alphabet books	animal stories

Later, you find an item about the impact Mother Goose rhymes have on children. Now *that's* what you'd like to research! Finally, you have a suitably narrowed subject:

The Impact of Mother Goose Rhymes on Children

Use a similar process to narrow your own broad subject to something manageable.

 Selecting a suitable subject is so vital that a few warnings are in order. Be critical enough to evaluate your proposed subject according to these possible pitfalls:

- The subject may be too broad. Even if you've been assigned a 1,500-word paper, keep in mind that most five-paragraph themes run over 700 words. Magazine articles run less than 3,000 words. So don't try to cope with a book-length subject in half the length of a magazine article.
- The subject may be too limited for research. Although you may have a special interest in a subject, if little or no research is available, you cannot write a successful research paper.
- The subject may be too technical. Unless you already have a good background in hydraulics, for instance, don't write a paper about the subject. In fact, unless a paper is for a technical class, avoid subjects that rely on technical terms.
- The subject may be too ordinary. Research should provide new information. To do research on the effects of sun lotion on skin exposed to ultraviolet rays will probably prove tiresome and dull unless, of course, you have just invented a revolutionary lotion.
- The subject may be too controversial. A highly contested issue may prove more than a single, carefully organized research paper can describe or evaluate. If volumes have already been written, chances are you have not chosen well.

Avoiding these pitfalls will help you select a workable, satisfactory subject.

STEP 2   **Prewriting • Listing the Possible Parts**
With your narrowed subject in mind, use logic and imagination to decide what to include. Make a list of possible topics. Then, to put yourself in the reader's seat. What do you want to know about this subject? What questions need answers? For example:

Suitable subject:
Impact of Mother Goose Rhymes on Children

Possible subtopics:
author of rhymes
publication of book
distinguishing fact from fiction
educational value
musical quality
teaching rhythm
promoting memorization
any negative aspects
characterizations
lulling to sleep
introduction to literature
classical allusion
stimulating imagination
translations

By listing topics, you can avoid wasting time later and avoid reading unrelated material. Of course, a preliminary list is just that—preliminary. It will change as you do your research. So, develop a list of possible subtopics to guide your early research.

STEP 3   **Prewriting • Writing the Thesis Statement**
Now you are ready to write a thesis statement. [*See* thesis statement *in the Glossary*.] Like the list, the thesis statement may change somewhat, but it will serve throughout your research. So write one now:

The Mother Goose nursery rhymes have a positive influence on children.

STEP 4   **Prewriting • Finding the Materials**
With your thesis and list of possible topics in place, select books, magazines, pamphlets, electronic, and other pertinent sources. Go to the library and check the computer catalog, the *Reader's Guide to Periodical Literature* (either a print or electronic version), the vertical file [*see* vertical file *in the Glossary*], and the various reference books and

electronic resources available, including *but not limited to* the Internet. Consider searching certain respected databases:

- *DIALOG* is a broad-based, highly respected database.
- *InfoTrak* includes over 1,000 business, technological, and general-interest periodicals, including *The New York Times* and the *Wall Street Journal*.
- *LEXIS/NEXIS* includes thousands of full-text articles.
- *MEDLINE* has information on medical topics.
- *ERIC* (Educational Resources Information Center) has information on education topics.
- *OCLC First Search* has many indexes for periodicals, media, and books in the United States and Canada.
- *VU/TEXT* is a newspaper database.

Be alert to publication dates. If you are doing historical research, the new electronic databases may not go back far enough to index the materials you need. Consult both print and electronic indexes.

As you search the Web, try several different search engines, such as *AltaVista, Cyberhound, HotBot, InfoSeek, Lycos, WebCrawler,* or *Yahoo!* Not every search engine calls up the same sources. Check out the search engine's online help to make your search most effective and least time-consuming.

STEP 5   Prewriting • Developing a Preliminary Bibliography

As you find seemingly useful materials, prepare bibliography cards for them. A bibliography is a list of sources and is an important part of your finished paper. The preliminary bibliography is the start of that component. Here's how to do it.

Prepare a separate 3" x 5" card for each source, including electronic sources and Web sites. Using this approach, you can throw away cards for sources that later prove useless. Similarly, you can alphabetize those that prove helpful. Follow these general instructions for making bibliography cards:

For books:

- List the call number in the upper left corner.
- List the author, last name first.
  - If there is an editor, list his or her name, followed by *ed.*
  - If there are two authors, list the name of the first author in reverse order but list the name of the second author in natural order.
  - If there are more than two authors, list the name of the first author in reverse order and follow it with *and others*.

- Write the title and underline it (or use italics if you are keyboarding).
- Give the publication information: city of publication, publisher, and year of publication.
- Add any notes that may be helpful to your later search (bibliography, illustrations, number of pages, and so on).
- If you use more than one library, note on the bottom line of the card the library in which you found this source.
- Number the card in the upper right corner. Begin with 1, and continue sequentially. Later, the numbers will help to quickly identify your sources.

[*See Step 12, later in this section, for a comprehensive list of sample bibliography entries.*]

For a book, then, a bibliography card may look something like this:

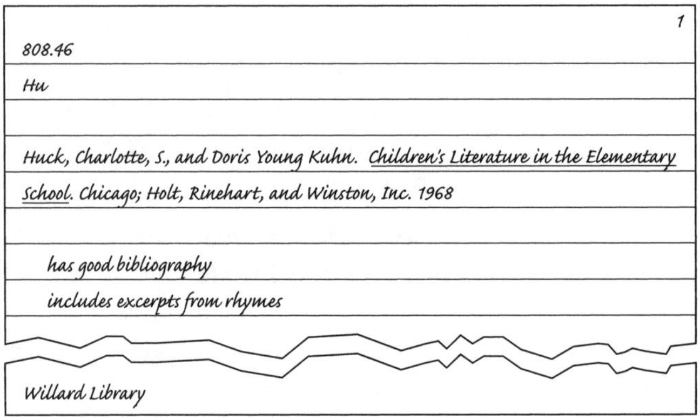

FIGURE 3.3

A bibliography card for books.

	1
808.46	
Hu	
Huck, Charlotte, S., and Doris Young Kuhn. *Children's Literature in the Elementary*	
School. Chicago; Holt, Rinehart, and Winston, Inc. 1968	
has good bibliography	
includes excerpts from rhymes	
Willard Library	

For an article:

- List the author, if there is one, last name first.
- List the title and enclose it in quotation marks.
- List and underline (or print in italics) the name of the magazine, newspaper, or encyclopedia in which the article appears.
- Include for magazines the volume number, page numbers, and date.
- Include for newspapers the section and page numbers and date.
- Include for encyclopedias the volume number, the page numbers, place of publication, publisher, and year of publication.

- Add any notes that may be helpful in locating or using the source.
- Number the card in the upper right corner.

A sample bibliography card for a magazine will look like this:

FIGURE 3.4

A bibliography card for magazines.

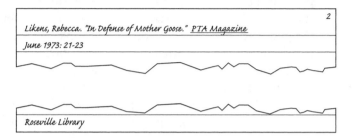

For electronic sources:

- List the author, last name first, or the sponsoring organization (many education and organization Web sites omit authors' names, but reputable sites will always indicate sponsorship).
- List the title of the article or document, in quotation marks.
- Give the title of the complete work (from the home page or CD-ROM title), if applicable, underlined.
- Add the date of publication or last update, if given.
- Copy the full URL (Web site address), enclosed in angle brackets.
- Give the date of your visit, in parentheses.

FIGURE 3.5

A bibliography card for electronic sources.

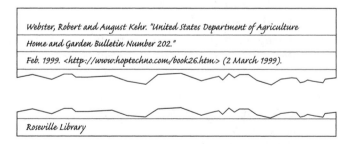

As you work, you will soon see which materials will be helpful and which will not. Before you cart home stacks of books and periodicals or spend hours fruitlessly searching electronic sources, check for usefulness. Here's how:

In books, look at tables of contents, indexes, and bibliographies. If nothing suggests information related to your topic, leave them. On the other hand, because you will be working primarily with nonfiction books, which are arranged on the library shelf by subject, look through books located near the ones you have found in the card or computer catalog. Perhaps one of them will be helpful.

Likewise, as you search through the *Reader's Guide* and other print and electronic periodical indexes, think of alternate headings under which to find sources. Sometimes the headings that appear in the guide are not the ones you might think of first. And don't hesitate to ask the reference librarian for suggestions.

Finally, for particularly obscure topics, you may wish to do a computer search through your local library. A computer search will say what information is available in computer-linked libraries all over the United States. This information is available through interlibrary loan. Check with your librarian for details.

STEP 6   **Prewriting • Shaping the Preliminary Outline**

Next, you must develop an outline from the list you wrote in Step 2. By now, as a result of your work with the preliminary bibliography, you have done additional skimming. You should be ready to think through the organization. [*For a thorough discussion of the process of outlining, see* Outlines: For a Paper *earlier in Part III*.]

While your first reaction may be to skip the preliminary outline, don't! You may have the typical reaction: How can I develop an outline when I haven't read all the materials available? The answer: How do you know which materials to read if you don't know what your paper will do? In other words, developing a preliminary outline now guides your reading in the future, saving hours of reading and avoiding stacks of useless notes.

So, do the outline now.

Using a list such as the example in Step 2, you could develop a preliminary outline that looks as follows:

I. Origins
   A. Author
   B. Publisher
II. Educational value
III. Literary introduction
   A. Fact or opinion
   B. Fun
   C. Rhythm
IV. Imagination

Your final outline will probably differ from the preliminary one in both content and organization. [By way of example, compare this preliminary outline with the final outline that appears with the Sample MLA Footnote Style Paper later in this section.]

STEP 7   Prewriting • Taking Notes

Now you are ready to begin reading seriously and taking notes. Remember, your reading will be guided by your outline, while your outline can be changed as you proceed.

Because you used 3" x 5" cards for your bibliography, you may wish to use 4" x 6" cards for your notes. The larger cards hold more and allow for easier reading, but above all, they cannot be accidentally mixed with the bibliography cards. If you are completing your cards at the keyboard, adjust your printer settings to accommodate different sized cards.

Regardless of the size, you will put only one idea from one source on a card. Why? Because when you write your paper, you will arrange the cards in the order in which you will use their respective bits of information. If you put more than one idea on a card, it will be useless in helping you arrange your ideas. If a card reflects more than one source, you won't be able to document its contents accurately.

Use the following guidelines for taking notes [*see also* Notes: For a Paper *earlier in Part III*]:

- Write the number of the bibliography card in the upper right corner of the note card. You will need this information later to document your paper. Because poor documentation is a serious shortcoming, early and ongoing precautions decrease the potential for error.

- List the page numbers from which you are about to take notes alongside the bibliography number. This information will also be essential for documentation. Be accurate and complete with your note cards; you will reduce the potential for error in your paper.

- Write the topic of the note (called the slug) on the top line of the card. The slug may be taken from your outline, or it may later become an outline topic. Do not use the Roman numerals and letters from your outline, however, as they may change, confusing your references. The slug lets you organize your notes by stacking all the cards with identical slugs together.

- Use a separate card for each idea from each source. Then, when you organize your note cards, each card will support only one topic.

- Take notes in your own words. You may use phrases, lists, key words, sentences, or paragraphs. [*See* Paraphrase, Precis, *and* Notes: For a Paper *elsewhere in Part III for more help with note-taking.*]
- When you find a particularly poignant passage, a phrase, or a sentence or two, copy it onto your note card exactly as it appears: comma for comma, letter for letter. Enclose the passage in quotation marks. If you omit words, or choose not to quote the complete sentence, show the omission by using ellipsis points. Use three points for the omission of a word or phrase; use a fourth point to represent a period at the end of a sentence.

 If you omit the quotation marks around words not your own, you are stealing. The act is called *plagiarism*, and it is such a serious error that some instructors will fail a paper that neglects to acknowledge sources accurately. So quote and document carefully.

- As you take notes, revise your preliminary outline as necessary. You will add sub-points, maybe even main points. Perhaps you will change the organization or rethink relationships among topics.
- You may need to find additional sources if gaps appear or you have no note cards for certain sections of the outline.

The following sample note cards illustrate some of the principles listed above:

FIGURE 3.6

Sample note cards for developing a research paper.

	3-2
Origins	
M.G. rhymes famous in France, America	
First published in England, 1765	
Author listed as Mistress Elizabeth Goose	

	6-287
Intro to Lit	
When child grows up with M.G., he's "apt to be a child who learns rapidly, who	
discovers early in life the commingling pleasures that words and pictures award to	
those who read books."	

Note that the first card, from page 2 of bibliography source 3, consists of fragments. The slug, *Origins*, comes from the preliminary outline. [*See Step 5.*] The second card, from page 287 of bibliography source 6, includes a direct quotation. Note the use of quotation marks. Again, the slug comes from the preliminary outline.

 As you take notes, try to avoid these potential trouble spots:

- Do not rely too heavily on any one source. In general, you should have about an equal number of note cards from each source. While it is not uncommon to find one source meeting most of your needs, your paper will be seriously weakened from a lack of broad research if you limit the variety of sources.
- If your subject permits, try to use book, periodical, and electronic references equally. To rely too heavily on books will date your paper. To rely too heavily on periodicals may result in cursory research, especially for a topic more thoroughly discussed in book-length sources. And to rely too heavily on the Internet will limit the perspective. Of course, the topic determines the appropriate sources. Television documentaries, public-radio talk shows, films, lecturers and the vast array of electronic resources are all legitimate sources. [*See also Step 8, Conducting Primary Research.*]
- If your subject is controversial, consult equally the sources supporting each side. If your paper is persuasive, you must answer the "other" side. If your paper is comparison and contrast, you must present both sides.
- Do not overuse direct quotations. You can usually summarize ideas in fewer words. Less than one-fourth of your cards should quote directly.
- Make absolutely certain that you have put quotation marks around any words not your own.
- Make absolutely certain that you have listed the bibliography card number and the page number(s) on each card.
- Be sure to include a single idea from a single source on each card.

STEP 8   Prewriting • Conducting Primary Research

Not every topic lends itself to primary research. [*See* primary research *and* secondary research *in the Glossary.*] Some topics, however, benefit from interviews, experiments, personal data gathering, and/or audience experience.

If, for instance, your subject deals with air pollution, excerpts from an interview with an EPA official or with an official from a power plant will add perspective. Books, magazines, and periodicals are never as immediate as firsthand experience. Similarly, if your subject deals with the psychological problems of nursing-home residents, interviews will give credibility to your paper. If your subject deals with the best methods for storing fresh vegetables, a tabulation of the results of your own experiments will add an important dimension to your paper.

Use primary research whenever the subject suggests.

STEP 9   **Prewriting • Creating the Final Outline**

Use the slugs to sort your cards into piles, each representing a topic in your revised outline. Next sort through each pile, thinking about order. Will chronological order be best? Spatial order? An order of importance? Will a comparison-and-contrast method of development determine order? Will a cause-and-effect method determine it? Put the cards in order. Expand or alter the outline as suggested by your cards. If you have not already done so, add subtopics to your outline as suggested by the slugs.

At this point, the final outline should nearly write itself. After referring to Outlines: For a Paper, elsewhere in Part III, complete the final outline for your paper.

 As you develop your outline, keep these points in mind:

- A full-length research paper probably should have no more than five or six main points. This means you should have no more than five or six Roman numerals in your outline. Too many main headings indicate fuzzy thinking.
- The outline divisions correspond to paragraph divisions or to subtopics within the paragraphs. To determine if the organization is logical, think through your outline in terms of paragraphs.
- The outline divisions, added together, must equal your thesis sentence. If they do not, make whatever adjustments are necessary.

STEP 10   **Writing • Developing the First Draft**

Next, you are ready to write the first draft. A research paper, like a good theme, begins with an introductory paragraph that states the subject and leads to the thesis sentence. The body of the paper follows the organization established in the outline, the divisions corresponding directly to the paragraphs. The conclusion wraps up the main ideas in a neat package. [*See* Writing a Multi-Paragraph Paper *in Part I for more on effective introductions, body organization, transitional devices, and conclusions.*]

Beyond the typical content and organization of a good theme, the first draft of a research paper also includes one feature peculiar to the form. Material from your note cards must be acknowledged by source, whether you put the idea in your own words or quote it directly. As a result, each time you refer to a note card in your first draft, add in parentheses the coded reference from the top right of your card (the bibliography source and page number). For example:

> The Mother Goose rhymes have survived because of their ageless quality of rhythm, rhyme, and motion. (4-3)

The idea is summarized in the writer's own words, but the information came from page 3 of bibliography source 4, details that will later go into the documentation. By using a code, you can move quickly through the first draft without having to develop exact documentation.

Complete the first draft as quickly as you can, getting ideas on paper. You need not write fine sentences or model paragraphs. Follow the outline, using the yo-yo approach, revising the outline, altering the methods of organization, and adding supporting details.

STEP 11   Revising • Polishing the Content

With your first draft completed, polish the content. [Refer to separate sections in this handbook for additional information as you need it.]

- Be sure the introduction gives a general statement about your subject and brings the reader from the general to the specific.
- Check the thesis statement for completeness and accuracy.
- Be sure the paper follows the organization established in the thesis sentence.
- Check for good paragraph development with clear topic and concluding sentences and supporting details. [*See* Revising: Sample Revision for Specific Detail *as well as the steps on checking structure in* Revising *in Part I.*]
- Make certain you have included a sufficient number of transitions within and between paragraphs. [*See* Revising: Sample Revision for Transition *in Part I.*]
- Reread for good sentence structure and variety. [*See* Revising: Sample Revision for Sentence Variety *as well as the section on checking sentence structure in* Revising *in Part I.*]
- Assure yourself that your subject is fully and carefully explained and is supported by adequate research.

- Be sure the conclusion reiterates the thesis and adds an appropriate clincher.

[*See also the general guidelines for revising any composition in* Revising *in Part I.*]

STEP 12   Revising • Preparing the Documentation

The forms of documentation will vary with the style manual preferred by the teacher or school. Most style manuals have changed recently, primarily as a result of electronic media.

Preparing Notes. In this section, you find five common research paper styles. Parts of the sample research paper are repeated to illustrate the five forms. These are

- MLA (Modern Language Association) parenthetical style: documentation notes appear parenthetically, within the text.
- MLA endnote style: documentation notes appear at the end of the paper, just before the list of works cited.
- MLA footnote style: documentation notes appear at the bottoms of the pages.
- MLA numbered bibliography style: documentation notes appear in numerical form, parenthetically, within the text.
- APA (American Psychological Association) style: documentation notes appear parenthetically, within the text.

Use whichever form of notation your instructor requires; or, if none is required, use the form easiest for you. In any case, be consistent throughout the paper. [*For additional comparison, note also that the sample papers for English and work-place writing in* Biography *earlier in Part III, and the sample paper in* Technical Report *later in Part III use parenthetical notes.*]

Endnotes and footnotes follow the same form. Note these peculiarities:

- Endnotes and footnotes are numbered consecutively.
- The numbers, both in the text and in the notes themselves, are raised, written as superscript.
- The notes are indented like paragraphs.
- They are followed by periods, as if they were complete sentences.
- Footnotes are single-spaced, with a double space between notes.
- Endnotes are double-spaced.

Sample note forms are listed later in this section, along with their corresponding bibliography entry forms.

Preparing a Bibliography. A bibliography is always part of a research paper. It may be one of two kinds: a list of those works cited in the paper, or a list of all works consulted, some of which may not have been cited. The advantage of the former is its brevity; the advantage of the latter is its demonstration of thorough research. Use whichever form your instructor prefers.

Note the following peculiarities of the bibliography in general.

- The bibliography begins on a new page at the end of the paper. The entries are arranged alphabetically by authors' last names.
- The bibliography uses hanging indentation: all lines but the first are indented. This format allows for ease in finding listings.
- Items in the bibliography are followed by a period, as if each were a sentence.
- Each note has a corresponding bibliography entry.
- The bibliography page is double-spaced.
- If two cited works are written by the same author, alphabetize by title. Omit the author's name in the second citation; instead, use a long dash (the equivalent of three hyphens).

Additional details of format are noted in the illustrations later in this section.

Note and Bibliography Forms. In general, a note or bibliography entry will include the author's name, titles, and publication information (city of publication, publisher, and date). The note will also include a page reference. The following samples show bibliography, parenthetical-note, and endnote forms. Footnotes are like endnotes but are single-spaced, with a double space between entries.

A book by one author:

Parenthetical note:
(Lannon 139)

Endnote:
[1]John M. Lannon, *Technical Writing* (Boston: Little, Brown and Company, 1992) 139.

Bibliography:
Lannon, John M. *Technical Writing*. Boston: Little, Brown and Company, 1992.

A book by two authors:

Parenthetical note:
(Gibaldi and Achtert 140)

Endnote:
[2]Joseph Gibaldi and Walter S. Achtert, *MLA Handbook for Writers of Research Papers.* 5th ed. (New York: The Modern Language Association of America, 1998) 140.

Bibliography:
Gibaldi, Joseph, and Walter S. Achtert. *MLA Handbook for Writers of Research Papers.* 5th ed. New York: The Modern Language Association of America, 1998.

Note that the preceding entries refer to the fifth edition of a book. The publisher is an organization.

A book by three or more authors:
Use *and others* to refer to all other authors or editors beyond the first. Or use *et al.* (Latin for *and others*) instead.

Parenthetical note:
(Frew and others 111–112)

Endnote:
[3]Robert Frew and others, *Survival: A Sequential Program for College Writing* (Palo Alto, California: Peek Publications, 1978) 111–112.

Bibliography:
Frew, Robert and others. *Survival: A Sequential Program for College Writing.* Palo Alto, California: Peek Publications, 1978.

A book with an editor:

Parenthetical note:
(Williams 925)

Endnote:
[4]Becky Hall Williams, ed., *1999 Writer's Market: Where to Sell What You Write* (Cincinnati: Writer's Digest Books, 1999) 925.

Bibliography:
Williams, Becky Hall, ed. *1999 Writer's Market: Where to Sell What You Write.* Cincinnati: Writer's Digest Books, 1999.

A signed encyclopedia article:

Parenthetical note:
(von Brandt)

Endnote:
[5]Andres R. F. T. von Brandt, "Fishing, Commercial," *Encyclopaedia Britannica: Macropaedia*, 1997 ed.

Bibliography:
von Brandt, Andres R. F. T. "Fishing, Commercial." *Encyclopaedia Britannica: Macropaedia*, 1997 ed.

An unsigned encyclopedia article:

Parenthetical note:
("Crowley")

Endnote:
[6]"Crowley, Robert," *Encyclopedia Americana*, 1999 ed.

Bibliography:
"Crowley, Robert." *Encyclopedia Americana*. 1999 ed.

A selection in an anthology:

Parenthetical note:
(Winters 59–60)

Endnote:
[7]Yvor Winters, "Robert Frost: Or the Spiritual Drifter as Poet," in *Robert Frost: A Collection of Critical Essays*, ed. James M. Cox (Englewood Cliffs: Prentice-Hall, Inc., 1962) 59–60.

Bibliography:
Winters, Yvor. "Robert Frost: Or the Spiritual Drifter as Poet." *Robert Frost: A Collection of Critical Essays*. Ed. James M. Cox. Englewood Cliffs: Prentice-Hall, Inc., 1962.

A translation:

Parenthetical note:
(Vergilius 48)

Endnote:
[8]Publius Vergilius Marc, *Virgil*, trans. H. Rushton Fairclough, rev. ed. (Cambridge: Harvard University Press, 1935) 48.

Bibliography:
Vergilius Marc, Publius. *Virgil.* Trans. H. Rushton Fairclough. Rev. ed.
    Cambridge: Harvard University Press, 1935.

A signed magazine article:

Parenthetical note:
(Rupp 67)

Endnote:
[9]Becky Rupp, "Home Schooling," *Country Journal* December 1998: 67.

Bibliography:
Rupp, Becky. "Home Schooling." *Country Journal* December 1998: 67–74.

An unsigned magazine article:

Parenthetical note:
("S.A.D. Truth" 123)

Endnote:
[10]"The S.A.D. Truth about Sunlight," *Harrowsmith* November/December 1986: 123.

Bibliography:
"The S.A.D. Truth about Sunlight." *Harrowsmith* November/December 1986: 123.

An article from a newspaper:

Parenthetical note:
(Reibstein 23)

Endnote:
[11]Larry Reibstein, "A Finger on the Pulse: Companies Expand Use of Employee
Surveys," *The Wall Street Journal* 27 October 1996, Midwest ed.: 23.

Bibliography:
Reibstein, Larry. "A Finger on the Pulse: Companies Expand Use of Employee
    Surveys." *The Wall Street Journal* 27 October 1996, Midwest ed.: 23.

A pamphlet:

Parenthetical note:
(Geologic Story 2)

Endnote:
[12]*Geologic Story of Turkey Run State Park,* (Bloomington, Indiana: State of Indiana Department of Natural Resources Geological Survey, 1977) 2.

Bibliography:
Geologic Story of Turkey Run State Park. Bloomington, Indiana: State of Indiana
   Department of Natural Resources Geological Survey, 1977.

A government publication:

Parenthetical note:
(U.S. Dept. of Commerce 8–9)

Endnote:
[13]United States Department of Commerce, Bureau of the Census, *Neighborhood Statistics from the 1980 Census* (N.p.: N.p., n.d.) 8–9.

Bibliography:
United States Department of Commerce. Bureau of the Census. *Neighborhood
   Statistics from the 1980 Census.* N.p., N.p.: n.d.

Electronic media, unsigned article:

Parenthetical note:
("Computers in Education")

Endnote:
[14]"Computers in Education," *Facts on File News Digest CD-ROM* (New York:
Facts on File, Inc., 1988) np.

Bibliography:
"Computers in Education." *Facts on File News Digest CD-ROM.* New York:
   Facts on File, Inc., 1988.

Electronic media, signed article:

Parenthetical note:
(Rosenberg 156)

Endnote:
[15]Victor Rosenberg, "Computers," *The New Grolier Electronic Encyclopedia*
(Danbury, CT: Grolier Electronic Publishing, Inc., 1999. CD-ROM) 156.

Bibliography:
Rosenberg, Victor. "Computers." *The New Grolier Electronic Encyclopedia.*
   Danbury, CT: Grolier Electronic Publishing, Inc., 1988. CD-ROM.

Electronic media, signed newspaper article:

Parenthetical note:
(Booth 13)

Endnote:

[16]William Booth, "Rebuilding Wetlands: Nature Proves a Tough Act to Follow" (*Washington [D.C.] Post* 30 Jan. 1990: Newsbank) ENV 5:C13–14.

Bibliography:

Booth, William. "Rebuilding Wetlands: Nature Proves a Tough Act to Follow." *Washington [D.C.] Post* 30 Jan. 1990, Newsbank ENV 5:C13–14.

Note: Because many electronic media exist, and because they do not always have authors or page numbers, follow a simple rule of thumb: Give enough information so that your reader can find your source.

Online material, signed article with complete work:

Parenthetical note:

(Kaplan)

Endnote:

[17]Lisa Faye Kaplan, "Workplace: On Job Interview," 28 Feb. 1997, <http://detnews.com/1999/accent/902/28/02280028.htm> (22 Aug. 1999) 3.

Bibliography:

Kaplan, Lisa Faye. "Workplace: On Job Interview." *The Detroit News.* 28 Feb. 1997. <http://detnews.com/1999/accent/902/28/02280028.htm> (22 Aug. 1999).

Online material, signed article, no complete work:

Parenthetical note:

(Henahan)

Endnote:

[18]Sean Henahan, "Wetlands under Siege in Cities across Nation," 7 July 1999, <http://www.gene.com/ae/WN/SU/wet596.html> (5 Sept. 1999) 2.

Bibliography:

Henahan, Sean. "Wetlands under Siege in Cities across Nation." 7 July 1999. <http://www.gene.com/ae/WN/SU/wet596.html> (5 Sept. 1999).

Online material, unsigned article, no complete work:

Parenthetical note:

("Defining Wetlands")

Endnote:

[19]"Defining Wetlands," 20 Feb. 1997, <http://www.ceres.ca.gov/wetlands/introduction/defining_wetlands.html> (27 July 1997) 2.

Bibliography:

"Defining Wetlands." 20 Feb. 1997. <http://www.ceres.ca.gov/wetlands/
introduction/defining_wetlands.html> (27 July 1997).

Online material, e-mail message:

Parenthetical note:

(Russ)

Endnote:

[20]Michael Russ <mkruss@evsc.k12.in.us> "Education URLs," 25 Aug. 1999, personal e-mail (25 Aug. 1999).

Bibliography:

Russ, Michael. <mkruss@evsc.k12.in.us> "Education URLs." 25 Aug. 1999.
Personal e-mail. (25 Aug. 1999).

Note: If you need more details for Internet documentation, turn to
the Internet itself. Search for *MLA Documentation*, and you will find
several URLs to meet your needs.

For a second endnote from the same source:

In the course of your paper, you will probably cite some sources
more than once. The primary endnote forms, illustrated above, are
simplified considerably for secondary endnotes. (Parenthetical notes
remain the same throughout the paper.)

First note:

David Powell, *What Can I Write About? 7000 Topics for High School Students*
(Urbana, Ill.: National Council of Teachers of English, 1981) 26.

Subsequent note:

Powell 38.

STEP 13   Revising • Making the Final Draft

The final draft demands careful attention to format details. Use these
general guidelines for typing your paper:

- The entire paper, including quotations, notes, and
  bibliography, is double-spaced.
- Except for page numbers, use one-inch margins on all four
  sides of each page.
- Use a running head to number all pages consecutively,
  including the bibliography page(s). To create a running head,
  type your last name and the page number a half-inch from the
  top of each page and flush with the right margin.

- All text begins a double space below the running head.
- On the first page of text, include the heading and title. At the left margin, type your name one inch from the top. On three subsequent double-spaced lines, type your instructor's name, the course title, and the date, using date-month-year order. Center the title a double space below the last line of the heading and capitalize only the first letter of appropriate words. Do not use quotation marks or underscores with the title. (If your instructor requires a title page, eliminate this step and see item on creating a title page later in this list.)
- Begin the text a double space below the title. Indent five spaces for each new paragraph.
- Insert parenthetical notes as necessary to credit sources of facts, ideas, statistics, and exact words. Parenthetical notes refer readers to the bibliography and include only the author's last name and page number(s). Use no punctuation between the name and number. If the author's name appears in the text, a page number is sufficient.
- If you use a quotation that requires more than four typed lines, set off the entire passage by indenting it ten spaces from the left margin. Type it double-spaced, without quotation marks.
- The bibliography page should have the title *Works Cited* (most common), *References*, or *Bibliography* (least common), centered. Double-space and begin the entries. Use hanging indentation, and double-space all entries.
- If you use endnotes, type the title, *Notes*, centered, one inch from the top of a new page. Begin the notes two spaces below the title. Indent each note five spaces, type the note number slightly above the line, skip a space, and begin the note. Any additional lines for a note appear at the left margin. Double-space all.
- If your instructor requires it, prepare a title page. (Do *not* use a title page along with the heading described earlier in this list.) Center from top to bottom and left to right the following five items: title of the paper, your name, the name of the course, the instructor's name, and the date. If you use a title page, repeat the title, centered, on the first page of the text, skip four spaces, and begin the text. Do not number the first page of the text.

- If your instructor requires it, type your final outline, in
  standard indented form, on a separate page. [*See* Outlines
  earlier in Part III.] Include the thesis statement at the head of
  your outline. If your instructor prefers, this outline may be
  rearranged to appear as a table of contents. [*See* Technical
  Report *later in Part III for an example*.] Number the outline
  page(s) with lower-case Roman numerals, centered, at the
  bottom of the page.

STEP 14   **Proofreading • Checking the Details**

In addition to the usual checks for spelling, mechanics, grammar, and
usage, you will want to check documentation forms carefully, period
for period and comma for comma. Check for italics and quotation
marks. Read carefully for typing errors. [*See also* Proofreading *in Part
I for additional guidelines*.]

The most important proofreading you will do for a research
paper, however, is quite different from that for any other paper. *Be
sure to check the use of quotation marks for any quoted material you
have included.* Remember, if you use another author's words as if they
were your own—even accidentally—you can suffer severe penalties.
(And that includes others' words taken from the Internet.) Plagiarism
is a serious error, almost a crime. You should check your original
sources against the ideas included in your paper just to be certain you
have not simply forgotten a set of quotation marks or neglected to
copy the quotation marks from your note cards onto your paper.

A NOTE ABOUT THE SAMPLES

Five research-paper samples follow.

MLA Parenthetical Style. The first sample, which is a complete
paper, illustrates one widely accepted form of documentation, the
MLA (Modern Language Association) parenthetical style, rapidly
becoming singularly popular.

[*For additional examples of a title page, table-of-contents page, parenthetical documentation, and an appendix, see the sample paper in*
Technical Report *later in Part III. Also see the sample papers for English and work-place writing in* Biography *earlier in Part III for slightly
different parenthetical documentation*.]

MLA Endnote Style. The second sample, an excerpt from the
first, illustrates the MLA endnote style, a common alternative to the
MLA parenthetical style.

MLA Footnote Style. The third sample is also an excerpt from the first and shows the MLA footnote style. The sample also illustrates a title page, an outline page, and footnote documentation.

APA Style. The fourth sample, another excerpt, illustrates the APA (American Psychological Association) style. Parenthetical documentation and mode of bibliography entries distinguish this style.

Numbered Bibliography Style. The fifth sample illustrates, in a brief paragraph, the MLA numbered bibliography style.

Certain style manuals suggest combining these basic formats. For instance, you may be asked to include a title page and a table of contents in a paper documented with endnotes. Thus, the five samples offer sound guidelines, no matter which format you are asked to follow.

If your instructor permits you to choose your own style, choose the easiest to prepare.

Combined, the five models flesh out the principles discussed in this section. The subsequent analyses point out details peculiar to the research process. Note particularly the combination of primary and secondary research going into this paper.

SAMPLE MLA PARENTHETICAL STYLE PAPER

The following sample illustrates the MLA parenthetical style. The paper illustrates a widely accepted style. Parenthetical style omits the use of superscript numbers as required in endnote and footnote styles.

Ann Commens

Instructor A. Kamp

Senior English II

18 January 20—

Mother Goose: A Devoted Teacher

Mother Goose has survived generations of critics. Perhaps the most trying test of all for Mother Goose has been through the honest and often unrestrained criticism by children (Grover 1). These rhymes have survived
because of their ageless quality of rhythm, rhyme, and motion (Arbuthnot 3).
They have been passed from parent to child for generations (Parker 46),
becoming such a part of the English-speaking world that it is a handicap for
a child not to know them (Becker 11). "The Mother Goose Page," hosted on
the Internet by Homework Central, attests to the continuing recognition of
their importance (Homework Central). The nursery rhymes of Mother Goose,
loved and recited by generations of children, help introduce children to good
literature, create fantasy friends, provide contentment, stimulate imagination,
and promote learning.

According to legend, Mistress Elizabeth Goose, known widely as
Mother Goose, lived in Boston 200 years ago. She is supposed to have
recited her varied rhymes to her numerous grandchildren. Her son-in-law,

Commens 2

Thomas Fleet, is said to have published her nursery rhymes in order to make some well-deserved money (Grover 2). Tourists and children still visit the site in Boston where Dame Goose is believed to be buried (Huck and Kuhn 62). Contrary to the Mother Goose legend, most authorities agree that Mother Goose appeared in 1697 as the title of a book of fairy tales by Charles Perrault. The original Mother Goose contained such popular tales as "Cinderella," "Red Riding Hood," and "Sleeping Beauty" (Huck and Kuhn 61). Mother Goose's fame spread from France to America and to England, where the first collection of rhymes was published under her name in 1765 (Grover 2). Many of the traditional nursery rhymes contained in this publication and those succeeding it were recited and sung long before they were ever written down. Most of the rhymes popular today have existed for so long that their actual author is unknown (Becker 13). The famous Mother Goose rhymes have been passed from parent to child, and both enjoy these rhymes together, the child for the first time and the adult once again in remembrance of his childhood (Parker 46).

In remembering their own exposure to the nursery rhymes, parents approve of Mother Goose, for she has proved to be a good influence upon a child. She serves as a child's first introduction to literature (Huck and Kuhn 104). Pre-school and primary-grade educators incorporate numerous activities by which youngsters of all backgrounds learn about Mary's lamb or Little Boy Blue even before they can read (Daycare, Parker 46), and it is the literature a child grows up with which greatly influences the type of an adult he will become (LaRoche 114). A child who grows up with Mother Goose is "apt to be a child who learns rapidly, who discovers early in life the commingling pleasures that words and pictures award to those who read books" (Huck and Kuhn 387). Although Mother Goose is not actually poetry, her rhymes provide a background for the child to accept and understand real poetry (Grover 2). The child who is exposed to Mother Goose will progress to other classics, such as Shakespeare, more easily because Mother Goose encourages a child to read good literature (Likens 22).

A child who grows up with Mother Goose not only learns the pleasures of reading, but he also discovers that the Mother Goose characters can become his friends. Many of the Mother Goose characters are reminiscent of real people, such as Mother Hubbard and her concern for her dog, Mary with her pet lamb, the Old Woman in the Shoe with her housing problem, and Little Bo Beep with her lost sheep. When the child reads about Jack and Jill and Peter, he is reminded of everyday people (Huck and Kuhn 99). A study of the history of children's literature clarifies that both the poetry and the illustrations accompanying Mother Goose helps children become familiar with major archetypes and motifs (Vandergrift 2).

In addition to providing a child with friends, Mother Goose rhymes provide a child with contentment and satisfaction. The rhymes remind the child of the happiness and family harmony in his life (Huck and Kuhn 99). One of

the most appealing qualities of Mother Goose is the humor the rhymes contain (Likens 23), which helps the child laugh and be happy (Mitchell 67).
Even the nonsense in Mother Goose cultivates a child's mind, because a
child must be able to recognize the nonsense in "the cow jumped over the
moon" (Huck and Kuhn 100) in order to think it funny. Mother Goose also
provides many amusing rhymes and riddles for a child to enjoy, such as
"There was a girl in our towne,/Silk an' satin were her gowne,/Silk an' satin,
gold an' velvet,/Guess her name, three times I've telled it" (Baring-Gould
271). The answer, of course, is "Ann." A child always enjoys telling the old
joke, "Adam and Eve and Pinch me/Went down to a river to bathe./Adam
and Eve got drownded,/Which one of the three was saved?" (Baring-Gould
261). The innocent listener pipes in, "Pinch me," and indeed gets just that
(Baring-Gould 261)!

The value of Mother Goose, however, is not only that the child learns to
laugh; he learns to build his imagination by changing and adding to the
familiar old Mother Goose rhymes (Rackham 2). The development of the
imagination is a very necessary factor in a child's life (Huck and Kuhn 331).

> Pretending, playing, making up stories about life, are some of the richest
> talents a person can develop when she or he is very small. Fantasy is at
> the root of all invention, both mechanical and social. No one would have
> developed airplanes if someone hadn't pretended that people could fly.
> No one would have formed the American Constitution if someone hadn't
> imagined that people could govern themselves (Rogers 39).

Commens 5

When a child grows up with Mother Goose, "he is a child who's apt to grow up with a mind wide open to new ideas" (Likens 23). And the ideas are plentiful. A quick check at Amazon.com shows 119 listings for Mother Goose poetry (Amazon.com).

Growing up with a mind wide open to new ideas provides opportunities for children to learn about poetry, to identify universal problems, to learn satisfaction, and certainly to exercise their imaginative expression. Together, these kinds of mind-opening opportunities permit authorities to name one more advantage to exposing children to Mother Goose: to promote learning.

Most authorities agree that Mother Goose stimulates a child's learning process. It has become evident that "the excitement of learning, the excitement of performing, can still begin with something so simple as the rhymes of Mother Goose" (Likens 22). Teachers use the child's knowledge of Mother Goose rhymes to help him want to learn to read, to participate, and to respond (Parker 46). Through the rhymes, a teacher can help the child memorize the day of the week without drills or boredom (Likens 23). Every child who knows "Solomon Grundy,/ Born on Monday,/Christened on Tuesday,/Married on Wednesday ..."(Mitchell 109) will be able to remember the days of the week. A child is introduced to his first lesson in numbers when he recites "One, two, three, four, five,/Once I caught a fish alive;/Six, seven, eight, nine, ten,/Then I let it go again" (Mitchell 115) and "1, 2, Buckle my

Commens 6

shoe,/3, 4, Knock at the door,/5, 6, Pick up sticks ..." (Baring-Gould 244). A

child remembers his Roman numerals through the rhyme "X shall stand for

playmates Ten;/V for Five stout stalwart men;/I for one ..." (Baring-Gould

244). A child easily learns his alphabet with "A, B, C, and D,/Pray, playmates

agree./E, F, and G,/Well so it shall be ..." (Baring-Gould 241) and "A was an

apple pie, / B bit it, / C cut it ..." (Baring-Gould 241). Mother Goose also

helps a child develop his language through tongue twisters and riddle

rhymes because between the ages of two and six is when the greatest part

of a child's language is developed (Huck and Kuhn 98). Mother Goose aids a

child in learning the numbers, in learning the alphabet, and in developing his

language.

The values of Mother Goose are many: as an introduction to literature,

as a child's companion, as a source of happiness and contentment, as a

stimulant to his imagination, and as a catalyst in the child's learning process.

> Mother and teacher agree that the best of these verses have an even
> more potent influence.... The healthy moral, so subtly suggested in
> many of the rhymes, is unconsciously absorbed by the child's recep-
> tive mind, helping him to make his own distinction between right and
> wrong, bravery and cowardice, generosity and selfishness (Grover 1).

Surely, then, it is no wonder the Mother Goose rhymes have survived

generations of critics. In fact, without the Mother Goose rhymes as part of his

childhood, a youngster may suffer a social if not an educational handicap.

Commens 7

Works Cited

Amazon.com. "Poetry – Mother Goose." 10 Jan. 2000.
   <http://www.amazon.com/New/Crawler/exec/ob...
   %20-%20Mother%Mother%20Goose> (20 Jan. 2000).

Arbuthnot, May Hill. *The Real Mother Goose*. Chicago: Rand McNally and
   Co., 1994.

Baring-Gould, William S., and Ceil Baring-Gould. *The Annotated Mother
   Goose*. New York: C.N. Potter, 1962.

Becker, May Lamberton, ed. *The Rainbow Mother Goose*. Cleveland: The
   World Publishing Company, 1974.

Daycare Provider. "Cindy's Cardfile – Circle, Craft and Activity Ideas:
   Rhymes." 6 March 1999. <http://www.icomm.ca/daycare/cardsb07.html>
   (20 Jan. 2000).

Grover, Eulalie Osgood, ed. *Mother Goose*. Chicago: M. A. Donahue and
   Company, 1915.

Homework Central Junior. "The Mother Goose Page." 7 Dec. 1998.
   <http://www.homeworkcentral.com/files.htp?fileid=13012> (20 Jan. 2000).

Huck, Charlotte S., and Doris Young Kuhn. *Children's Literature in the
   Elementary School*. 2nd ed. Chicago: Holt, Rinehart, and Winston, Inc.,
   1968.

LaRoche, Nancy E. "Save the Children," *Harper's* December 1973: 114–115.

Likens, Rebecca. "In Defense of Mother Goose," *PTA Magazine* June 1973:
   21–23.

Mitchell, Donald, ed. *Every Child's Book of Nursery Songs*. New York:
   Bonanza Books, 1967.

Parker, Patricia. "What Comes after Mother Goose?" *The Education Digest*
   October 1969: 46–49.

Rackham, Arthur. *Mother Goose Nursery Rhymes*. New York: Franklin
   Watts, Inc., 1969.

Commens 8

Rogers, Fred. "Three Classic Nursery Tales," *Redbook* December 1973: 39–44.

Vandergrift, Kay E. "History of Children's Literature." 18 May 1998. <http://www.scils.rutgers.edu/special/kay/history.html> (20 Jan. 2000).

 Analysis of the MLA Parenthetical Style Sample. The paper illustrates many of the important principles that should be evident in a research paper. While you can make many observations on your own about the approach the sample paper takes, note these specifics:

- The topic is interesting and narrowed appropriately for the length of the paper.
- The paper employs both primary and secondary research. The writer draws many of her comments directly from the rhymes themselves, rather using someone else's criticism of them. The two types of research enhance the quality of the paper and fulfill the requirement to write an evaluative paper.
- Quotations, especially those from the rhymes, support the writer's ideas. The few long quotations included offer insight into other critics' interpretations. Notice how quoted passages blend smoothly into the text, in some cases finishing sentences begun by the writer.
- Far more paraphrases appear than quotations. The writer avoids a paper that is little more than a string of quotations. Because of her paraphrasing, the paper reads evenly and reflects a thoughtful analysis of relationships among ideas.
- The paragraphs follow a clear organization. [*See the third Sample MLA Footnote Style Paper to compare the paper with the writer's actual outline.*] The paper includes a two-paragraph introduction (not part of the outline), and each of the remaining paragraphs corresponds to a main or subheading in the outline.
- The paper exhibits good sentence variety and sophisticated writing technique.

- Transitional words, phrases, and sentences move the reader smoothly from idea to idea, paragraph to paragraph. The seventh paragraph is transitional; it summarizes the main points covered so far and introduces the final point.
- The format, which includes accurate parenthetical notes and a list of works cited, follows the guidelines for good formatting. Long quotations are set apart from the rest of the text. The bibliography page is accurate and complete, citing only those sources used in the text.

By following carefully all the steps in the research process, you will be able to develop a satisfactory research paper. The precise form may well be determined by your teacher, department, or school policy.

SAMPLE MLA ENDNOTE STYLE PAPER

This excerpt illustrates another widely accepted style. The documentation appears in the text as raised numbers that refer to a list of notes at the end of the paper.

Commens 1

Ann Commens
Instructor A. Kamp
Senior English II
15 January 20—

Mother Goose: A Devoted Teacher

Mother Goose has survived generations of critics. Perhaps the most trying test of all for Mother Goose has been through the honest and often unrestrained criticism of children.[1] These rhymes have survived because of their ageless quality of rhythm, rhyme, and motion.[2] They have been passed from parent to child for generations,[3] becoming such a part of the English-speaking world that it is a handicap for a child not to know them.[4] The nursery rhymes of Mother Goose, loved and recited by generations of children, help introduce children to good literature, create fantasy friends, provide contentment, stimulate imagination, and promote learning.

Commens, page __

Notes

[1]Eulalie Osgood Grover, ed., *Mother Goose* (Chicago: M.A. Donahue and Company, 1915) 1.

[2]May Hill Arbuthnot, *The Real Mother Goose* (Chicago: Rand McNally and Co., 1944) 3.

[3]Patricia Parker, "What Comes after Mother Goose?" *The Education Digest* October 1969: 46.

[4]May Lamberton Becker, ed., *The Rainbow Mother Goose* (Cleveland: The World Publishing Company, 1974) 11.

 Analysis of the MLA Endnote Style Sample. The preceding excerpt illustrates endnote documentation. The bibliography page with endnote documentation is identical to that with parenthetical documentation.

SAMPLE MLA FOOTNOTE STYLE PAPER

The footnote style is still preferred by some. Most word-processing software includes formatting options to help with difficult page layout. It begins with a title page that is followed by an outline page.

MOTHER GOOSE: A DEVOTED TEACHER

By

Ann Commens

Senior English II

Ms. Aurelia Kamp

January 15, 20—

Statement of Purpose:

    The nursery rhymes of Mother Goose, loved and recited by generations of children, introduce children to literature, serve as fantasy companions, provide forms of contentment, stimulate imagination, and promote learning.

Outline:

I. Introduce literature
  A. Listening skills
  B. Poetry appreciation

II. Offer friends
  A. Mother Hubbard
  B. Mary
  C. Old Woman
  D. Little Bo Peep
  E. Jack and Jill
  F. Peter, Peter

III. Provide contentment
  A. Happiness
  B. Humor
  C. Riddles

IV. Stimulate imagination
  A. Alteration
  B. Fantasy

V. Promote learning
  A. Days
  B. Numbers
  C. Roman numerals
  D. Alphabet
  E. Language

Mother Goose: A Devoted Teacher

Mother Goose has survived generations of critics. Perhaps the most trying test of all for Mother Goose has been through the honest and often unrestrained criticism of children.[1] These rhymes have survived because of their
ageless quality of rhythm, rhyme, and motion.[2] They have been passed
from parent to child for generations,[3] becoming such a part of the English-
speaking world that it is a handicap for a child not to know the rhymes.[4] The
nursery rhymes of Mother Goose, loved and recited by generations of
children, help introduce children to good literature, create fantasy friends,
provide contentment, stimulate imagination, and promote learning.

According to legend, Mistress Elizabeth Goose, known widely as
Mother Goose, lived in Boston 200 years ago. She is supposed to have
recited her varied rhymes to her numerous grandchildren. Her son-in-law,
Thomas Fleet, is said to have published her nursery rhymes in order to
make some well-deserved money.[5]

---

[1]Eulalie Osgood Grover, ed., *Mother Goose* (Chicago: M. A. Donahue
and Company, 1916) 1.

[2]May Hill Arbuthnot, *The Real Mother Goose* (Chicago: Rand McNally
and Co., 1944) 3.

[3]Patricia Parker, "What Comes after Mother Goose?" *The Education
Digest* October 1969: 46.

[4]May Lamberton Becker, ed., *The Rainbow Mother Goose* (Cleveland:
The World Publishing Company, 1974) 11.

[5]Grover 2.

Analysis of the MLA Footnote Style Sample. The excerpt illustrates
a title page, an outline page (which could be altered to serve as a table
of contents), and footnotes. Notice that the footnotes appear at the
bottom of each page, separated from the text by a ten-space line from
the left margin and two double spaces. The footnotes are single-
spaced with double spaces between entries. The bibliography form
will be the same as that for endnotes, except single-spaced, with
two spaces between entries, to follow the pattern established in the
footnotes.

SAMPLE APA STYLE PAPER

The *Publication Manual of the American Psychological Association* describes a style, referred to as the APA style, primarily for psychology papers but used in other curricular areas as well.

- The title page includes the title, the author's name, and the author's school affiliation, double-spaced, centered left to right and top to bottom. A title requiring more than one line is also double-spaced. A running head, a shortened version of the title, appears at the top right margin with the page number a double space below and flush with the right margin. The head is repeated, without the page number, at the bottom.
- An abstract follows, summarizing the paper. The abstract page includes a shortened form of the title and a running head in the upper right corner. The title, Abstract, appears centered one inch from the top. The abstract is a single paragraph written in block form (that is, without indentation) beginning a double space below the title. The abstract should be 75 to 100 words for theoretical articles or reviews and 100 to 150 words for empirical papers.
- The first page of the paper repeats the title, centered, one inch from the top. Text begins a double space below the title.
- The parts of the paper are labeled (Method, Results, Discussion, References) in a manner similar to other technical reports. [*See* Technical Report *later in Part III.*] Headings of the same level are typed in the same format.
- All pages include a running head and are double-spaced.
- The notes are parenthetical and include the author's last name followed by a comma and the date of publication. When the author's name appears in the text, only the date appears in parentheses. If reference is made to a specific page or chapter, or if a quotation is included, the parenthetical note must also include a page or chapter number. Use the abbreviation *p.* or *pp.* preceding page numbers: (Smith, 1992, pp. 78–81).

- Instead of a bibliography, the APA style calls for a reference list. This list must include every citation in the text. Note, too, that the form for entries differs considerably from the MLA style. The use of surnames with only initials, the use of parentheses around the date of publication, the omission of capital letters in all but the first word and proper names of titles, the omission of quotation marks around periodical titles, and the underscoring of volume numbers of periodicals are some obvious differences. Note, too, that the entries are double-spaced with hanging indentation, the second line and following lines being indented only three spaces, rather than five as in the MLA style.

Mother Goose

1

Mother Goose Rhymes: Their Influence on Children's

Literary Introduction, Imagination, and Reading Readiness

Ann Commens

St. Philips College

Mother Goose

Mother Goose

2

Abstract

Mother Goose rhymes have been determined to be useful aids in developing educational readiness in preschool children. First, the rhymes introduce children to literature by helping them learn to appreciate sound and imagery in poetry. Second, as part of that introduction, children also learn to recognize the difference between real and imaginary friends. Third, the rhymes help children create their own contentment. Fourth, the combination of these elements stimulates imagination. The ultimate result, of course, is the promotion of learning by stimulating reading readiness in preschool children.

Mother Goose

3

Mother Goose Rhymes: Their Influence on Children's

Literary Introduction, Imagination, and Reading Readiness

Mother Goose has survived generations of critics. Some authorities (Grover, 1915, p. 1) profess that the most trying test of all for Mother Goose has been through the honest and often unrestrained criticism of children. These rhymes have survived because of their ageless quality of rhythm, rhyme, and motion (Arbuthnot, 1944, p. 3), and they have been passed from parent to child for generations (Parker, 1969, p. 46), becoming such a part of the English-speaking world that some believe (Becker, 1974, p. 11) it is a handicap for a child not to know the rhymes. The nursery rhymes of Mother Goose, loved and recited by generations of children, help introduce children to good literature, create fantasy friends, provide contentment, stimulate imagination, and promote learning.

According to legend, Mistress Elizabeth Goose, known widely as Mother Goose, lived in Boston 200 years ago. She is supposed to have recited her varied rhymes to her numerous grandchildren. According to Grover (1915, p. 2), Thomas Fleet, son-in-law to Dame Goose, published her nursery rhymes in order to make some well-deserved money. Today, tourists and children still visit the site in Boston where Dame Goose is believed to be buried (Huck & Kuhn, 1968, p. 62). Contrary to the Mother Goose legend, most authorities (Huck & Kuhn) agree that Mother Goose appeared in 1697 as the title of a book of fairy tales by Charles Perrault.

Mother Goose

7

References

Addams, C. (1967). *The Chas Addams Mother Goose*. New York: Windmill Books.

Arbuthnot, M. H. (1944). *The real Mother Goose*. Chicago: Rand McNally and Co.

Baring-Gould, W. S., and Baring-Gould, C. (1962). *The annotated Mother Goose*. New York: C. N. Potter.

Becker, M. L. (Ed.). (1974). *The rainbow Mother Goose*. Cleveland: The World Publishing Company.

De Angeli, M. (1954). *Book of nursery and Mother Goose rhymes*. Garden City: Doubleday and Company, Inc.

Grover, E. O. (Ed.). (1915). *Mother Goose*. Chicago: M. A. Donahue and Company.

Huck, C. S., and Kuhn, D. Y. (1968). *Children's literature in the elementary school* (2nd ed.). Chicago: Holt, Rinehart, and Winston, Inc.

LaRoche, N. E. (1973, December). Save the children. *Harper's*, pp. 114–115.

Likens, R. (1973, June). In defense of Mother Goose. *PTA Magazine*, pp. 21–23.

Mitchell, D. (Ed.). (1967). *Every child's book of nursery songs*. New York: Bonanza Books.

Parker, P. (1969, October). What comes after Mother Goose? *The Education Digest*, pp. 46–49.

Analysis of the APA Style Sample Paper. The APA style serves to provide logical, convenient documentation for psychological research. More complicated papers will take on the specific divisions (*Method, Results, Discussion*) after an initial introduction like that given earlier.

In this respect, the paper looks more like a technical report than it does a research paper. Compare the format of a technical report [*in Technical Report later in Part III*] with what you see here.

SAMPLE NUMBERED BIBLIOGRAPHY STYLE PAPER

Numbered bibliography style simplifies documentation. Some readers object to this style because they must flip to the bibliography to determine each source as it appears in the text. Other readers, especially those who place less emphasis on sources, prefer its uncluttered format. Writers generally like it because it eases documentation. Here's how you do numbered bibliography style:

- Before writing the final draft of the paper, prepare an alphabetical listing of sources used in the paper. Number the list consecutively, beginning with 1. (Note that other arrangements are also possible. For instance, scientific papers often list the sources in order in which they are first cited in the text. Use whichever arrangement works best for your purposes.)
- When you document a source in your text, refer parenthetically to the work by number. Follow the number with a comma and a space, and then add the page number. A numbered parenthetical note looks like this: (8, 32). In this case, *8* refers to the eighth source listed in the numbered bibliography and *32* refers to the page number within the source. A multiple-page reference looks like this: (12, 114–123).

The following excerpt illustrates numbered bibliography style:

Mother Goose: A Devoted Teacher

Mother Goose has survived generations of critics. Perhaps the most trying test of all for Mother Goose has been through the honest and often unrestrained criticism of children (6, 2). These rhymes have survived because of their ageless quality of rhythm, rhyme, and motion (2, 3). They have been passed from parent to child for generations (11, 46), becoming such a part of the English-speaking world that it is a handicap for a child not to know the rhymes (4, 11). The nursery rhymes of Mother Goose, loved and recited by generations of children, can have a combination of good and bad effects upon the children.

Works Cited

1. Addams, Charles. *The Chas Addams Mother Goose.* New York: Windmill Books, 1967.

2. Arbuthnot, May Hill. *The Real Mother Goose.* Chicago: Rand McNally and Co., 1944.

3. Baring-Gould, William S., and Ceil Baring-Gould. T*he Annotated Mother Goose.* New York: C. N. Potter, 1962.

 Analysis of the Numbered Bibliography Style Sample. Note that the format for the numbered bibliography is the same as for earlier MLA samples. The addition of numbers marks the only difference.

A Final Note: Reexamine the five forms. Note their differences and similarities, then follow the format that works best for you. In spite of the emphasis here on format, keep in mind that your instructor is more interested in content. Be sure that you use superior writing techniques and that your paper reflects thorough research. Accurate form will not substitute for careful research or polished writing.

Resume

A resume (pronounced *reh-zoo-may*) is a summary of your qualifications for a job. It usually includes your educational background, work experience, and references.

Submitted with a cover letter [*see* Letters: Business Letters, Sample to Accompany a Resume *earlier in Part III*], delivered either personally, by mail, or by e-mail, the resume may be your only opportunity to make a good impression. While formats vary considerably, all follow one of three patterns:

- Chronological organization: experiences are listed beginning with the earliest; the most recent experiences appear last.
- Reverse chronological organization: the most recent experiences appear first.
- Experiences grouped in relation to the job currently sought: little effort is made to show time relationships, but dates are included.

In seeking employment early in one's life, a reverse chronological pattern is usually most appropriate. We will follow this form in our discussion here.

CHARACTERISTICS

No matter its format, a resume will include these common characteristics:

- Your name, mailing address, e-mail address, phone number (including area code), and fax number, if you have one
- The position for which you are applying
- Your experience, including places, dates of employment and responsibilities or duties held
- Your education and special training
- References

In many cases, the resume is the only picture the personnel manager sees of you, so you must make the best impression you can without being dishonest or misleading.

PROCESS

The following process will help you develop a complete, accurate, and impressive resume.

STEP 1   **Prewriting • Analyzing the Employment Requirements**
Before you develop a resume, name the specific position you are seeking. Then make a list of the skills, duties, responsibilities, and education you think the job requires. If possible, ask for a job description and tailor your list from that.

The implications for doing this analysis are twofold:

- First, you will design a resume to best show your qualifications for the specific job.
- Second, you will design different resumes for different kinds of jobs.

Redesigning a resume to suit different positions may sound dishonest; in fact, it is not. You simply emphasize the experiences appropriate to the position. For instance, if you were applying for a job at a horticulture nursery, you would want to emphasize your experience with plants and your understanding of gardening. On the other hand, if you were applying for a position as an appliance salesperson where nobody cared what you know about gardening, you would emphasize your sales experience (even if the experience was selling plants) and your ability to relate well to other people.

So, yes, it is important to name the specific position and precisely determine its responsibilities so that your resume can be geared toward that goal.

STEP 2   **Prewriting • Analyzing Your Experience**

List your work experience. Jot down dates and employers. If you are young and lack job experience, do not hesitate to include volunteer work and major committee assignments. After all, it was work, even if you were not paid for it. It required responsibility and commitment; it shows willingness to work and achieve goals.

Once you have listed all the experiences you can, or all that seem appropriate, arrange them in reverse chronological order (that is, the most recent first).

STEP 3   **Prewriting • Meeting the Job Requirements**

For each experience listed, name the responsibilities you held or the duties you performed. List responsibilities and duties especially appropriate for the position you are seeking. If none seem especially appropriate, list the ones that show the greatest responsibility or skill.

If, for instance, you apply for the nursery job, the employer will be interested in knowing that you worked every spring preparing your neighbor's garden: fertilizing, planting, and mulching. On the other hand, the same job listed in a resume for the appliance salesperson might refer only to *seasonal yard work*, with duties listed merely as *responsible for developing necessary routine to maintain health and attractiveness of garden*. Thus, you show self-discipline and responsibility for a product, both important aspects of a sales job.

Now complete your own list.

STEP 4   **Prewriting • Meeting the Educational Requirements**

In a like manner, prepare details about your education and training. Emphasize anything directly related to the position sought, such as majors or minors or even specific courses. In addition, list any private lessons, seminars, workshops, and other noncredit classes you may have taken that add to your experience.

STEP 5   **Prewriting • Seeking References**

Most job applications request references. By including these on your resume, you will be better prepared to complete any application form the potential employer may request.

List two or three people, not relatives, who can vouch for your ability, especially as it relates to the position sought. The more responsible and credible your references, the more helpful their recommendations. Choose wisely, but make sure you choose someone who can honestly speak well for you. If a reference begins by saying to your potential employer, "I really don't know the applicant well, but ..." you have done yourself no favors.

Always get permission from anyone you list as a reference. To neglect getting permission is presumptuous, and your presumption may be just enough to earn a poor recommendation. After all, by neglecting to ask first, you have demonstrated a lack of responsibility.

Once you have selected the best references and gained their permission, write down their names, titles or positions, and addresses. In some cases, you will also include a home and/or business phone number.

STEP 6 **Writing • Following a Format**

As you begin to arrange your information into a resume, you should choose a logical format. While many exist, most center the applicant's name, address, and phone number at the top. The remainder of the resume is set in columns, the left listing the general headings, and the right giving the details:

Your Name
Your Street Address
Your City and State and Zip Code
Your Phone Number, Including Area Code

Position Sought: *Position named*

Experience: *List places, dates, and details of duties and responsibilities. Type single-spaced, but double-space between jobs. List the second job experience here.*

Education: *List education and any specific honors or leadership experiences appropriate for the position sought.*

References: *Give names, positions or titles, addresses, and phone numbers. Skip a line between individual references.*

If possible, limit your resume to a single page. Only when you are more experienced can you afford the risk of a multi-paged resume.

STEP 7   Revising • Evaluating Your Resume

Examine your resume as if you were a personnel manager. How does it read?

Next, look for ways to enhance your image. Ask these questions:

- Have I listed my most impressive duties or responsibilities as they relate to this position?
- Have I overlooked experience or abilities that would make me a better candidate? If so, how can I include them?
- Are the details accurate? Dates, places, names?
- Have I described my experience accurately? (The potential employer may check these details even though you do not list references connected with every position.)
- Can I make any revisions to improve my image without being misleading or dishonest?

STEP 8   Proofreading • Making a Sharp Impression

After you have typed the resume, look at the details. Is everything spelled correctly? Punctuated accurately? Is the grammar correct? Have you maintained standard usage and mechanics? [*See Part IV for rules and examples.*]

Now back off and take a critical look at the appearance. Keep in mind that this is your only chance for a first impression. The resume must be immaculate. Ask yourself:

- Is it neat?
- Is the format crisp and clean?
- Have I used good-quality white paper?

In other words, did you do everything possible to create a professional-looking resume? Your resume is your image to a potential employer.

SAMPLE RESUME

The following resume complies with the preceding suggestions:

Kevin L. McDermitt
12806 South Pike Road
Mt. Simon, Lousiana 23306-4441
(712) 877-5602

Position Sought: Consumer Computer Trainer

Experience: Community College, Computer Education Lab, Sept. 1998 to present. Supervisor: Dr. Clarence K. Elliott. Duties: tutoring students in word processing and spreadsheet work, using over 40 pieces of software with five major computer brands. Twenty-eight hours per week.

Computer Land, Dixon, Georgia, part-time sales, summers, 1995, 1996, and 1997. Supervisor: Jeannette Shovers. Duties: helping customers select software to meet specific needs and altering software to solve user and hardware compatibility problems.

Education: Community College, Mount Simon, Louisiana. Associate Degree in Business with minor in computer education, 1997. Special award for volunteer tutoring in area secondary school computer labs.

Rushing High School, Dixon, Georgia. Graduated with honors, 1984. President of Senior Class; Treasurer of Junior Achievement business group, 1983.

References: Dr. Clarence K. Elliott, Instructor, Community College, 100 North Judson, Mount Simon, Lousiana 23307-8211

Dr. Jeannette Shovers, Manager, Computer Land, 817 East Elm, Dixon, Georgia 27711

Mr. Rodney Tresseur, Junior Achievement Sponsor, Rushing National Bank, 1200 Bloom Street, Dixon, Georgia 27711-7003

Analysis of the Sample Resume. The sample includes all the characteristics suggested in the process. Note particularly these matters:

- The overall format is neat, clean, and crisp.
- The resume is limited to a single page.
- The spacing helps group the subject matter.
- The labels are clear.
- The content is clearly aimed at the position sought and extraneous material is omitted. For instance, there is no mention of athletic activities in high school or work backstage for dramatic productions at Community College.
- Honors and specific duties are included in the appropriate areas.
- References are related to the computer business or to the applicant's abilities.

Studying the process, sample, and analysis should help you develop a strong resume. Turn now to Letters: Business Letters, Sample to Accompany a Resume earlier in Part III so that you can develop an effective cover letter.

Best wishes for a good interview!

Review

Reviews of novels, films, concerts, scientific work, art exhibits, or plays often serve as an audience's introduction. The reader buys a book on the basis of an interesting review; the moviegoer takes in a Sunday afternoon matinee on the basis of a good review; the music lover saves the price of admission on the basis of a poor concert review.

But there is really very little we can say that will hold true for all reviews. They are free-form and highly personal, reflecting the opinions and experiences of the reviewer. As a result, then, in order to write good reviews, you must have broad experience in your chosen field. And you must have sound criteria with which to judge the work.

In spite of the minimal formal direction we can provide here, we will look at the general characteristics of reviews, examine the process by which they are written, and analyze a sample review.

CHARACTERISTICS

As you might guess, reviews have few strict characteristics, but good reviews almost always include certain elements and use certain techniques for development. A good review

- begins with an explanation that gives the work a frame of reference—including information about the author, background, genre, or general issues pertinent to the work,
- explains a work by indicating generally what it is about,
- includes material pertinent to the reader, aimed toward his or her interests,
- selects the most interesting, important, or thought-provoking ideas for discussion or examination,
- generates interest in the work, either positive or negative,
- describes strengths and weaknesses,
- concludes with an evaluation based on the points discussed,
- uses good style, sound sentence structure, and other techniques of excellent writing.

The remainder of this section focuses on one common kind of review, that for a literary work, particularly a novel. While reviews of literary works are not the same as literary analyses, reviews share certain techniques with them. Keep in mind, however, that reviews do not follow the typically thorough and technical nature of literary analyses. [*Refer to* Literary Analyses *earlier in Part III for comparison.*]

PROCESS

The following steps will help you develop a satisfactory review.

STEP 1 **Prewriting • Selecting the Focus**

In writing a literary review, you select interesting ideas that you can develop in the allotted space. To help you think about points worth discussing, ask yourself the following questions:

- What is the purpose of the work? What is its theme? What message does the author convey?
- Who are its major characters? What are they like? Can the reader identify with them?
- What problems do the characters face? Does the reader see the characters grow as a result of struggle? Is the main character a hero or an antihero?

- What is the setting? Is it important to the plot, the theme, or the characters' struggle?
- Are other literary elements (imagery, symbolism, personification, and so on) important in the work? If so, how are they used? [*See* imagery, symbol, personification, *and* figure of speech *in the Glossary*.]
- What is your reaction to the work? Do you like it, find it fascinating? Or would you prefer never to think about it again? Why?

Next, pick out the few questions that either touch on the most important aspects of the book or are likely to generate interest in the reader. That these two options should be the same is irrelevant. It may not be the case!

STEP 2   **Prewriting • Planning the Review**

Once you have selected the guiding questions, use them to create a list of ideas you want to include. Try these steps:

- First, determine your attitude toward the work. Do not allow yourself to be noncommittal; the reader may think you cannot make up your mind. Granted, you may be positive about some aspects and negative about others, but form an opinion either way.
- Next, use the responses from Step 1 to support your opinion. If you have both positive and negative reactions, then form two lists: one with details you liked and the other with details you disliked. Select the details that explain why you feel as you do.
- Third, state your idea in a single sentence. This is a tall order, and you may need to group items on the lists, but you must get a handle on where you are going. Consider the following example:

Positives	Negatives
peculiar setting	unbelievable relationships with scientific
learn about prehistory	research animals
heroic female character	too coincidental
alien culture	
spiritual rituals	
daily lives	
relationships	
living habits	

The positive list includes overlapping items. By grouping these together, the writer came up with a single sentence:

The novel's prehistoric setting, carefully researched, allows a heroic female to overshadow coincidences and bring readers a fascinating epic-like book.

The writer has sharpened his focus and can now see exactly what he wants to discuss:

Prehistoric setting couched in thorough research
Heroic female character
Coincidental events

The overall attitude will be favorable (two positives and one negative).

Now, formulate your own single sentence. [*See also* thesis statement *in the Glossary, and* Writing a Multi-Paragraph Paper *in Part I for additional details.*]

STEP 3 **Prewriting • Organizing the Plan**

Even though we said that reviews are free-form, they nevertheless follow an organization plan. Frequently, this organization is the most-to-least-important pattern [*see* order of importance *in the Glossary*]. But it may take almost any other pattern, such as cause and effect or comparison and contrast. [*See entries for each in Part II.*] Other kinds of reviews, particularly for performances, tend to follow a chronological order.

Decide on the best means of organizing your review. Look at the list and sentence you completed in Step 2. By putting them together, you should see which items will logically appear first, second, and so on. Put the list in order.

STEP 4 **Writing • Following the Plan**

Use the list of characteristics at the beginning of this section as a guide for writing your review. Begin with an introductory paragraph that puts the work in perspective. Include any information about the author, such as other works or follow-up plans. Identify the genre. And entice the reader. Somewhere in the introductory paragraph, include the thesis sentence. In fact, you may revise the sentence you wrote in Step 2 to this end.

Use good writing techniques to develop the body of the review. Support your opinions with examples drawn from the work, much as you would in an opinion paper or literary analysis. Hold to your plan so that the reader can follow your logic. Smooth the way with transitions. [*See* transitions *in the Glossary.*]

The conclusion gives a final evaluation of the work and either recommends or rejects it, based on the main ideas developed in the body of the review.

STEP 5   **Revising • Improving the Content**

As you revise, ask yourself the following questions:

- Have I introduced the work effectively? Will my reader understand the general idea of the work, its purpose, its message?
- Have I avoided giving away the plot? Or will the reader hate me for destroying the pleasure of discovering the outcome?
- Do the body paragraphs clearly support my opinion? Or have I muddled the supporting details with extraneous materials? [*See* Revising: Sample Revision for Specific Detail *in Part I.*]
- Have I clearly conveyed my attitude toward different aspects of the novel? Do my transitions help readers follow my thoughts? [*See* Revising: Sample Revision for Transition *in Part I.*]
- Recognizing that a review is a matter of opinion, have I been fair in my reactions? Have I been too hasty to applaud or criticize? Do I have a basis on which to commend or condemn the work?
- Have I maintained a good writing style, neither too flowery nor too blunt, showing features or flaws, not just telling about them? Are my sentences varied in length and structure? [*See* Revising: Sample Revision for Sentence Variety *and* Revising: Sample Revision for Emphasis *in Part I.*]

Revise accordingly. Then compare your review with the list of characteristics earlier in this section and revise as needed. Finally, refer to Revising in Part I for further guidance.

STEP 6   **Proofreading • Checking Technical Details**

A review, like any other piece of writing, follows the standards of grammar, usage, and mechanics. [*See Part IV for rules and examples.*] Finally, check spelling and word choice.

This process will help you write a successful review. Only by reading numerous magazine and newspaper reviews, however, will you fully understand the techniques used by professionals. For the sake of discussion, however, we have included below a review of a novel. Study it and its analysis before writing your own review.

SAMPLE REVIEW

The following review serves several purposes. It shows what a review can do. It enables you to compare a book review with a book report. And it lets you compare a book review with a literary analysis of a novel. The same novel serves as the topic for the sample book reports [*in* Book Report *earlier in Part III*] and the sample analysis of a novel [*in* Literary Analyses *earlier in Part III*]. A comparison of all three will help you develop a more effective review.

When Neanderthal-Reared Meets Cro-Magnon:
A Review of The Valley of the Horses

Whisked back 25,000 years to the last Ice Age, readers of Jean Auel's *The Valley of the Horses* land in prehistoric civilization peopled by cave-dwelling Neanderthals and tribes of Cro-Magnons. The second book in the Earth Children series, *Valley* alternately follows its two main characters until they ultimately meet. Ayla, the beautiful, willowy, orphaned Cro-Magnon girl raised by a Neanderthal tribe, has been exiled and separated from her son because she dared to dispute the word of the leader. Turned out alone, and with no provisions, to wander the Eurasian steppes, she uses her ill-gotten hunting skills and knowledge of medicinal plants to survive the loneliness and unrelenting environment for five years. She raises a foundling colt after she kills the mare for food. As a kind of surrogate mother to the colt, she develops a fond relationship with the animal which, when mature, provides transportation and labor for the young woman. A similar relationship develops with an injured lion cub. Together, the three of them form a kind of family. Eventually, Ayla meets Jondalar, an exceptionally handsome Cro-Magnon man astounded by Ayla's family, her beauty, her refined skills. He is the first non-Neanderthal man Ayla has ever seen. The remainder of the plot revolves around their efforts to learn to understand one another and to communicate. Ayla knows only the nonverbal communication skills of the Neanderthals; Jondalar never masters the subtle variations of her "primitive" language. Their biggest obstacle is Jondalar's unwillingness to accept Ayla's only filial attachment, the Neanderthals, as anything other than subhuman, animal-like flatheads.

Even without the fascinating characters who struggle with their social and cultural differences, the book provides superb reading. The scientific research evident in the book gives curious readers an insight into a world they would never take the time to study in biology, botany, anthropology, and archaeology books. Woven into a highly readable novel, however, the medicinal plants, woolly mammoths, cave lions, wild horses, glaciers, flint qualities, food preparation, hunting techniques, clothing construction, even sanitation habits of prehistoric tribes make for startling new perspectives on human evolution. While the fictionalized portions blend harmoniously with the obviously thorough scientific investigation, the result is pleasantly mind-stretching.

With a beautiful heroine and a strikingly handsome hero set in the midst of an unspoiled environment, Auel could have lapsed into a Garden of Eden paradise. But all does not go well; difficulties inherent in the uncivilized, lonely arena of *Valley* provide gripping episodes, a few tears, and satisfying joy. Only a few unlikely coincidences mar the otherwise delightful novel. That a young woman can stop a lion's attack in midair, even if she "knows" the lion, seems less than believable. That a young woman who happened to ride farther than usual also happened to arrive just as the lion was about to attack also seems preposterous. Because these incidents make up a major pivotal point in the plot, they present a significant weakness. With the remainder of the epic-like novel so carefully plotted and so logical in its possibilities, these incidents seem all the more unlikely.

For its insight into a world that preceded modern man, *The Valley of the Horses* offers an imaginative approach to how man—or, in this case, woman—came to think about riding a horse, how she may have learned to make fire with stones, how she may have learned to make medicine, how she may have learned to hunt animals that were too large or too fast to kill with a sling or a spear. That strange animals roamed the earth 25,000 years ago is no secret, but to see them roaming the grasslands, to watch their habits, to learn how prehistoric people relied on them for both food and protection—that is an eye-opener. Thanks to Auel, readers now have a delightful opportunity to learn about another world through the eyes of two arresting Cro-Magnon characters.

Analysis of the Sample Review. The review lets the writer express his opinion, supported by details. Note these specific characteristics:

- The opening paragraph places the book into perspective, establishing it as part of a series and summarizing its plot without giving too much away. In introducing the main characters, the author gives a brief description of their difficulties but rightfully omits any reference to the outcome of their struggles.
- The second paragraph elaborates on the best attributes of the novel. Detailed references to scientific research support the reviewer's opinion.
- The third paragraph, which begins positively, permits the reviewer to offer his only disparaging comments about the book. While admitting that one incident should not discredit an entire work, he indicates the pivotal importance of the incident. At the same time, he shows how other aspects of the book work so favorably that the criticism must be taken in their light.

- The final paragraph concludes favorably. Without directly saying so, the reviewer implies we should dash out, pick up a copy, and immediately read it.

Because this is a review, we know that a different reviewer might easily present a very different opinion.

Review writing is an art. The more you read reviews, and the works treated by them, the broader your own ideas will become as to what constitutes good practice. These guidelines should get you off to a good start.

Scripts

Scripts are used for all kinds of audio productions: plays, television dramas, radio shows, commercials, documentaries, pageants, ceremonies, and so on. Most scripts consist of two parts: a narration or dialogue (the spoken portion) and a set of directions for visual or sound effects (to enrich the spoken portion). The script for a play includes the lines for the actors and the stage directions to describe the setting, lighting, movement of characters, and so on. The script for a television play includes everything found in the stage play, plus camera directions and editing cuts.

Scripts are used in other media productions as well. PowerPoint or other technological presentations, for instance, may have either prerecorded narratives or printed scripts. Museum tours may have prerecorded audio presentations or written scripts for the guides.

Scripts vary less in how they present dialogue than in their format and technical vocabulary. As television or film script includes camera directions, it appears in two columns: audio and video. The drama script needs no camera cues; it appears in full-page format with italicized stage directions. The technical language varies as well.

We will limit our discussion here to three examples: drama, radio, and television.

DRAMA SCRIPTS

We have all read plays in literature textbooks and are accustomed to the elements they include. Drama is one of the oldest forms of human expression, and drama scripts, as a form, find their roots in equally remote times. Though the technical aspects of staging a play have altered somewhat over the centuries, the basic components and process for developing a play have not. Actors still speak lines, and the plot moves forward by showing, rather than telling.

CHARACTERISTICS

In a drama script, we expect to see

- a cast of characters, sometimes merely named, sometimes also identified by relationships,
- a setting in time and place,
- a description of the stage setting,
- a division of the play into acts and scenes,
- speeches, identified by character name,
- stage directions, to suggest characters' movements and changes in scenery and/or location.

In addition to these, we also expect the script to contain the essential dramatic elements. [*See* Literary Analyses: For Literary Works, Sample for a Drama, *and* Short Story, *both earlier in Part III, for a discussion of character, plot, setting, theme, and conflict.*]

The following elements appear in good dramatic productions:

- Characters who, in the course of their dialogue and interaction, tell the audience everything it needs to know
- Clearly developed characters, including at least one protagonist and antagonist [*see* protagonist *and* antagonist *in the Glossary*]
- Believable behavior and dialogue
- Motivation to account for behavior and attitudes
- Believable conflict [*see* conflict *in the Glossary*]
- Ample action
- Good plot or story line
- Rising action, crisis, climax, and falling action [*see each of these entries in the Glossary*]
- A theme [*see* theme *in the Glossary*]

PROCESS

To develop a drama script, you meld a number of writing skills. In one respect, you are writing a kind of short story, filled with action but lacking narration. In another respect, you are mapping character's actions within the confines of the stage. In still another, you are writing dialogue [*see* Dialogue *earlier in Part III*] and following the techniques of that creative art form. Along with these go concise descriptions of setting, staging, and direction. This complicated combination of writing skills requires attention to detail. The following process will help you develop the total script.

STEP 1 **Prewriting • Determining the Message**

Before you can write a drama script, you must decide what message, or theme, you hope to convey. [*See* theme, *as it relates to literature, in the Glossary.*] Think about what matters to you. If this is your first attempt at writing a drama, avoid dealing with world-impact messages. Instead, deal with something closer to home. Put your message in a single sentence.

Consider the following examples of one-sentence statements:

Showing responsibility develops trust.
Punctuality suggests responsibility.
We learn about people by watching how they treat animals.
Dishonesty usually ruins a friendship.

Each states a message on which a satisfactory drama could be based. Write your own message now.

STEP 2 **Prewriting • Planning the Plot**

Think about the action that will help the viewer understand your message. For instance, if you wish to show that dishonesty ruins a friendship, your plot should revolve around a friendship destroyed by lying. Certain necessary situations become immediately apparent:

The established friendship
The occurrence of the dishonesty
The discovery of the dishonesty
The deterioration of the friendship
The inability of the characters to mend the friendship as a result of lack of trust

Thus, these five items outline the drama. The problem, of course, is how best to show these occurrences. How can friendship be shown? What kind of dishonesty occurs? How does it occur? How is it discovered? What is the result of its discovery? Hurt feelings? Or something more serious, like physical injury? Does one friend try to mend the friendship? Who? How? What happens?

Asking these kinds of questions will help outline the plot. Develop your own outline now.

STEP 3   **Prewriting • Building the Characters**

As you outline the plot, you must simultaneously create characters. Some writers claim they develop characters before they begin plotting. In reality, characters and plot are so interdependent that the processes for developing them cannot easily be separated. For instance, if you decide the dishonesty occurs when one friend feigns illness to avoid going fishing with the other, then your character must pretend to enjoy fishing while actually preferring something else. How you develop a character determines the believability of his or her actions and, ultimately, that of the plot.

In order to create believable characters, start with a list of their traits. As you develop the plot, you can add or delete traits to clarify the characters in your own mind. Only when you see each character clearly will you be able to make him or her real for the audience. Consider the following:

First Female Character	Second Female Character
naïve	self-assured
honest to a fault	tells white lies
slightly paranoid	assertive
follows others	assumes leadership role
concerned for others	is introspective
is introspective	self-centered

Develop a list of traits for each character in your play.

STEP 4   **Prewriting • Selecting the Setting**

Where does the action take place? Picture it in your mind's eye. Can a producer build a set of the place within reasonable financial limits? Alter your vision as necessary, then develop a complete description of it. Include details that bear on the plot. For instance, if the characters discuss what they see out a window, describe the window's location. If a character makes a surprise entrance from an adjoining room, describe the room in relationship to the rest of the setting and describe the door's location.

If acts and scenes take place in more than one setting, develop similar descriptions of each.

STEP 5   **Writing • Putting the Plot into Script**

As you write, keep in mind that the audience knows only what the characters say or do. Without being blunt, you must have your characters clue the audience as to time, place, and situation. Dialogue tells all.

Follow the traditional form of scriptwriting. Note these techniques in particular:

- The name of the character speaking is listed first, followed by a colon. Following is the dialogue the character speaks.
- Quotation marks are omitted around a speaker's words. The identification of speaker by name eliminates the need for them.
- Stage directions appear in parentheses, printed in italics. Stage directions serve as general guidelines for blocking the play, the finer nuances being left to the director.

As you write, make every effort to include the items listed in the list of characteristics earlier in this section. Picture the action as you want the audience to see it.

Include sufficient directions to achieve that reality. Also keep in mind that stage directions should be written from the actor's point of view: hence, *stage left* is to the audience's right. Use the following chart to locate your characters onstage.

STAGE DIRECTIONS

Upstage Right	Upstage Center	Upstage Left
Right	Center	Left
Downstage Right	Downstage Center	Downstage Left
	Audience	

STEP 6   Revising • Polishing the Content

As you complete your script, you will, of course, improve plot and dialogue. Consider the following questions to suggest potential changes:

- Have I developed believable characters?
- Are their words consistent with their characters?
- Does the dialogue help the audience make deductions?
- Do the characters behave according to clearly defined motives?
- Does the plot develop smoothly, from rising action, through crisis and climax, to falling action? [*See entries for each in the Glossary.*]
- Is the plot believable, avoiding frequent coincidences and shaky cause-and-effect situations?
- Have I used good techniques to portray my characters, allowing the audience to see and hear them as well as hear what other characters have to say about them?
- Do I show rather than tell?
- Is my message clear by the end of the play?

In addition to content, you will need to make some final revisions with the script format. Note these specific details:

- Add a title to your script.
- Precede the script with a list of characters, perhaps stating their relationships to one another. Keep the identifications brief.
- Follow the cast of characters with a description of the setting: time, place, scene. Describe it clearly enough for a producer to stage your play. [*Use the information developed in Step 4.*]
- Identify each speaker as he or she speaks.
- Offset the stage directions with parentheses and print them in italics.
- Revise whatever you can to improve your script. Then go on to the next sections to make final adjustments.

STEP 7   Proofreading • Checking the Mechanical Details

As you proofread the final script, look for the usual kinds of errors: grammar, usage, mechanics, spelling, and word choice. In addition, look for certain details unique to scriptwriting:

- Have I used different print for the stage directions than for dialogue?
- Have I identified each speaker with a name followed by a colon?
- As the format identifies each speaker, have I omitted quotation marks?
- Do grammar and usage accurately reflect the character? [See Dialogue earlier in Part III for a discussion of nonstandard grammar and usage to build character.]

Finally, check spelling and word choice. Remember, no matter the characters' words, you, as a writer, must spell accurately. And remember, too, the right word choice can help develop character insight. Careful use of your thesaurus will strengthen your work.

SAMPLE DRAMA SCRIPT

The following example illustrates the format for a drama script. Compare it with radio and television scripts that follow.

THE LIE

CHARACTERS
Renee
Julianne
Mrs. Westbrook, Renee's mother
Mrs. Hollis, Julianne's mother
Walter, Westbrook's neighbor
Kathaleen
Janna

TIME: *The present.*

PLACE: *Middle-class suburban community.*

The Westbrook living room suggests nothing outstanding except an active teenager. The furnishings, generally traditional and colorless in beiges and greys, are decorated by Renee's school jacket, her cheerleader's uniform, a stack of books on the end table, and another on the floor by the sofa. Assorted shoes, sweaters, scarves, book bags, and tennis rackets litter the chairs and floor. The kitchen, offstage left, connects to the living room by a door center left. The upstairs bedrooms connect with the living room upstage center where the stairway enters. The only sense of quality is in the painting stage right of the stairway, a Flemish oil of obviously fine quality.

ACT I
Scene 1 : *Saturday morning.*

As curtain opens, Renee, dressed in an oversized shirt and floppy house shoes, enters from the kitchen munching a sweet roll. Her hair uncombed, she has obviously just awakened. Still eating, dropping crumbs across the floor, she flops on the only empty chair in the room, at downstage right.

Mrs. Westbrook: (*From the kitchen.*) Renee, are you eating in the living room again?

Renee: (*With obvious disdain.*) No, Mother. (*Licks her fingers and adds quietly to herself.*) Not anymore. (*She gets up, crosses to the sofa where she picks up her tennis racket and takes a few practice swings.*)

Mrs. Westbrook: (*Entering from the kitchen, wiping her hands on a towel.*) Is Julianne making her usual trek by here today, dear?

Renee: (*Continuing her practice swings.*) I suppose. I haven't talked to her today. (*She flops back in the chair downstage right, one leg draped over the arm.*) She hasn't called, and I'm not calling her.

Mrs. Westbrook: (*Looking carefully at her daughter.*) Oh? (*Renee does not respond. Mrs. W. shrugs.*) Well, whatever. At any rate, I want this living room straightened up. Pick up this mess and put it away. Looks like pigs live here. (*Mrs. W. exits upstage center toward bedrooms and then calls down.*) Oh, by the way, your father called about an hour ago. (*Mrs. W. reappears in the doorway.*) He said if you'd meet him at Weston's at noon, you could put in your two cents' worth on your new car.

Renee: (*With an explosion of excitement.*) Mom, really? Are you just kidding me? Is he really going to get me a car—a new one? (*Mrs. W. beams at her daughter.*) Mom, really? (*Renee dances around the furniture, over stacks of books, doing a ballet with the tennis racket.*) Whooppeeeee!

Mrs. Westbrook: Only if you get the living room straightened before you go. It's 10:30 now. (*She exits upstairs, then calls back.*) And don't forget to change the sheets on your bed this morning.

(*Renee begins furious activity. Stacking books, piling clothes and jackets in her arms, dropping some as she goes, she heads for the upstairs bedroom. In her scurry, she fails to hear the telephone ringing.*)

Analysis of the Sample Drama Script. The excerpt illustrates the form and style of this kind of writing. As you study it, note particularly these details:

- The cast list includes the relationships of three characters. The others need no such detail.
- The time, place, and setting are described, printed in italics to prevent their confusion with dialogue.
- As the first scene opens, the description of Renee's activities is printed in italics, again to prevent its confusion with dialogue.
- Characters' names, followed by a colon, precede their lines or any description of their actions.
- The stage directions appear in parentheses.
- The stage directions begin with a capital letter and end with a period, even when they are not complete sentences.
- Hanging indentation (all lines indented except the first) offsets the speakers' names, thus enabling players to find their lines easily.

These techniques, peculiar to drama scripts, serve a purpose: They help the producer, director, and players work effectively together. Granted, the techniques are gimmicks, but such gimmicks separate dialogue from instructions and clarify the sets of stage directions.

Use the sample and analysis to refine your own drama script.

RADIO SCRIPTS

The most frequent use of radio scripts is to provide continuity (materials that introduce and conclude programs, as well as provide transitions within them), commercial advertising, public-service announcements, and other spots. Because radio scripts differ significantly from drama scripts, we must first examine their general characteristics.

CHARACTERISTICS

Radio scripts rely solely on the sense of sound. Thus, the sound of words and phrases bears a greater importance than how they look on paper. Radio scripts, whether for commercials, continuity, or dramas, include certain characteristics. In general, radio scripts

- use short, concise sentences or phrases,
- rely on the listener's sense of sound,
- employ sensory images that affect the ear: repetition, alliteration, assonance, or onomatopoeia [see alliteration, assonance, and onomatopoeia in the Glossary],
- frequently take a conversational tone,
- often use an imperative mood [see imperative mood in the Glossary],
- are precisely timed to fill, for instance, a 60-second or 30-second spot.

In addition, the format of radio scripts follows certain specific characteristics. In general, radio scripts

- appear typed, double-spaced, on a continuity form (a special form used by radio stations),
- follow one of two formats: either material to be read typed in uppercase letters, or material not to be read typed in uppercase letters (the format is determined by the station or advertising agency),
- include all references to sound effects,

- rely heavily on nontraditional punctuation—dashes, exclamation points, and underlining—to indicate pauses and points of emphasis,
- use ellipses in a nontraditional way to indicate a pause or topping line (which interrupts, coming just a word or two prior to the end of the other speaker's words),
- spell difficult words phonetically.

Because the radio industry uses a vocabulary unfamiliar to the general public, you should learn the following terms:

across the board: advertisements or programs aired throughout the week at the same time every day

availability list: a list of the amount of air time that can be sold

cart: the shortened form of cartridge; a tape loop containing an advertiser's message which automatically returns to the start after playing

co-op copy: advertising copy in which both the sales store and the manufacturer's name are mentioned and for which both usually pay a portion of the advertising fee

donut: a commercial that begins with a jingle, has a hole for a spoken segment, and ends with a jingle

double spotting: using two commercials back-to-back with no commentary or music in between

down and under: to lower music to a background level so that the spoken voice becomes audible

fade in: to bring music gradually from zero volume to within acceptable balance

fade out: to bring music gradually from full level to zero sound

open-end transcription: a national program aired by a local station which allows room at the beginning and at the end for local advertising

outcue: the final words of a commercial spot, (often the same words for the same advertiser) that cue an on-the-air person to be ready for whatever is scheduled next

plug: an advertisement, often free, in the form of a public service announcement (PSA), to promote an activity or a business

prestige copy: advertising that promotes a positive image rather than a specific product

program log: a list required by the Federal Communications Commission (FCC), summarizing the announcements, commercials, and other broadcast materials aired by a given radio station, with reference to type of program or announcement, source of material (recorded, live, or other point of origin), and classification (record, tape, compact disc)

promo: promotional announcements advertising another program on the station

public service announcement (PSA): an announcement (or sometimes a longer broadcast) made without charge, in keeping with the Federal Communications Commission ruling that stations serve the public

punch: special emphasis placed on the delivery of certain words or even on an entire commercial (as opposed to a conversational tone)

ROS, or run of schedule: an advertisement that is scheduled by the station (rather than by the sponsor); often computer scheduled

signature: a piece of music played to introduce or conclude a program; sometimes called a theme song

sound effects (SFX): sounds to enhance a broadcast, either recorded live or made by substituting other sounds (for example, crinkling paper to sound like crackling fire)

spec: a speculation commercial used to try to attract a new advertiser

sponsor: an advertiser who pays for a program in return for advertising during that program

spot: a radio commercial

stand by: copy used as a backup

station ID: the identification of a radio station by its call letters and channel

sting: to bring music in at proper level

stinger: the process of bringing music in at proper level (as opposed to fade in)

tag: information added by the announcer to the end of a commercial: the name, address, and perhaps business hours of the advertiser

up and out: to increase the volume gradually to full and then fade it out

up full: to raise the volume to maximum

These terms will appear in work with radio programming. If you write scripts for radio, you may find yourself dealing with them.

PROCESS

Radio scripts require three essentials on the part of the writer: a good ear, a keen sense of brevity, and a well-developed technique for quickly gaining the listener's attention. Gaining attention amid daily distractions is no small challenge, especially as most radio listeners do not really listen: They merely want some background noise.

Try the following process to hone these three skills as we discuss the development of a typical radio script for a commercial:

STEP 1   **Prewriting • Sharpening the Focus**

In planning your script, you must first decide which features to emphasize. For a 30-second spot of co-op copy, you must know what the sponsor hopes the commercial to accomplish. [*See* Advertising *earlier in Part III.*] As a writer, you are responsible for finding this out, either from the station's salesperson or by your own inquiries. Does the sponsor want to advertise an upcoming sale on a particular brand of furniture? Does he pride himself on service and special orders? Free home delivery? Easy financing? Will the sale be on special-purchase inventory, overstock, or slightly damaged merchandise? Will the sale run three days or three weeks?

Focus on the commercial in two stages. First, determine its purpose. Second, list the main ideas the sponsor wants to emphasize. Consider the following example:

Purpose of commercial:

To encourage people to attend a new appliance store's open house

Main ideas to be included:

The open house will feature:
    5 door prizes valued at $100 each
    a grand prize valued at $500
    a gift for everyone who attends
    tours of the facility
    refreshments

Now write your own focus.

STEP 2   Prewriting • Planning the Approach

Consider the purpose of the message and how best to get the listener's ear. Because sound is your only tool, think of sounds that are attractive. Consider some of the following questions:

- Do I want a conversational tone?
- Will dramatic dialogue better serve the purpose?
- Could a dramatic or comic situation work well?
- Will background music suggest a tone or attitude that better conveys the message?
- Would other sound effects be better than music? Should the two be used together?
- Should I use a donut to capitalize on an already-familiar jingle?
- What other technique can I use to catch attention?

Try a test approach. Because success largely depends on creativity, you may need to try several before you finally decide upon one.

STEP 3 **Writing • Developing the Spot**

Now write the spot. Don't think about form, format, or the special techniques of scriptwriting. Just think about your message and the best means of conveying it. As you write, try some of these techniques:

- Read aloud what you have written. Let your ear tell you whether or not it works.
- Read at the pace best for the commercial, timing yourself. A normal pace is approximately 150 words a minute. If the ad calls for punch, the announcer can read at 170–180 words in a minute. Quiet conversation can be as slow as 100 words a minute. If you exceed the time limit, start cutting.
- Use your imagination to enhance the audio message.

STEP 4 **Revising • Polishing the Spot**

Radio commercials must grab attention and convey their message in a precise time. No matter how effective the spot may be, if it is too short or too long, it won't work. So, the first step in the revising process is to check the timing. Read the spot aloud at the desired pace and time yourself. The announcer and the director assume the final responsibility for getting the time right, but the script must set reasonable limits. Make any revisions necessary to adjust the timing

Second, since the radio commercial relies entirely on audio to convey its message, listen carefully to how the spot sounds. Ask yourself these questions:

- Is the spot appropriate to the product? That is, will the tone [*see* tone *in the Glossary*] attract the right listener?
- Have I used good word choice? Or can I convey the message more precisely by replacing weak adjectives and adverbs with strong nouns and verbs?
- Are my sentences varied? Or do they sound dull and monotonous? [*See* sentence structure *in the Glossary, and see* Revising: Sample Revision for Sentence Variety *in Part I.*]
- Do my sentences convey a proper emphasis? [*See* emphasis, in sentences *in the Glossary, and see* Revising: Sample Revision for Emphasis *in Part I.*]
- As commercials employ non-sentence word groups, have I used such groups effectively?
- Have I maintained accuracy? Or have I been distracted by technique?

Finally, as you work on the revision, reread your spot. Check the timing again and listen with a critical ear for anything needing improvement. Radio commercials are brief: Every word must be perfect. Revise carefully.

STEP 5   Proofreading • Attending to Details

Now you must attend to one last detail. Unlike other kinds of writing that follow traditional rules, radio scripts encourage nonstandard practices. Consider the following:

- If difficult-to-pronounce names appear, spell them phonetically so that the announcer does not misread them.
- Certain words may need emphasis. Underline those words.
- Similarly, certain parts may need the emphasis lent by a pause. Indicate such pauses with a dash or series of periods. Neither mark is used traditionally, but both are suitable in scriptwriting.
- Commas may also show pauses, even where traditional rules do not call for any punctuation.

Next, read the copy for anything misleading. Be sure you spell accurately (except in the phonetic spellings indicated above) to avoid confusing the announcer. And be sure your punctuation, including the nontraditional, enhances the copy.

Finally, prepare the typed copy. Use either of the formats illustrated in the following sample, and be consistent in style. Include references to any sound effects, but do not use sound effects just to be using them. Read the copy one last time to make sure everything is accurate and that you have omitted nothing.

SAMPLE RADIO SCRIPT

The following script is for a 30-second, ROS commercial. The script appears in both formats to highlight differences. Compare the radio script with the drama script, earlier in this section, and the television script, later in this section. You will find significant differences.

Format One

(Music down and under)

Announcer: ANIMAL LOVERS LOVE "THE ANIMAL STORE." WHETHER IT'S A POODLE PUPPY—A CUDDLY KITTY—OR EVEN A FEISTY FERRET YOU WANT, "THE ANIMAL STORE" HAS IT. AND TO PUT A SONG IN YOUR LIFE, STOP BY TO HEAR THE MELODIES OF CANARIES, FINCHES, PARAKEETS, AND COCKATOOS—ALL AT "THE ANIMAL STORE"... WHILE YOU'RE THERE, STOP BY TO SAY "HELLO" TO BARNEY ... HELLO, BARNEY!

Parrot voice: AWK, HELLO. HELLO THERE.

Announcer: NO, HE DOESN'T WANT A CRACKER—HE JUST WANTS SOMEBODY TO TAKE HIM HOME! ... "THE ANIMAL STORE"—WHERE EVERY ANIMAL LOVER FINDS SOMETHING TO TAKE HOME.

(Music up and out.)

Format Two

(MUSIC DOWN AND UNDER)

ANNOUNCER: Animal lovers love "The Animal Store." Whether it's a poodle puppy—a cuddly kitty—or even a feisty ferret you want, "The Animal Store" has it. And to put a song in your life, stop by to hear the melodies of canaries, finches, parakeets, and cockatoos—all at "The Animal Store".... While you're there, stop by to say "hello" to Barney.... Hello, Barney!

PARROT VOICE: Awk, hello. Hello there.

ANNOUNCER: No, he doesn't want a cracker—he just wants somebody to take him home! ... "The Animal Store"— where every animal lover finds something to take home.

(MUSIC UP AND OUT)

Analysis of the Sample Radio Script. This commercial illustrates many typical techniques of radio scriptwriting. Note specifically the following:

- The technical terms, such as *down and under* and *up and out*, tell the announcer, director, or engineer how to handle the sound effects. Note that, in reality, a spot will either name a specific piece of music or else be accompanied by prerecorded music that neither violates copyright nor necessitates royalties.
- The audio directions appear in parentheses.
- The announcer's lines appear as upper-case letters in the first format and lower-case letters in the second. Both are acceptable.
- The unusual punctuation indicates pauses (three periods and dashes) or emphasizes specific words (underlining).
- The use of *Barney the Parrot* appeals personally to animal lovers. The next spot could use *Pepper the Poodle* or *Doxie the Dalmatian* to appeal to dog lovers. Advertisers use such ongoing gimmicks to identify their product or store.
- The writer gives general directions; the director (or, occasionally, the announcer) adds further interpretation. The printed word is like a blueprint; the rest is artistic approach. A good radio announcer will read the above spot with significant vocal variety. While another voice may do the parrot, the announcer will assume a very personal approach as he or she asks listeners to stop by to say "hello" to Barney, a change in voice suggested by the three periods. The point is that the writer's responsibility ends with the preparation of the copy.

Now, check your own radio script against the information presented here. Make whatever revisions you find necessary to create a satisfactory product.

TELEVISION SCRIPTS

Because they must deal with both audio and video elements, television scripts have one part for each. A two-column format appears in virtually every television script, whether for a commercial, news broadcast, drama, or variety show.

CHARACTERISTICS

Television scripts vary significantly from those for radio or for drama, even when for television drama. In general, a television script

- appears in two-column format, the video directions in the left-hand column (one-third the width of the page) and the audio script in the right-hand column (two-thirds the width of the page),
- accounts for the limitations and abilities of the television camera,
- accounts for studio limitations,
- follows a careful time structure in accordance with FCC regulations regarding the number of commercial breaks per broadcast hour,
- includes technical terms appropriate to camera work [see those terms, listed and defined in the following list],
- takes a format similar to that of a radio-script.

The following technical terms are essential for accurate video directions. Study them until they become comfortable. Without them, no television script can succeed.

angle: the position of the camera; to angle on a character is to position the camera so that the character is emphasized

beat: a one-second pause in a character's speech or action

clip: a short piece of film or tape integrated into the program

close shot: a camera shot that eliminates everything except the person or item on which the close shot is made

close-up, or CU: a camera angle that shows a person's head or head and shoulders; an extreme close-up (XCU) may show only the eyes or mouth

cut, or cut to: an editing direction that requires the abrupt shift from one scene to another, as opposed to fade or dissolve

dissolve, or dissolve to: an editing direction that has one scene fading into another so that for a very brief moment the two scenes appear simultaneously

dolly in/out: to move the camera and mount to establish a closer or more distant shot

establishing shot: a broad shot of a large area, used to help set the scene

fade in: an editing direction that requires the picture to start from black (or some other color) and gradually become a full picture

fade out: an editing direction that calls for the picture to slowly go to black

full shot: a camera angle that shows all of a person or a scene, such as a yard, room, or football field

hold: to maintain a camera shot on an individual to emphasize his or her reaction or attitude

off-screen: a sound heard but whose source is not seen by the viewers

pan: to swing the camera from side to side without moving the base in order to show a broad scene; hence, pan right, pan left, and whip (meaning to pan quickly),

super: to superimpose, placing titles, credits, or images over the picture so that both are simultaneously visible

two shot: a camera shot of two characters; thus, a three shot is of three characters, and so on.

voice over: a voice that is heard though the speaker is not seen, especially used in newscasts and documentaries

wide angle: a camera shot made from a distance or with a wide-angle lens in order to show panoramic view

zoom in/out: to mechanically establish a closer or more distant shot by adjusting the lens of the camera.

Knowing and understanding these terms will help you direct the camera crew and make the most of their capabilities.

PROCESS

Television drama scripts closely parallel stage scripts; television commercials resemble radio commercials. Thus, for variety's sake, we'll examine here a short documentary.

Scripts for television documentaries require significant research. The short documentary modeled here shows the basic process and peculiar techniques of the form.

STEP 1   **Prewriting • Doing the Preliminary Research**

Assume you are preparing a ten-minute documentary on an aspect of your school or college, a video to be presented to incoming freshmen. Because you are active in the forensics program, you decide to deal with that subject. You'll begin by asking the kinds of questions your viewer will be likely to ask. These questions serve as a stable guide for developing this—and most any other—documentary:

- Why is this subject important?
- If the subject is not obviously important, how can I make it interesting and appealing?
- What kinds of things would a viewer want to know about the subject? Its beginnings? Its present situation? Its future?
- How can I personalize the subject?

- Who can best explain the subject?
- Are certain people a must for interviews?

Read or interview as necessary to develop a list of ideas for your documentary. A list for the school forensics documentary might look something like this:

Provides good training, no matter career choice
After-school activity
Extracurricular events good for experience
Good coach/friend
General activities for a school year
Specific activities of one team member
Kinds of events
Rewards: personal growth, friendships, scholarships, contacts in other schools

Certainly, this list is too long for a ten-minute documentary; still, too many ideas are better than too few. Stop now and make your own list.

STEP 2 **Prewriting • Planning the Video**

Begin thinking about what kind of video elements will enhance your subject. You may ask questions such as the following:

- What images will best show the aspects of the subject I hope to emphasize?
- What objects or which people should appear?
- Will I need still-life photographs to illustrate past events? If so, how can I make them look less static and more like film?
- How can I get the best action shots? Should I stage mock situations or shoot live on location?

Begin developing your list of video elements. Consider the following example for some general ideas, and then apply your creativity to your own list:

Interview with speech coach
Interview with award-winning debate-team members
Interview with award-winning speech-team members
Segments from a debate meet
Segments from a dramatic interpretation event
Footage from the all-school awards assembly
Shots of trophies and plaques
Interview with debate- or speech-meet judge
Interview with graduate participant
Interview with novice speech-team member

Segments from practice/coaching sessions
Shot of team member working with coach

Again, this list is too long for a ten-minute documentary. However, an extensive list allows you later to choose the most suitable and successful ideas.

So, complete your list now.

STEP 3   Writing • Developing the Audio Script

Once you have on paper what you hope to accomplish, begin writing the audio script. The following suggestions can help you get started:

- Begin with an attention-getting device. For instance, in the forensics documentary, you could show the excitement of winning a divisional speech tournament, make a startling statement about the impact of the program on individual students (scholarships, friendships, career opportunities), or provide something else to gain interest. Generally, television programs must catch a viewer's attention within 20 seconds.

- Allow yourself the freedom of interviews. Although you cannot script an interview, you should write out the questions in advance. Then, once the interview has been taped, edit it to include the most useful segments. These segments, called *clips*, become part of the final script.

- Always think from the point of view of your audience. What does it want or need to know about your subject? How can you best convey this information?

- Work for variety. If you include segments without visible action, intersperse them with activity. Obviously, don't add unrelated action for its own sake. Remember, too, altering camera angles suggests action and thus creates variety.

- Conclude satisfactorily, perhaps with something dramatic, fulfilling, or futuristic. Documentaries may point to an upcoming event or end with a summary. Sometimes a statement of impact or potential works best.

- Time your script carefully, to the second. Additional editing may be required to keep the program within the limit. Live programming, which cannot be edited, requires not only careful scriptwriting but also superb on-the-air talent who can adjust their performance on the spot. Because of these demands, very little television programming is live.

STEP 4   **Writing • Adding the Video**

With the audio script completed, turn to the video. Plan camera shots to best illustrate your topic. Rely on your creativity to develop video that really tells the story. (Watching televised programs similar to your own will give you additional ideas.) Specify the kind of camera work you want, using the right terminology.

STEP 5   **Revising • Checking the Script**

Now put the script in proper format. Use this simple guide:

- Draw a line, vertically, down a standard 8½" x 11" sheet of paper; leave one-third of the space on the left and two-thirds on the right.
- Label the left hand column *Video* and the right *Audio*.
- Enter the talent identification (*narrator, interviewee,* and so on) and the narration or dialogue in the right-hand column.
- Include sound effects in the audio column.

Give appropriate camera directions in the video column alongside their corresponding narration or dialogue. *Note:* Where you place the camera directions in the video column determines when the directions will be executed. As a rule of thumb, camera shots should change every 20 or 30 seconds. But creativity means that rules may be broken for a purpose. Keep your purpose in mind.

STEP 6   **Proofreading • Checking the Details**

Once the script is complete, reread it for accuracy. Ask yourself the following questions:

- Have I made typing errors that will confuse the technical director or on-the-air talent?
- Are words spelled accurately?
- Have I included phonetic spellings for difficult words?
- Is the script free from grammatical and usage errors? [*See Part IV for rules and examples.*]
- Finally, is it easy to read, both for the on-the-air talent and the technical director who must oversee the camera work? *Hint:* Never continue a sentence from one page to the next. It can cause the on-the-air talent to misread the script.

Polish your script using these preceding questions.

SAMPLE TELEVISION SCRIPT

The following sample represents a portion of a full-length script. It shows most of the significant characteristics of the genre.

Speech: Another Shawnee Team

Video	Audio
OPEN WITH FILM CLIP OF TEAM RECEIVING TROPHY AT AWARDS ASSEMBLY	NARRATOR (VOICE OVER): And the team with the most points, for first place in the divisional speech tournament . . . Shawnee Senior High School!
CLOSE SHOT OF STUDENT WITH TROPHY	(APPLAUSE; CHEERS; 6 SECONDS)
CUT TO CLOSE SHOT OF TEAM PRESIDENT ZOOM IN TO CLOSE-UP	STUDENT TEAM MEMBER: Hi! Welcome to Shawnee. I'm Robin Oaks, president of Shawnee Senior High Forensics Team. We love winning, but more than that, we love the challenge, the preparation, and the stimulation of good competition!
CUT TO MALE AND FEMALE WALKING HAND-IN-HAND	Every one of us has gained new friends in area schools and some of the friends have become . . . really good ones!
DISSOLVE TO BOY LEANING AGAINST DOOR, BACK TO CAMERA	Sure, we work hard, practice a lot, and (SLOWLY) sometimes we even lose. But doesn't everyone, at least sometimes?
CUT TO NARRATOR	NARRATOR: You've heard the adage that it's not whether you win or lose, but how you play the game that counts. Maybe that's the best way to describe the Shawnee forensics team.
CUT TO GROUP SHOT OF TEAM	The kids on this team specialize in their best areas, some in dramatic interpretation . . .

CUT TO CLOSE-UP OF STUDENT TWO AND MOVE TO TIGHT CLOSE-UP	STUDENT TWO (PRESENTING A DRAMATIC INTERPRETATION): . . . Don't make me lie to you. Just don't ask questions, please. You have to trust me, have faith that I'll make the right decision. Please . . .
SLOW DISSOLVE TO FOUR DEBATE TEAM MEMBERS	NARRATOR (VOICE OVER): . . . And other students excel in debate, putting their logic, research, and wit against one another.
ZOOM IN SLOWLY TO CLOSE-UP OF STUDENT THREE	STUDENT THREE: . . . And so my worthy opponents have left us little choice but to question the feasibility of such a radical, untried plan. Certainly, you must agree with the negative that the status quo will be financially more reasonable than the economically disastrous plan we've heard here today.
CUT TO ESTABLISHING SHOT OF NARRATOR AND COACH	NARRATOR: Dramatic interpretation, debate, and what else? Just what is forensics, Miss Calloway? You've coached the team to victory for the past three years. Tell us about this whole idea of forensics.
ZOOM IN TO CLOSE SHOT OF COACH	COACH: Forensics refers to debate or argumentation, but as we define it for national competition, it includes about a dozen kinds of speech activities—radio announcing, debate, comedy, original oratory, extempora-neous speaking—you name it and we probably do it.
CUT TO CLOSE SHOT OF NARRATOR	NARRATOR: How do students get involved in forensics?

DOLLY BACK TO TWO SHOT OF COACH AND NARRATOR	COACH: During a sign-up period early in the school year, we accept any student willing to work. We select areas most suitable to individual students and then begin gathering materials.
CUT TO FILM CLIP OF STUDENT WORKING WITH COACH	We do individual work with me working closely with the students until they are ready for the first team practice. . . .

Analysis of the Sample Television Script. The sample illustrates how television scripts differ from dramatic or radio scripts. Note, in particular, these details:

- The script includes two distinct portions, a *Video* portion on the left and an *Audio* portion on the right.
- The Video column gives specific directions in accurate technical terms printed uppercase.
- The Audio column, as in a radio script, includes narration and dialogue—here in lower-case letters, with speaker identification and directions in uppercase.
- The camera shots provide variety for the viewer and, at the same time, enhance the content and message of the audio portion.

Television probably offers the largest outlet for creative scriptwriting today. Serious students of television production recognize the extensive work—practice and analysis—needed to learn scriptwriting. As cameras and technical equipment become more sophisticated, the writer's options increase proportionately. These guidelines should help you begin to explore scriptwriting.

Short Answers

Short-answer responses are often required on tests, as well as on job, scholarship, and college applications. Sometimes we are asked for a brief response, short definition, or list. All are short answers. All require careful thought. A writer who jots down whatever comes to mind first may omit important, even critical, ideas. Thus, short-answers, whether to tests or requests for information, take planning and care, perhaps even more than do longer essays.

Although you may face the need for a variety of short-answer responses, most begin with phrases such as briefly explain, summarize the main points, list the general characteristics, define the main issues, state in a single paragraph, outline the principles, or give a brief review. In most cases, you are expected to provide a brief response, definition, or list. We will examine each of these three in turn.

BRIEF RESPONSES

Brief responses can follow any method of development: analogy, cause and effect, classification, comparison and contrast, definition, narration, opinion, or process analysis. [*See entries for each in Part II.*] They differ from other expository writing, however, in purpose. The reader wants highlights, not details.

CHARACTERISTICS

Brief responses generally

- run no longer than a short paragraph,
- limit themselves to main ideas, avoiding supporting details,
- follow a logical organization to clarify the relationship of main ideas,
- rely on strong nouns and verbs, avoiding weak and generally wordy modifiers,
- demand specificity [*see* specific detail *in the Glossary*],
- focus on the requested information, omitting unrelated matters.

PROCESS

Developing a brief response takes careful planning, concise writing, and critical revision. Frequently in test situations these steps must occur within strict time limits, so planning becomes essential.

STEP 1   **Prewriting • Analyzing the Question**
Before you begin writing, be sure you understand what to include. Look for clue words in the question or statement. The following are typical clue words:

summarize (give the main ideas)
outline (give the main ideas and show their relationships)
explain briefly (make clear)
give reasons (show why)

complete the sentence (finish the idea)
when (give date, historical period, or other time relationship)
why (give reasons)
how (explain the steps or stages)
where (give place)
who (identify person by name or position)
what (name the items)

STEP 2 **Prewriting • Planning Your Answer**

Brief responses of a word, phrase, or sentence need little planning; brief responses of several sentences take more.

In responding to a test question, use this quick line of questioning:

What are the key ideas? Write them in a list.
In what order should they be presented? Place them in order.
Is anything essential omitted? If so, what?

In completing an application, use the preceding guiding questions as well as the following ones:

Why is this question on the application? What is the reader trying to learn about me?
Are my ideas important to the reader or just to me?
As I respond, how can I show myself in the most favorable light?

As you develop your short-answer response for an application, you may have difficulty being objective about yourself, being either too modest or too complimentary. Take every opportunity to discuss your list with someone you trust. Your friend may have an insight into a qualification or characteristic you have overlooked.

STEP 3 **Writing • Completing the Brief Response**

As you list your answers to the questions in Step 2 and turn them into a written response, keep in mind these suggestions:

- Reread the question or request for information to make sure you have not strayed from your purpose. [*See* Revising: Sample Revision for Unity *in Part I.*]
- The amount of space provided for your response may be misleading. Use the space you need to give an accurate response, no more and no less.
- Be concise. Avoid wordy, rambling explanations. [*See* Revising: Sample Revision for Wordiness *in Part I.*]

- Use complete sentences unless otherwise directed.
- In a test situation, allot yourself a specific amount of time to complete the response. Then stick to the schedule. [*See also* Essay-Question Responses: Test Questions, *earlier in Part III for an illustration of planning time allotments.*]

STEP 4   **Revising • Checking the Focus**

In tests, the only revision you can afford is to check for focus. Reread the question or statement, thinking in terms of your response. Did you respond directly to the question or statement? Did you respond to every part of it?

On an application, you have time for careful revision; indeed, the reader expects polished work. Write your first draft on scratch paper, revise it, and enter the final draft on the application form.

The revision process for an application should deal with these possible weaknesses:

- Have I responded directly to the question or statement?
- Have I put myself in the most positive light without being inaccurate?
- Does my sentence structure reflect my personal maturity? [*See* sentence structure *in the Glossary, and see* Revising: Sample Revision for Sentence Variety *in Part I.*]
- Does my writing reflect my skill with the language? [*See* Revising: Sample Revision for Emphasis *in Part I.*]
- Is the vocabulary appropriate to my purpose?
- Have I focused on the aspects most important to the reader?

STEP 5   **Proofreading • Checking for Mechanics**

Before you hand in a test paper, reread it for spelling, grammar, usage, and mechanics. If you are permitted, use your dictionary to check questionable items.

On an application, take extreme care with your proofreading, perhaps even asking a friend to check your work, too. See Part IV of this handbook to see rules and examples to help with grammar, usage, and mechanics.

SAMPLE BRIEF RESPONSE

The following sample typifies the sort of brief responses called for by scholarship and college applications.

Question

Why do you want to attend Middletown College?

Response

Because Middletown College offers a nationally recognized equestrian program, I look forward to completing my associate degree there. Our family business involves breeding, training, and showing horses, as well as retailing trappings. As a result, my already deep personal involvement in my career has prepared me for the rigors of the curriculum.

 Analysis of the Sample Brief Response. The sample illustrates ways the writer can say things without really saying them. Consider these techniques:

- The writer compliments the college by acknowledging it is nationally recognized.
- He indicates a two-year stay at the college, to complete my associate degree. At the same time, he emphasizes his intent to fulfill requirements.
- He refers to a family business to stress his personal involvement in what the school offers.
- He clarifies that the curriculum requires hard work and emphasizes he is prepared to complete that work.

As a result of this writer's brief response, the college personnel will see certain characteristics they like. They want a student who plans to finish a degree, who comes to work not to play, who is motivated, and who shows maturity and a sense of direction. This writer's brief response shows all those characteristics.

DEFINITIONS

You can find an entire section on definition papers in Part II [*see* Definition]. Short-answer definitions contain certain specific characteristics that are quite unlike those of a full-length essay.

CHARACTERISTICS

Short-answer definitions usually

- identify the term to be defined,
- identify the class to which this term belongs,
- contrast the term with all others in its class,
- give this information in one sentence.

PROCESS

In order to develop a definition, use the following process.

STEP 1 **Prewriting • Identifying the Class and the Differences**
If asked to define a given term, you must first decide to what larger group, or class, the term belongs. Next you must show how the term differs from others in its class. Consider the following:

Term to be defined:
simile

Class:
figure of speech

Difference:
compares one thing to another, using like or as

In other words, the term *simile* belongs to the larger class called *figure of speech*. It is different from other figures of speech in that it compares one thing to another using "like" or "as."

STEP 2 **Writing • Putting the Definition into a Single Sentence**
Once you have established the class and difference, the rest is simple. Combine the ideas in a sentence, in this order:

Term to be defined
Class to which it belongs
Difference between the term and others in the class

Example: A simile (*term*) is a figure of speech (*class*) that compares one thing to another using like or as (*difference*).

STEP 3 **Revising and Proofreading • Checking Mechanical Details**
Once you have completed your definition, make sure you have included all three parts, in order, and that you have used accurate spelling, grammar, mechanics, and usage.

SAMPLES OF SHORT ANSWER DEFINITIONS

The following definitions can serve as examples for your own work.

> A lien is a claim on the property of another as security for the payment of a debt.
>
> An armadillo is a burrowing mammal of Texas and Central and South America that has an armor-like covering of bony plates over its body.
>
> A bulkhead is an upright partition dividing a ship or airplane into compartments to protect against the spread of fire or water in case of an accident.

 Analysis of the Sample Short Answer Definitions. The preceding definitions follow the pattern suggested. Each begins with a term and continues by giving the class identification. The remainder of the sentence contrasts the term with others in its class. Note the precision used:

Term	Class	Difference
lien	claim on property	as security for the payment of a debt
armadillo	burrowing mammal	has an armor-like covering of bony plates
bulkhead	upright partition	dividing a ship or airplane into compartments to protect against the spread of fire or water in case of an accident

This format guarantees precise and accurate definitions of virtually any term. [*If you need more than a short-answer definition, see* Definition *in Part II.*]

LISTS

While lists may seem easy to develop, too many students write them as mere groups of items. Lists that serve as short answers on tests and applications should reflect thought and show some sense of organization.

CHARACTERISTICS

While lists may be either a series of words or of phrases, carefully composed lists

- maintain parallel structure [*see* parallel structure *in the Glossary*],

- show evidence of logical order [*see* chronological order, spatial order, *or* order of importance *in the Glossary*],
- omit unrelated, extraneous items.

PROCESS

In order to develop a list, use these simple steps.

STEP 1 **Prewriting • Analyzing the Request for Information**
What does the question or statement really require from you? Look for clue words. Are you asked to list the most important facts, the most significant events, or the most influential activities? Or are you asked to list the activities, meaning, virtually all the activities? Be sure you know what is expected.

STEP 2 **Writing • Developing the List**
As you write, think about these questions:

For a test:

- Is the instructor looking for key words or phrases?
- What is the most logical order in which to list the key items? Chronological? Spatial? An order of importance?
- Is my list complete?

For an application:

- What is the reader hoping to learn about me? Am I including items that best reflect my personal characteristics and abilities?
- Have I arranged items in a logical order (for example, in an order of importance, with the most important first)?
- Is my list complete?

STEP 3 **Revising and Proofreading • Checking the List**
Certainly, a list leaves little room for grammar, usage, and mechanical problems. You still want to check spelling and word choice, though.

Punctuation usually causes some problems in lists written horizontally. Use commas to separate items, unless the items require internal commas. In that case, use semicolons.

In addition, check your list for logical arrangement. Remember, on an application you should list the most important items first, unless instructed otherwise. For other short-answer responses, use the organization most appropriate.

SAMPLE LIST

The following request for information resulted in this sample list:

Request Item

List your extracurricular activities. Indicate the number of years in which you participated in each.

Response List

Student Council, president 2 years; Mayor's Youth Council, 1 year; National Forensics League, debate team and individual categories, 3 years; Computer Club, 1 year; library assistant, 2 years; office assistant, 2 years; usher for auditorium events, 2 years.

Analysis of the Sample List. The list includes several details worthy of special attention:

- The writer shows his attitude toward his various activities. He sees his two-year stint as president of the Student Council as more important than his year with the Mayor's Youth Council. Likewise, he seems to think his library assistantship more important than his work in the office.
- Items are separated by semicolons because commas appear within most of them.
- The period denotes not the end of a sentence but the completion of the list.

Now you should be able to develop lists that show your knowledge, characteristics, or abilities, as well as your perception of their relative importance. Writing good lists shows far more responsibility and maturity than providing hodgepodges arranged in the order in which items were remembered.

Short Story

Whole books have been written to explain how to write short stories. As an imaginative literary form, the short story varies as much as its authors.

In its simplest form, a short story has a beginning, middle, and end. The characters meet and somehow resolve a conflict, thereby permitting the author to convey a message (otherwise called a *theme*).

Learning to develop the art form includes two steps, one simple, the other a lifelong effort. First, the potential short-story writer must learn the elements of the form. That is the easy part. Then, he must practice combining those elements until his skills are as finely honed as those of Edgar Allan Poe or O. Henry. That is the lifelong part.

CHARACTERISTICS

The short story has certain general characteristics. Although the approach to and interaction with these characteristics is the stuff by which short stories vary, certain elementary techniques will help a beginning writer develop a story. A short story, in general, should

- follow a consistent point of view [*see* point of view *in the Glossary*],
- develop believable characters with whom the reader can identify and whose motives the reader can understand,
- be placed in a setting consistent with the characters' personalities,
- develop a plot that includes conflict, rising action, climax, and resolution [*see* conflict, rising action, climax, *and* resolution *in the Glossary*],
- contain a theme, or message, for the reader [*see* theme *in the Glossary*],
- show, rather than tell, about characters, themes, and conflicts [*see* Narration *in Part II*],
- present concise, specific description [*see* Description *in Part II and* specific detail *in the Glossary*],
- include appropriate imaginative language and imagery [*see* figure of speech *and* imagery *in the Glossary*],
- employ other literary devices as appropriate: flashbacks, symbolism, foreshadowing [*see* flashback, symbol, *and* foreshadowing *in the Glossary*],
- use dialogue appropriate for the characters [*see* Dialogue *earlier in Part III*],
- maintain a consistent tone and mood [*see* tone *and* mood *in the Glossary*],
- be of appropriate length, from 200 to 10,000 words, but most likely 1,500 to 3,500,
- have each character, action, and word lead to a single end.

PROCESS

Developing the short story takes careful thought and planning. Not every writer works the same way. Some begin with plot and create characters to fill it. Others start by inventing characters and letting them interact; the plot grows from this interaction. Most writers, however, follow a kind of yo-yo process, changing characters as plot develops and altering scenes to improve characterization. No matter which process serves you best, you must reach a certain point in the prewriting stage before you begin to put words on paper. At that point, you should be able to put the specifics in this sentence:

> My fully developed characters will interact in these ways in order to achieve this resolution so that the reader will get this message.

In order to arrive at that point, you must thoroughly prepare. Try the following steps.

STEP 1   **Prewriting • Determining the Theme**

Before you can plan specific incidents in the story line, you must know what message you hope to convey. By setting characters against each other, what do you hope to tell the reader? Too early to know, you say? No! If you have no message, you have no story. You cannot reach your destination without a sense of direction. So stop now and write a sentence that expresses the message you hope to leave with the reader. Consider the following:

> Living by one's principles requires sacrifice.
> A winning attitude helps people climb the business ladder.
> Winning isn't important; it's how you play the game.
> Treat the land with respect and you will reap the rewards.

STEP 2   **Prewriting • Outlining the Plot**

Next, decide what conflict your characters will face to illustrate your message. You will not *state* the message in the story; your characters and plot must *reveal* the message. Begin by making a list:

- What events lead to the conflict?
- What initial conflict do they encounter?
- What are its results?
- How do the results build to additional, more complicated conflicts? In other words, what is the rising action? [*See* rising action *in the Glossary*.]
- What brings events to a crisis? [*See* crisis *in the Glossary*.]
- What is the crisis?

- What happens as a result of the crisis? In other words, what is the climax? [*See* climax *in the Glossary.*]
- What is the end result? Do the characters change? If so, what makes them change? Personal realization? The influence of other characters? In other words, what is the resolution? [*See* resolution *in the Glossary.*]

By answering these questions, you will outline the plot of your story.

STEP 3   **Prewriting • Developing the Characters**

Believable, motivated characters make or break a story. If the reader cannot understand or accept your story's characters, nothing else you do matters.

Before you begin writing then, sketch each of your characters. [*See* Character Sketch *earlier in Part III and* Narration *in Part II.*] Use the following guidelines:

- What does the character look like?
- What is the character's background? Family? Education? Business experience? Home life?
- What kind of surroundings does he or she like? Plush furniture? Luxury apartment? Bare walls? Rustic cabin? Disheveled office? Open water? Northern forest?
- What does the character think about? How does he or she react emotionally to frustrating situations? What does he or she value in life?
- How does he or she behave, move, respond?
- What does he or she sound like in speaking? What kind of vocabulary does he or she use?
- How do others react to the character? Do they all see the character in the same way? Does the character see himself or herself the way others do?

Now do one last thing. Look critically at your answers. Do your characters portray consistent, realistic behavior? Are their reactions a natural outgrowth of their backgrounds? Do their surroundings support their values? If not, do you have logical motives for uncharacteristic behavior? Will the reader accept those motives? Or do you need to alter the characters?

Few of your responses to these questions will actually appear in your story, as they are not directly related to your message. By answering them, however, you will force yourself to examine each character in turn, the only way to develop consistent, believable characters.

STEP 4   **Prewriting • Establishing the Setting**

By now you probably have a fairly good idea of where the story should take place. Jot down a brief description of the setting, notes to yourself. Picture it in your mind, listing as many details as you can. Imagine how it feels, smells, and sounds, not just how it looks. [*See* Description *and* Narration *in Part II.*]

STEP 5   **Prewriting • Selecting Point of View**

The reader identifies with the point of view from which the story is told, so how you tell things determines message. The cliche, "There are two sides to every story," is accurate only so far as it goes: There are as many sides as there are people involved. Even someone outside the conflict will have a perspective from which to relate the tale, though one which necessarily omits the personal reactions of the participants, which he or she has no way of knowing.

The story writer may select among three points of view. Consider each before choosing one for your own story.

Omniscient Point of View: The all-knowing, all-seeing point of view almost always represents the author as such. Only the author knows, sees, and understands all. Only he or she can tell what every character thinks and feels. For example:

> Jerod and Krista stood contemplating the stack of sales records to be com piled before they could call it quits for the day. Neither wanted to work late; that was understandable. But Jerod liked to ease back and let Krista assume the real burden. He hoped she'd make quick work of it tonight. Little did he know that Krista resented his mere presence.
>
> "Lazy rat," she thought. "He doesn't even know how to enter the basic data." Her stomach growled.

First Person Point of View: This uses *I, me, my,* and *our.* The first-person permits the author to tell the story from the point of view of a character, major or minor. Only those feelings, observations, and reactions that the character experiences appear in the story. For example:

> I stood there contemplating the stack of sales records to be compiled before we could call it quits for the day. I just wanted to go home, be with the kids, watch the ball game.
>
> I hesitated. "Well, Krista," I began, hoping she wouldn't be her usual grouchy self, "What do you want me to do first?"
>
> She frowned. "Why don't you sort the reports by department code?"
>
> She sounded cross. I thought I heard her stomach growl. I guessed she must be hungry.

Third Person Point of View: The third person uses *he, she, they, them,* and *their,* as well as people's names. The author tells the story, but he or she is more removed from the story than in the omniscient point of view. In fact, the story is told from only one character's point of view, describing only what that character can observe. For example:

> She stood there, contemplating the stack of sales records they had to compile before they could call it quits for the day. She just wanted to go home, have a quiet dinner with Tom, and curl up with a good book. She looked at Jerod.
>
> "Lazy rat," she thought, "he doesn't even know how to enter the basic data."
>
> "So what do you want me to do first," he asked. Krista thought he sounded almost willing to help. She hesitated, looked at him again, frowning, unsure why he seemed so helpful.
>
> "Why don't you sort the reports by department code?" she suggested. Silently she added, "And we'll see if you have any idea what you're doing."

Select the point of view that will best allow you to tell your story, reveal your characters, and convey your message. Maintain a consistent point of view throughout.

STEP 6 **Writing • Putting the Story Together**

Now you have a plot line and characters. You have placed them in a setting. You have selected a point of view. You are ready to write. As you begin, you may want to think about some of the following techniques:

- Dialogue adds life to characters. Allowing the reader to eavesdrop grants insight into your characters' thoughts, reactions, observations, and emotions.
- Showing, rather than telling, makes for a superior story. Allow the reader to discover your characters and their conflicts. [*See* Description *and* Narration *in Part II.*]
- Paragraphing in short stories bears no similarities to paragraphing in expository writing.
- Sentence structure should vary with character and action. [*See* Revising: Sample Revision for Sentence Variety *and* Revising: Sample Revision for Emphasis *in Part I.*]
- Description should be specific and concrete. [*See* Description *in Part II for additional help. Also see* specific detail *in the Glossary.*]

Writing is the tough part. Keep at it until you are done. Remember, you will be making revisions later, so aim now only for completion.

STEP 7   Revising • Polishing the Story

Once you have completed your story, you can begin to look for weaknesses. Try these questions:

- Have I avoided simply telling my reader about characters, motives, reactions? Instead, did I show these?
- Are my characters believable? Are their actions apt? Are their motives clear?
- Is the setting suitable?
- Does the conflict seem likely or contrived?
- Did I select the most appropriate point of view?
- Have I maintained a consistent point of view?
- Does the resolution grow naturally out of the conflict?
- Have I used effective sentence structure?
- Are my paragraphs appropriate to a short story?
- Are my descriptions specific rather than flowery?
- Have I included any of the finer points of literature: figurative language, imagery, foreshadowing, flashback, symbolism, and so on?
- Is my message clear? Have I avoided merely stating the message, making it, instead, evident through the action and resolution of the story?
- Have I selected an appropriate title that suggests some important element of the story?

Revise your story as many times as necessary to make it smooth, readable, and believable.

STEP 8   Proofreading • Polishing the Final Draft

No matter how "creative" you think your story may be, do not be creative with the standards of language. Characters may speak incorrectly to illustrate their lack of education, but your own writing must be accurate. [*See also* Revising *and* Proofreading *in Part I for guidelines and Part IV for rules and examples*.] Next, check word choice. Can you improve a description or enhance a character with a better word? Finally, check the spelling.

The process in this section should give you a running start in the development of your own short story. Before you complete your work, however, study the following sample and its analysis.

SAMPLE SHORT STORY

The following story serves as a model in which we can see many of the ideas listed in the preceding process section.

Spud

Emile looked up at the clock. Almost two. He was going to be late. After creeping down the broken stairs, he ducked into the kitchen, sneaked a potato from the burlap bag beneath the sink, and slipped out the side door into the alley. He ran between the crumbling buildings to an abandoned lot where the neighbor boys, lined up with their backs to the wind, were building a fire. They yelled at him across the field to hurry and to pick up some broken lumber for the fire along the way.

"Got your spud?" asked Melby.

"Yeah!"

"Throw 'er in."

They all tried their best to sneak away on Saturday afternoons with a potato or two. Then they sat around the hissing flames for an hour, discussing the cusses Mrs. Yakov had yelled down at her husband from their apartment window, or where Felix had been while he hookied, or who they thought Mrs. Brubaker was going to flunk in spelling, until the potatoes were thoroughly baked beneath the embers.

"Dibs on ya!" Emile yelled, as Melby accidentally uncovered his potato with his poking stick.

"No more dibs!" Melby yelled back, lest anyone else lay claim to a portion of his spud.

Every boy prepared to remove his potato as slyly as possible, scraping around in the coals to find them. Emile had this game all worked out. Instead of scraping the embers, he gently poked them, lowering the risk of accidentally exposing his spud as Melby had. Feeling the tip strike the spud's charred shell, he sidled it underneath and violently flipped the potato out of the fire with an accompanying rain of cinder and smoke that made his companion's eyes water.

"No dibs, no hunks!" he shouted while the potato was still in midair. Then he sat down to his meal.

In school, Mrs. Brubaker wrote long lists of words on the board while the class stared at the clock and yawned. Emile doodled in his spelling book. When Mrs. Brubaker turned around, the rest of the class straightened up, pretending to be awake, but Emile kept on doodling.

"Emile Gallois!"

He jerked upright. "Yes, Ma'am!" and fixed his gaze on the reflections in her spectacles. All at once, her face shifted and buckled, falling into a mosaic of angles and distortion. He averted his eyes.

"Look at me when I'm talking to you!"

Thankfully, the image had disappeared. "Yes, Ma'am."

"Spell 'attentive.'"

"A-t-t-e-n-t-i-v-e."

"Very good. Now be attentive."

She turned back to the board, and Emile turned back to his doodles. He drew her face as it had seemed, slipping her nose across the side of her cheek; skewing her eyes one way, her wire-rimmed spectacles the other; rolling her scalp forward and her right ear around until all sides of her head appeared superimposed on the flat surface of the page. He drew back to examine the drawing and slapped the book shut.

That weekend, he sneaked a potato as usual, but he didn't go to the field. He tiptoed back up to his room and flipped to the doodled page of his spelling book. With his rusty pocket knife, he began carving Mrs. Brubaker's head. He remembered the reflections in her eyeglasses and expanded them, projecting the ceiling beams into her brow, the ceiling panels onto her forehead, mixing the foliage of the window plants with the curl of hair about her ear, until her whole face was filled with foreign objects. Then he drizzled water color not too carefully onto her various parts—red on her brow, blue on her forehead, green on her lips—but left the majority of her surface to the yellow pallor of drying potato flesh. In the corner of his bottom drawer he nestled it—the first.

In homeroom Monday morning, Melby approached.

"Where were you?"

"Huh?"

"Saturday?"

"I didn't feel well."

"What?"

"I was sick."

"So. What'd you do, draw all day? You should have come."

"My mom wouldn't let me."

"Well, are you gonna play ball after school, or what?"

"Yeah, I'll be there."

"Good. Four o'clock."

At lunchtime, Emile picked at the peanut butter sandwich his mother had packed for him, and he ended up throwing it all in the trash. His stomach bothered him throughout the rest of the afternoon, and several times he was reprimanded for inattentiveness. His mind tossed about, settling momentarily on the shadowy image of a rugby ball, or Melby's ruddy face, or Mrs. Brubaker's carved head. He tried to concentrate, but succeeded only in sending a pile of half-formed images recoiling through the grey.

On the way to his last class, Emile stopped to heave up yellow stomach bile into the bathroom sink, then proceeded straight to his classroom desk where he laid his head. Did he want to go home? No. Or lie down in the cloakroom? No. He didn't stir until the bell rang the close of school. Then he lifted himself up and began the walk home.

On the edge of a run-down park, a rotten limb had fallen, and Emile stopped to examine its shattered length. He pulled free a short, fat segment near the base and chipped at its surface with his thumbnail. It was soft, but not yet rotting. Just then, Melby accosted him from the other side of the street.

"You're coming, right?"

"Yeah." He tucked the chunk of wood beneath his arm and continued on, parallel to Melby, but never glancing over or saying a word. At the end of the street, they turned in opposite directions, each proceeding down his own alley.

Emile walked through the empty house up to his bedroom and stuck the chunk of wood in his drawer. After changing into a dirty sweater, he returned downstairs, nibbled at a piece of biscuit, and started for the lot. Several others were already there, including Melby.

"Hurry up, Emile!" he shouted. "You and me are gonna be captains!"

After a half dozen more neighborhood kids had straggled in, the boys chose up sides and started the game.

It was a friendly game—tackle of course, but not too hard, especially because the lot was strewn with gravel and wood debris.

Emile, however, felt Melby was getting a little overzealous.

"Cool it," he told him.

The next play, Emile was passed the ball, and darting a glance to his left, he saw Melby fast approaching. Emile dished off the ball, but Melby didn't stop running, smothering Emile in his sweater as they rolled onto the ground. Emile didn't say a word, but the next play, he went straight for Melby, put his fist into his chest, grabbed his arm, and flung him to the ground. Melby skidded across the gravel on his stomach and then lay still, moaning. Everybody stopped where they stood and gaped. The ball wobbled unnoticed into the street. Emile smiled and pretended like he had done it in sport, but when he saw Melby's nose bleeding, he backed up a few steps, turned, and ran home.

He mounted the steps to his room and, curling into a ball, buried his head beneath his pillow. The images returned—the rugby ball, Melby, Mrs. Brubaker. He remembered the chunk of wood he had in his drawer, and pulling out his pocket knife, his hands went to work on it. He knew what he was carving, but he didn't let himself think about it, concentrating instead on the minuteness of the wood grain. The features began to pronounce themselves—a high, square forehead, a pair of dimpled cheeks, a broad flaring chin—and slowly, the hard lines melted into a point between the eyes ... where his blade came to a knot. He sawed at it with the blade's edge, bored at it with the tip, but the knot was like steel. In desperation, he gouged his blade beneath its edge in an effort to pry it out, but its roots ran deep, and the whole left side of the face splintered away. Underneath, invisible fungi were slowly eating their way outward, rendering the wood useless. A single saline drop splashed onto the rotten vein of wood as he walked to the window. Leaning over the window ledge, he let the half-carved head drop from his hands onto the cobblestones below. One by one, the stars awoke to a quiet street, where a young boy stared down at the scattered pieces of a chunk of wood.

Analysis of the Sample Short Story. This story includes all the essentials of the form. Note these details:

- The title suggests the significance of the potato, not only to the circle of boys who roast them but to Emile, who applies his artistic talents to it.
- The writer never says where the story takes place. The multi-ethnic names (Yakov, Gallois, and Brubaker) suggest a large city. References to an alley, crumbling buildings, and an abandoned lot suggest a poor neighborhood. The boys' first names (Melby and Felix) suggest the 1930s or 1940s.
- The only developed character is Emile. Melby, the antagonist, represents the boys in general, boys who cannot understand Emile's interest in art.
- The reader is not told about characters; the reader sees them in action—hears them, watches them interact. The result is consistent, believable characters.
- The dialogue is realistic. It includes grammatical errors and sentence fragments. Brevity, candor, and idioms all add to character development.
- The writer consistently uses a third-person point of view (in this case, Emile's).
- Two conflicts emerge from the story, the first within Emile, the second, between Emile and Melby. The inner conflict is undoubtedly the greater. Emile, whose artistic nature differentiates him from his schoolmates, must choose either to remain "one of the guys" or to develop his talent. Developing his talent brings ridicule, but remaining one of the guys results in internal frustration, even illness. Emile's attempt to integrate the two, by carving a realistic sculpture of Melby, fails. His is a talent requiring external and internal abstraction. He realizes his failure. The story concludes with Emile facing a choice between the two ways of life.
- The Picasso-like faces that emerge from his spelling book and the potato contrast with the realistic wooden carving he attempts.
- The story plot can be outlined as follows:
  - Emile realizes he is different, draws Mrs. Brubaker in his spelling book.
  - He experiments with the art, shirks his friends to carve the potato.
  - He tries to go back to his old way of life, plays football. The effort brings frustration.

- • He tries to integrate the two lives, carves the realistic wooden head. His effort fails.
  - • He realizes his failure, drops the carving out the window.
  - • He contemplates the choice, stares down at the scattered wood.
- The crisis occurs when Emile bloodies Melby's nose. The physical battle parallels Emile's inner conflict.
- Once the carving splinters (as a result of the fungus, which signifies, too, the rotting friendship between Emile and Melby), the climax leads quickly to the resolution. Emile realizes (as shown by his crying and his dropping of the carving) that he must choose between his friends and the life of an artist.
- By the end of the story, the potato has become symbolic. It carries Emile from childhood to the pain of self-discovery, from the roasting fire to the secret carving; from physical to spiritual value, from food to art. The potato now symbolizes Emile's growth.
- A message develops from Emile's actions: Often, those who deal with creative processes must choose between their buddies and their art. The choice is never painless.
- Thus, the imagery and figurative language are assets to the story.
- The plain sentence structure shows good variety and adds emphasis.
- The punctuation is accurate.
- The paragraphing is appropriate for dialogue.
- The description is concise, the narrative effective. Specific details show, rather than tell about, Emile's daily life.
- The tone and mood remain consistent throughout.
- The conclusion leaves the reader without a decision. But the world goes on; the stars come out. The reader is whisked from Emile's room to the street and to the larger world, where people face similar problems, perhaps without any more satisfactory solutions but with a recognition that life demands choices.

Certainly you will make other observations about the sample to arouse your interest and give you ideas for your own story.

The list of general characteristics, explanation of process, and ideas gleaned from the sample should help you write a successful story.

Summaries

Because summaries vary according to their purposes, this book deals with three kinds: *paraphrase, precis,* and *synopsis*. A paraphrase is nearly the same length as the original passage but reworded in simpler language. A precis reduces the original by about two-thirds while retaining its main ideas and general tone. A synopsis reduces a long work, like a book or play, into a short summary of a few paragraphs or pages.

[*See* Paraphrase, Precis, *and* Synopsis *elsewhere in Part III, for a complete description and analysis.*]

Synopsis

A synopsis is a summary. [*See* Paraphrase *and* Precis *earlier in Part III.*] The purpose of a summary is to give a shortened version of a passage. Frequently, a synopsis is a multi-paragraph summary of a chapter, book, article, or drama. Because it's a summary, a synopsis makes no effort to address every idea. The reader understands that it is necessarily subjective because the writer must select the items to be included. Thus, the synopsis shows editorial bias.

CHARACTERISTICS

A synopsis generally

- selects main ideas that, in the writer's opinion, best represent the original piece,
- reflects the style of the current writer, as opposed to the author of the original,
- gives sufficient details to clarify the main ideas,
- is sufficiently informative to aid further investigation,
- has a reporter's objectivity.

PROCESS

Use the following process to develop a synopsis.

STEP 1 **Prewriting • Reading the Material**

Quickly read the original passage without taking notes. Look for repeated themes and the general treatment of ideas. If unfamiliar names are difficult for you, you may want to list them for later reference, noting the correct spelling.

Once you've finished reading, jot down the three or four most important ideas. They will serve as the skeletal outline of your synopsis.

Remember, you will not cover all the ideas in a synopsis.

STEP 2 **Writing • Preparing the Synopsis**

Begin the synopsis by identifying in a single sentence the main idea. Weave the title and author into an early (though not necessarily the first) sentence. Follow with a brief description of the main ideas.

Follow the organization of the original.

Keep in mind that a synopsis will be short, maybe only a paragraph in length. Deal only with essentials.

STEP 3 **Revising • Improving the Content**

Your synopsis will almost invariably be too long. Begin cutting. Omit needless details. Shorten sentences. Use strong nouns and verbs in order to omit modifiers. Keep cutting. [*See* Revising: Sample Revision for Wordiness *in Part I for an illustration.*]

Try this challenge: If you had to summarize the original in a single sentence, what would you say? If you could add one more sentence, what would you say? Follow this progression until you have stated all the important ideas.

[*Finally, see* Revising *in Part I for guidelines for improving organization, sentence structure, unity, emphasis, and transition.*]

STEP 4 **Proofreading • Checking the Details**

Once you have completed the revision, check for spelling, punctuation, grammar, mechanics, and usage. [*See Part IV for rules and examples.*]

The preceding steps should enable you to develop a synopsis. Compare your own with the example that follows, and study the analysis that follows.

SAMPLE SYNOPSIS

The following synopsis summarizes a novel of nearly 550 pages.

> **Ice-Age Novel**
>
> *The Valley of the Horses* fictionalizes the beginning of civilization in the Asian area north of the Beran Sea. Like two of Jean M. Auel's other books, *The Clan of the Cave Bear* and *The Mammoth Hunters*, this one gets its foundation from archaeological research supporting the evolution of man. In this unusual historical novel, the reader follows Ayla, a child of the Others who has been reared by the Clan of the Cave Bear only to be ejected from the Clan when she violates customs she cannot understand or accept. In exile in the valley of the horses, she survives five years alone until she meets Jondalar, a man of the Others.
>
> Ayla faces a lonely struggle for survival after her death curse by the Clan. To solve basic survival problems, she must use logic: alone, how can she kill, butcher, and process an animal large enough to feed her through the severe winter; alone, how can she provide clothing, cooking utensils, sleeping skins, and shelter for protection; alone, how can she protect herself from the dangers around her? Her training as a medicine woman and her knowledge of hunting, coupled with the large brain characteristic of the Others allow her to succeed. Also, as a result of her background, she saves Jondalar's life after a lion mauls him and kills his traveling-companion brother. Jondalar is the first of the Others that Ayla has seen. After Ayla's medicinal powers help Jondalar regain his health, the two of them suffer from their inability to understand each other's customs. Jondalar finally teaches her to speak, however, and they are able to establish a strong bond, sharing their creative ideas to find solutions for both the physical and mental problems they face as a team.

 Analysis of the Sample Synopsis. The sample (which appears earlier in this handbook as part of the formal book report) illustrates most of the characteristics of a good synopsis:

- In two paragraphs, it summarizes a book of nearly 550 pages.
- The introductory sentence names the work and the author as part of a single sentence summary.
- The second sentence places the novel in its historical perspective, without adding details about the archaeological research, evolution, or the setting.
- The third sentence introduces the main character and explains why she is in the valley of the horses. We are given no details about the Clan or the Others, but the labels are sufficiently suggestive for the purpose of a synopsis.

- The second paragraph summarizes the plot and lists the problems facing Ayla. By using the colon and a list, the author condenses chapter after chapter into a simple series.
- Without elaborating, the writer alludes to problems facing Ayla and the male character, Jondalar.
- The introductory sentence names the work and the author as part of a single sentence summary.
- Simple clauses such as after a lion mauls him and after Ayla's medicinal powers help Jondalar summarize whole chapters.

Thus, the synopsis condenses the contents of a major work. The responsibility to select the most significant ideas weighs heavily on the writer.

Compare your own synopsis with this sample. Think through the analysis. You should now be able to analyze your own synopsis as effectively.

Technical Report

Technical reports present facts, clearly and objectively. Their purpose may be to inform or to persuade. In either case, they can help the reader solve a problem, make a decision, or analyze findings. The audience is usually specified.

A technical report differs from non-technical writing in two respects: First, its writing is objective and factual, reporting information without reflecting personal opinion. (Non-technical writing, on the other hand, may be subjective, reflective, or emotional.) Second, it uses headings and visual aids as a matter of course, which non-technical writing generally omits.

Virtually all professionals write technical reports. A foreman explains a new procedure to his workers. A scientist shows the results of a recent study. A computer programmer explains the operation of a new piece of software. A sales manager reports progress and problems in the marketplace. A chief executive officer convinces the board of directors of the importance of company expansion. All rely on technical writing to achieve their goals.

Many of the sections in Part II (Methods of Development) and Part III (Types of Writing) include technical writing samples. Most samples for mathematics also model technical writing.

CHARACTERISTICS

In general, a technical report

- uses comparison, contrast, description, cause, effect, classification, definition, and other methods of development [*see entries for each in Part II*],
- follows a chronological order, spatial order, or order of importance [*see entries for each in the Glossary*],
- uses clear, concise language,
- uses clear sentence structure,
- takes an objective, impersonal tone,
- uses a third-person point of view,
- uses denotative rather than connotative language [*see* denotation *and* connotation *in the Glossary*],
- generally omits figurative language and other literary devices [*see* figure of speech *in the Glossary*],
- directs the reader's attention with headings,
- includes visual aid in the form of charts, graphs, diagrams, tables, and/or illustrations,
- includes a table of contents and of charts, graphs, and illustrations,
- may include an appendix containing statistics or other supportive material too cumbersome or complex to include in the text,
- uses the technical language appropriate for the subject matter,
- may include documentation.

As a specific kind of technical report, a lab report includes all of these characteristics but also

- summarizes the proceedings of a laboratory experiment,
- presents the summary in clearly defined and clearly labeled sections of the paper,
- acknowledges sources used for background research.

PROCESS

The following steps outline the process of writing a technical report.

STEP 1 **Prewriting • Determining the Purpose**

Begin by pinpointing the purpose of your report. Are you convincing someone to take a certain course of action? Are you giving information? Are you reporting on an experiment and its results?

State the purpose of the report in a sentence or short paragraph. Try to avoid saying *the purpose of this report is*; instead say *this report provides . . .* or *this report presents . . .* or *this report summarizes . . .* or something similar.

STEP 2 **Prewriting • Analyzing the Audience**

Next, identify your audience. For instance, a salesman preparing a field report knows that the sales manager and engineering staff want to know different things. So determine your audience and decide what it needs. List the general ideas you think your audience wants or needs.

STEP 3 **Prewriting • Gathering Materials**

Obviously, technical reports report something, and you must collect that information or data. Reports usually omit secondary research, unless for background purposes such as in lab reports. [*See* secondary research *and* primary research *in the Glossary. See* Research Paper *earlier in Part III for detailed information on documenting secondary research.*] Rather, technical reports share the results of personal experience or primary investigation conducted by the writer or team of writers.

As you gather materials, consider what background information you need. Is the subject familiar to your readers? If so, leave out unnecessary details. If readers need basic background information, however, include it without "talking down."

With your knowledge of the audience as your guide, list the ideas you need to include. Do the ideas listed here support the list developed in Step 2?

STEP 4 **Prewriting • Planning the Development and Organization**

Technical reports set the introduction and conclusion apart from the main section. Other organizational matters are like those for similar non-technical writing. [*See* Prewriting *in Part I. Also, see the prewriting suggestions for specific methods of development in Part II and kinds of writing in Part III.*]

Choose a method of development that suits your purpose.

STEP 5   Prewriting • Selecting the Headings

With your method of organization in mind, decide on appropriate headings. List the three major divisions of your paper: the introduction, exposition, and conclusion.

The introduction must

- state your purpose in terms of audience [*from Step 2*],
- define any unfamiliar terms,
- state your purpose in terms of subject [*from Step 1*],
- summarize your findings.

The introduction in a lab report must

- include a statement of the problem, labeled as such,
- state your purpose in terms of the experiment,
- provide a one-sentence statement of the hypothesis.

The exposition, like the body of a theme, carries out the statement of purpose. For a lab report, the exposition includes two parts: procedure and data analysis.

The conclusion summarizes and clarifies the report's contents. A lab report's conclusion includes three parts:

- A single-sentence summary of findings
- A discussion of possible sources of error
- A single-sentence concluding statement

The divisions permit a busy reader to read only what he finds most important.

Now make your own list. Consider the following example for a technical paper comparing nesting success in two kinds of bluebird nesting boxes.

```
Introduction
     Purpose
     Definitions
     Comparisons
     Preference
Comparisons
     Construction
     Predator safety
     Cost
Conclusion
```

The list serves as an outline and later, with revision, provides the headings and subheadings for the final report.

STEP 6   **Writing • Preparing the First Draft**

Using the list prepared in Step 5, write a brief statement to support each of the headings. Be as concise and as objective as possible.

Plan visual aids (tables, charts, graphs, and illustrations) to replace narrative description as necessary. Use visual aids for the following purposes:

- To increase interest
- To emphasize certain data
- To condense information
- To show relationships among data

Refer to all visual aids in the text, pointing out their significance or summarizing their contents in a sentence or two.

As you work with the content of your report, feel free to revise the list/outline as often as necessary so that, as you follow it, and develop its headings and subheadings, the ideas flow smoothly.

STEP 7   **Writing • Developing the Appendix**

Sometimes statistics, narrative, or descriptive information is included in the appendix. Usually this information would be cumbersome in the text, and, while it adds strength or support to the results, it is not essential for every technical report.

A reference should appear in the text to any materials included in the appendix, and all materials in the appendix must be titled and labeled descriptively. Materials should be grouped into separate appendices (that is, Appendix A, Appendix B, and so on) if they support separate parts of the report.

STEP 8   **Writing • Preparing the Bibliography**

If you cite background sources in your report (a necessity only in a lab report but logical in some others), you must list the sources in a bibliography. Follow one of the documentation forms included with the Research Paper elsewhere in Part III.

STEP 9   **Writing • Adding the Final Touches**

Finally, the report needs a table of contents, a table of graphics, and a title page. Use the sample paper that follows as a model by which to develop these pages. Be sure to check for accuracy of pagination.

STEP 10   **Revising • Polishing the Content**

Reread your rough draft, asking yourself the following questions:

- Are all sections clearly labeled?
- Does the table of contents accurately reflect the sections of the report?

- Does the table of figures and charts reflect the graphics included in the report and in the appendix?
- Does the introduction clarify my report's audience, purpose, content, and findings? Will a reader, finishing the introduction, know all the main ideas in my report?
- Does the body deal with each topic separately under a separate subheading?
- Does the conclusion state my results clearly and concisely?
- Have I used appropriate vocabulary?
- Are my sentences simple and clear?
- Are my headings and subheadings logical and parallel? [*See* parallel structure *in the Glossary.*]
- Have I used visual aids effectively?
- Does my text treat the visual aids adequately, without repeating everything the reader will find in them?
- Are materials not essential to the content but relevant to the research included in the appendix?

[*For guidelines on improving writing techniques (structure, consistency, sentence variety, emphasis, transition, unity, and specific detail) see* Revising, *with its series of samples, in Part I.*]

STEP 11   **Revising • Developing the Visual Aids**

Prepare the visual aids neatly and professionally. Your word-processing software should allow you to produce visual aids neatly and professionally with a minimum of fuss.

Use the following guidelines for tables:

- Number the tables consecutively.
- Give each table a title.
- Give each table column a heading.
- Leave ample space around each table to offset it from the text.
- Refer to each table in the text and show its relation to the discussion.
- Place each table as near to the discussion as possible.
- Tables that give additional information, not directly related to the discussion, should be placed in an appendix.

Anything that is not a table is called a figure. For figures:

- Number the figures in the order of their appearance.
- Give each figure a descriptive title.
- Label both the horizontal and vertical axes of a graph.
- Place all labels horizontally on charts and diagrams.

- Include a legend, if necessary, to identify multiple lines, multiple bar patterns, or pie-chart patterns.
- Keep the figures simple. Show no more than three ideas per graph, and keep other figures as uncluttered as possible.
- Leave ample space around each figure to offset it from the text.
- Refer to each figure in the text, and show its relation to the discussion.
- Place each figure as near to the discussion as possible.
- Figures that give additional information, not directly related to the discussion, should be placed in an appendix.

STEP 12   Revising • Dealing with Format

The final draft of the technical report must include certain unique features. Follow these suggestions:

- Begin the first page with the word *Introduction*, centered, in capitals. Additional main headings will also be centered, in capitals.
- Place all subheadings, typed with initial capital letters and underlined, flush with the left margin.
- Indent the paragraphs five spaces.
- Place each table or figure close to the relevant text pages.
- Number the text pages in the upper right corner. Most lab reports require a running head that includes the writer's last name.
- Begin the appendix at the top of a new page. Center and type the word *APPENDIX* in capitals. Follow these specific suggestions for items in the appendix:
  - Place each table, figure, or other piece of information on a separate page, labeled as referred to in the text.
  - Place each piece of information in a separate appendix, headed Appendix A, Appendix B, and so on.
  - Do not include information in an appendix to which there is no reference in the text.
- If you include background information, add a bibliography after the appendix. If you include endnotes and a bibliography, place both after the appendix. [*See* Research Paper *earlier in Part III for proper parenthetical, endnote, and bibliography forms.*]

- Prepare a title page. Center the information, horizontally and vertically. Include a title for the report, your name, any specific meeting or occasion for which the report was prepared, and the date.
- Make a table of contents. Center the words *TABLE OF CONTENTS*. Then follow these suggestions:
  - Type in capitals any text heading that appears so in the text.
  - Indent and type in initial capital letters the text subheadings.
  - Double-space between main headings.
  - Use dots to help the reader find page numbers.
  - Use lower-case Roman numerals (i, ii, iii), centered, at the bottom of the page, to number the table of contents page(s).
- Prepare a list of tables and figures in a manner similar to that for the table of contents. Number the page(s) at the bottom, with lower-case Roman numerals, following sequentially after the table of contents page(s).
- Prepare an abstract. [*Usually lab reports omit abstracts. To see a model abstract, see* Research Paper *earlier in Part III, the APA style.*] The abstract may be a sentence or paragraph, but no more than a single page no matter how long the report. [*See Step 2.*] Center and type the word *ABSTRACT* in capitals. Number the page at the bottom with a lower-case Roman numeral, following sequentially after the list of tables and figures.
- Assemble the pages in the following order:

  Title page
      Table of contents
      List of tables and figures
      Abstract
      Body of the report
          Introduction
          Exposition
          Conclusion
      Appendix(es) [optional]
      Endnotes [optional]
      Bibliography [optional]

- Place the pages in a binder or staple them together, whichever best suits the occasion.

STEP 13   Proofreading • Checking Final Details

The final draft complete, proofread carefully. Check for errors of grammar, mechanics, and usage. [*See Part IV for rules and examples*.]

Check and recheck statistics. Have you miscopied any figures or made mistakes typing the visual aids? Does the information in the text agree with the latter?

Finally, read the entire report as if you were its intended audience. Make final revisions.

SAMPLE TECHNICAL REPORT

The following report is a lab report that follows the guidelines given in this section. Use it as a model.

THE EFFECTS OF ACID RAIN ON
THE GROWTH OF BULBOUS PLANTS

Jerome Welte

Senior Science Seminar

March 21, 20—

TABLE OF CONTENTS

LIST OF TABLES AND FIGURES

INTRODUCTION

Statement of Problem

For many years, acid rain has raised major concerns among environmentalists and conservationists as well as among the general public. Scientists have contended that rain-made acid from various sources has been
damaging trees, bridges, buildings, lakes, crops, and the world's most vital
resource, its soil. In fact, acid rain has become a problem of such magnitude
that the federal government has taken action. By creating the National Acid
Precipitation Assessment Program, the government is starting to search for
ways to halt this dangerous phenomenon.

Besides the damage to forests and lakes, a more serious and devastat-
ing result from acid rain is beginning to attract attention: the damage to common plants such as grasses, flowers, and crops. The extent of acid-rain
damage to crops will likely prove to be comparable to the extent of ozone
damage, or about 5% of the cash value (Peterson 7).

While acid-rain damage is subtle, it is nevertheless occurring, partially
through a gradual but steady increase in soil acidity. Acid rain takes nutrients
from the soil so that plants do not grow properly (Louisiana DEQ). According
to Lance Evans, however, most damage to plants caused by acid is the result
of foliar impact, not increased soil acidity. His discovery that broad-leaved

plants seem to be the most sensitive to acid rain supports his theory

(Schultz 57).

Unfortunately, the acidity of rain appears to continue to increase.

Researchers now believe that the normal pH for rainfall is closer to 5.0 than

to 5.6, the previously assumed value that reflected the amount of carbon

dioxide dissolved in water ("Acid Rain Annual Report"). According to these

statistics, then, since a pH below 5.6 is considered harmfully acidic, almost

any precipitation is potentially dangerous (Schultz 56).

In the Northeast, average rainfall has now reached a 4.2 pH value. At

first, according to Schultz, the 4.2 value was thought to be ten times more

acidic than normal (55). Recently, however, Chris Bernabo, executive direc-

tor of the National Acid Precipitation Program, determined that the rainfall in

the Northeast is only about 7 times more acidic than unpolluted rainfall

("Acid Rain Annual Report"). Best plant growth occurs in soils that are neu-

tral or only slightly acidic, with a pH of 6.0 to 7.0 (Wester 8).

Home gardeners can adjust the acidity of their soil by adding lime to

reduce acidity or organic matter and/or sulfur to increase acidity (Wester 9).

The rest of the earth's soil, however, needs attention. Something desperately

needs to be done to prevent future destruction, but exactly what measures

should be taken is still in question.

Welte, page 3

Purpose

The purpose of this experiment is to determine if acid rain has an effect on the growth and development of bulbous flowers through the forcing and growing periods, and to determine if water of varying pH values produces different effects on the growth of these bulbs.

Hypothesis

Water acidity hinders the growth of bulbous flowers.

PROCEDURE

On November 11, twelve each of five kinds of bulbs were planted in Baccto Potting Soil: Keizerkroon and Appeldoorn Elite tulips, Dutch Master daffodils, grape hyacinths, and crocuses. They were divided into three groups of four of each type of bulb, covered with layers of newspaper (for insulation purposes), then placed in an area in which the temperature ranged from -4°C to 5°C. This procedure was designed to force the bulbs.

Periodically they were checked and watered with their respective pH rain as needed. (See Table 1, Early Distribution of Water by Frequency and Volume.) The amount of water was measured carefully using measuring spoons or cups to ensure accuracy.

TABLE 1	Early Distribution of Water by Frequency and Volume

Date	Amount per Bulb
Nov. 23	30 ml
Dec. 1	15 ml
Dec. 15	15 ml

On January 7, after 57 days of simulated winter, all bulbs were brought

into an area that had a temperature range from 13°C to 18°C. The layers of

paper were not removed, thus slowing the beginning of bulb growth. This

procedure was followed in order to make the transition from winter to spring

conditions less drastic, a transition which otherwise may have had a limiting

effect on the growth of the bulbs.

After four days in this environment, the bulbs were placed in a warmer

area (18°C to 21°C), placed under artificial sunlight, and the paper removed.

Then, the bulbs were observed every day for growth and soil dryness. If

needed, the bulbs were watered with a predetermined amount per bulb.

(See Appendix A, Water Distribution by Frequency and Volume.) The plants

were misted with water with a relative pH value to simulate light rain or dew.

After 30, 42, and 55 days from January 7, the bulb's leaf growth was

measured. A meter stick was used to measure the leaf length from the bulb

to the top of the longest stem. These measurements were recorded.

The simulated acid precipitation was produced by using distilled water

in three separate containers in which concentrated sulfuric acid (HSO) was

added to produce the desired pH value. No sulfuric acid was added to the

pH 7 water. The solutions were mixed; then the pH reading was taken using

a calibrated pH meter.

If the pH reading was too high or too low, the solution was either diluted or subjected to more acid to obtain the desired pH 4 or pH 5 value.

DATA ANALYSIS

The following graphs illustrate the growth patterns and comparisons of each type of bulb as measured after 30, 42, and 55 days of growth. All growth was measured and averages were calculated to arrive at a mean height of the growth in the three different pH-value sets. (The data supporting these graphs appear in Appendix B.)

Taking all bulbs into consideration, those watered with the pH 5 solution produced the greatest height and appeared most hearty on the dates measured. However, the daffodils showed a deviation from the norm and produced the greatest height and appeared most hearty when watered with a pH 7 solution.

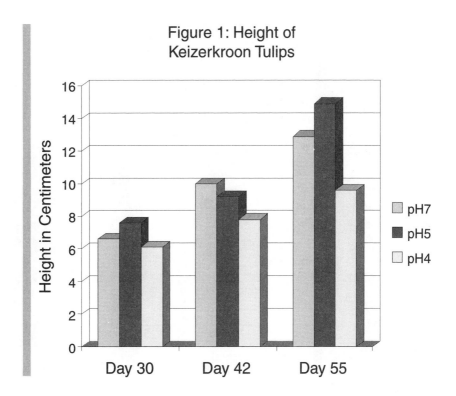

Figure 1: Height of Keizerkroon Tulips

Welte, page 7

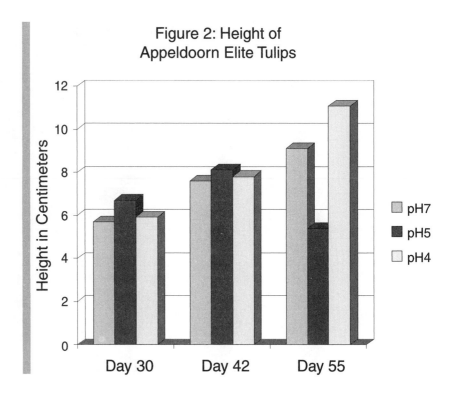

Figure 2: Height of
Appeldoorn Elite Tulips

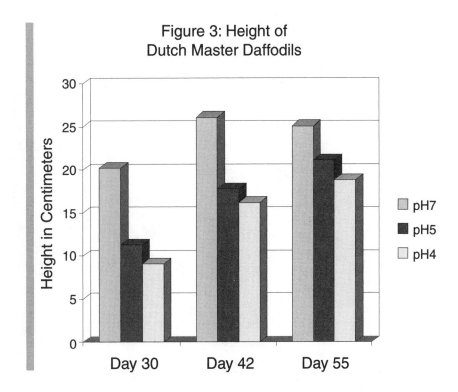

Figure 3: Height of
Dutch Master Daffodils

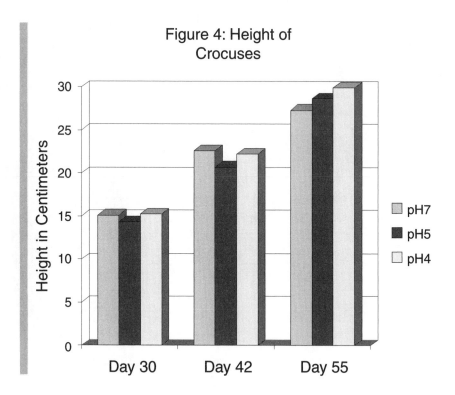

Figure 4: Height of Crocuses

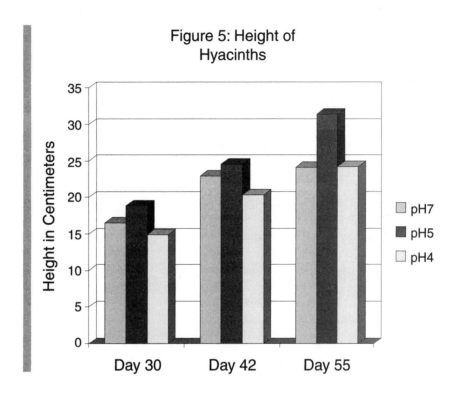

Figure 5: Height of Hyacinths

CONCLUSION

Summary of Findings

This investigation indicates that acid rain interferes with proper plant growth.

Possible Sources of Error

Even though every bulb was planted with at least one inch of surrounding area between bulbs, some bulbs had slightly larger surrounding space. This situation may have caused accelerated growth but would vary the obtained data only slightly.

Slight differences were recorded in the production of the artificial acid rain. The pH 4 solution actually ranged from 3.85 to 4.1; the pH 5 solution ranged from 4.9 to 5.1; and the pH 7 solution ranged from 6.8 to 7.0.

The use of sulfuric acid in preparing the rain solutions could cause slight differences in the growth of the bulbs, but not in that of the ones watered with the pH 7 solution. The sulfuric acid may produce differences from natural rain because natural rain is lowered to a pH of 5.6 from natural carbon dioxide in the air instead of from the sulfuric acid. The acidity in natural rain is increased as a result of sulfur dioxide from man-made pollution.

Concluding Statement

The hypothesis was correct. The data showed that the growth of bulbous flowers is deterred by water's increased acidity.

Welte, page 12

Appendix A

TABLE A-1   **Distribution of Water by Frequency and Volume**

Date	Amount per Bulb
Jan. 7	60 ml
Jan. 11	15 ml
Jan. 17	25 ml
Jan. 21	15 ml
Jan. 23	20 ml
Jan. 26	15 ml
Feb. 2	15 ml
Feb. 4	60 ml
Feb. 6	15 ml
Feb. 9	60 ml
Feb. 11	60 ml
Feb. 14	60 ml
Feb. 20	60 ml
Feb. 20	60 ml
Feb. 24	60 ml

Appendix B

Tables of Periodic Height Measurements and Averages of All Bulb Growth

TABLE B-1 **Height of All Bulbs and Averages in Centimeters after 30 Days**

Type of Bulb	pH7	pH5	pH4
Keizerkroon Tulips			
Bulb 1	5.1	8.9	6.4
Bulb 2	3.8	8.9	4.4
Bulb 3	12.1	5.1	7.0
Bulb 4	4.4	7.6	6.4
Averages	**6.4**	**7.6**	**6.1**
Appeldoorn Elite			
Bulb 1	5.1	7.0	5.7
Bulb 2	5.7	5.7	5.1
Bulb 3	6.4	7.0	5.7
Bulb 4	5.7	7.0	7.0
Averages	**5.7**	**6.7**	**5.9**
Daffodils			
Bulb 1	20.3	6.4	7.6
Bulb 2	5.7	5.7	5.1
Bulb 3	26.7	15.2	7.6
Bulb 4	27.9	17.8	15.9
Averages	**20.2**	**11.3**	**9.1**
Crocuses			
Bulb 1	14.0	12.7	15.2
Bulb 2	16.5	14.0	12.7
Bulb 3	14.6	14.0	17.8
Bulb 4	15.2	16.5	15.2
Averages	**15.1**	**14.3**	**15.2**
Hyacinths			
Bulb 1	15.2	16.5	17.8
Bulb 2	22.9	17.8	13.3
Bulb 3	15.2	22.9	12.1
Bulb 4	12.7	17.8	16.5
Averages	**16.5**	**18.8**	**14.9**

TABLE B-2   **Height of All Bulbs and Averages in Centimeters after 42 Days**

Type of Bulb	pH7	pH5	pH4
Keizerkroon Tulips			
Bulb 1	22.9	5.7	8.9
Bulb 2	5.1	11.4	5.1
Bulb 3	5.7	9.5	8.9
Bulb 4	6.4	10.2	8.3
Averages	**10.0**	**9.2**	**7.8**
Appeldoorn Elite			
Bulb 1	7.0	8.3	7.6
Bulb 2	8.3	7.6	7.0
Bulb 3	7.6	8.9	7.6
Bulb 4	7.6	7.6	8.9
Averages	**7.6**	**8.1**	**7.8**
Daffodils			
Bulb 1	33.1	20.3	17.8
Bulb 2	27.9	10.2	16.5
Bulb 3	36.8	26.7	15.2
Bulb 4	6.4	14.0	15.2
Averages	**26.1**	**17.8**	**16.2**
Crocuses			
Bulb 1	24.1	19.1	24.1
Bulb 2	20.3	20.3	21.6
Bulb 3	22.9	21.6	20.3
Bulb 4	22.9	21.6	22.9
Averages	**22.6**	**20.7**	**22.2**
Hyacinths			
Bulb 1	27.3	25.4	22.9
Bulb 2	22.9	24.1	16.5
Bulb 3	22.2	25.4	24.1
Bulb 4	19.1	22.9	17.8
Averages	**22.9**	**24.5**	**20.3**

TABLE B-3 **Height of All Bulbs and Averages in Centimeters after 55 Days**

Type of Bulb	pH7	pH5	pH4
Keizerkroon Tulips			
Bulb 1	27.9	17.8	10.2
Bulb 2	7.6	9.5	12.1
Bulb 3	8.9	15.9	5.7
Bulb 4	7.0	16.5	10.2
Averages	**12.9**	**14.9**	**9.6**
Appeldoorn Elite			
Bulb 1	9.5	10.8	8.3
Bulb 2	9.5	10.2	16.5
Bulb 3	8.3	22.9	7.6
Bulb 4	8.9	17.8	12.1
Averages	**9.1**	**15.4**	**11.1**
Daffodils			
Bulb 1	35.6	28.6	21.0
Bulb 2	31.8	24.1	17.8
Bulb 3	5.1	14.0	18.4
Bulb 4	27.9	17.8	17.8
Averages	**25.1**	**21.1**	**18.8**
Crocuses			
Bulb 1	22.9	30.5	22.9
Bulb 2	33.0	30.5	33.0
Bulb 3	30.5	30.5	33.0
Bulb 4	22.9	22.9	30.5
Averages	**27.3**	**28.6**	**29.9**
Hyacinths			
Bulb 1	27.9	27.9	26.7
Bulb 2	24.1	33.0	22.9
Bulb 3	23.5	30.5	22.9
Bulb 4	21.0	34.3	24.1
Averages	**24.1**	**31.4**	**24.2**

REFERENCES

Abelson, Philip H. "Acid Rain." *Science* 8 July 1993: 115.

"Acid Rain Annual Report." *Science News* 23 June 1998: 392.

Krug, Edward C. and Charles R. Fink. "Acid Rain on Acid Soil: A New Perspective." *Science* 5 August 1999: 520.

Louisiana Department of Environmental Quality. "Acid Rain." Jan. 2000. <http://www.deg.state.la.us/educate/acidrain.htm> (21 Feb. 2000).

Marshall, Eliot. "Acid Rain: A Year Later." *Science* 15 July 1999: 392–393.

— — — . "Acid Rain Researchers Issue Joint Report." *Science* 24 June 1995: 1359.

Peterson, Ivars. "New Reports Urge Action on Acid Rain." *Science News* 2 July 1997: 7.

Schultz, Warren Jr. "Is Acid Rain Eating Our Gardens?" *Organic Gardening* July 1997: 55–58.

Taylor, Ronald H. "The Plague That's Killing America's Trees." *U.S. News & World Report* 23 April 1984: 58–59.

Wester, Robert and August Kehr. "United States Department of Agriculture Home and Garden Bulletin Number 202." Feb. 1999. <http://www.hoptechno.com/book26.htm> (2 March 1999).

Analysis of the Sample Technical Report. The preceding sample follows the process outlined in the explanation for developing a technical report. You will note certain specifics that will further help you develop your own:

- The format, with sections clearly labeled, allows a reader to move quickly through sections of little interest.
- The Table of Contents and the List of Tables and figures clarify the organization and permit the reader to find specific sections or graphics quickly.
- While technical terminology is kept to a minimum, appropriate vocabulary appears throughout. Some reports may require a higher frequency of technical vocabulary.
- All measurements are given in the metric system.
- All data reported appear in logical order, both on the graphs and in the appendixes. For instance, Figures 1–5 report statistics in centimeters. The reader can move logically from the bottom of the chart to top to see increased growth. Likewise, the reader can move logically from left to right to follow the time span.
- The parenthetical documentation included within the text provides adequate but simple citation of reference materials. [*Compare this format with that in the samples for* Research Paper *earlier in Part III.*]
- The graphics, especially in the section titled *Data Analysis*, enhance or even replace text. Effective visual aids can provide significant support to all technical reports.
- The bibliography includes works consulted as well as works cited.

By using the steps outlined in this section, you should be able to prepare a technical report to meet the needs of virtually any situation.

PART IV

GRAMMAR, USAGE, AND MECHANICS

The revising and proofreading steps of the writing process require that you apply accurate grammar, usage, and mechanics to your paper. While lengthy books are available to describe the complexities of the English language, this section should suffice to answer most of the questions and solve most of the problems you encounter as you polish your writing for an audience.

This section functions in the following ways:

- As a basic grammar reference to help you classify the parts of speech and parts of a sentence
- As a reference for usage to help you clarify ways to solve problems with subject-verb agreement, pronoun usage, and adjective and adverb usage
- As a syntax reference to help you identify various kinds of phrases and clauses
- As a mechanics handbook to help you with rules and examples for punctuation

The index will help you locate items quickly; the glossary will provide short definitions.

Section A:
Classification of Words

PARTS OF SPEECH

Nouns

A noun is the name of a **person, place,** or **thing.**

> *Walking* in the *woods* is fun for *Jason*.
> (*Walking* is the **name of a thing;** *woods* is the **name of a place;** and *Jason* is the **name of a person.**)

Nouns **function** in one of three ways: as subjects, as objects (direct object, indirect object, object of a preposition, and object of verbal), and as predicate nouns.

> *Woodpeckers* hammer loudly.
> (*Woodpeckers*, a noun, is the **subject** of the verb *hammer.*)

> One woodpecker carved a *hole.*
> (*Hole*, a noun, is the **direct object** of the verb *carved.*)

> The woodpecker fed its *fledgling* some suet.
> (*Fledgling*, a noun, is the **indirect object** of the verb *fed.*)

> The woodpecker hammered on a dead tree *limb.*
> (*Limb*, a noun, is the **object of the preposition** *on.*)

> Do woodpeckers get headaches from hammering *trees*?
> (*Trees*, a noun, is the **object of the verbal** *hammering.*)

> Golden-shafted flickers are *woodpeckers.*
> (*Woodpeckers*, a noun, is the **predicate noun** after the linking verb *are.*)

A noun will have one or more (but not necessarily all) of the following **characteristics:**

Nouns are characterized by certain **endings.**

- Nouns can be made plural, so they have **plural endings,** usually *–s* or *–es*.

  > woodpecker, woodpeckers; box, boxes

- Some nouns have unique plural forms.

  woman, women; mouse, mice

- Nouns can show ownership, so they have **possessive endings.** An apostrophe and *–s* or apostrophe only shows possession. Note, however, that when a noun is possessive, it functions as an adjective.

  woodpecker, woodpecker's den; fledglings, fledglings' parents

Nouns are characterized by **noun markers,** certain words that often appear in front of nouns:

- First, the **articles** *a, an,* and *the* serve as noun markers.

  the woodpecker; *an* adult; *a* child

- Second, **adjectives** serve as noun markers. Adjectives are words that describe the shape, size, appearance, or number of a noun.

  round cavity nest (describe size and shape of noun *nest*)
  three immature mottled birds (describe number, kind, and appearance of the noun *birds*)

These characteristics serve as a test to decide whether a word is a noun. If words can be made plural (that is, you can count them), show ownership, or have *a, an,* or *the* in front, you can bet they are nouns.

Verbs

A verb shows **action** or **state of being,** a clear indication that there are two kinds of verbs, each with its own **function.**

Some verbs **show action.**

Speeders *cause* accidents.
(*Cause* shows action that the speeders are doing.)

Some verbs show **state of being** and link the subject to a predi-cate word.

Some speeders *are* drunk.
(Are is a linking verb that links speeders to drunk. Because drunk describes speeders, it is called a predicate adjective.)

Verbs show some combination of the following **characteristics:**

- The most important characteristic of verbs is that they **change time** (or *tense*). To find out whether a word can change time, add the word *yesterday* or *tomorrow* to the front of the sentence.

  > The cyclists were riding for exercise.
  > Yesterday, the cyclists were riding for exercise. (no change)
  > Tomorrow, the cyclists will ride for exercise.

  Thus, you know the words that changed, *were riding*, make up the verb.

- Because a verb changes time, it has certain characteristic **endings:** *-s, -ed, -en, -ing.* Don't confuse the *-s* ending on the verb with the *-s* ending on nouns. You add an *-s* to nouns to make them plural; you add an *-s* to verbs to make them singular.

  > The cyclists (plural noun) ride (plural verb).
  > The cyclist (singular noun) rides (singular verb).

- Because a verb changes time, it may have certain characteristic **helping verbs** (or **auxiliaries**): *do, does, did, have, has, had, is, am, are, was, were, be, been, being, could, would, should, may, might, must, will, shall.* The helping verb plus the main verb make up the complete verb phrase.

  > He could have been working overtime.

- Besides changing time, another characteristic is that most verbs **show action.** Action verbs have **voice.** The subject does something; the verb is said to be in **active voice.**

  > The eagle *hooked* a fish in its talons.

  The subject has something done to it: the verb is said to be in **passive voice.**

  > The fish *was hooked* by the eagle.

Verbs that do not show action are **state of being,** or **linking,** verbs. There are **two groups** of linking verbs.

- One group of linking verbs, when they are the main verbs, are **always linking:**

  > *is, am, are, was, were, be, been, being*

  (If verbs in this group are helping verbs, they are not linking.)

- The other group can be linking verbs or action verbs.

> seem, appear, remain, become, grow, stay, as well as the verbs of
> the senses: look, smell, taste, sound, feel

To determine whether these 11 verbs are linking or action verbs, substitute some form of *to be* (*is, am, are, was, were, be, been,* or *being*) for any one of them. If the substitution makes sense, that verb is linking.

> She *remained* calm.
> She *was* calm.

A form of *to be* makes sense, so *remained* is a linking verb.

Note that a form of *to be* can substitute for other verbs that will *not* be linking.

> The group *stood* on the corner.
> The group *was* on the corner.

But *stood* is not a linking verb, not one of the 11 listed earlier.

To know whether a verb is a linking verb followed by a predicate word or whether it's a verb phrase, insert the word *very*. If *very* makes sense, the verb is a linking verb with a predicate word.

> The gymnast was [very] dedicated to his sport.

If *very* does not work, it's a verb phrase.

> The memorial service was [very] dedicated to the survivors.

Adjectives

An adjective describes or modifies a noun.

An adjective **functions** to answer one of these questions about a noun:

Which one?

> The *yard* pond sported blooming lilies.
> (*Yard* describes which *pond*.)

What kind?

> The yard pond sported *blooming* lilies.
> (*Blooming* describes what kind of *lilies*.)

How many?

The yard pond sported *three* blooming lilies.
(*Three* tells how many *lilies.*)

Whose?

The *neighbor's* pond held water hyacinths.
(*Neighbor's* describes whose *pond.*)

Adjectives show two **characteristics.**

- First, adjectives characteristically can be **compared.** Certain **endings** show the comparisons that are characteristic of adjectives.

    Saundra is a *tall* girl, *taller* than her coach, the *tallest* athlete in the league.
    (*Tall* is the plain form of the adjective, used to describe one noun. *Taller* is the comparative form, comparing two nouns, Saundra and her coach. *Tallest* is the superlative form, comparing three or more nouns.)

  With adjectives of three or more syllables, use *more* instead of *–er* and *most* instead of *–est.*

    pretty, prettier, prettiest; beautiful, more beautiful, most beautiful.

- Also, **placement** characterizes adjectives. Adjectives usually appear in front of the nouns they modify.

    A *tall* athlete often plays basketball.
    (*Tall* describes *what kind* about the noun *athlete.*)

  Adjectives can follow a linking verb; these are predicate adjectives.

    She is *tall.*
    (*Tall* tells *what kind* about the noun *she* and follows the linking verb *is.*)

Adverbs

An adverb modifies a verb, an adjective, or another adverb.

Adverbs **function** to answer the following questions about verbs, adjectives, or other adverbs:

Where?

We flew *home.*
(*Home* tells *where* about the verb *flew.*)

When?

Our vacation ended *yesterday*.
(*Yesterday* tells *when* about the verb *ended*)

How?

The plane bounced *roughly* in the storm.
(*Roughly* tells *how* about the verb *bounced*.)

To what extent?

The pilot fought *really hard* to control the landing.
(*Really* tells *to what extent* about the adverb *hard*; *hard* tells *how* about the verb *fought*.)

Adverbs have two **characteristic endings** that help identify them:

- Adverbs, like adjectives, can be **compared** using the endings –*er* and –*est* or the words *more* and *most*.

     The athletes trained *hard* today, *harder* today than they did yesterday; but they trained the *hardest* on Saturday.
     (Use the comparative form *harder* to compare how they trained on two days; use the superlative form *hardest* to compare how they trained on three or more days.)

- Adverbs have a **common ending,** often –*ly*:

     He trained *methodically*.

  Not all words that end in –*ly* are adverbs; some are adjectives. Checking how the word functions determines whether it is an adverb or an adjective.

     The dog was *friendly*.
     (*Friendly* tells about the noun *dog*; thus it is an adjective, not an adverb.)

Prepositions

A preposition shows the relationship of its object to another word in the sentence. To find the **object of the preposition,** ask *who?* or *what?* after the preposition.

The children dashed *through the house*.
(Through shows the relationship between house and children; house answers what? about through and is the object of the preposition.)

The preposition, with its object, **functions** as a single word.

- The preposition can function as an **adjective.**

    The cat *with the bushy tail* chases birds.
    (The prepositional phrase *with the bushy tail* tells *which* about the-
    noun *cat*; thus, it functions as an adjective.)

- The preposition can function as an **adverb.**

    The child who fell *into the pond* needs dry clothes.
    (The prepositional phrase *into the pond* says *where* about the verb
    fell; thus it functions as an adverb.)

The following **characteristics** indicate prepositions:

- First, a preposition will always be followed by an **object,**
  which must be a noun.
- Second, a preposition is "any place a rat can run," that is, any
  word that describes a direction, destination, or state in which
  a rat runs. (The preposition *of* is the only exception.)

    A rat can run *across* the hall, *along* the wall, or *around* the corner.

PARTS OF THE SENTENCE

In order to determine correct usage, you must be able to identify the
parts of a sentence: subject, verb, direct object, indirect object, predicate word, and objective complement. These **eight easy steps to sentence analysis** can help you find the major parts of any sentence.

Step 1: Remove the **prepositional phrases.**

    A row *of boulders* blocks the driveway.
    A row . . . blocks the driveway. (prepositional phrase removed)

Step 2: Identify the word or words that change time, thus identifying
the **verb.**

    A row of boulders was blocking the driveway.
    A row . . . was blocking the driveway (prepositional phrase removed).
    Yesterday, a row . . . *blocked* the driveway; tomorrow a row *will block* the
        driveway. (*Blocks* is the verb.)

Step 3: Determine whether the verb is **action** or **linking.**

    Most of the road crew were hot and tired.
    Most . . . were hot and tired. (prepositional phrase removed).
    Tomorrow, most . . . *will be* hot and tired. (*Were* is the verb, a linking verb,
        one of the verbs *to be* that are always linking.)

Step 4: Find the **subject** by asking *who?* or *what?* in front of the verb.

> Many of the shoppers in the mall found bargains on Labor Day weekend.
> Many . . . found bargains . . . . (prepositional phrases removed).
> Tomorrow, many . . . will find bargains . . . . (*Found* is the verb. *Found* is an action verb.)
> *Who* or *what* found? *Many.* (*Many* is the subject.)

 Note that the subject is not always in front of the verb, so to find the answer to *who?* or *what?* you may have to look after the verb. Remember that *here* and *there* can never be subjects.

> There, peeping out from behind the door, stood Amity.
> There, peeping out . . . stood Amity (prepositional phrase removed).
> Tomorrow, peeping out . . . will stand Amity. (*Stood* is the verb. *Stood* is an action verb.)
> *Who* or *what* stood? *Amity.* (*Amity* is the subject.)

Step 5: If the sentence uses an **action** verb, ask *who?* or *what?* after the verb to check for a **direct object.** (A direct object must be a noun.) If the sentence uses a **linking** verb, skip to Step 8.

> A few of the travelers brought sack lunches with them.
> A few . . . brought sack lunches . . . . (prepositional phrases removed).
> Tomorrow, a few . . . will bring sack lunches . . . . (*Brought* is the verb. *Brought* is an action verb.)
> *Who* or *what* brought? *Few.* (*Few* is the subject.)
> Few brought *who* or *what*? *Lunches.* (*Lunches* is the direct object.)

 Not all action verbs have a direct object. A linking verb can *never* have a direct object.

Step 6: If the sentence uses a direct object, ask *to whom?* or *for whom?* after the direct object to check for an **indirect object.** (Without a direct object, there can be no indirect object.)

> The auto mechanic showed the SUV driver a diagram of the wiring system.
> The auto mechanic showed the SUV driver a diagram . . . . (prepositional phrase removed).
> Tomorrow, the auto mechanic will show the SUV driver a diagram. (*Showed* is the verb. *Showed* is an action verb.)
> *Who* or *what* showed? *Mechanic.* (*Mechanic* is the subject.)
> Mechanic showed *who* or *what*? *Diagram.* (*Diagram* is the direct object.)
> Mechanic showed diagram *to whom* or *for whom*? *Driver.* (*Driver* is the indirect object.)

In Step 5, there may be answers to both *who?* or *what?* In such a case, the word that answers *what?* is the direct object; the word that answers *who?* is the indirect object. The indirect object always follows the verb and precedes the direct object. The words *to* and *for* are prepositions, so if they appear in the sentence, check for a prepositional phrase, not an indirect object.

Step 7: If the sentence uses a direct object and a word that renames or describes the direct object, you have an **objective complement,** not an indirect object.

> The committee chose Juan chairman.
> The committee chose *who* or *what? Juan.* (*Juan* is the direct object.)
> What word renames or describes *Juan? Chairman.* (*Chairman* is the objective complement.)

Step 8: If the sentence uses a linking verb, the word that answers *who?* or *what?* after the verb is the **predicate word.** The predicate word can be a noun or an adjective.

> Richard's 1957 Chevy remains bright and shiny, in mint condition.
> Richard's 1957 Chevy remains bright and shiny . . . . (prepositional phrase removed).
> Tomorrow, Richard's 1957 Chevy will remain bright and shiny . . . . (*Remains* is the verb. *Remains* is a linking verb.)
> *Who* or *what* remains? *Chevy.* (*Chevy* is the subject.)
> Chevy remains *who* or *what? Bright* and *shiny.* (*Bright* and *shiny* are two predicate adjectives)

Any part of the sentence can be compound if joined by the words *and, but, or,* or *nor.*

Section B: Usage

AGREEMENT OF SUBJECT AND VERB

A singular subject takes a singular verb, and a plural subject takes a plural verb. As simple as that seems, five common errors related to subject/verb agreement can creep into writing.

The most common error occurs when the writer **chooses the wrong noun as the subject.**

- The writer may choose the wrong noun as the subject when words or phrases come between the subject and verb.

  > A package *of carrots* is in the refrigerator.
  > (The prepositional phrase *of carrots* may cause writers to incorrectly choose the verb *are* to agree with *carrots.* However, the singular subject *package* takes a singular verb *is.*)

- The writer may choose the wrong noun as the subject **when the subject comes after the verb.**

  > On the table were only old *magazines.*
  > (*Magazines* is the subject, not *table,* which is the object of the preposition *on*; thus the plural noun takes the plural verb are.)

- The writer may choose the wrong noun as the subject when a singular subject is followed by a plural predicate word, or vice versa.

  > The perfect dietary *combination is* chocolate cake and a diet cola.
  > Chocolate *cake and* a diet *cola are* a perfect dietary combination.
  > (Always make the verb agree with the subject, not the predicate word or words.)

Another common error occurs when a sentence includes indefinite pronouns.

- Some indefinite pronouns are **always singular** and take singular verbs:

  > *someone, somebody, anyone, anybody, everyone, everybody, each, one, nobody, no one, either, neither*
  > *Everyone is* on her target quota. (Think *every [single] one is . . . .*)

- Some indefinite pronouns are **always plural** and take plural verbs:

  > *several, few, both, many*
  > The desserts look wonderful, so surely *few are* calorie laden!

- Some indefinite pronouns can be **singular or plural.**

  > *some, any, all, none, most*
  > (The prepositional phrase that follows indicates whether these indefinite pronouns are singular or plural.)
  > *Some* of the *flour was* spilled; some of the *canisters have* loose lids.

A third common error occurs when the sentence has a compound subject.

- Two subjects joined by *and* take a **plural verb.**

  The *coach and* the *quarterback were conferring.*

- Two **singular** subjects joined by *or* or *nor* take a **singular verb.**

  The *coach or* the *quarterback will answer* questions from the media.

- A **singular** subject and a **plural** subject joined by *or* or *nor* take a **singular or plural verb,** depending on which subject is nearer the verb.

  The *coach nor* the *players are* happy about the call; the *players nor* the *coach finds* a satisfactory solution.

A fourth common error occurs **when the subject is a collective noun.** Collective nouns are words that represent a group, such as *team, jury, class, cast, crew, audience.* They can be singular or plural.

- Collective nouns are **singular** and take a singular verb when the group works together as a unit.

  The *orchestra is performing* admirably.

- Collective nouns are **plural** and take a plural verb when the members of the group are acting individually.

  The *cast* usually *collects* their own costumes.

A fifth common error occurs when words look plural but are not.

- Some words end in *–s* but represent a single thing and, therefore, take singular verbs:

  news, measles, mumps
  The *news is* sometimes about wonderful human-life sagas.

- Words that end in *–ics* are usually singular, especially when they refer to a study, science, or practice. They are plural only when they have modifiers in front.

  politics, mathematics, civics, ethics, economics, athletics
  Mathematics is her field of excellence.
  His mathematics are incorrect.

- Some English words retain their original foreign-language plural forms. Use a plural verb with the plural forms.

  datum, data; alumnus, alumni; memorandum, memoranda
  The *data are* overwhelmingly clear.

- Plural titles represent a single thing; use a singular verb.

    Great Expectations is one of Dickens' most famous novels.

- Nouns in the plural form that represent an amount, a fraction, or an element of time take a singular verb.

    Fifty dollars is too much to spend on my gift.

PRONOUN USAGE

Pronoun usage can be summarized in ten points.

First, use the **subjective form** of the pronoun for the **subject** of a sentence:

> *I, you, he, she, it, we, they*

Most errors occur when the pronoun is part of a compound subject. To avoid the error, consider the pronoun alone.

> Patricia and *she* visited over the weekend.
> (*She* visited over the weekend.)

Second, use the **subjective form** also for **predicate pronouns,** those that follow linking verbs.

> *I, you, he, she, it, we, they*
> It was *he* who made me smile.

Third, use the **objective form** for a pronoun used as **any object.**

> *me, you, him, her, it, us, them*

Most errors occur when the pronoun is part of a compound object. To avoid the error, consider the pronoun alone.

> The voters elected Jordan and *her* to the school board.
> (The voters elected *her* to the school board.)

Fourth, when a **noun immediately follows a pronoun,** blank out the noun to choose the correct pronoun.

> *We* students enjoyed the pep rally.
> (We . . . enjoyed the pep rally.)

Fifth, in a **comparison,** complete the comparison to choose the correct pronoun.

> Lewis is a better student than *I.*
> (Lewis is a better student than I [am].)

Sixth, use a possessive pronoun with *–ing* **nouns.**

my, mine, our, ours, your, yours, his, hers, its, their, theirs
His swearing was offensive.
(*Swearing* is an *–ing* noun, technically called a *gerund. See* Verbals and Verbal Phrases *later in this Part.*)

Seventh, in an appositive, use the same form for the pronoun as the word it renames. (An appositive is a noun that identifies another noun.)

The two injured players, Glenn and *I*, will sit on the sidelines.
(Read as . . . *I will sit on the sidelines. Glenn and I* renames *players*, the subject of the sentence; the pronoun takes the subjective form.)
The coach sent the two injured players, Glenn and *me*, to the showers early.
(Read as *The coach sent . . . me to the showers early. Glenn and me* renames *players*, the object of the verb *sent*; the pronoun takes the objective form.)

Eighth, use a compound pronoun only if the word it refers to is in the same sentence. The following are compound pronouns:

myself, yourself, himself, herself, itself, ourselves, yourselves, themselves
Mr. Kiegle *himself* announced the Kiegle Award winner.
(*Himself* refers to *Mr.* Kiegle.)
Those who won included Treena and *me*.
(Do not say Trenna and *myself*; no noun reference for the pronoun appears in this sentence.)

Ninth, use the pronouns *who* and *whom* the same way you would use *he* and *him*. Look at the way the pronoun is used in its own clause; ignore the rest of the sentence.

She didn't know (*who/whom*) to ask for money.
(Look at the clause, reword, and substitute: . . . ask (him) *whom* for money.)
We didn't understand (*who/whom*) had permission to leave.
(Look at the clause, reword, and substitute: . . . (he) *who* had permission to leave.)

Tenth, make pronouns agree in both number and gender with the words to which they refer.

All of the students were prepared with *their* homework, but *neither* of the absent students has turned in *her* homework.
(*All* and *their* are plural pronouns to agree with the plural *students*; *neither* is an indefinite pronoun that is always singular and so takes the singular pronoun *her*.)

One way to avoid sexist language is to use plural forms (*we, they, our, their, theirs, us, them*) as illustrated in the preceding example.

ADJECTIVE AND ADVERB USAGE

Adjectives must modify nouns; adverbs must modify verbs, adjectives, or other adverbs. The following enumerate common problems with adjective and adverb usage.

- Use **adverbs** to modify **action verbs.**

    He spoke *brilliantly*.
    (*Brilliantly* modifies the verb *spoke*.)

- Use **adverbs** to modify **adjectives.**

    His *convincingly* dramatic speech swayed the audience.
    (*Convincingly* modifies the adjective *dramatic*.)

- Use **adjectives** after **linking verbs.**

    The music sounded *moody*.
    (*Moody* is a predicate adjective describing *music*.)

- *Bad* is an adjective; ***badly,*** an adverb. Use the adjective, *bad*, after a linking verb.

    I felt *bad* (predicate adjective after a linking verb) that he played so *badly* (adverb modifying the verb *played*).

- *Good* is an adjective; ***well*** can be an adjective or adverb. As an adjective, *well* means *in good health, of good appearance, satisfactory*. *Well* as an adjective usually follows a linking verb.

    All is *well* (adjective after a linking verb) now that Ricardo made *good* (adjective) grades and gets along *well* (adverb) with his step-father.

- Use ***fewer*** to refer to countable things and ***less*** to refer to amounts.

    Use *less* coffee (an amount) for *fewer* cups (countable thing).

- Distinguish between the **comparative** and the **superlative** forms.

    Use the **comparative form** (words ending in *–er* or accompanied by the word *more*) when discussing two things.
    Jennifer is the *older* of the two sisters; she is also the *more outgoing*.
    Use the **superlative form** (words ending in *–est* or accompanied by the word *most*) when discussing three or more things.
    Jennifer is the *oldest* of the three sisters; she is also the *most outgoing*.

- Avoid double negatives.

  > Incorrect: We didn't get no mail.
  > Correct: We didn't get any mail.

- Avoid illogical comparisons.

  > Illogical: The white-throated sparrow's song is more welcome than any winter sound. (The song is a winter sound; thus the illogical comparison is that the song is more welcome than itself.)
  > Logical: The white-throated sparrow's song is more welcome than any other winter sound.

Section C: Phrases and Clauses

VERBALS AND VERBAL PHRASES

Verbals look like verbs, hence their name; but verbals function as nouns, adjectives, or adverbs. There are three kinds of verbals: infinitives, gerunds, and participles.

Infinitives

An infinitive is a verb-like word that combines a verb with the word *to*; thus *to* is a primary **characteristic.**

> *To liste*n to him talk is *to fall* asleep from boredom.
> (*To listen* and *to fall* are infinitives, each formed with a verb and the word *to*.)

Like verbs, verbals take modifiers and direct objects, and these words together make up the **infinitive phrase.**

> The losing political party wanted *to blame the outgoing mayor for the defeat.*
> (*Mayor* is the direct object of the infinitive *to blame*; *for the defeat* is a prepositional phrase modifying the infinitive.)

A verbal phrase **functions** as a **single word** in its sentence; thus, in the preceding example, the entire infinitive phrase is the direct object of the verb *wanted*.

 Not every use of the word *to* marks an infinitive. *To* plus a verb makes an **infinitive;** *to* plus a noun makes a **prepositional phrase.**

> Terrance wanted *to walk to the pond.*
> (*To walk* is an infinitive, *to* plus a verb; *to the pond* is a prepositional phrase, *to* plus a noun.)

An infinitive **functions** most of the ways that a noun, adjective, or adverb can function:

> subject, predicate word, appositive, direct object, noun modifier, verb modifier, adjective modifier, and adverb modifier

Gerunds

A gerund is a verb-like word that functions as a noun and is **characterized** by its *–ing* ending.

> *Identifying* birds is his forte.
> (*Identifying* looks like a verb but acts like a noun as subject of the sentence.)

A gerund can take objects and modifiers; together these words make up the **gerund phrase.**

> Paul's hobby is *identifying migrating birds in southern Indiana.*
> (*Birds* is the direct object of the gerund *identifying*; *in southern Indiana* is a prepositional phrase modifying *birds.*)

A gerund phrase **functions** as a **single word;** thus, in the preceding example, the gerund phrase is the predicate noun after the linking verb *is*, renaming the subject, *hobby.*

Not all words ending in *–ing* are gerunds, so always check the word's **function.** A gerund or gerund phrase always functions as a noun; thus, it can be a subject, predicate word, direct object, object of the preposition, or appositive.

> Not a gerund: Marilyn is *cutting* the grass. (*Is cutting* functions as the verb.)
> Not a gerund: Barry, *hoping* for a scholarship, kept up his grades. (*Hoping* functions as an adjective and modifies *Barry.*)
> Gerund: Marilyn loves *cutting* the grass. (*Cutting the grass* functions as the direct object of *loves*; and direct objects are nouns.)

Hint: If you can substitute the word <u>to</u> and the root word form for the *–ing* word and have a sentence that makes sense, the *–ing* word is a gerund:

> Marilyn loves *cutting* the grass.
> Marilyn loves *to cut* the grass. (The sentence makes sense; *cutting* is a gerund.)
> Mary is *cutting* the grass.
> Mary is *to cut* the grass. (The sentence does not make sense; *cutting* is not a gerund.)

Participles

Participles are verb-like words that take two forms, past participles and present participles.

Past participles are usually **characterized** by their *–ed* endings (the form of the verb you would use with helping words such as *have* or *has*, as in *have spoken* or *has rained*.

Present participles are usually **characterized** by their *–ing* endings, such as *speaking* or *raining*. While present participles *look* like gerunds, they don't function the way gerunds do.

Participles can have objects and modifiers, and these words together make up the **participial phrase.**

> The car *speeding down the interstate* scared other drivers.
> (*Down the interstate* is a prepositional phrase modifying the present participle *speeding*.)

A participial phrase **functions** as a **single word;** thus, in the preceding example, *speeding down the interstate* functions as a single adjective modifying the subject *car*.

Participles always **function** as **adjectives,** which, by definition, must modify nouns.

> The driver seemed *relaxed* behind the wheel.
> (The past participle *relaxed* is a predicate adjective following the linking verb *seemed* and modifying the subject *driver*.)

When the participial phrase appears at the **beginning of a sentence,** the phrase is followed by a **comma.**

> *Wandering the woods*, Kirsten identifies all the wild flowers.

Be sure the participial phrase modifies the noun that immediately follows it.

> Incorrect: Arriving late for dinner, the meal was over before I sat down. (The meal did not arrive late.)
> Correct: Arriving late for dinner, I missed the whole meal.

Clauses

Every clause has a subject and verb. That truth separates clauses from phrases, which do not have subjects and verbs. There are two kinds of clauses:

Main clauses (sometimes called *independent* clauses) can stand alone as sentences.

Subordinate clauses (sometimes called *dependent* clauses) cannot stand alone:

> . . . after the phone call came . . . .
> . . . when the stars came out . . . .

The three kinds of subordinate clauses are noun clauses, adjective clauses, and adverb clauses.

Noun Clause. A noun clause **characteristically** starts with a word called a *relative pronoun*:

> *who, whose, whom, which, what, that, whoever, whomever, whichever, whatever*
> The person most likely to win is *whoever least expects it.*
> (*Whoever* is the relative pronoun that begins the noun clause.)

The first word of the noun clause can also be its **subject.**

> We greeted *whoever came to the door.*
> (*Whoever* is the subject of the verb *came.*)

The first word of the noun clause can be an **object.**

> *What Jenny wants* Jenny gets.
> (*What* is the object of the verb *wants,* as in *Jenny wants what.*)

A noun clause must have a subject and verb but may also have **objects and/or modifiers.**

> *What I do for fun* makes my job less tedious.
> (*Do,* the verb of the noun clause, has *I* as its subject and *what* as its object; *for fun* is a prepositional phrase in the noun clause and modifies the noun *what.*)

A noun clause **functions** most of the ways a single **noun** functions: subject, predicate word, direct object, object of the preposition, appositive. To determine how a noun clause functions, think of the **clause** as a **single word** and use the sentence analysis described earlier in this part to determine sentence parts.

Adjective Clause. An adjective clause has a subject and a verb and is usually **characterized** by its *relative pronoun* openers, *who, whose, whom, which,* and *that.*

> The mystery book *that I've been reading* kept me awake all night.
> (*That I've been reading* opens with the relative pronoun *that.*)

Sometimes *when* and *where* can introduce an adjective clause.

> We visited the place *where the battle occurred.*

Other characteristics are similar to those of noun clauses.

An adjective clause **functions** the same way a **single adjective** functions and answers *which one? what kind?* or *how many?* about a noun.

> The author *whose work I most admire* writes only nonfiction.
> (The adjective clause describes the noun *author.*)

Confusion between adjective and noun clauses can occur because they can start with the same words. To decide which is which, think of the clause as a single word and then, using sentence analysis, find out how the clause functions in the sentence.

Adverb Clause. An adverb clause has a subject and verb and is **characterized** by words called *conjunctive adverbs* that begin most adverb clauses:

> *after, although, as, as if, as long as, as much as, as soon as, as though, because, before, even though, if, in order that, provided that, since, so that, than, though, unless, until, when, whenever, where, wherever, while*
> I'll come home *when I get off work.*
> (The conjunctive adverb *when* opens the adverb clause.)

Other **characteristics** are similar to those of noun clauses.

An adverb clause **functions** just as a **single-word adverb** and modifies verbs, adjectives, and other adverbs. It tells *when, where, why, how, to what extent,* or *under what conditions.*

> Ellen rides her bicycle to work *because she lives only three miles away.*
> (The adverb clause tells *why* about the verb *rides.*)

Some adverb clauses have **missing, but implied, parts.** Some have a missing, but implied, **verb.**

> The task is bigger *than I.*
> (The task is bigger *than I [am]*).

Some have a missing, but implied, **subject.**

> *When driving in the rain,* you should slow down.
> (*When [you are] driving in the rain,* you should slow down.)

Some **adverb clauses** can be confused with **prepositional phrases** because they can begin with the same words. An adverb clause must have a subject and verb.

After the football game, we went for pizza. (prepositional phrase)
After the football game was over, we went for pizza. (adverb clause)

Section D: Punctuation

COMMAS

Use a comma to separate **items in a series.** A series is made up of three or more nouns, verbs, modifiers, or phrases. If all items in the series are followed by *and* or *or*, omit commas.

Squirrel, rabbit, and venison are the three kinds of meat in burgoo.
Squirrel and rabbit and venison are the three kinds of meat in burgoo.

Use a comma to separate **coordinate adjectives.** Coordinate adjectives are two or more adjectives that equally modify the same noun.

The weak, tottery patient fell in his hospital room.

Omit the comma after *numbers* and after adjectives of *size, shape,* and *age*.

Six strong attendants carried him to his bed.

Use a comma to separate **two complete sentences joined by a conjunction** (*and, but, or, nor,* or *for,* and sometimes *yet* and *so*).

The CD player runs constantly, *so* I'm not surprised that it needs cleaning.

Before you use a comma in front of a conjunction, be sure that the conjunction joins **two sentences, not two other compound parts,** such as two verbs.

The Internet sites included good links, *and* Carolyn followed each one (connecting two sentences; use a comma with the conjunction).
The Internet sites included good links *and* led to some superb information (connecting two verbs; use no comma).

Set off **nonrestrictive verbal phrases or adjective clauses** with commas. *Nonrestrictive* means not essential or not needed to limit the noun.

> The man *wearing the red flannel shirt* won the hog-calling contest.
> (The verbal phrase is restrictive, or essential, to identify which man.)
> Mr. Talbert, *who is wearing the red flannel shirt,* won the contest.
> (The adjective clause is nonessential, or not needed, to identify Mr. Talbert.)

Set off **introductory elements** (words that introduce a sentence) with a comma. An introductory element can be a single word, a prepositional phrase of four or more words, a verbal modifier, or adverb clause.

> "*Yes*, we have no bananas," the song goes. (introductory single word)
> *Before sunset every summer evening*, we go to the beach to watch the sun sink. (introductory prepositional phrase of four or more words)
> *Warning her master*, the dog saved Gina from being trapped by the fire. (introductory verbal modifier, present participial phrase)
> *After the darkness descended*, the stars took on their brilliance. (introductory adverb clause)

Set off **interrupters** with commas. Interrupters, obviously, interrupt a sentence and create emphasis.

One kind of interrupter is the **appositive,** which is a noun that renames another noun.

> Bald eagles, *a once endangered species*, have made a comeback.

Another interrupter comes in the form of **words of direct address,** words used to speak directly to someone.

> Can you, *Mr. Goodaker*, take photographs of the race tomorrow?

A final kind of interrupter is the **parenthetical expression.** These expressions include, but are not limited to, the following:

> *of course, in fact, moreover, in the meantime, I believe, I hope, I think, on the other hand, therefore, however, consequently, for example, nevertheless, he said*
> Do you think, *in fact*, that he will win the scholarship?

Use commas to set of **dates and states.**

> August 15, 1943
> August 1943 (no comma needed)
> August 15, 1943, was her date of birth. (two commas needed)

Rochester, Minnesota
Rochester, Minnesota, can have brutal winters. (two commas needed)

SEMICOLONS

Use semicolons in three situations:

First, use a semicolon to separate two sentences when there is no coordinating conjunction such as *and, but, or, nor,* or *for.*

> **With coordinating conjunction:** Autumn leaves showered from the trees in multiple colors, and it looked like snow with a rainbow.
> **With semicolon:** Autumn leaves showered from the trees in multiple colors; it looked like snow with a rainbow.

If the two sentences are joined by a conjunctive adverb, such as *however, consequently, therefore,* or *moreover,* use a semicolon before the conjunctive adverb and a comma after it.

> Autumn leaves showered from the trees in multiple colors; consequently, we have a big job ahead of us raking them into compost piles.

Second, use a semicolon to separate two sentences joined with a coordinating conjunction when commas are contained within either of the sentences.

> Autumn leaves showered from the trees in red, gold, yellow, and brown; and it looked like snow with a rainbow.

Third, use a semicolon to separate items in a series if there are commas within the items.

> Mr. Johnson, my neighbor; Mrs. Addison, my aunt; and Ms. Ricardo, my music teacher, all came to the open house.

COLONS

There are three reasons to use colons.

First, use a colon for conventional items: giving the time, separating chapter from verse in Bible references, separating volume from page in bibliography references, and writing a salutation in a business letter.

> The alarm is set for 5:30 a.m.
> He read Luke 4:17-28.
> He cited an article in *National Geographic* 196:81 (that is, volume 196, page 81).
> Dear Madam:

Second, use a colon to introduce a formal list. Words such as *the following* or *as follows* frequently signal a formal list.

> The attendant made the following checks on my car: oil level, transmission fluid level, battery, tire pressure, and windshield washer fluid.

Third, use a colon to mean summary follows or explanation follows. The summary or explanation may be a complete sentence.

> The zoo faced a series of troubles: It lost accreditation, a keeper was attacked by a lion, a visitor was bitten by a monkey, and the director was fired.

OTHER PUNCTUATION

Use a **period** at the end of a statement or after an abbreviation.

> Dr. Ezra walked the hospital halls every evening.

Use an **exclamation point** to show excitement.

> Watch out!

Use a **question mark** to ask a direct question.

> Did you see the game last night?

Use an **apostrophe** to show ownership.

> The reporter's story missed few details. (singular possessive)
> The two reporters' stories each won journalistic awards. (plural possessive)
> Her sister-in-law's home was demolished in the tornado. (singular possessive)
> Her sisters-in-law's families are all safe. (plural possessive)

Use an **apostrophe** to show omission.

> Ingrid can't walk far in those high-heeled shoes.
> The blizzard of '86 was one for the records.

Use an **apostrophe** to show plurals of letters, signs, numbers, and words referred to as words.

> I think his last name has two *z*'s.
> His *7*'s look like *4*'s to me.

Use **italics** for foreign words, titles of long works (books, magazines, films), and for letters or words referred to as such.

> Geoffrey's goal is to graduate *cum laude*.
>
> I just finished reading *Random Passage* whose author won the Canadian prize for literature.
>
> I think his last name has two *z*'s.

Use **quotation marks** to set off someone's direct words, titles of smaller works, and the definition of a word.

> "Don't drink the water," Dr. Hazelit warned us.
>
> "African Marriage Rituals" appears in this month's issue of *National Geographic*.
>
> *Rambunctious*, meaning "wild, disorderly," fits my nephew perfectly.

GLOSSARY

A

abbreviation a shortened form of a word. A period after the shortened form indicates the abbreviation. **Example:** *Sat.* is the abbreviation for *Saturday; Ave.* for *Avenue.* **Note:** Many writers avoid abbreviations in formal writing.

absolute a phrase made up of a noun and a participle, which begins and modifies an entire sentence. **Example:** *The wind chill factor being below zero,* we bundled up to protect ourselves.

abstract **1.** nouns which name things that cannot be observed by the senses: hope, memory, belief. **2.** writing that lacks specific detail. **Example:** The weather was too cold for us to wait outside (abstract). **Revised:** With the temperature at 15 degrees below zero and the wind howling at 40 miles an hour, we could not safely wait outside 30 minutes for the bus (specific). [*See also* specific detail *in the Glossary and* Description *in Part II.*]

action verb shows the action of the subject. **Example:** We *wrote* letters (action). Letters from good friends *are* fun to receive (linking). Most experienced writers prefer action verbs to linking verbs. [*See also Part IV, Section A, and* verb *in the Glossary.*]

active voice refers to the verb whose subject is doing the acting. **Example:** Sheila ate an apple with her lunch. (*Ate* is in active voice; the subject *Sheila* is acting.) [*See also Part IV, Section A, and* passive voice *in the Glossary.*] **Note:** Because active-voice verbs make stronger sentences than do passive-voice verbs, most experienced writers prefer active voice. Exceptions are noted in Parts II and III under respective types of writing that often utilize the passive voice.

address a three-line indication of where one receives mail. It includes the person's name, street name and number, the city, two-letter abbreviation for the state, and zip code. **Example:** Dr. Chung Wong; 4274 Longshore Avenue; Lake Charlene, AR 33061. **Note:** For businesses, the address is sometimes four or more lines, the additional lines adding the person's title and company name. [*See also* Letters *in Part III.*]

adjective **1.** a word that modifies nouns or pronouns. **2.** a group of words functioning as an adjective, notably a prepositional, participial, or infinitive phrase, an adjective clause. **Example:**

Students *who work hard* succeed. (The adjective clause *who work hard* functions as an adjective to modify the noun *students*.) [*See also Part IV, Sections A and C and other Glossary entries:* phrase, preposition, participle, infinitive, verbal phrase, *and* clause, subordinate.]

adverb 1. a word that modifies a verb, adjective, or adverb. **2.** a group of words functioning as an adverb, notably a prepositional, participial, or infinitive phrase, or an adverb clause. **Example:** *After our team won the game,* we celebrated. (The adverb clause modifies the verb *celebrated*.) [*See also Part IV, Sections A and C and other Glossary entries:* phrase, preposition, participle, infinitive, verbal phrase, *and* clause, subordinate.]

agenda a chronological list of topics to be discussed at a meeting. An agenda serves several purposes: to give advance notice of topics so that the membership and/or the public can be prepared to speak, to keep the meeting organized, and to limit discussion.

agreement the correct grammatical use of words of like number and gender. Two kinds of agreement problems occur in everyday language. **1.** Pronoun-antecedent agreement requires a pronoun to agree in number and gender with its antecedent. [*See Part IV, Section B-2.*] **2.** Subject-verb agreement requires a subject and its verb to agree in number. [*See Part IV, Section B-1.*]

alliteration repetition of a beginning sound, usually of a consonant, in two or more words of a phrase, line of poetry, and so on. **Example:** *full fathom five thy father lies.*

allusion a casual or indirect reference. **Example:** By the end of the day, the apprentice was a virtual mad hatter. (The allusion, *mad hatter*, suggests to the informed reader the character from *Alice in Wonderland*.) **Note:** While the effectiveness of an allusion depends on an informed reader, its use adds considerable vitality and enrichment to written works.

ambiguity the quality or state of being unclear or uncertain in meaning. Ambiguity may result from **1.** unclear pronoun reference, **2.** vague or abstract words and phrases. [*See abstract in the Glossary.*] **Example:** Maggie asked Stacey to move her car. (The sentence is ambiguous because the reader doesn't understand whose car is to be moved.) **Revision:** Maggie, who does not own or drive a car, asked Stacey to move hers.

analogy a comparison in which two objects are compared, with the more complex explained in terms of the simpler. **Example:** The instructor complained that the manuals were not compatible with the computer. "It's like having a sewing machine manual to explain how to play a pipe organ." [*See also* Analogy *in Part II for a complete explanation and a series of sample papers.*]

analysis a careful examination of a cause, effect, process, or product. Sometimes referred to as *cause-and-effect analysis, process analysis,* or *critical analysis*, the term suggests precise thought and logic. [*See* Cause and Effect, Literary Analyses, *and* Process Analysis *in Part II for examples.*]

anecdote a short, entertaining story of some happening, usually personal or biographical, useful in introductions, both oral and written, as well as in supporting examples in less formal situations.

announcement a written, printed, or oral notice. [*See* Announcement *in Part III.*]

antagonist a character in a drama, novel, or story who opposes or fights with the protagonist. [*See* protagonist *in the Glossary.*]

antecedent the word, phrase, or clause to which a pronoun refers. **Example:** *Sue* likes frills, and she often trims her sleeves with lace. (The pronouns *she* and *her* refer to *Sue*, the antecedent.)

apostrophe a punctuation mark (') used to show **1.** omitted letters in a word, or **2.** the possessive case. [*See Part IV, Section D.*]

appositive a word, phrase, or clause that functions as a noun and explains another noun. **Example:** Mr. Jetson, *the mechanic*, is a wizard at repairing cars. (*The mechanic* explains the noun *Mr. Jetson* and is an appositive.) [*See Part IV, Section D, for punctuating appositives.*]

Arabic numerals the figures 1, 2, 3, 4, 5, 6, 7, 8, 9, and 0.

articles the words *a, an*, and *the. The* is a definite article; *a* and *an* are indefinite articles.

assonance 1. likeness of sound, especially of vowels, as in a series of words or syllables. **2.** a partial rhyme in which the stressed vowel sounds are alike but the consonant sounds are not, as in *late* and *make*.

attention-getter an introductory device that gains the reader's or listener's attention. Common devices include **1.** asking a question or questions **2.** making an unusual statement **3.** describing a scene **4.** repeating a conversation **5.** telling a brief story **6.** giving surprising or alarming statistics **7.** referring to an event, either historical or current **8.** showing a controversy or contradiction **9.** using a quotation, adage, or proverb **10.** stating an unusual opinion.

autobiography the story of one's own life. [*See* Autobiography *in Part III.*]

auxiliary verb a verb that helps form the tense, mood, or voice of another verb: *have, be, may, can, do, shall*, and so on. **Example:** She *must* work harder. (*Must* is an auxiliary verb accompanying the main verb *work*.) [*See Part IV, Section A, and* verb *in the Glossary.*]

B

bias a mental leaning for or against someone or something; partiality; prejudice; bent.

bibliography a list of books, articles, electronic media, and so on, referred to by an author. The list follows one of several formats. [*See* Research Paper *in Part III for form.*]

bibliography cards cards, usually 3" x 5", on which bibliographic information is recorded prior to the preparation of a bibliography. [*See* Research Paper *in Part III for a full explanation of preparing the cards.*]

biography the account of a person's life. [*See* Biography *in Part III for an explanation and examples.*]

body the main part of a paragraph or paper, in which ideas are developed and supported.

book report an essay that gives a brief summary of a book and a reaction to it. [*See* Book Report *in Part III for the process of developing a book report, including samples.*]

brackets punctuation marks [ ] used to enclose words and figures, such as those used for explanation.

C

capitalization the use of upper-case letters.

card catalog in a library, a file of cards that list books by title, author, and subject. The cards describe the book and give publication information.

case the inflected form taken by a noun, pronoun, or adjective to show its relationship to other words. **Example:** That is *his* watch. (*His* is a pronoun in the possessive case.) [*See Part IV, Section B,* Pronoun Usage.]

catharsis a relieving of the emotions, especially through art, as by watching a tragic play.

cause and effect a method of developing a paper showing **1.** what produced an effect or result; the reason for some action or feeling; or **2.** anything brought about by a cause; result; or **3.** both the producer and the result. [*For an explanation and examples, see* Cause and Effect *in Part II.*]

characterization the act of describing or showing a person's particular qualities or traits. **Example:** Tennyson characterized King Arthur as *wise and brave*. [*See* Character Sketch *in Part III.*]

chronological order an arrangement in the order in which things occur. Chronological order may move from past to present or, in reverse chronological order, from present to past.

classification a method of development in which objects are arranged according to class. [*For an explanation and examples, see* Classification *in Part II.*]

classified advertising advertising as in newspapers, under such listings as *help wanted* and *for sale*. [*See* Classified Ad *in Part III for an explanation and examples.*]

clause, main a group of words containing a subject and verb that can stand alone; also called an *independent clause,* or *sentence.* **Example:** After the celebration was over, *we had a big cleanup job.* (The main clause is *we had a big cleanup job.*) [*See Part IV, Section C.*]

clause, subordinate a group of words containing a subject and verb that depend on a main clause for meaning; also called a *dependent clause.* Three kinds of subordinate clauses function as modifiers and nouns: *adverb, adjective,* and *noun clauses*. [*See Part IV, Section C.*] **Example:** *After the celebration was over,* we had a big cleanup job. (The subordinate clause, *after the celebration was over,* functions as an adverb.)

cliché an expression that has become stale from too much use. **Example:** *as old as the hills.*

climax the decisive turning point of action, as in a drama.

coherence the quality of being logically consistent and intelligible, and of having all parts connected in a way that makes sense. Coherence is achieved by the effective use of transition. [*See* transitions *in the Glossary.*]

collective noun a noun that is singular in form but is the name for a collection of individuals (for example, *army, crowd*). A collective noun is treated as singular when the collection is thought of as a whole, and as plural when the individual members are thought of as acting separately. **Example:** The *crowd is* restless (singular). The *jury were* arguing over one piece of evidence (plural). [*See Part IV, Sections A and B-1.*]

colloquial expression words, phrases, and idioms found in everyday speech but avoided in formal writing; labeled in the dictionary as *Colloq.* **Example:** *John is on the beam* is a colloquial way of saying *John is alert and keen.*

colon a mark of punctuation (:) used **1.** before a long quotation, explanation, examples, series, and so on, **2.** after the salutation of a formal letter. [*See Part IV, Section D.*]

comma a mark of punctuation (,). [*See Part IV, Section D, for rules for using commas correctly.*]

comma fault the error of joining two main clauses by a comma instead of a semicolon or comma and coordinating conjunction. Sometimes called a *comma splice.* [*See Part IV, Section D for rules and examples.*]

common noun a noun that names a thing in general; as opposed to a *proper noun.* **Example:** Students in college take a wide range of courses (common nouns: *students, college, range, courses*). Students at the University of Colorado take Humanities (proper nouns: *University of Colorado, Humanities*).

comparative a form of adjective or adverb showing a greater, but not the greatest, degree in meaning. The comparative degree is usually indicated by the suffix *–er* (*harder*) or by the use of *more* (*more beautiful*). [*See Part IV, Section A,* Parts of Speech.]

comparison a method of development by which two subjects, seemingly different, are shown to be similar. [*See* Comparison and Contrast *in Part II for the organization and general techniques used to develop a comparison paragraph or multi-paragraph paper.*]

complement a word that completes the meaning of the predicate. It may be a direct or indirect object, or a predicate word. **Example:** We paid *him* (direct object). John gave *Miranda* a present (indirect object). Karen is *tall* (predicate word). **Note:** The object of a gerund, participle, or infinitive is also considered a direct object and is, therefore, a complement. **Example:** Watering her flower *garden* daily keeps Minnie busy (object of the gerund *watering*). [*See also Part IV, Section A,* Parts of the Sentence.]

complex sentence a sentence with one main clause and one or more subordinate clauses. The subordinate clause(s) may be noun, adjective, or adverb. **Example:** The child who performed the intricate ballet showed great promise (one main clause, *the child showed great promise,* and one noun clause, *who performed the intricate ballet*). [*See* Writing Sentences *in Part I. See also Part IV, Section C,* Phrases and Clauses.]

compound-complex sentence   a sentence with two or more main clauses and one or more subordinate clauses. The subordinate clause(s) may be noun, adjective, or adverb. **Example:** The child who performed the ballet showed great promise, so the choreographer gave her special attention (two main clauses, *the child showed great promise* and *the choreographer gave her special attention*; one subordinate clause, *who performed the ballet*). Compare with other kinds of sentences. [*See* Writing Sentences *in Part I. See also Part IV, Section C,* Phrases and Clauses.]

compound object   two or more direct or indirect objects following a verb or verb form. **Example:** They are *meat* and *vegetables* (compound direct objects of the verb *ate*). Mother bought *Betty* and *me* class jackets (compound indirect objects of the verb *bought*).

compound predicate   two or more complete verbs. **Example:** The canoe *rolled on its side* and *dumped us in the water.* [*Compare with* compound verb. *See also* verb *and* compound sentence.]

compound sentence   a sentence with two main clauses. **Example:** Tom made a touchdown and the crowd cheered (two main clauses: *Tom made a touchdown* and *the crowd cheered*). [*Compare with entries for* simple sentence, complex sentence, *and* compound-complex sentence. *See* Writing Sentences *in Part I. See also Part IV, Section C,* Phrases and Clauses.]

compound subject   two or more subjects. **Example:** Casting *rods* and spinning *reels* are useless together (two subjects: *rods* and *reels*). [*See also* subject *in the Glossary and* Parts of the Sentence *in Part IV, Section A.*]

compound verb   two or more simple predicates. **Example:** The canoe *rolled* on its side and *dumped* us in the water. [*Compare with* compound predicate. *See also* verb.]

compound word   a word made from joining two or more words: *sister-in-law; household.*

computer catalog   in a library, a computerized file that lists books by title, author, and key word. The computer display describes the book, gives publication information, and may show library location and availability.

conclusion a final statement that either summarizes or ties together the main points of a composition. May include a restatement of the topic or thesis sentence; may also include a clincher.

concrete designating a thing or class of things that are real or exist in material form; not abstract. *Tree* is a concrete noun. [*Compare with* abstract.]

conflict the fight, struggle, disagreement, or opposition on which a plot is based.

conjunction, coordinating a word used to show relationships between or among ideas of equal rank. Examples of coordinating conjunctions include *and, but, or, nor, for,* and sometimes *yet* and *so.* Used to join compound sentences and compound parts. [*See Part IV.*]

conjunction, correlative a pair of words used to express mutual relation: *neither . . . nor, either . . . or, both . . . and, not only . . . but also, whether . . . or.*

conjunctive adverb an adverb functioning as a conjunction that introduces an adverb clause: *accordingly, again, also, besides, consequently, finally, for example, furthermore, however, in addition, indeed, moreover, nevertheless, on the other hand, otherwise, then, therefore, thus.* [*See also Part IV, Section C,* Phrases and Clauses.]

connotation any idea suggested by or associated with a word or phrase, in addition to its basic or literal meaning, or denotation.

consistency agreement, following the same format or form.

consonant any letter of the alphabet not a vowel.

contraction a shortened word: *shouldn't, couldn't, can't, won't, weren't, wasn't,* and so on. **Note:** Formal writing usually omits contractions.

contrast a method of development that shows how seemingly similar subjects are, in fact, different. [*See* Comparison and Contrast *in Part II for an explanation and examples.*]

coordinate of equal order, rank, or importance, such as the *coordinate* main clauses in a compound sentence.

correlative expressing mutual relation; used in pairs such as *neither . . . nor*; correlative conjunctions.

crisis the turning point of a conflict, when it becomes clear how the conflict will be resolved.

critical writing aesthetic judgment based on analysis, most often applied to paragraphs or multi-paragraph papers written about a piece of literature.

D

dangling modifier a modifier with no clear reference. **Example:** His heart beating fast, the car sped away. (The participial phrase *his heart beating fast* seems to modify *car* but logically cannot. Thus, it is a dangling modifier.)

dash a mark of punctuation (—) used to indicate a sudden break in thought, as for something added or left out. Most experienced writers avoid dashes in formal writing.

declarative sentence a sentence that makes a statement, as opposed to *interrogative, imperative,* and *exclamatory sentences.* [*See Glossary entries.*] **Example:** Dogwood and redbud blossoms give the first hint of spring.

definition a method for developing an expository paragraph or multi-paragraph paper in which a term or idea is defined. [*See* Definition *in Part II for an explanation and examples.*]

demonstrative pronoun one of four pronouns that point: *this, that, these,* and *those.* [*See also* pronoun.]

denotation the basic or literal meaning; opposite of *connotation.*

dependent clause a clause that cannot stand alone but depends on an independent or main clause for its meaning; also called *subordinate clause.* [*See Part IV, Section C,* Phrases and Clauses.]

description a method of developing an expository paragraph or multi-paragraph paper by picturing something in words. [*See* Description *in Part II for an explanation and examples.*]

detail a small part, item, or particular used to support a main idea. [*See* Revising *in Part I for examples of writing with and without detail.*]

development, methods of means by which a subject can be supported or explained. Methods of development include *analogy, cause and effect, classification, comparison and contrast, definition, description, narration, opinion, persuasion,* and *process analysis.* [*See each of these detailed and illustrated in Part II.*]

dialogue 1. a written work in the form of conversation. **2.** the actors' lines in a play, story, and so on. [*See* Dialogue *in Part III for detailed explanations for writing dialogue as well as for example and analysis.*]

diction 1. the choice and arrangement of words. **Example:** The *diction* of everyday speech is different from that of a formal essay. **2.** manner of speaking or pronouncing words; enunciation. **Example:** An actor must have good, clear *diction.*

direct address a form of noun that names a specific person. **Example:** How are you, Mary? (*Mary* is a noun of direct address.) [*See Part IV, Section D, for rules and examples for punctuating nouns of direct address.*]

direct object a noun that tells who or what receives the action of a transitive verb. **Example:** Paul flew the *plane*. (The noun *plane* receives the action of the verb *flew*.) [*For comparison, see also* indirect object *and check Part IV, Section A,* Parts of the Sentence.]

direct question the exact words of another's question; as opposed to *indirect* question. **Example:** Mark asked, "Did you see many snakes?" (The words inside the quotation marks are Mark's exact words, a direct question.) [*For comparison, see* indirect question. *See Part IV, Section D, for rules and examples of quotation marks with direct questions.*]

direct quotation someone's exact words, either written or spoken. **Example:** Samantha explained, "These overcooked vegetables lack the vitamins of properly steamed vegetables." [*For comparison, see* indirect quotation. *See Part IV, Section D, for rules and examples of quotation marks with direct quotations.*]

documentation the supplying of supporting references by notation (*in-text parenthetical notes, endnotes,* and *footnotes*) and use of a bibliography. [*See* Research Paper *in Part III for a discussion and examples of each of the documentation styles.*]

E

editorial a statement of opinion in a newspaper or other publication, or on radio or TV, that gives the views of the owner, publisher, or others. [*See also* Editorial *in Part III.*]

ellipsis 1. the omission of a word or words necessary for complete grammatical construction but understood in the context. **Example:** *If possible* is understood to mean *if it is possible.* **2.** a mark of punctuation (. . .) indicating an intentional omission of words or letters or a lapse of time.

elliptical clause a clause in which grammatically necessary elements are omitted but implied by context. **Example:** Kelly is taller than she (implied: than she *is*).

emphasis, in sentences special attention given to a sentence part so as to make it stand out; importance, stress. **Example:** He contributed 50 dollars to the volunteer fire department (emphasis on fire department). To the first department, he contributed 50 dollars (emphasis on 50 dollars). [*For discussion and examples of various methods of emphasis, see* Revising *in Part I.*]

emphatic form a present or past tense in which a form of the verb *to do* is used as an auxiliary, for emphasis. **Example:** I *do care*.

endnote a reference or comment appearing at the end of a paper. A note with similar information appearing elsewhere in the paper is called a *footnote* or *in-text* or *parenthetical note*. [*See also* Research Paper *in Part III.*]

essay question a question, as on a test or application, that requires an organized, logical, well-developed answer. [*See* Essay-Question Responses *in Part III for a thorough discussion and examples.*]

essential modifier a word, phrase, or clause essential to the identification of the word it modifies. **Example:** The man *who ran the stop sign* hit the pedestrian. Compare with *nonessential modifier.* **Note:** Do not use commas to set off essential elements. [*See Part IV, Section D,* Commas, *for rules and examples about punctuating essential and nonessential elements.*]

evidence something that makes another thing easy to see or perceive; makes it clear, obvious, plain. In written work, evidence may take the form of illustrations, examples, analogies, and so on.

example a thing selected to show the nature or character of the rest; a sample. In written work, an example gives support and detail to a main idea.

exclamation point a mark of punctuation (!) used to express surprise, a strong feeling, and other strong emotions.

exclamatory sentence a sentence showing or using excitement or strong emotion. **Example:** Stop that thief! Compare also with *declarative, interrogative,* and *imperative* sentences. [*See Glossary entries for each.*]

explanation something that clarifies or interprets. In writing, an explanation may take the form of a definition, example, specific detail, and so on.

exposition writing that sets forth facts, ideas, and detailed explanations; as opposed to purely creative writing, such as short stories and poetry.

F

facts things that are actual. In writing, facts serve as evidence to explain or support a main idea.

falling action the part of the plot following the climax, when the conflict is resolved.

feature article a special story or article in a newspaper or magazine; shows human-interest side rather than straight news. [*See also* Feature Article *in Part III.*]

figure of speech an expression with an unusual or fanciful meaning used to add vividness to what is said. Figures of speech include *hyperbole, metaphor, personification, simile,* and *symbol.* [*See these entries in the Glossary.*]

final draft a complete, carefully revised and proofread copy.

finite verb a verb having limits of person, number, and tense.

five-paragraph theme a paper following a formal organization in which the first paragraph serves as an introduction and includes the thesis statement; the second, third, and fourth paragraphs develop a single topic from the thesis; and the fifth paragraph serves as a conclusion. [*See* Writing a Multi-Paragraph Paper *in Part I for a complete discussion and an example.*]

flashback the introduction into the events of a story of an episode that took place earlier.

focus in writing, a narrowed topic suitable for development into a paragraph or multi-paragraph paper.

footnote a comment or reference placed at the bottom of a page. Similar information appearing elsewhere may be called an *in-text, parenthetical note,* or *endnote.* [*See* Research Paper *in Part III for details.*]

foreshadowing a sign of something to come, a device used especially in short stories, plays, and novels.

formal language English usage that employs traditional rules of grammar and vocabulary; as distinguished from *colloquial language.*

formal style a characteristic manner of writing that incorporates formal language and avoids colloquialisms.

format 1. the physical layout of a paper. **2.** a general arrangement, as of a television program.

fragment an incomplete sentence used improperly, as if it were complete. **Example:** Running repeatedly around the track.

function the manner in which a part of speech behaves in a given sentence. **Example:** The girl is *tall*. (*Tall*, as an adjective, *functions* as a predicate adjective after the linking verb *is*.) **Note:** A word may function one way in one sentence and differently in another. [*See Part IV, Section A,* Parts of Speech, *for a complete discussion of function.*]

fused sentence two sentences joined improperly into a single sentence. **Example:** Glacial ice acted like a giant bulldozer it leveled hills and ridges as it moved south (two sentences fused into one). Sometimes called a *run-on sentence*. [*See* run-on sentence *and* comma fault.]

future perfect tense a form of verb that shows action in the future, prior to the completion of some other future action. **Example:** By the time I finish waxing the car, I *will have used* every good polishing rag we have. [*See also* verb.]

future tense a form of verb that shows action beyond the present, signaled by the auxiliaries *will* or *shall*. **Example:** He *will park* the car for us.

G

gender the classifying of nouns, pronouns, and adjectives into groups regarded as masculine, feminine, or neuter; in English, only some nouns (such as *actor* and *actress*) and all pronouns in the third person singular (as *he*, *she*, and *it*) are classified into these groups. [*See Part IV, Section B,* Pronoun Usage.]

generalization a statement that refers to a genus, kind, class, or order. Generalizations should be avoided unless well supported with specific details. [*See* Revising *in Part I for a discussion of specific details.*]

genre a kind or type. Literary genres include *short story, poetry, nonfiction, novel,* and *drama*.

gerund a verbal noun ending in *–ing* used like a noun but capable of taking an object or an adverbial modifier. **Example:** *Playing* golf is his only exercise. [*See Part IV, Section C,* Phrases and Clauses.]

grammar a body of rules for speaking and writing a given language.

H

hyperbole exaggeration used for effect, not meant literally. **Example:** He's *as strong as an ox.*

hyphen a mark of punctuation (-) used between the parts of a compound word (as *court-martial*) or the syllables of a divided word, as at the end of a line.

I

imagery **1.** mental images, as produced by memory or imagination. **2.** descriptions and figures of speech, as in the *imagery* of a poem. In writing, usually referring specifically to sensory images, that is, those created through the five senses.

imperative mood the mood of a verb that expresses a command or strong request. **Example:** *Open* that window now.

imperative sentence a sentence expressing a command or strong request. **Example:** Open that window now. Compare with *declarative* and *interrogative* sentences. [*See those entries in the Glossary.*]

incomplete constructions [*See* elliptical clause.]

indefinite pronoun a pronoun that does not specify, such as *any, someone, everyone,* and *each.* [*See Part IV, Section B, for rules and examples for using indefinite pronouns correctly.*]

independent clause a clause that can stand alone; a sentence; also called a *main clause.* [*See Part IV, Section D,* Phrases and Clauses.]

indicative mood designates that mood of a verb used to express an actual fact or state, or asks a question of fact. Compare with *imperative* and *subjunctive* moods. [*See entries in the Glossary.*]

indirect object the word or words identifying the person or thing that something (the *direct object*) is given to or done for. **Example:** Sid passed *Terry* the ball. [*See Part IV, Section A,* Parts of the Sentence *for additional details.*]

indirect question states a question but not the exact words. **Example:** He asked *if we were tired.* [*Compare with* direct question.] **Note:** Do not use quotation marks or a question mark with indirect questions.

indirect quotation reports the speaker's or writer's meaning without using his or her exact words. **Example:** Professor Clough said *that American literature merits careful study.* [*Compare with* direct quotation.]

infinitive a form of verb that expresses existence or action without reference to person, number, or tense; usually following the marker *to*. **Example:** He likes *to work*. [*See Part IV, Section C,* Phrases and Clauses *for details about infinitive phrases.*]

inflection a change of form by which words show number, case, gender, tense, comparison, and so on. For instance, the inflection of a noun can be singular (*car*), plural (*cars*), or possessive (*car's*).

informal language colloquial language, used on a daily basis for conversation and other informal communication.

informal style a manner of writing that relies on colloquial language and pays only casual regard to precise grammar. Informal writing, which is not to be confused with poor writing, permits the use of contractions, conversational language, and a first- or second-person point of view.

intensive pronoun pronoun ending in *–self* or *–selves* that emphasizes, or intensifies, the antecedent. **Example:** I'll take care of the work *myself*. [*Compare with* reflexive pronoun.]

interjection an exclamatory word or phrase, such as *ah!* or *good grief!* **Note:** Interjections are followed by exclamation marks.

interrogative pronoun a pronoun used to ask a question. **Example:** *What* did you say?

interrogative sentence a sentence that asks a question. **Example:** When did you arrive? Compare with *imperative, exclamatory,* and *declarative* sentences. [*See Glossary entries.*]

interview a meeting in which a person is asked about his opinions, activities, and so on, as by a reporter.

in-text note a comment or reference inserted parenthetically into the text of a paper, as opposed to a *footnote* or *endnote;* sometimes referred to as *parenthetical documentation*. [*See* footnote *and* endnote. *For specific details for form of in-text notes, see* Research Paper *in Part III.*]

intransitive verb a verb that does not require a direct object to complete its meaning. **Example:** He *shouted* with joy. Opposite of *transitive*. [*See* transitive verb.]

introduction the first part of a paragraph or multi-paragraph paper, which attracts the reader's attention and announces the subject. The introduction sets the tone and mood and, except in certain situations, tells the reader what ideas to expect. [*See* Writing a Paragraph *and* Writing a Multi-Paragraph Paper *in Part I for examples of introductions. Also see each type of writing in Parts II and III for sample introductions appropriate for the type.*]

irony 1. a method of humorous or sarcastic expression in which the meaning given to the words is the opposite of their usual sense. **Example:** She used *irony* when she said the stupid plan was clever. **2.** an event or result opposite to what might be expected. **Example:** That the fire station burned down was *ironic.*

irregular verb verb that does not follow the regular *–ed* ending for past tense and past participle. **Example:** *see, saw, have seen* (irregular verb); *walk, walked, have walked* (regular verb).

italic a printing type in which the characters slant upward to the right, used especially to call attention to words. **Example:** *This is italic type.* **Note:** In handwritten work, use an underscore to indicate italics.

L

laboratory report a summary of scientific findings; commonly called a *lab report.* [*For an explanation of format, content, and organization, see* Technical Report *in Part III.*]

letter a written or printed message, usually sent by mail. [*See* Letters *in Part III.*]

linking verb a verb that functions chiefly as a connection between a subject and its predicate complement. **Example:** He *seems* tired. [*See Part IV, Section A,* Parts of Speech.]

loose sentence a sentence that follows the usual subject-verb order so that the essential part of the sentence comes first, followed by additional details; probably the most common kind of sentence. **Example:** He drove the car home after the ball game. **Note:** A loose sentence can be simple, compound, complex, or compound-complex. Compare with *periodic sentence.* [*See* Revising *in Part I for a discussion of sentence variety. See* Writing Sentences *in Part I for a discussion of kinds of sentences.*]

lower case small letters, as opposed to *upper-case* or *capital* letters.

M

main clause a clause that can stand alone; a sentence; sometimes called an *independent* clause. [*Compare with* dependent clause *or* subordinate clause. *See Part IV, Section C,* Phrases and Clauses.]

mechanics the technical aspects of writing, including punctuation and capitalization.

metaphor a figure of speech that suggests likeness by speaking of one thing as if it were another. **Example:** Her moods are *the endless variations of a kaleidoscope.* [*Compare with* simile.]

meter rhythm in verse; regular arrangement of accented and unaccented syllables in each line.

minutes an official record of what was said and done at a meeting. [*See* Minutes of a Meeting *in Part III for a detailed explanation of how to write minutes.*]

misplaced modifier a phrase or clause placed away from the word it refers to, resulting in unclear meaning. **Example:** They made an announcement about the closing of school during the news report (sounds as if school is closed during the news report).

modifier a word, phrase, or clause that limits the meaning of another word or phrase. [*See* adjective, adverb, infinitive, participle, phrase, *and* clause, subordinate. *See also Part IV, Sections A and C.*]

monologue 1. a long speech, especially one that keeps anyone else from talking. **2.** a poem, story, or scene in which one character speaks alone or tells a story.

mood 1. the aspect of a verb that shows whether it is regarded as expressing a fact (*indicative mood*); a wish, desire, or possibility (*subjunctive mood*); or a command (*imperative mood*). **2.** the prevailing spirit or feeling in a piece of writing.

N

narration a method of developing a paragraph or multi-paragraph paper by means of telling a story. [*See* Narration *in Part II for details and examples.*]

news article an account of an event or situation written for the print media. [*See* News Article *in Part III for the process of writing a news article and for a sample new article and analysis.*]

nominative case the case of the subject of a verb and the words (*appositive, predicate adjectives,* and so on) that agree with it. *She, he,* and *who* are examples of pronouns in the nominative case. Compare with *objective* and *possessive case.* [*See Part IV, Section B,* Pronoun Usage.]

nonessential modifier a modifier not necessary to the identification of the word modified; sometimes called a *nonrestrictive modifier.* **Example:** Mrs. Heeger, *who is my neighbor,* is a superb seamstress. **Note:** Use commas to set off nonrestrictive modifiers. Compare with *essential modifier.* [*See Part IV, Section D.*]

notes brief written statements of facts as an aid to memory; a comment or explanation. [*See* Notes *in Part III.*]

noun any of a class or words naming or denoting a person, thing, action, quality, and so on. [*See Part IV, Section A.*]

number the change in form used to show whether one or more than one is meant; singular and plural forms show *number*. [*See* subject-verb agreement. *Also see Part IV, Section B.*]

O

objective case the case taken by an object. *Me, her, him,* and *whom* are examples of pronouns in the objective case. Compare with *nominative* and *possessive case*. [*See Part IV, Section B,* Pronoun Usage.]

objective complement word, phrase, or clause that completes the object. **Example:** The group named Christopher its *representative*. [*See Part IV, Section A,* Parts of the Sentence.]

omniscient point of view the point of view of an all-knowing, all-seeing speaker. [*See* Short Story *for examples and comparisons with other points of view.*]

onomatopoeia the formation of a word (such as *chickadee* or *tinkle*) by imitating the sound associated with the object or action.

opinion a method of developing a paragraph or multi-paragraph paper by which the writer expresses a personal belief. [*See* Opinion *in Part II for details, sample paper, and analysis.*]

order, in paragraph development the method of organizing a paragraph or multi-paragraph paper. The orders include *chronological, spatial,* and *order of importance*. [*See Glossary entries for each.*]

order of business the usual order in which business is conducted during a meeting. [*See* Minutes of a Meeting *in Part III for a list of the usual order.*]

order of importance a method of organizing a paragraph or multi-paragraph paper according to the relative significance of the subtopics. One standard arrangement is from most to least important; another is from least to most. A frequently used variation begins with the second most important idea, followed by the remaining details, listed from least to most important.

organization the way in which the parts of a paragraph or multi-paragraph paper are put together, with all parts properly connected. General plans of organization vary with the kind of writing. [*See individual listings in Parts II and III.*]

outline a plan for a paragraph or multi-paragraph paper, generally using letters and numerals to designate the relationships among and between topics. [*See* Outline *in Part III.*]

P

paragraph a section of a paper, letter, and so on, dealing with a particular point and made up of one or more sentences. A paragraph begins on a new line and is usually indented. [*See* Writing a Paragraph *in Part I.*]

paragraph development the means by which the main point of a paragraph is explained, supported, or detailed. [*See all of Part II*, Methods of Development.]

parallel structure like grammatical structures used for ideas of equal rank. **Example:** *Using computers* and *accessing databases* are second nature to him. (Two gerund phrases form parallel structures in compound subjects.)

paraphrase to put something spoken or written into different, more simple words having the same meaning. Used frequently in writing research and technical papers. [*See* Paraphrase *in Part III.*]

parentheses punctuation marks, always used in pairs, ( ) used to set off a word, clause, remark, and so on, added as an explanation of comment within a complete sentence. **Example:** The television special tomorrow night (Channel 9, 8:00 PM) will discuss laser surgery. **Note:** Parentheses rarely appear in formal writing.

parenthetical element a word, phrase, or clause added as an aside or additional comment within a complete sentence. **Example:** He is, *I'm convinced*, an honest person. **Note:** The parenthetical element is set off from the rest of the sentence with commas. [*See Part IV, Section D.*]

part-by-part organization a means of organization, particularly in a comparison or contrast paper, in which the similarities (or differences) or one point of both topics are discussed, followed by the similarities (or differences) of another point. Compare with *whole-by-whole organization*. [*See* Comparison and Contrast *in Part II for further illustration.*]

participial phrase a word group made up of a participle and its object(s) and any modifier(s). **Example:** The boy *wearing a baseball cap* must learn to take it off when entering a building. (The participle *wearing* includes an object, *cap*, and a modifier, *baseball*.) [*See Part IV, Section C*, Phrases and Clauses.]

participle a verbal form having the qualities of both a verb and an adjective. Participles are used as adjectives, either present (a *raving* beauty) or past (the *beaten* path). As a verb part, participles take auxiliaries to form a verb phrase. [*See Part IV, Section C,* Phrases and Clauses.]

parts of speech the eight terms given words according to their function: *noun, verb, adjective, adverb, preposition, conjunction, article, interjection.* [*See Part IV, Section A,* Parts of Speech.]

passive voice the voice or form of a verb whose subject is the receiver (object) of the action of the verb. **Example:** I *was hit* by the ball. Compare with *active voice.*

past participle a participle used **1.** with helping verbs to show completed action or a time or state gone by. **Example:** He *has worked.* **2.** as an adjective **Example:** He is a *grown* man. [*See Part IV, Section C,* Phrases and Clauses.]

past perfect tense a verb tense used to show an action completed in the past prior to some other past action. **Example:** He *had gone* before we arrived.

past tense any verb tense used to show an action completed before the present, including the simple past tense, present perfect tense, and past perfect tense.

perfect tenses the three verb tenses used to show relationships between actions, including present perfect tense (*have gone*), past perfect tense (*had gone*), and future perfect tense (*will have gone*). [*See entries in the Glossary.*]

period a mark of punctuation (.) used at the end of a declarative sentence or to indicate an abbreviation.

periodical a publication appearing at regular intervals.

periodic sentence a sentence so written that the full meaning cannot be understood until the end. **Example:** Under the porch, out of the sun, hidden from the prying eyes of mischievous little children, the old dog slept. Compare with *loose sentence.* [*See also* Revising *in Part I for a discussion of sentence variety.*]

personal pronoun any one of a group of pronouns divided into three sets: first person (*I, my*), second person (*you, your*), and third person (*he, her, their, it*). [*See Part IV, Section B,* Pronoun Usage.]

personification a figure of speech in which a thing or idea is represented as a person. **Example:** The sunshine *brushed my face with a warm hand.*

persuasion a method of development in which the writer attempts to convince the reader to agree with a certain position or to take a certain action. [*See* Persuasion *in Part II for process, sample, and analysis.*]

phrase a group of words conveying a single thought or forming a distinct part of a sentence but not containing a subject and predicate, including *prepositional, gerund, infinitive, participial, absolute, appositive,* and *verb* phrases. [*See Glossary entries and see Part IV, Section C,* Phrases and Clauses.]

plagiarism the act of stealing ideas or words from another and passing them off as one's own. To avoid plagiarism, a writer uses careful documentation. [*See* Research Paper *in Part III for an explanation of the documentation process.*]

plot the plan of action of a play, novel, short story, and so on.

plural of or including more than one. Because plural forms vary, consult *Webster's New World Dictionary* for irregular plural forms.

poem an arrangement of words having rhythm and, often, rhyme; usually set in imaginative or emotional language. Some poems are in meter, some in free verse. Common poetic forms include *ballad, blank verse, epic, dramatic monologue, elegy, epigram, free verse, haiku, light verse, limerick, ode, sonnet,* and *villanelle.*

point of view the place from which, or way in which, something is viewed; standpoint. [*See* Short Story: Step 5, Selecting Point of View, *in Part III for detailed explanation and examples.*]

possessive a case, form, or construction expressing ownership. **Example:** *Duane's* book is different from *mine.* [*See Part IV, Section D.*]

precis a concise summary. [*See* Precis *in Part III to learn how to develop an accurate precis.*]

predicate the verb or verbal phrase that says something about the subject of a sentence or clause. A predicate may be a verb (The wind *blows.*), a verb and an adverb (The wind *blows hard.*), a verb and its object (The wind *blows the leaves down.*), or a linking verb and its complement (He *is the happiest man I know.*). [*See Part IV, Section A,* Parts of the Sentence.]

predicate adjective an adjective that follows a linking verb and describes the subject. **Example:** He is *handsome.* [*See Part IV, Section A,* Parts of the Sentence.]

predicate noun a noun that follows a linking verb and identifies the subject. **Example:** Marcia is my *friend.* [*See Part IV, Section A,* Parts of the Sentence.]

preposition a relation word, such as *in, by, for, with,* and *to,* that connects a noun or pronoun, or a noun phrase, to another noun (the sound *of* rain), to a verb (went *to* the store), or to an adjective (late *for* the tea party). [*See Part IV, Section A,* Parts of Speech.]

prepositional phrase a word group formed by a preposition and its object(s) and any modifier(s); functions as an adjective or adverb. **Example:** She supervised children *on the playground* (functions as an adjective modifying the noun *children*). [*See Part IV, Section C,* Phrases and Clauses.]

present perfect tense a verb tense indicating an action or state as completed at the time of speaking but not at any definite time in the past. **Example:** He *has gone.*

present tense the verb tense that indicates current action or state of being. **Example:** He *walks.*

prewriting an activity used to prepare for writing, including reading, research, discussion, interviewing, brainstorming, journal writing, note-taking, list-making, outlining, and so on. [*See Part I,* Prewriting.]

primary research research conducted by the writer himself, including laboratory work, interviews, statistical analyses, surveys, and so on. Compare with *secondary research.* [*See* Research Paper *in Part III for the research process.*]

process particular method of doing something, in this case writing, in which there is a series of steps. [*See Part I for an overview.*]

progressive form a verb form showing continuing action. **Example:** I *am working.*

pronoun a word used to refer to or in place of a noun, including personal, reflexive, intensive, demonstrative, relative, indefinite, and interrogative pronouns. [*See Glossary entries.*]

pronoun agreement the agreement of number and gender of pronouns with their antecedents. [*See Part IV, Section B,* Pronoun Usage.]

pronoun reference the word to which a pronoun refers; antecedent.

proper noun a noun that names a specific individual, place, and so on, is not used with an article, and is normally capitalized, such as *Donald* and *Boston.* Compare with *common noun.* [*See Part IV, Section A,* Parts of Speech.]

protagonist the main character in a drama, novel, or story, around whom the action centers. Compare with *antagonist*.

purpose, statement of a sentence that states the topic and intended direction of a paper; thesis sentence. [*See* Writing a Multi-Paragraph Paper *in Part I.*]

Q

question mark a mark of punctuation (?) used to end interrogative sentences.

quotation the words or passage cited as an example or authority, as from a book or author. Enclosed in quotation marks. [*See* Research Paper *in Part III for a discussion of the proper use of quotations as supporting details.*]

quotation marks marks of punctuation (" ") used in pairs to enclose a direct quotation. Single quotation marks (') are used to enclose a quotation within a quotation.

R

redundancy the use of more words than are needed; wordiness. [*See* Revising *in Part I for eliminating wordiness.*]

reference, for research paper any book, periodical, or other media used as secondary research for the development of a research paper.

reflexive pronoun a pronoun ending in *–self* or *–selves* which refers to the antecedent. **Example:** I bought the book for *myself*. Compare with *intensive pronoun.*

relative clause a subordinate clause introduced by a relative pronoun, *who, whose, whom, which,* and *that*. **Example:** I wore the hat *that you bought*. [*See Part IV, Section C,* Phrases and Clauses.]

relative pronoun a pronoun used to introduce relative clauses: *who, whose, whom, which,* and *that*.

research a systematic study or investigation in a field of knowledge, to discover or establish facts or principles, including both *primary* and *secondary* methods of research. [*See Glossary entries.*]

research paper a paper that reports research, both primary and secondary, and includes documentation presented according to a specified form. [*See* Research Paper *in Part III.*]

resolution the part of a novel, play, story, and so on, in which the plot is explained or made clear.

resume a statement of a job applicant's previous employment experience and education. [*See* Resume *in Part III.*]

review a report, as in a newspaper, telling about a book, play, concert, and so on, and giving an opinion of it. [*See* Review *in Part III.*]

revision the act of correcting, improving, or bringing up to date as necessary. [*See* Revising *in Part I.*]

rhyme likeness of sound at the ends of words or lines of verse.

rhythm 1. the flow or movement having a regularly repeated pattern of accents and beats. **2.** the form or pattern of the regularly repeated stressed and unstressed or long and short syllables.

rising action in a play, novel, short story, and so on, the building action that occurs from the beginning of the work until its climax.

Roman numeral the Roman system of letters used as numerals: I = 1, V = 5, X = 10, L = 50, C = 100, D = 500, and M = 1,000.

rough draft an early version of a paragraph or multi-paragraph paper prior to revising and proofreading.

run-on sentence two main clauses improperly joined. **Example:** We ate too much we got sick (run-on sentence). We ate too much, so we got sick (corrected).

S

script the text of a play or movie. [*See* Scripts *in Part III.*]

secondary research research examining previously published findings. Compare with *primary research*. [*See* Research Paper *in Part III.*]

semicolon a mark of punctuation (;) showing more separation than a comma and less than a period; usually used between certain closely related independent clauses. **Example:** The door slammed shut; she was locked out. [*See Part IV, Section D.*]

sentence a word or group of words that states, asks, commands, or exclaims something, usually has a subject and predicate and which, in writing, begins with a capital letter and ends with a period, question mark, or exclamation mark. [*See* Writing Sentences *in Part I.*]

sentence outline an outline that states topics and subtopics in complete sentences. [*See* Outline *in Part III.*] **Note:** Sentence outlines should maintain parallel structure.

sentence structure the relation of phrases, clauses, and sentence parts within a sentence. [*See* Writing Sentences *in Part I.*]

series a number of similar grammatical structures appearing consecutively. [*See Part IV, Section D, for punctuating items in a series.*]

setting the time, place, and environment of an event, story, play, and so on.

shifts, confusing an unwarranted change of tense or viewpoint within a given segment of writing.

short answer a brief response to a test question, job application question, or college or scholarship application question. [*See* Short Answers *in Part III.*]

short story a short work of fiction developing a single theme of limited scope and number of characters. [*See* Short Story *in Part III.*]

similarities-differences pattern of organization a means of organizing a comparison-and-contrast paper in which all similarities are discussed in one part and all differences discussed in another. [*See* Comparison and Contrast *in Part II.*]

simile a figure of speech in which one thing is compared to another, using the word *like* or *as*. **Example:** His muscles were *as loose as last year's slingshot.* Compare with *metaphor.*

simple sentence a single main clause without any subordinate clauses. **Example:** The boy in the red shirt won the race without difficulty.

singular referring to only one.

slang coarse or highly informal language, avoided in formal speech and writing; it consists of new words and existing words given new meanings, and is usually fresh, colorful, or humorous for only a short time.

slant to write or speak so as to appeal to a particular point of view or to express a particular bias.

spatial order an arrangement according to space, from left to right, right to left, and so on.

specific detail supporting information that is concrete and non-general in nature. [*See* Revising *in Part I for examples of writing with and without specific detail.*]

split infinitive the separation of the marker *to* from the verbal form of the infinitive by inserting modifiers, as in *to boldly go* instead of *to go boldly*. Generally, good writers avoid split infinitives. [*See* infinitive.]

squinting modifier a modifier that could indifferently affect two or more references. **Example:** He ran down the hall with poor light. (*With poor light* could modify either *hall* or *ran*.) [*See* misplaced modifier.]

statistics numeric data arranged so as to show certain information.

subject 1. in a sentence, a noun, noun phrase, or noun clause about which something is said. **Example:** The *building* was vacant. **2.** in a paragraph or multi-paragraph paper, the main topic.

subject complement [*See* predicate adjective *and* predicate noun.]

subject-verb agreement agreement in number of a subject and verb. [*See Part IV, Section B*, Agreement of Subject and Verb.]

subjunctive mood the mood of a verb used to express supposition, desire, possibility, and so on, as opposed to actual fact. **Example:** If I *were* you, I'd go home.

subordinate clause a clause that cannot stand alone and depends on a main clause for its meaning; also called *dependent clause*. **Example:** The man *who came to dinner* is Dad's boss. [*See Part IV, Section C*, Phrases and Clauses.]

summary a brief report covering the main points. [*See* Synopsis *and* Precis *in Part III.*]

superlative degree a form of adjective or adverb that shows the greatest degree in meaning; the superlative degree is usually shown by the suffix —*est* or by the use of *most* (*most beautiful*). Compare with *comparative form*. [*See Part IV, Section A*, Parts of Speech.]

syllabify to form or divide into syllables, as in *syl-lab-i-fy*.

symbol a thing that stands for another thing; especially, an object that stands for an idea, quality, and so on.

synopsis a short outline or review of the main points, as of a story; summary. [*See* Synopsis *in Part III.*]

T

tense a form or set of forms of a verb that show the time. [*See* verb.]

theme **1.** a topic or subject, as of a lecture or essay. **2.** an idea or subject that is repeated or presented in a number of ways in a work of art or literature to unify it. **3.** a short essay, especially one written as a school assignment. [*See* Writing a Multi-Paragraph Paper *in Part I.*]

thesaurus a book containing synonyms and antonyms; also available in somewhat abbreviated form on most word-processing programs.

thesis sentence (or statement) the sentence that states the subject of a theme and states or implies the division of that subject into subtopics as they will be developed. [*See* Writing a Multi-Paragraph Paper *in Part I.*]

tone a way of wording or expressing things that shows a certain attitude.

topic the subject of a writing, speech, discussion, and so on.

topic outline an outline that uses parallel words or word groups for the topics and subtopics. Compare with *sentence outline.* **Note:** Do not use both sentences and topics in the same outline. [*See* Outline *in Part III.*]

topic sentence (or statement) a sentence that states the subject of a paragraph and may state or imply the attitude, time, and place of the subject. [*See Part I,* Prewriting *and* Writing a Paragraph.]

transitions words, phrases, or sentences that connect one idea with another either within or between paragraphs. [*See* Revising *in Part I for examples.*]

transitive verb a verb that requires a direct object to complete its meaning. **Example:** He *softened* the blow. Compare with *intransitive.*

U

understatement putting things more weakly than is warranted by truth, accuracy, or importance. **Example:** After a heavy rain, things are a *little damp.*

unity in a work of art or literature, an arrangement of parts so as to produce a single effect. [*See* Revising *in Part I for how to maintain unity in a composition.*]

upper case capital letters, as opposed to *lower case.*

usage the way in which a word or phrase is used in speaking or writing.

V

vagueness not clearly or exactly expressed or stated; not sharp. **Example:** We waited *a long time* (vague). We waited *32 minutes* (specific). Compare with *specific detail* and *concrete.* [*See also* Revising *in Part I for examples of writing with and without specific details.*]

verb a word expressing action, a state of being, or a happening, and forming the main part of a predicate. [*See Part IV, Section A,* Parts of Speech.]

verbal phrase a group of words made up of a main verb and its auxiliaries. **Example:** He *had been working* before lunch. [*See Part IV, Section A,* Parts of the Sentence.]

verse **1.** poetry in general, sometimes more specifically poetry of a light or amusing nature **2.** a stanza or short subdivision of a poem.

vertical file in a library, a file that contains bulletins, pamphlets, and other miscellaneous publications, usually located in the reference section.

voice a verb form showing the connection between the subject and the verb, either as performing (*active voice*) or receiving (*passive voice*) the action. [*See* active voice, passive voice, *and, in Part IV, Section A,* Parts of Speech.]

W

whole-by-whole organization in a comparison-and-contrast paragraph or multi-paragraph paper, a method of organization that treats all subpoints of one topic before moving on to treat all subpoints of the second topic. Compare with *part-by-part organization.* [*See* Comparison and Contrast *in Part II for a detailed explanation and examples.*]

wordiness the excessive use of words. [*See* Revising *in Part I for an example of wordiness and an explanation of methods for eliminating it.*]

INDEX